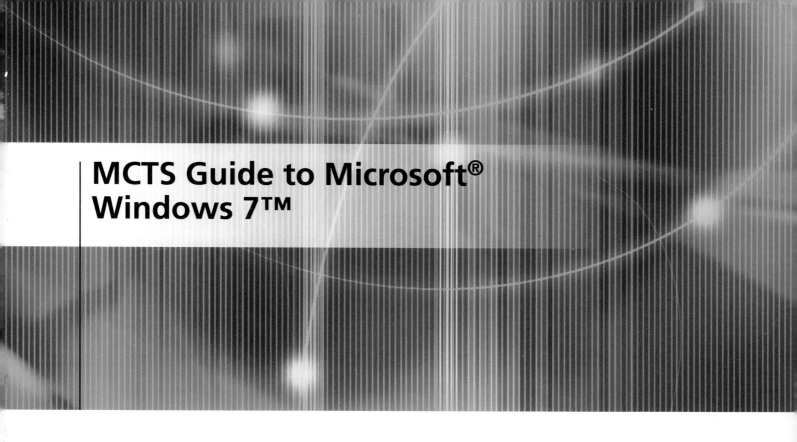

MCTS Guide to Microsoft® Windows 7™

Byron Wright
Leon Plesniarski

COURSE TECHNOLOGY
CENGAGE Learning™

Australia • Canada • Mexico • Singapore • Spain • United Kingdom • United States

P9-DUY-550

COURSE TECHNOLOGY
CENGAGE Learning

MCTS Guide to Microsoft® Windows 7™ (Exam # 70-680)
Byron Wright and Leon Plesniarski

Vice President, Career and Professional Editorial: Dave Garza

Director of Learning Solutions: Matthew Kane

Acquisitions Editor: Nick Lombardi

Managing Editor: Marah Bellegarde

Product Manager: Natalie Pashoukos

Developmental Editor: Jill Batistick

Editorial Assistant: Sarah Pickering

Vice President, Career and Professional Marketing: Jennifer Ann Baker

Marketing Director: Deborah S. Yarnell

Senior Marketing Manager: Erin Coffin

Marketing Coordinator: Shanna Gibbs

Production Director: Carolyn Miller

Production Manager: Andrew Crouth

Senior Content Project Manager: Andrea Majot

Senior Art Director: Jack Pendleton

Manufacturing Coordinator: Amy Rogers

Technical Edit/Quality Assurance: Green Pen Quality Assurance

Compositor: PreMediaGlobal

> For product information and technology assistance, contact us at
> **Cengage Learning Customer & Sales Support, 1-800-354-9706**
>
> For permission to use material from this text or product,
> submit all requests online at **cengage.com/permissions**
> Further permissions questions can be emailed to
> **permissionrequest@cengage.com**

Microsoft® is a registered trademark of the Microsoft Corporation.

Library of Congress Control Number: 2010933379

ISBN-13: 978-1-1113-0977-0

ISBN-10: 1-1113-0977-9

Course Technology
20 Channel Center
Boston, MA 02210
USA

Cengage Learning is a leading provider of customized learning solutions with office locations around the globe, including Singapore, the United Kingdom, Australia, Mexico, Brazil, and Japan. Locate your local office at: **international.cengage.com/region**

Cengage Learning products are represented in Canada by Nelson Education, Ltd.

For your lifelong learning solutions, visit **course.cengage.com**

Visit our corporate website at **cengage.com**

Microsoft and the Office logo are either registered trademarks or trademarks of Microsoft Corporation in the United States and/or other countries. Course Technology, a part of Cengage Learning, is an independent entity from the Microsoft Corporation, and not affiliated with Microsoft in any manner.

Printed in the United States of America
2 3 4 5 6 7 12 11

Brief Table of Contents

Table of Contents

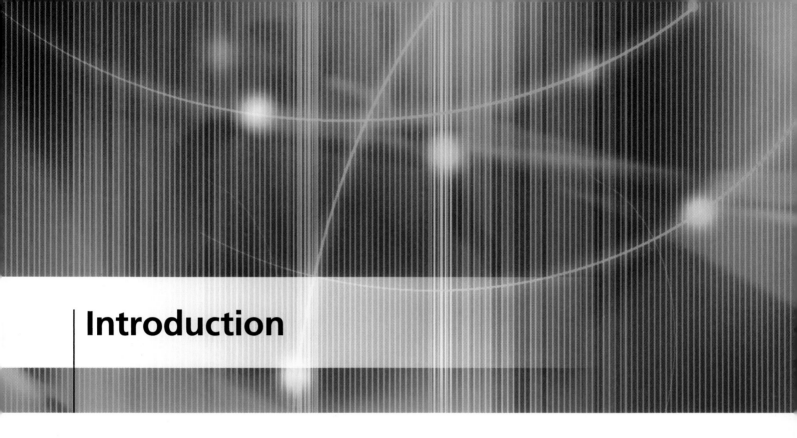

Introduction

Welcome to *MCTS Guide to Windows 7.* This book offers you real-world examples, interactive activities, and many hands-on activities that reinforce key concepts and prepare you for a career in network administration using Microsoft Windows 7. This book also features troubleshooting tips for solutions to common problems that you will encounter in the realm of Windows 7 administration.

This book offers in-depth study of all the functions and features of installing, configuring, and maintaining Windows 7 as a client operating system. Throughout the book, we provide detailed Activities that let you experience firsthand the processes involved in Windows 7 configuration and management. We then provide pointed Review Questions to reinforce the concepts introduced in each chapter and help you prepare for the Microsoft certification exam. Finally, to put a real-world slant on the concepts introduced in each chapter, we provide Case Projects to prepare you for situations that must be managed in a live networking environment.

Certification

MCTS Guide to Microsoft Windows 7 is intended for people getting started in computer networking as well as experienced network administrators new to Windows 7. To best understand the material in this book, you should have a background in basic computer concepts and have worked with applications in a Windows environment. The Microsoft Certified Technology Specialist (MCTS) certification allows technology professionals to prove their expertise in working with specific Microsoft technologies. This book prepares you to take exam 70-680: TS: Windows 7, Configuring, which leads to the MCTS: Windows 7, Configuration certification. After completing this book, you will not only be prepared to take the certification exam, but will also be prepared to implement and maintain Windows 7 in a business environment.

New to This Edition

The entire book has been updated from Windows Vista to Windows 7, covering the functions and features of installing, configuring, and maintaining Windows 7 as a client operating system. New activities, review questions, and case projects have been created to reinforce the concepts and techniques presented in each chapter and to help you apply these concepts to real-world scenarios. A new, full-color interior design brings the material to life and full-color screenshots provide a more detailed look at the Microsoft Windows 7 interface.

Chapter Outline

The topics covered in the 14 chapters of this book are comprehensive and organized as described in the following descriptions.

Chapter 1, "Introduction to Windows 7," outlines the versions of Windows 7 in the features available in each. It also introduces the new and improved features in Windows 7, including the updated user interface, hardware requirements, and system hardware support. New features for application support, connectivity applications, and enhanced networking models are also covered.

In **Chapter 2,** "Installing Windows 7," we discuss the deployment enhancements in Windows 7 and the considerations for choosing an installation method and installation type. We also explore transferring settings from one computer to another by using Windows Easy Transfer. Detailed explanations of attended and unattended installations are provided. Finally, imaging of Windows 7 by using the Windows Imaging Format is discussed.

Chapter 3, "Using the System Utilities," examines the tools used to manage Windows 7: namely, the Microsoft Management Console (MMC), Administrative Tools, Task Scheduler, and Control Panel applets. These tools are used to install and configure new hardware, power management, and the display.

In **Chapter 4,** "Managing Disks," we explore the differences between basic and dynamic storage and discuss the drive configurations supported by Windows 7. This chapter also introduces partition and volume management as well as the common disk management tools. The new virtual hard disk files available in Windows 7 are also discussed.

Chapter 5, "Managing File Systems," introduces the concept of files systems and describes the benefits and features of both FAT and NTFS. File system security is covered, including NTFS permissions and inheritance. Finally, accessing and restoring previous versions of files is discussed.

In **Chapter 6,** "User Management," we introduce the concepts involved in working with users, groups, profiles, and Parental Controls. This discussion includes setting up, naming, and managing local users and groups and default user and group accounts. User profiles and their role in user management are covered. User security in peer-to-peer and domain-based networks are evaluated. Finally the use of Parental Controls is explored as a method for controlling user access.

Chapter 7, "Windows 7 Security Features," teaches you about the security improvements in Windows 7, how to configure security by using the local security policy, and how to enable auditing. You will also learn about User Account Control, which is a way for user privileges to be managed. Malware security using Windows Defender and Microsoft Security Essentials is covered. Using Encrypting File System and BitLocker Drive Encryption for data protection is discussed. Finally, using Windows Update to automatically apply patches is covered.

Chapter 8, "Networking," describes the networking components and architecture of Windows 7. You learn about the TCP/IPv4 and TCP/IPv6 protocols. You also learn about file sharing, Internet connectivity, Windows Firewall, network bridging, and HomeGroup networks.

In **Chapter 9,** "Using Productivity Tools," we discuss Windows 7 printing and faxing. We also look at the new Windows Explorer libraries and search feature that make finding information easier. Finally, the new features and security of Internet Explorer 8 is discussed.

Chapter 10, "Performance Tuning," gives you the information you need to understand the performance and monitoring tools found in Windows 7. You learn performance tuning concepts that can be used for Windows 7 and other operating systems. Then you learn how to use the Performance Monitor along with Task Manager to monitor Windows 7. The performance ranking system in Windows 7 is discussed and you see some methods for optimizing system performance.

In **Chapter 11,** "Application Support," we discuss the Windows 7 architecture for supporting applications. The registry is also discussed. Support for applications compatibility including file and registry virtualization and compatibility tools are also discussed.

We introduce you to disaster protection and recovery concepts in **Chapter 12,** "Disaster Recovery and Troubleshooting." You learn about the general principals of troubleshooting that can be used to diagnose problems with any computer system. Tools used for information gathering are covered including Event Viewer and Problem Reports and Solutions. Also, you learn about the utilities that can be used for system maintenance and repair such as Windows Backup and the Advanced Boot Options Menu. Finally, you learn about advanced troubleshooting tools used for DirectX and the Windows 7 boot process.

Chapter 13, "Enterprise Computing" describes Windows 7 features and functions that are used in large companies. You learn how Active Directory and Group Policy can be used to manage hundreds or thousands of Windows 7 computers. As well, deployment planning and enterprise deployment tools for Windows 7 are described. Finally, you learn how Windows Server Update Services and Network Access Protection can be used to ensure that computers on your network have appropriate updates installed.

In **Chapter 14,** "Remote Access," we examine remote access. You learn how to use remote access under Windows 7, including how to use Remote Desktop and Remote Assistance. The new DirectAccess and BranchCache features are discussed. Finally, you learn about the Sync Center for mobile users.

Appendix A, "MCTS 70-680 Exam Objectives," maps each exam objective to the chapter and section where you can find information on that objective.

Features and Approach

MCTS Guide to Microsoft Windows 7 differs from other networking books in its unique hands-on approach and its orientation to real-world situations and problem solving. To help you see how Microsoft Windows 7 concepts and techniques are applied in real-world organizations, this book incorporates the following features:

Chapter Objectives—Each chapter begins with a detailed list of the concepts to be mastered. This list gives you a quick reference to the chapter's contents and is a useful study aid.

Activities—Activities are incorporated throughout the text, giving you practice in setting up, managing, and troubleshooting a network system. The Activities give you a strong foundation for carrying out network administration tasks in the real world. Because of the book's progressive nature, completing the Activities in each chapter is essential before moving on to the end-of-chapter materials and subsequent chapters.

Chapter Summaries—Each chapter's text is followed by a summary of the concepts introduced in that chapter. These summaries provide a helpful way to recap and revisit the ideas covered in each chapter.

Key Terms—All terms introduced with boldfaced text are gathered together in the Key Terms list at the end of the chapter. This provides you with a method of checking your understanding of all the terms introduced.

Review Questions—The end-of-chapter assessment begins with a set of Review Questions that reinforce the ideas introduced in each chapter. Answering these questions correctly will ensure that you have mastered the important concepts.

Case Projects—Finally, each chapter closes with a section that proposes certain situations. You are asked to evaluate the situations and decide upon the course of action to be taken to remedy the problems described. This valuable tool will help you sharpen your decision-making and troubleshooting skills, which are important aspects of network administration.

Text and Graphic Conventions

Additional information and exercises have been added to this book to help you better understand what's being discussed in the chapter. Icons throughout the text alert you to these additional materials. The icons used in this book are described as follows:

 Tips offer extra information on resources, how to attack problems, and time-saving shortcuts.

 Notes present additional helpful material related to the subject being discussed.

 Each Activity in this book is preceded by the Hands-On icon.

 Case Project icons mark the end-of-chapter case projects, which are scenario-based assignments that ask you to independently apply what you have learned in the chapter.

CertBlaster Test Preparation

The *MCTS Guide to Microsoft Windows 7 (Exam # 70-680)* includes an exam objectives coverage map in Appendix A. The guide also includes CertBlaster test preparation questions that mirror the look and feel of the MCTS exam. For additional information on the CertBlaster test preparation questions, go to ftp://ftp.certblaster.com/1/Course/.

Please follow these directions to install and launch your CertBlaster application:

1. Click the title of the CertBlaster you want to download.
2. Save the program (.EXE) file to a folder on your C: drive. (Warning: If you skip this step, your CertBlaster will not install correctly.)
3. Click Start and choose Run.
4. Click Browse and then navigate to the folder that contains the .EXE file. Select the .EXE file and click Open.
5. Click OK and then follow the on-screen instructions. In order to complete the installation, you will need the CertBlaster access code. The access code can be found inside the card in the back of your textbook.
6. When the installation is complete, Click Finish.
7. Click Start, choose All programs and Click CertBlaster.

Instructor Resources

The following supplemental materials are available when this book is used in a classroom setting. All the supplements available with this book are provided to the instructor on a single CD-ROM. All the information has been updated to cover Windows 7.

Electronic Instructor's Manual—The Instructor's Manual that accompanies this textbook includes additional instructional material to assist in class preparation, including suggestions for classroom activities, discussion topics, and additional projects.

Solutions—The solutions are provided for the end-of-chapter material, including Review Questions, and, where applicable, Hands-On Activities and Case Projects. Solutions to the Practice Exams are also included.

ExamView®—This textbook is accompanied by ExamView, a powerful testing software package that allows instructors to create and administer printed, computer (LAN-based), and Internet exams. ExamView includes hundreds of questions that correspond to the topics covered in this text, enabling students to generate detailed study guides that include page references for further review. The computer-based and Internet testing components allow students to take exams at their computers and also save the instructor time by grading each exam automatically.

PowerPoint presentations—This book comes with Microsoft PowerPoint slides for each chapter. These are included as a teaching aid for classroom presentation, to make available to students on the network for chapter review, or to be printed for classroom distribution. Instructors, please feel at liberty to add your own slides for additional topics you introduce to the class.

Figure files—All the figures and tables in the book are reproduced on the Instructor Resources CD, in bitmap format. Similar to the PowerPoint presentations, these are included as a teaching aid for classroom presentation, to make available to students for review, or to be printed for classroom distribution.

Companion Lab Manual

A companion lab manual is available with this book. It includes additional exercises for every chapter to complement the exercises in the book. The ISBN of the lab manual is 1-1113-0978-7.

System Requirements

Hardware

All hardware should be listed on Microsoft's Hardware Compatibility List for Windows 7. However, the Activities in this book have been designed to run with virtualization software such as Microsoft Virtual PC, Microsoft Virtual Server, Microsoft Hyper-V, VMWare Virtual Server, and VMWare Workstation.

Software

Microsoft Windows 7 Enterprise for each computer. Other versions can be used, but some activities may not be possible to perform. For example, the Parental Controls feature is not available in business versions of Windows 7. Students perform the installation of all necessary software during the course.

Software used during this course can be obtained at the following locations:

- Windows 7 Enterprise 90-day Trial—http://technet.microsoft.com/en-us/evalcenter/cc442495.aspx

Component	Requirement
CPU	1 gigahertz or faster, ×86 or ×64
Memory	1 GB of RAM (2 GB recommended for ×64)
Disk Space	40 GB hard disk
Video	Monitor supporting a resolution of 1024×768 DirectX 9 capable graphics processor with WDDM support (recommended)
Keyboard	Keyboard
Pointing Device	Microsoft mouse or compatible pointing device
Drives	A DVD-ROM drive
Networking	Internet connectivity recommended. Network connectivity required for some activities.
Cards	A Windows 7-compatible network adapter card and related cable

- Windows Automated Installation Kit for Windows 7—http://www.microsoft.com/downloads/details.aspx?FamilyID=696dd665-9f76-4177-a811-39c26d3b3b34&displaylang=en
- Windows Server 2008 R2 Trial—http://www.microsoft.com/windowsserver2008/en/us/trial-software.aspx

Set Up Instructions

To successfully complete the Activities, you need a computer system meeting or exceeding the minimal system requirements for Windows 7. Confirming those requirements and installing Windows 7 (along with available service packs) is covered in Chapters 1 and 2.

Acknowledgments

Byron and Leon would like to thank the entire team that we have worked with at Cengage Learning.

In particular we would like to thank Jill Batistick who patiently worked with us as we missed the occasional deadline during the writing process. We would also like to thank John Blackwood, Mike Fuszner, William Hilliker, Paulette Sibrel, and Pamela Kurtz, the reviewers who evaluated the first draft of our chapters and provided feedback on them. Your insights were a valuable contribution to this book. Finally, Leon would like to thank his loving wife, Angela, and his boys, Tyler and Terry, for sharing their family time with all the people who will use this book as part of their greater education. Byron would especially like to thank Tracey, Sammi, and Michelle for allowing him to maintain a sense of perspective when deadlines loom.

Reviewers

John Blackwood, MS, CCAI/CCNA, MCITP:
Enterprise Administrator, MCSE: Security, A+
Associate Professor
Umpqua Community College
Roseburg, Oregon

Mike Fuszner, CCAI
Computer Networking
Cisco Networking Academy
St. Charles Community College
Cottleville, Missouri

William E Hilliker, MSCIS, MBA, A+
Assistant Professor
Monroe County Community College
Monroe, Michigan

Pamella Kurtz, MBA
Keiser University, Fort Lauderdale Campus
Fort Lauderdale, Florida

Paulette Sibrel, Associate Professor
Illinois Central College
East Peoria, Illinois

About the Authors

Leon Plesniarski has been building with Microsoft products since 1984. After graduating with a Bachelor in Science in Computer and Electrical Engineering from the University of Manitoba in 1990, he applied his training as a Network Administrator and independent consultant. By 1996, he supplied Microsoft and Novell teaching services for the University of Manitoba Continuing Education Division as a Microsoft Certified Trainer (MCT), Certified Novell Instructor (CNI), and Certified Technical Trainer (CTT). This is where his passion grew for developing new certification course material, focusing his attention on details that enable students to enhance or gain employment.

Since joining Broadview Networks in 2001, he is leading his technical team's efforts to help companies design, deploy, and benefit from Microsoft technology. Leon continues to proudly direct and grow the skills of master consultants and enterprise architects employed at Broadview, students at the next level of applied knowledge. You can reach Leon at leon@broadviewnetworks.ca.

Byron Wright is a partner in Conexion Networks where he designs, implements, and maintains business computing solutions. He started working with Novell NetWare, but now works primarily with Microsoft products. His areas of expertise include network design, network security, Exchange Server, and Windows server and desktop operating systems.

Byron has worked extensively in the technical training industry, teaching courses to hundreds of corporate administrators. He also is a sessional instructor with the University of Manitoba teaching management information systems and networking for the Asper School of Business. Byron has authored and co-authored a number of books on Windows servers, Windows Vista, and Exchange Server, including the Windows Server 2008 Active Directory Resource Kit. You can reach Byron at byron@conexion.ca.

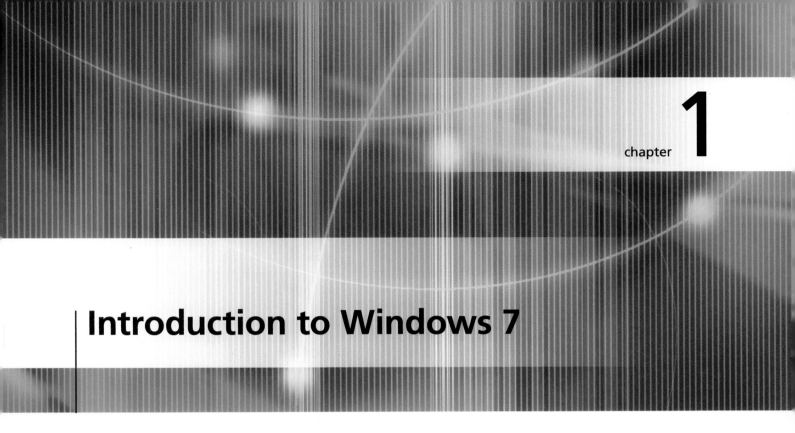

chapter 1

Introduction to Windows 7

After reading this chapter and completing the exercises, you will be able to:

- Describe the versions of Windows 7
- Discuss the new features in Windows 7
- Understand the Windows 7 user interface
- Define the hardware requirements and understand the hardware support of Windows 7
- Describe the application support built in to Windows 7
- Identify essential connectivity applications used in Windows 7
- Understand the networking models supported by different versions of Windows 7

The digital world has changed our lives and our expectations of the world around us. Our day-to-day life is often touched by the digital information created to describe, control, and experience it. More data exists than ever before, and people find themselves overwhelmed as they try to use it.

With its latest client operating system, Windows 7, Microsoft safely and reliably connects users with the information they need in the digital world, providing enhanced user interface and operating system features.

Windows 7 is the successor to Microsoft's previous client operating system, Windows Vista. Windows Vista built on the effectiveness of Windows XP and offer improvements in security, data handling, and portability. The computing community was slow to adopt Windows Vista due to the perception that it was slow and too restrictive in its attempts to protect the user. Windows 7 users can use their computers and see fewer security prompts than they did in Windows Vista, yet they are better protected than ever before.

Windows 7 maximizes performance on today's hardware which is very important as new computers no longer fully support Windows XP. For maximum performance, Windows 7 eclipses Windows Vista in many performance categories. These improvements together enable a Windows 7 user to concentrate on using their computer safely and productively.

This chapter outlines the versions of Windows 7 and the features available in each. This information enables users to determine which version is appropriate for their specific needs. The chapter also introduces new and improved features in Windows 7, including the updated user interface, hardware requirements, and system hardware support. Updated features for application support, connectivity applications, and enhanced networking models are also covered in the chapter.

Windows 7 Versions

Windows 7 is available in different versions to meet different consumer requirements. A consumer can upgrade from one version to another to get the extra features found in enhanced versions. Retail versions support this feature, called Windows Anytime Upgrade. The installed retail version has full support for all retail editions of Windows 7 already built-in. If the user purchases an upgrade key they can unlock an upgraded edition of Windows 7 on the computer in about 10 minutes.

If Windows 7 is pre-installed from the factory by the Original Equipment Manufacturer (OEM) of the computer, the Windows 7 license is tied to that computer hardware. This limits the operating system upgrade and downgrade rights to the terms specified by the OEM Windows 7 license. OEM licenses of Windows 7 are not transferable to new computer hardware.

In corporate environments, Windows 7 licenses may be purchased in bulk by purchasing a Volume License (VL) that entitles upgrades of computers with an existing operating system to a volume licensed version of Windows 7. Volume licensing has rules and limits that are subject to change, therefore the upgrade terms should be researched at the time of the sale.

The four mainstream versions of Windows 7 are:

- Windows 7 Home Premium
- Windows 7 Professional
- Windows 7 Enterprise
- Windows 7 Ultimate

Several additional specialized versions of Windows 7 are:

- Windows 7 Starter
- Windows 7 Home Basic
- Windows 7 N & K Editions

General descriptions of each product and new Windows 7 features are provided in the following sections.

Windows 7 Home Premium

Windows 7 Home Premium concentrates on enabling the home user to enjoy a rich productive multimedia experience. Business enhancements such as encrypted files, joining a domain, and processing Group Policy settings are not available unless the operating system is upgraded to a business-grade edition. This version includes the following:

- Full Aero interface
- Multiple monitors
- Support for up to 2 physical CPUs
- 32-bit and 64-bit versions
- 64-bit version supports up to 16 GB RAM
- Support for tablet PCs and MultiTouch controls
- Display personalization
- Desktop enhancements
- Windows Media Center capabilities
- Creation and use of HomeGroups
- Windows Mobility Center
- Network printing
- Internet Connection Sharing
- Fast user switching
- Games

Windows 7 Professional

In a corporate environment, the enhanced manageability of Windows 7 Professional allows a business to simplify its operations and concentrate on doing business. This version includes the features of Window 7 Home Premium and additionally:

- 64-bit version supports up to 192 GB RAM
- Multi-user fast switching
- Remote Desktop hosting
- Support for domain networking
- Location aware printing
- Dynamic disks
- Encryption File System
- Windows XP Mode with Windows Virtual PC
- Volume licensing

Windows 7 Enterprise

Windows 7 Enterprise is available only to customers who purchase **Software Assurance (SA)** from Microsoft. Software Assurance is available to medium- and large-scale customers who purchase Microsoft products at a volume level.

This version includes the features found in Windows 7 Professional and adds:

- Multiple Language User Interface for companies spanning the globe
- UNIX-based application support

- BitLocker Drive Encryption
- Enhancements to remote corporate data access

Windows 7 Ultimate

Windows 7 Ultimate provides the same feature set as Windows 7 Enterprise, combining all of the features of a home and business operating system. This is the only retail edition that provides functionality that is closely matched to Windows 7 Enterprise. There are no extra features added exclusively to Windows 7 Ultimate; however, the games included with the operating system are enabled in this edition by default.

Windows 7 Starter

The Windows 7 Starter edition is limited in features and reduced in cost to make it more attractive to buyers of computers with reduced hardware specifications. Types of computers commonly sold with the Starter edition are netbook computers. A netbook computer typically does not have a DVD drive, the CPU is limited to 32-bit processing, and the graphic capabilities are limited.

To lower the overall computer price point, some licensed software features are removed from the operating system. One example of this is software used to decode media played from a DVD. This limitation exists in the operating system by design, even if the hardware supports the ability to play DVD video.

One important limitation has been removed from this Starter edition. Previous versions restricted the user to only run 3 applications at the same time. If the user wanted to run another application they had to close one of those already open. Windows 7 Starter edition lets you run as many applications as possible, and desired, on the given computer hardware.

This version does not include:

- Aero Glass interface
- Support for multiple monitors
- DVD playback
- Ability to join a corporate network domain
- Ability to create a HomeGroup network
- Ability to personalize the display background, color scheme
- Windows Media Center and media streaming
- Windows XP Mode with Windows Virtual PC
- 64-bit version
- Support for more than two physical CPUs

Windows 7 Starter cannot be bought separately as a retail version; it can only be pre-installed by the manufacturer of the computer. It can be upgraded to a full retail version of Windows 7 if the user is willing to pay the upgrade price.

Windows 7 Home Basic

In some developing countries the marketplace needs an operating system capable of running on limited hardware at a competitive price point. Building on the features of the Windows 7 Starter edition, the Windows 7 Home Basic edition adds more functionality. Partial Aero functionality is added as well as multiple monitor support, Windows Mobility Center, network printing and Internet connection sharing. A 64-bit version is available but it is restricted to support a maximum of 8 GB of RAM.

The Windows 7 Home Basic edition is available from the original computer manufacturer and as a retail purchase, but it is not available for sale in developed countries such as Canada and the United States of America. It is designed to activate only in the countries it was meant to be sold in and not to operate if it detects it is outside of those countries.

Windows 7 N & K Editions

The N releases are sold in countries that do not allow Microsoft to bundle in Windows Media Player and other media software as part of the operating system. This is required by court rulings to allow fair competition for vendors who write similar software. Windows Media Player can still be freely downloaded and installed on this Windows edition by the user if desired.

The K releases are only sold in South Korea and also have some features, such as Windows Media Player, removed as well.

New and Enhanced Features of Windows 7

Microsoft has added several new and improved features to Windows 7 that make it more secure, reliable, and easier to use than earlier Windows operating systems. Not all features are available in all versions of Windows 7. The customer can buy the minimum version of Windows 7 that has the desired features. If the customer's needs expand they can upgrade to a different version to obtain the extra features. Several of these important features are:

- 32- and 64-bit Computing Support
- Aero
- .NET Framework 3.5
- Speech Recognition
- Internet Explorer 8
- User Account Control
- Fast User Switching Enhancements
- Windows Driver Foundation
- Repair and Restart Improvements
- Rapid Deployment
- Windows BitLocker Drive Encryption
- Trusted Platform Modules Services
- Network Connectivity

To help introduce some of these features and prepare for later chapters, you will now install Windows 7.

Activity 1-1: Installing Windows 7

Time Required: 30 to 60 minutes
Objective: Install Windows 7

Description: You have just received a new copy of Windows 7. You are considering deploying Windows 7 for your organization. To sell the management team on implementing Windows 7, you need to install the system and provide a demonstration of the new features. In this activity, you will install Windows 7 on your computer.

Your instructor may give you some additional steps to perform if the Windows 7 installation requires additional storage drivers.

1. Ensure that your computer is configured to boot from a DVD. The boot configuration of your computer is configured in the BIOS of your computer. Refer to the BIOS documentation specific to the computer to determine the steps to complete this requirement.

Many newer computers will boot from the DVD drive automatically if there is no operating system installed on the system's hard disk.

2. Place your Windows 7 DVD in the DVD drive of your computer.

3. Restart your computer.

4. If directed by the start-up screen, press any key to boot from DVD. This message will appear only if the hard drive has an existing bootable partition.

5. The system will proceed to load the first part of the installation program. When the Install Windows screen appears confirm the installation language, time and currency format, and keyboard layout are correct then click **Next**.

6. Click **Install now**.

7. Select the **I accept the license terms** check box, and click **Next**.

8. Click **Custom**. This is required to perform a new installation.

9. The next screen asks the question: "Where do you want to install Windows?". Click **Drive options (advanced)** to perform disk partitioning operations.

10. If necessary, install additional disk drivers as described by your instructor.

11. If there are any existing partitions, delete each partition using the following steps:

    a. Click the partition to select it.

    b. Click **Delete**.

    c. Click **OK** to confirm that you understand that all data on the partition will be deleted.

12. Examine the number in the **Free Space** column.

13. Click **Disk 0 Unallocated Space** and click **New**.

14. In the **Size** text box, enter a value that is no less than **30000** and that leaves at least 8 GB of disk space unallocated, and then click **Apply**.

15. In the warning window, click **OK** to acknowledge that additional partitions may be created. Windows 7 automatically creates a 100 MB system partition to support the use of BitLocker and other tools.

16. Click **Disk 0 Partition 2** to select it, and then click **Format**.

17. Click **OK** to confirm that all data on the partition will be lost when it is formatted. There is no data on this partition at this time.

18. If necessary, click **Disk 0 Partition 2** to select it, and click **Next**. Windows now copies system files to the hard drive, reboots, performs additional configuration tasks, reboots one or more times, and then asks for user input again. This portion of the installation takes up to 30 minutes. When your computer reboots, do not press a key to start from the DVD.

19. Under Type a user name, type **User**x, where x is a number assigned to you by your instructor.

20. Note that the computer name has already been filled in based on the user name and then click **Next**.

21. In the Type a password and Retype your password boxes, type **password**.

22. In the Type a password hint box, type **The password is listed in Activity 1-1** and then click **Next**.

23. If prompted to enter a product key, type the product key supplied by your instructor, clear the **Automatically activate Windows when I'm online** check box, and click **Next**. Note that this step is only necessary with some distributions of Windows 7.

24. Click **Use recommended settings**. This configures Windows 7 to automatically download and install updates.

25. Configure the correct time zone for your location, configure the correct time for your location, and click **Next**.

26. Windows 7 will attempt to enable network connections to establish connectivity to the Internet. Click **Public network** to select your computer's current location. This secures your network connection.

27. Wait for Windows 7 to prepare your desktop. This may take a few minutes.

28. After Windows 7 starts, Windows Update will complete installing updates. After the updates are successfully installed, click **Restart now**.

29. In the Password box, type **password**, and press **Enter**. When you log on for the first time a new profile is created for the user. This process may take a few minutes.

30. Click the **Start** button, and click the **Shut down** button.

32-Bit and 64-Bit Computing Support

Windows 7 comes in both 32-bit and 64-bit processor versions. The 32-bit version is limited to addressing 4 GB of RAM. If a computer has more RAM than 4 GB, the extra will not be available to the 32-bit edition. The 64-bit version is becoming popular as users are running applications that demand more RAM than the 32-bit version can use.

Depending on the version of Windows 7, the 64-bit editions can support up to 192 GB of RAM. The practical limit to how much RAM can be installed in a computer is usually a limit of the computer hardware design. Server class computers may support adding more RAM than desktop computers, but they will likely not support the installation of Windows 7 as an operating system. A better choice for server class computers is a server class operating system such as Windows Server 2008 R2.

The 64-bit version of Windows 7 has a greater theoretical limit for processing data, which may allow it to complete calculations faster than a 32-bit version, even on the same computer hardware.

Not all software and hardware is compatible with the 32-bit and 64-bit editions. Microsoft has created two tools to help the user decide if their existing computer system supports Windows 7, Windows 7 Upgrade Advisor and the Windows 7 Compatibility Center.

The Windows 7 Upgrade Advisor is a utility that can be downloaded from Microsoft to analyze the suitability of a computer to run Windows 7. It will report any issues it discovers with hardware and installed applications. The report gives a user the chance to address those issues before Windows 7 is freshly installed, or before the existing operating system is upgraded to Windows 7. Because the utility is examining all hardware it can find, make sure all devices that are typically connected to the computer are connected and turned on before the utility runs.

The Windows 7 Compatibility Center is a Web site that lists thousands of hardware and software products and their compatibility with Windows 7. Each product is separately documented for its compatibility with the 32-bit and 64-bit editions. If the product is not compatible there may be a recommended action listed that will tell the user what to do about it, such as upgrade the application or hardware that they are researching. Links to manufacturer Web sites are provided if updates, downloads, or special instructions are available to the user.

If the user determines that their computer hardware cannot use the 64-bit edition, they can upgrade their hardware or they can use a 32-bit edition of Windows 7 instead.

Aero

The Aero visual theme was first introduced with Windows Vista. Aero has been enhanced and continues to be the standard theme in Windows 7. All versions of Windows 7 except Windows 7 Starter and Windows 7 Home Basic support Aero. A visual theme is a standard look-and-feel that is applied to what you see on the screen, what you hear, and how you navigate between windows. The goal of Aero is to offer a pleasing user experience that is simple, easy to learn, and fun. The use of 3D effects, animation, and transparent visual features, called **Aero Glass** as shown in Figure 1-1, enhances this visually appealing look for Windows 7 and Windows applications.

To ensure optimal performance of Aero, Microsoft has limited the use of this advanced theme to computers that have adequate video hardware. The video card must have at least 128 MB of RAM, with 256 MB recommended. The graphics card driver—the software that lets the operating system use the graphics card hardware—must support a minimum of DirectX9.0 and the **Windows Display Driver Model (WDDM)**.

Figure 1-1 Transparent windows in Aero Glass
Courtesy Course Technology/Cengage Learning

For more information about graphics requirements, see the Hardware Requirements and System Hardware Support section later in this chapter.

If a computer does not meet these requirements, the user interface is automatically downgraded to a simpler version. If the user upgrades their graphics hardware, the new enhanced visual theme becomes available. Computers that have the ability to add new AGP and PCI-Express video cards are therefore preferable when purchasing new computers. AGP and PCI Express are different types of hardware expansion slots built in to some computers.

The Aero 3D effects require a great deal of data to be processed. If a computer has a slow video graphics system, the AGP or PCI-Express interface allows you to add a better graphics card. The AGP and PCI-Express expansion slots are high speed and can transfer data quickly between the graphics card and the main system. This helps to create smooth visual transitions. Graphics cards with a dedicated **Graphical Processing Unit (GPU)** allow Windows 7 to assign drawing operations directly to the GPU, freeing the processor for other operations.

.NET Framework 3.5

With the updated Windows look come new rules and methods for application developers to interact with it. Applications written to use the new look and features of Windows 7 use the .NET Framework 3.5 code model. This version comes with Windows 7 by default but new versions of the .NET Framework may be available for download in the future from Microsoft. Service packs and patches are routinely released by Microsoft to add and address features in the .NET Framework.

.NET Framework 3.5 defines multiple **Application Programming Interfaces (API)** that developers use as the programming foundation for their applications. This frees the application's developers from worrying about how their software will directly interact with the hardware or the operating system. The details are all hidden and the programmer can concentrate on their application's functionality instead.

The .NET Framework includes individual components that together provide features for enhanced applications. For example, this includes support for tools, templates, programming language enhancements, and protocols to transfer data. The .NET Framework 3.5 APIs are grouped into feature sets that include:

- Windows Presentation Foundation
- Windows Communication Foundation
- Windows Workflow Foundation
- Windows CardSpace

Windows Presentation Foundation

Applications can draw to the screen using standard methods defined in the Windows Presentation Foundation. The Windows Presentation Foundation (formerly code-named "Avalon") unifies the look and feel of the operating system for developers.

The Windows 7 visual interface offers stunning visual effects, but it also has to be easy for application developers to use. Programmers and applications can manipulate the graphical system with **eXtensible Markup Language (XML)** code, an industry standard used to communicate data.

Information presented to the user has an improved standardized appearance that maximizes its accessibility.

Windows Communication Foundation

Computers are more portable than ever, and people depend on them to safely and reliably connect with information. The boundaries of the computing environment have extended far outside the traditional office building, presenting greater challenges for collaborating with coworkers and partners.

Applications communicate with each other using the standard methods defined in the Windows Communication Foundation. The Windows Communication Foundation (formerly code-named "Indigo") enables applications to send messages to each other.

This API is used in Windows 7 for communication between standardized Web services, peer-to-peer sharing features, **Really Simple Syndication (RSS)** support, and new core networking services. It connects users and their applications to the services they need, when they need them, anywhere over a network.

Windows Workflow Foundation

The Windows Workflow Foundation allows developers to build applications that follow a logical sequence of events. The sequence of events, or workflow, a user takes to complete a task is guided by the business logic based on what they need to accomplish. The Windows Workflow Foundation is a programming model that allows developers to quickly build workflow-enabled applications. As multiple applications share in the processing of data, the Windows Workflow Foundation can help answer the question of "What happens next?"

Windows CardSpace Applications communicating across networks need to ensure the user's identity is protected. Windows CardSpace is a part of the .NET Framework 3.5 model that protects a user's digital identities. Windows CardSpace allows for applications to keep track of a user's security credentials (user ID and password) for one or more security systems. Each set of credentials becomes one information card assigned to the user. Windows CardSpace is specifically hardened to prevent identity theft and spoofing (pretending to be someone else).

Speech Recognition

Windows 7 includes a speech recognition system to add an input method beyond the keyboard and mouse. The speech recognition system is trainable, supports spoken corrections, and supports multiple languages. Commands to perform typical Windows operations such as starting programs and closing windows are built in.

Older applications designed to be accessible with Windows will inherit these basic speech recognition controls from the operating system without needing to be updated. Newer applications that are compatible with Windows 7's speech recognition system can offer enhanced dictation and input features.

Internet Explorer 8

The newest version of Internet Explorer is available with Windows 7. It includes many new features such as enhanced private browsing, Compatibility View, and Accelerators.

Internet Explorer 8 enhances the security of Internet browsing by restricting access to the operating system by default. This protected mode prevents malicious Web sites from damaging the user's system or settings.

User Account Control

Windows 7 has redefined the security levels that are available to grant access and control to user accounts (formerly User Account Protection). In older Windows operating systems, user accounts with limited access and control were often found to be too restrictive. Attempts to configure security rights that compromised between ordinary users and administrators (like the Power Users group) were not effective or popular.

In most home and business environments security is treated as a nuisance when changes are required for the computer; user accounts are often given permanent full administrative access to the computer. Exploits and malicious code can take advantage of this and make unwanted changes to the system.

The User Account Control system in Windows 7 allows the security level for an account to be fine-tuned, to the degree required, based on how trusted the user and computer environment are.

Instead of using the Run As feature, as found in earlier operating systems, standard users performing an administrative action can be prompted by Windows 7 for administrator approval to complete the action. Even administrators using their own computer are prompted by User Account Control during system-wide changes or suspicious installations to ensure that they are aware of the risk. This can reveal suspicious changes that might otherwise go unnoticed.

To avoid frequent administrative prompts by User Account Control for common user tasks that are not considered risky, Windows 7 has added privileges to the standard user account. The default User Account Control settings allow changes made to Windows settings by the user; however, changes made by applications will trigger a security prompt.

Activity 1-2: Limited Permissions for Users

Time Required: 15 minutes
Objective: Observe how users are prompted when performing administrative actions

Description: In this activity, you will change system settings relating to time to see which changes will cause Windows 7 to prompt for permission to make the change.

1. Start your computer and log on as **User*x*,** where *x* is the student number assigned by your instructor.

2. Click the **Start** button and click **Control Panel.**

3. In Control Panel, click **User Accounts and Family Safety.**

4. In the User Accounts and Family Safety window, click **User Accounts.**

5. In the User Accounts window, click **Change User Account Control settings.**

6. If the User Account Control dialog box appears, click the **Yes** button.

7. Note the slider control and its current position between the Always notify and Never notify settings. In the box next to the slider control Windows will display an explanation of what the current setting will do. Move the slider to each setting and note the description for each setting.

8. Move the slider up to the setting closest to **Always notify.**

9. Click the **OK** button. When the User Account Control dialog box appears click the **Yes** button.

10. On the left side of the User Accounts window, click **Control Panel Home** to return to the list of Control Panel options.

11. In Control Panel click **Clock, Language, and Region.**

12. In the Clock, Language, and Region window, click **Set the time and date.**

13. Make sure the Date and Time tab is selected.

14. Click the **Change time zone** button.

15. Note the time zone listed on the screen.

16. Note the clock time displayed at the bottom right of the screen.

17. Using the Time Zone drop-down menu, select a time zone that is different than the one currently selected.

18. Click the **OK** button to apply your changes. Notice that you are not prompted for permission to make this change.

19. Notice the new time displayed on the clock.

20. Reset your time zone back to its initial setting.

21. Make sure the **Date and Time** tab is selected.

22. Note that the Change Date and Time button has a shield displayed on the button. The shield indicates that this option is protected by User Account Control. Click the **Change date and time** button.

23. Notice that you are prompted by User Account Control for permission to make this change. Click the **Yes** button.

24. Change the time to add one hour to the current time. Click the **OK** button to save your change.

25. Notice that the system clock has changed.

26. Repeat the steps required to reset the time back one hour. Notice that you are prompted again for permission to make the change.

27. Close the **Date and Time** window.

28. Using the steps earlier in this exercise, return to User Accounts and change the User Account Control settings back to the default setting using the slider control. Save your changes by clicking **OK** button. Note that until this setting is saved, you are still prompted by User Account Control to accept the change. Click the **Yes** button to accept the change.

29. On the left side of the User Accounts window, click **Control Panel Home** to return to the list of Control Panel options.

30. In the Control Panel, click **Clock, Language, and Region**

31. In the Clock, Language, and Region window, click **Set the time and date**.

32. Make sure the Date and Time tab is selected.

33. Click the **Change date and time** button. Note that you are not prompted by User Account Control even though the button displays a shield. The default User Account Control setting does not prompt for Windows changes you make.

34. Click the **OK** button to close the Date and Time Settings window.

35. Close the Date and Time window. Close the Control Panel.

36. Click the **Start** button and type **CMD** into the *Search programs and files* search box. Press **Enter** to accept the found program which will start a command window.

37. In the command window, type the command **DISKPART** and press **Enter**.

38. Note that you are prompted by User Account Control to allow the program to make changes to your computer. Click **No**. Note that the command window displays the message "Access is denied." The default User Account Control setting prompts if a program attempts to change Window's settings.

39. Close the command window.

Fast User Switching Enhancements

User Account Control allows users to have more specific limits and greater freedoms within their own environment. But what if multiple people share a single computer? Users complain that it takes too long to switch users. They must shut down all applications, log out, log in as a different user, and then start a new set of applications. Windows XP introduced fast user switching, which is the ability for multiple users to log in to the same computer at the same time. The users can then toggle between themselves without having to log out or close applications.

With fast user switching, a user can lock their computing session and leave the computer. The session is preserved with their applications and data still running. Another user can securely connect and start a new session with different applications and data files open. The operating system protects and isolates one user's session from the other. A password is required to access and switch to a session left running. As users come and go, they can securely toggle between running sessions. A user can log out and leave the other sessions up and running for someone else to use.

Windows XP offered fast user switching in workgroup mode only. At home and in the small office, Windows XP users can operate in a workgroup setting using peer-to-peer methods to share files and printers. Windows Vista and 7 supports fast user switching in both the workgroup mode and the domain mode.

 For more information on workgroups and domains, see the "Networking Models" section later in this chapter.

In larger networks, computers are joined to a domain managed by central servers. Windows XP does not offer fast user switching in a domain environment. To allow generic workstation access for many users, companies typically create a single login account and all workers sharing the computer use that single account to log in.

Security settings for the single account represent a collection of security access levels based on the users that will share that account. Using this generic account facilitates multiple users' ability to work with the computer, but this compromise can grant some users more access than they require.

Windows 7 allows fast user switching even when the computer is joined to the domain. Users can securely toggle between domain accounts running simultaneously on the computer. Each account can run its own set of applications and security levels.

Activity 1-3: Fast User Switching

Time Required: 25 minutes
Objective: Observe how Windows 7 can switch between multiple user accounts running at the same time

Description: In this activity, you will create a new user account and observe how Windows 7 can manage more than one user account running at the same time.

1. If necessary, start your computer and log on.
2. Click the **Start** button and click **Control Panel**.
3. Under **User Accounts and Family Safety,** click **Add or remove user accounts**.
4. In the Manage Accounts window, click the **Create a new account** link.
5. Enter the name **Bob** in the New account name field.
6. Click the **Administrator** option button to make the account an administrator instead of a standard user.
7. Click the **Create Account** button.
8. Click the newly created icon that represents the user **Bob**.
9. Click the **Create a password** link.
10. In the New password field, enter the word **password**.
11. In the Confirm new password field, enter the word **password**.
12. Notice the statement on the screen that cautions the user that passwords are case sensitive.
13. In the Type a password hint field, enter the phrase **Just a simple password**.
14. Click the **Create password** button.
15. Close the **Change an Account** window.
16. Click the **Start** button, click **All Programs** and then click the **Accessories** folder.
17. Click **Notepad** on the menu.
18. Enter some random text into the Notepad editor.
19. Click the **Start** button, and click the arrow to the right of the shut down button, at the bottom right of the menu.
20. From the pop-up menu click **Switch User**.
21. Click the user icon named **Bob**.
22. Do not enter the correct password, but click on the arrow to attempt a logon. Notice that you are prompted that the credentials are not correct.
23. Click **OK** to close the error screen.
24. Notice the password hint is now displayed below the password entry box.
25. Enter the correct password of **password** and press **Enter** to log on. Because the user Bob has never logged in to this computer before a new user profile is created for the Bob user account. This may take a few minutes to complete.
26. Notice that Notepad is not currently running.
27. Click the **Start** button, and click the arrow to the right of the shut down button, at the bottom right of the menu.

28. From the pop-up menu, click **Switch User**.

29. Notice that the user selection screen now shows the phrase Logged on below those users that are currently logged on to the computer.

30. Click **User***x* and enter the password of **password** to log on again as your original account. Notice that Notepad is still running.

31. Click the **Start** button, and click the arrow to the right of the shut down button, at the bottom right of the menu.

32. From the pop-up menu, click **Log Off**. Notice that Notepad was left running. Notepad will prompt you to save your changes. Windows 7 will only wait for a brief time before displaying a screen that identifies applications that are interfering with the log off process. Click the **Cancel** button to abort the log off process.

33. Close **Notepad** without saving changes.

34. Log off using the steps detailed earlier in the activity. Because all applications are closed before you attempt to log off you are not prompted while the log off process completes.

35. Notice that the phrase **Logged on** no longer appears below the **User***x* icon.

36. Log off the **Bob** account.

Windows Driver Foundation

Windows 7 supports the **Windows Driver Foundation (WDF)** architecture that replaces the older **Windows Driver Model (WDM)** common to earlier Windows operating systems. WDF allows for greater improvements in device driver stability and performance.

WDM and WDF are standard methods used to define how device driver software operates. Device driver software controls how a piece of hardware can be used by the operating system. A poorly written device driver can lead to disaster by causing the operating system to malfunction and halt (crash).

WDM has evolved over time into a complex and difficult architecture where drivers spend much of their time interacting with the operating system instead of the hardware. Mistakes made by driver authors can lead to corruption and crashes at the core, or kernel, of the operating system. The kernel is a critical part of the operating system that directly manages how software interacts with the computer's hardware.

The operating system limits a driver's access to hardware and memory. Driver software has access to the computer's hardware at two distinct levels—kernel and user mode. Kernel mode drivers have direct access to all hardware and memory. Most hardware drivers for older Windows operating systems are kernel mode drivers. A kernel mode driver has the ability to corrupt memory and disable hardware, completely crashing the operating system.

User mode drivers have restricted access and must pass a request to the operating system to make a change to hardware. A driver that operates in user mode cannot directly crash the operating system. If a user mode driver crashes, the rest of the operating system is left intact. Unfortunately, drivers written to operate at the restricted user level in earlier Windows operating systems have no standard architecture such as WDM. This limits how such drivers interact with plug and play hardware or power management systems.

User mode driver architecture is defined under WDF, in addition to kernel mode drivers. If the user mode driver fails, it can be restarted without causing the core, or kernel, of the operating system to crash with it. Hardware developers can take advantage of the user mode drivers to help guarantee the stability of Windows 7.

The type of device connected to the computer typically guides the device developer's choice of user or kernel mode driver and how it will be used in the computing environment. The greatest improvement with WDF support in Windows 7 is that the developer has a choice.

Another advantage to WDF drivers is their support for distributed computing. As computers expand to include multiple processors and multiple core processors, there is a need to protect the stability of the core operating system while a given task is transferred from one processor to another. Running code must be portable across processors while keeping essential data together. WDF drivers designed for Windows 7 have more abstraction and portability to work specifically in these environments.

Hardware device drivers in WDF can concentrate on the hardware they manage—securely, portably, and in any computing environment.

Repair and Restart Improvements

Many services that fail in Windows 7 are designed to restart automatically without significantly disrupting service to the user. If multiple services depend on each other and one service fails, Windows 7 can restart the affected services without having to reboot the computer.

Windows 7 has improved self-diagnosing features, such as memory and disk diagnostic tools, to help determine why a failure occurred. Enhanced reporting services list pending failures and actions automatically taken to avoid disasters where possible.

If a computer fails to start properly, a tool called the **Startup Repair Tool** can be started by booting a disc with the utility from a CD/DVD drive to assist in the diagnosis and recovery of the system.

The Startup Repair Tool and other Windows 7 diagnostic tools are covered later in this book.

A common repair action is to update applications, drivers, and operating system code. Windows 7 tracks these updates as they are applied and determines when a restart is required. This helps to avoid having to reboot the computer after every update.

Rapid Deployment

Windows 7 uses an efficient strategy to deploy the operating system across many computers. The components are designed to be modular and selectable. The administrator can decide what components to install at the time of installation.

The files used to install Windows 7 are distributed using a Microsoft technology referred to as **Windows Imaging Format (WIM)**.

WIM and its use when installing Windows 7 are covered later in this book.

The files necessary to install Windows 7 or end user applications can be compiled into a single WIM file acting as a library. The files used to install the end user application are considered one image. The files used to install Windows 7 are a second image. These separate images can be combined into one image file to make it easy to distribute both Windows 7 and applications to new computers.

The WIM format offers many benefits when compared to other popular imaging software:

- The contents of the image files can be edited, added to, and deleted directly.
- Updates can be applied directly to the images without first having to install the image on a computer.
- The contents of the image files are typically compressed to save space.
- The WIM format supports single-instance file storage. A file can be referenced in multiple images, but it is only stored once in the image file.
- WIM image files can be deployed from many media types (such as DVD, network share).
- One image file can be used on a variety of computers.
- WIM image files can be used with scripted installations.

Windows BitLocker Drive Encryption

Windows 7 has added security for computers that contain highly confidential data. Windows 7 Ultimate and Windows 7 Enterprise Edition include BitLocker Drive Encryption.

BitLocker Drive Encryption adds the ability to securely encrypt the hard drive's contents at a hardware level. Without the correct pieces in place to decrypt the hard drive, the hard disk by itself is useless. One of those pieces can be an external smart card or memory key (see the "Trusted Platform Module Services" section that follows). If the hard disk is stolen or sold with the data intact, even a skilled professional cannot mine the hard drive and access sensitive data. Windows 7 has extended the BitLocker protection to portable flash memory and external hard drives with a technology called BitLocker To Go. Contents of a portable device can only be encrypted by versions of Windows 7 that fully support BitLocker but any version of Windows 7 can decrypt and read contents if the correct authentication is provided.

Trusted Platform Module Services

Windows 7 includes support for the Trusted Computing Group (*www.trustedcomputinggroup. org*) and its **Trusted Platform Module (TPM)** architecture.

The TPM architecture defines options for adding firmware and hardware to computers to detect low-level tampering before the operating system starts. A computer vendor can build a computer to TPM specifications during its design phase. TPM support is not typically an add-on technology for a computer. If you need TPM support from a computer, it should be one of your criteria when you are comparing computers for purchase.

Optional hardware such as smart cards and USB keys holding digital identification can be used as part of the TPM solution to make sure that stolen computers can't be started or have their hard drive decrypted (see BitLocker Drive Encryption above). The required hardware key must be present to start the computer. BitLocker encryption in Windows 7 only supports the use of TPM version 1.2 and above. If the computer's version of TPM is too old, a firmware upgrade from the computer manufacturer is required to upgrade it, if an upgrade is available.

Since February 2006, many American military and government contracts have required the presence of TPM hardware in computers supplied to departments requiring secure computing.

Network Connectivity

Several features are available that enhance network connectivity. Some of the key networking areas with new features include:

- TCP/IP Networking
- Network Location Awareness Service
- Windows Firewall
- Location Aware Printing

TCP/IP Networking   In Windows 7 the standard protocol for computers to format and exchange data across a network is TCP/IP. TCP/IP is a global protocol that defines several key networking architecture features. For example, it defines how computers identify themselves with an address and how data is broken into blocks of data called packets and delivered between computers.

TCP/IP networking is enhanced in Windows 7 to support a newer version of TCP/IP, IPv6. The older standard of IPv4 has been the most commonly implemented form of TCP/IP. IPv4 suffers from a lack of features that limit what applications and computers can accomplish. The only way to eliminate those limits is to use the enhanced IPv6 standard.

TCP/IP network settings used by Windows 7 are covered later in this book.

Not all computers that support TCP/IP support IPv6. In those cases where people want to use new features enabled by IPv6, such as HomeGroups, they may have to consider how they will upgrade and implement translation systems between IPv4 and IPv6. To understand IPv6, IT administrators will have to learn new IP addressing techniques, translation tools, and network protocols.

Knowing that it will take time for network systems to change from IPv4 to IPv6, Microsoft has provided a software client to support IPv4 to IPv6 translation called Teredo. The Teredo client is supported in all versions of Windows Vista, Windows 7, and Windows Server 2003 SP1 plus later server editions.

Network Location Awareness Service

Computer networks have become more complicated and variable. The operating system and its applications must be aware of the networks around them. One computer can have more than one network available to send and receive data from. An application may require only one of those connected networks, and it should avoid the others.

To help application designers, the **Network Location Awareness Service (NLA)** is available in Windows 7. Applications can track what network services are available using the NLA service as a central reference.

Not only can applications use the service to be aware of available networks, but NLA can also report the status and performance of each network. This enables applications to adapt to changing networks. Applications can change which network they are using if a change in network services is reported. If network performance increases or drops, an application could alter the quantity of data it tries to transfer to better match the link speed and the user's experience.

When a new network connection is enabled, it is assigned one of four network locations types, also known as network location profiles, which categorize its location and applicable settings. The four network locations are Home, Work, Public, and Domain. The Home network is trusted and Windows allows your computer and devices to be seen by other computers on that network. The Work network allows the computer to be seen on the network but disables some networking features only required in a home network. Public networks are not trusted and the computer is hidden as well as possible on that network. Domain networks are a special type of Work network where settings are managed by corporate administrators and cannot be changed locally. If the network location profile for a new network connection is not obvious, Windows 7 will prompt the user to identify which one to use.

When a computer had multiple network connections in Windows Vista, all connection shared the same active network location profile. For example, if a computer had two network connections—one wireless connection to a Public network and one wired connection to a Home network—the user could only select one network profile to apply to both. In that case, if the user selected a Home network profile, their computer could be insecure on the wireless Public network. In Windows 7 each network connection can have its own network location profile, and they do not need to be the same one.

Windows Firewall

The Windows firewall software is enhanced to restrict network connections in both directions—incoming and outgoing. Each type of network location profile in Windows 7 can have its own customized Windows firewall settings. Older versions of Windows firewall would restrict connections that started from outside the computer. The new firewall also allows the administrator to restrict connections that start from the computer itself. Connections can be defined as permitted or restricted when traffic is inspected by the Windows firewall. Windows Firewall settings can be configured as part of an administrative policy and applied throughout an organization.

The Windows Firewall is covered later in this book.

Location Aware Printing

Most computers only use a single network connection at a time. As the user moves from home to work, or to a public location like an airport, their computer connects to a new network location each time, Windows 7 can assign a new default printer based on the network location when the network connection is established. Once printers are mapped to locations, Windows automatically configures the default printer. This is an optional enhancement supported in Windows 7 Professional, Enterprise, and Ultimate Editions. If this is not desirable behavior, it can be set to only use one default printer at all times regardless of the active network location.

User Interface

The user interface of Windows 7 has been updated to present a fresh new look for tools used to interact with the operating system. Several new or improved features in this area include:

- Start Menu
- Windows Help and Support
- Search Interface
- Gadgets
- Taskbar
- Notification Area
- Advanced Window Management

Start Menu

The Start Menu made popular by Windows Vista has been changed to present an updated look for the Start button in Windows 7. When the cursor hovers over the start orb a highlight effect is displayed, as shown in Figure 1-2.

Figure 1-2 The Start button
Courtesy Course Technology/Cengage Learning

When browsing the Start Menu, as shown in Figure 1-3, two columns of information are displayed. The right-hand column identifies the currently logged in user at the top and lists a series of useful links to the user's data folders and common system tools below that. The shutdown icon at the bottom of the column has been replaced with a button that displays the default action using text, eliminating the uncertainty of what will happen if the button is clicked. Clicking on the arrow next to the shutdown button will present a full menu of applicable shutdown commands to choose from.

A key goal of the Start Menu is to stop the menu from sprawling across the user's screen as they navigate from one level of program listings to another. As the user moves from one level to another, the list above the Start button is replaced with the next selected level's program icons. To go back one level, the user can select the Back menu option. If a Start menu item has an arrow shown to the right of its name, then it has a Jump List associated with it.

Jump Lists are a new feature introduced in Windows 7 that identify what content was recently opened by that application, or what content is automatically linked to the menu item. If a user clicks on an item on the Jump List the content or listed application is opened. When the cursor is moved over a Start menu item with a Jump List, the right-hand side of the Start menu is widened and replaced with the associated Jump List. If nothing is selected and the cursor is moved, the right-hand side of the Start menu returns to its normal appearance.

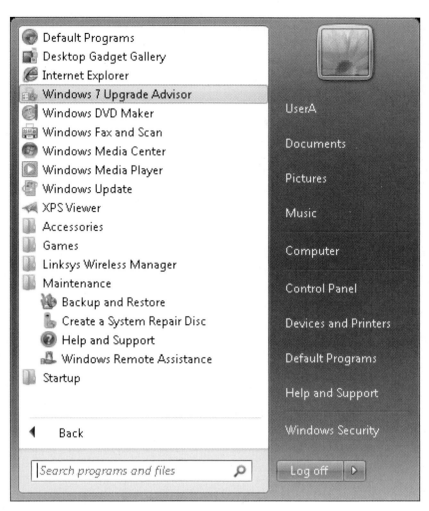

Figure 1-3 Browsing the Start Menu
Courtesy Course Technology/Cengage Learning

Windows Help and Support

Windows Help and Support is designed to include more methods in one utility to help users find the solution they need. This includes the ability to search for help content on the local computer (Figure 1-4) and when connected to the Internet. Additional information is collected from Windows Assistance Online.

If users can't find the solution they need, the Help and Support interface allows them to:

- Initiate a Remote Assistance call
- Post a question to a newsgroup
- Search other databases
- Look up phone numbers for Microsoft support

Search Interface

A search tool is tied in to all areas of the user interface. The search tool can be launched from the Start menu and from any computer browser window, as shown in Figure 1-5.

Gadgets

Windows 7 allows the user to add Gadgets to the desktop (shown in Figure 1-6) as helpful tools to aid the user. A Gadget is considered a mini-application that will provide information, perform

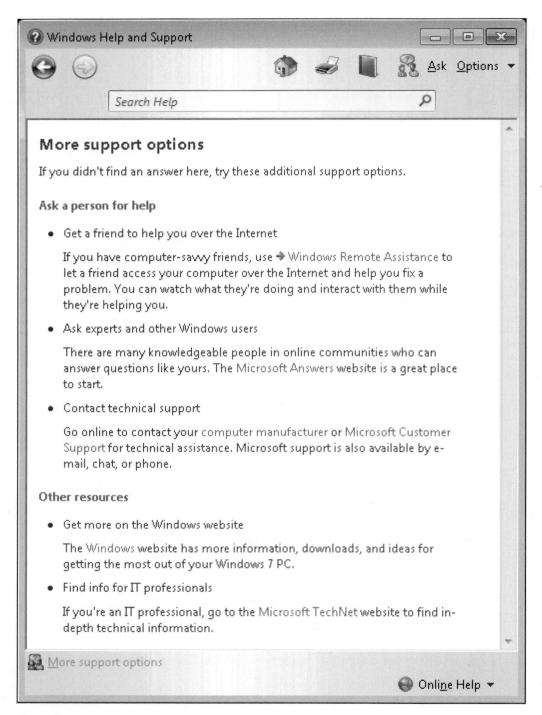

Figure 1-4 Help and Support window
Courtesy Course Technology/Cengage Learning

a useful task, or link to enhanced Web services such as RSS. In Windows Vista a Gadget could only be displayed using a special utility called the Sidebar. Windows 7 no longer uses the Sidebar application since a Gadget can now be placed anywhere on the desktop.

Gadgets are covered later in this book.

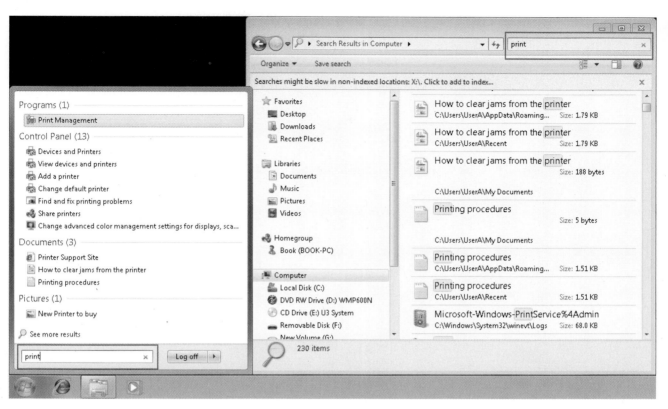

Figure 1-5 Search interface
Courtesy Course Technology/Cengage Learning

Taskbar

The taskbar is a horizontal bar located at the bottom of the screen by default. It contains the Start button to the left and the notification area to the right. In the middle is an area to keep track of open windows (see Figure 1-7).

When multiple windows are open, the screen can get cluttered and screens overlap each other. To organize what windows are open, a button is placed on the taskbar with an icon representing the running application. Note that there is no text included with the icon on the taskbar. Hovering the mouse over an icon will list the windows that application has open. Clicking on one of the names in the list will activate that window and bring it to the front of all other windows.

If the Aero interface is active, instead of a simple list, a preview of each window the application has open will be displayed above the taskbar button. By hovering the cursor over a preview window, all windows will become transparent and only that window will be shown on the desktop. This is known as the Aero Peek feature, where a user can conveniently peek at an active window without having to fully switch to it. If the mouse is moved away from the preview window without selecting it, the desktop will go back to as it was before the preview. If the user clicks on the preview window that window comes to the front of all other windows.

Taskbar buttons can represent a shortcut to an application, even if it isn't actively running. Application icons can be pinned to the taskbar and Start menu to make it easy to launch a popular application. When an application icon is pinned to the taskbar, it does not have an outlined box drawn around the taskbar button. Once it is used to open a window, the outlined box will appear around the taskbar button. When all of the application's windows are closed, the outlined box will disappear and the icon will remain on the taskbar. If an application is not pinned to the taskbar the taskbar button for that application will disappear when all of that application's windows are closed.

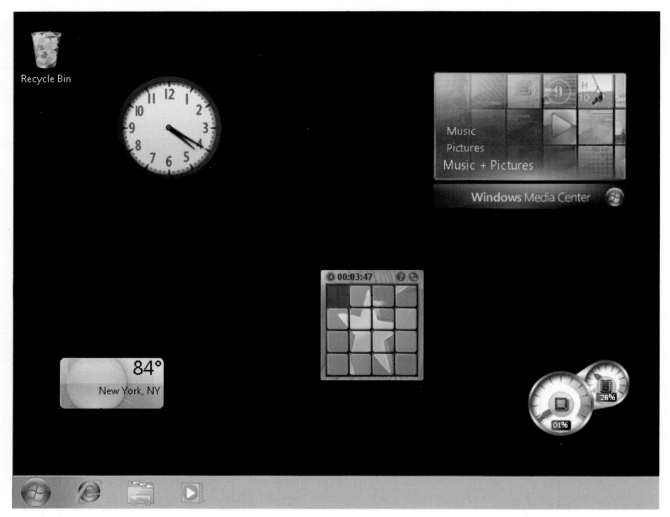

Figure 1-6 Gadgets on the desktop
Courtesy Course Technology/Cengage Learning

Notification Area

The notification area is located to the right of the taskbar in the bottom right-hand side of the Windows 7 screen (see Figure 1-8). In previous versions of Windows this area was called the system tray. Many users complained that the area could easily get cluttered with notifications and icons from multiple applications and the operating system. The notification area has been simplified by default to display the clock and icons for volume, network connectivity, power, and Action Center notifications.

The Action Center notifications list important operating system messages in one convenient place. The user should periodically check this area to see if there are new notifications of problems or solutions that Windows 7 has discovered.

Other applications can add icons to the notification area, but they are not displayed automatically. The extra icons are viewed by clicking the up-arrow icon at the left-hand side of the notification area. A window will pop up to display other notification icons that may be active. Control panel settings can be used to change what icons are displayed in the notification area.

Advanced Window Management

Individual windows can be difficult to organize on the screen. To help with this, Windows 7 has an advanced window management features called Snap and Shake.

Snap allows windows to quickly be resized by having the user click on the title bar of the window and drag it to the top, sides, or middle of the screen. If the window is dragged to the top of

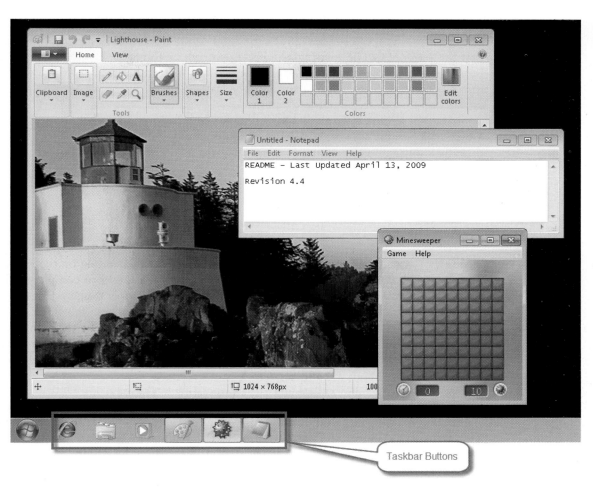

Figure 1-7 Windows taskbar
Courtesy Course Technology/Cengage Learning

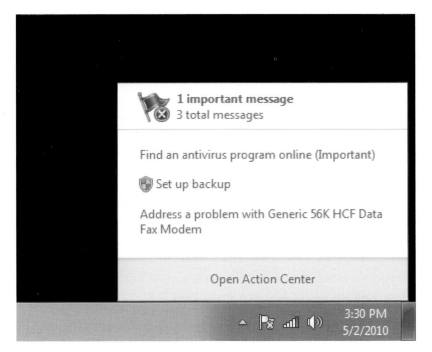

Figure 1-8 Taskbar notification area
Courtesy Course Technology/Cengage Learning

the screen, an outline will be drawn showing that the window will be resized to fill the screen. If the window is dragged to the right or left sides of the screen, an outline will be drawn showing that the window will be resized to fill half the screen on that side. If the window is left inside the borders of the screen it will resume the last size and shape it had before being docked to a side or top of the screen. Note that it is not until the user lets go of the mouse button that the screen will actually resize and lock itself into position.

Shake is a feature only available in versions of Windows 7 that are using the Aero theme. If a user clicks on the title bar of a window and shakes the mouse from side to side, all other windows will automatically minimize. Repeating the shake will restore all other windows to their original size and location.

Hardware Requirements and System Hardware Support

Windows 7 is designed to provide a different look and feel depending on the version of the operating system and the capabilities of the system's hardware. A user or company only has to purchase the version and hardware they require. If desired, the operating system can be upgraded from one version to another if the need for enhanced features arises.

The degree to which a computer can be upgraded is determined by the manufacturer and its consideration for expandability and upgradeability. It is the consumer's responsibility to make sure the features of the computer they buy can be changed or expanded, or to determine that a nonupgradeable system will suit their needs.

Consumers have many computers and components to choose from. How do they know what will work with Windows 7? Microsoft has tried to simplify the choice by creating a testing program for computer hardware. Component manufacturers that want their product to be tested with Windows 7 can submit their solution to the **Windows Hardware Quality Labs (WHQL)**. After it is thoroughly tested and deemed compatible, their solution will be publicly catalogued and recognized by Microsoft.

In the past, Microsoft maintained a **Hardware Compatibility List (HCL)** to keep track of which products would work with each operating system. The HCL was replaced with the Windows Catalog Web sites for products newer than Windows NT 4. Server class operating systems still have certified products listed on the Web at *www.windowsservercatalog.com*.

Legacy HCL lists and links to current compatibility Web sites, including Windows 7, can be found at *www.microsoft.com/whdc/hcl/*.

To help shoppers differentiate products, Microsoft has incorporated a logo program as part of the WHQL testing process. A vendor can display special "Compatible with Windows 7" logos on their hardware and software packaging to help the consumer make a better choice.

To add security and validity to the tested solutions, Microsoft will also include digital signatures as part of the hardware's drivers. Windows 7 will be able to recognize the digital signature and determine if it is safe to trust the driver. In a business environment, administrators can restrict the installation of drivers based on those digital signatures.

Even when a product passes initial testing and gets a Windows 7 logo, it may encounter difficulty and crash as the user adds patches, products, or makes configuration changes to their computer. Microsoft collects this information from the Windows Error Reporting (WER) tool built in to the operating system. When a crash occurs, a summary of what was happening on the computer is compiled and the user is asked if he or she wants to send this to Microsoft. The product's manufacturer can collect this data and find out more about their product stability.

Microsoft compiles a rating system for the manufacturer's drivers that scores how often people have problems with the driver and how many people it impacts. If the manufacturer maintains a low score for too long, Microsoft can revoke their logo status. To assist the manufacturer with distributing a patch, manufacturers who obtain logo status can distribute updated drivers through Windows Update—Microsoft's standard Web site for distributing patches and upgrades.

For WER tool users, the manufacturer can also send back a response to the user pointing them to the manufacturer's Web site for advice and updates.

Table 1-1 lists Window 7's minimum hardware requirements.

Table 1-1   Minimum hardware requirements for Windows 7

System Component	Recommendation
CPU	32- or 64-bit processor, 1 GHz or faster
System RAM	1 GB (2 GB for a computer with a 64-bit CPU)
Disk Space	16 GB for 32-bit editions, 20 GB for 64-bit editions
Video Card Drivers	DirectX 9 graphical processor and WDDM 1.0 (or higher)

Processor Support

Processing support in Windows 7 is designed for modern 32- and 64-bit processors. Processors that do not meet minimum recommendations may still be able to run Windows 7, but with some impact on features, performance, or stability. To enhance the performance of Windows 7, Microsoft has built-in support for several enhanced processor configurations.

Processes and Threads   The actions performed by a **Central Processing Unit (CPU)** are defined by the instructions it is given. Programmers compile a list of instructions to build their applications. These instructions are typically grouped into units of code called **threads**. A thread is spawned, or started, by a process. The process itself is created by the applications and the operating system as they run. Threads and processes are common terms used to describe what the CPU is working on. To visualize what a thread and process represent, consider the following breakdown of an application.

A single application can be described by the tasks it must accomplish. For instance, we can describe the tasks a user is experiencing with a word processing application. The user will open a new document and type in text at the keyboard. The user wants the application to format a visual representation of the document, perform a spell check and grammar check, highlight errors it finds, and periodically save a copy of the text to disk. The word processing application in this case is the process. Formatting, spell check, and saving to disk are each executed by a different thread, or unit of code.

A single program that performs all of these tasks would be difficult to write and hard to maintain. The old DOS operating system ran applications that were essentially one big program with a single process running one thread at a time. To switch between threads, the DOS applications would typically need a trigger, such as the user pressing a key on the keyboard or a signal from the computer's clock. Typically, all of the application's code was written into a single file with a .COM or .EXE file extension. To switch between processes, a user would terminate one application and start another.

With the introduction of Windows, the idea of multitasking became popular. **Multitasking** gives the appearance that the computer is running multiple applications or processes at the same time. The operating system is switching from one thread to another very quickly, giving the illusion that all processes and their threads are running concurrently. In our word processing example, the user can see all those tasks happen at the same time while they type.

Applications designed to run in Windows run as one or more processes. A single **process** in Windows represents a collection of data, files, and instructions with a specific purpose while it is running. One or more application tasks can be assigned to a single process. In our example, the spelling and grammar check with suggested fixes can be part of one process; the auto-save to disk can be part of another.

Processes are typically described in Windows by the application they service, the user who launched them, and other attributes. The operating system uses its own processes to perform system actions such as managing files and network connections.

When a process executes a single task it will run a small block of code, a thread, for that task alone. The programmer decides what a single thread should do. Windows assigns that single thread to the CPU for execution.

For multitasking to work, a single task cannot take over the CPU for an extended period of time. In early versions of Windows, typically Windows 3.X, the applications and the operating system cooperated to share the CPU. This is called **cooperative multitasking**. The problem with this scheme is that a single task could take over the CPU and make it appear that the computer has stopped responding.

Preemptive multitasking was introduced as an improvement over cooperative multitasking in later versions of Windows and is used by Windows 7. This allows a single process to be interrupted by another process, even if the first process has not completed. To control the interruptions, Windows uses a system of priority levels and time windows to control scheduling of the processes and threads.

Each thread is given a window of time to execute in before the operating system checks to see if the CPU should switch to another thread. If the thread has not finished its task, it must wait for its next turn. The time window a thread is allowed to run in is known as a **quantum**. The thread can be preempted by another thread before its quantum is over—even before it has started processing.

To help determine which thread gets to go next, and which threads are allowed to preempt others, the threads and processes are assigned a priority level. The higher the priority level, the greater the chance that the process will preempt the current thread or get the next quantum. If there are no threads that are ready to run, there is an operating system process (the Idle Process) always ready to run.

If a thread is not finished running, perhaps because it had to wait or it was preempted, it is typically restarted on the same processor that previously ran it. This is known as **processor affinity**, where the thread is restricted to which CPU can run it.

When multiple processes and threads are running, it doesn't make sense for a programmer to write all of the instructions for an application into a single file. Windows programs are usually written in a modular nature, with different files holding different pieces of the application. Code modules are saved in **Dynamic Link Library files (DLLs)**. Code modules in the DLLs can be shared between applications. Updates to applications can replace individual DLLs instead of the entire application.

Activity 1-4: Switching between Applications

Time Required: 5 minutes
Objective: Observe how to switch between running applications

Description: In this activity, you will start multiple applications and use the application switcher feature of Windows 7 to quickly change which application is in the foreground.

1. If necessary, start your computer and log on as **User***x***,** where *x* is the student number assigned by your instructor.

2. Start **Notepad** and enter some random text.

3. Start **Internet Explorer** and leave it at the starting page.

4. Hold down the **Alt** key and press the **Tab** key once. Do not release the **Alt** key.

5. Notice that each running application has its active content displayed in a miniature preview window.

6. Press the **Tab** key repeatedly to cycle the highlighted box from one application to the next.

7. Press the **Tab** key until Notepad is highlighted. Release the **Alt** key.

8. Notice that the **Notepad** application becomes the foreground application.

The remainder of the activity requires the Windows Aero interface to be active on your computer.

9. Hold down the **Windows** key on the keyboard and press **Tab** once. Do not release the **Windows** key.

10. Notice that each running application is displayed in a 3D preview window.

11. Press the **Tab** key repeatedly to cycle the 3D windows. Press the **Tab** key until the Notepad window is the top window. Release the **Windows** key.

12. (Optional step). If your mouse has a scroll-wheel control you can test the following. Press the **Windows** and **Tab** keys as in Step 9. While you are holding down the **Windows** key scroll the wheel on the mouse to cycle through the 3D preview windows. Release the **Windows** key when Notepad is the top window.

13. Close all applications without saving any changes and log off.

Activity 1-5: Working with Task Manager

Time Required: 20 minutes
Objective: Observe how to start and stop applications with Task Manager

Description: The operating system is constantly starting and terminating processes as required. The Task Manager tool enables users to monitor and manage this activity. In this activity, you will start Task Manager and use it to start and stop applications and processes. You will see how Task Manager can filter which processes are shown to the user and how to sort the list of running processes.

1. If necessary, start your computer and log on.

2. Start **Notepad** and enter some random text.

3. Start **Internet Explorer** and leave it at the starting page.

4. Right-click the system clock at the bottom right of the screen.

5. Select **Start Task Manager** from the pop-up menu.

6. Notice that if this is the first time Windows Task Manager is opened the **Applications** tab is initially selected. Windows Task Manager will remember the last tab that was opened and make it the default to view the next time the program is launched. If the Applications tab is not already selected click it to select it.

7. Highlight the **Untitled—Notepad** application and then click on the **End Task** button. Note that you are prompted by notepad to save your work. A new window will appear called End Program – Untitled – Notepad. Click the **End Now** button to force Notepad to close.

8. Notice that Notepad is no longer running.

9. In the Windows Task Manager window, click the **New Task . . .** button.

10. In the Open field, enter **notepad** and click on the **OK** button.

11. Notice that Notepad has started in the background and is now listed on the Applications tab. By default the Task Manager window is always displayed on top of all running application windows.

12. Click the **Processes** tab in Windows Task Manager.

13. Click the **Image Name** column header to sort the list of processes by name.

14. Find and highlight the process with the name **notepad.exe**.

15. Right-click the **notepad.exe** process.

16. Notice the pop-up menu items to Set Priority and Set Affinity. . . .

17. Point to the **Set Priority** menu item and notice the options. Do not change the default setting of Normal. The Set Priority option allows you to increase or reduce how often the multitasking system pays attention to that process.

18. Select the **Set Affinity** menu item and notice the options. The Set Affinity option allows you to limit which processors can run the selected process. Click **OK** to close the Processor Affinity window.

If your computer only has a single processor and it does not support hyper-threading or multiple cores (discussed below), the Set Affinity option may not be available. This option may also be unavailable if Windows 7 is running as a virtual machine.

19. Right-click the **notepad.exe** process and select **End Process** from the pop-up menu.

20. Notice that you are prompted with a warning when you try to terminate the program from the list of processes. An application can spawn multiple processes, and terminating just one might leave the others in an unstable state.

21. Click the **End process** button and notice that Notepad has closed.

22. Click the **CPU** column header to sort the list of processes by CPU utilization. Notice that the number in this column is indicating how much of the CPU's time is spent on that process. Note the process that is taking the most CPU time.

23. Click the **Show processes from all users** button.

24. If you are prompted by User Account Control for permission to use this program click the **Yes** button.

25. Notice the check box next to **Show processes from all users** is currently selected.

26. Sort the list of running processes by CPU time.

27. Notice the System Idle Process is now listed as taking the most CPU time. The Image Name column may not be wide enough to display the full process name. The column can be made wider by clicking on and moving the column divider.

28. Close the **Windows Task Manager** window.

29. Close all applications without saving any changes and log off.

Multiple Processor Support   Windows 7 includes processor support for multiprocessor systems. Multiprocessor systems have more than one physical CPU. Each additional CPU allows the computer to process instructions in parallel, at the same time. Most Windows 7 Editions support a maximum of two physical processors. The Windows 7 Starter and Home Basic Editions support only one physical processor.

Hyper-Threading Support   Some processors produced by Intel include a technology called **Hyper-Threading**. These CPUs have extra hardware built in to allow more than one thread to be processed at the same time on a single CPU.

When a single thread is running, it may have to pause and wait for an external event, such as fetching a value from memory. During that pause another thread can receive attention from the CPU to maximize the amount of work done by the CPU. Each thread processed by the Hyper-Threading environment runs in its own virtual space, keeping the threads independent.

Threads are created by the operating system and the applications the user runs. The operating system and the applications have to be aware of Hyper-Threading to maximize the flow of processing between threads. Windows 7 is designed to support Hyper-Threading.

Multi-Core Support A CPU feature such as Hyper-Threading can boost performance if the operating system and its application processes are written to be aware of it. Unfortunately, that is not always the case.

Threads created by applications can limit themselves so that only one thread can execute and the CPU cannot use its extra hardware to work on another thread in parallel. Any performance benefits while running those tasks is lost. The threads would have to be redesigned by the programmer to remove the bottleneck.

Rather than redesign how the threads share a CPU and work together in those applications, a performance boost can be obtained by introducing multi-core CPUs. The CPU package physically looks like one CPU, but internally contains multiple CPU cores.

Each CPU core is capable of running its own thread, even if the thread is not aware of the other cores. This is similar to having multiple CPUs in the computer, but each core is part of a single CPU package.

The cores share some connections to the rest of the computer, so performance will occasionally suffer as shared resources are managed. Compared to a single-core CPU, performance for running parallel threads can be greatly enhanced on a multi-core CPU.

Plug and Play

Windows 7 monitors its total environment—what hardware components it is using, when they are available, and what types of programs are running to use that hardware.

The hardware components (devices) are defined by the type of service or resource they represent. They interact with the operating system through a software module called a device driver. The **device driver** is made up of programming code written by a developer and supplied as one or more files.

Like Windows XP, Windows 7 is designed to support plug and play technology. Hardware devices are not always available to the operating system: Components can be powered down to save power, others are unplugged, some are wireless and are out of range.

Plug and Play technology assumes that hardware components can be connected or activated at any time while the operating system is running. The device driver will be automatically loaded by the plug and play system and, after a brief initialization period, the hardware is available for use.

Plug and Play technology is not new, but Windows 7 attempts to be more aware of what the user is doing with this hardware and what the operating system can do to maximize the user's experience. The goal is to make the hardware work for the user, not the other way around.

Power Management

Windows 7 is designed to work in a diverse range of physical environments. Many of those environments impose limits on how much power is available. Computers powered by Windows 7 and meeting the latest hardware power standards can consume less power than ever before. This power economy can translate into laptops that can run longer on battery power, and buildings full of computers that will reduce companies' energy bills significantly.

Much of this power savings is realized by exposing more power management features to device drivers and allowing those drivers to better integrate with the operating system. New low-power sleep modes use a combination of deactivating hardware components and buffering the current state of the computer to disk (that is, hibernating) to maximize power savings.

Tablet Hardware

In the past, Windows XP required a special edition of the operating system to support tablet computers. Windows 7 Home Premium, Professional, Enterprise, and Ultimate Editions include support for tablet computers as a standard feature.

A tablet computer is similar to a laptop in its portability, but it does not rely on a traditional keyboard for data entry. Instead, it typically uses a specially designed pen, otherwise known as a stylus, and a touch-sensitive screen for input.

A MultiTouch compatible tablet or monitor does not require a stylus to use the tablet enhancements. MultiTouch supports the use of one or more fingers, touching the screen at the same time to recognize gestures such as: zoom in, zoom out, scroll, rotate, and right-click.

Handwriting recognition is improved in Windows 7 so it can learn the personal writing style of a user. Frequent menu actions can be assigned to specific flicks of the input pen to simplify the command interface. Windows 7 works with the user to maximize their productivity, unlike older Windows operating systems that were less flexible in adapting to the user.

Media Hardware

Windows 7 Home Premium, Professional, and Ultimate Editions support Windows Media Center, which allows the computer to become part of a full entertainment system. This can include music devices, TV, game consoles such as the Xbox 360, and online entertainment such as Internet TV. In the older Windows XP, this was part of a specialized version of the operating system, Windows XP Media Center Edition.

Media, such as music, videos, and pictures stored on a computer, are accessible remotely from another computer, even if it isn't in the same location. A remote Windows 7 computer can access the media stored on the home system and stream it over the local network, or Internet, using Windows Media Player 12. Windows Media Player 12 is the default media player application in Windows 7.

Multiple Monitor Support

Multiple monitor support has been enhanced to enable less user involvement when multiple displays are detected. The screen hardware can provide **EDID (Extended Display Identification Data)** information to the computer about its preferred resolution and aspect ratio to automatically enable a recognized display using its recommended settings. The user can customize multi-monitor settings to extend the display to the monitor, duplicate the main monitor, or blank the screen.

Video hardware and device driver software installed to operate it must be compatible with Windows 7 to fully operate as a multi-monitor setup. If a monitor cannot be enabled with multi-monitor support then its device drivers or the video hardware might need to be replaced.

Networking Technologies

Data moves in a dynamic way from one computer to another over networks. Many networking improvements in Windows 7 are focused on:

- Network cards
- Wireless networks

Network Cards Windows 7 has redesigned networking support for the large data streams users will see in both home and business applications. This includes the ability to use network cards that have a Network Processing Unit to perform simple tasks that do not require the full abilities of the CPU.

A further performance boost is seen if the computer has multiple CPUs. Windows 7 is designed to deploy network processing across all CPUs at the same time. This is essential for media-playing software to provide a smooth, glitch-free experience.

Wireless Networks Wireless networking in older versions of Windows was typically developed as an extension to Ethernet network card technology. Because it was an add-on, developers encountered many limitations that were difficult to avoid. In Windows 7, wireless networking built on Wi-Fi standards is considered native to the operating system. Wi-Fi stands for wireless fidelity, a term used to describe wireless networks built in IEEE 802.11 standards. The programming code to support Wi-Fi in Windows 7 is new and specific to wireless technology.

Wireless connections support the new Network Diagnostic Framework, which will aid in automatically diagnosing problems with the wireless connection and assist with repairing or reporting the problem.

Wireless connections can be configured with command line utilities and administrative policies set by network administrators—a feature not possible in earlier versions of Windows prior to Windows Vista.

As the state of the user's connection changes, perhaps as the user is traveling, the Network Awareness Service in Windows 7 will track these changes and report them to applications that are sensitive to them.

Disk Technology

Physical disk storage can be connected to a computer internally or externally, using connection technology such as: IDE, SATA, SCSI, or USB. In addition to physical disks, virtual hard disks are supported by Windows 7. To the user and the operating system the virtual disk appears as just another physical disk attached to the computer, however it is not. A virtual disk's contents are stored inside a single file on a real physical disk. As long as there is space, one physical disk can contain many active virtual disks.

Disk technology supported by Windows 7 is covered later in this book.

Disk Partition Styles

When a computer is first started, firmware, which is built in code to initialize the hardware and load an operating system, starts first. That code looks to an attached device, typically the hard drive, to locate and load an operating system. The oldest style of firmware, BIOS, recognizes the MBR partition style. A newer and alternate type of firmware, UEFI, recognizes the GPT partition style. The partition style tells the firmware where to look next on the device to access valid data and ultimately, load the operating system.

Disk partition styles supported by Windows 7 is covered later in this book.

Types of Disk Partitions

Desktop computers commonly have a single hard disk that stores the operating system, applications, and user data. The space on the disk is organized and grouped into blocks called partitions or volumes. The strategy to organize the partitions and volumes was first developed for the original IBM PC and that type of disk partitioning hasn't evolved very much. Disks using this older partition organization strategy are called Basic disks.

For advanced partition options, the Basic disk scheme can be replaced by a Microsoft partitioning scheme called Dynamic disk. Not all editions of Windows 7 support Dynamic disks. Because this is seen as a business-class feature, only the Windows 7 Professional, Enterprise, and Ultimate Editions support dynamic disks.

Partition types supported by Windows 7 are covered later in this book.

File Systems

Windows 7 supports several file systems to organize files and directories within a disk partition (FAT16, FAT32, exFAT, NTFS, CDFS, and UDF). They are discussed in the following sections.

File systems supported by Windows 7 are fully covered later in this book.

FAT16 The **File Allocation Table (FAT)** file system is an older file system that is supported for backward compatibility. The FAT16 file system was originally created for the DOS operating system and its 16-bit computing environment. If the computer is designed to boot more than one operating system and the second operating system is older, such as Windows 95 SR1, a FAT16 partition will be required to hold its files because the older operating system doesn't support any of the newer file systems.

The older FAT16 file system has limitations. There is no support for file or folder security. There is no support for quotas, encryption, or compression. Files are stored in chained blocks of data. No complicated indexing scheme is used to organize the file and folder data. No fault tolerance schemes are built-in to automatically protect file data.

Traditional FAT16 supports partition sizes up to 2 GB in size. Windows 7 also supports an enhanced FAT16 data block size, which increases the limit to 4 GB.

FAT32 Windows 7 also offers support for the FAT32 file system, which was introduced as an enhanced version of FAT with Windows 95 OSR2. Earlier operating systems, such as MS-DOS, do not support direct access to FAT32 partitions.

The FAT32 file system uses a 32-bit numbering system to increase the number of data blocks that can be managed and organized as part of a single partition. The FAT32 theoretical partition size limit is 2048 GB.

Unfortunately, the method used to organize the clusters in such a large partition is inefficient and not necessary, as better alternatives exist. The maximum partition size supported for FAT32 in Windows 7 is 32 GB. For larger partitions, the NTFS or exFAT file system must be used.

exFAT Portable flash memory devices with more than 32GB of space cannot use FAT32. For these devices Microsoft has licensed exFAT as a variant of the FAT file system to manufacturers. exFAT supports extremely large memory devices but does not add much functionality to the basic FAT file system.

NTFS A new version of **NT File System (NTFS)** is supported in Windows 7. NTFS was introduced originally with Windows NT and has been revised with each successor (that is, Windows 2000, Windows XP, and Windows Server 2003). Older operating systems such as MS-DOS, Windows 95, 98, and ME do not support direct access to NTFS partitions natively. Some third-party tools exist that allow those older operating systems to access NTFS file systems, but Microsoft does not support them.

NTFS has support for organization and management features that do not exist in FAT-based file systems. Files and folders are represented in a more virtual and expandable format using metadata to represent their data and attributes. The metadata is the detailed information that the operating system uses to display and organize the files and folders. Instead of a File Allocation Table, NTFS stores the metadata in a Master File Table (MFT). The MFT itself is a database that has a record for every file and folder on an NTFS partition.

NTFS partitions are theoretically limited to 256 Terabytes (TB, 1 TB = 1024 GB), but the practical limit is lower. Basic disks using the old IBM standard for partitions are restricted to 2 TB. Newer dynamic disk partitions are limited to 16 TB.

Because of the disk space required to manage the NTFS file system, floppy disks always use a FAT file system.

NTFS file systems offer several enhancements over FAT technology.

Secured Storage Access to folders and files can be limited based on permissions and rights that can be individually configured for each file and folder.

File Names Stored in Unicode Format The names of files and folders can be stored in many different languages following the Unicode character standard. This is an improvement over the limitation of using the traditional ASCII English character set.

File and Folder Compression Any file or folders can be compressed or decompressed automatically using built-in compression technology to conserve disk space.

Disk Space Quotas by User The administrator can set space limits for individuals allowed to store files on the NTFS partition.

Alternate Data Streams A single file can contain more than one stream of data. The main stream is used to store the actual file data and optional alternate data streams can be created to store extra information with the main data stream. For example, this can be used by an application to store a thumbnail for a larger image.

File Encryption The contents of a file can be encrypted using the **Encrypted File System (EFS)** as an additional safeguard.

Volume Mount Point A folder can be created in an NTFS partition to act as a gateway to another partition accessible to the operating system. The space on that partition then becomes available as part of the original NTFS partition.

Fault Tolerance The NTFS file system uses a log-based system to track changes that are made to the file system. When a low-level error occurs, or the system crashes, NTFS has the ability to repair incomplete transactions by rolling the changes back to the last known good point.

   If a part of the disk goes bad, NTFS has the ability to try and move any valid data from that part of the disk to another spot on the disk, and to automatically map the defective area as bad to avoid using it in the future.

   Depending on the number of disks available, NTFS supports storing file data redundantly across multiple disks to increase the chance that data will still be available in the event of a disk failure.

Transactional NTFS Transactional NTFS allows applications to monitor the sequence of events used to save data to NTFS files and folders. If an application decides not to finish writing changes to a file, it can use Transactional NTFS to roll back the changes made to that file.

CDFS The **CD-ROM File System (CDFS)** was introduced with Windows NT 4 and has been replaced with UDF as a preference for formatting removable media such as CDs and DVDs.

UDF The **Universal Disk Format (UDF)** is a third-party standard that defines how to store data on removable media such as DVDs. Windows 2000 provided support to read UDF media and Windows XP introduced support for read and write. Windows 7 improves on Windows XP native support for writing and troubleshooting DVDs.

Application Support

The core of Windows 7 has been redesigned by Microsoft architects to provide application features that could not be achieved in earlier versions of Windows. Windows 7 achieves many of these new features by implementing features in new ways that are not compatible with older applications. Those older applications have a few options to try and run successfully under Windows 7.

Compatibility Settings

Compatibility settings are available as a property of an application after it is installed. Windows 7 is directed by the compatibility settings to emulate an environment for that application that is based on an older operating system. The older operating systems to simulate include:

- Windows 95
- Windows 98/ME
- Windows NT 4 Service Pack 5

- Windows 2000
- Windows XP Service Pack 2
- Windows XP Service Pack 3
- Windows Server 2003 Service Pack 1
- Windows Server 2008 Service Pack 1
- Windows Vista
- Windows Vista Service Pack 1
- Windows Vista Service Pack 2

Some legacy applications were written with the assumption that the user running them has administrator privileges to the entire computer. For this reason, the compatibility settings allow the option of granting administrator privileges to a legacy application while it runs. This must be used with caution for applications that are not truly trusted.

Program Compatibility Wizard

If the user is not comfortable selecting compatibility settings, a wizard is available to assist them. The Program Compatibility Wizard is a tool that can be started by right-clicking a program icon and selecting Troubleshoot compatibility from the pop-up menu. This wizard has the ability to guide the user through different compatibility settings and, if that doesn't work, report the results to Microsoft.

Application Compatibility Toolkit

The **Application Compatibility Toolkit (ACT)** is a free tool provided by Microsoft to help IT administrators discover which of their existing applications are compatible with Windows 7. The toolkit by itself does not guarantee that an application can be made to run on Windows 7.

Windows XP Mode with Windows Virtual PC

It is possible that, even with compatibility settings, an application will not run on Windows 7. In this case, there are a few options that chiefly apply to the larger corporate environment.

The Windows Virtual PC product is free from Microsoft and allows the creation of a virtual computer system that runs as an application hosted on Windows 7 Professional, Ultimate, and Enterprise Editions. Windows Virtual PC allows a user to run an older version of Windows XP inside the virtual computer. The virtual computer shares the computer's hardware with Windows 7. The legacy application is unaware that Windows 7 is running and runs in the virtual computer, using the older compatible operating system to run those applications that otherwise would not work with Windows 7. The computer running Windows XP Mode with Windows Virtual PC will need at least 1 GB of RAM above the minimum recommended specifications for Windows 7 and at least 15 GB of free disk space before it is installed.

Windows XP Mode allows the applications installed in the Windows Virtual machine to show up on the Windows 7 Start Menu as if they were installed on Windows 7 itself. When a user selects the application from the Start Menu, the Windows XP virtual machine runs the application and the user is not aware that a second operating system is actually running it. Resources such as drives, printers, the clipboard, and attached USB devices are shared between Windows 7 and the virtual instance of Windows XP.

If Windows Virtual PC is not a practical solution, customers can try loading the legacy application on a Windows Server 2003 or 2008 terminal server and share the application over the network. Not all applications are compatible with terminal services, but many are. Terminal servers require special licensing, a server-class operating system, and dedicated server hardware. If this is not possible or practical, then a dedicated workstation computer to run the legacy software may be required.

Kernel and User Mode Enhancements

To provide better application isolation, Microsoft architects have redesigned the security levels for core components of the operating system.

The terms kernel mode and user mode are often mentioned as key terms in describing the stability and impact of a software component.

A software component that has **kernel mode** access has total access to all of the computer's data and its hardware. Most operating system software requires this level of access. Some software in earlier Windows operating systems required this level of access to work as designed. Print drivers are a good example of a driver that required kernel mode access to function correctly.

If a kernel mode component performs a bad operation that crashes the computer, there is little the operating system can do to stop it or recover. The phrase **"blue screen of death"** (BSOD) came to describe the error screen displayed by the operating system when it realized that a component has performed an action that is considered bad enough to force the operating system to halt. Using the example of a print driver above, a bad operation by a simple print driver could crash the computer. If this was unacceptable, what could the IT administrator do? The answer was very little other than to obtain a fixed print driver or avoid using the printer.

Software can run at a reduced privilege level. It can be restricted so that it only has access to its own private space and nothing else. This is the **user mode** access level. A user mode application that crashes cannot crash the computer, but it can crash itself. If this happens, the user mode application can be shut down and restarted within its private space. This is similar to rebooting just the application.

Windows 7 architects have redesigned the kernel to support more types of software running at a user level instead of a kernel level. Print drivers are an example of software that has moved from almost an exclusively kernel mode driver to a supported user mode driver. Print drivers in Windows 7 are no longer allowed to use kernel level access.

The CPU itself makes the switch between kernel and user mode. The CPU can load and unload virtual environments to run each thread it processes. As it switches from one context to another it can also change security levels. Any application that violates the limits of its security level will cause an exception in the CPU. The exception causes the CPU to stop what it is doing and run a clean-up routine. The exception details are passed on to the error-handling routines and they determine the actions required to clean up the error.

The terms user mode and kernel mode are also used to describe security levels in the operating system itself. The term **ring level** is used to describe security levels at the CPU hardware level. The least restricted security level is called Ring 0. The most restricted security level is Ring 3. Ring 1 and Ring 2 exist but are seldom used. Kernel mode and user mode map to Ring 0 and Ring 3, respectively.

Virtual PC Hypervisor

Windows 7 has been written to work together with products such as Windows Virtual PC to create a virtual computer within the computer. Those virtual computers can run other operating systems and their own applications. The virtual computers do not even have to be running a Windows operating system. This is important to Enterprise customers who are looking at ways to simplify their environment.

The shift in Windows 7 to limit access to the kernel, or Ring 0, poses a problem with limiting virtual computer access to Ring 0. Operating systems and applications running in the virtual machine expect access to Ring 0. Advances in CPUs and Virtual PC design allow the creation of a virtual security level with more permissions than Ring 0, called Ring –1.

At Ring –1, a hypervisor program runs with a higher security level than any operating system. The computer can be running one or more operating systems that think they have the highest security level. In fact, the hypervisor program is managing those operating systems and their applications. If those "kernel mode" operating systems and applications crash, they still can't crash the computer.

An example of a hypervisor in Enterprise server environments is the Windows Server 2008 Hyper-V role, which allows multiple virtual servers to run on one physical machine.

Connectivity Applications

Instead of fortifying the idea that a user only works on their own computer, Windows 7 provides several tools to help connect one person to other computers and resources that they can leverage. Several of these connectivity applications are:

- Remote Desktop
- Remote Assistance
- Network Projection
- HomeGroups

Remote Desktop

Remote desktop is included with Windows 7 Professional, Enterprise, and Ultimate Editions. Remote desktop allows a user to remotely connect to their computer using the remote desktop client over TCP/IP. Once connected, the user can log on and begin running applications.

   Remote Desktop is covered later in this book.

Remote Assistance

Remote Assistance is now a stand-alone application included with all versions of Windows 7. A user can ask for help from a trusted professional over the network using e-mail, file transfer, or use the Easy Connect service. Easy Connect allows a computer to be discovered over the Internet using a generated password and the IPv6 network protocol. This is accomplished by establishing a live connection between the computer and public servers configured to support this service. The password uniquely identifies your computer on the public server. The professional service provider can connect to chat, transfer files, run diagnostics, and reconnect across reboots.

   Remote Assistance is covered later in this book.

Network Projection

Windows 7 Professional, Ultimate, and Enterprise Editions include support for connecting to network-attached projectors over wired and wireless networks. This will enable the user to spend less time worrying about how to connect to a projector and more time on making their presentation.

HomeGroups

HomeGroups provide a mechanism to easily share printers, pictures, music, videos, and documents with other Windows 7 computers using a shared wired or wireless network at home. Each computer that joins the HomeGroup system must present a valid HomeGroup password to communicate with other members. Each computer can be configured with limits on what content, ot type of content, is shared with other HomeGroup members.

Networking Models

Multiple computers can connect together and share data over a network. A network model details a logical framework for sharing, securing, and managing data across that network. Just as there are different versions of Windows 7 to meet the differing needs of customers, there are also different network models available to connect computers. Some networking models support more computers and offer greater administrative control. Other models try to simplify the framework for simpler and smaller environments. The specific networking features of Windows 7 are covered later in this book. The networking models supported by Windows 7 and covered here include:

- Workgroup Model
- Domain Model
- Windows Peer-to-Peer Networking

Workgroup Model

When a computer is first connected to a network, it typically is configured as a member of a workgroup. A workgroup is a loosely knit collection of peer computers on a network where no computer has control or superior role to any other computer. The peers share resources with each other over the network. This can be useful for a small number of computers in a typical home or small business network.

Each computer is identified by its name and address on the network. The workgroup itself is identified by an assigned name. The default workgroup name is typically WORKGROUP.

Workgroup membership rules are simple; a computer can be a member of only one workgroup at a time. More than one workgroup can coexist on the same network. Being a member of a workgroup helps a computer find shared resources such as files and printers on its peers, but it does not restrict it from accessing resources located outside its own workgroup.

The workgroup design is traditionally known as a peer-to-peer networking model; however Microsoft has introduced Windows Peer-to-Peer Networking technology with Windows XP SP2 to extend the boundaries of the traditional workgroup. These enhancements will be covered later in the chapter.

The workgroup design has strong advantages in informal environments. Its simple design and function allow easy sharing of files and printers. Even in the small office setting, the workgroup model can be effective at sharing information quickly among members. The factors for business to determine if the workgroup model is appropriate are the degree of computer management required and the need to centralize data into a central location.

Managing a workgroup can be difficult because each computer is in control of its own resources, its own users, and the permissions and actions assigned to them. A new user who will access shared files and printers on multiple machines on the network will need an account created on each workgroup machine that they require access to. Each of those machines will then need permissions configured to allow that user to access the required resources.

This can become a management nightmare, especially when changes or removal of access is required. Because separate users control each computer, each user must receive training on the care and control of their computer. When changes are required in security settings, each user must be monitored to ensure the changes are made throughout the workgroup.

The computers in a workgroup are usually part of a single local area network operating with direct access between each computer. Network routers typically act as physical boundaries of the workgroup. Network addressing is a logical boundary, as all workgroup members typically have the same network address. It is not typical to see a workgroup span outside a single local area network. This is altered with the introduction of the Windows Peer-to-Peer Networking technology.

Microsoft recommends that workgroups should not be used for more than 10 to 20 computers. There is a practical limit to sharing resources from workstation class computers. All Windows 7 Editions are limited to support a maximum of 20 simultaneous connections.

Note that this does not limit the number of members in the workgroup, only the number of computers accessing a shared resource simultaneously. If the shared resource needs to be accessed by more users at the same time, then the domain model becomes a better solution.

Domain Model

The Domain Model is a client/server strategy that allows central administrative management of its members. A domain is a collection of computers and users that are identified by a common security database. The database is stored on one or more dedicated servers called **Domain Controllers (DC)**. Computers that are part of the domain can reference the domain database and read the user and computer accounts contained within. Member computers can access shared resources on other computers from the same domain, using the security information referenced by the DC to restrict access.

 The Domain Model is covered later in this book.

Each member of the domain can take on a client or server role. Servers host centralized resources and the clients access those shared resources.

The major differences between workgroup and domain models are how the members are managed and the limits to sharing resources. A Windows 7 computer can be used as a server in a domain, but the connection limits mentioned in the workgroup model still apply. Server class operating systems, such as Windows Server 2003, can theoretically have an unlimited number of clients access a shared resource simultaneously. The practical limit with centralized servers becomes overall performance and licensing.

Domain networking is typically employed in business environments, so not all editions of Windows 7 have support for it. Windows 7 Ultimate, Professional, and Enterprise Editions support joining a domain networking system. The Home and Starter editions do not.

When a server shares a resource it can define permissions to access the resource based on the domain user and computer names stored on the DC. If a new user is added to the domain, each domain computer can directly reference the new domain user name by verifying it with the domain controller. Likewise, if a domain user account needs to be removed, it only has to be removed from the domain database on the domain controller and not each domain member computer.

A computer can be a member of a workgroup or a domain, but not both at the same time. A computer cannot be a member of more than one domain at the same time. The computer and the domain must be identified by unique names.

Access to shared resources in other domains and workgroups is still allowed, but the user has to authenticate to those resources. The user would be prompted to provide a user ID and password for the foreign system.

More than one domain can coexist on a network, with the domain defining a security boundary. Changes made to the security or configuration of a domain usually only impact domain members. However, it is possible for different domains to trust each other to allow shared access between domains. The limits of how domains trust each other depend on the type of domain in use.

Windows NT Domains The original Microsoft Domain Model was introduced with Windows NT. The database of computer and user accounts was stored on dedicated servers called DCs (Domain Controllers). Two types of DCs exist for a Windows NT domain, the **Primary DC (PDC)** and a **Backup DC (BDC)**. The PDC is allowed to make changes to the domain database and the BDC maintains a read-only copy of the database.

The NT domain model has limitations when compared to current domain technology, but it served its purpose when it was first introduced. NT Domains are designed to support up to a few thousand computers per domain. NT Domains also use an older naming technology called NetBIOS to identify themselves. This restricted the domain name to 15 characters or less.

This model was considered appropriate, given the size of networks at the time and their localized nature. The expectation was that if you had more computers, or distinct geographic regions, the administrator would create separate domains and then configure those domains to share resources between them. Unfortunately, this was difficult to configure and did not work well on a global scale. To address this, Microsoft introduced Active Directory Domains with Windows 2000.

Active Directory Domains With the introduction of Windows Server 2000, Microsoft introduced a new domain model generally referred to as **Active Directory (AD)**. The Active Directory model still represents a central database of user and computer accounts and centralized tools to manage them. The domain database is still stored on dedicated Domain Controller (DC) servers, but there is no longer a Primary and Backup designation. All DCs are capable of updating the database and replicating those changes to the other DCs in the domain. This is commonly referred to as **multi-master replication**.

Active Directory systems use a different naming strategy based on TCP/IP based **Domain Name System (DNS)** technology, using names that appear similar to common Internet names, such as "microsoft.com". This was done to better support the TCP/IP network protocols that link networks around the globe today.

Active Directory can define more than one domain as part of the same system. Those multiple domains implicitly trust each other. Each domain will have its own unique DNS and NetBIOS name. This collection of trusting domains is called an Active Directory forest.

Each domain in the forest will have one or more domain controllers. At least one domain controller is required for each domain. A domain controller can only belong to one domain. Fault tolerance and load balancing can be achieved by adding more domain controllers to the domain. The domain controllers from each domain within the forest will securely communicate with each other to automatically establish the trusts required.

The effect for a client is that they can transparently access resources in other domains within their AD forest as long as they have permission to do so. This means they do not have to keep typing in a user ID and password to get access; they only have to do so when they first log on.

From an administrator's perspective, another advantage to Active Directory is the ability to manage the user and computer environment of its members. The administrator can use Active Directory Group Policy to define items such as installed applications, security settings, environment settings, and limits. The Group Policy settings are stored as part of the Active Directory database and are visible to all members of the Active Directory forest. The Active Directory administrator can define specific criteria that control to what computers or user the settings apply.

Each new operating system enhances the administrator's flexibility with Group Policy by introducing support for new settings and controls that did not exist before. Windows 7 introduces several hundred new Group Policy settings. The client operating system must understand what a single Group Policy setting is before it can apply it.

Windows 7 can be a client of a domain, but it can never be a Domain Controller. To create an Active Directory domain, you are required to purchase and install Windows Server 2008 or Windows Server 2003 on a dedicated computer. Likewise, domain Group Policy settings only apply if the Windows 7 computer is a member of the domain.

Windows Peer-to-Peer Networking

Microsoft has introduced Windows Peer-to-Peer Networking as a client operating system enhancement for Windows XP SP2, and all versions of Windows Vista and Windows 7.

This technology is similar in concept to the traditional workgroup model, but the technical details about how it operates are unique. The traditional workgroup is usually limited by the physical and logical boundaries of a basic network—respectively, the routers and network addresses assigned to computers. The traditional workgroup requires computers to share a common network addressing scheme and the same physical Local Area Network (LAN).

This places a limit on sharing content across larger networks. Companies and individuals are forced to implement centralized servers to enable sharing technologies in these environments. This restricts ad hoc collaboration between users and companies as some type of preplanning and infrastructure deployment in advance is required.

The new Windows Peer-to-Peer Networking technology tries to remove these limits and make peer-to-peer infrastructure scalable from the LAN to the Internet. It does this by first removing the old restrictions of router and network addressing by basing communications on the new TCP/IP IPv6 protocol.

The IPv4 standard defines traditional TCP/IP communication between computers. IPv6 is a new standard for TCP/IP communication that resets the limits as they apply to peer-to-peer computing. Windows Peer-to-Peer Networking clients anywhere on the Internet can talk to each other and form a peer-to-peer network, as long as they communicate using IPv6. The problem is that most of the Internet is designed to support only IPv4 traffic.

For IPv6 traffic to make it across the Internet, some form of translation between IPv4 and IPv6 is required. This translation requires the use of special transition devices and software. Microsoft has included its own translation software, called Teredo, as part of the Windows 7 operating system.

Teredo allows IPv6 traffic to be embedded in legacy IPv4 traffic and make it across the Internet to another Teredo client or Teredo relay, where it is turned back into IPv6 traffic. The Teredo client is supported in Windows XP SP2, all versions of Windows Vista, all versions of Windows 7, and Windows Server 2003 SP1 or later server Editions.

Once Windows Peer-to-Peer Networking clients establish communication with each other, they can interact to securely share resources—without a central server.

There is no reliance on central server technologies such as DNS, Active Directory, or Certificate Authorities; the Windows Peer-to-Peer Network clients manage themselves with technologies and techniques specific to Windows Peer-to-Peer Networks. For example, Peer Name Resolution Protocol (PNRP) is used by Windows Peer-to-Peer Networking clients to discover each other.

Applications such as Remote Assistance and HomeGroups take advantage of this new peer-to-peer infrastructure to allow users to find each other, exchange data, and share the processing of data in real time. Note that the scope of allowed connectivity depends on the application, not the peer-to-peer protocol itself. For instance, Remote Assistance can enable a user on the Internet to connect to a home computer and offer support. That home computer can also connect to other home computers using HomeGroups to share content; but it cannot connect using HomeGroups to computers over the Internet. This limitation is designed into HomeGroups because the solution is only supposed to help connect home-based networks.

Chapter Summary

- Windows 7 is available in five versions: Windows 7 Starter, Windows 7 Home Premium, Windows 7 Professional, Windows 7 Ultimate, and Windows 7 Enterprise. There are several special versions: Windows 7 Home Basic, and the Windows 7 N and K Editions.

- This chapter introduced the new and enhanced features of Windows 7 and how they help you organize and access information. The Aero style adds an exciting visual element that applications can take advantage of using the .NET Framework 3.5 code model. Input technologies such as speech recognition let you interact with Windows 7 in a richer multimedia environment. Users can securely interact with Windows 7 using new access levels controlled through User Account Control, fast user switching, TPM services, and BitLocker drive encryption. Security is heightened in built-in applications such as Internet Explorer 8 to limit the exposure of the computer while it connects users to Web resources. Windows 7 comes in 32- and 64-bit versions.

- Windows 7 offers a streamlined Start menu interface that does not sprawl across the screen. Searching has been enhanced as a key feature to aid the user in accessing and organizing data. New tools are available as mini-application Gadgets that can be added to and launched anywhere on the desktop. The application environment supports multitasking, multithreading, multiple processors, application compatibility emulation, and virtual computing. The networking environment has been enhanced to support ad-hoc networks, network projection, mobile and wireless support, and network location awareness.

- Minimum hardware requirements must be met with Windows 7. Compatible hardware is listed on the Windows Marketplace tested products list, a replacement for the older Hardware Compatibility List used for earlier operating systems. Hardware products can distinguish themselves with the Windows Logo program that ensures that a product meets the compatibility tests of the Windows Hardware Quality Labs. Certified products digitally sign their device drivers and distribute updates through the Windows Update Web service. Windows 7 includes support for faster processors, plug and play technology, efficient power management, and portable tablet and media center hardware that connects through advanced network connections to provide a rich user experience. Data is stored locally using backward compatible file systems such as FAT16, FAT32, and CDFS, while still providing newer file systems such as exFAT, NTFS, and UDF for today's diverse multimedia content.

- Application support in Windows 7 is designed to work on more than one level to give the user options and choices. A program can take advantage of basic compatibility settings, or the Program Compatibility Wizard can guide the user through the choices. When planning which applications are compatible, tools such as the Application Compatibility Toolkit can organize and simplify the task. If an application cannot be made to work with Windows 7, then XP Mode on Windows Virtual PC can provide a legacy operating system environment for Windows 7 Enterprise users. All applications can benefit from the kernel and user mode enhancements that protect running applications and device drivers from one another.

- Networks enable the sharing of data between computers, but Windows 7 also enables the user to share computers and resources through tools such as Remote Desktop, Remote Assistance, network projection, and HomeGroups. The emphasis is connecting users to the tools they need, even if they are not local.

- Windows 7 can participate in the workgroup or domain networking models. The workgroup model has been enhanced with the addition of TCP/IP IPv6 and Windows Peer-to-Peer Networking technology to extend the boundaries of the workgroup beyond the traditional local area network.

Key Terms

Active Directory (AD)   A domain security database of user and computer information that is stored on domain controllers and referenced by domain member computers. This database is stored on multi-master replicating domain controllers running Windows 2000 or Windows 2003 for an operating system. The older Windows NT domain controllers cannot hold Active Directory security databases.

Aero Glass   A visual effect that is part of the Aero theme of Windows 7. Many graphical elements have a semitransparent appearance to allow users to see other windows under the active one. This is done to allow the user a better feel for what other applications are doing in the background without being too distracting.

Application Compatibility Toolkit   A collection of tools, advice, and methodologies that guides the IT administrator in determining which legacy applications are compatible with Windows 7. It does not make those applications compatible; it merely helps the IT administrator use a structured method of testing and tracking compatibility information.

Application Programming Interface (API)   A set of rules and conditions a programmer follows when writing an application to allow the program to interact with part of the operating system. The program is guaranteed to work if they follow the API rules published by the authors of a feature in the operating system.

Backup DC (BDC)   A specialized Windows NT server that is responsible for holding a read-only copy of the domain security database.

BitLocker Drive Encryption   An encryption method used to protect an entire hard disk. Without proper credentials a hard disk will remain encrypted, even if the disk is removed from the computer.

blue screen of death (BSOD)   A common term used to describe an error condition in the operating system that has resulted in a full halt of the operating system due to a critical error. The error screen is usually white text on a blue background, hence the name.

CD-ROM File System (CDFS)   A file system introduced with Windows 95 and Windows NT to organize files and folders on a CD-ROM disk. The CDFS file system is considered adequate for older CD-ROM disks but not for rewritable CD-ROMs or newer DVD media formats. For those newer media technologies, UDF is the preferred file system.

Central Processing Unit (CPU)   A device responsible for the actual execution of instructions stored in applications and operating system code. Windows 7 supports 32- and 64-bit. CPUs.

cooperative multitasking   A method for applications to share the CPU. All applications rotate access to and do not monopolize the CPU. If an application does not release control of the CPU, the computer may appear stalled or other applications appear very sluggish.

device driver   Software written by the developer of a hardware component that tells the operating system how to talk to and control the hardware.

Domain Controller (DC)   A server responsible for holding a domain security database which contains a list of user and computer account security data.

Domain Name System (DNS)   A standard service in the TCP/IP protocol used to define how computer names are translated into IP addresses.

Dynamic Link Library files (DLLs)   A file that holds application code modules. These modules are shared among applications, so the file is also called a library. DLL files can be replaced to update an application without having to replace the entire application.

EDID (Extended Display Identification Data)   A standard that defines how the monitor hardware can pass details about its abilities to the graphics card and ultimately the operating system. Details such as preferred refresh rate and screen resolution can be set by the monitor manufacturer and EDID will allow this information to be passed to the operating system. The operating system can use that information to configure the optimum view on the monitor without having to ask the user for those settings. This provides a simpler user-friendly experience when setting up new monitor hardware.

Encrypted File System (EFS)   A component of the NTFS file system that is responsible for encrypting individual files. Those files are not readable without the correct digital identification.

eXtensible Markup Language (XML)   A standard for formatting data that is exchanged between applications. By using a standard, application developers do not have to write custom data translators for every product with which their applications share data.

File Allocation Table (FAT)   An older method of organizing files and folders in a hard disk partition. Files are stored in blocks of data that point to each other in a chain-like structure. The blocks that are used in the partition and the link from one to another are stored in a master table called the FAT.

Graphical Processing Unit (GPU)   A hardware component, similar to the CPU, that is added to video cards to calculate how to draw complex shapes on the screen. Because the GPU can perform the complex operations on its own, the CPU is free to work on other tasks.

Hardware Compatibility List (HCL)   A legacy method of determining if hardware is compatible with the operating system. This has been replaced by the Windows Catalog and the Windows Marketplace Web site.

Hyper-Threading   A technique used in certain Intel processors to improve their overall performance by working on more than one thread at a time. When one thread is waiting for an operation to complete a second thread can use some of the processor's hardware instead of the processor just idling. This extra work is done inside the processor's hardware and is specific to the design of the processor itself. Programmers writing application threads and the operating system that schedules those threads to run must be aware of the benefits and limits of the Hyper-Threaded processor to take best advantage of any performance gain that might be possible.

kernel mode   An access mode for applications while they are running on the CPU that allows full access to all hardware devices and memory in the computer.

multi-master replication   When a domain has multiple domain controllers, all domain controllers are capable of making changes to the security domain database they share. The changes are replicated from one domain controller to another.

multiprocessor   A term used to refer to a computer with more than one CPU.

multitasking   A term used to describe the appearance of more than one application sharing the CPU of the computer. To the user, the applications all seem to be running at the same time.

Network Location Awareness Service (NLA)   A service that allows applications to track the state of the network connections available to the computer. An application can track how much data can be sent over a connection, if it is available, or if new connections appear. Based on this information, the application can modify its attempts to communicate over the network.

NT File System (NTFS)   A standard for organizing files and folders on a hard disk partition. This standard is more complex than FAT but adds more management features. This is the preferred standard for storing files on a hard disk.

Plug and Play technology   A general term used to describe hardware that can be plugged in to the computer system and removed at any time. The computer will recognize the hardware dynamically, load a device driver for it, and make it available to the user in a short period of time.

preemptive multitasking   A method for applications to share a CPU and appear that they are all running at the same time. This method adds time limits and priority levels to determine how long an application can use the processor and which application gets to go next. An application can also be preempted by another application if it has a higher priority level.

Primary DC (PDC)   A specialized Windows NT server that is responsible for holding a writeable copy of the domain security database.

process   A term used to describe the files, memory, and application code that combine together to form a single running application. Each application running on a multitasking system is referenced by a single process.

processor affinity   A standard in which a process that starts in a computer with more than one CPU is usually assigned to that CPU again the next time it runs.

quantum   The amount of time allocated to a program running in a preemptive multitasking environment. Once a program's quantum has expired, it must wait for the next available quantum.

Really Simple Syndication (RSS)   A Web-based service used on the Internet to distribute updates about new content, articles, and news on Web sites and provide links to those sites. A user can subscribe to a particular feed or type of update to stay up to date and informed on the latest content available in an area or site that interests them.

ring level   A security level in the CPU that is used to determine a program's degree of access to memory and hardware. The ring levels are used to set user and kernel mode access in the operating system.

Software Assurance (SA)   An option when purchasing Microsoft software that allows you to automatically receive the latest version of a product. For example, if you purchased Windows XP with Software Assurance you would automatically be able to upgrade to Windows 7.

Startup Repair Tool   A tool provided in Windows 7 to help users determine why their computer failed and what they should do to repair it.

thread   A piece of code that performs a specific single task. An application is written as one or more threads, each of which performs a specific task within the application. The thread is typically seen as a unit of work for the CPU to perform.

Trusted Platform Module (TPM)   A third-party standard to define a method of trusting the computer environment before an operating system is started. This helps to prevent the theft of a hard disk and placement of the disk in a foreign system to steal data.

Universal Disk Format (UDF)   A third-party standard that defines how data is stored on removable media such as DVD disks.

user mode   An access mode for applications while they are running on the CPU that allows restricted access to all hardware devices and memory in the computer. This mode makes it difficult for the running application to corrupt and crash the operating system. System-level applications may need more access than is allowed and must use kernel mode instead.

Windows Display Driver Model (WDDM)   A standard API for writing device drivers that are compatible with the newer graphical subsystem that is part of Windows 7.

Windows Driver Foundation (WDF)   A standard for writing device drivers that interact with Windows 7. This standard replaces WDM and adds new features such as support for user mode device drivers.

Windows Driver Model (WDM)   An older standard for writing device drivers that interact with Windows. Device drivers that use this standard are still supported, but should be replaced with drivers that use the new WDF architecture.

Windows Hardware Quality Labs (WHQL)   A service provided by Microsoft to hardware developers and vendors to test their hardware with different versions of Windows. This testing only validates that a device works with Windows; it does not compare devices.

Windows Imaging Format (WIM)   A format to store images of applications and operating systems in image files. These images represent customized installations that can be distributed to other computers and installed using a scripted solution.

Review Questions

1. A friend has asked you which version of Windows 7 should be purchased to start a new multimedia-based home entertainment system. Your friend will not require business support features, but will require support communicating with an Xbox 360. Which version of Windows 7 do you recommend?

   a. Windows 7 Ultimate

   b. Windows 7 Home Basic

   c. Windows 7 Home Premium

   d. Windows 7 Enterprise

2. Windows 7 supports only cooperative multitasking. True or False?

3. The _____ Processing Unit is a hardware component capable of quickly drawing items to the screen.

4. A graphics card capable of running the Aero Theme must have drivers certified to which standard (select two)?

   a. DirectX

   b. WDDM

   c. WDF

   d. WDM

   e. Vendor

5. All device drivers are considered safe to install if they are _____ by Microsoft.

   a. compiled

   b. certified WDDM

   c. digitally signed

   d. reviewed by WHQL

6. You are considering purchasing a USB microphone. You are not sure it is compatible with Windows 7. What type of logo should you look for on the product packaging?

   a. WHQL

   b. compatible with Windows 7

   c. WDDM driver

d. Vendor certified

e. Ultimate

7. Your workstation is running Windows 7 Professional and you decide to share a folder on your computer. Twenty-two? people in your office are trying to connect to that folder at the same time over the network. The first 20 people can connect, the other two cannot. To fix this you could _____.

a. buy a computer, software, and licenses to run Windows Server 2003

b. restart your computer

c. make sure the network card is using WDF device drivers

d. none of the above

8. Computers that belong to the same domain can access a common security database of user and computer account information. This type of database on Windows 2003 domain controller servers is also known as a(n) _____ database.

a. primary

b. workgroup

c. jet

d. Active Directory

e. backup

9. Which of the following is an advantage of domain networking?

a. no central security database

b. built in to every version of Windows 7

c. centralized security management

d. support for up to 10 simultaneous shared connections

10. A new company will have 30 workstations in one building sharing a single network. All users must be able to share files and printers with each other. Access to shared information must be secure and simple to administer. The best technology for this system is:

a. Workgroups

b. Windows Peer-to-Peer Networking

c. People to People

d. Domain Networking

11. Your computer is capable of starting more than one operating system. Windows 7 Ultimate and Windows 2003 are both installed, but to different hard disks in the computer. A third hard disk will be used to hold data that is used by both operating systems. To make this disk accessible in both operating systems, you decide to format it as (select all that apply):

a. UDF

b. NTFS

c. FAT32

d. FAT16

12. Your computer is capable of starting more than one operating system. Windows 7 Ultimate and Windows 95 SR1 are both installed, but to different hard disks in the computer. A third hard disk will be used to hold data that is used by both operating systems. To make this disk accessible in both operating systems you decide to format it as:

a. UDF

b. NTFS

c. FAT32

d. FAT16

13. The main network protocol used to communicate between Windows 7 computers is:

     a. TCP/IP

     b. X.25

     c. SLIP

     d. Peer-to-Peer

     e. Teredo

14. Window 7's version of TCP/IP supports the newer standard called _____.

     a. IPv4

     b. IPv6

     c. Teredo

     d. WDDM

     e. IPv8

15. A feature of Windows 7 designed to provide easy access to helpful mini-applications and utilities is called _____.

     a. Start button

     b. HomeGroups

     c. Search

     d. Teredo

     e. Gadgets

16. Which networking component included with Windows 7 supports sending IPv6 traffic over IPv4 networks?

     a. Teredo

     b. Windows Plug and Play Networking

     c. TCP/IP

     d. X.25

     e. .NET Framework 3.5

17. A driver that has full access to all hardware and the memory of the computer has what type of security level?

     a. digitally signed

     b. kernel mode

     c. user mode

     d. WHQL tested

     e. WDDM

18. A hardware vendor's product has passed Microsoft testing and has received a certified logo. Updated drivers for the hardware can be obtained from the manufacturer and from which Microsoft Web site?

     a. Windows Marketplace

     b. Windows Driver Distribution

     c. Microsoft Support

     d. Windows Update

19. Some hardware can be added to the computer without having to restart or power down the computer. After a short period of time the device driver automatically loads and the hardware is available to applications and the user. This type of hardware is considered compatible with what type of technology?

    a. Teredo

    b. WDDM

    c. Plug and Play

    d. Legacy

20. You have purchased a new 72 GB disk drive and would like to format it in Windows 7 with a single partition that uses up all the space on the drive. You can format the file system on the partition as (choose all that apply):

    a. FAT16

    b. FAT32

    c. CDFS

    d. NTFS

21. Software assurance customers can take advantage of extra applications provided with Windows 7 Enterprise edition. What feature included with this edition will allow legacy applications to run at the same time as other Windows 7 applications?

    a. BitLocker drive encryption

    b. NTFS

    c. UNIX native application support

    d. XP Mode

    e. Terminal Services

22. Which of the following is an advantage of HomeGroup computing?

    a. requires one or more expensive servers

    b. supports 20 workstations

    c. no security enforced

    d. simple to set up initially

23. A thread represents the files, data, and instructions that make up a single running task or application. True or False?

24. After a computer crashes and restarts, what tool automatically runs and tries to determine a solution to the problem?

    a. Startup Repair Tool

    b. Network Awareness Service

    c. Network Repair Tool

    d. Windows Boot Repair Services

25. Which of the following is a disadvantage of workgroup computing?

    a. requires one or more expensive servers

    b. supports an unlimited number of workstations

    c. no centralized security management

    d. simple to set up initially

Case Projects

Case Project 1-1: Selecting Windows 7 Versions for a Small Organization

Master Motors has 18 computers. They are replaced only as necessary due to hardware failure or new software requirements. No server is in place to centrally manage resources or security and no plan exists to add one in the next three months. Master Motors has no multimedia requirements at this time. Two computers have recently failed and require replacement. Which version of Windows 7 should be purchased with the new computers?

Case Project 1-2: Selecting Computers for Secure Computing

Superduper Lightspeed Computers builds over 100 computers per week for customers. A government contract bid has been received and is due in five days. The company is required to list all security advantages provided by their hardware and operating system solution. The hardware must meet industry standards. What combination of hardware and Windows 7 features would provide a secure computing environment?

Case Project 1-3: Dealing with Application Compatibility for Large Organizations

Gigantic Life Insurance has 4,000 users spread over five locations in North America. They have hired you as a consultant to identify the different options for deploying Windows 7 to the desktops in their organization. They are concerned that there are too many legacy applications to consider deploying Windows 7 within their company. List several tools that could be used to help you audit each application's compatibility with Windows 7. For those applications that cannot run with Windows 7, provide other options for running these applications.

chapter 2

Installing Windows 7

After reading this chapter and completing the exercises, you will be able to:

- Describe the deployment enhancements in Windows 7
- Choose a method for installation
- Choose a type of installation
- Use Windows Easy Transfer
- Perform an attended installation of Windows 7
- Perform an unattended installation of Windows 7
- Use and manage Windows Imaging Format image files

Before you can begin using Windows 7, you must install it. From the user perspective, the installation of Windows 7 is similar to Vista and differs little from installing Windows XP. However, from the perspective of a network administrator, there are many changes to how Windows 7 is installed. Like Windows XP, Windows 7 still offers the option for attended or unattended installation, but that is where the similarities end.

Windows Vista introduced a new installation method that uses Windows Imaging Format image files to apply installation files to the chosen partition. In addition, the installation process is performed by using Windows PE, a limited version of Windows that replaces DOS as an installation environment. Windows PE allows you to use current Windows drivers for network connectivity and mass storage controllers when you are creating bootable media to start the installation. Windows 7 uses the same installation process as Windows Vista.

In Chapter 1, you performed an attended installation to get your computer going and view some of the new features in Windows 7. In this chapter, you learn about the new deployment features in Windows 7, different installation sources, attended installations, and unattended installation. You also will learn about using Windows Imaging Format image files.

Deployment Enhancements in Windows 7

Home users are typically not concerned with how an operating system is deployed or the tools used for deployment. Many home users buy a computer preconfigured with an operating system and never need to install the operating system themselves. Other home users who do like to install the operating system are not greatly inconvenienced by an inefficient deployment process because they perform installations only occasionally.

Conversely, network administrators are much more concerned than home users with how operating systems are deployed. Network administrators are responsible for deploying operating systems to many computers; inefficiencies in the deployment process can extend the length of deployment projects and cost their companies additional staff time. Long projects and additional staff time result in higher costs.

Microsoft has introduced many new enhancements in Windows 7 to streamline deployment. These enhancements make it easier to deploy Windows 7 in corporate environments and can be considered in two categories:

- Design improvements
- Tool and technology improvements

Design Improvements

The design improvements in Windows 7 and Windows 7 deployment are all designed to make the installation of Windows 7 easier to manage. These improvements include:

- Modularization
- Windows Imaging Format
- XML-based answer files
- Installation scripts
- File and registry redirection

Modularization Windows 7 has been designed to be more modular than Windows XP. This is not readily apparent to users and administrators because it does not affect the user interface. Modularization is implemented behind the scenes in Windows 7 code and primarily makes modification of Windows 7 easier for Microsoft developers.

Modularization has the following benefits:

- Simplified addition of drivers and other updates, to make managing installation easier
- Simplified development of service packs, to reduce the risk of implementing service packs and updates
- Simplified implementation of multiple languages

Windows Imaging Format The installation of Windows 7 is done from a **Windows Imaging Format (WIM) image file**. You can modify existing WIM **images** and create your own WIM images. Some of the benefits you receive from using WIM images for deployment are:

- The ability to add and remove components directly from the image file
- The ability to add updates directly to the image file
- The ability to add and remove files directly from the image file
- A single image for multiple hardware platforms
- A single image file for multiple images with varying configurations

XML-Based Answer Files Windows XP required multiple text-based **answer files** for **unattended installations**. An unattended installation reads configuration information from the answer files rather than requiring user input. Having multiple answer files was confusing because it was difficult to remember which options were available in each answer file. The confusion was compounded by some options being available in more than one answer file.

To reduce confusion, Windows 7 uses a single XML-based answer file to perform automated installations. In addition, **Windows System Image Manager (WSIM)** is the only tool used to create and edit answer files for Windows 7 installation.

Installation Scripts Using scripts to manage the installation process ensures consistency. If the installation process requires you to prepare images, partition disks, and select components, then it is possible to make a mistake at any point in each process. Scripts can be used to automate installation tasks to ensure that they are performed in exactly the same way each time.

File and Registry Redirection Network administrators faced a challenge when securing previous versions of Windows. To enhance the stability of desktop computers, it is important to limit computer users to the minimum system rights possible. This prevents them from installing malicious software. However, to run properly, many common business applications required users to be either Administrators or Power Users. The Administrator or Power User privileges were required because the applications wrote information to restricted parts of the registry or the Windows directory.

Windows 7 eliminates this problem with file and registry redirection. When applications attempt to write information to the Windows folder or restricted parts of the registry, the requests are redirected to a virtual Windows folder or virtual registry location. This "tricks" the application into running, without requiring users to have elevated privileges.

Tools and Technology Improvements

To manage and use the design improvements in Windows 7 deployment, you must have certain required tools and technologies. Some of the tools are updated versions of tools that were available for previous versions of Windows. Other tools are brand new and created to take advantage of new technologies.

The new and improved tools and technologies for deployment included in Windows 7 are:

- Application Compatibility Toolkit
- User State Migration Tool
- ImageX
- Windows System Image Manager
- Windows PE
- Windows Deployment Services

Application Compatibility Toolkit Computer hardware and operating systems do not add value to an organization; applications are the tools that bring value to organizations. It is essential that the applications that ran on an older operating system still run properly on a new operating system. The **Application Compatibility Toolkit** helps organizations quickly identify which applications are compatible with Windows 7 and which applications are not.

Updated features in the Application Compatibility Toolkit include:

- A new agent that tests for compatibility when deploying service packs and hotfixes
- Centralized agent configuration
- Centralized data collection
- Data analysis to generate reports
- Automated updates of compatibility data
- Automated issue resolution to centrally fix known application compatibility problems
- The Online Application Community to share and resolve application compatibility problems

User State Migration Tool The User State Migration Tool (USMT) moves desktop settings and applications from one computer to another. Some features of USMT are:

- XML files
- Migrate encrypting file system (EFS) certificates with the /copyraw option
- Create a configuration file by using the /genconfig option
- The use of hard links to simplify data migration on the same computer

ImageX ImageX is a command-line tool for managing WIM images. ImageX is included in the **Windows Automated Installation Kit (WAIK)**, a collection of utilities and documentation for automating the deployment of Windows 7.

You can use ImageX to:

- Create images that include applications
- Split images into multiple files
- Compress images
- Mount images to a folder for adding or removing files

Windows System Image Manager WSIM is a graphical tool for configuring unattended installs creating distribution shares. WSIM is also included in the WAIK.

You can use WSIM to:

- Create answer files for unattended installations
- Add device drivers and applications to an answer file
- Create and add files to a distribution share

Windows PE Windows PE is a limited and non-GUI version of Windows based on Windows 7 technologies that can be used for installing, troubleshooting, and repairing Windows 7. In the past, an MS-DOS boot disk would be used for many of these tasks. Configuring MS-DOS boot disks for network connectivity was particularly cumbersome. Windows PE includes networking components and allows you to use current Windows drivers for network connectivity rather than searching for older MS-DOS drivers.

When you boot from the Windows 7 installation DVD, Windows PE is the operating system that controls the installation process. This is an improvement over previous versions of Windows, where the installation was a very limited, character-based version of Windows. Windows

PE provides more flexibility during the installation process. Without the feature-rich installation environment provided by Windows PE, the installation process could not use WIM.

Deployment Image Servicing and Management (DISM)
DISM is used to perform offline servicing of WIM images. This tool replaces the functionality provided by Package Manager (pkgmgr.exe) for Windows Vista. You can use DISM to service WIM images for Windows Vista and Windows 7.

Offline servicing is typically used by large organizations that want to apply windows updates or drivers to an image. However, it can also be used to update Windows PE images. DISM can use answer files created by WISM to define which updates should be applied. Only the offline servicing section of the answer file is used.

Windows Deployment Services
Windows Deployment Services (WDS) is an updated version of **Remote Installation Services (RIS)**. WDS is the server side component that can be used to manage the deployment of images over the network. Desktop computers can be booted to the network using a **Preboot eXecution Environment (PXE)** network card to perform an installation.

Activity 2-1: Installing the Windows Automated Installation Kit

Time Required: 10 minutes
Objective: Install the Windows Automated Installation Kit (WAIK).

Description: The WAIK includes most of the new and improved installation tools for Windows 7. Some of the tools included are documentation on automated installations, ImageX, and Windows System Image Manager. In this activity, you install WAIK on your computer. You can download WAIK for Windows 7 from the Microsoft Download Center at http://www. microsoft.com/downloads/details.aspx?displaylang=en&FamilyID=696dd665-9f76-4177-a811-39c26d3b3b34.

1. If necessary, start your computer and log on.

2. Place the **WAIK DVD** into your computer.

3. Click **Run StartCD.exe** in the Autoplay dialog box. If you are prompted by User Account Control for permission to continue click the **Yes** button.

4. In the Welcome to Windows Automated Installation Kit window, click **Windows AIK Setup**. Windows Installer begins preparing to install.

5. In the Welcome to the Windows Automated Installation Kit Setup Wizard screen, click **Next**.

6. In the License Terms screen, click **I Agree**, and click **Next**.

7. Click the **Disk Cost** button. Notice the WAIK requires approximately 1.2 GB of disk space.

8. Click **OK** to close the Windows Automated Installation Kit Disk Space window.

9. Click **Next** to accept the default installation location of C:\Program Files\Windows AIK\ and the default availability of Everyone.

10. Click **Next** to start the installation. Installation will take a few minutes.

11. Click **Close** on the Installation Complete screen.

12. Close the **Welcome to Windows Automated Installation Kit** window.

13. Click the **Start** button, point to **All Programs**, click **Microsoft Windows AIK**, and click **Documentation**. You can see that Windows System Image Manager and the documentation are installed, as shown in Figure 2-1.

Figure 2-1 Windows AIK
Courtesy Course Technology/Cengage Learning

Windows 7 Installation Methods

Windows 7 supports a number of different installation methods. Which method you choose varies depending on the number of computers in your organization, the speed of your network, and the level of customization that is required.

The three most common installation methods for Windows 7 are:

- DVD boot installation
- Distribution share installation
- Image-based installation

DVD Boot Installation

The **DVD boot installation** method is the least suitable method for a large volume of computers. It requires you to visit each computer with a DVD and to leave the DVD in the computer during the installation process. This method is suitable for small organizations that only occasionally install Windows 7.

The degree of customization performed with a DVD boot installation is low because it includes only the drivers and components included on the Windows 7 installation DVD. It does not include additional applications or updates. However, you can add drivers during installation by using a floppy disk, USB drive, or other removable storage media.

Distribution Share Installation

A **distribution share installation** requires computers to be booted into Windows PE from removable storage and then run the Windows 7 installation from a distribution share. The removable storage could be a CD-ROM or flash drive. The installation files on the distribution share are created by WSIM.

The speed of a distribution share installation varies because all of the files must be transferred across the network. An installation over a 100 Mbps network is typically slower to access than a DVD drive. However, over a 1 Gbps network, the installation may be faster than when using a DVD boot installation.

The level of customization for a distribution share installation is higher than a DVD boot installation because the installation image on the distribution share can be customized by WSIM or ImageX. This means you can add updates or additional drivers. However, you cannot include installed applications in the installation image.

Image-Based Installation

Image-based installation requires the creation of a customized image that you apply to each computer. After the customized image is created using ImageX, it is placed on a distribution share by using WSIM. This installation type requires computers to be booted into Windows PE from removable storage and then copying the customized image onto the computer.

An image-based installation is the fastest type of installation because all configuration is already complete. However, you may need several images for different types of users. In larger organizations it is reasonable to put forth the effort required to develop multiple images.

The highest level of customization is achieved by using image-based installations. Image-based installations can include service packs, updates, additional drivers, and even installed applications.

Windows 7 Installation Types

When an organization moves to a new desktop operating system, the network administrators must decide whether to upgrade existing systems or perform **clean installations**. A clean installation is an installation of Windows 7 performed on a computer that does not have existing data or applications. Most organizations choose to perform clean installations because the computers tend to be more stable afterwards. If clean installations are performed, then there must be a plan for migrating user settings and files from the old operating system to the new operating system. In some cases, you may choose to perform a dual boot of Windows 7 with another operating system.

Clean Installations

Most Windows 7 installations are clean installations. Home users typically get Windows 7 when they buy a new computer. A new computer always has a clean installation. Even in corporate environments, new operating systems are often implemented when new computers are purchased. Using new computers ensures that they are powerful enough to run the new operating system.

Network administrators in corporate environments often prefer clean installations on existing computers rather than upgrades because clean installations tend to be more stable than upgraded computers. Over time, operating systems become less stable due to additional software being installed. The additional software may be full applications, but it can also be ActiveX controls from Web sites, Web browser plug-ins, helper applications in the system tray, or even maintenance utilities that run in the background. A clean installation eliminates all of the extra software that has been installed over time.

When a clean installation is performed on an existing computer, the hard drive of the computer is usually wiped out and reformatted to erase the contents before installation. This raises concerns about losing files stored on the local hard drive of the computer.

Clean installations can be performed by any installation method. This includes the DVD boot, distribution share, or image-based installation methods.

In most corporate environments, computer usage rules dictate that users cannot store any files on their local hard drive. However, in practice many users store important files on the local hard drive despite the usage rules. Network administrators are therefore always concerned about locally stored data as part of performing a clean installation on an existing computer.

Even when a clean installation is performed on a new computer, there are concerns with data migration. When a user gets a new computer, they often want to retain files and settings from their old computer.

Upgrade Installations

An **upgrade installation** is also referred to as an in-place migration. Upgrade installations automatically migrate the user settings, files, and applications that exist in the previous operating system to the new operating system on the same computer. For example, when you perform an upgrade from Windows Vista to Windows 7, the user settings and files are retained. All of the applications are retained as well.

Only Windows Vista with at least Service Pack 1 can be upgraded to Windows 7. Also, a Windows Vista version can only be upgraded to the equivalent version of Windows 7 or better. For example, Windows Vista Business can be upgraded to Windows 7 Professional, Windows 7 Enterprise, or Windows 7 Ultimate. For a complete list of allowed upgrade paths see Windows 7 Upgrade Paths (*http://technet.microsoft.com/en-us/library/dd772579(WS.10).aspx*) on the Microsoft TechNet Web site.

You cannot use image-based installation when you perform an upgrade to Windows 7. You must run Setup.exe to properly upgrade an existing computer. Only DVD boot installations and distribution share installations use Setup.exe.

The biggest benefit of performing an upgrade installation instead of a clean installation is the time saved by automatic migration of user settings, files, and applications. The potential downside is less stability on an upgraded computer.

The upgrade process for Windows 7 is slightly different from the upgrade process used by Windows XP. The Windows XP upgrade process copied files over an existing Windows installation and reused the same configuration files. Because the Windows 7 installation is image based, the upgrade process captures settings from the Windows Vista installation instead and applies them after Windows 7 is installed. You can see this during the upgrade process. A potential downside to this process is that the upgrade may not migrate all settings and applications because settings stored in a nonstandard way may be missed.

Before upgrading to Windows 7, you should verify that your computer hardware and software are compatible with Windows 7. The simplest way to test compatibility is by using the Windows 7 Upgrade Advisor. You can download the Windows 7 Upgrade Advisor from the Microsoft Web site at *http://www.microsoft.com/windows/windows-7/get/upgrade-advisor.aspx*.

Windows Anytime Upgrade allows you to upgrade to a more full-featured version of Windows 7 at any time by purchasing a license from a Microsoft partner site or the Microsoft Store.

Migrating User Settings and Files

Deploying Windows 7 should not affect the ability of your users to perform their jobs. To provide a consistent experience when Windows 7 is implemented, Windows 7 must have all of the same user settings as the previous operating system.

Windows 7 stores user settings in user profiles. Each user profile is stored as a folder in the C:\Users\directory. For example, the user profile for the user Joe is stored in C:\Users\Joe. In this folder are a number of subfolders that hold information such as Start button configuration, Desktop icons, My Documents, and the Internet Explorer cache. In addition, this folder contains a registry file named Ntuser.dat that holds user-specific registry information related to application configuration and some Windows configuration settings for that specific user.

Windows XP stores user profiles in the "C:\Documents and Settings" folder.

During an upgrade from Windows Vista to Windows 7, profiles are automatically upgraded and settings within the profile are retained. When a clean installation is performed, there must be a process in place to migrate user profiles to the new computer. You can migrate user settings from Windows XP or Windows Vista to a clean installation of Windows 7.

You can use the following applications to migrate user settings and files:

- Windows Easy Transfer
- User State Migration Tool

Windows Easy Transfer is a graphical utility suitable for migrating user settings and files from one computer at a time. The User State Migration tool is a command-line utility that can be scripted to migrate user settings and files from many computers at the same time.

There is no automated method to migrate applications from one operating system to another. Applications must be installed on the new computer when a clean installation is performed.

Dual Boot Installations and Virtualization

When two operating systems are installed on the same computer and you can switch between them, it is referred to as a **dual boot installation**. To perform a dual boot installation, the boot loader of an operating system must support dual boot installations. The boot loader of an operating system is the first component loaded from the hard drive during the boot process and is responsible for starting the operating system. The Windows 7 boot loader supports dual boot installations.

Dual booting is typically required for two purposes:

- *Using unsupported applications*—Some older custom applications are not written in a way that is compatible with newer versions of Windows. The security in newer versions of Windows stops them from running properly. If you require an application that can only be run using Windows XP, then you may want to perform a dual boot of your computer between Windows XP and Windows 7. You would boot into Windows XP only to run the specific application that is not supported in Windows 7.

- *Keeping configuration data separate*—Sometimes network administrators and developers have a dual boot installation for testing purposes. One installation is used as a standard operating system for performing daily tasks, and the other operating system is used for testing new service packs, drivers, or software. This ensures that the new test software does not affect their daily work if it is unstable.

Windows 7 can perform a dual boot with almost any operating system. The main requirement is to install Windows 7 on a **disk partition** that is separate from other operating systems. This is required for the following reasons:

- *Partition type compatibility*—Different operating systems have different requirements for partition types and formatting. For example, Linux does not use the NTFS disk format that Windows 7 requires. Therefore, Linux and Windows 7 cannot be installed on the same partition.

- *Application file compatibility*—Installing multiple versions of Windows in the same partition can lead to problems with application files getting mixed up. For example, there may be different versions of an application for Windows XP and Windows 7. However, both applications could install to the same directory in C:\Program Files. By installing the Windows XP and Windows 7 versions of the application in different partitions both versions of the application can be run from the same computer, just not at the same time. A downside to this idea is the extra disk space required to store the extra operating system and the two application installations.

When you configure a dual boot installation for Microsoft operating systems, the rule of thumb is to install the operating systems in their order of release. For example, to dual boot Windows XP and Windows 7, you would install Windows XP first.

Windows 7 includes support for booting from a virtual disk file. In some cases, this can simplify dual booting by eliminating the requirement for separate partitions.

Most network administrators and developers now use **virtualization software** rather than dual boot installations. Virtualization software uses the main operating system as a host to run as many guest operating systems as you need. Each guest operating system is a completely separate virtual machine that is also separate from the host operating system. Virtualization software has the following advantages over dual boot installations:

- *Faster access to other operating systems*—A virtual machine can be up and running while you use the host operating system. You can access other operating systems almost instantly instead of shutting down your computer and restarting in another operating system.

- *Multiple virtual machines at the same time*—A single host operating system supports running multiple virtual machines at the same time. This allows you to set up complex testing environments, including networking.

- *Simpler disk configuration*—Virtual machines do not require additional disk partitions. Each virtual machine has one or more virtual disk files that can be stored on any existing partition that the host operating system has access to.

- *Snapshots and undo disks*—Snapshots and undo disks let you choose whether to save or delete the changes you have made to a virtual machine. For example, if after installing a software update on a virtual machine the virtual machine is unstable, you can revert to a snapshot made before the software update was applied.

- *Virtualized hardware*—When using new hardware it is sometimes difficult to get drivers for older operating systems. However, virtual machines have widely supported virtual hardware that is independent from the host operating system hardware. For example, a new computer may have a network card that is not supported by an older version of Windows. The virtual machines simulate older network cards that are supported by older versions of Windows, or the drivers are available from the virtualization vendor.

The two major virtualization products are VMWare Workstation and Microsoft Virtual PC. Both products are capable of running Windows 7 in a virtual machine. However, VMWare officially supports other products such as Linux that are not supported by Virtual PC. For more information about VMWare, see the VMWare Web site at *www.vmware.com*. For more information about Virtual PC, see the Microsoft Web site at *www.microsoft.com/windows/virtualpc/default.mspx*.

To support legacy applications that do not run properly under Windows 7, you can download Windows XP Mode for Windows 7 from the Microsoft Web site at *http://www.microsoft.com/ windows/virtual-pc/download.aspx*. Windows XP Mode is a Windows XP virtual machine that runs inside of Microsoft Virtual PC.

Windows Easy Transfer

Windows Easy Transfer is a graphical application included in Windows 7 for migrating settings and files from one computer to another. Settings and files can be migrated directly from the old computer to the new computer over a network or temporarily stored on a disk.

Windows Easy Transfer can migrate:

- *User accounts*—Only local user accounts are migrated. If the computer is part of a domain, then local user accounts are typically not used.
- *Folders and files*—Includes My Documents and other specified locations.
- *Program settings*—Includes program settings from the registry.
- *Internet settings and favorites*—Includes all of the Internet Options from Internet Explorer and favorites.
- *E-mail settings, contacts, and messages*—Includes configuration settings for Outlook Express or Outlook, address books, and files storing mail messages.

The graphical interface of Windows Easy Transfer simplifies the migration of user settings and files by leading you through all of the steps required to migrate files and settings. In small environments where user settings and files are only migrated occasionally, Windows Easy Transfer is an excellent tool. However, in corporate environments during a large deployment project, Windows Easy Transfer is too staff intensive because a person must be at the computer to perform each step of the Wizard.

Using Windows Easy Transfer requires four steps:

1. Copy Windows Easy Transfer to the old computer
2. Select a transfer method
3. Select what to transfer
4. Transfer user settings and files to the new computer

Copy Windows Easy Transfer

To collect user settings and files from your old computer, you must run a copy of Windows Easy Transfer on the source computer (your old computer). As seen in Figure 2-2, you can copy Windows Easy Transfer to USB flash drive, external hard disk, or a shared network folder so that your old computer can access and run Windows Easy Transfer.

Windows Easy Transfer is copied to the location that you specify and can be run directly from that location. A shortcut is created in the specified location for starting Windows Easy Transfer. Use this shortcut to avoid identifying the specific executable file that you need to run.

On the destination computer (your new computer), Windows Easy Transfer stays up and running to accept information from the source computer. This is required if you are transferring user settings and files directly from the source computer to the destination computer over the network or by using a USB cable. If you are not transferring user settings and files directly from the source computer to the destination computer over the network or a USB cable, then you can close Windows Easy Transfer on the destination computer at this point.

Select a Transfer Method

You can run Windows Easy Transfer on Windows XP or Windows Vista to migrate user settings and files to the Windows 7 destination computer. Windows Easy Transfer cannot migrate system and program settings from Windows 2000. When you run Windows Easy Transfer on the old

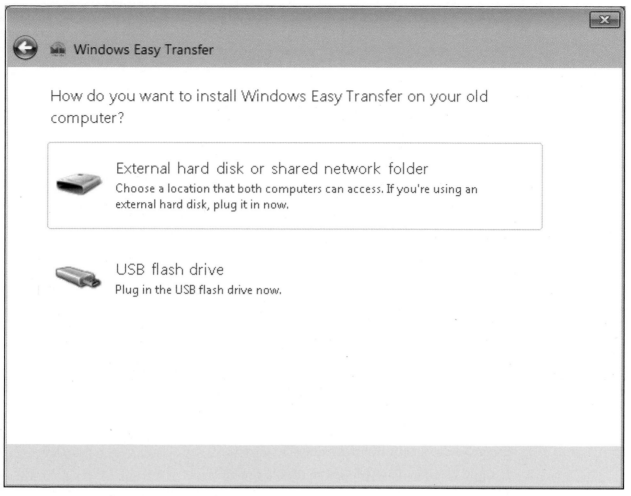

Figure 2-2 Windows Easy Transfer copying options
Courtesy Course Technology/Cengage Learning

computer you choose how to transfer user settings and files from the source computer to the destination computer, as shown in Figure 2-3.

Your options for transferring user settings and files are:

- *An Easy Transfer Cable*—Use this option only if the computers are physically close together and network connectivity is not available. The Easy Transfer Cable is a special USB PC-to-PC cable provided by the new computer vendor or it can be purchased separately.

- *A network*—This is the recommended option if both computers are on the same network because it does not require any additional configuration. After this option is selected, the source computer scans the network for the destination computer. The destination computer must have Windows Easy Transfer running and waiting for the connection.

- *An external hard disk or USB flash drive*—This option is required if the destination computer is not yet available. For example, if the source computer is getting a clean installation of Windows 7, then the user settings and files must be stored in a different location while the source computer is erased and Windows 7 is installed. After Windows 7 is installed, the user settings and files can be restored. Floppy disks are not supported as valid removable storage with Windows Easy Transfer.

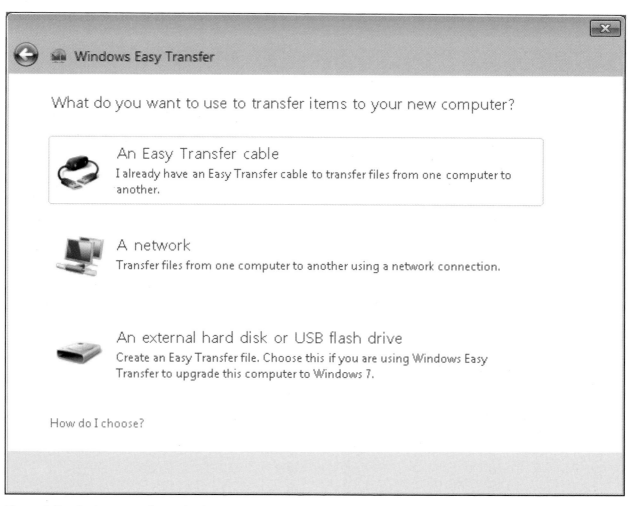

Figure 2-3 Selecting a transfer method
Courtesy Course Technology/Cengage Learning

You have the option to password-protect user settings and files when Windows Easy Transfer saves them to removable storage or a network folder.

Select What to Transfer

When you are collecting data from your older computer, Windows Easy Transfer presents you with a list of user accounts from which you can transfer data as shown in Figure 2-4. By default, all users and the shared items are selected for transfer. In many cases, you want to transfer the data for only a single user rather than all users. For example, if Bob is the only person that uses the computer on a regular basis, then only his data needs to be transferred.

For each user, you can customize the specific data that is transferred. The basic customization allows you deselect Documents, Music, Pictures, Videos, and Windows Settings. If users in your organization do not store documents locally, then you can migrate only the Windows Settings. This saves time during the migration process.

You can also perform advanced customization. When you select Advanced customization, you can identify specific folders within Program Files that you want to transfer. You can also customize the specific folders that are transferred within each user profile.

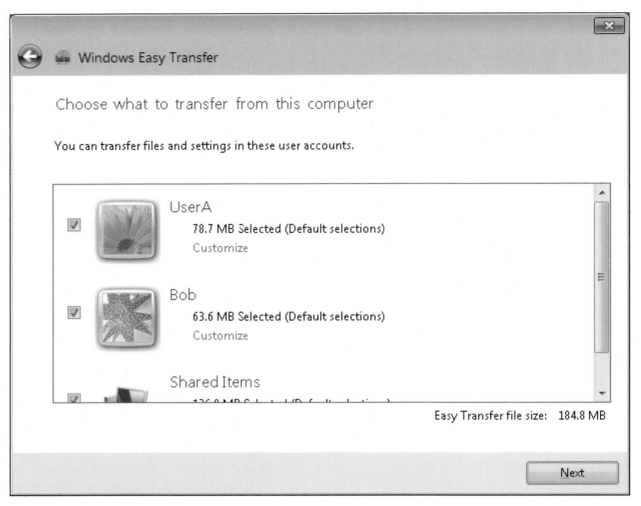

Figure 2-4 Selecting what to transfer
Courtesy Course Technology/Cengage Learning

You have the option to secure the data being transferred with a password. This allows you to protect any passwords that may be stored in user profiles during the migration process. It also allows you to protect any documents that are included in the data transfer.

 Windows Easy Transfer migrates application settings to a new computer, but does not migrate the applications. The applications must be installed on the new computer.

Transfer User Settings and Files

The detailed steps for transferring user settings and files varies depending on the method selected. When transferring settings and files on an external hard disk or network folder, you perform the following steps:

1. Enter the encryption password to protect the transferred data, if desired.
2. Specify the location of the MIG file that contains the data being transferred.
3. Match the user accounts on the old computer with existing accounts on the new computer, or create new user accounts on the new computer.
4. Begin the transfer.

One of the Advanced options available when importing the transfer data is mapping user accounts, shown in Figure 2-5. This feature allows you to create user accounts on the new computer automatically as part of the migration process. This feature also allows you to migrate settings to a user profile with a different name, in case the user account has been named differently on the new computer. If user accounts are created automatically, users are prompted for a new password the first time they log on. You could also migrate the same user settings and files to multiple accounts by performing the process several times to create a consistent user profile for several users.

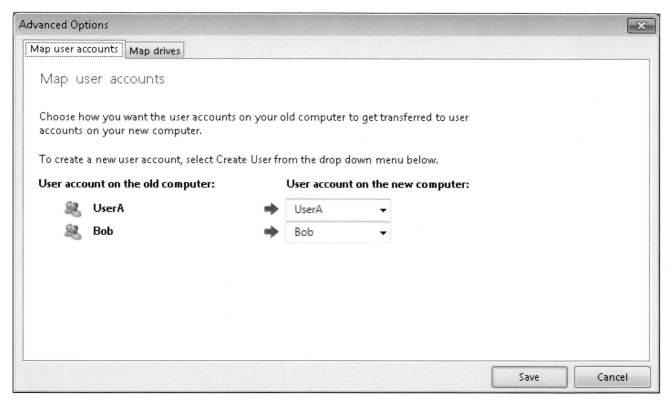

Figure 2-5 Mapping user accounts
Courtesy Course Technology/Cengage Learning

After the migration of settings is complete, Windows Easy Transfer generates reports that you can view. The reports provide a summary of user data that was transferred. This can be useful to verify that user settings were migrated. The reports also provide a summary of applications that were installed on the old computer and whether the application was found on the new computer. This can be useful to identify any application that should be installed on the new computer.

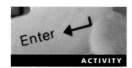

Activity 2-2: Using Windows Easy Transfer

Time Required: 20 minutes
Objective: Use Windows Easy Transfer to migrate user settings and files.

Description: You have ordered new computers for your organization to replace some older Windows XP Professional computers. The new computers are running Windows 7. You have confirmed with the users that they do not have any files stored on their computers, but all of the users want to retain their settings. Before deploying the new workstations, you want to test Windows Easy Transfer. In this activity, you use Windows Easy Transfer to save and then import your settings.

Due to the constraints of a lab environment, you are exporting and importing settings on the same computer. However, typically the settings would be exported from one computer and imported on another.

1. If necessary, start your computer and log on.

2. Close all programs that opened automatically at startup.

3. Click the **Start** button, point to **All Programs**, click **Accessories**, click **System Tools**, and click **Windows Easy Transfer**.

4. On the Welcome to Windows Easy Transfer page, click **Next**.

5. Click **An external hard disk or USB flash drive.**

6. Click **This is my old computer.**

7. Wait while the computer is scanned, read the items that Windows Easy Transfer has selected for migration and then under UserA, click **Customize**. Notice that you can select the type of data to migrate.

8. In the UserA window, click **Advanced**. Here you can select any folder on the computer to migrate.

9. In the Modify your selections window, click **Cancel**.

10. On the Choose what to transfer from this computer page, click **Next**.

11. On the Save your files and settings for transfer page, in the Password and Confirm Password boxes, type **password** and then click **Save**.

12. In the Save your Easy Transfer file window, double-click **Local Disk (C:)**, and then click **Save**.

13. After the settings have been saved, click **Next**.

14. On the Your transfer file is complete page, click **Next** and then click **Close**.

15. Right-click an empty space on the **Desktop** and click **Personalize**.

16. Click **Desktop Background.**

17. Click a new picture for the desktop background, and click **Save changes**. Setting a new desktop background allows you to confirm that the settings restore performed in the next few steps is successful.

18. Close the **Personalization** window.

19. Click the **Start** button, point to **All Programs**, if necessary, click **Accessories**, if necessary, click **System Tools**, and click **Windows Easy Transfer**.

20. On the Welcome to Windows Easy Transfer page, click **Next**.

21. Click **An external hard disk or USB flash drive.**

22. Click **This is my new computer.**

23. Click **Yes** to indicate that you already have access to your Windows Easy Transfer file. You would click No if you wanted help on how to obtain the settings from your old computer.

24. In the Open an Easy Transfer File window, double-click **Local Disk (C:)**, click **Windows Easy Transfer – Items from old computer**, and then click **Open**.

25. In the text box, type **password** and then click **Next**.

26. Click **Transfer** to accept the default copying of all account settings on the old computer to the new computer.

27. On the Your transfer is complete page, click **Close**. Notice that the original desktop background has returned.

28. Click the **Start** button, point to **All Programs**, click **Accessories**, click **System Tools**, and then click **Windows Easy Transfer Reports**.

29. In the User Account Control window, click **Yes**.

30. Read the information available on the Transfer report tab.

31. Click the **Program report** tab and read the information that is available.

32. Close Windows Easy Transfer Reports.

Attended Installation

An **attended installation** requires you to manually start and perform the installation. You start the installation by running Setup.exe. You perform a DVD-based installation and run Setup.exe from the Windows 7 DVD or perform a distribution share installation and run Setup.exe from a network share. For a single PC in a nonstandardized environment, the simplest method is to boot from the Windows 7 DVD, which automatically runs Setup.exe for you.

The process for performing an attended installation is much improved over Windows XP. Windows XP asked for configuration information at various points during the installation process. This forced you to stay with the computer during most of the installation process to enter additional information.

Windows 7 minimizes user involvement during installation. You enter information only at the very beginning and very end of the installation. The middle portion of the installation requires no intervention by you. This installation process allows you to spend a few minutes starting an installation, leave to perform other tasks, and then spend a few minutes finishing the installation.

In Activity 1-1, you performed a clean installation of Windows 7 by booting from the Windows 7 DVD. Please refer back to it for the steps that were performed.

An attended installation does not ask for any network configuration information. A new attended installation installs TCP/IP for networking and uses DHCP to obtain its IP address and configuration. Any additional network configuration, such as joining a domain or setting a static IP address, must be performed after installation is complete.

Setup.exe in Windows Vista and Windows 7 replaces the Winnt.exe and Winnt32.exe files used to install Windows XP.

Product Activation

Product activation is a process put in place by Microsoft to reduce piracy. If an installation of Windows 7 is not activated within 30 days, then Windows 7 displays a Windows Activation dialog box that reminds the user to activate Windows 7. The desktop background is also changed to solid black. However, Windows 7 functionality is not impaired.

Product activation requires very little additional work on the part of a computer user and significantly reduces piracy. It is now designed to inform a user that an unscrupulous retailer is selling illegitimate copies of Windows 7 rather than to punish the user.

If you are using an evaluation copy of Windows 7 Enterprise and do not activate it, then after 10 days the evaluation copy will shut down after one hour.

You can activate Windows 7 from the System applet in Control Panel, as shown in Figure 2-6. The System applet also shows you the current activation status of Windows 7.

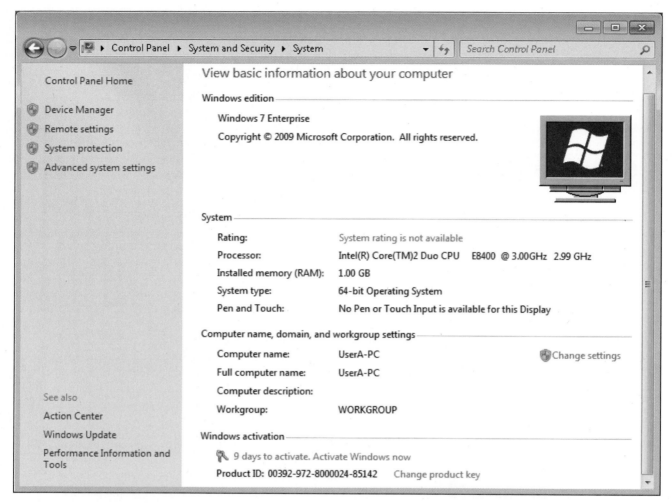

Figure 2-6 The System applet in Control Panel
Courtesy Course Technology/Cengage Learning

When Windows 7 is activated, the product key used during installation is associated with the specific computer that is performing the activation. Unique information about the hardware in the computer is used to generate a unique identifier that is sent as part of the activation process. No personal information is sent as part of the activation process. If another attempt is made to activate a different computer using the same product key, the attempt is denied.

If you perform significant hardware changes to your computer, you may be forced to reactivate Windows 7 because Windows 7 calculates that it is installed on a new computer. Reactivation is not forced for simple upgrades such as an additional hard drive or additional RAM. However, installing a new motherboard may require reactivation.

In practice, at the time of this writing, Microsoft has been allowing two automatic product activations before requiring users to phone the Activation Center. This is useful when moving your copy of Windows 7 to a new computer. If you do need to phone the Activation Center, Microsoft confirms your license information and the reason for an additional installation before giving you an activation code.

For more information about activation, see the Microsoft Product Activation Web page at *http://www.microsoft.com/piracy/mpa.aspx*.

Smaller organizations typically obtain Windows 7 when they purchase a new computer (OEM) or at a retail store. Both OEM and retail software activate over the Internet or by phone as described previously. Larger organizations typically purchase Windows 7 through a volume license agreement. A volume license agreement allows for two types of keys:

- *Multiple Activation Key (MAK)*—This type of product key functions the same as an OEM or retail product key that can be activated over the Internet or by phone. However, a MAK can be used on specific number of computers rather than just once. This simplifies key management for mid-sized organizations.

- *Key Management Service (KMS)*—This type of product key requires you to install KMS on a computer to act as a central point for product registration on your internal network. Product keys are installed on the KMS server and activated by having the KMS server communicate with the Internet. Computers activate by communicating with the KMS server on the Internet network. This scenario simplifies key management in very large organizations. It also allows activation to occur in scenarios where the client computer is not able to directly perform activation due to firewalls.

For more information about volume activation, see the Frequently Asked Questions About Volume License Keys Web page at *http://www.microsoft. com/licensing/existing-customers/product-activation-faq.aspx.*

Activity 2-3: Activating Windows 7 Online

Time Required: 5 minutes
Objective: Activate Windows 7.

Description: You were concerned about privacy during your initial installation of Windows 7 and selected not to activate online during the installation. However, after further research you realize that there are no privacy concerns with activation. In this activity, you activate Windows 7 over the Internet.

1. Click the **Start** button, and click **Control Panel**.
2. Click **System and Security**.
3. Click **System**.
4. If necessary, scroll to the bottom of the page to read the information under the Windows Activation heading. Notice that your product ID is listed here. You can also change your product key here if necessary.
5. Click **XX day(s) to activate. Activate Windows now.**
6. Click **Activate Windows online now.**
7. Click **Close.** Your copy of Windows 7 is now activated.
9. Close the System window.

Unattended Installation

Unattended installations do not require administrator intervention. The entire process can be automated using an answer file. An answer file is an XML file that contains settings used during the Windows installation process. Installation settings are read from the answer file instead of requiring administrator input during installation. Unattended installations are faster than attended installations and can be more consistent when the same answer file is used each time.

Using an unattended installation gives you a wider range of configuration options than can be performed during an attended installation. For example, an attended installation does not allow you to configure network settings. An unattended installation allows you to configure network settings and many other settings by putting the necessary information in the answer file.

To perform unattended installations of Windows 7, you must understand:

- Answer file names
- Configuration passes
- Windows System Image Manager

Answer File Names

When you perform a basic unattended installation you can specify the name of the answer file or allow Setup to find the answer file automatically. You specify the name of the answer file by using the /unattend switch when you run setup. The /unattend switch allows you to specify the path and name of the answer file.

If you do not specify the name of an answer file, then Setup will search for an answer file. This allows you to perform unattended installations by putting an answer file on removable media and then booting from DVD. Removable media includes floppy disks, USB drives, CD-ROMs, and DVDs.

The name of the answer file searched for varies depending on the configuration pass being performed. When performing a full setup without using Sysprep, you need to use an **autounattend. xml** file. Configuration passes and the required answer file name are listed in Table 2-1. If an autounattend.xml file is used, then it is cached to disk as unattend.xml for use by later configuration passes.

Table 2-1   Configuration passes and answer file names

Configuration Pass	Answer File Name
windowsPE	Autounattend.xml
offlineServicing	Autounattend.xml
Specialize	Unattend.xml
Generalize	Unattend.xml
AuditSystem	Unattend.xml
AuditUser	Unattend.xml
oobeSystem	Unattend.xml

Setup also looks in multiple locations for an answer file. The most common locations used are removable storage or the sources folder in the Windows 7 distribution directory. Table 2-2 shows the order in which locations are searched for answer files.

It is important to realize that answer files are cached in the %WINDIR%\panther directory and are reused during later actions that look for an answer file. For example, if an answer file is specified during initial Windows 7 installation, then it is cached to %WINDIR%\panther. Later, if Sysprep is run, the cached unattend.xml is reused before searching removable media or the sysprep folder. To resolve this problem, you can specify a specific answer file when running Sysprep, remove the unwanted unattend.xml file from %WINDIR%\panther, or place the new unattend. xml file in a location that is higher in the search order. The variable %WINDIR% represents the installation directory for Windows 7, typically C:\Windows.

Configuration Passes for a Basic Installation

Previous versions of Windows required different answer files during each phase to complete an unattended setup. Windows 7 still has multiple phases of setup, but a single answer file is used for all configuration passes.

2

Table 2-2 Answer file search locations in order

Location	Notes
Registry key HKLM\System\Setup!UnattendFile	The registry key points to the location of the answer file. This is suitable for upgrade installations or when using Sysprep. You specify the name of the answer file.
%WINDIR%\panther\unattend	This location is not searched when Windows PE is used to perform the installation.
%WINDIR%\panther	Answer files are cached here during installation for use during multiple configuration passes.
Removable read/write media in order of drive letter	The answer file must be located in the root of the drive. Subfolders are not searched.
Removable read-only media	The answer file must be located in the root of the drive. Subfolders are not searched.
\sources directory in a Windows distribution	Valid only for the windowsPE and offlineServicing passes. The file must be named autounattend.xml.
%WINDIR%\system32\sysprep	Valid for all configuration passes except the windowsPE and offlineServicing passes. The answer file must be named unattend.xml
%SYSTEMDRIVE%	Typically not used.

Different portions of the answer file are used for different configuration passes. Some settings can be configured in multiple configuration passes. However, only the last applied setting is effective.

The overall process for a simple unattended installation, booting from DVD, uses configuration passes in the following steps:

1. Windows PE starts.

2. Setup.exe starts and reads the answer file (autounattend.xml).

3. The windowsPE configuration pass is performed.

4. The specified Windows image is copied to the local hard drive.

5. The offlineServicing configuration pass is performed.

6. The computer reboots.

7. Windows 7 starts.

8. Perform basic system configuration.

9. Perform specific configuration including security ID (SID) generation and plug and play components.

10. The specialize configuration pass is performed.

11. The computer reboots.

12. Windows 7 starts.

13. The oobeSystem configuration pass is performed.

14. Windows Welcome is displayed.

Additional configuration passes are triggered when Sysprep is used to configure Windows 7.

NOTE

The windowsPE Configuration Pass Most network administrators expect to perform tasks like partitioning before running an automated install. However, with Windows PE you can automate this early portion of the installation process, just as you can automate the installation and configuration of Windows 7 components. Windows PE is a limited version of Windows that is loaded from DVD during the Windows 7 Setup process.

The **windowsPE configuration pass** is used at the start of the installation to:

- Partition and format the hard disk before installing Windows 7. Including this information ensures that you do not need to manually partition and format the hard disk before installing Windows 7.
- Specify a specific Windows image to install.
- Specify credentials for accessing the Windows image. This is useful when accessing the Windows image from a network share.
- Specify the local partition to install Windows 7 on.
- Specify a product key, computer name, and administrator account name.
- Run specific commands during Windows Setup.

The offlineServicing Configuration Pass The **offlineServicing configuration pass** is used to apply packages to a Windows 7 image after it is copied to the computer hard drive, but before it is running. The packages can include language packs, device drivers, and security updates.

The benefits of applying packages to a Windows image offline are:

- *Faster installation*—It is faster to install multiple packages offline than after installation is complete. This is particularly true if some packages require system reboots when performed online.
- *Enhanced security*—Applying security updates after the system is up and running leaves the system vulnerable until the updates are applied. Applying security updates offline ensures that the system is never vulnerable to the exploits fixed by the update.

When you are applying an image rather than installing from DVD or distribution share, you can use the Deployment Image Servicing and Management utility to apply offline updates.

The specialize Configuration Pass A wide variety of settings related to the Windows interface, network configuration, and other Windows components can be applied during the specialize configuration pass. This is the most common configuration pass to implement settings. The settings in the **specialize configuration pass** are applied after the SID is generated for the local computer and hardware is detected by using plug and play.

The oobeSystem Configuration Pass The **oobeSystem configuration pass** is applied during the user out-of-box experience (OOBE). The user out-of-box experience is the portion of the installation where users are asked for information after the second reboot. Information requested includes time zone, administrator name, and the administrator password.

Many of the settings you can apply during the oobeSystem configuration pass are the same as the settings you can apply during the specialize configuration pass. Therefore, it makes no difference whether you configure a component during the specialize configuration pass or during the oobeSystem configuration pass for a basic unattended installation.

The distinction between using the oobeSystem configuration pass and the specialize configuration pass is relevant when using Sysprep to prepare workstations. This is discussed in the Sysprep Configuration Passes section.

Sysprep Configuration Passes The **Sysprep** utility is used to manage Windows 7 installations that are imaged. Depending on the use scenario, additional configuration passes are triggered by Sysprep.

The configuration passes that can be triggered by Sysprep are:

- *The* **generalize configuration pass**—Used only when Sysprep is used to generalize an installation of Windows 7 by removing specific information such as the computer name and SID. This is done before imaging to allow the image to be used on multiple computers.

- *The* **auditSystem configuration pass** *and* **auditUser configuration pass**—Used only when Sysprep is used to manage or audit an installation of Windows 7 that has just been imaged. The auditSystem settings apply before user logon, and the auditUser settings apply after user logon.

- *The* **oobeSystem configuration pass**—Used when Sysprep is used to trigger the Windows Welcome after reboot. This may be done just before a new machine is delivered to a client.

The configuration passes triggered by Sysprep integrate with the configuration passes used by a basic installation. Figure 2-7 shows how the configuration passes triggered by Sysprep relate to the configuration passes triggered by Setup.exe

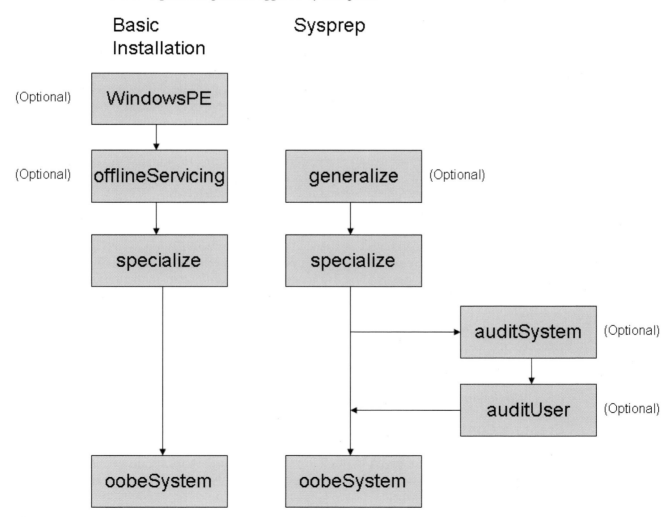

Figure 2-7 Configuration passes
Courtesy Course Technology/Cengage Learning

Windows System Image Manager

WSIM is the utility that allows you to create and modify answer files that are used for unattended installations. You can also perform a variety of other installation related tasks. Common tasks you can perform with WSIM include:

- Create or update an answer file
- Add device drivers or applications to an answer file
- Create a configuration set

Create or Update an Answer File
WSIM allows you to create an answer file to control the installation of Windows. The installation can be from a distribution share, the Windows 7 DVD, or an image you have created. WSIM reads the configurable settings for an image either directly from the image or a **catalog file**.

A catalog file lists all settings and packages included in an image. The states of all the settings are also included in the catalog file. For example, if the image has configured the screen saver to lock the system after 10 minutes, this will be reflected in the catalog file. Using a catalog file is faster than scanning the image directly. However, catalog files are not updated automatically. You must manually update the catalog file for an image after you update the image. The Windows 7 installation DVD includes catalog files for the versions of Windows 7 included on the DVD.

After an answer file is created, you can easily update it by opening the existing answer file with WSIM and modifying it. When you modify the existing answer file, WSIM ensures that all of the settings are still valid based on the catalog file or the image.

Some answer file settings are required for a completely unattended installation with no user intervention. Table 2-3 lists the settings and provides a description for each.

Add Device Drivers or Applications
Windows 7 ships with a large number of device drivers that support most hardware available at the time of release. However, as new types of hardware are released, there is a need to install additional drivers or updated versions of drivers. You must create a **distribution share** to hold a copy of device drivers you are installing.

A distribution share contains two folders for updating drivers:

- *OEM*—The drivers located in this folder are used during the initial setup of Windows 7 when Setup.exe is run from installation DVD or a distribution share. These drivers will be available for Windows when plug and play hardware is detected.

- *Out-of-Box Drivers*—The drivers located in this folder can be used either during the windowsPE configuration pass or the auditSystem configuration pass. The windowsPE configuration pass is performed for all unattended installations where Windows PE is used to run Setup.exe. The auditSystem configuration pass is only performed when the Sysprep utility is used to prepare images. Adding drivers during the auditSystem configuration pass allows you to add drivers to an existing Windows image without running Setup.exe from the installation DVD or a distribution share.

WSIM allows you to create a distribution share and then specify applications and device drivers from the distribution share that are to be installed during an unattended installation. The path to the distribution share should always be referred to by the **Universal Naming Convention (UNC)** path to ensure that it can be accessed over the network during unattended installations. For example, a distribution share on a server should always be referred to by a path such as \\server\share.

Create a Configuration Set
A distribution share typically has device drivers and packages that are used by multiple answer files. For example, a company might have only a single distribution share for all of its Windows 7 installations, but the various answer files are used to build workstations for different user types. Each answer file uses only some of the files on the distribution share.

A **configuration set** is the subset of files in a distribution share that are required for a particular answer file. For example, a retail store might have an answer file that includes a special

Table 2-3 Required settings for unattended installation

Configuration Pass	Setting	Description
windowsPE	Microsoft-Windows-International-Core-WinPE	UILanguage	The default language used for the installed operating system.
windowsPE	Microsoft-Windows-International-Core-WinPE	SetupUILanaguage	UILanguage	The default language used during Windows Setup
windowsPE	Microsoft-Windows-Setup	UserData	AcceptEula	Accepts the license agreement.
windowsPE	Microsoft-Windows-Setup	UserData	Product Key	Key	The Windows 7 Product Key. Does not prevent asking for the key during the specialize configuration pass.
windowsPE	Microsoft-Windows-Setup	ImageInstall	OSImage	InstallToAvailablePartition	Installs Windows to the first available partition. Alternatively, you can specify the disk and partition to install to by using other settings.
specialize	Microsoft-Windows-Shell-Setup	ProductKey	The product key used for activation.
specialize	Microsoft-Windows-Shell-Setup	ComputerName	The computer name for the Windows installation. To generate a random computer name set this value to *.
oobeSystem	Microsoft-Windows-International-Core	InputLocale	The default input locale for the Windows installation.
oobeSystem	Microsoft-Windows-International-Core	SystemLocale	The default system locale for the Windows installation.
oobeSystem	Microsoft-Windows-International-Core	UILanguage	The default UI language for the Windows installation.
oobeSystem	Microsoft-Windows-International-Core	UserLocale	The default user locale for the Windows installation.
oobeSystem	Microsoft-Windows-Shell-Setup	OOBE	HideEULAPage	Avoids displaying the license agreement.
oobeSystem	Microsoft-Windows-Shell-Setup	UserAccounts	The user accounts that are created during installation.
oobeSystem	Microsoft-Windows-Shell-Setup	UserAccounts	AdministratorPassword	Specifies the password for the local Administrator account.
oobeSystem	Microsoft-Windows-Shell-Setup	ProtectYourPC	The protection level of the Windows installation (recommended, only important updates, disabled).
oobeSystem	Microsoft-Windows-Shell-Setup	TimeZone	The time zone of the Windows installation.
oobeSystem	Microsoft-Windows-Shell-Setup	NetworkLocation	The network location of the computer (home, work, other).

scanner driver for the computers running the cash registers. A configuration set for that answer file would include the special scanner driver, but not any of the other drivers and packages in the distribution share that are not referenced by the answer file.

It is best to use a configuration set when workstations cannot access the distribution share. A configuration set allows you to minimize the amount of data that is placed on DVD or copied to a remote location. The answer file created when you create a configuration set uses relative paths so that the configuration set can be moved without introducing errors in the answer file.

Apply Offline Updates to a Windows Image Offline updates are software packages containing device drivers or security updates that are applied to an image during the offlineServicing configuration pass of the installation. If offline updates are included as part of the installation process, they are installed before Windows is functional.

Installing software updates before Windows 7 is running ensures that problems are fixed before the system is functional. This is particularly important for security updates which could be exploited between the time of system installation and installing the security updates.

Packages used for offline updates are included in a configuration set, as are other software packages required during an unattended installation.

 You can also apply offline updates to a Windows image by using Deployment Image Servicing and Management. This applies the update once to the image file, rather than each time during installation.

Activity 2-4: Creating an Answer File

Time Required: 30 minutes
Objective: Create an answer file that can be used for an unattended installation.

Description: You would like to streamline the process you use for installing new Windows 7 workstations. The biggest problem you run into when deploying new installations of Windows 7 is finding the proper product key. In this activity, you will create an answer file that automatically enters in the product key for you during configuration.

1. If necessary, place the Windows 7 DVD in your computer.

2. Click the **Start** button, point to **All Programs**, click **Accessories**, and click **Command Prompt**.

3. Type **md c:\wininstall** and press Enter.

4. Type **xcopy d:*.* c:\wininstall\ /s** and press **Enter**. This command assumes that the DVD drive on your computer is assigned the drive letter D:. If the DVD drive letter is different, replace **d:** with the appropriate letter. This copies the contents of the Windows 7 DVD to your hard drive. This step will take some time to complete.

5. When copying is complete, close the command prompt.

6. Click the **Start** button, point to **All Programs**, click **Microsoft Windows AIK**, and click **Windows System Image Manager**.

7. In the Windows Image pane, right-click **Select a Windows image or catalog file**, and click **Select Windows Image**.

8. Browse to **C:\wininstall\sources**, click **install.wim**, and click **Open**.

9. If the WIM file contains multiple images, you are prompted to select an image. If prompted to select an image, click an image and then click **OK**. This lab assumes that Windows 7 Enterprise is selected.

10. Click the **File** menu, and click **New Answer File**. A new untitled answer file has been created in the answer file pane, as shown in Figure 2-8. Notice that it lists the configuration passes in the components, and also lists packages.

11. In the Windows Image pane, if necessary, expand **Windows 7 ENTERPRISE**, and expand **Components**. This lists the categories of settings that you can configure in the answer file.

12. Expand **x86_Microsoft-Windows-Setup_6.1.xxxx.xxxxx_neutral** (.**xxxx.xxxxx** represents a subversion number that will change depending on the revision version of Windows 7), and expand **UserData**.

13. Click **ProductKey**. Notice that the upper right pane is now labeled ProductKey Properties and shows information about the ProductKey setting. You can see that the only configuration pass that this setting can be used in is the windowsPE configuration pass.

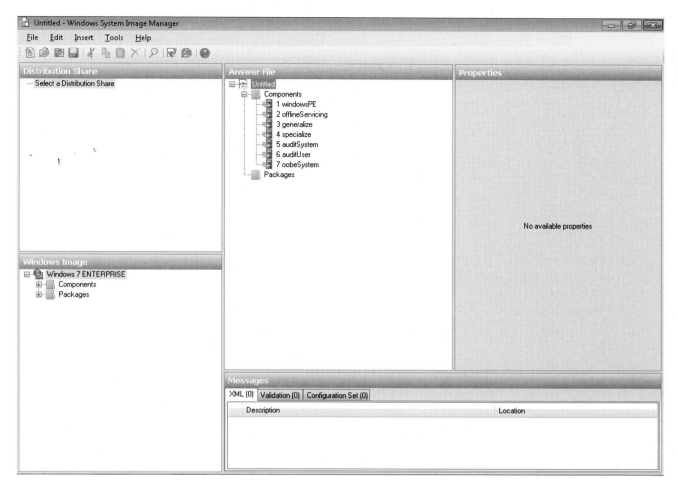

Figure 2-8 New answer file
Courtesy Course Technology/Cengage Learning

14. In the Windows Image pane, right-click **ProductKey**, and click **Add Setting to Pass 1 windowsPE**. This adds the setting to the currently opened answer file, and selects it in the Answer File pane.

15. In the ProductKey Properties pane, double-click **Key**. This allows you to edit the product key.

16. Type the product key for Windows 7, including the dashes(-), and press **Enter**. If you do not have a product key for Windows 7, then type **12345-12345-12345-12345-12345**.

17. Click **WillShowUI**, click the drop-down arrow, and click **OnError**, as shown in Figure 2-9. This configures the product key entry screen to be displayed only if an error is encountered with the product key in the answer file.

18. Browse through some of the other settings available in the **Windows Image** pane. Take note of which configuration passes the different settings can be configured in.

19. Click the **File** menu, and click **Save Answer File As**.

20. In the File name text box, type **autounattend** and click **Save**. This file can be copied to removable storage or another appropriate location for use during an unattended installation.

21. Close **Windows System Image Manager**.

22. Click **Internet Explorer** on the taskbar.

23. In the Address bar, type **C:\wininstall\sources\autounattend.xml**, and press **Enter**.

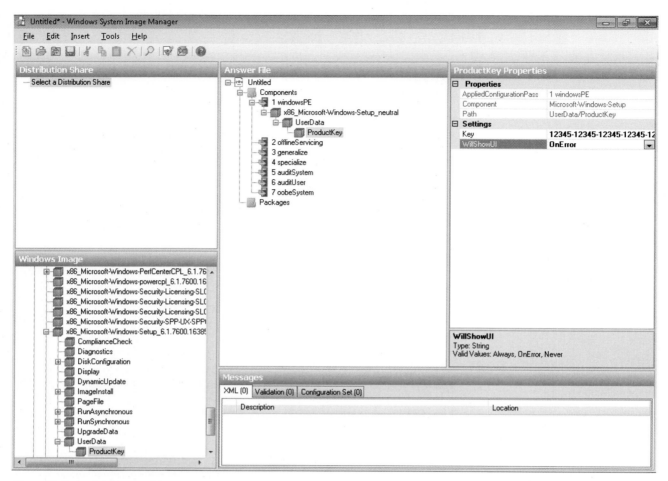

Figure 2-9 ProductKey configuration
Courtesy Course Technology/Cengage Learning

24. You can now see the structure of the XML file you created with Windows System Image Manager. It shows the product key you entered and the OnError choice for showing the user interface.

25. Close **Internet Explorer**.

Activity 2-5: Creating a Distribution Share

Time Required: 5 minutes

Objective: Create a distribution share that can be used for installing Windows 7.

Description: After receiving some new computers, you find that they are only able to display a resolution of 800 × 600 with 256 colors when Windows 7 is installed from DVD. After doing some research, you realize that Windows 7 does not include the correct video driver for the new computers. To avoid manually updating the video driver after installation, you decide to create a distribution share that you can place the appropriate video drivers in. In this activity, you create a distribution share.

This activity creates a distribution share on the local C drive due to hardware restrictions. The distribution share would normally be located on a server and accessible over the network.

1. Click the **Start** button, point to **All Programs**, click **Microsoft Windows AIK,** and click **Windows System Image Manager.**

2. In the Distribution Share pane, right-click **Select a Distribution Share,** and click **Create Distribution Share.**

3. Click **Open** to select the C:\wininstall\sources folder.

4. In the Distribution Share pane, expand **C:\wininstall\sources.** Notice that three folders are listed, as shown in Figure 2-10. These folders are used to store device drivers and packages that can be added to the Windows 7 installation. You must copy any device drivers and packages into these folders to make them available.

5. Close **Windows System Image Manager.**

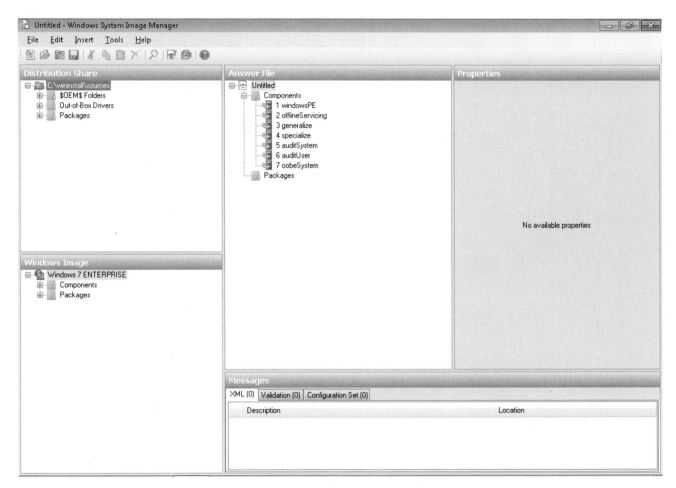

Figure 2-10 Distribution share
Courtesy Course Technology/Cengage Learning

Image-Based Installation

In a corporate environment, you need a quick and easy way to deploy workstations. Even with the improvements in Windows 7, attended installations take too much time to be practical. Unattended installations are better suited to a multiworkstation environment, but after installation, you still need to install additional applications and customize them to meet corporate standards. Image-based installation allows you to quickly deploy Windows 7 to workstations, complete with applications and customizations.

Corporate environments have been using imaging for many years as a method to quickly deploy workstation operating systems and applications. Sysprep has long been included as a deployment utility to support third-party imaging software. However, until now, corporations have been forced to rely on third-party tools to perform imaging operations. The Windows Automation Installation Kit includes the ImageX utility for capturing, modifying, and applying images.

The overall imaging process is as follows:

1. Install and configure Windows 7 and applications on a source workstation.

2. Use Sysprep to generalize the source workstation for imaging.

3. Boot the source workstation using Windows PE.

4. Use ImageX to capture the image from the source workstation and store it in a distribution share.

5. On the destination workstation, use Windows PE to connect to the distribution share.

6. Use ImageX to apply the image in the distribution share to the destination workstation.

Sysprep

In a corporate environment the most common use for Sysprep is preparing workstations to capture an image. This process is known as **generalization**. Generalization removes system-specific data from Windows. System-specific data includes the computer name, computer SID, and hardware information. After generalization is complete, the workstation image is captured and placed on a distribution share.

You can specify an answer file to use during generalization. If you do not specify an answer file, then Sysprep will search for **unattend.xml** to use as an answer file. If an unattend.xml file was used during the initial Windows 7 setup, then it is cached to the local hard drive and will be found when Sysprep is run.

 The generalize configuration pass is performed only when Sysprep is used to generalize an installation.

When a generalized image is applied to a workstation, that workstation creates all of the system specific data that is required, including the computer name and computer SID. It also detects the plug and play hardware and loads drivers for the detected hardware. After the system-specific information is generated, the computer is either put into audit mode or the Windows Welcome is run.

In order to properly use Sysprep, you need to understand the following:

- System cleanup actions
- Sysprep limitations
- Sysprep command-line options

System Cleanup Actions When you run Sysprep to generalize an image, you must also select a system cleanup action, as shown in Figure 2-11. The system cleanup action determines the behavior of Windows 7 after configuration. The two available system cleanup actions are:

- Enter System Out-of-Box Experience (OOBE).
- Enter System Audit Mode.

Out-of-Box Experience In most cases, you will choose the **System Out-of-Box Experience (OOBE) cleanup action** when generalizing an image. This configures the image so that on first boot, Windows Welcome is launched to collect any necessary information from the user before the configuration is finalized.

The oobeSystem configuration pass is performed when Windows Welcome is launched and will use an unattend.xml answer file if one is available. If the answer file is properly configured, the entire Windows Welcome can be automated.

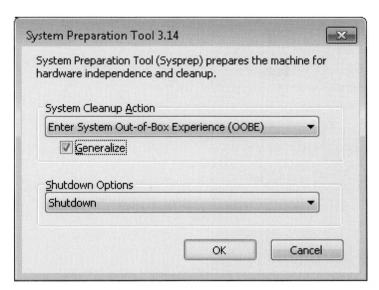

Figure 2-11 Sysprep selecting a cleanup action
Courtesy Course Technology/Cengage Learning

Audit Mode Audit mode is used by organizations that wish to perform additional modifications to an image before distributing it to users. In audit mode, you can install additional drivers or applications for users, then use Sysprep to trigger Windows Welcome on the next boot. You can also use audit mode to verify that the workstation is properly configured before delivery to the end user. To enter audit mode, select the **System Audit Mode cleanup action**.

Using audit mode is helpful when you want to continue using the same base image for many different varieties of hardware and end users. A single base image is applied to the computers, and then audit mode is used to add any specific drivers required by that model of computer and any specific applications required by the end user. Using audit mode prevents the OOBE from running. The process for using audit mode is shown in Figure 2-12.

The ability to continue using the same base image is particularly important for organizations that must perform significant testing on workstations to ensure quality. When a consistent base image is used, the testing for the functionality in the base image needs to be performed only once. Only the additional modifications need to be tested.

The auditSystem and auditUser configuration passes for unattended installations are performed only when audit mode is used. The auditSystem configuration pass runs before user login. The auditUser configuration pass runs after user login. Both configuration passes can be used to automate customizations performed in audit mode, rather than requiring manual intervention. Automating tasks performed in audit mode reduces testing requirements, as the automated process only needs to be tested once, rather than on each computer.

Sysprep Limitations Sysprep is a very useful tool, and a requirement for deploying Windows 7 by imaging. However, like any tool, Sysprep has a few limitations you should be aware of, particularly those restrictions related to hardware.

Unlike with Windows XP, the **Hardware Abstraction Layer (HAL)** can be different on the source and destination computers when imaging Windows Vista and Windows 7. In the boot configuration, you can use the detecthal option to allow the proper HAL to be loaded.

Sysprep limitations include the following:

- Drivers must be available to support plug-and-play hardware of the destination computer. However, the hardware does not need to be identical.

- Sysprep generalization resets the activation clock a maximum of three times. This limits the number of times Sysprep can be used on derivative images before activation is forced. For example, a computer manufacturer may make multiple modifications to an

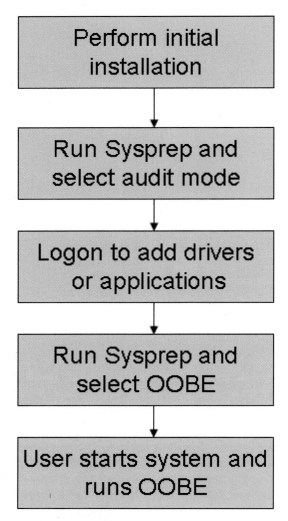

Figure 2-12 Audit mode process
Courtesy Course Technology/Cengage Learning

image and run sysprep after each modification to prepare the workstation for imaging. Activation is only cleared from the computer three times. On the fourth time, an error is generated.

- Sysprep does not perform imaging operations. You must use either ImageX or third-party disk imaging software to capture and apply images.

- If a computer is a member of a domain, running Sysprep removes the computer from the domain.

- Sysprep will not run on upgraded computers.

- After running Sysprep, encrypted files and folders are unreadable because the encryption certificates are lost when user profiles are removed.

Sysprep Command-Line Options Sysprep has both a command-line interface and a graphical interface. In most cases, network administrators prefer to use the graphical interface because it is more intuitive. To run Sysprep in graphical mode run C:\Windows\System32\Sysprep\Sysprep.exe without specifying any options. In high volume situations, you may prefer to use Sysprep in batch files. Running Sysprep in batch files requires you to use command-line options. The command line options for Sysprep are listed in Table 2-4.

Table 2-4   Sysprep command-line options

Option	Description
/audit	On reboot, the computer starts in audit mode. Cannot be used with /oobe
/generalize	Removes system specific information from the computer, such as computer SID
/oobe	On reboot, the computer starts Windows Welcome. Cannot be used with /audit
/reboot	The computer reboots after Sysprep completes. This is useful for immediately testing the post boot experience. Cannot be used with /shutdown or /quit
/shutdown	The computer shuts down after Sysprep completes. This is useful to prepare for imaging. Cannot be used with /reboot or /quit
/quiet	Prevents Sysprep from displaying dialog boxes. This is useful when Sysprep is used in batch files.
/quit	The computer continues running when Sysprep completes. Cannot be used with /reboot or /shutdown
/unattend:*answerfile*	Specifies an answer file to use for unattended setup

Activity 2-6: Generalizing Windows 7 by Using Sysprep

Time Required: 30 minutes
Objective: Use Sysprep to generalize Windows 7 for imaging.

Description: After using unattended installations for a period of time, you decide that you would like to include applications automatically as part of the Windows 7 installation to new workstations. You have not used Sysprep before, and you want to see what the user experience is like after Sysprep is performed to ready a workstation for image capture. In this activity, you use Sysprep to generalize Windows 7 for imaging, then you restart Windows 7 to see the user interface that is presented when the image is applied to new workstations.

1. Click **Windows Explorer** on the task bar.

2. In the Address bar, type **C:\Windows\System32\sysprep** and press **Enter**.

3. Double-click **sysprep**.

4. In the System Cleanup Action box, select **Enter System Out-of-Box Experience (OOBE)**. This option is used to prepare a computer for delivery to an end user.

5. Check the **Generalize** check box. This option removes computer specific information such as SID and computer name.

6. In the Shutdown Options box, select **Shutdown**. This turns off the computer after Sysprep is complete, so that an image can be captured from it.

7. Click **OK**. Sysprep looks for an unattend.xml file to process during the generalize configuration pass, generalizes Windows 7, and shuts down Windows 7. After Windows 7 is shut down, it is ready for an image to be captured. To capture an operating system image, you would boot Windows PE from removable storage and run ImageX to place the image on external storage or a network share.

8. Start your computer. Notice that the startup screen is the same as that seen during installation. Windows 7 now detects plug and play hardware, reboots, and then starts the out-of-box experience. If an unattend.xml file is found, then the settings for the oobeSystem configuration pass are applied.

9. Click **Next** to accept the default settings for Country or region, Time and currency, and keyboard layout.

10. In the Type a user name box, type **User***x* and then click **Next**. Notice that you cannot reuse the same local username because sysprep did not remove the existing user account. You need to enter a new user account to continue. You can avoid being forced to create a new user account by using an answer file.

11. In the Type a user name box, type **NewUser***x*.

12. In the Type a computer name box, type **User***x***-PC** and then click **Next**.

13. On the Set a password for your account page, in the Type a password and Retype your password boxes, type **password**.

14. In the Type a password hint box, type **Just a simple password** and then click **Next**.

15. If prompted for a product key, type the product key provided by your instructor and then click **Next**.

16. Select the **I accept the license terms** check box and then click **Next**.

17. On the Help protect your computer and improve Windows automatically page, click **Use recommended settings**.

18. Click **Next** to accept the existing time zone information.

19. Click **Public network.**

20. Click the **Start** button. Notice that you are automatically logged on as NewUser*x*

21. Log off and then log on as **User***x*.

22. Click **Start** and then click **Control Panel**.

23. Under User Accounts and Family Safety, click **Add or remove user accounts.**

24. Click **NewUser***x* and then click **Delete the account.**

25. In the Delete Account window, click **Delete Files.**

26. In the Confirm Deletion window, click **Delete Account.**

27. Close the Manage Accounts Window.

28. If required, use the instructions in Activity 2-3 to reactivate your computer.

ImageX

Most corporations are already using third-party imaging tools to deploy operating systems and applications to desktop computers. ImageX is included as part of the WAIK to create, modify, and apply workstation images. This tool is unique and offers advantages over third-party imaging tools.

Features and Benefits   The ImageX tool includes a number of features and benefits:

- A single image file (.wim) can hold multiple images. Within each image file, single instance storage is used. That is, if multiple images in the same image file have the same file, it is stored only once. This means that for each image added to an image file, the size increase is minimized.

- File-based imaging lets you capture images from one partition type and restore them on another. It also eliminates problems with mass storage controllers and matching HAL layers.

- Images can be taken of an entire partition or just a particular folder. This means you can use images to capture information for backup, such as databases. This can be useful when you are moving applications to a new computer.

- Images can be applied to an existing hard drive without destroying the existing data. However, this method cannot be used to apply operating system updates or application updates.

- Using imaging for initial setup is significantly faster than the xcopy-based file copy used in previous versions of Windows.

- Images can be compressed with either fast compression or maximum compression. This allows you to optimize images for speed or size depending on your environment. When multiple images are stored in the same file, they must use the same compression type.

- Images can be mounted to a folder in an NTFS partition for modification.

- When ImageX is combined with Windows Deployment Services (WDS), you can completely automate the deployment process to include partitioning and formatting hard drives. ImageX does not perform partitioning or format hard drives.

ImageX is capable of working only with .wim files. It cannot interact with images created by third-party imaging applications.

Image Capture After a workstation is prepared for image capture, you must shut down the computer before imaging. Shutting down the computer ensures that there are no open files when imaging is performed. You can boot the computer using Windows PE to perform the imaging operation.

The syntax for capturing an image is:

```
ImageX /capture image_path image_file "description"
```

The /capture option specifies that an image is being copied from disk to an image file. This option assumes that no image file already exists. To add an image to an existing image file, use the /append option instead.

The *image_ path* defines the source files that are to be captured as part of the image. To capture an entire partition, specify the root of the partition. For example, specifying C:\ would capture the entire C drive.

The *image_file* defines the .wim file that will hold the image. If you do not specify the full path to the .wim file, it will be created in the same directory with ImageX.

When multiple images are stored in a single image file, you should include a *description* for each image. Each image in an image file is uniquely identified by a number. The description is used as an easy way to identify the contents of each image, and can be used in place of the image number when accessing the image.

Table 2-5 lists other options that can be used when capturing images.

Table 2-5 ImageX options for capturing images

Option	Description
/boot	Marks a volume image as bootable. This is applicable only to Windows PE images that can be booted directly from the image file.
/check	Checks the integrity of the image file
/compress [maximum | fast | none]	Specifies the level of compression used when capturing a new image file. This option is not available when appending an image to an existing image file. Compression speed primarily affects image creation, not application. Fast is the default compression type used if none is specified.
/config configuration_file.ini	A configuration file for ImageX has three headings. The heading [ExclusionList] specifies files and folders to exclude from a capture or append action. The heading [CompressionExclusionList] specifies files and folders to exclude from compression. Wildcard characters can be used to exclude files from compression. The heading [AlignmentList] specifies files to align on a 64K boundary. The default action is to align files on a 32K boundary. A 64K boundary is required by some security programs.
/scroll	Displays output to screen. Typically, the output is redirected to a file.
/verify	Checks for errors and file duplication. File duplication is typically introduced when you modify the contents of an existing image.

Activity 2-7: Capturing an Image

Time Required: 10 minutes

Objective: Create an image by using ImageX.

Description: After confirming how Sysprep is used to generalize Windows 7 for imaging, you want to try capturing an image. To keep your test manageable in scope, you are only imaging part of the file system rather than the entire C drive. In this activity, you will image the C:\ Program Files\Windows AIK folder.

When imaging the entire C drive including the operating system, you must boot from Windows PE to ensure that all files are closed. When imaging data files, ImageX can be run from Windows 7. This activity allows you to perform the basics of imaging without using Windows PE.

1. Click the **Start** button, point to **All Programs**, click **Microsoft Windows AIK**, right-click **Deployment Tools Command Prompt**, and then click **Run as administrator**. ImageX must be run using administrator privileges and does not automatically elevate privileges by using UAC.

2. In the User Account Control dialog box, click **Yes**.

3. Type **md \images** and press **Enter**. In a production environment, you would typically store images on a network server rather than a client computer.

4. Type **ImageX /capture "C:\Program Files\Windows AIK" C:\images\WAIK.wim "WAIK"** and press **Enter**, as shown in Figure 2-13. This takes an image of the Windows

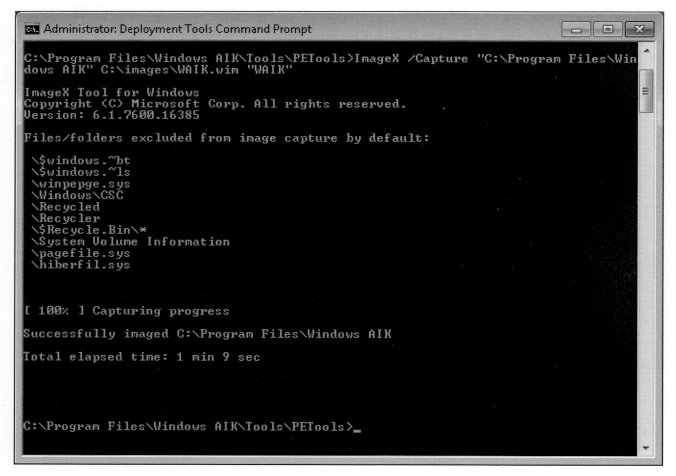

Figure 2-13 Capturing an image
Courtesy Course Technology/Cengage Learning

AIK folder and creates the WAIK.wim image file. The image is given the description WAIK. Any options with spaces must have quotes around them.

5. Type **dir \images** and press **Enter**. The file WAIK.wim is approximately 1 GB.

6. Type **ImageX /append "C:\Program Files\Windows AIK\Tools" C:\images\WAIK. wim "WAIK Tools"** and press **Enter**. This command images the Tools folder and places it in the same WAIK.wim image file. The image is given the description WAIK Tools.

7. Type **dir \images** and press **Enter**. As shown in Figure 2-14, notice that the file WAIK. wim is still approximately 1 GB because of the single-instance file storage used by WIM files. The Tools folder contains about 1 GB of data.

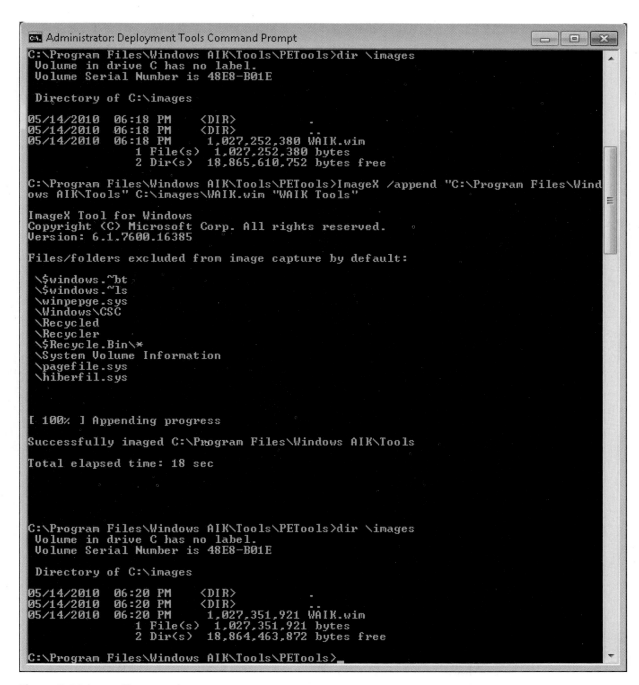

Figure 2-14 Image file comparison
Courtesy Course Technology/Cengage Learning

8. Type **ImageX /append "C:\Program Files\Windows AIK\Docs" C:\images\WAIK. wim "WAIK Docs"** and press **Enter**. This command images the Docs folder and places it in the same WAIK.wim image file. The image is given the description WAIK Docs.

9. Close the Deployment Tools Command Prompt.

Image Application   When you are using ImageX to deploy images with operating systems and applications, you must boot using Windows PE and connect to the distribution share holding the image file. After you are connected to the share, you can use ImageX to apply an image to the local workstation.

It is important to remember that ImageX cannot create or format partitions. Partition management must be performed manually or scripted within Windows PE.

The syntax for applying an image file is:

```
ImageX /apply image_file [image_number | image_name] image_path
```

The /apply option indicates that an image is going to be placed on a local hard drive from the *image_file*. The *image_number* or *image_name* is used to specify which image from *image_file* is applied. The *image_path* specifies the location on the local drive where the image will be placed. For example, C:\ indicates that the image will be placed at the root of the C drive.

If the image has been split into multiple files, then you must include the /ref option. The /ref option is used to specify the name and location of additional.swm files. For example, if the first of three split image files is BaseImage.swm, then /ref BaseImage2.swm BaseImage3.swm ensures that ImageX finds all three files.

Activity 2-8: Applying an Image

Time Required: 10 minutes
Objective: Apply a WIM image to a computer.

Description: One of the unique benefits of the WIM format is the ability to add files to an existing computer when an image is applied. Applying an image does not remove the existing files on a partition. You want to test this functionality. In this activity, you apply the WAIK Tools image to restore missing files.

1. Click the **Start** button, point to **All Programs**, click **Microsoft Windows AIK**, right-click **Deployment Tools Command Prompt**, and then click **Run as administrator**.

2. In the User Account Control dialog box, click **Yes**.

3. Type **ImageX /info C:\images\WAIK.wim** and press **Enter**. This displays information about the images included in WAIK.wim, as shown in Figure 2-15. Notice that image number 2 is named WAIK Tools. You can refer to images by their name or index number.

4. Type **rd "C:\Program Files\Windows AIK\Docs" /s /q** and press **Enter.**

5. Type **dir "C:\Program Files\Windows AIK"** and press **Enter**. You can see that the Docs folder is not there.

6. Type **md "\Program Files\Windows AIK\Docs""** and press **Enter**. This recreates the Docs folder so that the Docs image can be placed in it.

7. Type **ImageX /apply C:\images\WAIK.wim "WAIK Docs" "C:\Program Files\Windows AIK\Docs"** and press **Enter.**

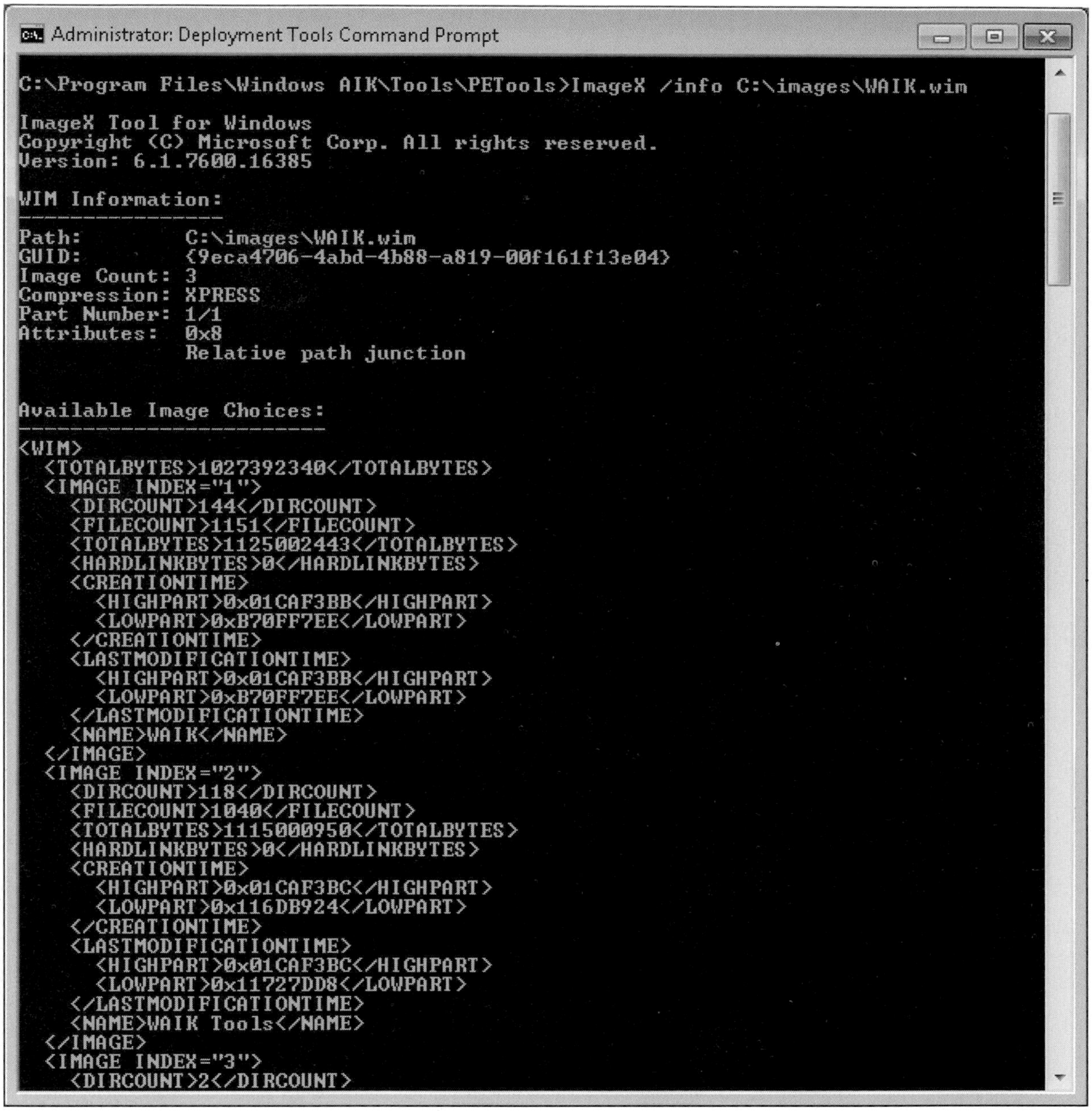

Figure 2-15 Information about a wim file
Courtesy Course Technology/Cengage Learning

8. Type **dir "C:\Program Files\Windows AIK\Docs"** and press **Enter.** You can see that the files have been restored to the Docs folder.

9. Close the **command prompt.**

Other Image Management Tasks ImageX is capable of performing additional image management tasks. Table 2-6 describes the additional options for ImageX that can be used to manage images.

Image Maintenance

When you use images to deploy Windows 7, you can include a preconfigured installation of Windows 7 and applications. When you build the image, you include any necessary applications and updates that are available at that time. Maintaining images requires you to apply software

Table 2-6   ImageX additional options

Option	Description
/delete	Used to delete a specified image in an image file, however, only metadata information and XML about the image are removed. The image file is not optimized and may contain unneeded information.
/dir	Lists the files and folders contained in an image
/export	Copies a specified image from one image file to another
/split	Splits a single wim file into multiple parts. This can be useful when storing a large image on DVDs.
/mount	Mounts an image in a wim file to an empty folder for viewing.
/mountrw	Mounts an image in a wim file to an empty folder for modification.
/remount	Refreshes the data mounted from a wim file. If used without options to specify a wim file, then all mounted images are listed.
/commit	Commits changes to an image that was mounted as read/write. If you do not commit changes, then they are never written back to disk.
/unmount	Unmounts an image from an empty folder
/cleanup	Frees all resources associated with a mounted image. The cleanup process is performed automatically when you unmount an image.

updates to those images and possibly modify Windows 7 features that enabled in the image. You can maintain an image by using DISM or Sysprep with audit mode.

DISM allows you to perform a wide variety of maintenance tasks on a Windows 7 or image while it is offline. An offline image is still stored in a wim file and not applied to a computer. Maintaining an image offline simplifies maintenance, but you are limited in the tasks you can perform. DISM can also modify an operating system that is running as an alternative to graphical tools. Windows 7 includes DISM as a utility.

Some common scenarios for using DISM for offline maintenance include:

- Add device drivers. As your organization purchases new computers that require new drivers, you can add those drivers to an existing image. This ensures that all hardware is properly detected when the image is applied.

- Apply Windows updates. Over time, additional updates for Windows 7 are released that are not included the image. Deploying Windows 7 without the latest updates is a security risk because some malware takes advantage of computers without security updates. Applying updates before an image is applied reduces the security risk. Windows updates must have an msu or cab extension. Service packs cannot be applied by using DISM.

- Enable Windows features. After initial development of an image, you may find that a specific feature that is needed for users has not been enabled. Rather than modifying the configuration of each computer after an image is applied, you can use DISM to enable the feature.

- Identify the need for application updates. To determine whether applications in an image need to be updated with a specific application update, you can use DISM to query whether a specific msp file is applicable. However, application updates cannot be applied by using DISM. Application updates must be delivered after the image is applied.

If you are using DISM to add multiple device drivers and install multiple Windows updates, performing the maintenance at a command-line can be quite time consuming. Each driver and Windows update requires a command to be entered separately. As an alternative, you can use an answer file with DISM. First, you build an answer file by using WSIM that includes the necessary drivers and Windows updates in the offlineServicing portion of the answer file. Then run DISM and specify the answer file. DISM uses only the offlineServicing portion of the answer file.

For detailed information about the capabilities and syntax for using DISM, see the Deployment Image Servicing and Management Technical Reference in WAIK or on the Microsoft TechNet Web site at *http://technet. microsoft.com/en-us/library/dd744256(WS.10).aspx.*

The only way to have complete control over the update of an image is to apply that image to a computer, make any necessary modifications, and then capture the image again. This is time consuming, but it allows you to apply any type of software updates, including applications and service packs.

Typically, you run Sysprep to generalize an image just before capturing it. However, each time you run Sysprep to generalize an image, it requires reactivation. Windows 7 can be reactivated only three times and then sysprep will cease to function. You must carefully consider this as you update images.

Windows PE Boot Media Creation

An operating system on a hard drive cannot be running while an image is being taken or applied. You need an alternative way to get access to the data on the hard drive and run ImageX. Windows PE is a small version of Windows that can be installed on a CD or a USB drive. You can use Windows PE as part of the imaging process. Windows PE is included as part of WAIK.

To create a Windows PE boot CD that you can use for imaging, complete the following steps:

1. Run **copype.cmd** to create the folder structure with the necessary files

2. Copy **winpe.wim** to ISO\Sources\boot.wim.

3. Copy **ImageX.exe** and other desired files to the ISO folder.

4. Run **oscdimg.exe** to create an ISO file that you can burn to CD.

5. Burn the ISO file to CD or DVD.

For detailed information about creating Bootable Windows PE RAM Disks, see Deployment Tools Walkthroughs in Windows AIK or on the Microsoft TechNet Web site at *http://technet.microsoft.com/en-us/library/ dd744287(WS.10).aspx.*

If you need to customize Windows PE for your hardware, you can use DISM add any necessary drivers. For example, new hardware may require you to add a new network driver to the Windows PE image.

Activity 2-9: Creating a Windows PE Boot CD

Time Required: 10 minutes
Objective: Create a Windows PE boot CD.

Description: To enable imaging, you need to have a portable operating system with the ability to run ImageX. In this activity, you create an ISO file that can be burned to a CD and used for imaging operations.

1. Click the **Start** button, point to **All Programs**, click **Microsoft Windows AIK**, and click **Deployment Tools Command Prompt**.

2. Type **copype.cmd x86 C:\bootcd** and press **Enter**. This command creates the necessary folder structure for the 32-bit version of Windows PE in the C:\bootcd folder. For a 64-bit version of Windows PE, use the option amd64 instead of x86.

3. Type **copy C:\bootcd\winpe.wim C:\bootcd\ISO\sources\boot.wim** and press **Enter**. This command copies and renames the bootable image of Windows PE. The ISO folder is the content that is used to create the ISO file.

4. Type **copy "C:\Program Files\Windows AIK\Tools\x86\imagex.exe" C:\bootcd\ISO** and press **Enter**. Notice that ImageX is being copied from an architecture specific directory. You need to ensure that copy the version ImageX that matches the architecture selected when you ran copype.cmd.

5. Type **oscdimg –n –bC:\bootcd\etfsboot.com C:\bootcd\ISO C:\bootcd\WinPEboot. iso** and press **Enter**. This command creates WinPEboot.iso by using the contents of the ISO folder and etfsboot.com. For EFI-based computers (instead of BIOS), you need to substitute efisys.bin for etfsboot.com.

6. WinPEboot.iso is now ready to be burned to a CD or DVD.

Chapter Summary

- Windows 7 has many enhancements that make deployment easier. Design improvements include modularization, WIM-based installation, XML-based answer files, installation scripting, and file and registry redirection. Tool and technology improvements include the Application Compatibility Toolkit, User State Migration Tool, ImageX, and WSIM.

- The three primary ways to install Windows 7 are DVD boot installation, distribution share installation, and image-based installation. DVD boot installations have low customization and are only suitable for infrequent installations. Distribution share installations allow you to add extra drivers and packages. Image-based installations can include installed and configured applications along with operating system.

- Clean installations are preferred over upgrade installations by most network administrators because a clean installation results in a more stable operating system. However, clean installations require user settings and data to be migrated from the old computer to the new computer. Upgrades automatically migrate user settings and data.

- Windows 7 can perform a dual boot with almost any other operating system. However, most network administrators now use virtualization software to create virtual machines rather than performing a dual boot.

- Windows Easy Transfer is a graphical wizard that leads you through the process of migrating user settings and files from an old computer to Windows 7. User Settings and files can be migrated from Windows XP or Windows Vista.

- An attended installation requires you to answer questions during the installation.

- Unattended installation uses an answer file to pass configuration to Setup, with a network administrator answering questions. The two most common names for answer files are autounattend.xml and unattend.xml.

- During a basic installation, the windowsPE, offlineServicing, specialize, and oobeSystem configuration passes are performed. When Sysprep is used, then the generalize, auditSystem, auditUser, and oobeSystem configuration passes can be triggered.

- WSIM is used to create answer files, add device drivers or packages to an answer file, create a configuration set, or apply offline updates to a Windows 7 image.

- Sysprep is used to prepare computers for imaging. After Sysprep is run, Windows 7 can be configured to enter audit mode or start the out-of-box experience. Windows 7 is much more portable to varying hardware platforms than previous versions of Windows.

- ImageX is used to capture, modify, and apply WIM images. WIM is file-based imaging and allows you to store multiple images in a single image file. Single-instance storage reduces the size of an image file.

- DISM is used to maintain Windows 7 images. DISM can be used to apply Windows updates and enabled features.

- You can create a bootable CD, DVD, or USB drive to perform imaging operations. The necessary files are included with WAIK.

Key Terms

answer file   An answer file is used during an unattended setup to provide configuration to Setup.exe. Windows 7 answer files are in an XML format and are created by using Windows System Image Manager.

Application Compatibility Toolkit   A set of utilities and resources from Microsoft to help organizations run legacy software on Windows 7.

attended installation   An installation when a network administrator must be present to answer configuration questions presented during Windows 7 installation.

auditSystem configuration pass   This configuration pass is performed before user logon when Sysprep triggers Windows 7 into audit mode.

auditUser configuration pass   This configuration pass is performed after user logon when Sysprep triggers Windows 7 into audit mode.

autounattend.xml   An answer file that is automatically searched for during the windowsPE, offlineServicing, and specialize configuration passes.

catalog file   WSIM uses catalog files to read the configurable settings and their current status for an WIM image.

clean installation   An installation that is performed on a new computer, or does not retain the user settings or applications of an existing computer.

configuration set   The subset of files from a distribution share that are required for a particular answer file. A configuration set is more compact than a distribution share.

DVD boot installation   An installation of Windows 7 that is started by booting from CD or DVD to run Setup.exe.

Deployment Image Servicing and Management (DISM)   A command-line tool that can be used to service Windows 7 images offline or online.

disk partition   Hard disks are subdivided into logical units called partitions. Each partition is then formatted and represented as a drive letter in Windows.

distribution share   A share configured through WSIM to hold drivers and packages that can be added to Windows 7 during installation.

distribution share installation   An installation of Windows 7 that is started by running Setup.exe over the network from a distribution share.

dual boot installation   A computer with two operating systems installed at the same time. The user selects an operating system during start up.

generalization   A process performed by Sysprep to prepare a computer running Windows 7 for imaging. The computer SID, computer name, user profiles, and hardware information are removed during generalization.

generalize configuration pass   This configuration pass is performed when Sysprep is run to generalize Windows 7.

Hardware Abstraction Layer (HAL)   A low-level system driver in Windows 7 that controls communication between Windows 7 and the computer hardware.

image   A collection of files captured using ImageX and stored in an image file.

image-based installation   An image-based installation that uses ImageX to apply an image of an operating system to a computer. The image can include applications as well as the operating system.

image file   A file that stores one or more images. The size of an image file is minimized through the use of single-instance storage when a file exists in multiple images.

ImageX   A new command-line tool for managing WIM images.

offlineServicing configuration pass   The second configuration pass that is performed after the Windows image has been copied to the local hard drive. This configuration pass applies packages such as security updates and service packs before Windows 7 is started.

offline update   An offline update is applied to Windows 7 during installation before Windows 7 is started. The packages used for offline updates are supplied by Microsoft.

oobeSystem configuration pass   The final configuration pass before installation is complete. This configuration pass is typically used in conjunction with Sysprep and ImageX.

Preboot eXecution Environment (PXE)   A standard used by network cards to boot directly to the network and download an operating system. Once that operating system is started, tasks such as imaging can be performed.

product activation   A process put in place by Microsoft to reduce piracy. Unique information about your computer is sent to Microsoft to ensure that the package of Windows 7 purchased is installed on only a single computer.

Remote Installation Services (RIS)   The server-based system available in Windows Server 2003 SP2 and later versions for deploying desktop operating systems automatically over the network.

specialize configuration pass   The configuration pass that is performed after hardware has been detected. This is the most common configuration pass to apply settings.

Sysprep   A tool that is used to generalize Windows 7 and prepare computers for imaging.

System Audit Mode cleanup action   An option in Sysprep that triggers the computer to enter Audit mode and run the auditSystem and auditUser configuration passes on reboot.

System Out-of-Box Experience cleanup action   An option in Sysprep that triggers the computer to run the oobeSystem configuration pass and start Windows Welcome on reboot.

unattend.xml   An answer file that is automatically searched for during the generalize, auditSystem, auditUser, and oobeSystem configuration passes.

unattended installation   An installation that does not require any user input because all necessary configuration information is provided by an answer file.

Universal Naming Convention (UNC)   A naming system used by windows computers to locate network file shares and network printers. The format is \\servername\sharename.

upgrade installation   An installation that migrates all of the settings from a preexisting operating system to Windows 7.

User State Migration Tool (USMT)   A set of scriptable command-line utilities that are used to migrate user settings and files from a source computer to a destination computer. USMT is typically used by large organizations during deployments of desktop operating systems.

virtualization software   Software that allows you to run multiple operating systems on a single computer at the same time. One operating system functions as the host, while others are guest operating systems that run on the host.

Windows Automated Installation Kit (WAIK)   A collection of utilities and documentation for automating the deployment of Windows 7.

Windows Deployment Services (WDS)   A server-based system for deploying desktop operating systems automatically over the network. PXE is used to connect the computers to WDS.

Windows Easy Transfer   A graphical wizard for migrating user files and settings from Windows 2000 Professional, Windows XP, or Windows Vista to a new Windows 7 computer.

Windows Imaging Format (WIM)   A file-based image format developed by Microsoft to create and manage WIM files using ImageX.

Windows PE   A limited version of Windows that can be used to perform recovery tasks and install Windows 7.

windowsPE configuration pass   The first configuration pass performed during setup, which can be used to perform tasks such as disk partitioning and entering the product key.

Windows System Image Manager (WSIM)   A utility that is used to create answer files for Windows 7 unattended installations. WSIM can also create distribution shares and configuration sets.

Review Questions

1. Which Windows 7 design improvement over Windows XP simplifies the development of service packs and therefore reduces the risk of implementing service packs?

   a. modularization

   b. Windows Imaging Format

   c. XML-based answer files

   d. installation scripts

   e. file and registry redirection

2. Which Windows 7 design improvement allows applications that require administrative privileges to run even when the user running the application does not have administrative privileges?

   a. modularization

   b. Windows Imaging Format

   c. XML-based answer files

   d. installation scripts

   e. file and registry redirection

3. Which task cannot be performed by using ImageX?

   a. Create an image.

   b. Add files to an image.

   c. Add service packs to an image.

   d. Delete an image.

   e. Apply an image.

4. What server-side component is used to manage the deployment of Windows 7 over a network?

   a. Windows Deployment Services

   b. Remote Installation Service

   c. Preboot eXecution Environment

   d. ImageX

   e. distribution share

5. Which utility is used to create answer files for unattended installations?

   a. ImageX

   b. Windows PE

   c. Windows System Image Manager

   d. Windows Deployment Services

   e. Preboot eXecution Environment

6. Which utility is used to prepare computers for imaging by removing specific information, such as the computer name and computer SID?

   a. ImageX

   b. Windows PE

   c. Windows System Image Manager

   d. Windows Deployment Services

   e. Sysprep

7. Which installation methods require booting into Windows PE before Windows 7 starts? (Choose all that apply.)

    a. DVD boot installation

    b. distribution share installation

    c. upgrade installation

    d. image-based installation

8. Which installation method can be used to distribute Windows 7 with applications already installed?

    a. DVD boot installation

    b. distribution share installation

    c. unattended installation

    d. image-based installation

    e. attended installation

9. The _____ installation method is best suited to small organizations that install Windows 7 only occasionally.

10. A clean installation of an operating system is typically considered to be more stable than an upgrade installation. True or False?

11. Which methods can you use to migrate user settings from a previous operating system to Windows 7? (Choose all that apply.)

    a. Copy the user profile from the old computer to the new computer.

    b. Perform an upgrade over the top of the old operating system.

    c. Use Windows Easy Transfer.

    d. Use the User State Migration Toolkit.

    e. Use Remote Desktop to copy to files.

12. Which folder is used to store user profiles in Windows 7?

    a. C:\Documents and Settings

    b. C:\Profiles

    c. C:\Windows\Profiles

    d. C:\Users

    e. C:\Documents and Settings\Profiles

13. Which methods can you use to place applications from a previous operating system on Windows 7? (Choose all that apply.)

    a. Copy the applications from the previous computer to the new computer.

    b. Perform an upgrade over the top of the previous operating system.

    c. Use Windows Easy transfer.

    d. Use the User State Migration Toolkit.

    e. Reinstall the applications on the new computer.

14. When installing Windows 7 as a dual boot installation with another operating system, it is recommended to keep Windows 7 on the same partition as the other operating system. True or False?

15. In which situation is dual booting required because virtualization is not able to perform the task?

    a. installing and testing new applications

    b. installing and testing new device drivers

c.   installing and testing service packs

d.   installing and testing security updates

16. Which of the following are benefits of virtualization over dual booting? (Choose all that apply.)

a.   running multiple operating systems at the same time

b.   free operating system licenses

c.   simpler disk configuration

d.   last known good is never required for system recovery

e.   snapshots and undo disks

17. Which operating systems can Windows Easy Transfer migrate user settings and files from? (Choose all that apply.)

a.   Windows NT

b.   Windows 98

c.   Windows 2000 Professional

d.   Windows XP

e.   Windows Vista

18. Windows Easy Transfer can migrate the user settings and files for multiple users in a single pass. True or False?

19. Which utility can be used update drivers in an existing Windows 7 image?

a.   WISM

b.   ImageX

c.   DISM

d.   Package Manager

e.   Windows Update

20. Which configuration passes automatically search for an autounattend.xml file, if an answer file is not specified? (Choose all that apply.)

a.   windowsPE

b.   offlineServicing

c.   specialize

d.   generalize

e.   oobeSystem

21. Which configuration pass can be used to perform disk partitioning operations?

a.   windowsPE

b.   offlineServicing

c.   specialize

d.   generalize

e.   oobeSystem

22. Which configuration pass is performed by Sysprep?

a.   windowsPE

b.   offlineServicing

c.   specialize

d.   generalize

e.   oobeSystem

23. A WIM image file containing two Windows 7 images will be approximately twice as big as a WIM image file containing one Windows 7 image. True or False?

24. Which options must be used with ImageX to save changes to an image? (Choose two.)

    a. /mount

    b. /mountrw

    c. /unmount

    d. /commit

    e. /save

25. Which of the following are benefits of ImageX? (Choose all that apply.)

    a. WIM image file size is minimized by single instance storage.

    b. Images can be taken of an entire partition or just a single folder.

    c. Partitions can be created automatically.

    d. Images are always compressed to save disk space.

    e. There is no charge to use ImageX for Windows 7 imaging.

Case Projects

Case Project 2-1: Installation for a Small Organization

Buddy's Machine Shop has 30 computers. Computers are replaced only as required by hardware failure or new software requirements. Jeff performs network administration tasks for Buddy's machine shop 25% of the time and spends 75% of his time doing computer-automated design work. What is the best way for Jeff to start implementing Windows 7 for Buddy's Machine Shop?

Case Project 2-2: Using Image-Based Installation

Superduper Lightspeed Computers builds over 100 computers per week for customers. The computers use a wide range of hardware depending on whether they are built for gaming, home use, or office use. Create a plan for Superduper Lightspeed Computers to start using imaging, including audit mode, to install Windows 7 on their new computers.

Case Project 2-3: Migrating User Settings and Files

Hyperactive Media Sales has 10 Windows Vista laptop computers used by sales people in the organization. Each laptop computer has several customized applications that are used during the sales process as well as customer relationship management software. All of the applications on the laptops are difficult to configure and have large data files. If all of the laptops have current hardware, what is the easiest way to install Windows 7 on them?

Case Project 2-4: Installation for a Large Organization

Gigantic Life Insurance has 4,000 users spread over five locations in North America. They have hired you as a consultant to identify the different options for deploying Windows 7 to the desktops in their organization. List several ways Windows 7 could be deployed for Gigantic Life Insurance, the benefits and drawbacks for each, and your recommendation.

chapter 3

Using the System Utilities

After reading this chapter and completing the exercises, you will be able to:

- Understand and use the Control Panel applets
- Understand the Administrative Tools
- Manage hardware components
- Understand and configure power management
- Configure the display
- Use Task Scheduler

Windows 7 includes a wide range of system utilities in Control Panel and in Administrative Tools. A thorough knowledge of these utilities can help you manage, tune, and improve your system. Some of the more advanced tools are Microsoft Management Console (MMC) snap-ins. A snap-in is the standardized format for creating system management utilities in Windows 2000 and later versions of Windows.

This chapter provides an overview of Control Panel applets and Administrative Tools. There is also a description of the Microsoft Management Console. As well, there is in-depth coverage of how to manage hardware components, configure power management, configure the display, and use Task Scheduler.

Control Panel Overview

As with previous Microsoft operating systems, Windows 7 includes **Control Panel** as a central location for management utilities. Windows 7 uses the same Control Panel design as Windows Vista with a few new management **applets**. An applet is a small application or utility that is used to perform management tasks in Windows 7.

By default, Control Panel uses the Category view, as shown in Figure 3-1. This offers an intuitive way for less experienced computer users to find the Control Panel applet necessary to perform a specific task. Some applets appear in multiple categories because they perform functions in multiple categories. For example, Ease of Access Center appears in the Appearance and Personalization category and the Ease of Access category.

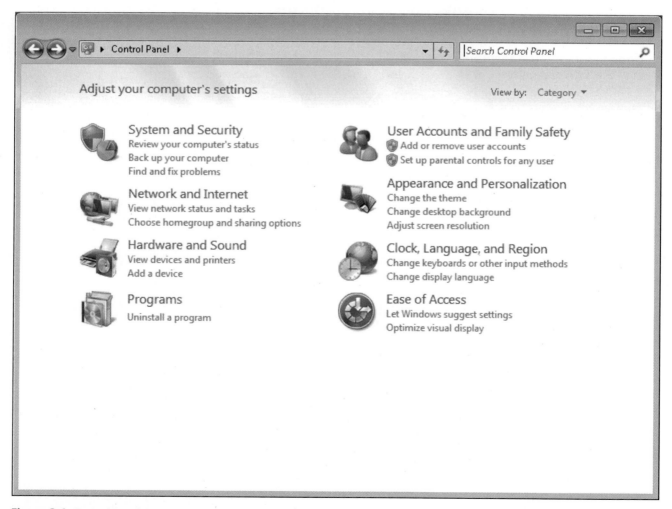

Figure 3-1 Control Panel Category view
Courtesy Course Technology/Cengage Learning

The categories available in Control Panel are:

- System and Security
- Network and Internet
- Hardware and Sound
- Programs
- User Accounts and Family Safety
- Appearance and Personalization
- Clock, Language, and Region
- Ease of Access

Beyond organizing Control Panel applets, Category view also uses wizards that help you perform tasks. The wizards are graphical tools that lead you through the process of performing a particular task by asking you for all of the necessary information. Within each category, the wizards for performing tasks are listed below the name of each applet. All of the tasks performed by using a wizard can also be performed by using Control Panel applets.

The applets in Control Panel can also be viewed in a single list by selecting Large icons or Small icons view, shown in Figure 3-2. This is the view preferred by most network administrators because they can see all of the Control Panel applets at once and quickly select the applet they want. Throughout this chapter, you will use Category view to ensure that you are familiar with it and can relay instructions to end users when required.

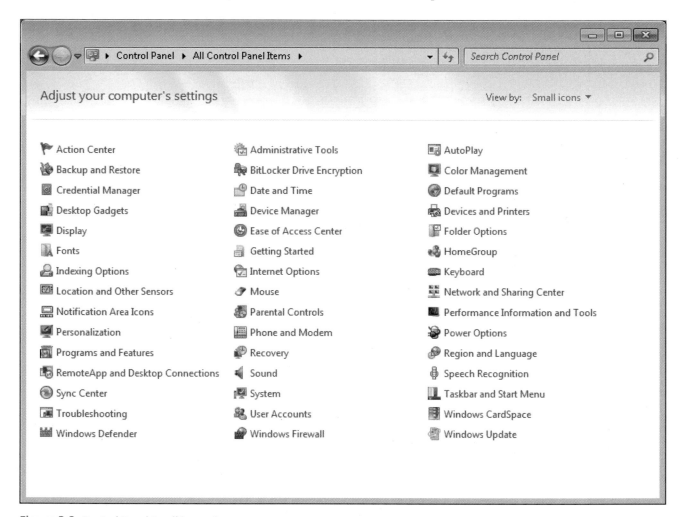

Figure 3-2 Control Panel Small icons view
Courtesy Course Technology/Cengage Learning

System and Security

The System and Security category in Control Panel includes a wide range of applets for managing Windows 7. Some of the applets are used to configure Windows 7, while others are used for troubleshooting.

Control Panel applets in the System and Security category are:

- Action Center
- Windows Firewall
- System
- Windows Update
- Power Options
- Backup and Restore
- BitLocker Drive Encryption
- Administrative Tools

Action Center, shown in Figure 3-3, is a place where you can review and resolve system messages. The system messages presented by Action Center are categorized as Security or Maintenance. Security messages are related to settings such as Windows Firewall, Windows Update, or virus protection. Maintenance messages are related to settings such as backup or overall system

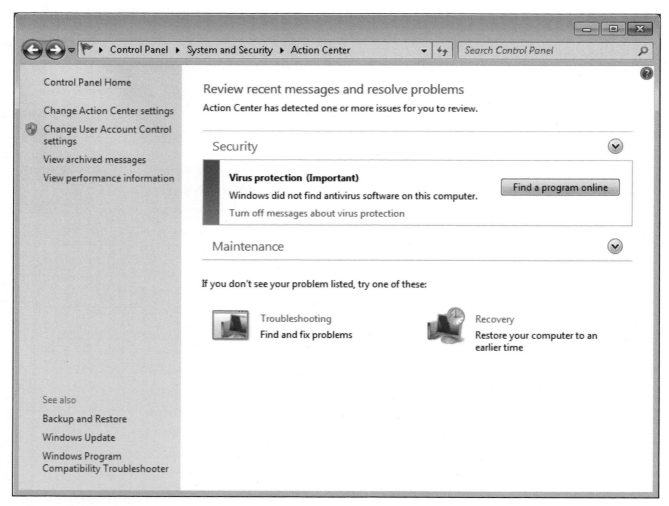

Figure 3-3 Action Center
Courtesy Course Technology/Cengage Learning

reliability. There are also tools for troubleshooting and system recovery. Action Center is new in Windows 7 and replaces the Security Center found in Windows Vista and Windows XP.

Detailed information about Action Center is covered in Chapter 7, Windows 7 Security Features

Windows Firewall protects your computer by controlling communication between your computer and the network. The Windows Firewall applet allows you to configure the settings for Windows Firewall. You can configure which local programs are allowed to accept network communication, configure specific ports to allow or block, and select which network cards are protected by Windows Firewall. Windows Firewall is updated from the version in Windows XP but similar to the version in Windows Vista.

Detailed information about Windows Firewall is covered in Chapter 8, Networking.

The **System applet,** shown in Figure 3-4, shows basic information about your computer and provides links that allow you to configure system properties. The basic information about

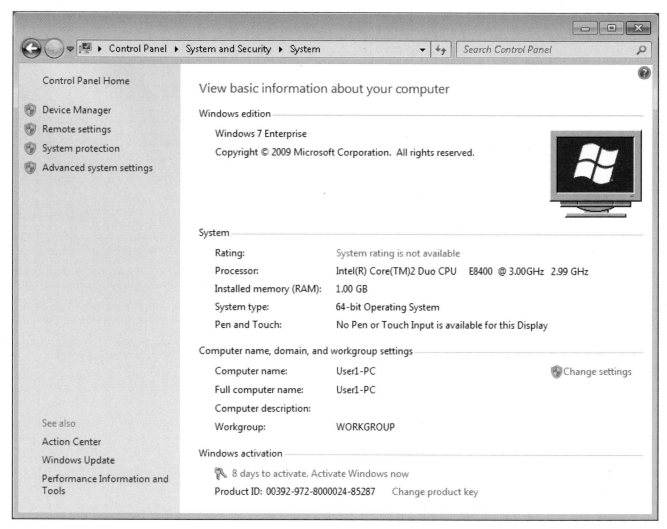

Figure 3-4 System applet

Courtesy Course Technology/Cengage Learning

your computer includes the Windows edition, system information such as performance rating, computer name, and activation status. In Advanced system settings you can configure hardware, Remote Assistance and Remote Desktop, restore points, performance, user profiles, and startup and recovery settings.

Detailed information about Remote Assistance and Remote Desktop are covered in Chapter 14, Remote Access; user profiles are covered in Chapter 6, User Management; and startup and recovery settings and restore points are covered in Chapter 12, Disaster Recovery and Troubleshooting. Hardware configuration is covered later in this chapter.

Windows Update is a service in Windows 7 that automatically downloads and installs service packs and security updates. In addition, you have the option to download device driver updates.

Detailed information about Windows Update is covered in Chapter 7, Windows 7 Security Features.

You can use the **power plans** available in Power Options to minimize power usage or maximize computer performance. If the default power plans are not sufficient, you can create your own. In addition to power plans, you can configure what the power button does, when the computer is turned off, and when the computer goes to sleep. The Power Options are similar to Windows Vista, but have been significantly modified compared to Windows XP.

Detailed information about Power Options is covered later in this chapter.

Backup and Restore provides access to Windows recovery tools for files and the system. Windows Backup can be used to back up and restore files. In addition, you can use System Restore backup and restore to create a system repair disc.

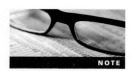

Detailed information about Windows Backup and System Restore is covered in Chapter 12, Disaster Recovery and Troubleshooting.

BitLocker Drive Encryption is a method for securing the data on a hard drive or portable media. When BitLocker Drive Encryption is enabled, all of the data on a hard drive or portable media is encrypted. So, even if a hard drive or portable media is lost or stolen, the data cannot be read. The BitLocker Drive Encryption applet lets you configure BitLocker Drive Encryption. BitLocker Drive Encryption is enhanced in Windows 7.

Detailed information about BitLocker Drive Encryption is covered in Chapter 7, Windows 7 Security Features.

The **Administrative Tools** are used to manage Windows 7. Some of these tools are **Computer Management**, Event Viewer, Performance Monitor, System Configuration, and Task Scheduler.

Detailed information about Administrative Tools is covered later in this chapter.

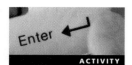

Activity 3-1: Performing System and Maintenance Tasks

Time Required: 10 minutes

Objective: Perform system and maintenance tasks.

Description: The System and Maintenance category in Control Panel includes a wide variety of tools for managing Windows 7. In this activity, you use some of those tools to view system status and performance.

1. If necessary, start your computer and log on.
2. Click the **Start** button, and click **Control Panel**.
3. If necessary, in the View by box, click **Category** and then click **System and Security**.
4. Click **System**.
5. Read the information that is displayed in the System window. Information about your computer is located here, such as processor type and speed, memory, and computer name. There are also links at the left side to manage your computer.
6. In the left column, click **Advanced system settings**.
7. Click the **Environment Variables** button. This displays environment variables that are used by Windows to keep track of information, as shown in Figure 3-5. For example, the TEMP variable is configured to be the \AppData\Local\Temp folder inside the user profile. Windows programs use this as a temporary storage location for files.

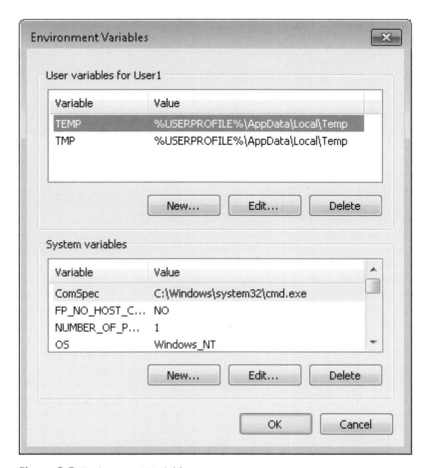

Figure 3-5 Environment Variables
Courtesy Course Technology/Cengage Learning

8. Click **Cancel** to close the Environment Variables dialog box and click **Cancel** to close the System Properties dialog box.

9. In the System window, in the System area, click **System rating is not available**. If you have previously rated this computer, click **Windows Experience Index**.

10. In Performance Information and Tools, click **Rate this computer**. If you have previously rated this computer, click **Re-run the assessment** instead.

11. If Windows 7 is running in a virtual machine, an error message will be displayed. Click **Close** to close the error message and skip to step 14.

12. After waiting a few moments for the overall rating to be calculated, read the overall rating for your computer. The overall rating is typically based on the least powerful component being rated. For example, if your Graphics are rated 1.0, then the overall rating is 1.0.

13. Close the **Performance Information and Tools** window.

Network and Internet

The Network and Internet category in Control Panel, shown in Figure 3-6, contains applets for configuring network communication. The applets included in this category are updated from Windows Vista and very different from the options available for configuring Windows XP.

Control Panel applets in the Network and Internet category are:

- Network and Sharing Center
- HomeGroup
- Internet Options

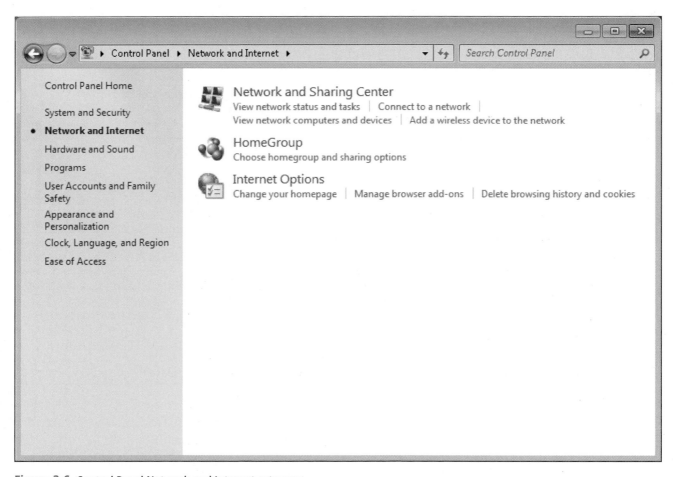

Figure 3-6 Control Panel Network and Internet category
Courtesy Course Technology/Cengage Learning

Network and Sharing Center, shown in Figure 3-7, is a central location for viewing network status and detailed network information. The detailed network information includes the name of the network, what is accessed through that network, the network category, and the connections used to access the network. There are also links to manage network devices and network connections. Finally, you can configure options for sharing and discovery of network resources. This applet is updated in Windows 7.

Detailed information about the Network and Sharing Center is covered in Chapter 8, Networking.

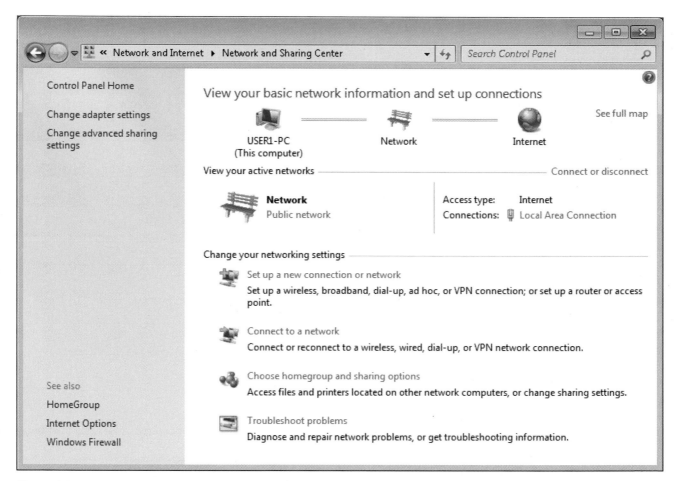

Figure 3-7 Network and Sharing Center
Courtesy Course Technology/Cengage Learning

HomeGroup is a new feature in Windows 7 that is used to configure file and printer sharing for small peer-to-peer computer networks. A password is created for the HomeGroup rather than requiring user accounts to be synchronized between computers.

Detailed information about HomeGroup is covered in Chapter 8, Networking.

Internet Options gives you access to a wide variety of settings for Internet Explorer, including security settings. Some of the settings you can configure for Internet Explorer include the home page, browsing history, appearance, security, privacy, content controls, proxy servers, and helper programs.

Detailed information about Internet Explorer is covered in Chapter 9, User Productivity Tools.

Hardware and Sound

The Hardware and Sound category in Control Panel, shown in Figure 3-8, lets you configure a wide range of hardware settings in your system. However, for most device types, it does not allow you to configure device drivers. Instead, you can configure settings such as how fast the cursor blinks or whether CD-ROMs automatically play when inserted into your CD-ROM drive.

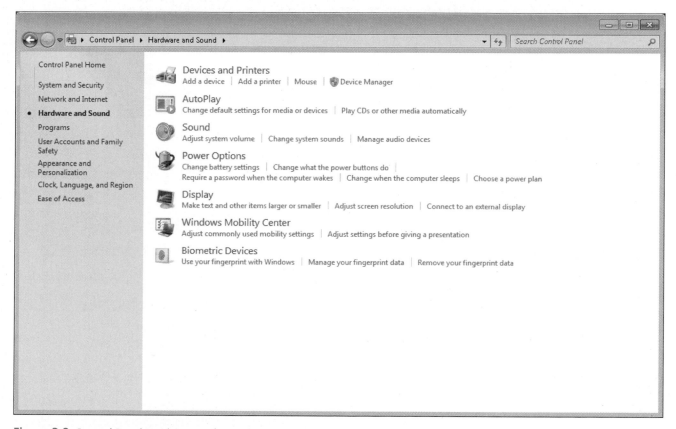

Figure 3-8 Control Panel Hardware and Sound category
Courtesy Course Technology/Cengage Learning

Control Panel applets in the Hardware and Sound category are:

- Devices and Printers
- AutoPlay
- Sound
- Power Options
- Display
- Windows Mobility Center
- Biometric Devices
- Tablet PC Settings

The Devices and Printers applet in Control Panel lets you install, configure, and manage various devices and printers. Not all devices are listed here. The main device types are: USB devices, wireless devices, portable devices such as a music player, and some network enabled scanners and storage. You can also manage faxing by using the Devices and Printers applet.

AutoPlay is a feature that automatically performs an action when new media is inserted into a removable device such as a DVD player or a USB drive. In Windows 7, AutoPlay supports different default actions for different types of media that are inserted. For example, you can specify that an audio CD is automatically played, but no action is performed when a blank DVD is inserted. A wide variety of different media are supported as shown in Figure 3-9. This functionality is not available in Windows XP.

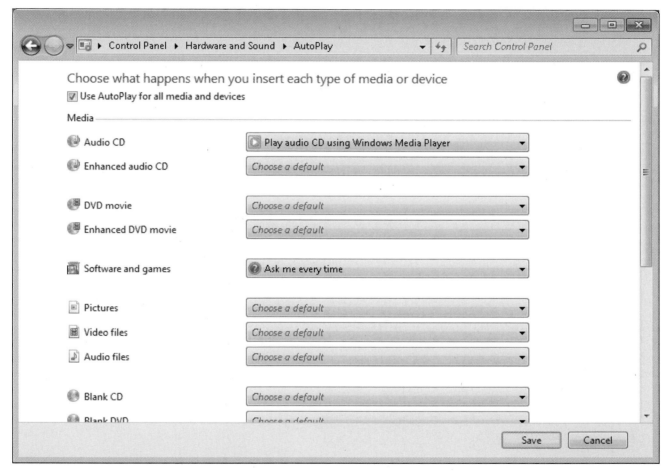

Figure 3-9 AutoPlay
Courtesy Course Technology/Cengage Learning

The **Sound applet** lets you view and configure the properties for the audio devices in your system and configure a sound scheme. When you configure audio devices, you can adjust the volume level of your speakers or the input levels of microphones or videos. You can also configure the format of the sound used by that device. For example, you can specify that your sound card uses CD quality (16 bit, 44100Hz) sound. Sound schemes are groups of predefined sounds that are associated with system events in Windows. For example, a specific audio file is played when Windows 7 is shut down. You can choose whichever sound scheme you prefer.

The **Display applet** gives you links to adjust the screen resolution, calibrate color, change display settings, adjust ClearType text, and set a custom text size. The links to the screen resolution and change display settings both provide access to the same options for changing the screen resolution. The calibrate color link lets you optimize the display of colors for your specific monitor to ensure that the correct colors are displayed. Color calibration is done primarily by design professionals who need precise color matching between their monitor and printer to ensure that what they see on the monitor is what is produced by the printer.

You can adjust the display of text by using ClearType or a custom text size. ClearType is used to enhance the readability of text on LCD displays and can be enabled to smooth the edges of fonts. You can set a custom text size to increase the size of text displayed by Windows and most applications. However, you should be aware that this may result in some older applications not displaying text properly. For example, if you increase the text size, then an older application may cut off some of the text because the window does not adjust properly for the increased text size.

 Detailed information about display configuration is covered later in this chapter.

Windows Mobility Center, shown in Figure 3-10, is available only for mobile computers such as laptops or a tablet PC. It provides quick access to settings commonly used on mobile computers, such as power options, wireless networking, external display settings, and synchronization settings.

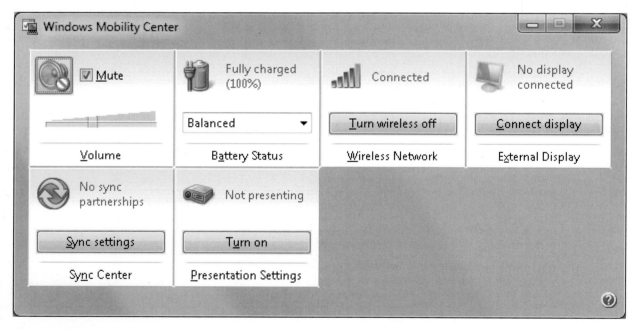

Figure 3-10 Windows Mobility Center
Courtesy Course Technology/Cengage Learning

The **Biometric Devices applet,** shown in Figure 3-11, is available only for computers with a biometric device attached. It is used to manage both the biometric devices and the authentication data associated with the biometric devices.

The **Tablet PC Settings applet** lets you configure settings that are specific to a tablet PC. The General tab lets you configure which side of the screen menus appear on and calibrate the pen. The Handwriting Recognition tab lets you configure how Windows 7 learns to recognize your handwriting. The Display tab lets you change the screen orientation between landscape and portrait. This applet is only available on a computer with a touch screen.

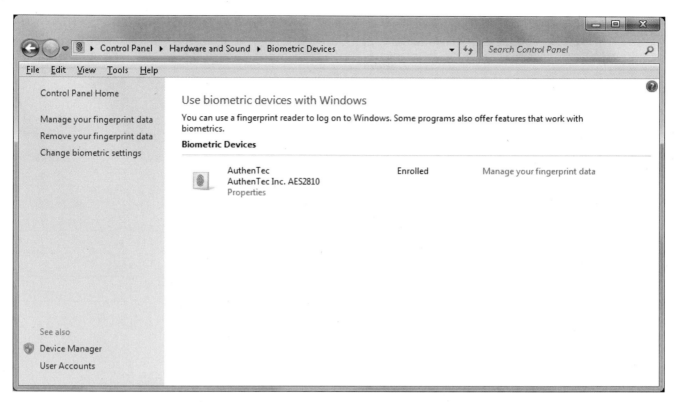

Figure 3-11 Biometric Devices applet
Courtesy Course Technology/Cengage Learning

Activity 3-2: Configuring Hardware

Time Required: 10 minutes
Objective: Configure hardware settings for Windows 7.

Description: The Hardware and Sound category of Control Panel lets you configure many hardware and sound characteristics. However, this category is not used to configure device drivers for hardware. In this activity, you configure AutoPlay and sound.

1. If necessary, start your computer and log on.
2. Click the **Start** button, and click **Control Panel**.
3. Click **Hardware and Sound**.
4. Click **Devices and Printers**. Notice that your computer is one of the devices displayed.
5. Right-click **User*x*-PC**, where *x* is the number assigned to you by your instructor, and read the options available in the context menu.
6. Click the **back** arrow.
7. Click **AutoPlay**.
8. In the Audio CD option box, select **Play audio CD using Windows Media Player**.
9. Click **Save**.
10. If you have an audio CD, to test the change you just made:
    a. Insert the audio CD in the CD-ROM drive of your computer.
    b. After Windows Media Player begins playing the music from the audio CD, close Windows Media Player.

11. In the Hardware and Sound window, click **Sound**.

12. Click the **Communications** tab. Notice that you can automatically adjust the sound settings when windows 7 detects communications activity, as shown in Figure 3-12.

13. Click **Cancel** and close the **Hardware and Sound** window.

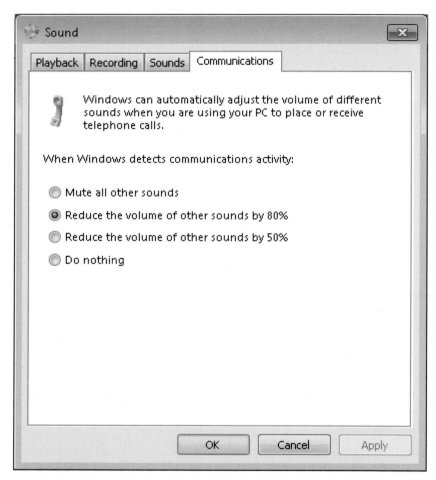

Figure 3-12 Communications tab for Sound configuration
Courtesy Course Technology/Cengage Learning

Programs

The Programs category in Control Panel, shown in Figure 3-13, has applets that are used to install, manage, and uninstall applications. You can also get a list of Windows Updates that have been installed and configure Windows Defender.

Control Panel applets in the Programs category are:

- Programs and Features
- Default Programs
- Desktop Gadgets

The Programs and Features applet, shown in Figure 3-14, gives you a list of installed applications. From this list you can see the names of the applications, the publisher names, when the applications were installed, the size of each application, and the version. You can also remove applications. Options for viewing and removing updates are also accessed from this applet. This applet is similar to Windows Vista.

Default Programs is another subcategory that provides access to additional applets. The Set your default programs applet lets you configure an application to be the default application for all file types and programs it can open. The Associate a file type or protocol with a program

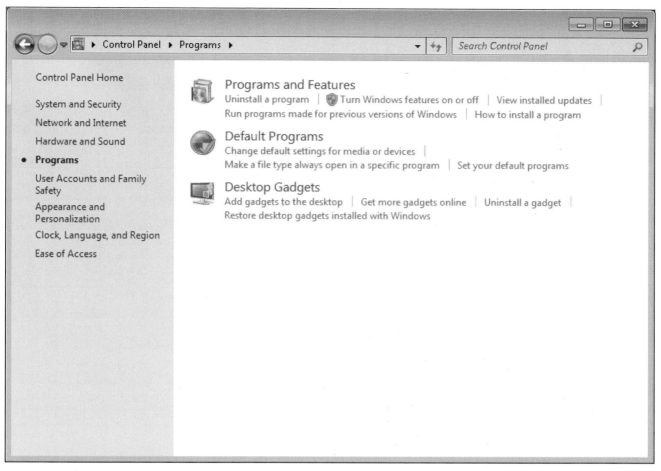

Figure 3-13 Control Panel Programs Category
Courtesy Course Technology/Cengage Learning

applet lets you configure the default application that is used to open each file type based on the file extension. Change AutoPlay Settings modifies the same settings as the AutoPlay applet in Hardware and Sound. The Set program access and computer defaults applet configures default programs to use for Web browsing, e-mail, media playing, instant messaging, and a virtual machine for Java, if users have not configured personal preferences.

Desktop Gadgets is a method for displaying small applications called gadgets at the side of the screen. Gadgets can include information such as clock, RSS feeds, or weather updates. This is an update to the Windows Sidebar that first appeared in Windows Vista.

Detailed information about Desktop Gadgets is covered in Chapter 9, User Productivity Tools.

Activity 3-3: Managing Programs

Time Required: 10 minutes
Objective: Manage programs by using Control Panel applets.

Description: The Programs category in Control Panel contains applets that let you manage the installation and removal of applications and Windows components. In this activity, you view the installed applications and Windows components.

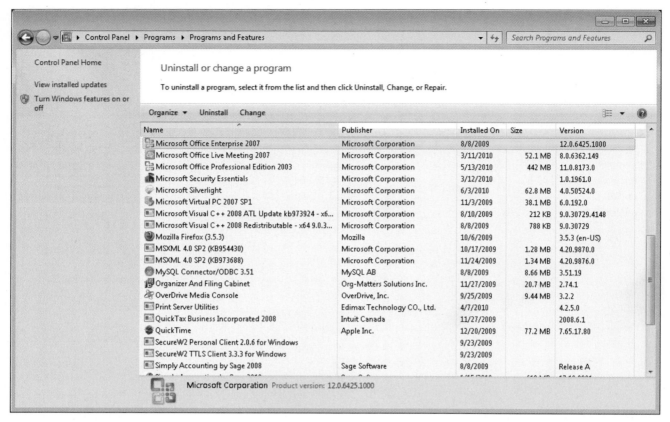

Figure 3-14 Programs and Features applet
Courtesy Course Technology/Cengage Learning

1. If necessary, start your computer and log on.

2. Click the **Start** button, and click **Control Panel**.

3. Click **Programs**.

4. Click **Programs and Features**. This is the screen that is used to view and remove applications that are installed on your computer. The WAIK is listed here because you installed it during Activity 2-1.

5. Click **View installed updates**. This is the screen that is used to view and remove updates that are installed on your computer. The contents of this screen will vary depending on your classroom environment. Updates may or may not be displayed at this time depending on whether your computer has access to the Internet and has installed updates.

6. Click the **back arrow** twice.

7. Click **Default Programs**. This is the screen that is used to associate a file type or protocol with a program. You can also change autoplay settings here.

8. Click **Associate a file type or protocol with a program**. This applet displays a list of file extensions and the default program used to open those files, as shown in Figure 3-15. Notice that .bmp files are opened using the Windows Photo Viewer.

9. Click **.bmp** and click the **Change program** button.

10. Click **Paint** and click **OK**. Now .bmp files will be opened by default in Paint instead of in the Windows Photo Viewer.

11. Click **Close**.

12. Close the **Default Programs** window.

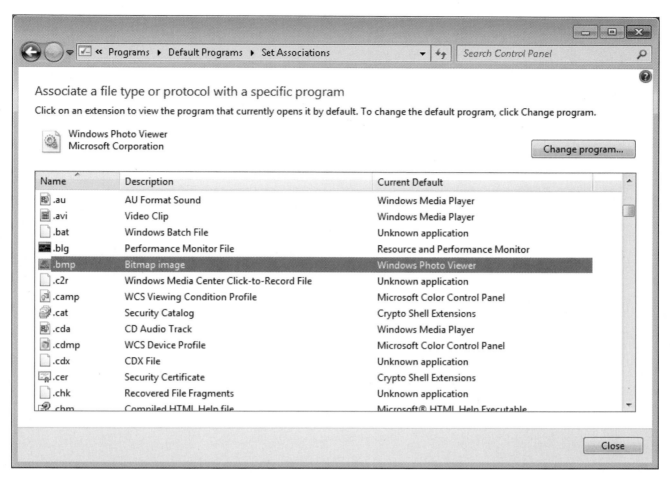

Figure 3-15 Setting file associations
Courtesy Course Technology/Cengage Learning

User Accounts and Family Safety

The User Accounts and Family Safety category in Control Panel, shown in Figure 3-16, lets you configure user accounts and **parental controls**. User accounts are required to log on to the computer. Parental controls are used to control access to Web sites through Internet Explorer.

Control Panel applets in the User Accounts and Family Safety category are:

- User Accounts
- Parental Controls
- Windows CardSpace
- Credential Manager

The User Accounts applet is used to create and manage Windows 7 user accounts. You can change passwords, change the picture for an account, change the account name, or change the account type. In addition, there are links to create a password reset disk, link online IDs, and manage file encryption certificates. This applet is similar to the one in Windows Vista.

 Detailed information about user accounts is covered in Chapter 6, User Management.

Parental controls are a feature that was first available in Windows Vista. Parental controls allow you to restrict when a computer can be used and which applications can be used. You can

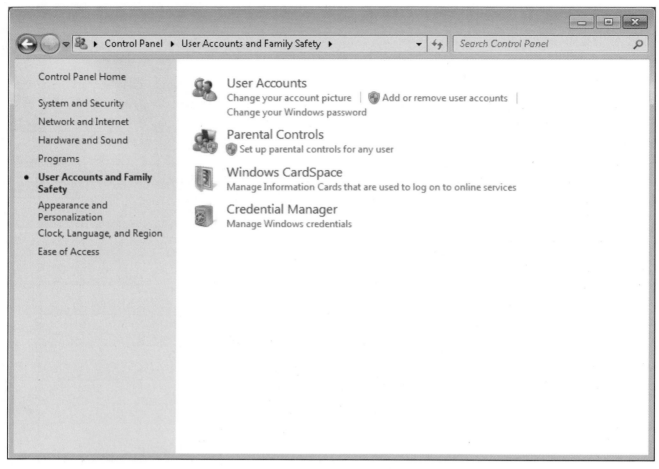

Figure 3-16 User Accounts and Family Safety
Courtesy Course Technology/Cengage Learning

configure individualized settings for each user. Parental Controls are available only for computers in a workgroup rather than a domain.

Detailed information about Parental Controls is covered in Chapter 6, User Management.

The Windows CardSpace applet is used to store and manage log on credentials for Web sites. This allows you to visit Web sites that require passwords without entering the password each time. You can also enter in other information such as your address that can be used to fill in Web forms automatically. All personal information stored in Windows CardSpace is encrypted to keep it secure.

Credential Manager is a place where you can store authentication credentials for logging on to other computers remotely. The computers may have file shares or Web sites. In addition to a username a password, you can also configure certificates to be used for authentication. Unlike Windows Cardspace, Credential Manager is only used for authentication credentials and cannot be used to store additional information.

Appearance and Personalization

The Appearance and Personalization category in Control Panel, shown in Figure 3-17, lets you modify the user interface for Windows 7. Modifying the user interface lets you maximize your productivity by configuring Windows 7 to behave the way you prefer. For example, you can configure Windows Explorer to display folder contents as a list by default instead of icons.

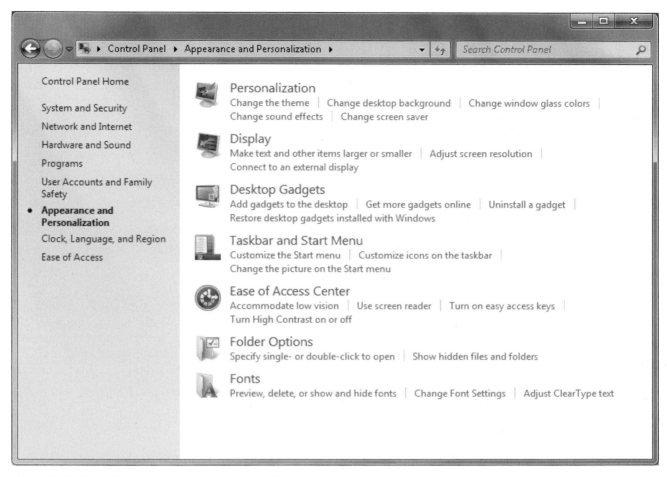

Figure 3-17 Control Panel Appearance and Personalization category
Courtesy Course Technology/Cengage Learning

Control Panel applets in the Appearance and Personalization category are:

- Personalization
- Display
- Desktop Gadgets
- Taskbar and Start Menu
- Ease of Access Center
- Folder Options
- Fonts

The Personalization option gives you links to adjust themes, color schemes, the desktop background, screen saver, sound effects, and mouse pointers. Themes are preconfigured collections of visual and sound elements such as mouse pointers, startup sounds, and windows colors. Color schemes control the color of windows and menus. You can personalize the desktop background by selecting a picture included with Windows 7 or using one of your own. The screen saver settings include options such as how long the computer is idle before displaying a screen saver and whether authentication is required to exit the screen saver. The sounds configuration allows you to define the sounds associated with Windows events.

The **Taskbar and Start Menu applet** is used to configure the behavior of the taskbar and Start menu. The Taskbar tab lets you configure how the taskbar displays information, such as auto-hiding the taskbar customizing the notification area. The Start Menu tab lets you customize detailed options about how the Start menu looks, the power button action, and choose whether recently opened programs appear in the Start menu. The Toolbars tab lets you configure which toolbars are displayed on the taskbar, such as Address, Links, and Tablet PC Input Panel.

The **Folder Options applet** lets you configure the display and behavior of Windows Explorer. The General tab lets you configure whether opening a new folder opens a new window, and whether you need to single-click or double-click to open an item. The View tab has many settings, such as whether to show hidden files, whether to hide system files, and whether to show file extensions for known file types. The Search tab lets you configure settings for search including whether file contents and subfolders are searched from Quick Search, whether partial matches are performed, whether natural language search is used, and how nonindexed files are searched.

The Fonts applet lets you manage fonts that are installed in Windows 7. You can install new fonts, view the properties of existing fonts, or remove fonts. There are also links to change font size and configure ClearType.

Activity 3-4: Personalizing Your Computer

Time Required: 10 minutes
Objective: Personalize your computer's operations.

Description: The Appearance and Personalization category in Control Panel has settings to control how Windows 7 interacts with you. You can change display characteristics, customize the taskbar and Start menu, configure folder options, and more. In this activity, you customize the taskbar. In addition, you modify the folder options to display hidden files and file extensions for known file types.

1. If necessary, start your computer and log on.
2. Click the **Start** button, and click **Control Panel**.
3. Click **Appearance and Personalization**.
4. Click **Taskbar and Start Menu**.
5. Check the **Use small icons** check box and click **Apply**. This reduces the size of the icons in the task bar and allows you to have a bit more screen space for applications.
6. Uncheck the **Use small icons** check box and click **Apply**.
7. Click the **Customize** button for the notification area.
8. Check the **Always show all icons and notifications on the taskbar** check box and click **OK**. Depending on the programs that are installed on your computer, you may notice that several more icons are displayed in the Notification Area at the right side of the toolbar.
9. Click the **Customize** button for the notification area.
10. Uncheck the **Always show all icons and notifications on the taskbar** check box and click **OK**.
11. Click the **Toolbars** tab.
12. Check the **Links** check box and click **Apply**. This displays a links toolbar that can be used to access Web pages similar to the Favorites in Internet Explorer. The links are actually part of the Internet Explorer favorites.
13. Uncheck the **Links** check box and click **Apply**.
14. Click **Cancel**.
15. Click **Folder Options**.
16. Click the **View** tab.
17. Click the **Show hidden files, folders, and drives** option button.

18. Uncheck the **Hide extensions for known file types** check box. Windows Explorer will now display the full filename for all files.

19. Click **OK**.

20. Click the **Start** button, click **Computer**, and double-click **Local Disk (C:)**. Notice that the ProgramData folder in the root of the C drive is faded out. A faded out folders is hidden.

21. Double-click **Windows** and scroll down to the files. Notice that you can see all of the file extensions for these files, as shown in Figure 3-18.

22. Close Windows Explorer.

23. Close the Appearance and Personalization window.

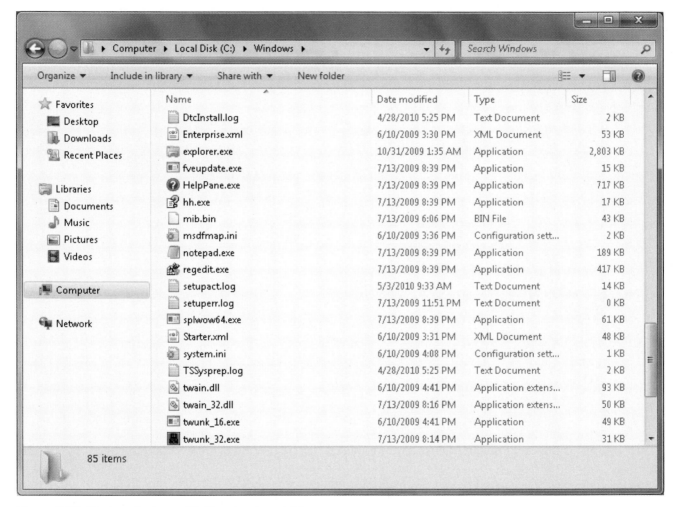

Figure 3-18 Windows Explorer with file extensions visible
Courtesy Course Technology/Cengage Learning

Clock, Language, and Region

The Clock, Language, and Region category in Control Panel, shown in Figure 3-19, includes applets for configuring time, regional format, and language settings. Some of the settings available here include the time zone and display formats for numbers and dates.

Control Panel applets in the Clock, Language, and Region category are:

- Date and Time
- Region and Language

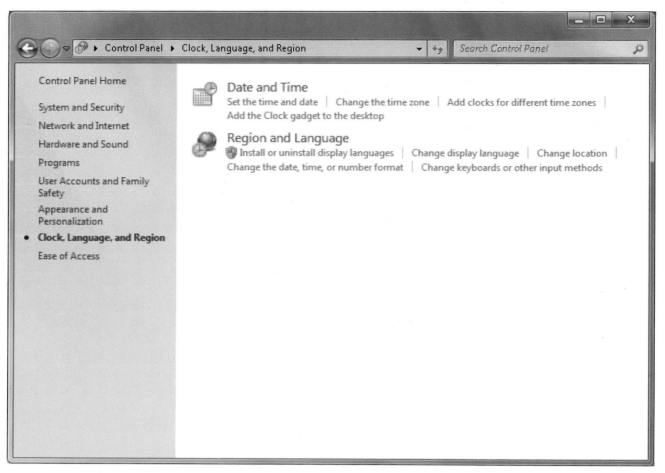

Figure 3-19 Control Panel Clock, Language, and Region category
Courtesy Course Technology/Cengage Learning

The Date and Time applet lets you configure the date and time settings. The Date and Time tab is used to configure the date, the time, and time zone. The Additional Clocks tab lets you select up to two additional time zones that Windows 7 displays when you hover over the taskbar clock. Configuring additional clocks can be useful when your coworkers are in different time zones. The Internet Time tab is used to configure a Network Time Protocol (NTP) source to get accurate time information. NTP is a protocol used to synchronize time from very accurate time sources on the Internet such as atomic clocks. By default, Windows 7 is configured to get time from the Microsoft server *time.windows.com*.

When Windows 7 is part of a corporate network and joined to a domain, it will obtain time from the PDC emulator for the domain rather than a time server on the Internet.

The Region and Language Options applet is used to configure display and input options to support different languages and regions. The Formats tab lets you configure the format used to display numbers, currency, time, short date, and long date. The Location tab lets you select a country as your location so that certain applications can provide you with relevant information such as local news. The Keyboards and Languages tab lets you select a keyboard layout and choose the language that is used in Windows menus and dialog boxes. The Administrative tab lets you configure the language that is used for nonunicode programs and apply regional and language settings to system accounts and the default user account. Nonunicode programs use only a single byte to store character information and are unable to display extended character sets required for some languages such as Chinese or Japanese.

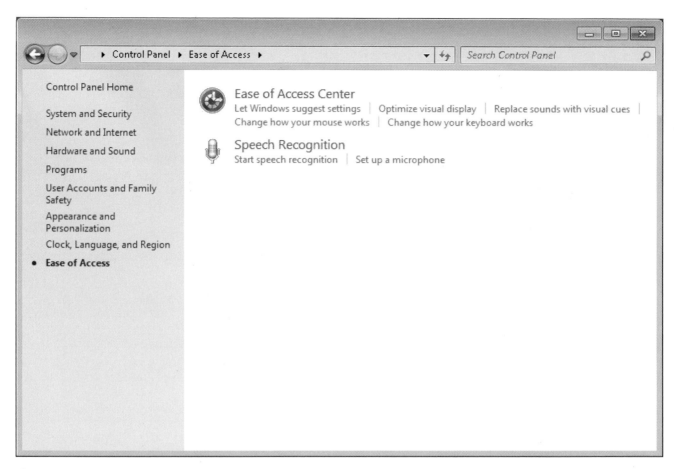

Figure 3-20 Control Panel Ease of Access category
Courtesy Course Technology/Cengage Learning

Ease of Access

The Ease of Access category in Control Panel, shown in Figure 3-20, is used to make Windows 7 easier to use. Many of these settings are used by those with visual or hearing impairment. However, other options such as speech recognition can be useful to anyone.

Control Panel applets in the Ease of Access category are:

- Ease of Access Center
- Speech Recognition Options

The Ease of Access Center applet, shown in Figure 3-21, has a wide range of settings that makes Windows 7 easier to use for those with motor, visual, or hearing impairment. Some of the options available here are Magnifier, to increase the size of a portion of the screen, and Narrator, to read menus that are displayed on the screen. There are also detailed settings for display, input devices, and sounds. This applet replaces the Accessibility Options in Windows XP.

Windows 7 is capable of using speech recognition as an input device. This means that you can dictate to Windows 7 rather than typing. The Speech Recognition Options applet lets you configure all of the settings for speech recognition. The tasks for speech recognition include initial configuration, microphone configuration, and training speech recognition for your voice. This feature was not available in Windows XP.

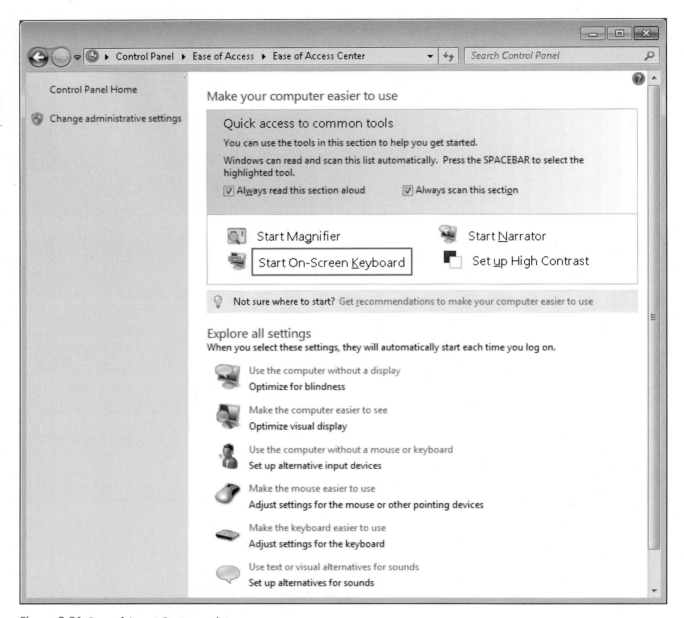

Figure 3-21 Ease of Access Center applet
Courtesy Course Technology/Cengage Learning

Activity 3-5: Using the Ease of Access Center

Time Required: 10 minutes

Objective: Use the Ease of Access Center to configure features for users with disabilities.

Description: The Ease of Access Center contains a number of options to make using a computer easier for people with disabilities. In this activity, you enable some of the options in the Ease of Access Center to see how they work.

1. If necessary, start your computer and log on.
2. Click the **Start** button, and click **Control Panel**.

3. Click **Ease of Access**.

4. Click **Ease of Access Center**.

5. Click **Start On-Screen Keyboard**. This displays a keyboard on the screen so that you can type with a mouse. This can be useful for someone with limited hand movement who cannot use a regular keyboard.

6. Close the On-Screen Keyboard.

7. Press **left SHIFT+left ALT+PRINT SCREEN**, click **Yes** to enable high contrast viewing. High Contrast helps people with visual impairments see the screen better.

8. Press **left SHIFT+left ALT+PRINT SCREEN** to disable high contrast.

9. Click **Start Magnifier**. This option magnifies screen, as shown in Figure 3-22, and is useful for people with visual impairments.

10. The magnifier dialog box is minimized on the taskbar, close the **Magnifier** dialog box to stop the Magnifier.

11. Close the **Ease of Access Center** window.

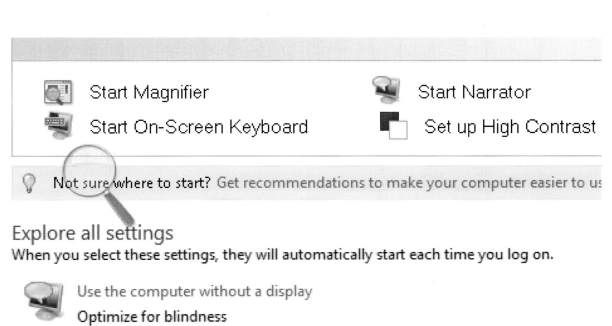

Figure 3-22 Magnifier
Courtesy Course Technology/Cengage Learning

Administrative Tools

Windows 7 includes a collection of system configuration utilities that are grouped in a category called Administrative Tools and found in System and Security in Control Panel. Most of the tools in this category use the **Microsoft Management Console (MMC)**. The MMC is a framework that simplifies the development of administrative tools.

The utilities included in the Administrative Tools category are:

- Component Services
- Computer Management
- Data Sources (ODBC)
- Event Viewer
- iSCSI Initiator
- Local Security Policy
- Performance Monitor
- Print Management
- Services
- System Configuration
- Task Scheduler
- Windows Firewall with Advanced Security
- Windows Memory Diagnostic
- Windows Powershell Modules

Component Services is used to configure settings for some applications. It includes settings for COM+, DCOM, and Distributed Transaction Coordinator. Typically, these settings are only modified if you receive instructions from an application developer or as part of a troubleshooting document.

Data Sources (ODBC) is used to configure data sources for applications that require access to a database. Open Database Connectivity (ODBC) is a standard mechanism for applications to access databases. Applications written to use ODBC can communicate with any supported database such as Microsoft SQL Server, Microsoft Access, or Oracle databases. A network administrator must then configure an ODBC data source to communicate with the proper database. This isolates the application from the database, makes application development easier, and provides greater flexibility when choosing a database.

Event Viewer is used to view messages from applications or Windows 7. These messages are useful for troubleshooting errors. The version of Event Viewer in Windows 7 is significantly enhanced over the Event Viewer included with Windows XP.

Detailed information about Event Viewer and the enhancements introduced in Windows 7 are covered in Chapter 12, Disaster Recovery and Troubleshooting.

The **iSCSI** protocol allows computers to communicate with external disks over standard Ethernet networks. External storage devices that support iSCSI are known as iSCSI targets. The computers that access iSCSI targets are iSCSI initiators. The iSCSI Initiator tool lets you configure Windows 7 to communicate with iSCSI targets and use the iSCSI targets as external disks over the network. The iSCSI protocol is used only in corporate environments and mostly on servers rather than workstations.

For more information about iSCSI, see Help and Support in the Windows 7 start menu.

The Local Security Policy tool allows you to edit a wide variety of security settings on the local computer. Some of the settings include password policies, account lockout policies, auditing policies, user rights assignment, and software restriction policies. When Group Policies are used in a corporate environment, the group policy settings configured centrally by the administrator override the settings configured locally.

 Detailed information about the Local Security Policy tool is covered in Chapter 7, Windows 7 Security Features.

Performance Monitor is used to monitor and troubleshoot performance issues in Windows 7. It includes the ability to monitor many system resources including the processor, disk, memory, and the network. Performance Monitor can log resource status over time and generate reports. Performance Monitor replaces the Performance tool in Windows XP.

 Detailed information about Performance Monitor is covered in Chapter 10, Performance Tuning.

Print Management is a tool that was new in Windows Vista for monitoring and managing printers. In a single view you can monitor and manage local and network printers.

System Configuration gives you access to boot configuration, service startup, startup applications, and system tools. The General tab, shown in Figure 3-23, lets you select the type of boot you want to perform. The Boot tab lets you configure boot options such as Safe Mode. The Services tab lets you enable or disable services. The Startup tab lets you see and disable all of the applications that Windows 7 is starting automatically. The Tools tab gives you easy access to a variety of system tools such as the Registry Editor.

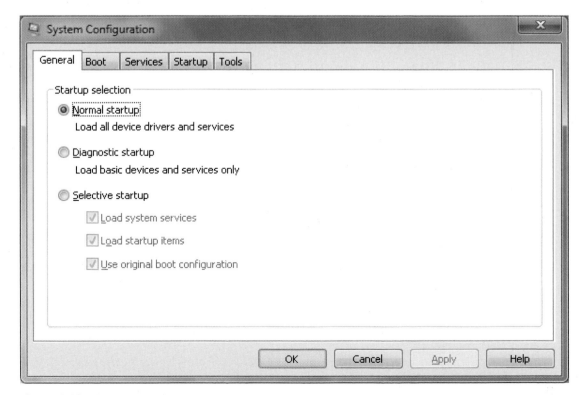

Figure 3-23 System Configuration
Courtesy Course Technology/Cengage Learning

Services allows you to configure Windows 7 services. You can also start and stop services if required for troubleshooting. This functionality is also available in Computer Management.

Task Scheduler lets you create system maintenance tasks that are performed on a regular schedule or when system events occur. The Task Scheduler in Windows 7 is greatly enhanced over Windows XP. New features include a history log and additional trigger mechanisms.

Detailed information about Task Scheduler is covered later in this chapter.

Windows Firewall with Advanced Security is an advanced editor for configuring Windows Firewall. It is able to configure advanced settings for Windows Firewall that are not available through the Windows Firewall applet in Control Panel. In addition, Windows Firewall with Advanced Security can also configure IPSec settings. IPSec is a protocol used to encrypt data communication over the network. This tool was new in Windows Vista.

The **Windows Memory Diagnostics Tool** was new in Windows Vista and is used to perform tests on the physical memory of a computer running Windows 7. The physical memory of a computer cannot be tested when Windows 7 is running because the memory diagnostics tool needs access to test all of the memory, including the memory used by Windows 7. So, when you choose to use the Memory Diagnostics Tool, your computer reboots to run the tool without Windows 7 in memory.

Windows PowerShell Modules is a way for you to organize **Windows PowerShell** scripts and functions in order to make them easier to distribute to other users and computers. Windows PowerShell is an enhanced command-line interface that can be used to perform administrative tasks.

Microsoft Management Console

The MMC is a graphical interface shell that provides a structured environment to build management utilities. The MMC provides basic functionality, such as menus, so that management utility developers do not have to. This also provides a consistent user interface for all management utilities, which makes network administrators more productive.

Network administrators use **MMC consoles** with **MMC snap-ins** to perform management tasks. A console is like a document window; one or more consoles can be loaded into the MMC at a time. Each console can host one or more snap-ins. A snap-in is a component that adds control mechanisms to the MMC console for a specific service or object. For example, the Disk Management snap-in is used to manage hard disks. Within a snap-in there are typically multiple functions. For example, the Disk Management snap-in can partition and format hard disks.

An MMC console, shown in Figure 3-24, is composed of a console menu bar, console tree, details pane, and an Actions pane. The contents of the Action and View menus in the console menu bar change based on the snap-in that is active in the console. The console menu bar also contains a mini-icon toolbar of shortcuts to common tasks in the Action and View menus. The console tree is the left pane of the console and displays the snap-ins that are loaded into the console. The details pane is the right pane of the console and displays the details of the item selected in the console tree. The Actions pane is used to provide easy access to the options in the Action menu.

The actions pane is now favored by Microsoft over the taskpad views available in previous versions of the MMC. Snap-ins written for MMC 3.0 do not support taskpad views. Creation of taskpad views using snap-ins written for MMC 2.0 is still supported.

You can create a customized MMC console by adding the snap-ins you want to a single console and then saving the console as an .msc file. You can share .msc files between users and computers. This allows network administrators to be more productive.

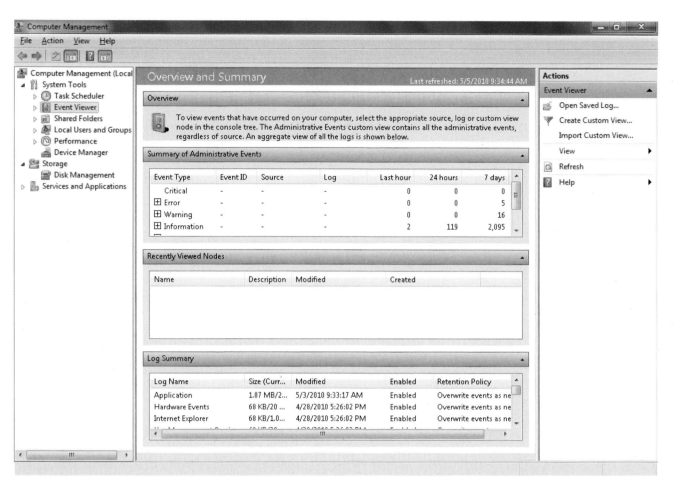

Figure 3-24 MMC console for Computer Management
Courtesy Course Technology/Cengage Learning

When you share MMC consoles, you may wish to restrict the ability of others to modify them. This ensures that the MMC consoles are consistent each time they are used. To prevent modification of an MMC console, you can change the console access mode. All of the available console access modes are listed in Table 3-1.

Table 3-1 MMC console access modes

Console Access Mode	Description
Author mode	Full customization of the console is allowed. This is the default console access mode.
User mode–full access	Removes the ability to add or remove snap-ins, change snap-in console options, create Favorites, or create taskpads
User mode–limited access, multiple window	Limits access to only the portion of the console tree that was visible when the console was saved. Users are able to create new windows, but not close existing windows.
User mode–limited access, single window	Limits access to only the portion of the console tree that was visible when the console was saved. Users are not able to create new windows or close existing windows.

Limiting access to MMC consoles is not an effective security mechanism. You must limit user rights and permissions to limit a user's ability to perform administrative tasks.

Computer Management

Computer Management is an MMC console that serves as a common troubleshooting and administrative interface for several snap-ins. The Computer Management console is divided into three sections: System Tools, Storage, and Services and Applications.

The System Tools section contains:

- *Task Scheduler*—Used to schedule programs to run at a particular time or when a particular event occurs.

- *Event Viewer*—This is another way to access the same information as is found in the Event Viewer administrative tool.

- *Shared Folders*—Used to view the shared folders on the local system. The Shares folder lets you see all shares, including hidden shares, the path of each share, and the number of clients connected to each share. The Sessions folder lets you view which users are connected to the local system over the network, how many files they have open, and the computer they are using. The Open Files folder lets you see which files are open and which user has each file open.

- *Local Users and Groups*—This is a way to access similar information as the Users applet found in the User Accounts and Family Safety category. However, this option is more advanced, and provided additional options.

- *Performance*—This is another way to access the same information as is available in the Performance administrative tool.

- *Device Manager*—Used to view and modify the configuration of hardware devices in your computer.

The Storage section contains:

- *Disk Management*—Used to manage hard disks. You can partition and format hard disks.

The Services and Applications section contains:

- *Services*—Used to enable, configure, and disable Windows 7 services.

- *WMI Control*—Used to back up and restore, control security, and specify a default namespace for Windows Management Instrumentation (WMI). WMI is used to perform remote monitoring and management of Windows.

Activity 3-6: Using Computer Management

Time Required: 5 minutes
Objective: Use the Computer Management MMC console.

Description: The Computer Management MMC console is one of the most commonly used administrative tools. It has several useful snap-ins such as Event Viewer, Disk Management, and Services. In this activity, you open Computer Management using two different methods.

1. If necessary, start your computer and log on.
2. Click the **Start** button, and click **Control Panel**.
3. Click **System and Security** and click **Administrative Tools**.
4. Double-click **Computer Management**. Notice that there are a number of options to manage Windows 7 using this single MMC console, as shown previously in Figure 3-24.

5. In the left pane, expand **Services and Applications** and click **Services**. This is the same information you can see in the Services MMC console that is available in Administrative Tools.

6. Close Computer Management.

7. Close the **Administrative Tools** window and close the **System and Security** window.

8. Click the **Start** button, right-click **Computer**, and click **Manage**. This is another way to start the Computer Management MMC console.

9. Close Computer Management.

Services

A **service** is a type of Windows application that runs in the background without user interaction. Services typically perform tasks for other software applications or perform housekeeping tasks for Windows 7. For example, the DHCP Client service is responsible for communicating on the network to get a network address that allows Windows 7 to access servers and the Internet. Windows Firewall also runs as a service.

The **Services administrative tool**, shown in Figure 3-25, is used to manage Windows 7 services. The details pane of Services has a standard view and an extended view that can be selected from tabs at the bottom of the console. The extended view shows the description of the selected service at the left side of the details pane and includes shortcuts for starting and stopping the selected service.

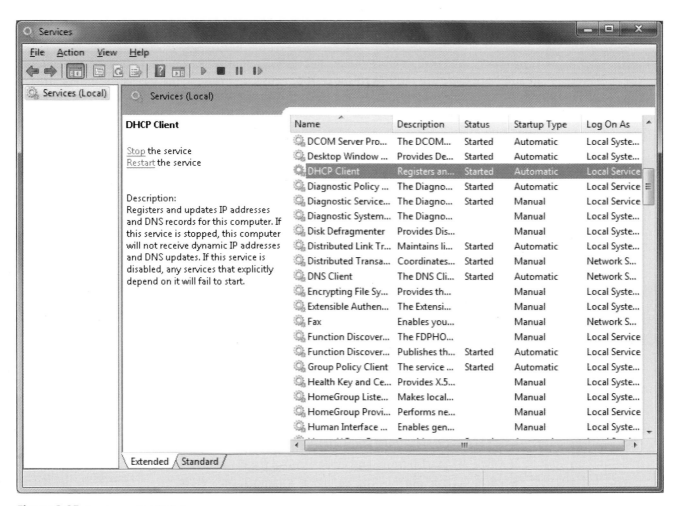

Figure 3-25 Services extended view
Courtesy Course Technology/Cengage Learning

Both views show the following service information:

- *Name*—Each service is given a name to identify it. You can modify the name of a service, but it is not recommended. If you call a vendor for support, they expect services to be using standard names.

- *Description*—The description of a service provides information about what tasks the service performs. Descriptions for Windows services are provided by Microsoft, while descriptions for other services are provided by the vendor.

- *Status*—The status of a service indicates whether it is started or stopped. In rare cases a service may have a status of starting or stopping if the service is experiencing problems during startup or shutdown.

- *Startup Type*—Services with an automatic startup type are started when Windows 7 boots. Services with a manual startup type must be started manually by a user, or by another application. Services with a disabled startup type cannot be started.

- *Log On As*—Each service logs on to Windows to determine its permissions to perform tasks such as file manipulation. Services can log on as the Local System account, which has full access to Windows 7 or a specific user account. Most Windows 7 services log on as Local System. However, logging on as a specific user account is more secure. Some Windows 7 services log on as Network Service or Local Service. Both of these accounts are more limited than Local System.

When you view the properties of a service, you can see additional information about it. You can also modify characteristics of the service. A Properties dialog box of a service includes the following tabs:

- *General*—Displays the service name, description, path to executable, and start parameters. In addition, there are buttons to start, stop, pause, and resume the service. Stopping and starting a service is often performed when the service has experienced an error. Pausing and restarting a service is typically done when testing service functionality.

- *Log On*—Allows you to specify the account name used by a service to log on to perform its tasks.

- *Recovery*—Allows you to specify which action is taken after first, second, and subsequent failures. The actions include taking no action, restarting the services, running a program, and restarting the computer.

- *Dependencies*—Shows you which other services require this service to be running before they can start. In addition, this tab shows you the other services that must be running for this service to start.

Activity 3-7: Managing Services

Time Required: 10 minutes
Objective: Manage Windows 7 Services by using the Services MMC snap-in.

Description: Windows 7 has a number of services that run in the background performing system tasks. As part of a troubleshooting process, you often need to verify the status of services and occasionally stop or start services. In this activity, you manage services by using the Services MMC snap-in.

1. If necessary, start your computer and log on.
2. Click the **Start** button, and click **Control Panel**.
3. Click **System and Security** and click **Administrative Tools**.
4. Double-click **Services**.
5. Click the **Computer Browser** service. The extended view in the Services snap-in shows a description of the service at the left side of the window. This description can also be viewed when you are looking at the properties of a service.

6. Click the **Standard** tab at the bottom of the window. This view removes the service description and makes it easier to see information about the services.

7. Right-click **DHCP Client** and click **Restart**. This stops and starts the DHCP Client service. It is occasionally necessary to stop and start a service if it is not functioning properly.

8. Double-click **DHCP Client**. The General tab, shown in Figure 3-26, shows mostof the same information that was visible in the summary of services you have already been viewing. Notice that this tab shows the executable file that runs as a service.

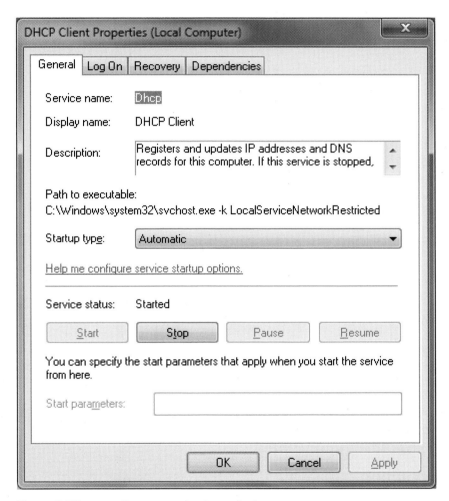

Figure 3-26 DHCP Client Properties General tab
Courtesy Course Technology/Cengage Learning

9. Click the **Log On** tab. If a service is configured to run as a particular user account to limit its permissions, then the credentials are entered here.

10. Click the **Recovery** tab. This tab contains settings for the actions to be taken if this service fails one or more times. Notice that this service is automatically restarted after each of the first two failures, as shown in Figure 3-27.

11. Click the **Dependencies** tab, as shown in Figure 3-28. Notice that the DHCP Client service requires several services to run properly, and the WinHTTP Web Proxy Auto-Discovery Service depends on the DHCP Client service.

12. Click **Cancel**.

13. Close **Services**, close the **Administrative Tools** window, and close the **System and Security** window.

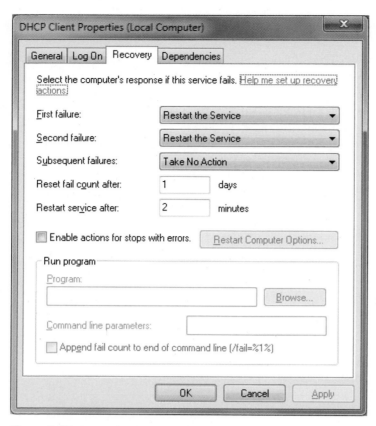

Figure 3-27 DHCP Client Properties Recovery tab
Courtesy Course Technology/Cengage Learning

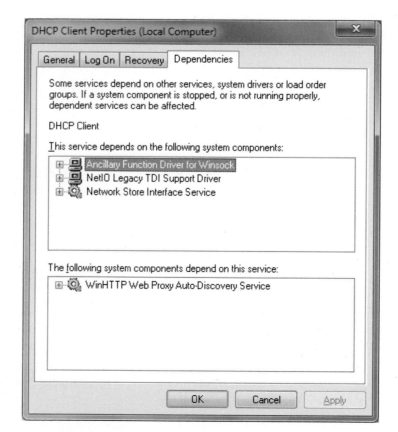

Figure 3-28 DHCP Client Properties Dependencies tab
Courtesy Course Technology/Cengage Learning

Hardware Management

Managing and maintaining computer hardware is a task performed regularly by network administrators. Windows 7 supports a wide variety of internal and external hardware components that you should be familiar with. Internal hardware components include network cards, video cards, and hard disk drives. External components are typically peripheral devices such as a mouse, printer, or USB drive.

Windows 7 requires **device drivers** to manage and communicate with hardware components. Device drivers are written specifically for a particular type and model of component. For example, a 3C905 network card driver is different from an E1000 network card driver.

The **Windows 7 Compatibility Center** is a list of software or hardware and associated device drivers that have been tested with Windows 7. If a device is certified as "Designed for Windows 7" then you are assured that Microsoft has tested the hardware component and device driver to ensure they work properly with Windows 7. Hardware components and device drivers that are not certified by Microsoft may work properly, but are not supported by Microsoft.

 To identify whether hardware is compatible with Windows 7, you can search for a hardware device at the Windows 7 Compatibility Center at http://www.microsoft.com/windows/compatibility/windows-7/en-us/default.aspx.

To manage hardware in Windows 7 you should understand:

- Device drivers
- Device driver compatibility
- Device Manager
- Device driver signing
- Procedures for adding new hardware components

Device Drivers

Hardware devices such as modems, network adapter cards, and video cards are manufactured by a wide variety of vendors. The capabilities and functions of these devices vary depending on the model and manufacturer. A device driver is software that allows Windows 7 to properly communicate with and use the functionality of a device.

Device drivers act as intermediaries between a hardware component and an operating system such as Windows 7. A device driver contains the instructions on how to use the full capabilities of a device properly. After they are installed, device drivers load automatically as part of the boot process each time Windows 7 is started.

In some cases, a device driver not specifically designed for a hardware component may allow that component to function. For example, the SVGA display driver works with almost all video cards. If an incorrect device driver works, it is because the basic functionality of a class of hardware devices, such as video cards, is similar. However, installing the wrong device driver for a hardware component results in poor performance and does not let you use the advanced features of a device. Using the incorrect device driver for a hardware component may also make Windows 7 unstable.

Vendors regularly release updated device drivers. Device drivers are updated to improve performance, add additional features, or fix flaws. It is a best practice to use the latest device drivers that are available from the manufacturers Web site. When a device is not working properly, installing the latest device driver should be one of the first troubleshooting steps.

 Some device drivers can be obtained through Automatic Updates. They are distributed as optional updates.

Device Driver Compatibility

Some device drivers designed for previous versions of Windows do not work properly with Windows 7. The driver incompatibility is due to changes that make Windows 7 more stable and secure. If a driver does not function properly in Windows 7, you must get an updated driver from the device manufacturer.

Some potential device driver compatibility issues are:

- A 32-bit version of Windows 7 requires 32-bit drivers and a 64-bit version of Windows 7 requires 64-bit drivers.

- All driver files referenced in an INF file must be part of the driver installation package. In previous versions of Windows this was preferred, but not enforced. This may cause the installation of some drivers to fail.

- Installers cannot display a user interface during installation. Some device drivers display a user interface during installation to request configuration information. You must obtain an updated device driver from the manufacturer that does not present a user interface during installation.

- Digital signatures are required for 64-bit drivers that run in kernel mode. The 64-bit version of Windows XP allowed unsigned drivers to be installed. You must obtain a signed version of 64-bit drivers from the device manufacturer if a driver is not included with Windows 7.

- Driver user interfaces may not appear properly. Windows 7 isolates services in session 0 and runs applications in other sessions. Processes running in session 0 cannot access the display driver to display a user interface. This is most likely to be a problem with printer drivers.

- Registry management changes for 64-bit Windows 7 may prevent drivers from updating settings properly. The 64-bit Windows 7 registry supports ownership of keys. This may result in a user other than the original installer being unable to change device driver settings.

- Video drivers written for Windows 2000 or Windows XP cannot support the new **Aero Glass** interface. You must obtain a new device driver that meets the requirements of the Windows Display Driver Model (WDDM).

- Windows 7 uses the NDIS 6.20 interface for network devices. Network drivers for Windows XP are NDIS 5.x and are translated, which reduces performance. To ensure the best performance, obtain an NDIS 6.0 or newer network driver.

- Kernel mode printer drivers cannot be used in Windows 7. Replace Kernel mode printer drivers with newer, user mode drivers from the printer manufacturer. This affects a very small number of printer drivers. Affected printer drivers are typically specialized devices used in manufacturing environments, such as barcode printers.

By using only devices certified as Designed for Windows 7, you can ensure that appropriate device drivers are available.

Device Manager

Device Manager is the primary tool for managing device drivers. The main purpose of Device Manager is to allow you to view and modify hardware device properties. Some of the tasks that can be performed with Device Manager are:

- Determining whether installed hardware is functioning correctly
- Viewing and changing hardware resource settings
- Determining and changing the drivers used by a device
- Enabling, disabling, and uninstalling devices

- Configuring advanced settings for devices
- Viewing and printing summary information about installed devices

After installing Windows 7, you should use Device Manager to confirm that all devices are working properly. After installing a new hardware component, you should use Device Manager to confirm that the specific component is functioning properly. Any hardware component that is not functioning correctly is displayed with a yellow exclamation mark. A hardware component that has been manually disabled is displayed with a down arrow, as shown in Figure 3-29.

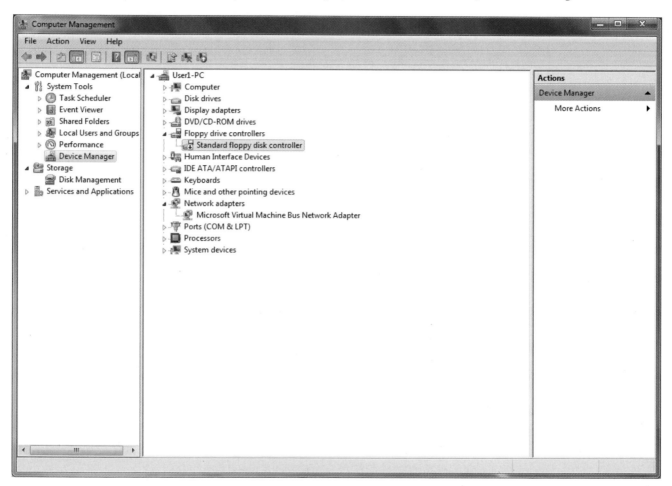

Figure 3-29 Device Manager
Courtesy Course Technology/Cengage Learning

If a hardware component is not functioning properly, you should install an updated driver for it. You can install an updated device driver from the Driver tab in the Device Properties, shown in Figure 3-30. You can also install an updated device driver by using the Hardware Update Wizard that is accessible by right-clicking the device.

Although vendors perform extensive testing, occasionally an updated device driver causes problems. You can roll back a device driver to the previous version when an updated device driver causes problems.

Activity 3-8: Using Device Manager

Time Required: 10 minutes

Objective: Use Device Manager to configure hardware components and device drivers.

Description: Device Manager is an MMC snap-in that can configure hardware components and device drivers. You can use it to install updated drivers and disable devices that are not functioning properly. In this activity, you view the status of the network card in your computer.

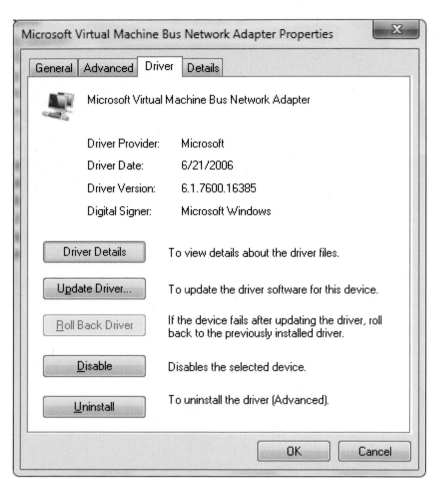

Figure 3-30 Device Properties Driver tab
Courtesy Course Technology/Cengage Learning

1. If necessary, start your computer and log on.

2. Click the **Start** button, right-click **Computer**, and click **Manage**.

3. Click **Device Manager**. If some devices are listed with a yellow question mark, it means that no device driver is loaded for those devices.

4. Expand **Network adapters** and double-click your network card (the name of the network card will vary depending on your hardware). The General tab gives general information about your network card including its status.

5. Click the **Advanced** tab. The contents of the Advanced tab vary depending on the model of network card. The settings are defined by the device driver.

6. Click the **Driver** tab. This shows information about the device driver including date, version number, and the publisher. You can also update drivers here.

7. Click the **Driver Details** button. This displays the files that are used as part of the device driver.

8. Click **OK** and click the **Details** tab. The Details tab has an option box that lets you select and view all the device driver details.

9. Click the **Property** option box and browse through the list of details you can view.

10. If present, click the **Resources** tab. You can view and modify the resources used by a device on this tab. This tab may not be available if your Windows 7 installation is virtualized.

11. If present, click the **Power Management** tab. You can this tab to control how the network adapter interacts with power management. This tab may not be available if your Windows 7 installation is virtualized.

12. Click **Cancel**.

13. Close Computer Management.

Device Driver Signing

Windows 7 uses file signatures on system files to ensure system stability. Device drivers can also be signed. **Device driver signing** ensures that a driver for a specific hardware component has been verified by Microsoft to be from a known software publisher (meaning it is authentic). Device driver signing also ensures that the device driver has not been modified in any way since it was signed (meaning it has integrity). Viruses are unable to spread by using device drivers because digital signing shows an infected device driver as corrupted.

If you attempt to install an unsigned device driver in Windows 7, one of the following messages will appear:

- *Windows can't verify the publisher of this driver software*—This message appears when no digital signature is present, or the digital signature cannot be verified as valid. You should install unsigned drivers only if you are confident it is from a legitimate source.

- *This driver software has been altered*—This message appears if the device driver has been altered since the developer added the digital signature. In most cases, this message indicates that the original device driver has been infected by a malicious program and it should not be installed.

- *Windows cannot install this driver software*—This message appears only on the 64-bit versions of Windows 7. The 64-bit versions of Windows 7 do not allow unsigned device drivers to be installed by default. However, for testing purposes, you can disable the check for driver signing by using bcdedit.exe.

You can verify that existing drivers and system files are signed by running the **File Signature Verification utility** (sigverif.exe). The filename, location, modification date, and version number are returned for each unsigned file. You can then investigate whether signed versions of these files are available. It is a best practice to use only signed device drivers.

 A signed device driver does not indicate that Microsoft has performed stability or quality testing. Only devices in Windows 7 Compatibility Center have undergone testing by Microsoft.

Hardware Component Installation

When hardware components are installed in a computer, they are assigned resource settings that allow them to access the system processor and memory in different ways. Each type of hardware component has different requirements.

The four main resources a hardware component might use are:

- *Direct memory access (DMA) channels*—A legacy method for allowing devices to communicate directly with system memory instead of passing data through the processor. Typically used for sound cards.

- *Input/output (I/O) ranges*—Addresses at which a device can be communicated with. A single device can have several addresses, with each address allowing access to a particular device feature or component.

- *Interrupt request (IRQ) lines*—A mechanism for devices to request time from the CPU.

- *Memory address ranges*—Address ranges in system memory that are dedicated to the device.

Windows 7 no longer supports legacy **Industry Standard Architecture (ISA)** devices, which sometimes required manual configuration of resources. Newer **Peripheral Component Interface (PCI)** devices support **plug and play**, which automatically assigns resources to devices. Universal Serial Bus (USB) devices are also plug and play. Only settings for legacy ports such as parallel ports and serial ports may require manual configuration of resources in Windows 7.

 The loss of support of ISA devices is not important for most users since current computers do not have ISA slots. However, some specialized software, such as equipment monitoring software, may rely on ISA devices and be incompatible with Windows 7.

To install a plug and play device:

1. Install or attach the new hardware component.

2. Windows 7 automatically detects the new device.

3. A device driver is loaded automatically if Windows 7 contains an appropriate device driver.

4. If Windows 7 does not contain an appropriate device driver, you are prompted to provide one.

 Windows 7 may not contain the latest device driver for your hardware component. You can update the device driver after installation, if required.

To simplify the location of device drivers, you can make them available to computer by staging the drivers in the **driver store** or by providing a location to search. Windows 7 contains a driver store with a large set of device drivers included on the Windows 7 installation media. You can add new drivers to the driver store by using pnputil.exe. By adding a device driver to the driver store, you ensure that Windows 7 is able to find and install the driver when the matching hardware is attached. For example, you could stage the driver for a new USB printer on all Windows 7 computers. Then, when that printer is attached to any Windows 7 computer in the office, the appropriate driver is automatically loaded without asking the user to locate the appropriate driver.

 Activity 9-2 Modifying the Printer Driver Store has you use pnputil.exe to add a printer driver to the driver store.

You can also store drivers in a centralized network location. If you store drivers in a network location, you need to modify a registry key on the Windows 7 computers to configure the computers to search in that location when looking for drivers. Edit the following registry key: HKLM\Software\Microsoft\Windows\CurrentVersion\DevicePath. Generally, you should use an automated tool to updated this registry key on all of the computers to simplify deployment.

Power Management

Power management is becoming a major concern for corporate and personal owners of computers. Hardware manufacturers have started to address this concern by focusing on reduced power consumption in their new products. However, a computer and monitor can still easily consume over 100 watts of power while they are running.

Minimizing power usage is driven by both cost and environmental factors. To address power management concerns Windows 7 has a power management structure that was introduced in Windows Vista.

Windows 7 relies on power management capabilities built into a computer to perform power management. Computers must meet the specifications of the **Advanced Configuration and Power Interface (ACPI)** standard to be managed by Windows 7. All current computers meet this standard.

The ACPI standard defines power states for global power management and individual devices. Power states define which devices are drawing power in the system. Power states can be implemented at different times based on the power plan you have configured. For multimedia computers, away mode provides a way to have instant power-on, similar to other consumer electronics such as a television.

 Power management can be centrally controlled by using Group Policy in a corporate environment.

ACPI States

The ACPI standard defines a number of global power management states. However, not all states are used by Windows 7. Table 3-2 lists the ACPI power states used by Windows 7.

Table 3-2　ACPI power states used by Windows 7

Power state	Description
S0 (or G0) Working	This power state is the fully functioning computer. While in this state, individual devices, such as the processor and hard disks, can be in varying power states. For example, the spinning of a hard disk can be stopped after a few minutes of inactivity to reduce power usage.
S3 Sleep	This sleep state is also known as suspend to RAM. In this state, all system devices are powered down except the RAM. The RAM retains the state of all running applications. Returning from S3 to S0 requires only that the hardware be reinitialized. This state is known as Standby in previous versions of Windows.
	If power is lost while the computer is in the S3 state, all data from memory is lost. This is equivalent to losing power while the computer is running.
S4 Sleep	This sleep state is also known as suspend to disk. In this state, the contents of RAM are saved to disk and all devices including RAM are powered off. During restart the contents of RAM are loaded from disk rather than booting the operating system. When a computer system has a large amount of RAM, restarting from the S4 state can take a long period of time. For example, a computer with 2GB of RAM needs to load 2GB of data from disk during startup from the S4 state. This state is known as Hibernate in previous versions of Windows.
	If power is lost while the computer is in the S4 state, all data is unaffected. Because the contents of memory are stored on disk, a power failure does not affect the S4 state.
S5 (or G2) Soft Off	In this state, the operating system is not running. This is the power state triggered when the operating system is shut down. Minimal hardware functionality is maintained, such as the ability to start booting the computer by using Wake on LAN. To start a computer from this state, the operating system must go through a complete boot up.
G3 Mechanical Off	In this state, the operating system is not running and no power is supplied to any devices in the computer. This is the only state in which hardware can be serviced. A computer that is in the G3 state can be unplugged and not be affected. The only power consumption for a computer in the G3 state is from a small battery that maintains BIOS settings and the clock.

Sleep Mode in Windows 7

Windows XP had two sleep states. **Standby** put the computer in the **S3 state** and **Hibernate** put the computer in the **S4 state**. Windows 7 also includes a combination of the S3 and S4 states called **hybrid sleep**.

Hybrid sleep saves the contents of memory to disk when entering the S3 state. Effectively this means the computer is in the S3 state, but prepared for the S4 state. Hybrid sleep is disabled by default.

Hybrid sleep provides a number of advantages:

- If power is lost in the S3 state, the computer can recover from the S4 state on reboot. No data is lost when there is a power outage in the S3 state.

- Eliminates the requirement to leave Standby mode to enter hibernation. Windows XP required a laptop in the S3 state to wake up to the **S0 state** to move down to the S4 state. If there was a problem entering the S4 state, then the laptop would stay in the S0 state, fully running, and potentially overheat while in a carrying case. As well, the laptop may run out of battery life and lose data.

Windows XP commonly had problems with computers either transitioning into sleep states, or coming out of sleep states. After experiencing errors, users often stopped using power management for fear of system crashes and losing their work.

A major source of sleep state transition errors in Windows XP was poorly written device drivers and services. Windows XP let drivers and services veto entering a sleep state, and many developers had their software veto sleep states unnecessarily. To prevent sleep state transition problems, Windows 7 does not let user mode services veto sleep states. In addition, Windows 7 includes diagnostics for troubleshooting sleep state errors.

Other enhancements to power management over Windows XP include:

- Resume from S3 state in less than 3 seconds
- Resume from S4 state in less than 10 seconds
- Updated USB hub driver that initializes faster
- Optimized use of processor power management
- Support for additional devices such as graphics cards and wireless network cards
- Support for screen brightness in policies
- Enhanced hard drive management by extending the time a hard drive is off
- Closing a laptop case can trigger sleep mode
- Sleep mode as default shutdown option to speed startup

Power Plans

Windows 7 uses power plans to control how your computer implements power management. There are three default power plans. Some of the details of each default power plan for a laptop computer are listed in Table 3-3. In addition, you can create your own power plans. The options available to you when creating or modifying a power plan vary depending on the capabilities of your computer hardware. For example, settings for running on battery power only apply to portable computers with a battery.

 In Windows XP, power plans were known as power schemes.

Table 3-3   Default power plans

Parameter	Balanced		Power saver		High performance	
	AC	Battery	AC	Battery	AC	Battery
Turn off display after	10 min	5 min	5 min	2 min	15 min	10 min
Turn off hard disk after	20 min	10 min	20 min	5 min	20 min	20 min
Minimum processor state	5 %	5 %	5 %	5 %	100 %	5 %
Maximum processor state	100 %	100 %	100 %	100 %	100 %	100 %
Sleep after	30 min	15 min	15 min	10 min	Never	Never
Hibernate after	360 min	360 min	360 min	360 min	Never	Never

Activity 3-9: Configuring a Power Plan

Time Required: 5 minutes

Objective: Configure a power plan to reduce power consumption.

Description: Windows 7 includes three default power plans to maximize performance, maximize power saving, and provide balanced power saving and performance. Most office computers do not need to maximize performance; it is more beneficial to maximize power savings. In this activity, you configure your computer to maximize power savings.

1. If necessary, start your computer and log on
2. Click the **Start** button, and click **Control Panel**.
3. Click **System and Security** and click **Power Options**.
4. Under Preferred plans, click the **Power saver** option button.
5. At the left side, click **Choose what the power button does**. If your computer is not ACPI compliant, then the only option for the power button is Shut down. However, if your computer is ACPI compliant, the default is Sleep. If you are on a mobile computer, then you have additional options as shown in Figure 3-31.
6. Click **Cancel**.

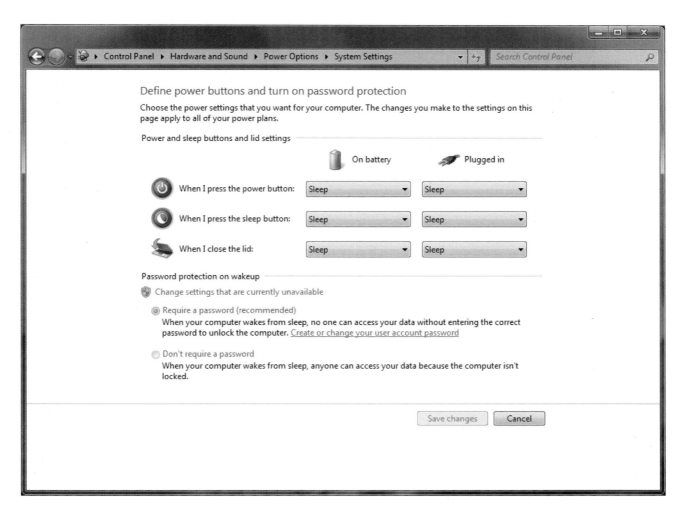

Figure 3-31 Laptop power button options
Courtesy Course Technology/Cengage Learning

7. Under the Power saver plan, click **Change plan settings**. Notice that when using the Power saver plan the display turns off after 5 minutes. The content displayed here will vary depending on whether your computer is ACPI compliant. An ACPI compliant computer will also have a setting for when the computer goes to sleep, as show in Figure 3-32.

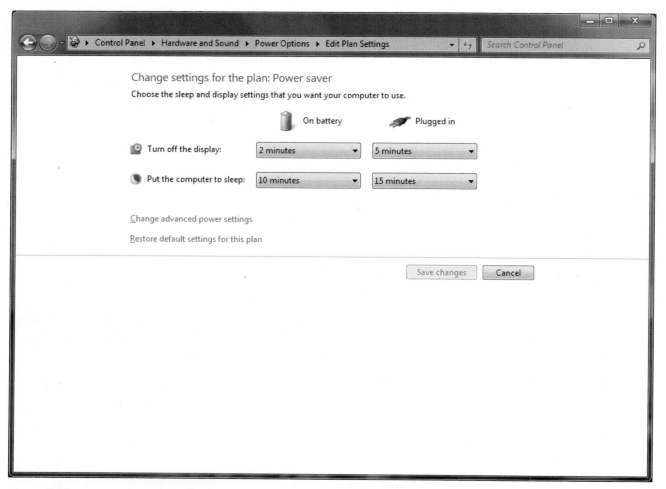

Figure 3-32 Laptop power plan settings
Courtesy Course Technology/Cengage Learning

8. Click **Change advanced power settings**. This allows you to see more detailed information about the power plans.

9. Expand **Processor power management** and expand **Minimum processor state**. The minimum processor state is 5%. A virtualized version of Windows 7 may not have this setting.

10. Expand **Maximum processor state**. The maximum processor state is 100%. You could reduce the maximum processor state to reduce battery utilization, but it will also decrease system performance.

11. Click **Cancel** and close the **Edit Plan Settings** window.

Away Mode

In some situations, even resuming from the S3 state in five seconds or less is not fast enough. Computers that are used for services such as media streaming or as a personal video recorder need almost instant functionality. **Away Mode** is designed for these types of devices. Away Mode is not designed to be implemented on most computers. The default power management configuration is a better option in most situations.

Away Mode is not a different power state. Computers in Away Mode are still in the S0 state. However, the computer looks and sounds like it is off. Away Mode maximizes all of the device level power savings while continuing to work in the background if required.

After Away Mode is enabled, it replaces Standby requests. For example, if shutdown normally puts the computer in the S3 state, it now puts the computer in Away Mode instead.

Away Mode has the following characteristics:

- Video is blanked

- Audio is muted

- Keyboard and mouse input is filtered out

- S0 power state

- May still idle to sleep based on the power plan

For detailed information about away mode and how to enable it, see Away Mode in Windows Vista on the Microsoft Web site at http://www.microsoft.com/whdc/system/pnppwr/powermgmt/awaymode.mspx.

Display

Windows 7 has an entirely new system for graphics presentation when compared with Windows XP. Developers now use Windows Presentation Foundation to control how applications draw windows on the screen. Enhanced features that can be used by developers include transparency and the ability for menu buttons to overlap each other.

As a network administrator, your main concern is the display drivers that are required for Windows 7. Windows 7 is able to use display drivers from Windows XP. However, to use the Aero Glass interface, you must have a display driver that supports the Windows Display Driver Model (WDDM) and DirectX 9.0c. If your video card and video driver do not support the Aero Glass interface then the basic interface is displayed. The basic interface is similar to the Windows XP interface.

The Aero Glass interface makes extensive use of advanced graphics functionality. However, this functionality is not just about looking pretty. The features in Aero Glass are designed to help you be more productive on your computer.

In addition to transparency of windows, Aero Glass provides:

- *Live taskbar thumbnails*—If you hold the mouse pointer over a minimized item on the task bar, a small version of the application window is displayed. This allows you to quickly see exactly what the application is. For example, you may have several graphics files open for editing, with each graphic in its own window. The live taskbar thumbnail for the applications will show you each graphic file so you can easily move back and forth between them.

- *Windows Flip*—In the basic interface of Windows, you can use ALT-Tab to move between open Windows. When you move between the windows, you select an icon that represents the application. However, if you have multiple windows open for the same application, it is difficult to be sure you have selected the correct window. **Windows Flip** offers similar functionality but provides a live thumbnail of each window, which makes it easier to select the correct window.

- *Windows Flip 3D*—A further enhancement to Windows Flip, **Windows Flip 3D** lets you view all of your open windows and scroll through them using the mouse wheel. For each open Window, you see a version larger than a thumbnail, but still reduced in size so that you can see the contents of each window.

Aero Glass is enabled by default if your video card and video driver support it. If Aero Glass is not enabled and your video card is relatively new, check the manufacturer's Web site to see if a WDDM driver is available.

In addition to Aero Glass, you should understand the following display settings and functions:

- Display settings
- Visual Effects
- Themes
- Desktop backgrounds
- Screen savers
- Multiple monitors

Display Settings

The Screen Resolution applet, shown in Figure 3-33, allows you to configure the **screen resolution** for your display. Other more complex options such as screen refresh rate and **color depth** are available in the Advanced Settings.

Figure 3-33 Screen Resolution
Courtesy Course Technology/Cengage Learning

The screen resolution is the number of **pixels** that are displayed on your monitor or LCD panel. A pixel is a single dot on the screen. The resolution is expressed as the number of horizontal pixels by the number of vertical pixels. For example, a resolution of 1024 × 768 means that there are 1024 pixels across the screen and 768 pixels up and down the screen.

The optimal screen resolution varies depending on the display you are using and your video card. In general, LCD panel monitors should be used at their native resolution. The native resolution for your LCD panel can be found in the documentation that came with it, but for most non-widescreen 17-inch or 19-inch LCD panels the native resolution is 1280 × 1024. If you set your screen resolution at less than the native resolution, the display will appear fuzzy. Older cathode ray tube (CRT) monitors have better flexibility for varying resolutions. You can get good display quality from a CRT monitor at any resolution up to the display maximum.

Advanced Settings allows you to access additional information about your video card and monitor. On the Adapter tab, you can see the Chip type, DAC type, memory size, and BIOS information. You can also list all of the modes your video card is capable of in combination with your monitor. Each mode is a combination of display resolution, color depth, and refresh rate.

Color depth indicates how many bits of information are used to store color information about each pixel in the display. The most common setting for color depth is 32-bit, which is easily supported by current video cards. Some older video cards with very limited memory benefit from reducing the color depth to 16-bit. This reduces the amount of memory required for each pixel by half. In most cases, however, reducing color depth to 16-bit has no benefit.

The refresh rate of a display is critical. If the display rate is set too low, the monitor may flicker and cause users to get headaches. Flicker is caused by displays refreshing at 60 Hz, which is the same frequency as fluorescent lights. Ideally, the refresh rate should be set to 70 Hz or higher.

Current displays support plug and play, which allows them to communicate their capabilities to Windows 7. If the display supports plug and play, Windows 7 limits your ability to set the refresh rate to those rates which the display is capable of without being damaged. In some cases, you may need to install a driver for your monitor to set the display appropriately.

Activity 3-10: Configuring Display Settings

Time Required: 5 minutes
Objective: Configure the screen resolution and color resolution for your computer.

Description: Windows 7 automatically selects display settings based on the display device that is connected to your computer during installation. However, you may wish to modify the display settings to suit your own preferences. Or, you may wish to modify the display settings after getting a new display such as a 19-inch LCD panel. In this activity, you will change the screen resolution and color resolution of your display.

1. If necessary, start your computer and log on.
2. Right-click the **Desktop** and click **Screen Resolution**.
3. Configure the resolution to be **800 by 600 pixels** and click **Apply**. Your screen resolution changes and all of the graphics become larger on the screen. If your screen resolution is already at 800 by 600 pixels, select a different resolution.
4. Click **Revert** to prevent the keeping of the settings.
5. Click the **Advanced Settings** link. The Adapter tab shows general information about your graphics card, as shown in Figure 3-34.
6. Click the **List All Modes** button. This displays all of the screen resolution, color depth, and refresh rate combinations that your display and video card are capable of providing.
7. Click **Cancel**.
8. Click the **Monitor** tab. This tab shows you what type of monitor is installed and allows you to configure the screen refresh rate and the color depth.
9. Click **Cancel** to close the Advanced Settings and click **Cancel** to close the Screen Resolution window.

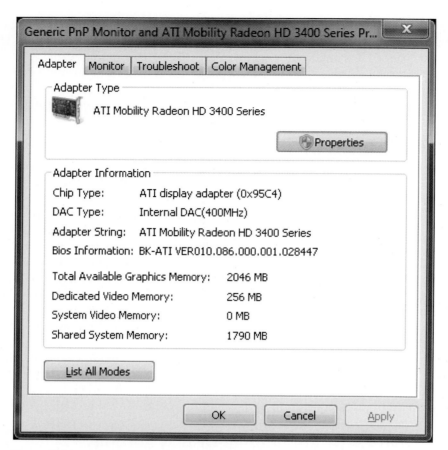

Figure 3-34 Advanced display settings, Adapter tab
Courtesy Course Technology/Cengage Learning

Visual Effects

The performance options for Windows 7 includes a variety of visual effects that can be enabled or disabled, as shown in Figure 3-35. In most cases, you should use the "Let Windows choose what's best for my computer" option. When this option is selected, Windows enables and disables specific options based on the performance capabilities of your computer.

Disabling the effects in Windows 7 may make third-party remote control programs such as VNC and PC Anywhere run faster. The Remote Desktop function in Windows 7 is typically not affected by these features, or they can be disabled in the Remote Desktop client.

Themes

The Personalization applet lets you select from several predefined themes that control the color of windows, backgrounds, sounds and screen saver. Some of the themes are high contrast to help people with visual impairments see information better.

The Windows color option lets you precisely control the color settings for your desktop. Instead of selecting a color scheme, you can configure the color of windows yourself. In the Advanced appearance settings you can also select the fonts that are used for menu and window titles. However, the advanced appearance setting only applies when an Aero theme is not selected.

Desktop Backgrounds

Personalizing the desktop background is one of the most common actions users want to perform when receiving a new computer. Some corporate environments dictate that a standard desktop background must be used. However, standardizing the desktop background has no effect on the performance of a computer.

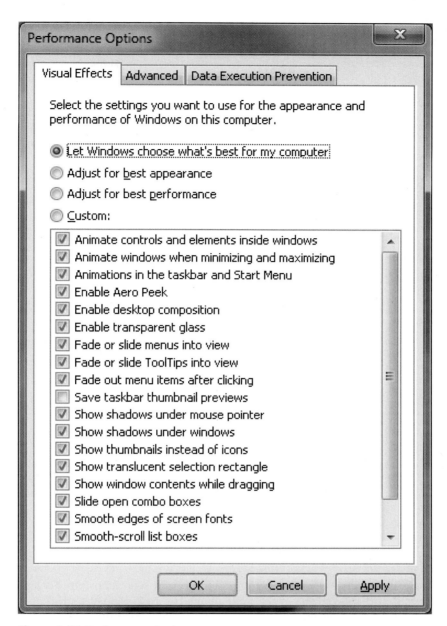

Figure 3-35 Performance Options
Courtesy Course Technology/Cengage Learning

Windows 7 comes with a number of desktop backgrounds for you to choose from. However, most people want to use their own pictures for a desktop background. This is the computer equivalent of putting a picture on your desk. When you use your own picture for a desktop background it must be in bitmap (bmp), Joint Picture Experts Group (jpeg, jpg), Graphics Interchange Format (gif), or Portable Network Graphics (png) format.

When you select a desktop background, you must also select how the graphic is laid out on the page. You can choose to stretch the picture to the size of the screen, center the picture on the screen, or tile the picture. Stretching the picture distorts the image if the original graphic is not the same proportion as the screen. Centering the picture ensures that the image is not distorted, but may leave blank spaces around the picture. Tiling the picture repeats the image if the size of the picture is less than the screen resolution.

New in Windows 7 is the option to configure a slideshow for your background, as shown in Figure 3-36. If you select more than one picture for you background, it automatically becomes a slideshow. You can define how often the pictures are changed and use the Shuffle option to randomize how they are displayed.

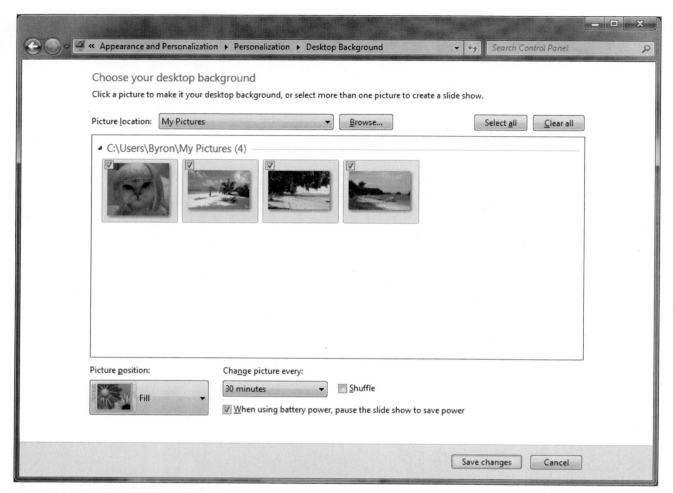

Figure 3-36 Desktop Background configuration
Courtesy Course Technology/Cengage Learning

Screen Savers

At one point in time, screen savers were used to prevent screen burn in. Screen burn in occurred in monitors that displayed the exact same image for an extended period of time. After screen burn in occurs, a ghosted image appears on the screen. Screen savers were meant to combat screen burn in by constantly changing the information displayed on the screen.

Screen savers are no longer required to prevent screen burn in. Modern displays are much less susceptible to screen burn in than older devices. In addition, power saving features in modern computers turn off displays quite quickly, often the same time frame you would configure a screen saver to turn on.

Screen savers are now a security mechanism for locking a computer. By default, no screen saver is configured in Windows 7 and the screen does not lock. To increase security, you should enable the On resume, display logon screen option. After you enable this option, you can define how many minutes of inactivity are required before the screen saver starts. If no screen saver is selected, the screen is blanked instead. When you resume using the computer, you are forced to log on again. This ensures that if you leave your computer unattended no one can access your work.

Multiple Monitors

Like Windows XP, Windows 7 supports **multiple monitors** attached to a single computer. When you use multiple monitors there are three configuration options; each option is useful in different scenarios.

- *Mirrored*—The default option for multiple monitors is to mirror the desktop on both displays. This is most useful when one display is a projector and you are performing a presentation or demonstration.

- *Extended*—When the desktop is extended onto the second display, you have additional screen space to perform your work. You can move windows back and forth between the two displays and even stretch windows across both monitors. While this does not sound important if you have not used it before, it is a very handy feature. A network administrator can perform remote desktop operations on one display, while reading documentation on the other display. Office workers can perform Internet research on one display while creating a document on the other display. Productivity is greatly increased by eliminating or reducing window switching.

- *External display only*—When you are running a laptop on batteries, it is useful to turn off the LCD panel display and use only an external projector during presentations and demonstrations. This may also be required if a laptop can only display video on a single display.

The hardware requirements for multiple monitors vary depending on whether your computer is a laptop computer or a desktop computer. Most laptop computers allow the external video connector to be used for multiple monitors. Desktop computers require either multiple video cards to be installed, or a multihead video card. A multihead video card has connectors for multiple monitors on a single card.

When you have multiple displays, you can configure which display is primary. The primary display is the one that displays the taskbar and Start button. Both displays are shown in the Display Settings applet. The resolution and color depth can be configured for each display independently if the extended configuration option is used.

Task Scheduler

Network administrators seldom have enough time to visit workstations and perform preventive maintenance. In most cases, the only time a network administrator sees a workstation is after it is already having problems.

Task scheduler allows you to be proactive about computer maintenance. You can schedule a task to run at a particular time or after a particular event. For example, you could trigger disk maintenance to be performed each day at noon, when the network users are typically having lunch. If the computer is in standby, it wakes up, performs the scheduled task, and then goes back into standby.

Task Scheduler in Windows XP had a number of limitations. The version of Task Scheduler introduced in Windows Vista, and retained in Windows 7, has addressed many of these limitations. Many Windows maintenance tasks are now performed automatically by the Task Scheduler instead of relying on services to remain running. Table 3-4 compares pre-Vista versions of task scheduler to the version of task scheduler in Windows 7.

Activity 3-11: Using Task Scheduler

Time Required: 10 minutes
Objective: Use Task Scheduler to schedule a task.

Description: The Task Scheduler is used extensively by Windows 7 to run background processes. As a network administrator, you may want to add your own scheduled tasks to Windows 7 to perform maintenance. In this activity, you view a scheduled task that defragments your computer hard drive.

1. If necessary, start your computer and log on.

2. Click the **Start** button, right-click **Computer**, and click **Manage**.

Table 3-4   Task scheduler comparison

Windows XP Limitations	Windows 7 Enhancements
The credentials used by each task were stored locally. If the password for a user was changed, tasks would no longer run and the network administrator had to update the password on each task that used that set of credentials.	Scheduled tasks no longer need to store credentials locally in most cases. The Service for Users (S4U) and Credential Manager can be used to manage credentials. S4U eliminates the need to store credentials locally in a corporate environment where domains are used. CredMan stores passwords locally, but ensures that each password needs to be updated only once for each set of credentials.
Recent versions of Windows required administrator rights to add and schedule tasks. This enhanced security but limited the ability of users to create tasks on their own computers.	The Task Scheduler in Windows 7 allows all users to create scheduled tasks. Security is not compromised because Task Scheduler has been redesigned to remove vulnerabilities that were present in Windows XP.
Only the most recent success or failure of scheduled tasks could be monitored. There was no way to view the status of multiple tasks if they ran in succession.	The Task Scheduler Summary shows the status of previously run and currently active tasks. In addition, each task has a history tab that allows you to view detailed information about that particular task.
Limited triggers. A scheduled task could be triggered based on a specified time or a limited set of system conditions.	You can still schedule a task to run at a particular scheduled time. However, there are now many additional triggers including at log on, at startup, on idle, on an event, on registration, on Terminal Server session connect, on Terminal Server session disconnect, on workstation lock, and on workstation unlock. If multiple triggers are specified, then all triggers must be activated to run the task.
Each scheduled task could perform only a single action. If multiple actions were required, multiple scheduled tasks had to be created or a batch file used.	You can now include multiple actions in a single task. When multiple actions are specified they are completed in order. This allows you to complete an entire process that has multiple actions that must be performed in a particular order. Each action can run a program, send an e-mail, or send a message.
Conditions for running scheduled tasks were limited to only a few states, such as an idle CPU.	Conditions have been enhanced to include power states and network conditions. Power states let you specify that certain tasks are run only when the computer is or is not in a sleep state. Network conditions let you specify that the task should only be run if certain network connections are available.
The additional settings allowed you only to specify stopping the task if it had run for a certain period of time.	Other settings are available to control how tasks behave when they start or fail. For example, you can configure a task to restart every few minutes if it fails. You can also control whether the task can be run manually regardless of the triggers and conditions that are in place.

3. In the left pane, click **Task Scheduler**. This displays the Task Scheduler Summary in the middle pane, which shows the status of currently running tasks and previously run tasks. As well, all tasks scheduled to run in the future are listed under active tasks, as shown in Figure 3-37.

4. In the left pane, expand **Task Scheduler**, expand **Task Scheduler Library**, expand **Microsoft**, expand **Windows**, and click **Defrag**. You can see in the left pane that many categories of tasks have been created for system maintenance. ScheduledDefrag is one task.

5. In the middle pane, click the **Triggers** tab. You can see that the ScheduledDefrag task runs each week starting Wednesday at 1:00 am.

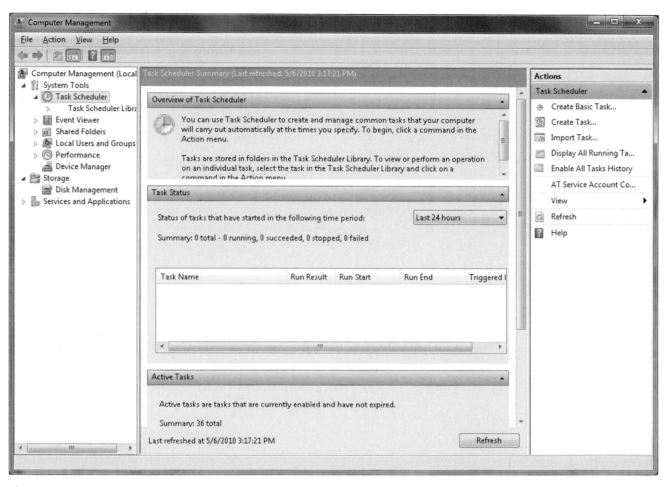

Figure 3-37 Task Scheduler
Courtesy Course Technology/Cengage Learning

6. Click the **Actions** tab. You can see that this task runs the program defrag.exe.

7. Click the **Conditions** tab. You can see that this task runs only if the computer is on AC power. If the computer switches to battery power, then the task will stop.

8. Click the **Settings** tab. You can see that if the computer is turned off when the task is configured to run, then the task will start as soon as possible once the computer is turned on.

9. Click the **History** tab. This shows you all of the event log entries for this task including when it was started, when it completed, and if there were any errors.

10. Close Computer Management.

Chapter Summary

- Control Panel is a central location for management utilities. Category view is the default configuration for Control Panel and divides applets into logical groupings to make finding a particular setting more intuitive. Experienced network administrators will likely change to a list view, which shows all Control Panel applets in a single window.

- Administrative Tools is a collection of system maintenance utilities. All of the Administrative Tools are MMC consoles. Two of the most commonly used Administrative Tools are Computer Management and Services.

- Windows 7 uses device drivers to properly communicate with various hardware components in a computer. To be sure your hardware component is compatible with Windows 7, you should check the Windows 7 Compatibility Center or ensure that it has the "Designed for Windows 7" logo. Most device drivers designed for Windows 2000 and newer versions of Windows are compatible with Windows 7.

- Device Manager is the MMC snap-in that is used to manage device drivers and hardware components. You can use Device Manager to update drivers, roll back to previous driver versions, or view the resources a hardware component is using.

- Windows 7 will allow 32-bit systems to install unsigned device drivers, but will warn you that the driver publisher cannot be determined. The 64-bit versions of Windows 7 require signed device drivers.

- Power Management has been enhanced in Windows 7 to make using the sleep feature easier. Power plans are used to define how power management is implemented for various devices.

- To use the Aero Glass interface, you must have a video card and video driver that support the WDDM and DirectX 9.0c. Aero Glass helps users work more efficiently and includes live taskbar thumbnails, Windows Flip, and Windows Flip 3D. Multiple monitors can also be used to increase employee efficiency.

- The display on a Windows 7 computer can be customized by controlling the display resolution, color depth, and refresh rate. The optimal configuration for display settings varies depending on the display device. Themes control the color of windows, backgrounds, sounds and the screen saver. Desktop backgrounds let you display a picture on your desktop. Screen savers are used to implement security.

- Task Scheduler has been enhanced with security improvements for credentials, improved logging, and expanded triggers for starting tasks. Multiple actions are allowed per task, and additional conditions can be required for a task to run.

Key Terms

Action Center   A place where you can review and resolve security and maintenance messages.

Administrative Tools   A group of MMC consoles that are used to manage Windows 7. Computer Management, Event Viewer, and Services are the most commonly used.

Advanced Configuration and Power Interface (ACPI)   The current standard for power management that is implemented in Windows 7 and by computer manufacturers.

Aero Glass   A visual effect that is part of the Aero look-and-feel of Windows 7. Many graphical elements have a semitransparent appearance to allow users to see other windows under the active one. This is done to allow the user a better feel for what other applications are doing in the background without being too distracting

applet   A tool or utility in Control Panel that is focused on configuring a particular part of Windows 7.

AutoPlay   Automatically performs a configurable action when new removable media is inserted into the computer.

Away Mode   An instant-on power saving mode that keeps the system in the S0 state.

Backup and Restore   Recovery tools for files and the overall operating system. Backup and System Restore can be found here.

Biometric Devices applet   A Control Panel applet that is used to configure biometric devices and the authentication data associated with them.

BitLocker Drive Encryption   Encrypts all of the data on a hard drive to keep data secure even if a hard drive is stolen.

color depth   The number of bits that are used to store the color information for each pixel in the display.

Computer Management   One of the most commonly used Administrative tools. This MMC console contains the snap-ins to manage most Windows 7 components.

Control Panel   A central location for Windows 7 Management utilities. Most system settings are configured here.

Data Sources (ODBC)   Used to configure data sources for applications that require access to a database.

device driver   Software that manages the communication between Windows 7 and a particular hardware component.

device driver signing   A system that ensures that a device driver is from a known publisher and that the device driver has not been modified since it was signed.

Device Manager   An MMC snap-in that is used to manage hardware components and their device drivers.

Display applet   A Control Panel applet that gives you links to adjust the screen resolution, calibrate color, change display settings, adjust ClearType text, and set a custom text size

driver store   A central location in Windows 7 where drivers are located before they are installed. A large set of drivers is included with Windows 7.

Ease of Access Center applet   A collection of settings to make Windows 7 easier to use for those that have visual or hearing impairment.

Event Viewer   An MMC console that is used to view messages generated and logged by Windows 7, applications, and services.

File Signature Verification utility   A utility that verifies the digital signature on operating system files and device drivers.

Folder Options applet   Configures the behavior of Windows Explorer, including whether file extensions are hidden for known file types, and whether hidden files are displayed.

hibernate   See S4 state.

HomeGroup   A new feature in Windows 7 that is used to configure file and printer sharing for small peer-to-peer computer networks.

hybrid sleep   The sleep method used by Windows 7 that combines the S3 state and S4 state. When the computer moves to the S3 state, it also saves the memory file required for the S4 state.

Industry Standard Architecture (ISA)   A legacy standard for connecting expansion cards to the motherboard in computers.

Internet Options   Settings to control Internet Explorer, including security settings.

iSCSI   A protocol for transferring files between a computer and external disk storage over an Ethernet network.

Microsoft Management Console (MMC)   A graphical interface shell that provides a structured environment to build management utilities.

MMC console   A collection of one or more snap-ins that are saved as an .msc file for later use.

MMC snap-in   A small software component that can be added to an MMC console to provide functionality. An MMC snap-in typically manages some part of Windows.

multiple monitors   Attaching two or more displays to a single computer. The information can be exactly the same on each display, or each display can be used independently by using extended mode.

Network and Sharing Center   A central location used to view network status and detailed network information.

parental controls   Used to restrict user access to Web sites and view activity reports on Web site access.

Performance Monitor   An MMC console used to monitor and troubleshoot the performance of your computer.

Peripheral Component Interface (PCI)   A current standard for connecting expansion cards to a computer motherboard. PCI devices are plug and play.

pixel   A single dot on the display.

plug and play   A standard for devices, BIOSes, and operating systems to interact and automatically assign resources to devices.

power plan   A set of configuration options for power management. The Balanced, Power save, and High performance power plans are created by default.

Region and Language Options applet   Used to configure display and input options to support different languages and regions. Settings include time, date, and number formats.

S0 state   An ACPI power saving mode that disables power to specific devices as requested by the operating system, but keeps the overall system running.

S3 state   An ACPI power saving mode that disables power to all devices except RAM.

S4 state   An ACPI power saving mode that saves the contents of RAM to disk and then disables power to all devices including RAM.

screen resolution   The number of pixels that are displayed on your display.

service   A Windows application that runs in the background without user interaction.

Services administrative tool   An MMC console used to manage Windows services.

Sound applet   Configures the properties for the audio devices in your system and configures a sound scheme

Speech Recognition Options applet   Configures how Windows 7 performs speech recognition, and allows you to train speech recognition for your voice.

standby   See S3 state.

System applet   Shows basic information about your computer, such as Windows edition, performance rating, and activation status. Links are provided to configure system properties.

System Configuration   The Administrative Tool that gives you access to control the boot configuration, service startup, application startup, and system tools.

Tablet PC Settings applet   Configures settings that are specific to tablet PCs such as screen menu locations and handwriting recognition.

Task Scheduler   A utility that allows you to schedule tasks to run at a particular time or based on specific events occurring.

Taskbar and Start Menu applet   Configures the behavior of the taskbar and Start menu, including which toolbars are displayed on the taskbar.

Windows 7 Compatability Center   A list of software or hardware and associated device drivers that have been tested with Windows 7.

Windows Firewall   Protects your computer by controlling the communication between your computer and the network.

Windows Flip   Displays a live thumbnail of each open Window as you use ALT-Tab to select a window.

Windows Flip 3D   Displays each open Window in a three-dimensional list and allows you to scroll through the windows using the mouse wheel.

Windows Memory Diagnostics Tool   A utility used to perform tests on the physical memory of a computer.

Windows Mobility Center   A single location that you can use to configure the mostly commonly used settings on mobile devices.

Windows PowerShell   An enhanced command-line interface that can be used to perform administrative tasks.

Windows Update   A service that automatically downloads and installs service packs and security updates.

Review Questions

1. Which Control Panel applet shows basic information about your computer and provides links to configure system properties?

   a. Action Center

   b. System

   c. Problem Reports and Solutions

   d. Performance

   e. Administrative Tools

2. Which of the following accurately describe the Administrative Tools available in Control Panel? (Choose all that apply.)

   a. Most are MMC consoles.

   b. You can schedule tasks.

   c. You can change the screen resolution.

   d. You can change power options.

   e. You can manage device drivers.

3. Which Control Panel applet is a centralized panel to view security and maintenance information for Windows 7?

   a. Action Center

   b. System

   c. Windows Firewall

   d. Parental Controls

4. Which Control Panel applet allows to install and remove optional components of Windows 7?

   a. Default Programs

   b. System

   c. Programs and Features

   d. Desktop Gadgets

5. A _____ is a type of Windows application that runs in the background without user intervention.

6. Which Control Panel applet lets you control the size of fonts? (Choose all that apply.)

   a. Taskbar and Start Menu

   b. Folder Options

   c. Fonts

   d. Ease of Access Center

   e. Display

7. While speech recognition can operate without any configuration, you can train it to more accurately recognize your voice. True or False?

8. The _____ administrative tool is used to configure data sources for applications that require access to a database.

9. Which of the following are found in Administrative Tools? (Choose all that apply.)

   a. Event Viewer

   b. Windows Memory Diagnostic

   c. Computer Management

    d.   Installed Programs

    e.   Task Scheduler

10.   You can build a customized MMC console by adding _____ to the console.

11.   Which MMC access mode allows users to create new windows, but prevents them from viewing some of the console tree?

    a.   Author mode

    b.   User mode—full access

    c.   User mode—limited access, multiple window

    d.   User mode—limited access, single window

12.   Which snap-ins are available in Computer Management? (Choose all that apply.)

    a.   Task Scheduler

    b.   Folder Options

    c.   Services

    d.   Security Configuration Management

    e.   Device Manager

13.   Which tasks can you accomplish using the Services administrative tool? (Choose all that apply.)

    a.   Stop a service

    b.   Configure a service to start automatically

    c.   Configure the credentials for a service

    d.   Schedule the time when a service will start

    e.   Configure the dependencies for a service

14.   A _____ is software used to manage communication between hardware components and Windows 7.

15.   To find a list of hardware components certified to run on Windows 7, you should consult the Hardware Compatibility List. True or False?

16.   Which task can you perform in Device Manager? (Choose all that apply.)

    a.   Determine which devices do not have a driver loaded

    b.   Disable devices

    c.   Install new hardware

    d.   View hardware resource configuration

    e.   Roll back device driver

17.   In Device Manager, a device with a red "x" is missing the correct driver. True or False?

18.   With a signed device driver, which of the following can Windows 7 do? (Choose all that apply.)

    a.   Determine if a driver has been modified

    b.   Determine if a driver has been adequately tested

    c.   Determine if the publisher is valid

    d.   Determine if the driver is 32-bit or 64-bit

    e.   Automatically download updates

19.   Which legacy devices are no longer supported in Windows 7?

    a.   ISA devices

    b.   PCI devices

c.   Plug and play devices

d.   USB devices

e.   Game controllers

20.   Hybrid sleep is a combination of which ACPI power states? (Choose two.)

a.   S0

b.   S3

c.   S4

d.   S5

e.   G3

21.   Away Mode puts the computer in which ACPI power state?

a.   S0

b.   S3

c.   S4

d.   S5

e.   G3

22.   Which requirements must be met to use the Aero Glass display theme? (Choose all that apply.)

a.   Minimum 256 MB of RAM on the video card

b.   Support for WDDM

c.   Support for DirectX 9.0c

d.   Do not use Windows 7 Starter Edition

e.   Computer is certified as "Designed for Windows 7"

23.   Which display setting can cause users to get headaches if it is not configured correctly?

a.   Screen resolution

b.   Color depth

c.   Refresh rate

d.   Desktop background

e.   Color scheme

24.   The primary purpose of a screen saver is to prevent screen burn in. True or False?

25.   Windows 7 supports attaching more than two monitors to a computer and extending the desktop across all of them. True or False?

Case Projects

Case Project 3-1: Mobile Users

All of the sales people in Hyperactive Media Sales use laptops, so that they can take their applications and data on the road to client sites. One of the sales people, Bob, has a docking station so that his laptop easily connects to a printer and external monitor when he is in the office. What should you do to ensure that Windows 7 uses the proper device drivers when Bob is in and out of the office?

Case Project 3-2: Saving Money by Using Power Management

Gigantic Life Insurance is always looking for ways to save money. This month the saving theme at the managers meeting was power consumption. The operations manager has proposed changing some of the incandescent lighting to fluorescent lighting. As the IT manager, what can you propose for Windows 7 computers?

Case Project 3-3: Fuzzy Displays

Superduper Lightspeed Computers sells LCD panel displays to their customers. One of those customers phoned complaining that his display looks fuzzy. He is very upset that his new display actually looks worse than his old display. What might you be able to do to fix the fuzzy display?

Case Project 3-4: Accessibility Options

Over the last few months the accountant for Buddy's machine shop has been having problems reading his computer display, but has been too embarrassed to tell anyone. Today, he finally lets you know about his problem and asks if there is anything you can do to help him. The accountant is using Windows 7 on his computer. What can you suggest?

Case Project 3-5: Managing Device Drivers

One Windows 7 computer in the Engineering department of Way North University has been having network connectivity problems. This computer is a different brand and model than all of the other computers because it was purchased directly by a professor as part of a research project. As a result, you are not sure whether the problem is hardware or software. You were able to test that the network cabling is functioning properly. What can you suggest for solving this problem?

chapter 4

Managing Disks

After reading this chapter and completing the exercises, you will be able to:

- Understand common disk technology and related partition styles
- Understand basic and dynamic disk storage technology
- Understand typical disk management tools and tasks
- Understand partition and volume management
- Understand VHD disk management

When a computer is turned off, applications and their data must be stored in a nonvolatile location. The operating system files must be available the next time the computer is started. Many types of devices are used to store nonvolatile information and organize the data into individual files. Examples of those devices include USB memory keys, recordable optical disks, Solid State Disk (SSD), battery-backed RAM, and electromechanical hard disk drives.

The details about how files are organized and managed are similar for most long-term file storage devices. This chapter will look at how disks are managed by Windows 7 using basic or dynamic disk architecture. It will look at how the disk space is divided into partitions and volumes that are formatted with file systems to store data to help you decide on and guide your storage solution needs.

Windows 7 supports many different disk interface technologies. The common interface types include SAS, SATA, IDE and SCSI. These interface technologies apply limits for how disk hardware connects to the computer, and depending on the disk technology used, there are limits on how you can use them with Windows 7.

Disk Technology

When long term storage for files is described as disk storage, it usually brings to mind the idea of a spinning disk inside an electromechanical hard drive. As technology has advanced, the term disk storage is better applied to any device capable of storing files for a long period of time. The device may indeed have a spinning disk, it may be made entirely from electronic circuitry without any moving parts, or it may be a virtual device presented to Windows 7 as if it were a physical disk drive.

Disk technology can be categorized by how it is connected to the computer and how it is presented to Windows 7. When you are reviewing disk technology available on a computer for use with Windows 7, consider these disk technologies:

- Internal Disk
- External Disk
- Virtual Hard Disk (VHD)
- Multiple Disks as One Logical Disk

Internal Disk

Computers that run Windows 7 are usually designed with desktop technology and not server-grade components. Typical internal disk interface types include IDE, SATA, and SCSI. Nonremovable fixed disks are attached to these internal interfaces and provide a suitable location to store operating system files required to start the computer.

The firmware built in to the computer is designed to recognize supported internal disk storage and boot from at least one of the installed internal disk devices.

External Disk

External interfaces are used to connect removable portable disk storage. Typical external disk interface types include USB, eSATA, SCSI, and FireWire (IEEE 1394). An external disk is useful for expanding a computer's bulk file storage to contain application and user data files, but it is not suitable for operating system files that are essential and must always be present.

It is best practice to avoid using external disks as a location for operating system files. Windows 7 should not be installed on removable disk media, and it will identify the disk as unsuitable during installation if it recognizes the media as removable.

Virtual Hard Disk (VHD)

The **Virtual Hard Disk (VHD)** image format specification is publicly available from Microsoft for use by any third-party company for free. Windows 7 is the first version of Windows to natively support Virtual Hard Disk operations. Files can be stored in a VHD storage location just like any other disk technology once the VHD is made available in the Windows 7 operating system. All file data stored in a VHD is actually stored in a single file on the file system of a real disk drive. A VHD may contain thousands of individual files from the user's perspective, but it still only appears as one physical file on the real disk drive.

Before the files in a VHD are available to Windows 7, the VHD file must be opened using a specific process. The required steps are covered later in this chapter.

All versions of Windows 7 support VHD operations, but only Windows 7 Ultimate and Windows 7 Enterprise support the ability to natively boot from a VHD. The ability to boot from a VHD is useful in managed desktop environments where business staff must maintain a large number of computers.

Multiple Disks as One Logical Disk

A logical disk appears to the Windows 7 operating system as if it is one disk drive. Single internal, external, and VHD disks can all be examples of logical drives. Multiple physical drives can be grouped together to appear as one logical drive. There are two reasons for doing so: (1) creating a logical drive that has more combined space than one physical drive alone can have and (2) adding fault tolerance that allows for a physical drive to fail without losing access to the logical drive.

Windows 7 can combine multiple disks as one logical disk using software built into the operating system. The combination of disks and how they store data is defined by RAID standards covered later in this chapter. RAID is an acronym for Redundant Array of Inexpensive Disks. This is a collection of disk management strategies to either combine data space from multiple disk drives to look like one bigger drive or provide fault-tolerance so individual disks can fail without losing data. Some advanced RAID strategies provide fault-tolerance and disk space aggregation at the same time. RAID technology implements complex operations to manage the data disks involved. Either the operating system or a dedicated hardware controller can run the code necessary to manage different types of RAID. Windows 7 can implement RAID operations through software but the performance may be limited by how busy the processor is while it is also running applications.

Instead of using operating system software to combine space from multiple drives, multiple disks can be connected to an advanced hardware based RAID disk controller. Not all computers have an advanced hardware-based RAID disk controller or have the option of adding one. They are more often found in high-end business-class desktop computers. The use of an advanced hardware-based disk controller in a computer is possible only if Windows 7 has a supported device driver installed that defines how the operating system can interact with that disk controller and the disks attached to it.

The physical drives are managed by the disk hardware controller directly and management operations are done with the management software that comes with the third-party hardware. The disk hardware controller can implement hardware-based RAID arrangements without Windows 7 knowing it is doing so. From the perspective of the operating system, Windows 7 would see the combined multiple disks as one logical drive.

The advantage of an advanced hardware-based disk controller implementing RAID is that it may be faster than having Windows 7 implement the same RAID-based logical drive through software. Hardware based disk controllers can also implement RAID modes that Windows 7 cannot implement in software, such as RAID 5. The disadvantages include increased hardware cost, compatibility issues with operating system device drivers, and having to learn a third-party management tool to configure and maintain the attached disks.

There may be problems with using an advanced hardware-based disk controller as a boot device. For the controller to be used as a boot device, the computer's firmware must be able to recognize the disk controller as a valid boot device. Windows 7 must also be able to recognize the logical drive presented by the controller as a valid location for installation. If the logical drive is visible to Windows 7, but cannot host the Windows 7 system or boot files, it may still be used for storing general application and data files.

Partition Styles

Windows 7 can organize data on disk drives using one of several partition styles. When a blank disk is first configured for use by Windows, one of these styles must be selected:

- Master Boot Record (MBR)
- GUID Partition Table (GPT)

Master Boot Record (MBR)

For most computers, the standard used for accessing hard disk data is based on old BIOS conventions that were introduced with the first personal computers. When a computer is first started, its BIOS firmware is responsible for initializing the computer. The computer must find and load the operating system after required boot hardware components are tested and initialized by the BIOS's Power On Self Test (POST) routine. The BIOS design introduced the concept of a Master Boot Record (MBR) enabled disk. The MBR disk partition style defines where the BIOS examines the disk drive to determine where data is stored on the disk and the types of data it contains.

MBR disk technology is still common today because the startup routines for most **x86** 32-bit and **x64** 64-bit computers are based on it. The computer's BIOS looks to the first hard disk it finds and loads a small program from the very first block of space on the disk. That small block of data, or sector, is called the **boot sector**. The boot sector is the first part of the **Master Boot Record (MBR)**. The boot sector code is typically written when the operating system is first loaded on the computer and the MBR is created.

The MBR includes the boot sector and a data table that identifies how sections, or partitions, of space on the disk are used to store files. The boot sector is essential as part of the process to load an operating system from one of those partitions.

MBR disk technology is limited to organizing partitions on a single logical drive up to 2 terabytes (TB) in size (discussed in Chapter 5). If the drive is larger than 2 TB, the space beyond 2 TB is visible in Windows 7 but is not able to be used for any purpose.

GUID Partition Table (GPT)

As hardware capacity has grown and technology has improved, the old BIOS standard has become a limitation that manufacturers struggle with. Intel created a new standard in the 1990s to replace the traditional BIOS with a new standard called **Extensible Firmware Interface (EFI)**. Intel still holds the copyright on it but has given the specification to a trade organization to develop and promote as the **Unified Extensible Firmware Interface (UEFI)**.

To support EFI/UEFI, the computer's firmware must be designed to that specification by the computer's manufacturer. Like the older BIOS standard, the EFI/UEFI firmware controls the startup process of the computer and eventually loads the operating system. Very few computers designed to run Windows 7 have firmware designed to the EFI/UEFI specifications.

Part of the EFI/UEFI specification defines the **GUID Partition Table (GPT)** as a replacement for MBR specifications. The partitions of a GPT disk are each identified with a unique coded label called a **GUID (Globally Unique Identifier)**. One of the primary advantages to using the GPT partition style instead of MBR is that it supports drives larger than 2 TB. However, the GPT partition style is restricted to certain computer configurations.

Only computers designed with EFI/UEFI firmware running the 64-bit Editions of Windows Vista or Windows 7 can boot from a disk drive that is using the GPT partition style. If a computer's firmware is using the older BIOS specification it can boot only from a MBR disk.

Even though a BIOS-based computer must use one MBR-based drive to boot, additional disk drives can be added. This means that an extra disk drive configured with GPT can be used only as a data disk and not a boot disk. To take advantage of the GPT support for disks larger than 2 TB, the computer must be running the ×64 64-bit Editions of Windows Vista or Windows 7.

A disk using the GPT partition style can be converted to MBR, but only if it is empty and does not contain any file data. Troubleshooting tools and utilities designed for MBR cannot be used with GPT disks as they will not recognize it.

Types of Disk Partitions

Once a partition style has been decided on and applied to a drive, the empty space on the drive can be organized using two different methods in Windows 7: basic disk storage and dynamic disk storage.

Basic Disk Storage

A hard disk initialized to use basic storage technology is referred to as a **basic disk**. Basic disk storage provides a simple means to logically organize disk space. When a new hard disk is added to a computer it is initially configured as a basic disk. Many operating systems support basic disk storage.

All versions of Windows and MS-DOS support MBR-style basic disk storage and understand how to interpret basic disk data. Because basic disks have been in use for so long, many people and most computer utilities understand how to work with basic disks.

A basic disk can have its space organized into one or more defined areas of storage called partitions. Each partition is identified by its size and the type of data it is supposed to hold. Most of these partition attributes are stored in a data table on the disk that is part of the MBR or GPT specifications. This table is commonly called the **partition table**.

The partition type is used by the operating system to determine what the purpose of a partition is. Different operating systems recognize different partition types. Windows 7 recognizes three partition types on a basic disk:

- Primary partitions
- Extended partitions
- Logical partitions

Primary Partitions Primary partitionsare the only type of basic disk partitions designed to store files that are used to load an operating system. A basic disk usually contains only one primary partition, but it could have more. A single MBR-style basic disk can contain a maximum of four primary partitions limited by the partition table design. Windows 7 will only allow the creation of three primary partitions with the graphical Disk Management tool in Computer Management. The fourth partition to be created on a basic MBR-style disk will automatically be configured as an extended partition that will in turn contain logical drives. The command-line tool diskpart will not automatically create the extended partition if three primary partitions already exist; this advanced disk administration tool can create a fourth primary partition if desired. Diskpart is covered later in this chapter. A GPT-style basic disk can contain a maximum of 128 primary partitions. Basic GPT disks are not commonly encountered as boot disks but they use primary partitions to store files.

If a single MBR-style basic disk contains up to four primary partitions, then in theory it could start at least four different operating systems, perhaps more. If there are multiple primary partitions on a single basic disk, the MBR standard allows for only one primary partition on that drive to be marked as active and capable of starting an operating system. This partition is referred to as an **active partition**. If a basic disk is not part of the boot process, then none of its primary partitions are required to be marked as active.

If a computer has multiple basic disks, then each disk can have one active primary partition. The computer picks only one of the active partitions to load the operating system. The exact drive selection logic depends on the computer's firmware and options used to control the search order for boot devices.

Each primary partition that is formatted with a file system is represented in the operating system by a **drive letter** (e.g. "C:") or a specific folder path called a **mount point**. Mount points are covered in Chapter 5, Managing File Systems.

Extended Partitions A single MBR-based basic disk can contain no more than one **extended partition**. The extended partition, if used, takes the place of one of the primary partitions that can be created on the basic disk. This means that if a basic disk has an extended partition, then a maximum of three primary partitions can exist on the same disk. GPT-based disks do not use or support extended partitions.

The extended partition does not have a drive letter or specific folder path assigned to it. The only purpose of an extended partition is to reserve space for and hold logical partitions.

An extended partition cannot be deleted without first deleting all logical partitions it contains.

Logical Partitions   A **logical partition** can only be created using the free space inside an extended partition. Windows 7 refers to logical partitions as logical drives in disk administration utilities. The terms logical drive and logical partition can be used interchangeably. If an extended partition does not have any free space, a new logical drive cannot be created inside the extended partition. The free space inside the extended partition is the only limit to how many logical partitions can be created inside it.

A logical partition can be formatted using a file system to store files. Only drive letters can be assigned to logical partition file systems. Note that even though the number of logical partitions within an extended partition is theoretically unlimited, there is a practical limit. If a computer runs out of available drive letters, any logical partitions created after that point cannot be properly formatted with a file system.

Dynamic Disk Storage

A hard disk initialized to use dynamic storage technology is referred to as a **dynamic disk**. Dynamic disk storage provides the flexibility to logically organize disk space across one or more disk drives. Both MBR and GPT partition styles can be configured as dynamic disk storage. Dynamic disks were first introduced with Windows 2000 as an alternative strategy to basic disk technology. Dynamic disk technology exceeds and avoids limits that are part of the older basic disk technology. Only Windows 2000, Windows XP, Windows Server 2003, Windows Server 2008, Windows Vista, and Windows 7 can understand dynamic disk storage. Earlier operating systems such as MS-DOS, Windows 95, Windows 98, Windows Millennium Edition (Me) and Windows NT cannot access dynamic disks. Not all versions of Windows 7 support dynamic disk technology. Only Windows 7 Ultimate, Windows 7 Enterprise, and Windows 7 Professional can work with dynamic disks.

Dynamic disks use a different method to organize how blocks of space are reserved on a hard disk. On dynamic disks, the blocks of space are called **volumes** instead of partitions. Details about the volumes are stored in a hidden database on the dynamic disk instead of a partition table. A disk requires at least 1 MB of space to store the hidden database. The dynamic disk's volume database stores information about all the volumes available to the computer, not just the ones stored on that disk. All other dynamic disks in the computer are known to each other and identified as members of a group that belongs to that computer. Each volume that is formatted with a file system is represented in the operating system by a drive letter (e.g. "C:") or a specific folder path called a mount point. Mount points are covered in Chapter 5, Managing File Systems.

Dynamic disk technology is not appropriate for **removable disk storage** because the membership is tracked for all dynamic disks in the computer. If a disk was removed, the remaining disks could be impacted.

A dynamic volume must be aware of the other dynamic volumes on the computer because some types of dynamic volumes interact with each other. This can increase file system capacity or provide fault tolerance through the operating system. Basic disks do not provide this functionality. Dynamic disks support five volume types:

- Simple
- Spanned
- Striped
- Mirrored
- RAID 5

4

Simple A **simple volume** exists on just a single dynamic disk. With basic disks, a single contiguous block of disk space is assigned a partition type and is treated as a unique partition. With dynamic disks, a simple dynamic volume can consist of one or more blocks of space from the same disk. The blocks of space do not have to be contiguous on the disk.

A simple volume is not fault tolerant, and a failure of the dynamic disk will result in data loss. All versions of Windows 7 that support dynamic disks support simple volume types.

Spanned A **spanned volume** exists on two or more dynamic disks. Blocks of space from multiple dynamic disks are linked together to form one spanned volume. The blocks of space can be any size. The operating system presents the sum total of all linked blocks of space as one volume. When a file is saved to a spanned volume it can reside on any linked block of space. As one block fills up, the operating system adds new files to the next available block of space.

A spanned volume is not fault tolerant, and a failure of any linked block of space from a dynamic disk will result in the loss of the entire spanned volume.

All versions of Windows 7 that support dynamic disks also support spanned volume types.

Striped A **striped volume** exists on a minimum of two dynamic disks, up to a maximum of 32 dynamic disks. Blocks of space from multiple dynamic disks are linked together to form one striped volume. The operating system presents the sum total of all linked blocks of space as one volume. This sounds similar to a spanned volume, but it differs in how a file is written to the disks. A striped volume is a **RAID 0** solution.

When a file is saved to a striped volume it is broken down into smaller blocks of data, usually 64 K in size, that are stored to each of the striped volume's member disks in turn. The first block of data is stored to the first physical disk that is a member of the striped volume. The next block of file data is stored on the next physical disk in the striped volume. The process continues with each physical disk; when the last disk is written to, the process repeats—starting with the first member of the striped volume. This can result in a performance increase when reading and writing data because the task is spread across multiple disks.

The space used from each disk in a striped volume cannot exceed the smallest block of space used from a single disk. For example, if four 20 GB disks and one 10 GB disk are used to create a single striped volume, the largest block of space that can be used from each disk is 10 GB. The size of the striped volume is the sum total of all blocks of space used from each drive. In the example above, this would be five 10 GB blocks of space, or 50 GB. To get the most efficient use of disk space, the striped volume's disk members are usually the same size.

A striped volume is not fault tolerant, and a failure of any linked dynamic disk will result in the loss of the entire striped volume.

All versions of Windows 7 that support dynamic disks also support striped volume types.

Mirrored A mirrored dynamic volume can only be created with two dynamic disks. A block of space on one dynamic disk must be matched to an identically sized block of space on a second dynamic disk. The operating system presents the space of just one block as the total space available in the **mirrored volume.**

A mirrored volume is a fault-tolerant design. It is also known as a **Redundant Array of Independent Disks (RAID)** 1 solution, indicated as just **RAID 1.** When a file is saved to a mirrored volume it is written to both dynamic disks. Depending on the computer hardware this can take just as long as writing the file to one disk, or even longer because it has to be written to two disks. There is usually an increase in performance when reading a file because one of the disks may be available while the other disk is busy.

A mirrored volume is fault tolerant, and a failure of any single linked dynamic disk will not result in data loss. The remaining dynamic disk will continue to function and provide access to the data. Repairing the mirrored disk is covered later in this chapter in the Partition and Volume Management section. Note that a failure in a common hardware component such as a disk controller or cable can disable both dynamic disks, which would result in the loss of the entire mirrored volume.

It is possible that each hard disk could be placed on its own interface controller and data cables so that the two disks are relatively independent. This increases the cost but also the reliability of the mirrored disks. This fully redundant form of mirrored disks is commonly referred to as a **duplexed mirror**.

All versions of Windows 7 that support dynamic disks also support mirrored volumes.

RAID 5   A **RAID 5** dynamic volume can only be created with three or more dynamic disks. Similar to a striped dynamic volume, the RAID 5 volume will stripe data and error-correcting information about the data across each of the dynamic disk members.

A RAID 5 volume is a fault-tolerant design. When a file is saved to a RAID 5 volume the operating system must break down the data into fixed-size blocks. For each block of data, it also calculates error-correcting information about the data. The error-correcting data can be used to detect and repair faults in the data.

The data blocks and the error-correcting data are written across the physical disks in such a way that the failure of any one disk allows the operating system to calculate the missing data. This is possible because the error-correcting data is spread across all disks and does not reside on a single disk. If more than one disk fails, the volume's missing data can no longer be calculated and the volume is considered failed.

Calculating the error-correcting data can place a considerable drain on the computer's performance, therefore writing a file can take just as long (or longer) than writing the file to a single disk. There is usually an increase in performance when reading a file because the data is being read from multiple devices at the same time. In the event a single disk fails, the missing data must be calculated from the remaining data on all of the surviving members. This can make the RAID 5 volume's performance very slow when a single disk fails.

Dynamic volume RAID 5 is calculated by the operating system, so it is known as software RAID 5. A hardware-based controller can be purchased to offload the calculations required for RAID 5 storage. Hardware-based RAID 5 solutions use the same error-correcting technique as software RAID 5, but this does not make the resulting storage a dynamic disk. The resulting space appears to the operating system as a single logical disk that can be formatted as a basic or dynamic disk. The operating system does not know that RAID 5 is being used at all. Any maintenance steps or fault-tolerance features will be determined by the vendor of the hardware-based solution. This chapter will focus on software-based RAID 5.

A RAID 5 volume's space is calculated by examining the size of the free space on each disk and the number of disks involved. Data is striped across all of the RAID 5 volume's member disks. Each block of space must be the same size on each physical disk. For example, if a 20 GB disk and two 100 GB disks are combined into a RAID 5 volume, the space used from each disk cannot exceed the size of the smallest free block of space from any one disk—in this case 20 GB. Consequently, 20 GB of space from each of the disks can be combined to create a new RAID 5 volume. The rest of the disk space cannot be added to this RAID 5 volume. To get the most efficient use of disk space, the RAID 5 volume's member disks are usually the same size.

Some of the disk space is used to store error-correcting data, so the sum total of all space is not the volume's size. You must subtract the space used on one drive from the total used on all drives to calculate the space available to store files. In the example above, you would subtract 20 GB from the total space used on all drives (60 GB) to calculate the available RAID 5 volume space for files as 40 GB.

As the number of disk members used to build a RAID 5 volume increases, the space lost to error-correcting data does not exceed the space used on one drive. For example, if four 20 GB drives were combined into a RAID 5 volume, 60 GB would be available to the operating system (25% of the disk space is used for error-correction data). If ten 20 GB drives were combined into a RAID 5 volume, 180 GB would be available to the operating system (10% of the disk space is used for error-correcting data). This makes larger implementations of RAID 5 cost effective when compared to mirrored disks, which require that every drive is fully duplicated (50% of the disk space is always used for error-correcting data).

A RAID 5 volume cannot be spanned or expanded after it is created.

RAID 5 dynamic volumes are considered a server-class technology and cannot be created on a Windows 7 based computer. Currently only Windows 2000 Server, Windows Server 2003, and Windows Server 2008 fully support implementing RAID 5 dynamic volumes in software.

Disk Management Tools

After the operating system is installed, the computer's disks are usually managed from within Windows 7 with two tools: Disk Management and DiskPart.

Disk Management

The **Disk Management console** is an MMC console snap-in that is usually found as part of the Computer Management utility. Disk Management provides a graphical interface that allows a member of the Administrators group to observe and make changes to the computer's disk configuration.

The Disk Management console allows changes to be made interactively and usually takes effect immediately without requiring the computer to be restarted.

As shown in Figure 4-1, the Disk Management console is divided into two views, a top view and a bottom view. The top view defaults to a summary of the volumes and partitions on the computer. The bottom view defaults to a graphical view of the disks and the volumes/partitions they contain.

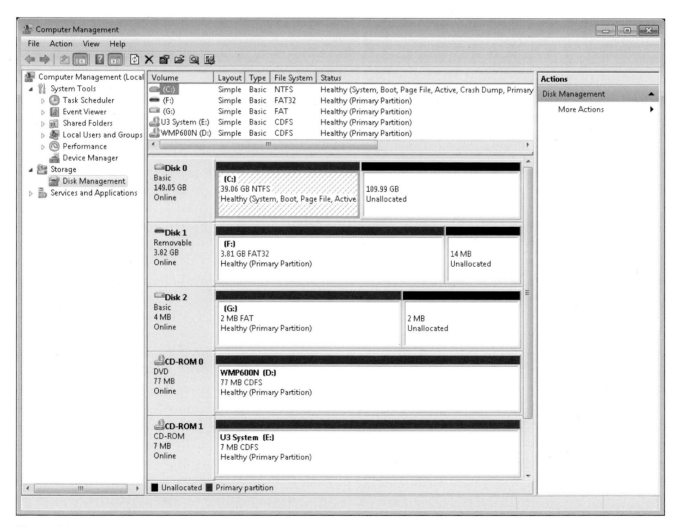

Figure 4-1 Disk management console
Courtesy Course Technology/Cengage Learning

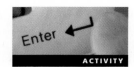

Activity 4-1: Customizing Disk Management

Time Required: 15 minutes

Objective: Open the Disk Management console and modify the default view.

Description: In this activity, you will change display settings for the Disk Management console and note key information provided by the utility.

1. If necessary, start your computer and log on.
2. Click the **Start** button to open the Start menu.
3. Right-click the **Computer** Start menu item.
4. Click **Manage** from the pop-up menu.
5. If you are prompted by User Account Control for authorization to run this program, click the **Yes** button.
6. In the left-hand console navigation pane, click the **Disk Management** item below Storage to highlight it.
7. In the bottom view, note the Disk number of the first disk. ___
8. In the bottom view, note the default disk type of the first hard disk (Basic or Dynamic). ___
9. At the bottom of the bottom view, read the color legend for the partition types. Note the color used for primary partitions. ___
10. Open the **View** menu.
11. Click **Settings** on the menu.
12. Make sure the **Appearance** tab is selected in the Settings window that opens.
13. Select **Primary partition** in the list under Disk region.
14. In the Color drop-down list, select **Red**.
15. Click the **OK** button to save your selection. Note that the graphical display in Disk Administrator has updated to reflect the selection. When you close the Computer Management window at the end of the exercise the original display color will be restored.
16. Open the **View** menu and point to the **Top** menu item to open the side menu.
17. Click **Disk List** and note that the top view has changed to provide a brief list of the computer's disks and their properties.
18. In the top view, what is the **Partition Style** for Disk 0? ___
19. Open the **View** menu and point to the **Top** menu item to open the side menu.
20. Click **Volume List** and note that the top view has returned to its default view.
21. Open the **View** menu and point to **Bottom** to open the side menu.
22. Click **Hidden** and note that the bottom view is no longer visible.
23. Open the **View** menu and point to **Bottom** to open the side menu.
24. Click **Graphical View** and note that the default bottom view has returned.
25. Open the **View** menu.
26. Click **Settings** from the menu.
27. Click the **Scaling** tab in the Settings window that opens.
28. Click **All as the same size** under Display disk regions.
29. Click **OK** to save your selection.
30. Close the **Computer Management** window.

DiskPart

DiskPart, shown in Figure 4-2, is a command-line tool that allows disk and volume operations to be performed from a text-based screen interactively or from within a scripted file.

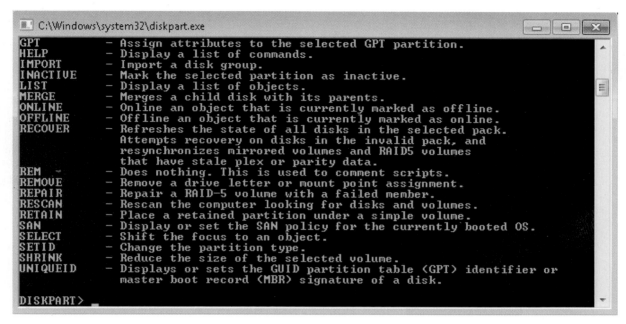

```
C:\Windows\system32\diskpart.exe
GPT        - Assign attributes to the selected GPT partition.
HELP       - Display a list of commands.
IMPORT     - Import a disk group.
INACTIVE   - Mark the selected partition as inactive.
LIST       - Display a list of objects.
MERGE      - Merges a child disk with its parents.
ONLINE     - Online an object that is currently marked as offline.
OFFLINE    - Offline an object that is currently marked as online.
RECOVER    - Refreshes the state of all disks in the selected pack.
             Attempts recovery on disks in the invalid pack, and
             resynchronizes mirrored volumes and RAID5 volumes
             that have stale plex or parity data.
REM        - Does nothing. This is used to comment scripts.
REMOVE     - Remove a drive letter or mount point assignment.
REPAIR     - Repair a RAID-5 volume with a failed member.
RESCAN     - Rescan the computer looking for disks and volumes.
RETAIN     - Place a retained partition under a simple volume.
SAN        - Display or set the SAN policy for the currently booted OS.
SELECT     - Shift the focus to an object.
SETID      - Change the partition type.
SHRINK     - Reduce the size of the selected volume.
UNIQUEID   - Displays or sets the GUID partition table (GPT) identifier or
             master boot record (MBR) signature of a disk.

DISKPART>
```

Figure 4-2 DiskPart command-line tool
Courtesy Course Technology/Cengage Learning

Operations in the DiskPart utility are driven by a sequence of commands. Each command must have a specific object to focus its action on. For example, before a partition can be created, the DiskPart utility must be told which disk the partition will be created on. Items such as disks and partitions are usually numbered, with the first disk or partition object starting at 0.

 To see a list of DiskPart commands, type **help** at the diskpart command prompt. To see more detail about a specific diskpart command, type **help** *command_name*, where *command_name* is the command of interest.

The DiskPart utility is powerful; it can contain a series of maintenance or repair commands that can be executed as part of a scheduled task or automated response on the local computer or remotely on another computer. It is considered an advanced tool that is not normally used for day-to-day administration.

Activity 4-2: Using DiskPart

Time Required: 15 minutes
Objective: Start the DiskPart utility, browse its help menu, and use DiskPart to explore fundamental disk properties.

Description: In this activity, you will start the DiskPart utility, browse its help utility, and try out basic DiskPart commands.

1. If necessary, start your computer and log on.
2. Click the **Start** button to open the Start menu.
3. Click the **Computer** Start menu item.
4. Navigate to the **C:\WINDOWS\SYSTEM32** folder.

5. Scroll to and double-click the **diskpart.exe** file.

6. If you are prompted by User Account Control for permission to run this program, click the **Yes** button.

7. Type **help** and press **Enter** to see a list of DiskPart commands.

8. Type **help select** and press **Enter** to see information about the select command.

9. Type **help select disk** and press **Enter** to see information and examples for the select disk command.

10. To see what disks can be selected, type **list disk** and press **Enter**.

11. The DiskPart utility has not been focused on a particular disk yet, so some commands will not be able to run. Type **list partition**, press **Enter**, and note the error message.

12. To focus attention on the first disk, type **select disk = 0** and press **Enter**.

13. Type **list partition**, press **Enter**, and note that the error message is gone now that a disk has been specifically identified and selected.

14. To see what volumes are visible to the DiskPart utility, type **list volume** and press **Enter**.

15. To leave the DiskPart utility, type **exit** and press **Enter**.

16. Close **Windows Explorer**.

Note that the CD-ROM is included in the volume listing, which does not rely on the selected disk.

Disk Management Tasks

When disks are installed in a computer, several administrative tasks must be carried out to make them useable and keep them functional. The major activities for proper disk administration include:

- Preparing hard disks
- Disk cleanup
- Checking disk health
- Defragmenting disks
- Moving disks
- Converting disk types
- Managing fault tolerance

Preparing Hard Disks

A hard disk can be connected to the computer using many different connection technologies; SATA and USB are two common examples. The hard disk may be responsible for loading the operating system or it may just provide a location for bulk data storage. For those drives that provide bulk storage and that are physically portable, it is common that they use plug and play technology to connect. These hard disk devices must be prepared to work with the computer before data can be stored on them by ensuring that three tasks are performed:

- Scan for new hardware changes
- Scan for disks
- Initialize new disks

Scan for New Hardware Changes A hard disk is a singular device, but the hardware used to connect it to the computer may consist of many individual components. For example, a USB-connected hard disk has a USB controller between itself and the computer that must be working correctly before the hard disk is visible to the operating system. A hardware-based RAID solution typically has a dedicated controller between the disks and the computer that hides the physical disk arrangement from the operating system.

If these intermediate devices are not functional, or if the drivers and their settings are not operational, the disks are not useable. It is also possible that the hardware is based on plug and play technology and the computer has not detected the new device when it was added.

When adding new hard disks, the Device Manager utility is used first to detect device driver issues and trigger a manual scan for hardware changes if the plug and play system did not detect the change.

Scan for Disks Once all connection technologies for hard disks are properly detected and their corresponding device drivers are fully functional, the hard disks should be visible. The operating system may not see the new disks immediately. Windows 7 can be forced to manually recheck all of the connected hardware for a change in disk availability by using the Disk Management console.

Initializing New Disks When a new hard disk is installed on the computer, it cannot be used until it is initialized with a fundamental structure to identify the disk and prepare it to hold data. This process is called disk initialization and is supposed to be performed by Windows 7 when it sees a blank new hard disk for the first time.

If the initialization process cannot complete automatically, the Disk Management console can be used to trigger the process manually. An administrator can right-click the unknown disk in the Disk Management console and select **Initalize Disk** from the pop-up menu to trigger the process. Once a disk is initialized, any data it may have held is lost.

Until a new disk is initialized, its status is reported as **Unknown** and the disk cannot be used to store data. Once the disk is initialized, it becomes a basic disk without any partitions defined on it.

Activity 4-3: Scanning for New Disks

Time Required: 10 minutes
Objective: Scan the computer for new disks.

Description: In this activity, you will perform the typical steps required to check for new hard disks on a computer.

1. If necessary, start your computer and log on.
2. Click the **Start** button to open the Start menu.
3. Right-click the **Computer** Start menu item.
4. Click **Manage** from the pop-up menu.
5. If you are prompted by User Account Control for authorization to run this program, click the **Yes** button.
6. In the left-hand console navigation pane, click the **Device Manager** item below System Tools to select it.
7. In the details pane, right-click the computer name at the top of the device list and click **Scan for hardware changes** from the pop-up menu.
8. In the left-hand console navigation pane, click the **Disk Management** item below Storage to select it.

9. Right-click **Disk Management** and click **Rescan Disks**. This will force Windows 7 to scan for disks attached to any new hardware found in step 7.

10. In the lower view of the Disk Management console, make sure no disks are reported as **Unknown**.

11. Close the **Computer Management** window.

Disk Cleanup

The partitions and volumes that are formatted with a file system and identified with a drive letter are treated as individual disks by the operating system. Some utilities, such as Disk Cleanup, also treat partitions and volumes as distinct disks.

Disk Cleanup is available by selecting the Disk Cleanup button when viewing the general properties of a drive (see Figure 4-3).

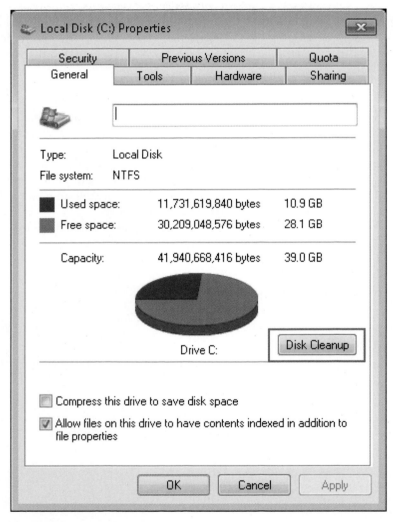

Figure 4-3 Disk Cleanup button on a disk's General properties tab
Courtesy Course Technology/Cengage Learning

The Disk Cleanup utility (see Figure 4-4) helps the user identify common sources of data that can be purged from the disk to recover disk space. Items selected in this screen will be purged when the user clicks OK. Clicking the **Clean up system files** button activates a second tab with more disk cleanup options.

Figure 4-4 Disk Cleanup options
Courtesy Course Technology/Cengage Learning

The Disk Cleanup **More Options** tab (see Figure 4-5) allows the user to trigger additional methods to recover disk space, such as uninstalling files and removing data used to restore prior application and operating system functional states. These options are considered extreme measures and are not typically used to recover disk space unless absolutely necessary. This tab is only available when you are performing cleanup with Administrator privileges.

Checking Disk Health

A hard disk can have physical areas that become damaged and therefore corrupt data stored in those locations. A disk area that is damaged this way is typically reported as bad sectors on the disk. Even if the disk is physically okay, misbehaving device drivers, applications, or intermittent faults in the hardware itself can logically corrupt a file that is written to the disk.

If a user suspects a problem with the way data has been stored to the disk, several utilities are available to check for problems. From the perspective of the utilities, a disk is a partition or volume that is accessible via a drive letter or mount point.

Disk health can be checked by selecting the **Check Now** button on the Tools tab of the properties of a volume (see Figure 4-6).

The **chkdsk** command-line utility is also available for use at the command prompt or from within a script. Partition and volume error checking requires Administrator permission.

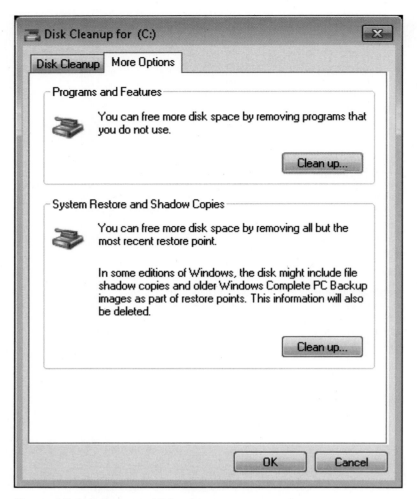

Figure 4-5 Disk Cleanup additional space recovery options
Courtesy Course Technology/Cengage Learning

Activity 4-4: Checking Drive C: for Errors

Time Required: 20 minutes
Objective: Scan drive C for disk errors.

Description: In this activity, you will check the integrity of drive C and the files it contains. Because the files on drive C are in use, not all of the files are accessible. This exercise will require a restart of the computer to complete a full integrity check of drive C.

1. If necessary, start your computer and log on.
2. Click the **Start** button to open the Start menu.
3. Click the **Computer** Start menu item.
4. Right-click the **Local Disk (C:)** graphical icon and click **Properties** from the pop-up menu.
5. Click the **Tools** tab to select it.
6. Click the **Check Now** button.
7. If you are prompted by User Account Control for authorization to run this program, click the **Yes** button.
8. Note that the Check Disk Local Disk C: window opens. Deselect all options in the **Check disk options** area.

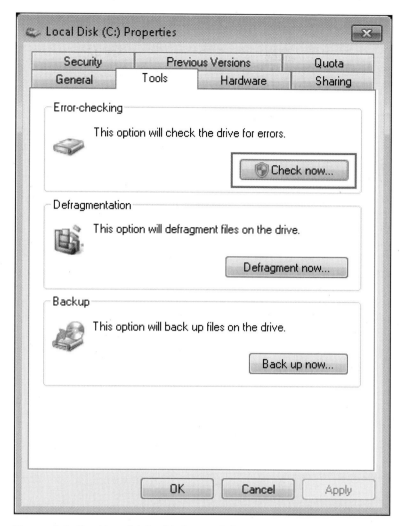

Figure 4-6 Checking disk health from a disk's properties, Tools tab
Courtesy Course Technology/Cengage Learning

9. Click the **Start** button to begin the scan of drive C. This scan will find disk errors but not fix them.

10. When you are prompted that the disk check is complete, click the **Close** button to close the message window.

11. Click the **Check Now** button from the Tools tab of the drive C: properties window again.

12. If you are prompted by User Account Control for authorization to run this program, click the **Yes** button.

13. Note that the Check Disk Local Disk C: window opens. Select the check boxes next to **Automatically fix file system errors** and **Scan for and attempt recovery of bad sectors**.

14. Click the **Start** button to begin the scan of drive C.

15. Note that you are prompted that the operation could not be completed because some files are in use by the operating system. The optional steps selected for this scan require complete access to all files on the drive. If an application or the operating system has a file opened and locked for exclusive use, you are asked if you want to schedule the scan to run at startup the next time the computer is started. Click **Schedule disk check** to schedule the scan for the next startup of the computer.

16. Click **OK** to close the **Local Disk (C:) Properties** window.

17. Restart the computer and note that a disk health check automatically runs on drive C before the logon screen is presented.

Defragmenting Disks

Files are stored in partitions and volumes on the physical disk. From the perspective of the **defragmentation** utility, a disk is a partition or volume that is accessible via a drive letter or mount point. The type of file system determines how that data is organized in sectors and **clusters** within the partition or volume. Regardless of the file system used, the sectors and clusters that are used by a file can become distributed throughout the physical disk's read/write surfaces.

This can have a significant impact on the performance of the computer when the physical disk is a spinning electromechanical drive. In an electromechanical drive, moving parts must reposition themselves to read and write data. The time it takes the physical components to position and activate can be minimized if the blocks of data read or written to the drive are sequentially organized on the device.

Consider a file that is spread throughout a volume in such a way that little of the data is sequentially stored on the physical disk. As the file is accessed, the computer has to wait as the mechanical mechanism used to update the file moves from one part of the disk to another. Mechanical components are relatively slow to move and must wait for the disk to spin around to the required section being accessed. Compared to RAM, these physical devices can be several thousand times slower. If the file being accessed is widely distributed over the surface of the physical disk, the cumulative access delays become significant.

A file that is stored in sequential sectors occupies the same general area of the physical disk. Ideally, the mechanical components used to access the data will barely have to move, and the delay to wait for the disk to spin to the right part of the disk's surface is minimized. Rewriting a file that is spread all over the volume to make it sequentially accessible is a process called defragmenting the file.

Defragmentation is a "best effort" utility that tries to improve the layout of files within a disk but not perfect it. It is common to find that some files cannot be moved by the defragmentation utility or there is not enough room to rearrange a file's contents. If a disk is reported as heavily fragmented, the expectation is that the computer's performance will improve after the disk is defragmented. In some cases that improvement can lead to a significant performance gain.

In older Windows operating systems, such as Windows XP, users typically did not know they should defragment their disks or they would forget to do so. To improve on this, the defragmentation utility in Windows Vista and Windows 7 is designed to run automatically on a periodic basis for all volumes.

The automatic defragmentation control utility, shown in Figure 4-7, is available by clicking the Defragment Now button on the Tools tab when viewing the properties of a drive.

The defragmentation utility does not add a significant drain on the computer's performance while it rewrites files on the disk, however it does have some impact. The best times to schedule the utility to run is when other operations such as virus scans and backups are not running.

To see a report of fragmented files and changes made by defragmenting a disk, use the command-line utility defrag.exe or the graphical defragmentation utility shown in Figure 4-7. Windows 7 has added reporting to the graphical defragmentation utility that Windows Vista did not show. The status of drives that can be defragmented is shown with details including percent fragmentation and the last time the drive was defragmented. Any drive with more than 10% fragmentation should be considered for defragmentation.

Windows 7 regularly defragments eligible drives automatically on a scheduled basis, as part of a "set it and forget it" management concept. Using the graphical defragmentation administration utility an administrator can disable the defragmentation schedule, change when and how often it runs, or manually trigger a defragmentation of selected disks before the next scheduled defragmentation. The graphical utility also allows the administrator to analyze the current fragmentation level of each drive on demand to make sure the fragmentation data is up to date.

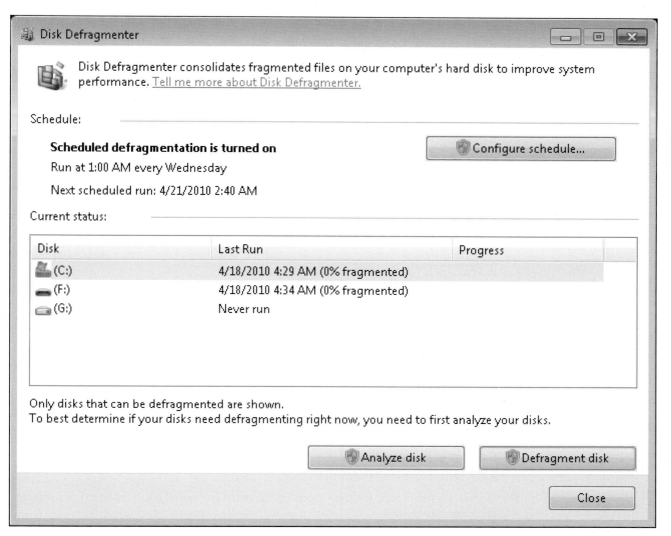

Figure 4-7 Disk defragmentation control utility
Courtesy Course Technology/Cengage Learning

Improvement made to Windows 7 defragmentation includes the ability to defragment multiple drives in parallel, instead of one drive at a time. This allows the defragmentation to complete in a shorter window of time which makes picking a maintenance interval easier. To maximize the life of computer hardware, defragmentation is automatically disabled for a drive if Windows 7 detects that a logical drive is hosted on a SSD disk device. This avoids accelerating the failure of the SSD device, which has a finite number of times that data can be written to it before the device fails.

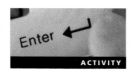

Activity 4-5: Defragmenting Disks

Time Required: 10 minutes
Objective: Change the automatic defragmentation schedule and review a report of drive C fragmentation.

Description: In this activity, you will perform the typical steps required to change the scheduled interval for automatic defragmentation and generate a report of fragmentation statistics for drive C.

1. If necessary, start your computer and log on.
2. Click the **Start** button to open the Start menu.

3. Click the **Computer** Start menu item.

4. Right-click the **Local Disk (C:)** graphical icon and click **Properties** from the pop-up menu.

5. Click the **Tools** tab to select it.

6. Click **Defragment now** to open the Disk Defragmenter window.

7. Click the **Configure schedule** button to open the Disk Defragmenter: Modify Schedule window.

8. Click the drop-down list next to **Frequency:** and if necessary click **Weekly** in the list of choices.

9. Click the drop-down list next to **Day:** and click **Saturday** in the list of choices.

10. Click the drop-down list next to **Time:** and click **6:00 AM** in the list of choices.

11. Click the **OK** button to close the Disk Defragmenter: Modify Schedule window. Note that if you do not make any changes to the schedule choices the OK button will be grayed out.

12. In the Disk Defragmenter window click C: in the **Current status:** portion of the window to highlight and select the drive.

13. Click the **Analyze disk** button and note that activity is reported in the Progress column as Windows checks the selected drive's fragmentation status. When the defragmentation analysis is complete, note that the Last Run date and time has updated.

14. Click the **Close** button to close the Disk Defragmenter window.

15. Click **OK** to close the Local Disk (C:) Properties window and then close Windows Explorer.

16. Click the **Start** button, point to **All Programs**, click **Accessories**, and right-click **Command Prompt**.

17. Click **Run as administrator** in the pop-up menu.

18. If you are prompted by User Account Control for permission to run this program, click the **Yes** button.

19. In the resulting command window, type **defrag.exe /?**, press **Enter**, and note the generated help text.

20. In the same command window, type **defrag.exe C: /A**, press **Enter**, and note the fragmentation report.

21. Close the **Administrator: Command Prompt** window.

Moving Disks

Physical disks can be moved from one computer to another, but the partitions and volumes they contain require special consideration. When a basic disk is moved from one computer to another, the drive letters assigned to its logical and primary partitions will be assigned the next available drive letters on the destination computer. When a dynamic disk is moved the volume's drive letters are retained if they are not already in use on the destination computer.

All dynamic disks have a database that identifies all volume components on all dynamic disks in that computer. The database also stores the name of the computer that the dynamic disk belongs to. When a dynamic disk is moved to a different computer, this computer identification in the database must be changed.

To change this name in the moved disk's database, the dynamic disk must be removed as a member of the source computer and imported into the destination computer's current dynamic disk database with either the Disk Management console or the DiskPart command-line utility. This will update the database on the moved disk and on every other dynamic disk that might already exist in both computers.

The Disk Management console will report the status of the disk as a **Foreign Disk** when it recognizes that the disk does not belong to that computer. You must right-click the disk in the graphical portion of Disk Management and select **Import Foreign Disk** from the pop-up menu to initiate the import process.

If a dynamic disk contains a volume that is spread across multiple dynamic disks, such as a striped or spanned volume, then all member disks must be moved at the same time. Failure to do so will leave the volume broken even if the dynamic disk's computer membership is correctly updated.

Because there is some risk in moving a dynamic disk between computers, it is always best practice to ensure that a backup copy of the volume data exists before the move is performed. Before a disk is moved its status should report as healthy in the Disk Management console.

Importing dynamic disks requires Backup Operator or Administrator-equivalent permission.

Converting Disk Types

A physical disk can have its space organized into partitions or volumes using basic or dynamic technology, respectively. Basic disk technology is common to all versions of Windows. Enhanced volume types that span multiple disks are available with dynamic disks. Those versions of Windows 7 that support dynamic disks can convert between basic and dynamic disk formats.

Conversion between basic and dynamic disk formats can be performed with the Disk Management console or the DiskPart command-line utility. Converting disk types requires Backup Operator or Administrator-equivalent permission.

When a basic disk is converted to a dynamic disk, all primary and logical partitions it contains are converted to simple volumes. The disk will obtain a copy of the dynamic disk database that records all other dynamic disks and their volumes on that computer. If the basic disk being converted contains the system or boot partitions, the computer will require multiple restarts to complete the conversion.

To convert a basic disk to a dynamic disk there must be at least 1 MB of unpartitioned disk space. This space is used to hold the dynamic disk database that tracks volume locations.

When a dynamic disk is converted to a basic disk, all volumes contained on that disk are destroyed. If the data they contain must be preserved, it must be backed up or moved somewhere temporarily before the conversion takes place. If the volumes on the disk being converted are part of a spanned or striped volume, those volumes will be destroyed when the disk is converted. The data will be inaccessible on the other disks that contain the remaining parts of those volumes, even if those dynamic disks remain dynamic disks.

Managing Fault Tolerance

Basic disks are not fault tolerant by design. If the data is not backed up, the loss of a basic disk will result in permanent data loss.

Windows 2000 Server, Windows Server 2003, and Windows Server 2008 are server operating systems that support fault-tolerant dynamic volumes. Dynamic disks support two types of fault-tolerant volumes: mirrored and RAID-5. Mirrored volumes consist of identical data mirrored across two dynamic disks. RAID-5 volumes consist of striped data and parity information across three to 32 dynamic disks. Versions of Windows 7 that support dynamic disks only support mirrored volumes.

If a single disk fails in a mirrored set, the mirror can be broken using the Disk Management console or the DiskPart command-line utility. Breaking a mirror means that the remaining disk is told that it no longer has a partner to replicate with. The volume that was being mirrored reverts to just a simple volume. Once a replacement disk is added back into the computer as a dynamic disk, the simple volume can be converted back into a mirrored volume.

If both disks fail in a mirrored set, such as when a common component like a data cable fails, then the mirrored volume is unavailable. If neither disk can be revived, the mirror set has to be rebuilt from scratch and the volume's data is then restored from a backup copy.

If a single disk fails in a RAID-5 array of disks, the RAID-5 volume will continue to operate in a degraded mode. A replacement dynamic disk drive must be added to the computer and a repair operation initiated with the Disk Management console or the DiskPart command-line utility.

If more than one disk fails in a RAID-5 array of disks, the entire RAID-5 volume becomes unavailable. In this case, the RAID-5 array would have to be rebuilt from scratch and the data restored from a backup copy.

Partition and Volume Management

Partitions and volumes are terms used to describe a block of disk space used to store files. These blocks of space must be reserved for a particular partition or volume and cannot be shared between other partitions and volumes. (Partitions and volume types were described earlier in this chapter in the Disk Types section.) Before the partitions or volumes on a hard disk can store files they must be formatted with either a **FAT** or **NTFS** file system. File systems are covered in Chapter 5, Managing File Systems.

The terms **boot partition** and **system partition**, or boot and system volume, are labels used to identify which partitions or volumes are used in the boot process. These are not types of partitions or volumes. The system partition contains the hardware-specific files necessary to start Windows. The boot partition contains the files necessary to load the main Windows operating system itself.

The term *partition* is used when describing reserved regions of space on a basic disk. The term *volume* is used when describing regions of reserved space on a dynamic disk. There can be some confusion because the term *volume* is used interchangeably to describe partitions or dynamic volumes in some utilities and documentation. In a discussion about volumes, you must determine the nature of the disk by determining if the disk is functioning as a basic or dynamic disk. Dynamic and basic disk formatting is a logical construct and not a physical property of the disk.

Not all dynamic volume types are supported in Windows 7 because some of the volume types are considered server-class technologies. Windows 7's support for partition and volume types is summarized in Table 4-1.

Common administrative tasks for partitions and volumes include:

- Creating partitions and volumes
- Deleting partitions and volumes
- Extending partitions and volumes
- Shrinking partitions and volumes

Table 4-1 Volume types supported by disk type in Windows 7

Volume Type	Dynamic Disk	Basic Disk
Primary partition	No	Yes
Extended partition	No	Yes
Logical partition	No	Yes
Simple	Yes	No
Spanned	Yes	No
Striped	Yes	No
Mirrored	Yes	No
RAID-5	No (restricted to servers)	No

Creating Partitions and Volumes

Partitions and volumes can be created using either the Disk Management snap-in or the DiskPart command-line utility. Partition and volume changes can only be made by a Backup Operator or Administrator-equivalent user account.

Free space must be available on the disk and the types of partitions and volumes that can be created on the disk are limited based on disk type (basic or dynamic).

Creating Basic Disk Partitions Basic disks follow simple partition rules. Only primary, extended, and logical partition types can exist on a basic disk. The rules for the existence and creation of these partition types are summarized in Table 4-2.

4

Table 4-2   Basic Disk Partition Creation Rules

Partition Type	Rules
Primary	A maximum of four primary partitions can exist on one basic MBR-style disk. The Disk Management tool in Windows 7 will only allow the creation of three primary partitions before the fourth partition is created as an extended partition. A maximum of 128 primary partitions can exist on one GPT-style disk.
	A primary partition is required to start the load sequence of an operating system.
	A primary partition can only be used as part of the load sequence of an operating system if it has been flagged as the active primary partition.
	If a single disk contains multiple primary partitions, only one of them can be flagged as active.
	If a basic disk contains primary partitions and none of them are used to start the operating system then none of the primary partitions have to be flagged as active. This assumes that a second disk exists in the computer and is responsible for starting the operating system.
Extended	An extended partition can take the place of one of the primary partitions on a single basic MBR-style disk.
	Only one extended partition can exist on a single basic MBR-style disk.
	An extended partition is not required unless logical partitions are required on a disk.
Logical	A logical partition can exist only inside an extended partition.
	The number of logical partitions is only limited by the availability of free space in an extended partition.

Creating Dynamic Disk Partitions Dynamic disk technology supports five types of volumes, some of which can use multiple disks and provide fault tolerance. Windows 7 versions that support dynamic disks fully support simple, spanned, mirrored and striped volumes. Fault tolerant RAID 5 volumes are supported only in server-class operating systems.

The number of dynamic volumes supported on a disk is limited by the space in the database used to track dynamic volumes. A copy of the database is kept on each dynamic disk on the computer and takes up 1 MB of disk space on each disk. The database has enough room to store details about several thousand individual volumes. The rules for the existence and creation of dynamic volume types are summarized in Table 4-3.

Activity 4-6: Creating Disk Partitions

Time Required: 20 minutes
Objective: Create disk partitions.

Description: In this activity, you will perform the typical steps required to create new disk partitions using free space on the computer's startup hard disk.

1. If necessary, start your computer and log on.
2. Click the **Start** button to open the Start menu.

Table 4-3   **Dynamic Disk Volume Creation Rules**

Volume Type	Rules
Simple	A simple volume exists only on one dynamic disk.
	A simple volume can be made up of one or more regions of disk space on the single dynamic disk.
	If multiple regions of disk space are used on a single dynamic disk, they are not required to be contiguous on the disk.
Spanned	A spanned volume consists of pooled regions of disk space from multiple dynamic disks.
	A simple volume becomes a spanned volume if extra space is added to a simple volume from another dynamic disk.
	The total space available to store files is the sum total of all linked regions of disk space.
Striped	Equally sized blocks of space are pooled across multiple dynamic disks.
	The total space available to store files is the sum total of all linked blocks of disk space.
	Striped volumes support a minimum of two and a maximum of 32 dynamic disks.
Mirrored volume creation	Equally sized blocks of space are linked across two dynamic disks. Data is written identically to both blocks of space.
	The total space available to store files is the size of a single block of disk space.
	Mirrored volumes require only two dynamic disks.
RAID 5	Equally sized blocks of space are pooled across multiple dynamic disks.
	The total space available to store files is the sum total of all linked blocks of disk space minus one block of disk space for parity data.
	RAID 5 volumes support a minimum of three and a maximum of 32 dynamic disks.

3. Right-click the **Computer** Start menu item.

4. Click **Manage** from the pop-up menu.

5. If you are prompted by User Account Control for authorization to run this program, click the **Yes** button.

6. In the left-hand console navigation pane, click the **Disk Management** item below **Storage** to highlight it.

7. In the lower view of the Disk Management console, identify disk space on Disk 0 or the disk identified by your instructor as **Unallocated**.

8. Note the size of the unallocated disk space. _____

9. Calculate one-quarter of that amount. _____ If the amount is greater than 500 MB then use 500 MB for partition sizes later in this activity.

10. In the lower view of the Disk Management console, click on the unallocated space to select it. Notice that the graphical view of the unallocated space changes its appearance to indicate that it has been selected.

11. Right click on the unallocated space and notice that the pop-up menu has a **New Simple Volume** option. <u>Do not select it.</u>

12. With the unallocated space selected, click the **Action** menu and point to **All Tasks**.

13. Click **New Simple Volume** from the side menu. This starts the New Simple Volume Wizard.

14. Click **Next** to skip the introduction screen.

15. On the volume size screen, change the volume size to use a quarter of the available unallocated disk space (use the amount determined in step 9) then click **Next**.

16. On the assign drive letter screen, leave the default settings and note the drive letter that will be assigned to the new partition, then click **Next**.

17. On the Format Partition screen, change the default **Volume label** of **New Volume** to **DataVol1** and click **Next**.

18. Review the summary screen and click **Finish** to create the new partition. Notice that Disk 0 is a basic disk. The wizard refers to volumes but has created partitions because the disk is a basic disk, not a dynamic disk. The partitions created by the New Volume Wizard up to this point are primary partitions. You should now have three primary partitions on Disk 0: a 100 MB System partition, the C: partition, and DataVol1.

19. Repeat steps 12 to 18 on the remaining unallocated space and create a new volume using one quarter of the original unallocated space (use the amount determined in step 9). Note the new partition drive letter and label the new volume **DataVol2**. Note that you were not prompted for the partition type, which was determined automatically by the wizard.

20. Since this is the fourth partition on the basic disk, note that the new partition just created is not a primary partition. Compare the graphical color-coding of the partitions to the legend at the bottom of the Disk Management console. Disk Management has used all of the remaining disk space to create an extended partition and the new volume is created as a logical drive within the extended partition. This ensures that there is no unusable disk space caused by the four partition limit on disks.

21. Repeat steps 12 to 18 on the remaining unallocated free space and create a new volume using the remainder of the unallocated space. Note the new partition drive letter and label the new volume **DataVol3**.

22. In the lower view of the Disk Management console, click on the **DataVol1** space to select it. Note that this is a primary partition.

23. Right-click the **DataVol1** space and select **Mark Partition as Active**.

24. Note the warning that marking a primary partition active without a valid operating system installed on it could leave the computer unable to start. Select **No** to exit the prompt and avoid making the change.

> If you select **Yes**, your computer will be unable to restart.
>
> **NOTE**

25. Close the **Computer Management** window.

26. Close all **Windows Explorer** windows.

Deleting Partitions and Volumes

Dynamic volume and basic disk partitions can be deleted using the Disk Management MMC console or the DiskPart command-line utility. Partition and volume changes can only be made by an Administrator-equivalent user account.

Deleting a volume or partition will result in the loss of the data it contains unless the data is saved to another disk or backup device first.

Extended partitions cannot be deleted unless all of the logical partitions they contain are deleted first.

Activity 4-7: Deleting Disk Partitions

Time Required: 5 minutes
Objective: Use Disk Management to delete a partition.

Description: In this activity, you will perform the typical steps required to delete a partition or volume from the computer's hard disk.

1. If necessary, start your computer and log on.

2. Click the **Start** button to open the Start menu.

3. Right-click the **Computer** Start menu item.

4. Click **Manage** in the pop-up menu.

5. If you are prompted by User Account Control for authorization to run this program, click the **Yes** button.

6. In the left-hand console navigation pane, click the **Disk Management** item below Storage to highlight it.

7. In the lower view of the Disk Management console, click the **DataVol3** space to select it.

8. Right-click the **DataVol3** space and click **Delete Volume**.

9. Select **Yes** to continue on the warning that all data on that volume will be lost. If you are prompted that the drive is currently in use and would you like to force the deletion of the partition, click **Yes**. In a non-lab setting this would not be the recommended action. The recommended action would be to first close all applications and windows which may have the drive or its files open.

10. Close the **Computer Management** window.

Extending Partitions and Volumes

When a partition or volume is created it is a specific size. In some cases, extra space can be added to increase the size of the partition or volume, as long as specific rules are observed.

Dynamic volumes and basic partitions can be extended using the Disk Management MMC console or the DiskPart command-line utility. Partition and volume changes can only be made by an Administrator-equivalent user account.

The rules for extending a partition or volume depend on the disk type (basic or dynamic).

Extending Basic Disk Partitions
Basic disk technology allows for several different partition types: primary, logical, and extended. Primary and logical partitions can be expanded, extended partitions cannot. Before a partition on a basic disk is expanded, consider the following:

- The system and boot partitions can be expanded
- Free space must be available that is not assigned to another partition
- The free disk space must be contiguous with the partition being expanded
- The partition being expanded must have either no file system or is formatted with the **New Technology File System (NTFS)**
- The partition expansion is immediate and does not require a reboot of the computer to complete

Extending Dynamic Disk Volumes
Dynamic disks are designed to support a multidisk environment. Not all dynamic volumes can be extended once they are created. Only simple and spanned volumes can be extended. Before one of these dynamic volumes can be extended, consider that:

- The system and boot volume can be expanded
- A simple volume can be extended using any free disk space on the same physical disk and remain a simple volume
- The free disk space used to extend a simple volume does not have to be contiguous with the volume on the same physical disk
- If a simple volume is extended with free space from another physical disk, it becomes a spanned volume
- A spanned volume cannot be used to create a larger striped or fault-tolerant volume
- The volume expansion is immediate and does not require a reboot of the computer to complete.

Activity 4-8: Extending Disk Partitions

Time Required: 5 minutes

Objective: Use the Disk Management console to extend a basic disk partition.

Description: In this activity, you will perform the typical steps required to extend a partition using the Disk Management console.

1. If necessary, start your computer and log on.
2. Click the **Start** button to open the Start menu.
3. Right-click the **Computer** Start menu item.
4. Click **Manage** in the pop-up menu.
5. If you are prompted by User Account Control for authorization to run this program, click the **Yes** button.
6. In the left-hand console navigation pane, click the **Disk Management** item below Storage to highlight it.
7. Note the size of **DataVol2** and the free space next to it.
8. In the lower view of the Disk Management console, right-click **DataVol2**.
9. Click **Extend Volume** in the pop-up menu.
10. Click the **Next** button when the Welcome to the Extend Volume Wizard starts.
11. In the Select Disks page, change the value next to **Select the amount of space in MB:** to 500.
12. Click the **Next** button to continue.
13. Click the **Finish** button to complete the Extend Volume Wizard.
14. Note that the size of **DataVol2** has increased and the free space next to it has shrunk.
15. Close the **Computer Management** window.

Shrinking Partitions and Volumes

When a partition or volume is created, it is a specific size. In some cases, extra space can be removed to decrease the size of a partition or volume, as long as specific rules are observed.

Dynamic volume and basic disk partitions can be shrunk using the Disk Management snap-in or the DiskPart command-line utility. Partition and volume changes can only be made by an Administrator-equivalent user account.

The following rules apply to shrinking partitions and volumes:

- Free space must exist within the partition equivalent to or greater than the amount of disk space being removed from the partition or volume.
- Files are automatically moved within the partition as required.
- Some files, such as the swap file or shadow copy storage, cannot be moved and may limit the amount of disk space that can be recovered by shrinking a partition or volume to less than the free disk space available.
- The partition or volume either has no file system or is formatted with NTFS.
- If there is a high number of bad sectors detected on the disk, the shrink may be unsuccessful, and you should replace the disk.

The change is immediate and does not require a reboot.

ACTIVITY

Activity 4-9: Shrinking Disk Partitions

Time Required: 5 minutes
Objective: Use DiskPart to shrink a partition.

Description: In this activity, you will perform the typical steps required to shrink a partition or volume on a computer's hard disk. This exercise assumes that the computer has only one disk and the earlier exercises have been successfully completed. You will shrink the logical partition DataVol2 that was created earlier by 500 MB. Because the partition contains no files and is formatted with NTFS, this can be performed.

1. If necessary, start your computer and log on.
2. Click the **Start** button to open the Start menu.
3. Click the **Computer** Start menu item.
4. Navigate to the **C:\WINDOWS\SYSTEM32** folder.
5. Scroll to and double-click the **diskpart.exe** file.
6. If you are prompted by User Account Control for permission to run this program, click the **Yes** button.
7. To focus attention on the first disk, type **select disk** = 0 and press **Enter**.
8. Type **list partition** and press **Enter**. You should see five partitions listed. Note that if you have multiple hard disks in your computer, the disk number in step 9 may have to be modified to select the correct disk.
9. Type **list volume**, press **Enter**, and note the size and volume number of the partition labeled **DataVol2**.
10. To focus attention on DataVol2, note the volume number from step 9. That volume number will uniquely identify that volume given the current disk configuration. In the following command, it is assumed that the volume number is 4. If your volume number is different, change the value 4 in the following commands to match your value. Type **select volume 4** and press **Enter**.
11. Type **shrink desired** = **500** and press **Enter** to shrink DataVol2 by 500 MB.
12. Type **list volume**, press **Enter**, and note the size of DataVol2 has been reduced by 500 MB.
13. To leave the DiskPart utility, type **exit** and press **Enter**.
14. Close all open windows and log off.

Virtual Disk Management Tasks

Windows 7 introduces native support for working with Virtual Hard Disks (VHDs):

- Creating VHDs
- Attaching VHDs
- Detaching VHDs
- Advanced VHD Management

Creating VHDs

A VHD in Windows 7 is created as a single file on an attached physical disk drive. All versions of Windows 7 support the ability to create a VHD. VHDs can be created using the Disk Management snap-in or the DiskPart command line utility. Administrator or Backup Operator permission is required to complete the operation.

To create a VHD you must specify the following information:

- *Location*—The name and physical location of the file that will hold the VHD data
- *Virtual Hard Disk Size*—A value specified in MB, GB, or TB (limited to 2 TB)
- *Virtual Hard Disk Format*—Specify either as dynamically expanding or fixed size

If you specify that the VHD can grow dynamically, it will grow as files are added to the VHD, up to the maximum size specified. This can be useful when application developers create multiple VHD files and they want to conserve as much disk space as possible on the physical drive. Write performance can be slow because the physical file must grow as new files are added to the VHD. If the physical disk runs out of free space before the VHD reaches its maximum size, the VHD will fail to grow and any new write operations will fail. Dynamically sized VHD files do not automatically shrink when file data is deleted from the VHD.

When fixed size VHD files are created, they create a file on the physical disk that is as large as the Virtual Hard Disk Size specified. If the VHD size specified is 100 GB, then a file that size is created on the physical disk. The time is takes to write a large VHD file may be considerable, but the write performance to the VHD will be greatly improved. If there is not enough free disk space to create the VHD file using the size specified, the creation request will fail.

VHD disks created through the graphical Disk Management utility will automatically attach to the operating system and appear as a new operational disk drive. The drive must be initialized, just like a new hard drive, before it can be configured with partitions to store files. VHDs are restricted to basic disk technology due to their transient existence in the operating system.

Activity 4-10: Creating VHD Disks

Time Required: 15 minutes
Objective: Create a dynamically expanding VHD disk with the graphical Disk Management utility.

Description: In this activity, you will perform the typical steps required to create a new VHD disk hosted on drive C: using the Disk Management utility

1. If necessary, start your computer and log on.
2. Click the **Start** button to open the Start menu.
3. Click the **Computer** Start menu item.
4. Double-click **Local Disk (C:)** and create a new folder called **VHD Storage** on C:. This folder will be used to store the VHD file that will be created later in this activity.
5. Click the **Start** button to open the Start menu.
6. Right-click the **Computer** Start menu item.
7. Click **Manage** from the pop-up menu.
8. If you are prompted by User Account Control for authorization to run this program, click the **Yes** button.
9. In the left-hand console navigation pane, click the **Disk Management** item below Storage to select it. This will focus the Computer Management utility on this storage tool.
10. In the left-hand console navigation pane, right-click the **Disk Management** item below Storage to open a side menu. In the side menu select **Create VHD**.
11. Click the **Browse** button and navigate to **C:\VHD Storage**. In the File name: field, enter the text **Version1AppFiles** and click the **Save** button to close the Browse Virtual Disk files window. This will define the name and location of the VHD file.
12. In the Create and Attach Virtual Hard Disk window enter the value **50** in the Virtual hard disk size field, leaving the size drop-down list set to **MB**.

13. Select **Dynamically expanding** under Virtual hard disk format to allow the VHD file to grow as required with a maximum size of 50 MB.

14. Click the **OK** button to create the VHD and automatically attach it. Note that a new disk appears in the graphical disk view with an Unknown disk type and a status of Not Initialized. The free space on the drive appears as 50 MB of unallocated space and the graphical drive icon next to the disk identifier is light blue.

15. Right-click the 50 MB of unallocated space from the VHD disk and note the available volume creation options.

16. Right-click the disk name next to the blue drive icon to open a side menu. Select **Initialize Disk** from the side menu. Note in the Initialize Disk window which partition styles are available for use with the VHD disk.

17. Click the **OK** button to complete the initialization of the VHD disk.

18. Right-click the unallocated space from the VHD disk and note the available volume creation options. Select **New Simple Volume** from the pop-up menu.

19. Complete the typical steps to create a NTFS based volume but change the default Volume label of New Volume to **VHDVOL**. Note the drive letter assigned to this new volume when the volume creation completes. Note the size of the newly created partition in Disk Management.

20. Switch to the Windows Explorer computer browser window and browse to **C:\VHD Storage**. Note the size of the VHD file in that folder.

21. In the Windows Explorer computer browser window, right-click the drive letter assigned to the VHD disk and select **Properties** from the pop-up menu. Note the Used space and Capacity values shown on the General tab. Compare this to the actual size of the VHD file noted in step 19.

22. Click the **OK** button to close the drive properties window.

23. Close the Computer Management window.

24. Close all Windows Explorer windows.

Attaching VHDs

A VHD must be attached, or mounted, to be available to the operating system and the user. When a VHD is attached it can be managed with typical disk and partition operations. All versions of Windows 7 support the ability to attach an existing VHD file. VHDs can be attached using the Disk Management snap-in or the DiskPart command line utility. The attached VHD appears as just another disk in Disk Management but the drive icon for the disk is highlighted in blue, as seen in Figure 4-1. Administrator or Backup Operator permission is required to complete the operation. When a VHD file is attached, it can be optionally opened in read-only mode. Using this option means that the file's content can only be read and ensures that it cannot be accidentally modified.

When a computer is restarted, the VHD files currently attached will not automatically reattach. They will have to be manually attached again after the computer restarts. The only time a VHD automatically mounts as the computer starts is the special case where Windows 7 is configured to boot from a VHD file. Even in that case, if other VHD files were attached before the computer is restarted, they will not automatically attach.

Detaching VHDs

A VHD must be detached, or dismounted, to make it unavailable to the operating system and the user. All versions of Windows 7 support the ability to detach an existing VHD file. VHDs can be manually detached using the Disk Management snap-in or the DiskPart command line utility. Administrator or Backup Operator permission is required to complete the operation. When a computer is restarted the VHD files currently attached automatically detach.

When a VHD is detached the files it contains cannot be accessed by the user or the operating system. To the operating system the detached VHD file appears as just another data file. This can be useful if a backup utility is backing up the physical drive hosting a VHD file. The backup utility will fail to back up the VHD file if it is currently in an attached state because it is considered an open file. To avoid the error, the VHD can be detached until the backup operation is complete. Once the backup operation is complete the VHD can be attached again. This may be necessary to guarantee that the VHD file information backed up by the backup utility will be recoverable and functional.

Advanced VHD Management

The Disk Management snap-in is limited in what management operations can be done with VHD files. The DiskPart command line utility allows for advanced management operations such as:

- *Compact VHD*—Decrease the maximum size of a dynamic or fixed size VHD
- *Expand VHD*—Increase the maximum size of a dynamic or fixed size VHD
- *Detail VHD Properties*—Display detailed information about a VHD

Other utilities and administration software is available to work with VHD files for deployment to multiple desktops and hosts running virtual machines. These advanced tools are beyond the scope of this chapter.

Activity 4-11: Managing VHD Disks

Time Required: 5 minutes

Objective: View VHD attributes and detach a VHD using DiskPart.

Description: In this activity, you will use DiskPart to view a VHD's details, detach it, and confirm that it is no longer visible as an active disk in the Disk Management graphical utility.

1. If necessary, start your computer and log on.
2. Click the **Start** button to open the Start menu.
3. Click the **Computer** Start menu item.
4. Navigate to the **C:\WINDOWS\SYSTEM32** folder.
5. Scroll to and double-click the **diskpart.exe** file.
6. If you are prompted by User Account Control for permission to run this program, click the **Yes** button.
7. Note that after a brief delay, the diskpart utility will start with an interactive command prompt visible as **DISKPART>**. To focus attention on the VHD, type **select vdisk file="C:\VHD Storage\Version1AppFiles.vhd"** at the prompt and press **Enter**.
8. Type the command **detail vdisk** and press **Enter** to display detailed information about the VHD. Note the Virtual size and Physical size attributes listed in the output of the command.
9. With DiskPart still focused on the selected VHD, type the command **detach vdisk** and press **Enter** to dismount the VHD.
10. To leave the DiskPart utility, type **exit** and press **Enter**.
11. The Disk Management utility will now be used to confirm that the VHD file is no longer visible as a disk to the operating system. Click the **Start** button to open the Start menu.
12. Right-click the **Computer** Start menu item.
13. Click **Manage** from the pop-up menu.

14. If you are prompted by User Account Control for authorization to run this program, click the **Yes** button.

15. In the left-hand console navigation pane, select **Disk Management** below Storage to open the Disk Management utility.

16. Note that the VHD disk is no longer shown in the bottom graphical disk view.

17. Close all open windows and log off.

Chapter Summary

- In this chapter, you learned that Windows 7 supports MBR and GPT partition styles that use basic and dynamic disk technology to organize data into partitions and volumes on physical disks. Basic disks use primary, logical, and extended partitions on a single physical disk. Dynamic disks use simple, spanned, striped, mirrored, and RAID-5 volumes that can involve multiple physical disks. Dynamic disks identify the computer they belong to and are aware of all other dynamic disks installed in the computer. Basic and dynamic disks are managed using the Disk Management console or the DiskPart command-line utility. Basic disks can be converted to dynamic disks without losing data, but converting dynamic disks to basic disks requires that all data be removed from the dynamic disk before the conversion.

- Disk management activities include preparing new disks for use, cleaning up wasted space, checking the disk health, minimizing access delays, and moving disks. Disks that are added to the computer might not be immediately recognized and Windows 7 can be told to check for new hardware and disks. Wasted space can be recovered using the disk cleanup wizard. Defragmenting disks will minimize the time it takes to access data on the physical disk. When disks are moved from one computer to another the drive letters they use may have to change. Dynamic disks must be imported when moved to update their membership with other dynamic disks that belong to a computer.

- The disk type limits partitions and volumes created on a disk. Once a partition or volume is created, it is possible to extend and shrink them if specific conditions apply.

- Virtual Hard Disks (VHDs) are natively supported by Windows 7 and can be managed as a basic disk once the VHD is attached in the operating system. VHD files can either be a fixed size or allowed to grow dynamically to a maximum size. When a computer is restarted, the VHDs mounted before the reboot are not automatically attached. Windows 7 has the ability to boot from a VHD file.

Key Terms

active partition   A primary partition that is indicated in the partition table as the partition to use when loading the rest of the operating system. If a basic disk has multiple primary partitions, only one primary partition can be marked as active at a time. The primary partition's boot sector is used to load the rest of the operating system.

basic disk   An older, IBM-originated method used to organize disk space for x86 computers into primary, extended, and logical partitions. Basic disk technology is supported by many legacy operating systems and may be required in certain multiboot configurations.

boot partition   The partition or volume used to load the operating system from a hard disk. The system partition is processed before the boot partition. The boot partition can be the same partition as the system partition.

boot sector   A term used to describe a special-purpose block of data on a disk or partition essential to the boot process of an x86 computer. The computer's BIOS will process the boot sector of the MBR initially to find a partition to continue the boot process. The first sector of that partition or volume contains a boot sector with code responsible for beginning the operating system load process from a partition or volume.

cluster   A unit of storage for reading and writing file data in a file system. The cluster size is determined when a partition or volume is first formatted with a file system. Cluster size is based on the sector size of a disk and the number of sectors used per cluster. Cluster sizes typically range from 512 bytes to 64 KB.

defragmentation   The process of ordering data on the hard disk in a contiguous fashion to minimize the delays in reading or writing data. This attempts to minimize the mechanical delay caused by having to move read/write mechanisms from one region of the disk to another.

Disk Management console   An MMC console snap-in used to administer hard disks in Windows 7.

drive letter   A letter of the alphabet assigned to a formatted partition or volume as a reference point for future access by the user or their applications.

duplexed mirror   A RAID 1 implementation that uses one hardware controller for the first disk in a RAID 1 pair, and a second different hardware controller for the second RAID 1 disk. This increases fault tolerance in the case where a disk controller fails instead of a single disk. IDE and SCSI implementations of RAID 1 would typically use one hardware controller to manage both RAID 1 members. In this case the hardware controller would be a single point of failure.

dynamic disk   A new method used to organize disk space into volumes. First introduced with Windows 2000, the dynamic disk method is seen as an improvement over basic disk technology. Not all operating systems support the dynamic disk method of organizing disk space. This may restrict multiboot configurations. Dynamic disk technology supports simple, spanned, striped, mirrored, and RAID 5 volumes. All dynamic disks in a computer are identified with a group membership ID personalized for the computer they belong to. Volume information is stored in a database that is replicated to all other dynamic disks in the computer. The volume information database is stored in the last 1 MB of each disk.

Extensible Firmware Interface (EFI)   A standard initially created by Intel to replace the BIOS based computer firmware

extended partition   A reserved block of space on a basic disk. No more than one extended partition can exist on a single basic disk. Logical partitions are created within the extended partition. Extended partitions cannot be formatted with a file system directly.

File Allocation Table (FAT)   A file system used to organize files and folders in a partition or volume. A master File Allocation Table is used to indicate what files and folders exist within the file system. The FAT table entries point to the beginning cluster used to store a file's data. The first cluster points to the next cluster used to store the next part of the file's data. The file's data is stored in a chain of clusters, with the last cluster marked with an end-of-file identifier. The FAT table stores the name and attributes of the files and folders on the disk, their starting cluster, and which clusters link to the next. The number of addressable clusters determines the size of the FAT table. The limit for how many addressable clusters exist is based on the size of the binary number used to address each cluster. The number of bits used for the cluster address distinguishes the different versions of FAT. The common versions of FAT include FAT16 and FAT32.

FAT   See File Allocation Table.

Foreign Disk   A dynamic disk that is recognized as not belonging to the computer it is currently installed in. Until the disk is imported, to change its dynamic disk computer membership, the volumes it contains are not accessible.

GUID (Globally Unique Identifier)   A label that identifies an item with a unique name or code that is used to tell it apart from similar items. Software typically uses a coded number or value to represent a unique identifier.

GUID Partition Table (GPT)   A disk partitioning style that allows more partitions and advanced partition information when compared to the older MBR style disk partition scheme. Desktop computers only use GPT in specialized and limited cases due to its limited applicability.

logical partition   A reserved block of space on a basic disk. Logical partitions can only be created within an extended partition. As long as free space exists in an extended partition, a new logical partition can be created. Logical partitions can be formatted with a file system directly.

Master Boot Record (MBR)   The Master Boot Record exists at the very first sector of an IBM-formatted hard disk. It contains code to start the load process for an operating system from a partition or volume on the disk, a partition table to indicate what space has been reserved as partitions, and a signature sequence of bytes used to identify the disk to the operating system. When the disk is used as a basic disk, the partition table is used to identify primary, extended, and logical partition types. When the disk is used as a dynamic disk, the partition table is filled with placeholder values and the volume information is actually held in a 1 MB dynamic volume database at the end of the drive.

mirrored volume   A RAID 1 implementation using dynamic disks.

mount point   An empty folder in an NTFS-formatted file system that is used to point to another FAT, FAT32, or NTFS partition.

New Technology File System (NTFS)   A file system introduced with Windows NT. NTFS supports advanced features to add reliability, security, and flexibility that file systems such as FAT and FAT32 do not have.

NTFS   See New Technology File System.

partition table   A data structure contained in the MBR that is used to identify reserved areas of disk space for hard disks formatted for x86 computers. The partition table holds a maximum of four entries originally tasked to point to a maximum of four primary partitions, or three primary and one extended partitions.

primary partition   A reserved region of disk space on a basic disk that is capable of loading an operating system. The first sector of the primary partition is also known as a boot sector and stores the code for beginning the operating system load process from that primary partition.

RAID 0   A collection of disks that combine their storage capacity by striping data across all drives. Data is written in a fixed block size, typically sized in KB, in a sequential fashion to each disk. The first block of data for a file is written to the first disk, the second block of data to the second disk, and so on until the last drive is reached. The next block of data starts over with the first drive and the process continues with each subsequent block of data written to the next disk. This type of storage is not fault tolerant and the failure of a single disk will result in the loss of all file data. This type of storage will generally improve write and read performance when compared with a single disk. The number of disks that can be pooled this way is limited by the operating system or hardware controller used to pool the disks.

RAID 1   Two disks are used to store a single copy of file data in a fault-tolerant fashion. An exact copy of the data is written to each disk. If one disk fails, the other copy allows continued operation. Performance is similar to a single disk where reads are generally faster and writes can be slower. Both disks can be on a single controller, which introduces a common point of failure. If the hardware used to control each disk is fully duplicated into independent channels, the system is referred to as a duplexed mirror.

RAID 5   A collection of disks that combine their storage capacity by striping data and error-correcting parity information across all drives. The parity information is calculated from the data itself and can be used to identify and regenerate damaged or missing data. The data and parity information is striped in the same fashion as RAID 0 data. RAID 5 is fault tolerant in that a single disk in the collection may fail and the missing data can be calculated from the remaining data and parity information distributed across the remaining disks. A multiple disk failure will result in the loss of all data in the collection. The disks space cost for parity information is approximately the same as the size of disks space contributed from one disk member. For example, if five 10 GB disks are collected into a single RAID 5 solution then the space of one disk, 10 GB, is consumed by parity information. The remainder of 40 GB is available for file storage. A minimum of three disks is required to build a RAID 5 solution.

Redundant Array of Independent Disks (RAID) Also known as Redundant Array of Inexpensive Disks. A standard reference to a collection of disks grouped to store data. The RAID level indicates the type of grouping and is indicated by a number following the term RAID. Common RAID levels are RAID 0 striped storage, RAID 1 mirrored storage, and RAID 5 striped storage with error-correcting information.

removable disk storage A mass storage device that can be removed from the computer, either by powering down the computer first or while the computer is running. This includes floppy disks, portable hard disks, and cartridge-based disk storage.

sector A single unit of storage for a hard disk that represents the smallest block of data that can be read or written to the disk. The typical hard disk sector size is 512 bytes.

simple volume A reserved area of space on a single dynamic disk. A simple volume can be formatted with a file system. The areas of space reserved for a simple volume do not have to be contiguous on the dynamic disk.

spanned volume A reserved area of space combined from two or more dynamic disks. A spanned volume can be formatted with a file system. Files are written to each disk's reserved area of space until that area is full. Additional file data is then written to the next available reserved area of space on the next disk that is part of the spanned volume. The capacity of the spanned volume is the total of all reserved areas of space from each disk that is a member of the spanned volume. Loss of a single disk that holds part of the spanned volume will result in the total loss of the volume.

striped volume A RAID 0 implementation using dynamic disks.

system partition The partition or volume used to initiate the boot sequence for a computer from a hard disk. The system partition is processed before the boot partition, which loads the remainder of the operating system. The system partition can be the same partition as the boot partition.

Unified Extensible Firmware Interface (UEFI) An open standard that builds on the proprietary EFI standard started by Intel to replace the legacy BIOS firmware design.

Virtual Hard Disk (VHD) Disk space that stores files and folders in a formatted file system. The disk space is not an actual physical device; it is actually stored in a single file. That file will have the extension ".vhd". Once the vhd file is created it can be attached, or opened for use. The operating system can use the space inside the file as if it was an actual disk device, but it is really a virtual disk. The vhd file itself is stored on a real physical device.

volume A term used to refer to a region of disk space reserved to store file data. The term is used to generically refer to both dynamic disk volumes and basic disk partitions.

x64 A generic term used to refer to Intel and AMD CPU processors capable of 64 bit operations that are compatible with the Windows operating system.

x86 A generic term used to refer to computers based on Intel CPU processors. These CPUs include 8086, 80286, 80386, 80486, the Pentium family and Pentium compatible processors from other companies such as AMD.

Review Questions

1. If a RAID 5 array is composed of 4 disks with 100 GB of storage each, then what is the total capacity of the RAID 5 array for data storage?

    a. 100 GB

    b. 200 GB

    c. 300 GB

    d. 400 GB

2. A VHD has been created using the Disk Management Utility. Before the newly created VHD can be used to store files it must be _____.

    a. detached

    b. configured as a spanned dynamic disk

    c. set to GPT partition style

    d. initialized

    e. set to MBR partition style

3. The _____ partition hosts the main Windows 7 operating system files.

4. When viewing the properties of a drive, the Tools tab allows access to which of the following? (Select all that apply.)

    a. Defragmentation

    b. Disk Cleanup

    c. Classic Sharing

    d. Error Checking

    e. Advanced Security

5. You have just plugged a USB hard drive into an older laptop and the disk has not appeared as available. You are concerned that the hard disk hardware has not been recognized by the computer. What utility would you use to verify?

    a. DiskPart

    b. Disk Management console

    c. USB Management console

    d. Device Manager

    e. none of the above

6. You have recently added a new USB portable hard disk to your computer. You have received a notice that new hardware has been detected. The disk does not appear as a storage location. Which utility would you use to verify that the hard disk's logical disk information is scanned by Windows 7? (select two.)

    a. DiskPart

    b. Disk Mangement console

    c. USB Management console

    d. Device Manager

    e. none of the above

7. The maximum number of primary partitions that can exist on a MBR-style basic disk is _____.

    a. 0

    b. 3

    c. 4

    d. unlimited

8. A mirrored volume is also known as a RAID _____ implementation.

    a. 0

    b. 1

    c. 3

    d. 5

    e. The volume is not a RAID implementation.

9. A data volume containing important documents has been deleted. You must recover the accidentally deleted file data. This can be accomplished by _____.

   a. using DiskPart to recreate the volume with the same name and the recovery option enabled

   b. using Disk Management console to undelete the volume

   c. using DiskManagement console to recreate the volume with the same name and the recovery option enabled

   d. using DiskPart to undelete the volume

   e. creating a new volume and recovering the files from a backup source

10. Your computer currently runs the Windows 7 operating system. You have added a second 20 GB hard disk drive to your computer to hold research data for a project you are working on. You have created a single simple volume on the data hard drive that takes up all the free space on the disk. After formatting the simple volume with the FAT32 file system and copying 10 GB of data to the volume you realize that you need 8 GB of unpartitioned disk space on the data disk drive. The next step you should take to free space on the data disk drive is to _____.

   a. shrink the existing simple volume using the DiskPart command-line utility

   b. shrink the existing simple volume using the Disk Management MMC console

   c. convert the 20 GB data disk to a basic disk

   d. delete the existing simple volume and create a new one using the correct size

11. The maximum number of logical drives that can exist within a single extended partition is _____.

   a. 23

   b. 4

   c. 21

   d. only limited by the availability of free space in the extended partition

12. Before a new hard disk can be managed through the Disk Management console in Windows 7, it first must be _____.

   a. formatted

   b. partitioned

   c. erased

   d. initialized

13. You are attempting to inspect the partition information for an existing hard disk using DiskPart utility. After issuing the LIST PARTITIONS command, you receive an error message stating that no disk is selected for the action. Assuming the disk is the first hard disk in the computer, which command should you issue next?

   a. SELECT DISK = 0

   b. SELECT DISK = 1

   c. FOCUS DISK ANY

   d. FOCUS DISK = 1

   e. none of the above

14. A basic disk contains 3 logical partitions. How many of these partitions can be marked as active?

   a. 0

   b. 1

    c. 2

    d. 3

    e. 4

15. You have recently added a new USB hard disk to your computer. The hardware has been detected and you have verified that the disk is visible to Windows 7. You are unable to store data files to the new hard disk. What is the first step you must perform before you can store data on the disk?

    a. initialize the disk

    b. scan for new hard disks

    c. create partitions or volumes

    d. convert the disk to a dynamic disk

    e. format the disk

16. You decide to move a hard disk from your computer to another computer that is also running Windows 7. The disk is currently configured as a dynamic disk. The file data it currently contains must be accessible on the destination computer. Before moving the disk you should _____.

    a. convert the disk to basic storage

    b. use the Disk Management console to initialize the disk as a Foreign Disk

    c. use DiskPart to flag the disk as a Foreign Disk

    d. back up the disk's data contents

    e. lock the disk using the Disk Management console

17. A basic disk contains 3 partitions. How many of these partitions can be primary partitions?

    a. 0

    b. 1

    c. 2

    d. 3

    e. 4

18. Upon opening the Disk Management console, you notice a disk whose status is reported as Foreign Disk. This is most likely because _____.

    a. the disk's Unicode property is enabled

    b. the disk has been corrupted

    c. the disk is shared on the network

    d. the disk was moved from another computer

19. The _____ partition contains the computer hardware specific files required to start Windows.

20. The maximum number of primary partitions that can exist on a dynamic disk is _____.

    a. 0

    b. 3

    c. 4

    d. unlimited

21. An existing hard disk contains a second primary partition that is currently used to store data files. You are running out of space and would like to expand the data partition. There is only 8 MB of unpartitioned disk space available on the hard disk. You have added a new

hard disk and have verified that the new disk is properly recognized by the operating system. You would like to span the data partition across to the new hard disk. To do this you must first _____.

    a.   back up the original partition data, create a new dynamic volume that spans the two disks, and restore the data

    b.   link the two disks using the Disk Management console

    c.   link the two disks using the DiskPart utility

    d.   create a primary partition on the new hard disk the same size as the original data partition

    e.   convert the disk holding the primary partition to a dynamic disk

22.   You suspect that the data partition known as drive E on your system is unhealthy. To check the health of drive E, what should you do next?

    a.   Open the properties of drive E:

    b.   Issue the command CHECK DISK = 1 in the DiskPart utility

    c.   Run the Disk Scan Tool from Control Panel

    d.   Run the Disk Scan Tool from the Accessories folder in the Start menu

    e.   none of the above

23.   File throughput performance when reading and writing large files is typically better for striped volumes than simple volumes. True or False?

24.   The data files contained inside a VHD file cannot be browsed with Windows Explorer in Windows 7. True or False?

25.   A data partition you have recently formatted using FAT32 is larger than required. You decide to decrease the size of the partition by shrinking it. This can be accomplished by _____.

    a.   using the Shrink tool

    b.   using DiskPart

    c.   backing up the existing files, deleting the partition, creating a smaller partition using a smaller size, and restoring the file data from backup

    d.   converting the disk to a dynamic disk and then using DiskPart to shrink the partition

Case Projects

CASE PROJECTS

Case Project 4-1: Dealing with Running Out of Space

Your computer has several mission-critical applications installed that are hard-coded to use drive C as the location of their data files. Unfortunately, drive C is running out of space. The single hard disk in the computer is formatted as a basic disk and cannot be converted to dynamic. The boot partition of the computer is formatted with NTFS. No unpartitioned space remains on the hard disk. What action could you take to remedy the crisis?

Case Project 4-2: Improving Disk Performance

A friend is complaining that their gaming experience with a Windows 7 Ultimate computer is too slow. Upon examining the system you note that constant disk activity is slowing down the user's applications. The current disk is a basic disk with two primary partitions, one for the operating system and one for game data. What suggestions could be made to boost disk performance?

chapter 5

Managing File Systems

After reading this chapter and completing the exercises, you will be able to:

- Understand file system features and limits in Windows 7

- Understand file system management tasks

- Understand file and folder attributes used in the FAT and NTFS file systems

- Understand file and folder permissions, permission scope and inheritance, plus the impact of ownership and moving or copying content

- Understand how to use previous versions of files

Files are stored on many different types of devices; floppy disks, hard drives, CD/DVDs, USB memory sticks, and more. File systems are used to store and organize files on each of those devices. The user has different file storage requirements for different devices. For example, some files must be portable and interchangeable with other operating systems while other files must be secure and efficiently stored. Some devices, such as hard disks, support multiple file systems on one device. This chapter identifies the common file systems used in Windows 7, the properties of files stored on them, securing those files, and how to access previous versions of files.

Supported File Systems

A file system allows the operating system to store and organize files on a hard disk. Hard disks store data on a sector-by-sector basis. File systems group sectors into units of storage called a cluster. The file system uses the clusters to form the files, folders, and data structures used to manage those files and folders. The choice of file system can limit the total amount of data stored in a partition or volume, the number of files, the size of the files, their names, attributes, and other properties. Windows 7 supports five file systems:

- File Allocation Table
- NT File System
- Universal Disk Format
- CDFS File System
- Extended File Allocation Table

The choice of basic or dynamic disk technology has no impact on file system features described in this section.

File Allocation Table

The earliest file system used for hard disks by the MS-DOS operating system is the **File Allocation Table (FAT)**. All Microsoft operating systems since MS-DOS support a version of this file system. Three different versions of **FAT** exist: FAT12, FAT16, and FAT32. The number after the FAT label indicates the number of binary bits used to address blocks of data, or clusters, in the file allocation table. The larger the number, the more distinct addresses are available for identifying blocks of file data, generally resulting in the ability to store more data.

FAT12 was introduced with early versions of MS-DOS. A 12-bit address for a FAT entry allows up to 4096 addresses. The cluster size for FAT12 can range from a single sector up to 4 KB. This allows for a maximum partition size of 16 MB. Windows 7 only uses this file system for floppy disks.

FAT16 is common to earlier operating systems where the partition size did not exceed 2 GB. A 16-bit address for a FAT entry allows up to 65,536 addresses. The cluster size for FAT16 is limited depending on the version of Windows. Windows NT, Windows 2000, Windows 2003, Windows Server 2008, Windows 7 and Windows Vista support a maximum cluster size of 64 KB with FAT16, which allows a maximum partition size of 4 GB. All other operating systems that support FAT16 only support a maximum cluster size of 32 KB, which allows a maximum partition size of 2 GB with FAT16.

FAT32 was introduced with Windows 95 OSR2 to support hard disks that were becoming much larger than 2 GB in size. The 32-bit address used for a FAT entry allows for more than 2 million addresses. The problem introduced by so many addresses is that the table used to keep track of them becomes very large and inefficient to manage. Windows XP, Windows Vista, and Windows 7 will not use FAT32 as a file system for new partitions or volumes larger than 32 GB. Additionally, files larger than 4 GB cannot be stored in a FAT32 file system.

Pre-existing partitions or volumes that are larger than 32 GB and formatted with FAT32 are still accessible to Windows 7.

Regardless of which version of FAT is used, the limits of FAT are similar:

- Limited fault tolerance—There is no provision for fault-tolerance in FAT, except for the fact that two copies of the FAT table are stored in the partition.

- Inefficient storage—When a file's data is written to a cluster, the entire cluster is unavailable for any other file to store data in, even if the entire cluster is not used. Large cluster sizes can lead to a lot of wasted space.

- Limited security—Simple attributes are used to mark files as system files, hidden, or read only; no user-based security is available.

Despite its limits, the FAT file system does offer some benefits:

- Supported by many legacy operating systems, which may be required if partitions are shared in a multi-boot configuration

- Simple technology that is well understood and supported by third-party utilities

- Adequate when file and folder requirements are simple and do not require complex security

- Suitable for removable media such as digital camera memory, media players, and USB memory sticks

To provide enhanced features for security, usability, and larger partitions, NTFS provides a more suitable alternative.

New Technology File System

The **New Technology File System (NTFS)** was first introduced with Windows NT and is supported by Windows 7. NTFS was introduced as a secure and efficient file system that is commonly used in business computing environments. Several operating systems introduced after Windows NT include support for earlier versions of NTFS including Windows 2000, Windows XP, and Windows Vista. MS-DOS, Windows 3.x, and Windows 95/98/ME do not support the NTFS file system.

NTFS partitions are theoretically limited to 256 **Terabytes** (TB, 1 TB = 1024 GB), but the practical limit is lower. Basic disks using the old IBM standard for partitions are restricted to 2 TB. Newer dynamic disk partitions are limited to 16 TB.

Each operating system that supports NTFS is designed for a specific version of NTFS. If a partition is moved or shared between two different operating systems, problems may occur with the operation and management of the partition. Because partitions are more likely to be shared over the network instead of locally as part of a multi-boot setup, this is not typically a problem.

NTFS stores files and folders in a way that looks very similar to the FAT file system. The difference is in how that data is secured, reliably managed, and allowed to grow. NTFS supports partition sizes above the 32 GB limit imposed on FAT32.

The major advantages of NTFS include:

- Log file and checkpoint consistency checks

- Automatic bad cluster management

- Transactional NTFS

- File names stored in Unicode and 8.3 DOS format

- Alternate data streams

- Encrypting File System (EFS)

- File and folder permissions

- Compression
- Disk quotas
- Shrinkable/extendable partitions and volumes
- Volume mount points
- Symbolic links
- Sparse files

Log File and Checkpoint Consistency Checks The FAT file system has little support for validating that data stored to the FAT table itself is actually valid. Only the most basic form of error checking, using checksums and signature bytes, is typically performed. NTFS uses a more advanced system to incrementally update the directory information about files and folders stored on the NTFS partition.

Information about files and folders stored on the disk is kept in a special file called the Master File Table (MFT), which is named $MFT on the disk. Many different NTFS system files are used to manage the data and features of a specific NTFS partition or volume. This is an improvement over the simplistic FAT table because a richer amount of detail and control structures can be implemented as virtual constructs for each file and folder. The MFT is the most important NTFS system file because it is a relational database that provides the starting point for accessing any file on the NTFS partition.

These system files are hidden from general browsing and are not visible to the user. It is not necessary to know the details of these files for typical day-to-day management of an NTFS volume. In advanced scenarios, some of these system files are reported and tweaked by system tools. It is sufficient to know that these files exist. The system files are placed on the volume when it is formatted with the NTFS file system.

To safeguard this richer information base, the NTFS system files are protected by a transactional file system. Any changes that are made to the system files are recorded in log files. The log files keep a record of changes that were made; in the event of a failure or problem, changes made to the NTFS system files can be rolled back to a known good state.

This is possible because as changes are completed, a record of checkpoints and sequence numbers are committed in the system files. Updates to the NTFS system files can be replayed or rolled back if they have not completed. Note that this transactional system is designed to protect the NTFS system files and information about the files and folders stored on the partition, but not the data inside those files and folders.

The process of managing the log files and checkpoints is automatic and performed by the operating system itself. No administrative changes or monitoring are typically required.

Automatic Bad Cluster Management This is an automatic feature built into the NTFS file system. An NTFS system file called the Bad Cluster File keeps a record of all the clusters that are considered unusable by the file system within that volume. When the operating system detects that a cluster cannot be trusted to store data, the cluster's identification will be automatically added to this file. If the bad cluster is currently used by a file or folder to store data, the operating system will try to move that data to a different cluster. The move is transparent to the user and does not require user intervention.

Transactional NTFS Transactional NTFS is similar to the transactional system used to protect NTFS system files, such as $MFT, but it is used in Windows 7 to protect file data. Updates using a transactional system utilize change logs and checkpoints to validate that updates have successfully completed. If there is a problem with the updates to a file, the changes can be replayed or rolled back to a known good state.

This is a feature first introduced in Windows Vista that is available to application developers who write applications for Windows 7. If the application does not use the transactional system to write to a file, then the file data is not protected by transactional NTFS.

File Names Stored in Unicode and 8.3 DOS Format Files and folders on an NTFS file system in Windows 7 can use Unicode characters in the file name. This allows a file to use characters from many different international languages, not just the English-based ASCII character set. Each file has two names assigned to it, a **long file name** and an **8.3 file name** compatible with MS-DOS. The long file name is limited to 255 characters and can contain any valid Unicode character. The 8.3 DOS name contains a maximum of eight characters followed by a period and a maximum of three characters that act as the **file extension**.

The 8.3 DOS name, or alias as it is also known, uses only the ASCII character set for naming files. Windows 7 will automatically convert the long file name to a simplified 8.3 DOS name. The procedure to do so is:

1. Remove all invalid 8.3 file name characters from the long name.

2. Remove all blanks from the long name.

3. Remove any extra periods so that no more than one period exists at the end of the name.

4. Use the first six characters in the remaining name as the start of the 8.3 DOS name.

5. Append the '~' character and a sequence number starting at 1 (for example, ~1).

6. Append the period and a maximum three-character extension used by the long file name.

7. The calculated 8.3 DOS file name is compared to existing aliases in the folder that will store the file.

8. If there is a conflict because the 8.3 alias is already in use, the first part of the name is recalculated. The sequence number after the '~' is incremented and the file is checked for uniqueness again.

9. If the alias is already in use, the sequence number is incremented to a maximum of four.

10. If no unique file name could be created in the folder using the preceding steps, the format of the eight character alias changes again. Only the first two characters of the file name are used, instead of six, and a four-digit hash is calculated to represent a unique hexadecimal number to add after the two characters.

The '~' character and a sequence number of 1 is appended as before to complete the eight characters required.

This method allows over 300,000 different 8.3 aliases to co-exist in the same directory. The alias names created in this fashion are dependent on the order that long file names are written to a folder, making the name assigned to the file difficult to anticipate. The same long file name stored to multiple folders can have different 8.3 DOS names calculated for each folder. When a long file name is deleted from a folder, its alias is also deleted, making the alias available for re-use by another long file name created in that folder.

To see the alias names assigned in a folder, open a CMD window and change the directory to the target folder. The command **dir /X** will show both the alias and the long file names for all files in that folder.

Alternate Data Streams A file stored on an NTFS file system can have multiple streams of data associated with it. Each stream is a sequence of data bytes. Every file has one unnamed stream that is used to store the byte data typically associated with the file and visible to users and applications. Files stored on the FAT file system would only have the data associated with the unnamed stream.

Applications can create additional named streams and link them to the file in addition to the unnamed stream. This is only visible and useful to the application itself, as the user does not have direct access to the named streams.

Applications create the named streams and refer to them using the file name and the name of the stream to interact with the correct data. The use of the data is determined by the application designer. A common example is a named stream that could be used to store a thumbnail of a large image for quick and easy previews within a graphic application. The file name becomes a pointer to multiple related data streams instead of just one.

Encrypting File System

Files that are stored on an NTFS file system can have their contents encrypted to protect the information from unauthorized users that gain access to the file. Even though a user obtains access, they require additional security information to decrypt and access the file's contents. The **Encrypting File System (EFS)** is the part of the operating system that handles these operations.

EFS is a valuable form of protection for local file access. If a malicious user gains direct access to the hard disk, unencrypted files can be compromised. The user could gain direct access by physically removing the hard disk or booting the computer with a different operating system that allows direct access to the NTFS partition. With EFS encryption enabled for a file, the malicious user would not be able to decrypt the data they have access to. EFS is a local-access protection tool; when an encrypted file is sent across the network or in an e-mail, it is sent in its unencrypted form.

A user is authorized to access the file's contents if they are the original user that encrypted the file, an additionally authorized user, or a specific user assigned as a recovery agent. A recovery agent is usually assigned as part of a domain-wide group policy to ensure that files can be recovered even if the local user accounts on a computer are deleted.

Digital encryption keys from each user are implemented to encrypt and decrypt the file's contents. Without the correct key the file's contents are inaccessible. Even an administrator with full permissions to the file will not have access unless their encryption key is one of the recognized accounts.

Files that are encrypted with EFS will stay encrypted until an authorized user disables encryption on the file or copies the unencrypted contents to a storage device that does not support EFS (for example, a floppy disk).

The first time a user encrypts a file, they are prompted by Windows 7 to back up their encryption key to a file. This file should be moved to a protected and safe location off of the computer.

Encryption of files as an attribute of the file is examined later in this chapter.

File and Folder Permissions

Each file and folder on an NTFS file system has its own list of permissions that determine the actions that users or groups are allowed to perform with that item. This list of permissions is known as the Access Control List (ACL).

The ACL permissions are stored in NTFS system files hidden on the partition itself. This makes NTFS permissions local to the partition. ACL data is an attribute of the file while it exists in that NTFS partition. When a file or folder is moved or copied to a different NTFS partition, the permissions are reset based on the destination location's default permissions.

NTFS permissions are examined later in this chapter.

Compression

Files can be compressed to save space on NTFS volumes. The compression process is transparent to the user and their applications. From the user's perspective, the file takes up its uncompressed amount of space on the disk. When a compressed file is accessed, Windows 7 will decompress the file and present it to the user and their applications. When the file is closed, it is compressed once again.

Not all files should be compressed. Each time a file is compressed or uncompressed the CPU performs the calculations required. This impacts the computer's performance to some extent. If many compressed files are being accessed, the impact to performance may be significant.

To maximize the speed with which files are compressed, Windows 7 will only enable file compression if the cluster size for an NTFS partition is 4 KB or less.

Compression of a file is controlled by an attribute of files and folders. Compression attributes and their operation are examined later in this chapter.

Disk Quotas The amount of disk space used by a user can be restricted to ensure that one user does not exhaust or monopolize available space in an NTFS partition. By default, **disk quota** limits are not enabled for NTFS partitions.

Disk quotas are set using the Disk Management console, the Computer browser window, or with the command-line file system management utility fsutil. Administrative permissions are required on the computer to access the quota settings. By viewing the NTFS volume's properties from within Disk Management or in a Computer browser window, an extra tab called **Quota** will appear. This tab displays quota settings for that partition or volume (see Figure 5-1).

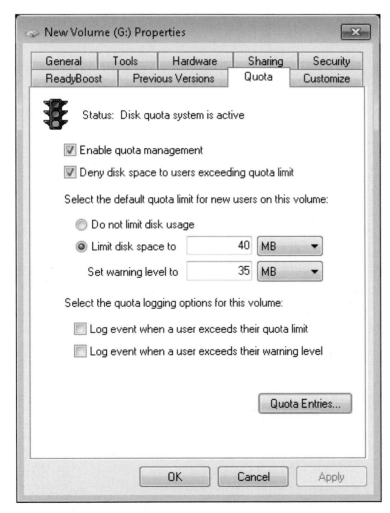

Figure 5-1 NTFS Formatted Disk Properties, Disk Quota Tab
Courtesy Course Technology/Cengage Learning

Once disk quotas are enabled for a partition, the operating system tallies the amount of disk space used by each unique owner listed for all files on the volume. The first time quota management is turned on, the system will take some time to identify all the owners and count up all the file sizes attributed to each owner.

Compressed files count against the disk quota based on their uncompressed size, not their compressed size.

Even if disk quotas are enabled, the initial configuration only reports the amount of data in use by different owners; no limits or warnings are enforced. The options on the Quota tab allow for limits to be configured as a default setting for all users.

As users approach those limits, warnings can be issued; when they finally reach the maximum limit, they are denied additional disk space within the partition. Warnings to users can be ignored, misinterpreted, and not noticed by administrators, so the warnings can be optionally recorded to the application event log as a permanent reference of the event.

Some users may require special consideration and should have a different warning or deny limit in place. The **Quota Entries** button on the **Quota** tab in Figure 5-1 opens a Quota Entries window (see Figure 5-2) where user-specific limits can be defined that override the default settings.

Quota Entries for New Volume (G:)

Quota   Edit   View   Help

Status	Name	Logon Name	Amount Used	Quota Limit	Warning Level	Percent Used
OK		BUILTIN\Administrators	72 KB	No Limit	No Limit	N/A
OK		NT AUTHORITY\SYSTEM	4 MB	No Limit	No Limit	N/A
OK		Lab-PC\UserA	11.28 MB	45 MB	40 MB	25

3 total item(s), 1 selected.

Figure 5-2 NTFS Formatted Disk Properties, Disk Quota Tab, Quota entries by owner
Courtesy Course Technology/Cengage Learning

Changes in the ownership of a file change the amount of data that is considered to belong to a user.

Activity 5-1: Enabling Disk Quotas for an NTFS Partition

Time Required: 10 minutes
Objective: Format a partition with NTFS and enable disk quotas for that partition.

Description: In this activity, you will format DataVol2, a pre-existing volume created in an earlier activity. This volume will be used to store bulk data files for users in the future. You decide to enable disk quotas now for this volume to record how much data users are storing. In the future, the collected data will provide a reference to support decisions on implementing storage limits.

1. If necessary, start your computer and log on.
2. Click the Start button to open the Start menu.
3. Right-click the **Computer** Start menu item.
4. Click **Manage** in the pop-up menu.
5. If you are prompted by User Account Control for authorization to run this program, click the **Yes** button.
6. In the left-hand console navigation pane, click the **Disk Management** item below Storage to highlight it.

7. In the upper view of the Disk management console, click **DataVol2**.

8. Right-click **DataVol2** in the upper view and click **Format** in the pop-up menu.

9. In the File system drop down list, click **NTFS**, if necessary.

10. Check the **Perform a quick format** check box, if necessary.

11. Click **OK** to continue.

12. Click **OK** to acknowledge the warning.

13. Wait for the status of DataVol2 to become **Healthy**.

14. In the lower view of the Disk Management console, identify **DataVol2** on Disk 0.

15. Right-click on **DataVol2** and click **Properties** in the pop-up menu.

16. In the DataVol2 (F:) Properties window, click the **Quota** tab to bring it to the front.

17. Note that the traffic light indicator on the quota tab is red and that the status is reported as **Disk quotas are disabled**.

18. Select the check box next to **Enable quota management**.

19. Click the **Apply** button to activate the quota system for this volume.

20. A warning will appear that enabling the disk quota system will take some time to complete. Click on the warning window's **OK** button to continue.

21. Note that the traffic light indicator on the quota tab is yellow and that the status is reported as **Rebuilding disk quota information**. Depending on the speed of your system, you may not see this status stage.

22. Note when the traffic light indicator on the quota tab turns green and the status is reported as **Disk quota system is active**.

23. Click the **Quota Entries** button on the quota tab.

24. Note that the Quota Entries for DataVol2 (F:) window appears and lists the current owners that have files on the volume. The Logon Name column will initially be populated with the Security Identifiers (SIDs) of the owners found on the volume. After a period of time, the SID codes will be resolved into their friendly names. Depending on the speed of your system, you may not see the SIDs.

25. Close the Quota Entries for DataVol2 (F:) window.

26. Close the **DataVol2 (F:)** Properties window.

27. Close the **Computer Management** window.

Shrinkable/Extendable Partitions and Volumes

If a partition or volume is formatted with NTFS, the file system can adapt when the partition or volume is resized. Partition and volume resizing are covered in Chapter 4.

Volume Mount Points

A partition or volume has a finite amount of space available. The partition or volume can be extended or spanned but in some cases this is not an option. Volume mount points allow an empty folder in an NTFS-formatted file system to point to another partition or volume in the local computer. Volume mount points are also known as junction points and are created with the Disk Management console. The user performing the task must have Administrator privileges on the local computer.

To the user, it appears they are accessing a folder in the original NTFS partition but in fact they are accessing the file system on the other partition. The partition connected via the volume mount point can be formatted with FAT, FAT32, or NTFS. Note that the FAT option in the new volume wizard refers to the FAT16 file system. The disk space reported for the NTFS volume hosting the mount point does not increase; the volume mount point is just a pointer. The free space and control of the target pointed at by the volume mount point is separately reported and managed.

A partition or volume accessed via a volume mount point can also have its own drive letter directly assigned to it. Carefully consider that combinations like this do not confuse the user.

From the user's perspective, the partition connected via the volume mount point is known by the folder name used to link to it. A folder must be empty before it can be converted into a volume mount point. A single volume mount point can only point to one partition or volume. Different volume mount points can point to the same target partition or volume. Volume mount points can be added or removed for a partition but they cannot be modified.

If a partition or volume is deleted and it is pointed to by one or more mount points, those mount points revert to empty folders.

Activity 5-2: Managing Mount Points

Time Required: 30 minutes

Objective: Link additional space to an existing volume using volume mount points and observe the changes to the view in Explorer.

Description: In this activity, you have decided that the volume DataVol2 does not have enough drive space to store user files. You decide to format DataVol2 with the NTFS file system as drive X and create a mount point to a new volume called DataVol3. DataVol3 will be formatted with the FAT32 file system. Once the mount point has been created, you will use Explorer to verify that the space is available from DataVol2. After you have completed verifying that the mount point works as planned, you will remove the mount point.

1. If necessary, start your computer and log on.
2. Click the Start button to open the Start menu.
3. Right-click the **Computer** Start menu item.
4. Click **Manage** in the pop-up menu.
5. If you are prompted by User Account Control for authorization to run this program, click the **Yes** button.
6. In the left-hand console navigation pane, click the **Disk Management** item below Storage to highlight it.
7. In the upper view of the Disk management console, identify **DataVol2**.
8. Right-click **DataVol2** and click **Format** in the pop-up menu.
9. Ensure that the option for **File system** is set to **NTFS**.
10. Select the check box next to **Perform a quick format**.
11. Click **OK** to continue.
12. Click **OK** to acknowledge the warning.
13. Wait for the status of DataVol2 to become **Healthy**.
14. Right-click **DataVol2** and click **Change Drive Letter and Paths** in the pop-up menu.
15. Note the current drive letter assigned to DataVol2 and click the **Change** button.
16. In the Change Drive Letter or Path window, click **X** in the drop-down menu **Assign the following drive letter**.
17. Click the **OK** button to save your changes and click **Yes** to acknowledge the warning.
18. Note that the name of DataVol2 is now followed by the name (**X:**) in the Disk Management console.

19. Right-click the free space on Disk 0 and select **New Simple Volume** from the pop-up menu. Click **Next** and enter a volume size of **100 MB**, then click **Next** again to set the size of the new volume.

20. In the Assign Drive Letter or Path window, click **Mount in the following empty NTFS folder.**

21. Click the **Browse** button next to the empty folder name box.

22. In the Browse for Drive Path window that opens, click the drive icon labeled **X:** and click the **New Folder** button.

23. Replace the **New Folder** text in the new folder name with the name **Overflow**.

24. Click the **OK** button to save the change.

25. Note that the path listed for the mount point folder is now **X:\Overflow**. Click **Next**.

26. Change the file system selected to format the drive from NTFS to **FAT32**. Change the volume label from "New Volume" to **DataVol3**. Click **Next** and then click the **Finish** button to create the volume. Notice that support for lowercase volume names is not available when a volume, such as DATAVOL3, is formatted with a FAT based file system.

27. Click the Start button and click **Computer.**

28. In the left pane, double-click **DataVol2 (X:).**

29. Right-click an empty area in the right pane, point to **View**, and click **Medium Icons.**

30. Note the icon used to identify the **Overflow** folder. This icon represents a mount point. However, applications access it exactly like a normal folder.

31. Right-click an empty area in the right pane, point to **New**, click **Folder**, type **Just Empty**, and press **Enter.**

32. Note the difference in the appearance of the **Overflow** and **Just Empty** folder icons.

33. Right-click an empty area in the right pane, point to **View**, and click **Details.**

34. Note the difference in the size of the **Overflow** and **Just Empty** folders.

35. Double-click the **Overflow** folder to open it.

36. Right-click an empty area in the right pane, point to **New**, click **Text Document**, type **Testing**, and press **Enter.**

37. Right-click an empty area in the right pane and click **Properties.**

38. Note that the Overflow Properties window opens and that the General tab is displayed. Note that the **Type** is listed as **Mounted Volume** and that the **Target** is **DATAVOL3.**

39. Close the **Overflow Properties** window.

40. Click **Start** and type in **cmd** in the search programs and files field and press **Enter** to open a command window.

41. In the command window, at the prompt type the command **X:** and press Enter to switch the focus to drive X:. Enter the command **dir** and press **Enter**. Note that the folder "Overflow" is listed as a junction point and the folder "Just empty" is listed as a simple directory.

42. Go to the Disk Management console again.

43. Right-click **DATAVOL3** and click **Change Drive Letter and Paths** in the pop-up menu.

44. In the Change Drive Letter and Paths for **DATAVOL3** window, click **DataVol2 (X:) \ Overflow**, and click the **Remove** button.

45. A warning message will appear stating that users will no longer be able to access this partition through the existing mount point. Click the **Yes** button to proceed.

46. Switch to the Computer browser window and click **DataVol2 (X:)** in the left pane. Note that the appearance of the **Overflow** and **Just Empty** folder icons is now the same in the Computer browser window.

47. Right-click the **Overflow** folder and click **Properties** in the pop-up menu.

48. Note that the Overflow Properties window opens and that the General tab is displayed. Note that the **Type** is listed as **File Folder** and that the **Location** for the folder is **X:**.

49. Switch to the command window currently displaying the X:\> prompt. Enter the command **dir** and press **Enter**. Note that both folders are now listed as simple folders.

50. Close all open dialog boxes and windows.

Symbolic Links Windows Vista introduced support for symbolic links with its version of NTFS. Windows 7's implementation of NTFS continues to support symbolic links. Symbolic links were originally added to support UNIX-based POSIX applications that are redesigned to run under Windows. Symbolic links are not restricted to that use alone. By default, only Administrators can create symbolic links using the command line utility **mklink**.

A symbolic link is stored in the directory of a folder as a file system object. The purpose of a symbolic link is to point to a file or folder located somewhere other than that folder. To applications and the user, the linked file or folder appears to be located in the folder that contains the symbolic link.

This is different from a shortcut because a shortcut is a file that defines how Windows Explorer can locate content somewhere else. To other applications, the shortcut appears as just another file with a **.lnk** extension. Symbolic links appear as a file or folder with a given name that may be different or the same as the target. The majority of applications would be "oblivious" to the fact that the file or folder being accessed is located somewhere else.

A symbolic link can point to a file or folder on the local computer or to a remote location identified with a UNC path. If the target is remote, then the other computer hosting the target must also support symbolic links. There are two special types of symbolic links known as hard links and junction points.

Windows 7's support for symbolic links includes a special type of symbolic link called a hard link. A hard link can only point to a file on the same partition or volume as the hard link object. Hard links cannot be used with folders.

A regular symbolic link points to the directory or directory entry of a target in its target location. A hard link is a duplicate directory entry that points to the *contents* of a target file. When a user or application accesses a hard link, they believe the file content exists in the folder holding the hard link.

Multiple hard links can point to the same target file. If the hard link's target file is deleted from the target's original location, the content can still be accessed through any hard link that still points to the content. The file's content is preserved until the original file and all hard links that point to it are deleted.

A junction point is a special type of symbolic link that points to folders only. The path to the target folder must be specified using an absolute path. The absolute path points to a target that can be located without needing to know the location of the original junction point object. Volume mount points are an example of how Windows 7 can use junction points. Junction points are also used by Windows 7 to organize content in user profile folders.

A general purpose symbolic link can use a relative or absolute path to point at a target. A relative path defines how to find the target given the current location of the symbolic link object. The symbolic link may be broken if the symbolic link or target move. In that case, it can be corrected by restoring the relative locations of the symbolic link and its target. For the symbolic link to work, it does not necessarily have to go back to its starting locations, only its position relative to each other.

When a target is deleted, a general purpose symbolic link will still exist but fail to find its target. If another file or folder with the same name is created in the correct target location, the symbolic link will work again but point to the new content.

One common mistake made with symbolic links is the failure to consider how many unique files must have symbolic links created for an application to work. An administrator might create a symbolic link to a single executable file but forget to create similar links to related application files. When the user attempts to run the executable in its linked location he or she receives an error and the program fails to run. It is not the symbolic links that have failed but rather the design of *what to link* that has broken the application. The executable likely cannot find its related application files in the folder or subfolders containing the symbolic link.

A Windows Explorer shortcut defined as an .lnk file includes extra information in its properties to help Windows Explorer start the application so it can find the rest of its application files, symbolic links do not. Consider the use of symbolic links carefully with an application to avoid overcomplicating its implementation.

Symbolic links are commonly used to point to target folders located on another volume or remote location where data can be centralized or preserved. For example, suppose application developers must create a folder and file system on C: to test their new application. Some of those folders may be data folders that take a long time to fill with test data. As part of their testing, the developers must wipe the partition holding C: and reinstall Windows 7. Instead of reloading all their data on the new build of C:, they could use symbolic links instead. The data could be stored on another partition or volume that is not erased when the partition holding C: is. Once Windows 7 is reinstalled, a symbolic link is created on C: that transparently links to the preserved partitions holding test data. Their application would think the data folders actually exist on C: and testing could rapidly resume.

Sparse Files A file can be stored with a special attribute to mark it as a sparse file. Large portions of a sparse file contain bytes with the value of zero. Instead of storing long strings of zeros, the sparse attribute tells NTFS to track the ranges of empty data. The sparse file will then contain nonzero data and a list that identifies where ranges of empty data occur between the nonzero data.

If a sparse file contains 50 MB of nonzero data and 200 MB of zero data, the file size will be just over 50 MB with the sparse attribute set. The same file copied to a FAT partition would require 250 MB of disk space.

When a sparse file is copied over the network, it is copied as its full size. In the example above, the 50 MB sparse file would be transferred as a 250 MB data file. Windows 7 allows some applications, such as backup programs, to directly back up the sparse data in its minimal state.

Universal Disk Format

The Universal Disk Format (UDF) is a file system defined by the Optical Storage Technology Association (OSTA). The OSTA was created to promote the use of recordable optical technologies and products. UDF was developed as a standard to allow file interchange between different operating systems. This makes it ideal for storing files on portable CD-ROM and DVD media. Some manufacturers will use the UDF file system with portable flash memory, but it is formatted at the factory and not by Windows 7.

UDF is an evolving specification and several versions are defined by the OSTA. Windows 95 and Windows NT 4.0 do not support UDF as a file system. Windows 98, Windows 2000, Windows XP, and Windows Server 2003 support UDF versions in a read-only capacity. Windows Vista and Windows 7 support both reading and writing of files to the UDF file system.

CDFS File System

The CD-ROM File System (CDFS) is a legacy file system for read-only CD-ROM media. Windows Vista supports CDFS for compatibility with older CD-ROM media. The CDFS standard closely follows the ISO 9660 standard and was first introduced with Windows 95 and Windows NT 4.0. CDFS is no longer the preferred format for CD media because it is limited by file names, folder depth of its directory structure, and limited support by newer operating systems. UDF is the current preferred file system for CD media.

Extended File Allocation Table

As removable memory devices such as USB memory sticks grow in maximum capacity, the choice of a file system becomes an issue. **Extended File Allocation Table (exFAT)** is a new file system that can be used by the manufacturer for these large portable memory devices. exFAT is supported by Windows 7 and mobile operating systems such as Windows Embedded CE. Support for exFAT can be added to older operating systems such as Windows XP or Windows Vista by downloading and installing an exFAT file system driver update package from Microsoft. If support for exFAT is not present in an operating system the file system will appear as unknown. The exFAT technology is not an open standard; it must be licensed by a memory device manufacturer from Microsoft.

The larger memory device sizes available push the boundries of older file systems. Many removable memory devices use the FAT or FAT32 file system. Many operating systems support and can immediately use these file systems. Of these two, FAT32 has the greatest capacity but is still limited to a maximum volume size of 32 GB and a maximum file size of 4 GB. exFAT is recommended for volume sizes of 512 TB or less but can theoretically support a volume size equivalent to the sum total of a billion blocks sized at 64 TB each.

A robust file system such as NTFS could be used but introduces complexity and conditions that limit what operating systems the device's data is compatible with. This would complicate and limit the use of the manufacturer's device, thereby limiting sales. Manufacturers need a simpler file system that works with the greatest number of operating systems.

Microsoft introduced native support for exFAT with Windows Vista Service Pack 1 and continues to license the technology to memory device manufacturers. As memory device sizes exceed 32 GB, exFAT will likely be the file system the device will be pre-formatted with at the factory. The command **format** *volume* **/FS:exFAT** will format a connected volume with the exFAT file system.

File System Tasks

After a partition of volume is formatted with a file system, few changes to its base configuration are possible. The most common file system changes are changing the assigned drive letter and converting the installed file system.

Changing Drive Letters

Drive letters are used by applications and users as a quick reference to locate files. A **drive letter** points to a partition or volume formatted with a file system.

Once a drive letter has been used to reference a particular group of files, the user and their applications expect the same drive letter to be used when the files are accessed again. In some instances, the drive letter assigned to a partition or volume must change. For example, a new application may be installed that requires a specific drive letter to access data files, perhaps to mirror old settings hard-coded into the application. In another example, a CD-ROM may be using a drive letter on one computer that is different than the CD drive letter on another computer. The user or application may be confused by the drive letter difference.

It is possible to change the drive letter, or assign a new one, to a partition or volume using the Disk Management console.

When a new partition or volume is created, one of the New Simple Volume Wizard's tasks will ask if a drive letter should be assigned (see Figure 5-3). Any unused drive letter can be selected. A single drive letter can only be assigned to one partition or volume.

After a drive letter has been assigned to a volume or partition it can be changed to a different available drive letter, but some applications may become confused. If this happens, the applications will require modifications to update their drive letter expectations.

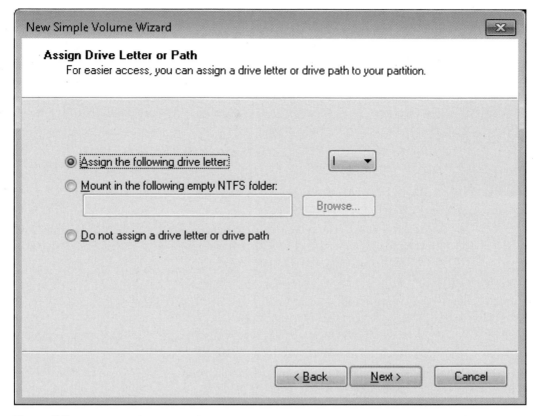

Figure 5-3 Assigning a drive letter during partition creation
Courtesy Course Technology/Cengage Learning

Drive letters can also be removed from a partition or volume. If a drive letter is removed, the files may become inaccessible to the user.

The number of drive letters is limited (that is, A–Z) and some drive letters are reserved for specific purposes. For example, C is reserved for the boot partition.

Converting File Systems

NTFS and FAT file systems can be converted from one form to another. The process to do so depends on the direction of the conversion.

To convert an NTFS file system to FAT, perform the following steps:

1. Back up the data on the partition.
2. Reformat the partition with FAT or FAT32.
3. Restore the data originally backed up from the NTFS partition.

To convert a FAT file system to NTFS, perform these steps:

1. Back up the data on the partition.
2. Ensure free space remains on the partition.
3. Convert the partition using the **convert** command-line utility.

Any file system conversion has a risk of failure. The backup of the original data should be verified as correct and accessible before the conversion begins.

The convert command-line utility has the syntax of **convert *drive_id* /FS:NTFS.**

The *drive_id* is the drive letter, mount point, or volume name used to identify which partition to convert. The command line option **/FS:NTFS** tells the utility to convert the existing file system to NTFS.

For example, the command to convert drive N: to NTFS is **convert N: /FS:NTFS.**

Converting a partition requires that the convert utility runs with full Administrative access to the local computer. If the file system is currently in use, the computer may have to reboot several times to complete the conversion process.

Activity 5-3: Changing Drive Letters and Converting File Systems

Time Required: 10 minutes

Objective: Add, change and remove drive letters assigned to DataVol3 and change its file system from FAT32 to NTFS and back again

Description: In this activity, you have decided that the volume DataVol3 should be accessible to local users as drive Y. You decide to convert the file system from FAT32 to NTFS but then change your mind and want to change it back to FAT32.

1. If necessary, start your computer and log on.

2. Click the **Start** button to open the Start menu.

3. Right-click the **Computer** Start menu item.

4. Click **Manage** in the pop-up menu.

5. If you are prompted by User Account Control for authorization to run this program, click the **Yes** button.

6. In the left-hand console navigation pane, click the **Disk Management** item below Storage to highlight it.

7. In the upper view of the Disk management console, identify **DATAVOL3** and note it is not currently assigned a drive letter.

8. Right-click **DATAVOL3** and click **Change Drive Letter and Paths** in the pop-up menu.

9. In the Change Drive Letter and Paths for DATAVOL3 window, click the **Add** button.

10. In the Change Drive Letter or Path window, click **Y** in the drop-down menu next to **Assign the following drive letter.**

11. Click the **OK** button to save your changes. Note that the file system of drive Y: is currently FAT32.

12. Open the Computer browser window and create a text document in Y:\ called **Memo. txt** that contains a few lines of random text. Close Notepad once the content is created and save your changes to the file.

13. Click **Start** and type in **cmd** in the search programs and files field. Right-click **cmd** in the search results and select **Run as administrator.** When User Account Control prompts your for permission to continue click on **Yes.** Note that a command window has now opened.

14. Enter the command **convert Y: /FS:NTFS** and press **Enter.** Notice that you are prompted for the current volume label for Y:. Enter the name **DATAVOL3** and press **Enter.**

15. When the message **Conversion complete** is displayed, open a Computer browser window and verify that the text file Memo.txt still exists. The contents of the drive have been preserved during the conversion. Switch to the Disk Management console and note that the file system for Y: is now shown as NTFS.

16. To convert **Y:** back to FAT32, the volume must be formatted. Right-click **Y:** in the Disk Management window and select **Format** from the pop-up menu.

17. In the Format Y: window make sure that the file system selected for DATAVOL3 is **FAT32** and click on **OK**. Respond **OK** to the warning that the volume contents will be erased. Note that unlike the convert command, the Memo.txt document stored on Y: will be lost unless it has been backed up somewhere else before the volume is formatted.

18. Close all open windows.

File and Folder Attributes

The FAT and NTFS file systems use attributes to describe general information about a file or folder. To see the general attributes of a file or folder, view the properties of the item in Windows Explorer. The General tab displays basic attributes such as dates and times the item was created, last accessed, and last modified. The General tab also reports the size, location, and control attribute settings.

The details reported for the properties of a file or folder change slightly depending on the type of item, file, or folder, and the file system (FAT or NTFS).

The details on the General tab for a file on a FAT file system include (see Figure 5-4):

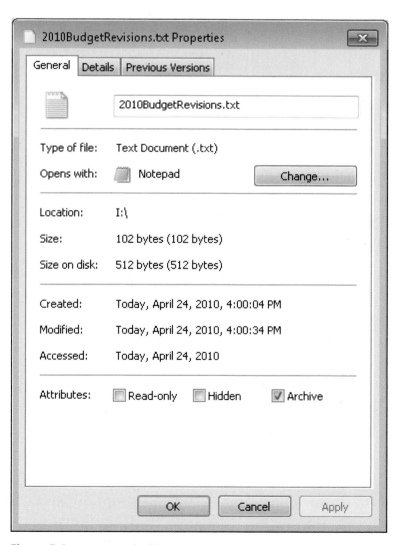

Figure 5-4 Properties of a file on a FAT file system, General tab
Courtesy Course Technology/Cengage Learning

- *Name*—An editable box displaying the name of the file
- *Type of file*—If the file extension is recognized, its type is displayed here, otherwise the extension itself is listed.
- *Description (application files only)*—The description associated with the application
- *Opens with (nonapplication files only)*—Lists of applications used to open the file
- *Change (nonapplication files only)*—Button to change which application is used to open the file
- *Location*—The path to the file
- *Size*—The number of data bytes contained in the file
- *Size on disk*—The disk space used by clusters on disk to store the file's data
- *Created*—Creation date and time of the file
- *Modified*—Modified date and time of the file
- *Accessed*—Last accessed date and time of the file
- *Read-only attribute*—Check box to restrict updates to the file
- *Hidden attribute*—Check box to hide the file from general browsing
- *Archive attribute*—Check box to indicate the file has changed since the last backup

The details on the General tab for a folder on a FAT file system include (see Figure 5-5):

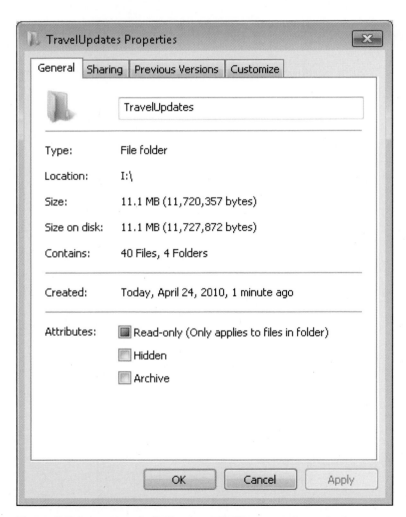

Figure 5-5 Properties of a folder on a FAT file system, General tab
Courtesy Course Technology/Cengage Learning

- *Name*—An editable box displaying the name of the folder
- *Type*—Object type (For example, File folder)
- *Location*—The path to the folder
- *Size*—The number of data bytes contained in the folder, including the files and folders it contains
- *Size on disk*—The disk space used by clusters on disk to store the folder's data
- *Contains*—Counts the number of files and folders contained in the folder
- *Created*—Creation date and time of the folder
- *Read-only attribute*—Check box to restrict updates to the folder, not used
- *Hidden attribute*—Check box to hide the folder from general browsing
- *Archive attribute*—Check box to indicate the folder has changed since the last backup

The details for a file on an NTFS file system include the properties of a file on a FAT file system plus advanced attributes and an additional security tab (see Figure 5-6). The archive attribute is moved to the advanced attributes screen.

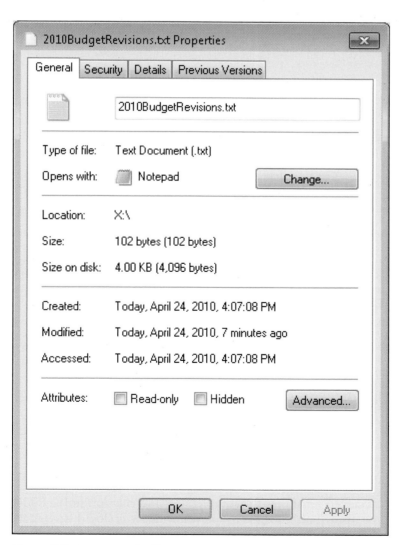

Figure 5-6 Properties of a file on a NTFS file system, General tab
Courtesy Course Technology/Cengage Learning

Advanced attributes for a file on a NTFS file system include (see Figure 5-7):

Figure 5-7 Properties of a file on a NTFS file system, General tab, Advanced Attributes
Courtesy Course Technology/Cengage Learning

- *File is ready for archiving*—Check box to indicate that the file has changed since the last backup.

- *Allow this file to have contents indexed in addition to file properties*—Check box to enable or disable including the file in the indexing process.

- *Compress contents to save disk space*—Check box to enable or disable compression of the folder.

- *Encrypt contents to secure data*—Check box to enable or disable encryption of the file.

- *Details*—Button used to view which accounts are configured to access the file when encrypted

The details for a folder on an NTFS file system include properties of a folder on a FAT file system plus advanced attributes and an additional security tab (see Figure 5-8). The archive attribute is moved to the advanced attributes screen.

Advanced attributes for a folder on an NTFS file system include (see Figure 5-9):

- *Folder is ready for archiving*—Check box to indicate the folder has changed since the last backup.

- *Allow files in this folder to have contents indexed in addition to file properties*—Check box to enable or disable including the folder and its contents in the indexing process.

- *Compress contents to save disk space*—Check box to enable or disable compression of the folder.

- *Encrypt contents to secure data*—Check box to enable or disable encryption of the file.

- *Details*—Button used to view which accounts are configured to access the file when encrypted

Changes to advanced attributes for compression and encryption for folders are only saved after you click the Apply button or the properties window is closed (see Figure 5-9) by clicking the OK button. You are prompted to apply your changes to the folder alone or to the folder and all of its contents (see Figure 5-10).

Changes to the folder alone will apply the setting to all new files created in the folder. Existing files in the folder will keep their original setting.

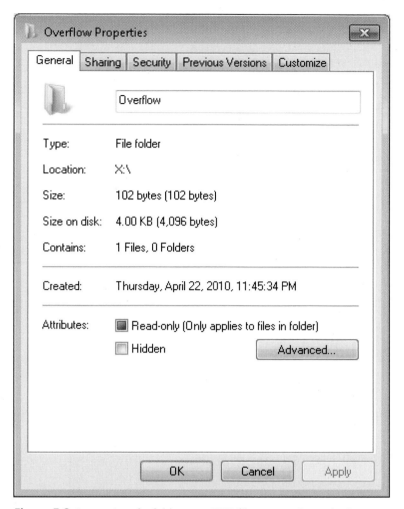

Figure 5-8 Properties of a folder on a NTFS file system, General tab
Courtesy Course Technology/Cengage Learning

Attribute Flags

Each file and folder has its own attribute flags to control some aspects of how the operating system interacts with the object. Most attribute flags can be viewed in Windows Explorer as part of the object's properties. The attrib command-line utility is used to manage the *System* and *Not content indexed* attribute flags which cannot be accessed by using Windows Explorer. The compression and encryption attribute flags cannot be managed by using attrib. The compact command-line utility is used to manage the compress attribute flag and the cipher command-line utility is used to manage the encrypt attribute flag. The main attribute flags are:

- Read only
- Archive
- Hidden
- System
- Compress
- Encrypt

Read Only Files and folders use the read-only attribute flag differently. Files that have the read-only flag set will block changes to the contents of a file.

Folders that have the read-only attribute flag set trigger special behavior in Windows Explorer. Folders are not marked as read only to protect their contents; Windows Explorer largely ignores

Figure 5-9 Properties of a folder on a NTFS file system, General tab, Advanced Attributes
Courtesy Course Technology/Cengage Learning

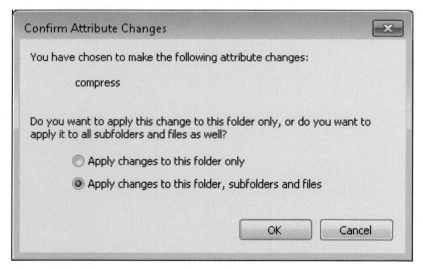

Figure 5-10 Confirm scope of advanced attribute change for a folder
Courtesy Course Technology/Cengage Learning

this setting. Instead the read-only flag is used to indicate that the folder is a system folder and should be treated differently. That is why when viewing the properties of a folder (see Figures 5-5 and 5-8), the read-only setting is blocked out by default.

Archive   The archive attribute flag is set by the operating system when a file or folder changes. This is used as a signal to the user and backup applications that the contents have changed since the last time the file was backed up. The next time the backup runs, the backup program can clear this attribute flag to avoid repeatedly backing up the same file or folder when its contents have not changed.

Hidden   The hidden attribute flag is set by the user or the operating system to hide folders and files from the user. To view hidden files and folders in Windows Explorer, change the Folder View options in Control Panel (see Figure 5-11).

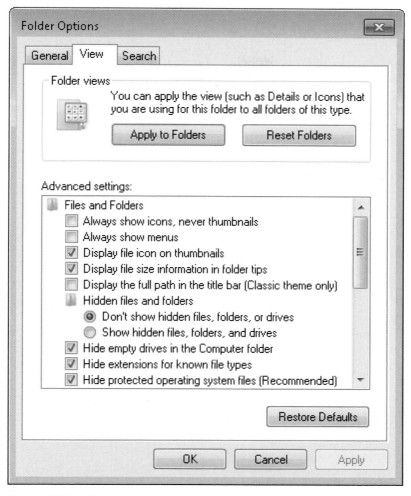

Figure 5-11 Folder view options to view hidden files and folders
Courtesy Course Technology/Cengage Learning

To see all objects in a command prompt window, including hidden files and folders, use the command **dir /a**.

To see only hidden objects in a command prompt window use the command **dir /ah**.

System The system attribute flag is set by the operating system for specific folders and files. The system attribute flag is not exposed through Windows Explorer. The attrib utility must be used to view or change this attribute. A file or folder that has this attribute flag set is typically important to the operation of the computer and hidden from the user.

Compress The compress attribute is only supported on volumes and partitions formatted with the NTFS file system. A folder or file that is set to the compressed state cannot be encrypted. By default, compressed files and folders are displayed in an alternate color in Windows Explorer.

A folder that is set as compressed does not take up less space on the disk. The compress attribute flag for a folder indicates the default setting for new files created in that folder. A file that is set as compressed will immediately become compressed on the disk.

Moving Compressed Files NTFS attributes for a file are stored in NTFS system files within the partition's file system. Each NTFS-formatted partition has its own set of NTFS system files.

When a file is moved from its current location to a new location in the same NTFS partition, its attributes do not change. This means the compress attribute on the file remains the same regardless of what the target folder default setting is set to.

When a file is moved from its current location to a new location in a different NTFS partition, new attributes are created in the destination's NTFS system files. This means the compress attribute on the file becomes the same as the target folder's compress attribute setting.

When a file is moved to a destination folder that does not support compression (formatted with the FAT file system), then the file will be uncompressed.

Copying Compressed Files   When a file is copied, the original file is left in its old location and a new file is created in the target folder. The newly created file will always receive new attributes in the NTFS system files. This means the compress attribute on the file becomes the same as the target folder's compress attribute setting. This is true whether the destination folder is in the same NTFS partition or another NTFS partition.

When a file is copied to a destination folder that does not support compression (formatted with the FAT file system), then the copy of the file will be uncompressed.

Encrypt

The encrypt attribute is only supported on volumes and partitions formatted with the NTFS file system. A folder or file that is set to be encrypted cannot be compressed. By default, encrypted files and folders are displayed in an alternate color in Windows Explorer.

A folder that is set as encrypted is not encrypted itself. The encrypt attribute flag for a folder indicates the default setting for new files created in that folder. A file that is set as encrypted will immediately become encrypted on the disk.

Only users with valid digital security keys can decrypt and access an encrypted file's contents. The Details button of a file or folder's advanced attribute settings (see Figures 5-7 and 5-9) allows users to be granted access to the encrypted file (see Figure 5-12).

If a user is not on the list of users who can access the encrypted file, they will not be able to access the encrypted file's contents, even if they are an Administrator of the computer. The recovery agent is a special user account(s) set by domain policy to allow access to encrypted content in case the local users with access are accidentally deleted.

Figure 5-12 Managing users with access to an encrypted file or folder
Courtesy Course Technology/Cengage Learning

Moving and Copying Encrypted Files Once a file is encrypted it will remain encrypted unless the encrypt attribute is disabled or the file is saved to a destination volume that does not support encrypt.

If an encrypted file is saved to a destination device that does not support encryption, the user will receive a warning message to indicate that the security will be lost (see Figure 5-13).

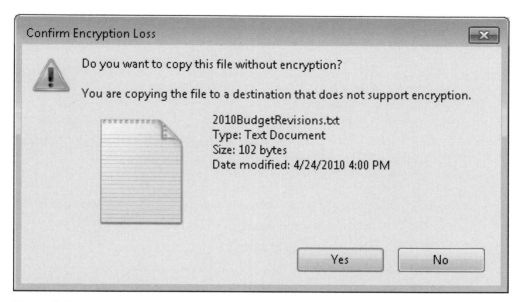

Figure 5-13 Warning that encryption will be lost saving encrypted file to a FAT formatted volume
Courtesy Course Technology/Cengage Learning

Activity 5-4: Managing File and Folder Attributes

Time Required: 30 minutes
Objective: Verify compressions and encryption attribute settings for files and folders that are moved and copied between different partitions.

Description: In this activity, you will format three partitions: DataVol1, DataVol2, and DATAVOL3. DataVol1 and DataVol2 will be formatted with NTFS, DATAVOL3 with FAT32. Various files and folders will be created as part of the exercise and copied or moved to different folders and partitions. You will observe the effect of the move and copy operations on compression and encryption attributes. You will also examine the certificate used to encrypt the files and verify its suitability for this purpose.

1. If necessary, start your computer and log on.
2. Click the **Start** button to open the Start menu.
3. Right-click the **Computer** Start menu item.
4. Click **Manage** in the pop-up menu.
5. If you are prompted by User Account Control for authorization to run this program, click the **Yes** button.
6. In the left-hand console navigation pane, click the **Disk Management** item below Storage to highlight it.
7. In the upper view of the Disk management console, identify **DataVol1**.
8. Right-click **DataVol1** and click **Change Drive Letter and Paths** in the pop-up menu.
9. In the Change Drive Letter and Paths for E: (DataVol1) window, click the **Remove** button. Click **Yes** when warned the change will limit access to the partition.

10. Right-click **DataVol1**, click **Change Drive Letter and Paths,** and click the **Add** button.

11. In the Add Drive Letter or Path window, click **H** in the drop-down menu next to **Assign the following drive letter.**

12. Click the **OK** button to save your changes.

13. Repeat steps 7 to 12 for **DataVol2** but assign DataVol2 drive letter **I.**

14. Repeat steps 10 to 12 for **DATAVOL3** but assign DataVol3 drive letter **J.**

15. Right-click **DataVol1** and click **Format** in the pop-up menu.

16. In the **File system** drop down list, click **NTFS.**

17. Select the check box next to **Perform a quick format.**

18. Click **OK** to continue.

19. Click **OK** to acknowledge the warning. If you are prompted that the partition is currently in use click the **Yes** button to force a format of the volume.

20. Wait for the status of DataVol1 to become **Healthy.**

21. Repeat steps 15 to 20 for **DataVol2.**

22. Repeat steps 15 to 20 for **DATAVOL3** but change step 16 to be **FAT32** instead of NTFS.

23. Click the **Start** button and click **Computer.**

24. In the left pane, click **DataVol1 (H:).**

25. Create a new folder called **Private Documents** in H:\.

26. Open the folder **Private Documents** and create a new text document called **Budget Mistakes.txt.**

27. Double-click **Budget Mistakes.txt,** enter some random text, click the **File** menu, click **Save,** and close Notepad.

28. Right-click the **Budget Mistakes.txt** file and click **Properties** in the pop-up menu.

29. Note that the read-only and hidden attribute flags are clear.

30. Click the **Advanced** button.

31. Note that the File is ready for archiving and Index this file for faster searching attribute flags are set and that the Compress contents to save disk space and Encrypt contents to secure data options are clear.

32. Click Cancel twice to close the Advanced Attributes and Budget Mistakes.txt Properties windows.

33. In the left pane of Windows Explorer, click **DataVol1 (H:).**

34. Right-click the **Private Documents** folder and click **Properties** in the pop-up menu.

35. Note that the Read-only attribute flag is blocked out and the hidden flag is clear.

36. Click the **Advanced** button.

37. Note that the options **Compress contents to save disk space** and **Encrypt contents to secure data** are clear.

38. Select the check box next to **Encrypt contents to secure data.**

39. Select the check box next to **Compress contents to save disk space.** Note that the check box next to **Encrypt contents to secure data** automatically clears.

40. Click **OK** to close the Advanced Attributes window.

41. Click **OK** to close the Private Documents Properties window.

42. Select **OK** to apply the changes to this folder and its contents.

43. Note that the name of the folder changes color to light blue in the Windows Explorer window. The new color identifies the folder as a compressed folder.

44. Double-click the **Private Documents** folder and note that the Budget Mistakes.txt file name is also a light blue color.

45. Right-click **Budget Mistakes.txt**, click **Properties**, and click the **Advanced** button. Notice that this file is compressed.

46. Click **Cancel** twice to close the Advanced Attributes and Budget Mistakes.txt Properties windows.

47. In the left pane of Windows Explorer, click **DataVol1 (H:)** and create a new folder in H:\ called **Public Documents**. Note that the new folder name is the standard color of black.

48. Create a new text document in the Public Documents folder called **Holiday Schedule.txt**.

49. Double-click **Holiday Schedule.txt**, enter some random text, click the **File** menu, click **Save**, and close Notepad.

50. Note that the **Holiday Schedule.txt** file is currently uncompressed.

51. Right-click the **Holiday Schedule.txt** file and click **Cut** in the pop-up menu.

52. In the left pane, click **Private Documents**, and then paste the **Holiday Schedule.txt** file into it. Note that because the file was moved within the same NTFS volume, it retained its original uncompressed state.

53. Create a new file in the folder **H:\Private Documents** called **Budget Ideas.txt**. Note that the new file has taken on the folder's compression attribute and is also compressed.

54. In the left pane, click **DataVol2 (I:)**.

55. Create a new folder called **Compressed Documents** in I:\.

56. Create a new folder called **UnCompressed Documents** in I:\.

57. Right-click **Compressed Documents**, click **Properties**, click the **Advanced** button, select **Compress contents to save disk space**, and click **OK** twice to save the changes.

58. Copy the file **H:\Private Documents\Budget Ideas.txt** to **I:\Compressed Documents**.

59. Notice that the copy of **Budget Ideas.txt** in **I:\Compressed Documents** remains compressed because it has taken on the destination folder's compression attribute.

60. Copy the file **H:\Private Documents\Budget Ideas.txt** to **I:\UnCompressed Documents**.

61. Note that the copy of **Budget Ideas.txt** in **I:\UnCompressed Documents** is uncompressed because it has taken on the destination folder's compression attribute.

62. In the left pane of Windows Explorer, click **DataVol3 (J:)**.

63. Create a new folder called **FAT Documents** in J:\.

64. Copy the file **H:\Private Documents\Budget Ideas.txt** to **J:\FAT Documents**. Note that the copy of **Budget ideas.txt** in **J:\FAT Documents** is uncompressed because files on FAT formatted partitions cannot be compressed.

65. In the left pane of Windows Explorer, click **Private Documents**.

66. Right-click **Budget Mistakes.txt**, click **Properties**, click the **Advanced** button, and select **Encrypt contents to secure data**.

67. Click **OK** to close the Advanced Attributes window.

68. Click **OK** to close the Budget Mistakes.txt Properties window.

69. In the Encryption Warning window, click the **Encrypt the file only** option and click **OK** to save your changes.

70. Note that the file color changes to light green in the Windows Explorer window. This color indicates that the file is encrypted.

71. Copy the file **H:\Private Documents\Budget Mistakes.txt** to **H:\Public Documents**.

72. Notice that the file retained its encrypted file setting even though the target folder did not have the encryption attribute enabled.

73. Copy the file **H:\Private Documents\Budget Mistakes.txt** to **I:\UnCompressed Documents**.

74. Notice that the file retained its encrypted file setting even though the target folder did not have the encryption attribute enabled.

75. Copy the file **H:\Private Documents\Budget Mistakes.txt** to **J:\FAT Documents**.

76. Notice that you are warned that the encryption of the file will be lost, this is because the destination file system is FAT and does not support all NTFS attributes. Click **Yes** to proceed.

77. In the left pane of Windows Explorer, click **Private Documents**, right-click **Budget Mistakes.txt**, and click **Properties**.

78. Click the **Advanced** button to open the Advanced Attributes window.

79. Click the **Details** button to open the User Access to H:\Private Documents\Budget Mistakes.txt window.

80. Note your user name listed under **Users who can access this file**.

81. Click the **Add** button. This window can be used to select the certificates of additional users who are granted access to this file.

82. Click your user name in the Encrypting File System window and click the **Click here to view certificate properties** link.

83. Notice that the certificate purposes listed on the certificate's **General** tab includes **Allows data on disk to be encrypted**.

84. Close all open windows.

File and Folder Permissions

Every file and folder stored on an NTFS partiton has its own **Access Control List (ACL)**. The ACL is a collection of **Access Control Entries (ACE)** that identify a specific security identifier (that is, who) can perform a given action (that is, what) to a file or folder. The ACL is used to specify what a user or group is allowed to do with the file or folder. Files and folders stored with other file systems such as FAT or FAT32 do not have an ACL. The UDF file system specification supports the concept of an ACL, but it is not implemented in current versions of Windows 7.

NTFS permissions apply security to files and folders that impact any user trying to access the object. This applies equally to local users and network users. If the ACL in a file system has denied access to a file, then access is denied regardless of how the file is being accessed.

Windows 7 applies specific default permissions to folders when a partition is first formatted with the NTFS file system.

Default Folder Permissions

The first level of folder in an NTFS partition is the root folder. The default permissions assigned to this folder on the C: drive are:

- Members of the computer's Administrators group have full control.
- The operating system has full control.
- Members of the computer's Users group have the ability to read and execute programs.
- Authenticated users have the ability to create folders in this folder.
- Authenticated users have the ability to create files and write data in subfolders only.

Users by default cannot create files in the root folder of an NTFS-formatted drive.

To see the permissions for the root folder of an NTFS-formatted volume, view the Security tab of the drive's properties (see Figure 5-14).

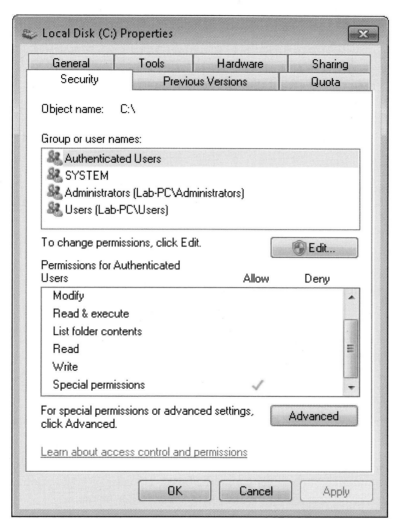

Figure 5-14 Security tab for a drive's properties
Courtesy Course Technology/Cengage Learning

The default permissions assigned to subfolders on the C: drive and the root folder on all other NTFS partitions are:

- Members of the computer's Administrators group have full control.
- The operating system has full control.
- Members of the computer's Users group have the ability to read and execute programs.
- Authenticated users have the ability to create, modify, and delete files and folders in this folder and its subfolders.

As additional folders and files are created, they inherit permissions from the parent object that contains them. Inheritance allows a permission setting to be configured at a higher level in the file system and have it propagate to lower subfolders and files.

NTFS permissions are assigned using two formats:

- NTFS standard permissions
- Individual NTFS permissions

NTFS Standard Permissions

Standard NTFS permissions represent a collection of predetermined individual NTFS permissions. Individual NTFS permissions are discussed later in this chapter. The combination of individual permissions provides a general level of access specific to the type of standard permission assigned. For example, the standard NTFS permission of Modify is a collection of individual NTFS permissions that allows a file to be read, written to, renamed, or deleted. The names of standard NTFS permissions are meant to be intuitive and easy to understand.

The standard NTFS permissions for folders and files are:

- Write
- Read
- List folder contents
- Read & execute
- Modify
- Full control
- Special

Write This permission used for folders allows new files and folders to be created in the current folder. The folder attributes can be changed and the folder's ownership and security can be viewed.

This permission used for files allows file data to be rewritten. The file's attributes can be changed and the file's ownership and security can be viewed.

Read This permission used for folders allows files and folder data, attributes, ownership, and security to be viewed.

This permission used for files allows the file's data, attributes, ownership, and security to be viewed.

List Folder Contents This permission only applies to folders. Without this permission, the files and folders contained in a folder cannot be listed. The user or application can still access the files if they have permission and know the exact file or folder name.

Read & Execute This permission used for folders allows read access to files and folders below this point. This is the equivalent of enabling Read and List Folder Contents.

This permission used for files allows read access to the file's information and, if it is an executable file, the user is allowed to run it. This permission automatically includes the Read permission.

Modify This permission used for folders allows the same actions as Write and Read & Execute permissions combined. The folder can also be deleted.

This permission used for files allows the same actions as Write and Read & Execute permissions combined. Files can also be deleted.

Full Control This permission used for folders allows the same actions as Modify plus the ability to change permissions and allow a user to take ownership of the folder.

This permission used for files allows the same actions as Modify plus the ability to change permissions and allow a user to take ownership of the file.

Ownership of a file or folder is important because the owner automatically receives Full Control permission to their own data.

Special Special permissions are the individual permissions that can be assigned when the predefined standard permissions are not adequate to achieve desired results.

Individual NTFS Permissions

Many individual NTFS permissions exist to fine-tune access and control for files and folders. The list of individual permissions is only visible when editing a permission entry in the advanced security view (see Figure 5-15).

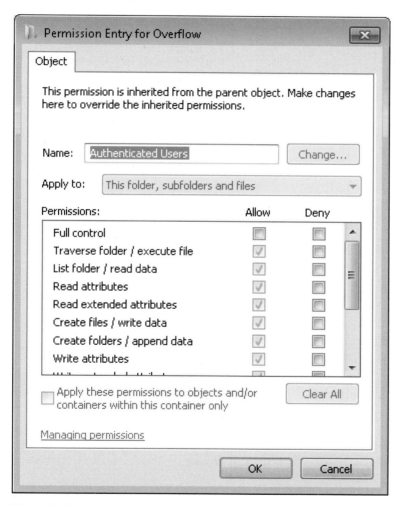

Figure 5-15 Editing a permission entry in the advanced security view
Courtesy Course Technology/Cengage Learning

Individual NTFS permissions are not typically used to apply security to files and folders directly. The name and purpose of the individual permissions is often not intuitive. It is a best practice to use standard NTFS permissions wherever possible. This avoids complex special security settings that are unnecessarily difficult to manage.

Permission Scope

When an NTFS permission setting is applied to a file or folder, it also has a scope assigned. The scope determines what other objects are impacted by the assigned permission.

For files, the scope is limited to **this object only**, which is just the file itself.
For folders, the scope can be set to:

- This folder only

- This folder, subfolders, and files

- This folder and subfolders

- This folder and files

- Subfolders and files only

- Subfolders only

- Files only

The permission scope is visible as Apply To information when viewing the Advanced Security
Settings view (see Figure 5-16) or editing a permission entry in the advanced security view
(see Figure 5-15).

The permission scope must be carefully considered to obtain the desired
effect.

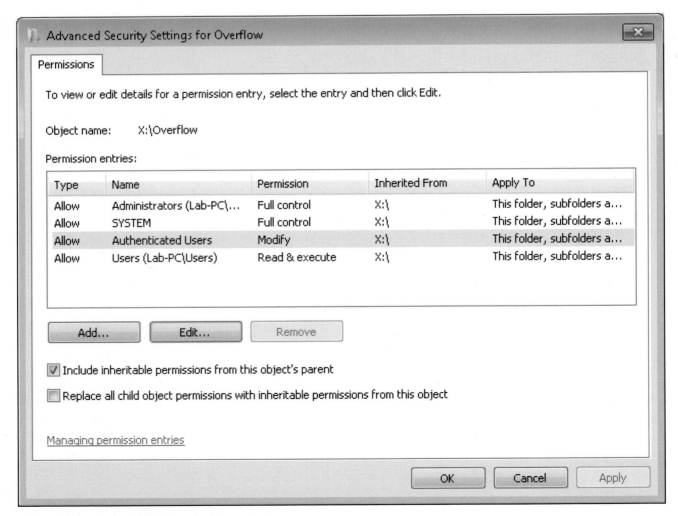

Figure 5-16 Advanced security settings for a folder
Courtesy Course Technology/Cengage Learning

Permission Inheritance

NTFS permissions for folders apply to the first folder on which they are used. The permission then propagates to all folders below that point. When viewing the advanced security settings for a folder, the Inherited From column shows where a permission setting was first applied (see Figure 5-16). Further changes to those permission assignments will automatically propagate through folders and files below that point. Any files created in those folders will inherit permissions from the folder in which they are located.

Inheritance of permissions is convenient but it may not be desired for all situations. Each file or folder has an option called Include inheritable permissions from this object's parent in the Advanced Security Settings view to enable or disable inheritance at that object (see Figure 5-16). The option to inherit permissions from the parent is enabled by default.

Disabling this option will block inheritance at the object. Once inheritance is blocked, the object needs new permissions assigned to it. When inheritance is blocked, a prompt appears asking if the old inherited permissions should be copied to the object or removed entirely. If the permissions are copied, they provide a starting point and can be customized to meet any requirements. If the permissions are removed, new permissions must be configured from scratch.

Any file or folder can have additional permissions assigned directly to the object that combine with the inherited permissions.

Effective Permissions

Permissions on files and folders can be difficult to analyze. Many items have an impact on calculating permissions:

- Permissions can be inherited or directly assigned.
- Each permission has a scope that determines what range of objects it applies to.
- Permissions can be allowed or denied.
- Permissions can be applied to groups, and any member of that group receives those permissions.
- Users can be members in multiple groups that have different permissions to the same object.
- Owners of a file or folder have full control of the object.

To simplify the analysis, the advanced security view for any file or folder includes a tab called Effective Permissions (see Figure 5-17).

A group or user name can be selected for analysis. The window will show which individual NTFS permissions are effective for that group or user for that object. This tool does not show how those effective permissions were obtained; it only shows what they are.

Ownership

Each NTFS file or folder has an owner assigned to it. The owner of a file or folder always has the ability to assign permissions to that file or folder, regardless of what existing permissions are assigned. This ensures that the owner can always assign himself full control permission and modify a file.

The current owner of a file or folder is visible by viewing a file or folder's Advanced Security Settings view and selecting the Owner tab (see Figure 5-18).

Members of the Administrator group have the right, by default, to assign or take ownership of a file or folder. Users with the Full control standard permission or the individual NTFS permission Take ownership can also assume ownership of a file.

Once a user is the owner of a folder or file, they implicitly have full control of the object.

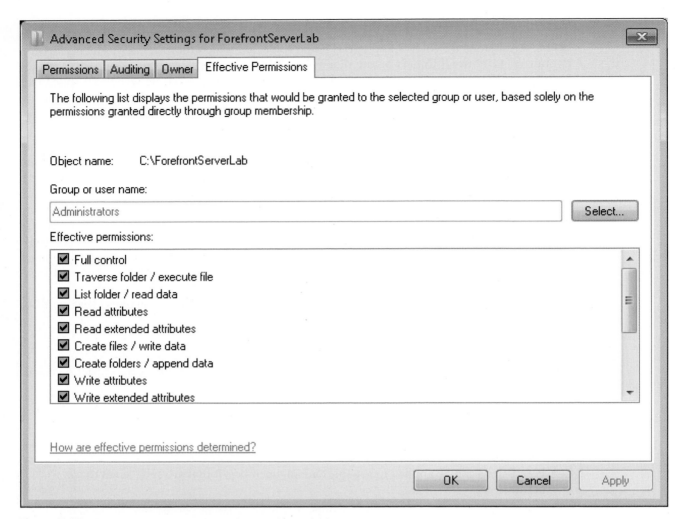

Figure 5-17 Effective Permissions tab in advanced file or folder security view
Courtesy Course Technology/Cengage Learning

Permission Changes When Content Is Copied or Moved

When files and folders are first created in a volume that is NTFS formatted, they inherit the permission settings of the folder in which they are created. Copy operations always create new versions of the content that is being copied. Those new versions will inherit the permission settings of the target location, which may be different than the permission settings of the source content. Move operations affect permissions differently depending on the destination location relative to the source location.

Each single volume or partition formatted with the NTFS file system has its own database to track permissions and attributes for each file and folder it stores. When files and folders are moved from one location on the volume to another location on the same volume, new content is not created; only pointers to the content are moved in the database. In that case, the destination content keeps whatever permissions it originally had, regardless of the destination folder's permissions.

When files and folders are moved from one volume to a different volume formatted with NTFS, new content is created in the destination location. Just like a copy operation, the new content inherits the permission settings of the target location. Any permission settings originally assigned to the source content are lost.

Permission Strategy Considerations

A poorly designed permission strategy can quickly lead to problems such as users having too much access to content, not enough access, inconsistent access to files in the same folder, and confusing differences in access at different levels of a folder structure. When designing a permission strategy for files and folders, there are several best practices to consider.

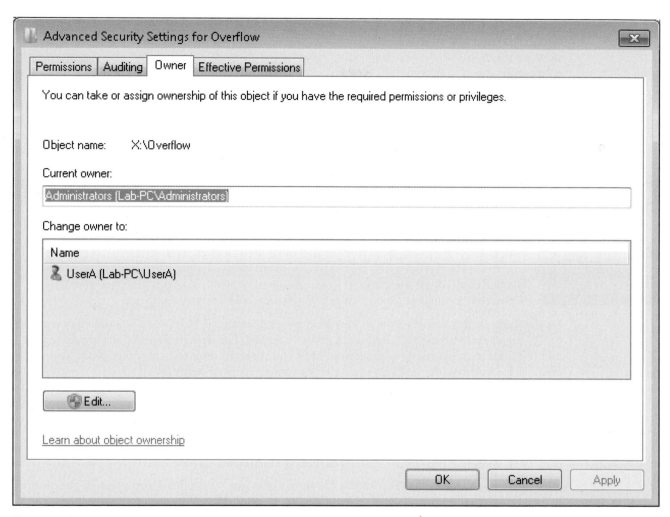

Figure 5-18 Owner tab in advanced file or folder security view
Courtesy Course Technology/Cengage Learning

A folder structure should be designed so that permissions can easily flow down from the top folder to the bottom. The most restrictive permissions are applied at the top of the folder structure; the most permissive permissions are applied toward the bottom. If the most permissive permissions were applied to the top of a folder structure it could require the use of blocking inheritance to restrict permissions lower in the folder structure. This can work but it can be difficult to understand and maintain without good design documentation.

A folder structure should have a specific permission strategy before users are allowed to store files in it. If permissions are applied as an afterthought, the existing organization of files and folders might not lend itself to convenient management concepts such as inheritable permissions.

Specific permissions can be applied to a file or folder for a given user or group of users. Applying permissions based on identifying a specific user can make a permission strategy difficult to manage. If an auditor asks you to explain all the places that you have assigned a user permission to files and folders, you may have to spend a lot of time looking for unique permission assignments.

Strategically placing permissions based on identifying a specific group is easier to document and explain. Each group can grant or deny permission to the file system. Being a member of the group will grant a user those permissions. Reporting the groups that a user belongs to can quickly summarize what files and folders that user is restricted from or has access to.

Exceptions to permissions can be made with specific assignments to files and folders that combine with inheritable and group permissions. Any exceptions should be documented to explain why they exist. Some exceptions to a permission management strategy may be unintentional. For example, this can happen when files are copied or moved without regard to the impact it can have on permissions.

Some exceptions are subtle and may be hard to find. Users may be able to update content in a folder in which they should not have access by design. An administrator would have to consider all mechanisms by which the user receives permissions to access the content, starting by confirming effective permissions to the content itself. A commonly missed consideration is that the user may be the creator of the original content, and thus receive full access to that content as the creator and owner.

Many subtle exceptions are missed because the administrator makes assumptions about what they know instead of confirming actual settings in the file system and the user environment. A simple problem such as a person logging in with a different user ID than expected can frustrate an administrator trying to troubleshoot a user's access to files and folders.

All folder permissions strategies should be tested before users are allowed to access and store files. Unexpected effective permissions may provide unexpected access to sensitive content otherwise.

Activity 5-5: Managing File and Folder Permissions

Time Required: 30 minutes

Objective: Configure a new folder with unique NTFS security settings.

Description: In this activity, you will create a new folder called Marketing Documents on an NTFS-formatted partition created in an earlier exercise. The default permissions are removed and replaced with permissions that allow only your user account to access the folder. You will create a file in the folder and investigate its resulting inherited permissions.

1. If necessary, start your computer and log on.

2. Click the **Start** button and click **Computer**.

3. In the left pane, click **DataVol1 (H:)**.

4. Create a new folder called **Marketing Documents** in H:\.

5. Right-click the **Marketing Documents** folder and click **Properties** in the pop-up menu.

6. Click the **Security** tab.

7. Click the **Advanced** button on the Security tab.

8. Click the **Effective Permissions** tab.

9. Click the **Select** button to open the **Select User or Group** window.

10. Type your user name, click **Check Names** to verify the name, and click **OK** to continue.

11. On the Effective Permissions tab, notice which individual NTFS permissions have a check mark next to them. You have all available permissions because your account is a local administrator.

12. Click the **Owner** tab.

13. Note the current owner of the folder. Your account is the owner of the folder because you created it.

14. Click the **Permissions** tab.

15. Click the **Change Permissions** button to open a new window that allows you to change the folder's permissions.

16. Clear the check box next to **Include inheritable permissions from this object's parent**.

17. In the Windows Security warning dialog, click the **Remove** button to start with blank security settings for the Marketing Documents folder.

18. Click the **Add** button in the Advanced Security Settings for Marketing Documents window to open the **Select User or Group** window.

19. Enter your user name, click **Check Names** to verify the name, and click **OK** to continue.

20. In the Allow column, place a check next to the **Full control** permission. Note that all other individual permissions are automatically assigned and that the permission scope is set to **This folder, subfolder and files**.

21. Click **OK** to continue. Note the new permission entry on the **Permissions** tab in the Advanced Security window. Notice that the **Inherited From** column shows as **<not inherited>** for the directly assigned permission.

22. Click **OK** twice to close both Advanced Security Setting for Marketing Documents windows. Notice the new permission setting and the simpler view on the **Security** tab of the folder's properties.

23. Click **OK** to close the Marketing Documents Properties window.

24. Create a new text document called **First Quarter Report.txt** in the **H:\Marketing Documents** folder.

25. Right-click **First Quarter Report.txt**, click **Properties**, and click the **Security** tab. Notice that the permissions from the Marketing Documents folder are inherited by this file.

26. Click **Cancel** and close **Windows Explorer**.

Previous Versions

Windows 7 includes a Previous Versions tab, shown in Figure 5-19, when viewing the properties of a file or folder. You can use this tab to restore a previous version of a file after it has been modified or deleted. Previous versions of a file on the local computer are generated by a backup or **shadow copies**. Previous versions of a file on a network server are generated only by shadow copies.

Shadow copies are a system in which the computer takes a snapshot of files at a specific point in time, and then tracks changes to those files. If you restore a shadow copy, the file changes are removed and the older version of the file is restored. Be aware that shadow copies cannot replace backups for data security. A shadow copy does not store a complete copy of the file, just changes. If the original file is lost due to data corruption or disk failure, you are not able to restore a shadow copy, but you can restore the file from a backup.

On Windows servers, you can schedule how often shadow copies are taken and the amount of file system space that is allocated for them. In Windows Vista, taking a shadow copy is integrated into the process of creating a restore point. In most cases, a restore point is created automatically each day. However, you can manually trigger the creation of a restore point as well.

Shadow copies are taken only for disks that are protected by System Protection. This is enabled by default for the C: drive, but not other partitions. Only NTFS formatted partitions can be protected by System Protection.

Activity 5-6: Using Previous Versions

Time Required: 10 minutes
Objective: Use Previous Versions to restore a file.

Description: You can use Previous Versions to restore an older version of a file from backup or a shadow copy. This can be useful if a file is accidentally modified and saved. In this activity, you enable shadow copies for a partition and then test the functionality of Previous Versions.

1. If necessary, start your computer and log on. Click the **Start** button and click **Computer**. Copy the **Marketing Documents** folder and all of its contents from H:\ to C:\.

2. Click the **Start** button and click **Control Panel**.

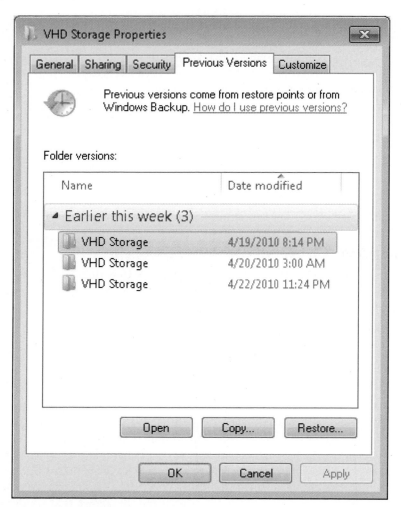

Figure 5-19 Previous Versions tab of a file
Courtesy Course Technology/Cengage Learning

3. Click **System and Security**, and then click **System**.

4. In the Tasks list on the left side of the System window, click **System protection**.

5. In the **Available Drives** area, select **Local Disk (C:) (System)** and then click the **Configure** button.

6. Note the Max Usage reported as a percentage of current disk space. Increase the maximum space available to system protection by moving the slider control to the right until the percentage of disk space is displayed as **15%**.

7. Click the **OK** button to save your changes. Click the **Create** button to create a new restore point immediately.

8. When you are prompted for a description of the restore point, type **Shadow Copy 1** and click **Create**. It will take a few minutes to create the restore point.

9. After the restore point is created, click **Close**.

10. Click **OK** to close the System Properties window.

11. Close the **System** window.

12. If necessary, open Windows Explorer.

13. In the left pane, expand **Local Disk (C:)** and click **Marketing Documents** to display the folder contents.

14. Double-click **First Quarter Report.txt** to open it.

15. Create a new line at the top of the file and type **After Shadow Copy**.

16. Click the **File** menu and click **Save**.

17. Close Notepad.

18. Double-click **First Quarter Report.txt** to open it, verify the text **After Shadow Copy** is present, and close Notepad.

19. Right-click **First Quarter Report.txt** and click **Restore previous versions**. Notice that one version of the file is listed.

20. Click the previous version of **First Quarter Report.txt** to select it and click the **Open** button. This opens the previous version so you can view it without affecting the current version. Notice that the text After Shadow Copy is not present in the file because the shadow copy was taken before you added the text.

21. Close Notepad.

22. Click the **Restore** button.

23. Read the warning and click the **Restore** button.

24. Click **OK** to acknowledge that the file has been successfully restored to the previous version.

25. Note that the list of previous file versions no longer includes an instance of the file because you have already rolled it back. Click **OK** to close the First Quarter Report.txt Properties window.

26. Double-click **First Quarter Report.txt** to open it, verify the text **After Shadow Copy** is not present, and close Notepad.

27. Close all open windows.

Chapter Summary

- The primary file systems used to format bulk storage are FAT, NTFS, and UDF. The NTFS file system is preferred in Windows 7 because it supports advanced features such as security, disk quotas, compression, and encryption that FAT does not. Legacy operating systems in a multiboot configuration and small partitions can still benefit from the legacy support and simplicity of FAT. UDF is a suitable file system for CD/DVD media. For flash memory devices larger than 32 GB the exFAT file system may be suitable.

- Users and applications can use drive letters or mount points to access partitions and volumes. Mount points are features available only with NTFS-formatted volumes. A mount point allows an empty folder in an NTFS partition to link to another volume or partition without changing the drive letter the user is using to access the data. To the user, it appears that the original partition has extra capacity.

- NTFS allows special support for larger partitions, alternate data streams, sparse files, file names with special characters, and transactional reliability.

- NTFS allows the use of file system objects called symbolic links that transparently point to files and folders in other locations. Symbolic links can point to content that is located relative to the symbolic link's location or else at a specific absolute location. A volume mount point is a special type of symbolic link called a junction point. Hard links that point at files are duplicate directory entries that point at the content of a target file. Hard links are limited to point to content on the same volume as the one holding the hard link itself.

- Files stored in FAT and NTFS partitions use attributes to control and limit file access. NTFS supports additional attributes for advanced features such as compression and file encryption. Encryption and compression can not both be enabled for a file. Compression and encryption processing is automatic for file data. Encrypted files are protected even if the local disk is stolen or accessed by starting the computer with a different operating system.

- Given a NTFS formatted source location, a copy operation will create content in a destination location. A move operation will only create content in a destination location when the destination is in a different NTFS volume. Newly created content will take on the permissions of the destination folder they were created in.

- NTFS files and folders are protected by standard permissions. Standard NTFS permissions are made out of more complex individual NTFS permissions. NTFS permissions have a scope applied to limit what type of data they apply to. NTFS permissions are inherited from higher levels to lower levels. If desired, inheritance can be blocked at a file or folder. It is difficult to manually analyze NTFS permissions, so an Effective Permissions tool is available for each file and folder. Owners of a file or folder always have the ability to update permissions on the object they own.

- Permissions strategies should be carefully considered and documented before they are implemented. All permission strategies should be tested before users are allowed to use them. Permissions are best assigned by group membership instead of directly assigning permission to a user. Inherited permissions are best designed with restrictive permissions at the top of a folder structure and less restrictive permissions or exceptions at the bottom. Examining a user's effective permissions should be done by looking at actual settings, not making assumptions given the known permission strategy.

- The Previous Versions tab can be used to restore files from backup or shadow copies. Shadow copies are created as part of a restore point. Only the C: drive is included by default.

Key Terms

8.3 file name   A standard for naming files first introduced with MS-DOS operating systems. The numbers indicate the maximum number of characters that can be used for that part of the name, eight characters and three characters respectively. The period is a separator character between the two names. The three-character field is also known as the file extension.

Access Control Entries (ACE)   A specific entry in a file or folder's ACL that uniquely identifies a user or group by its security identifier and the action it is allowed or denied to take on that file or folder.

Access Control List (ACL)   For those file systems that support ACLs for files and folders, such as NTFS, the ACL is a property of every file and folder in that file system. It holds a collection (that is, list) of ACE items that explicitly defines what actions are allowed to be taken on the file or folder to which it is attached.

Disk quota   A system of tracking owners for file data within an NTFS-formatted partition or volume and the total disk space consumed by each owner. Limits or warning can be established to restrict disk space usage.

Drive letter   A letter of the alphabet assigned to a formatted partition or volume as a reference point for future access by the user or their applications.

Encrypting File System (EFS)   A component of the NTFS file system that is responsible for encrypting individual files. These files are not readable without the correct digital identification.

Extended File Allocation Table (exFAT)   A proprietary Microsoft file system used with external storage media to organize files and folders using a technology similar to FAT but without the space limitations of FAT32. Volume sizes over 32 GB are fully supported.

FAT   A generic term that refers to early versions of the FAT file system (FAT12, FAT16) or to any FAT file system in general, also see File Allocation Table.

File Allocation Table (FAT)   A file system used to organize files and folders in a partition or volume. A master File Allocation Table is used to indicate what files and folders exist within the file system. The FAT table entries point to the beginning cluster used to store a file's data. The first cluster points to the next cluster used to store the next part of the file's data. The file's data is stored in a chain of clusters, with the last cluster marked with an end-of-file identifier. The FAT table stores the name and attributes of the files and folders on the disk, their starting cluster, and which clusters link to the next. The number of addressable clusters determines the size of the FAT table. The limit for how many addressable clusters exist is based on the size of the binary number used to address each cluster. The number of bits used for the cluster address distinguishes the different versions of FAT. The common versions of FAT include FAT16 and FAT32.

File extension   Typically a three-character name at the end of a file name that is used to indicate the type of data contained in the file. Common extension examples include DOC for documents and EXE for executable programs.

Long file names   File names that can be a maximum of 255 characters in length.

New Technology File System (NTFS)   A file system introduced with Windows NT. NTFS supports advanced features to add reliability, security, and flexibility that file systems such as FAT and FAT32 do not have. NTFS is the preferred file system for use with Windows 7.

Shadow copy   A snapshot of the file system that tracks changes to files and allows the restoration of previous file versions.

Terabyte   A unit of data that consists of 1024 gigabytes. Commonly abbreviated as TB.

Review Questions

1. A user would like to secure files stored on a floppy disk. Which file system should they select to format the disk?

    a. NTFS

    b. UDF

    c. FAT

    d. CDFS

2. A hard link can point to a folder on a different computer. True or False?

3. When assigning NTFS permissions, an ACE entry can explicitly define who is denied access to a resource. True or False?

4. A user would like to secure files stored on a hard disk. Which file system should they select to format the disk?

    a. NTFS

    b. UDF

    c. FAT16

    d. FAT32

    e. SECF

5. A user is given Read permission to a file stored on an NTFS-formatted volume. The file is then copied to a folder on the same NTFS-formatted volume where the user has been given Full Control permission for that folder. When the user logs on to the computer holding the file and accesses its new location via a drive letter, what is the user's effective permission to the file?

    a. Read

    b. Full control

    c. No access

    d. Modify

    e. none of the above

6. A user has been granted Full control to an NTFS folder on your computer in which she has created all the documents that exist in it. Another administrator accidentally adds a permission setting denying the Write Permission to her. The next time she logs in, opens the file, and tries to save her changes to it, will she notice?

    a. The changes to the file are written as expected

    b. Access to save the changes is denied

    c. User Access Control will prompt her to allow administrative access

    d. The permissions will automatically update to allow her access

    e. A shadow copy is created

7. A user is given Read permission to a file stored on an NTFS-formatted volume. The file is then moved to a folder on the same NTFS-formatted volume where the user has been given Modify permission to that folder. When the user logs on to the computer holding the file and accesses its new location via a drive letter, what is the user's effective permission to the file?

    a. Read

    b. Full control

    c. No access

    d. Modify

    e. none of the above

8. A user is given Read permission to a file stored on an NTFS-formatted volume. The file is then moved to a different folder on a different NTFS-formatted volume where the user has been given Full Control permission to that folder. When the user logs on to the computer holding the file and accesses its new location via a drive letter, what is the user's effective permission to the file?

    a. Read

    b. Full control

    c. No access

    d. Modify

    e. none of the above

9. A portable flash memory device with 64 GB of storage is attached to a computer through a USB connection. The device allows the user to store music and other media files in its internal memory by presenting it to the user as a hard disk. Which file system would be appropriate when formatting the device?

    a. NTFS

    b. CDFS

    c. WMA

    d. FAT

    e. exFAT

10. A large database file containing 100 MB of data is reported as taking up only 64 MB of disk space. The difference in size is likely due to _____.

    a. compression

    b. encryption

    c. cluster size

    d. file corruption

11. A 40 GB partition can be formatted with which file systems? (Choose all that apply.)

    a. FAT12

    b. FAT16

    c. FAT32

    d. NTFS

12. A 4 GB partition can be formatted with which file systems? (Choose all that apply.)

    a. FAT12

    b. FAT16

    c. FAT32

    d. NTFS

13. A volume formatted with NTFS must be converted to FAT32. To preserve the files it currently contains, you must _____.

    a. do nothing at all, volume conversions do not alter volume contents

    b. run the command **convert** *<drive letter>***/FS:NTFS**

    c. manually trigger a shadow copy

    d. run the command **convert** *<drive letter>***/FS:FAT32**

    e. back up the volume's contents

14. A user is assigned Read permission to the NTFS folder C:\ACCOUNTING. They must not have access to C:\ACCOUNTING\ADMIN. This can be accomplished by _____.

    a. blocking permission inheritance at C:\ACCOUNTING\ADMIN and not assigning the user any permission to C:\ACCOUNTING\ADMIN

    b. blocking permission inheritance at C:\ACCOUNTING and not assigning the user any permission to C:\ACCOUNTING\ADMIN

    c. assigning the user deny Read permission to C:\ACCOUNTING\ADMIN

    d. assigning the user deny Read permission to C:\ACCOUNTING and setting the permission scope to apply to subfolders

    e. not possible

15. When assigning a new NTFS permission what two factors must first be considered? (Select two.)

    a. permission

    b. compression

    c. inheritance

    d. permission scope

    e. ownership

16. A user checks the free space in a folder, Y:\BusReports, and notices that 3 GB of disk space is reported as available. When the user checks free space in Y:\BusReports\Archive, he notices that 5 GB of disk space is reported as available. The difference in available disk space is probably because the folder Y:\BusReports\Archive is _____.

    a. archived

    b. compressed

    c. encrypted

    d. dynamic

    e. mount point

17. A user is assigned Read permission to the NTFS folder C:\ACCOUNTING. They require full access to C:\ACCOUNTING\FORMS. This can be accomplished by _____.

    a. not possible

    b. blocking permission inheritance at C:\ACCOUNTING\FORMS and assigning the user Full control to C:\ACCOUNTING\FORMS

    c. assigning the user Full control to C:\ACCOUNTING

    d. blocking permission inheritance at C:\ACCOUNTING and assigning the user Full control to C:\ACCOUNTING\FORMS

    e. assigning the user Full control to C:\ACCOUNTING\FORMS

18. A user has been granted Read permission to an NTFS folder. It is discovered that they can update a text file in that folder even though they have not been given explicit permission to do so. The reason for the is most likely because _____.

    a. the user cannot update the file

    b. the permission is marked as hidden

    c. the user is the owner of the file

    d. the user is the administrator of the local computer

19. You can reliably use shadow copies to replace a system backup. True or False?

20. A computer running Windows 95 cannot access a UDF-formatted DVD disk. This is because _____.

    a. compatibility mode was not selected during the creation of the DVD

    b. Windows 95 does not support UDF

    c. the disk is corrupt

    d. the UDF file system must first be converted to CDFS

21. A user is given read permission to a file stored on an NTFS-formatted volume. The file is then moved to a different folder on a different NTFS-formatted volume where the user has been given Modify permission for that folder. The file is then moved to a folder on a FAT32-formatted volume. When the user logs on to the computer holding the file and accesses it via a drive letter, what is the user's effective permission to the file?

    a. Read

    b. Change

    c. Full control

    d. Modify

    e. No permissions apply

22. In addition to shadow copies, previous versions of files can be restored from a _____.

23. A file stored on an NTFS-formatted volume is currently compressed. For security reasons, the file is required to be encrypted. The file can be both compressed and encrypted. True or False?

24. A backup program will only back up those files that have recently changed. You do not want a large accounting database to be backed up on the next backup job. What file attribute should you modify?

    a. read only

    b. compress

    c. backup allowed

    d. archive

25. Which of the following are attributes only of NTFS files and folders and not FAT files and folders? (Select all that apply.)

   a. owner

   b. security

   c. compress

   d. encrypt

Case Projects

Case Project 5-1: Selecting a File System and Security Settings

You decide to share the annual report for your company from your computer. You decide that the data will be stored in its own partition, so you create a 20 MB logical partition for the report. If a user logs on to your computer locally, they must have read-only access to the files. What file system would you select for the partition? What security settings would you use to achieve the desired results?

Case Project 5-2: Designing a Shared File System with Security

You are responsible for creating a shared file system to support a new branch office. The manager has requested shared locations for branch staff to access files. An area is required for all staff to access common forms and notices. Staff members are required to have read-only access to this location but the manager will require full access to all content. A different area is required for all staff to share files without restrictions. The last area required is for the manager's private files, and only the manager has access to this location. A second manager will be hired in the next month to share the current manager's duties for job training. Both managers will require the same access throughout the file system. Only the IT administrator should have the ability to change file and folder permission settings for any area. Network permissions are not a concern because they will be configured appropriately based on the NTFS permissions you select. What groups would you create to simplify permission assignment? What folder structure and corresponding file-level permission settings would you use to achieve the desired results?

User Management

After reading this chapter and completing the exercises, you will be able to:

- Describe local user accounts and groups
- Create and manage user accounts
- Manage Profiles
- Describe Windows 7 integration with networks
- Configure and use Parental Controls

User accounts are the most basic level of Windows 7 security. Authenticating as an individual user account is the basis for all other Windows 7 security mechanisms. In this chapter, you learn about local user accounts and groups, including how to create and manage user accounts.

Each user has customized settings, such as desktop and program configuration data, stored in a user profile. Profile management is a key aspect of managing Windows 7. In addition, the creation of user accounts for different network environments is important for efficiently controlling security. Finally, for home users, Parental Controls let you monitor and control computer usage to ensure that all activity for a specific user or group account is age appropriate.

User Accounts

User accounts are required for individuals to log on to Windows 7 and use resources on the computer. Each **user account** has attributes that describe the user and control access. Some user account attributes are:

- Name
- Password
- Group membership
- Profile location

The user accounts created in Windows 7 are **local user accounts**. This means that they exist only on the local computer. Local user accounts cannot be used to access resources on other computers in a workgroup or a domain. For example, if you are accessing a shared folder on the network, a local user account does not have the necessary permissions to access the shared folder.

 Detailed information about how user accounts are used on networks and in domains is covered later in this chapter.

Local user accounts are stored in the **Security Accounts Manager (SAM) database** of Windows 7. Each time a user logs on locally, the SAM database is used to verify logon credentials. However, the SAM database is not used when the user account and Windows 7 computer are part of a domain.

Within the SAM database, each user account is assigned a **Security Identifier (SID)**. Windows 7 uses the SID when assigning permissions to resources. For example, when a user is assigned permissions to access a folder, the SID is written to the folder access control list, not the user account name. Using a SID for security ensures that accounts can be renamed without losing security information. The SID for each user account is unique.

To fully comprehend user accounts, you should understand the following:

- Logon methods
- Naming conventions
- Default user accounts
- Default groups

Logon Methods

Users must log on to Windows 7 before they can access resources and interact with the system. How each user logs on varies depending on how Windows 7 is configured. Windows 7 supports the following configurations:

- *Standalone*—This is a Windows 7 computer without network connectivity. All user accounts are local accounts.

- *Workgroup member*—This is a Windows 7 computer that has network connectivity. Workgroups are logical groupings of Windows computers on the network. All user accounts are local accounts with no synchronization of accounts between computers.

- *Domain client*—This is a Windows 7 computer that has network connectivity and is a member of a domain. Most of the time a user logs on by using a domain user account, but local user accounts are still supported when required.

Windows 7 supports several log-on methods; which method you choose depends on your requirements as network administrator, user needs, and whether the computer is a member of a domain.

The available logon methods are:

- Windows Welcome
- Secure logon
- Fast user switching
- Automatic logon

Windows Welcome Windows Welcome shown in Figure 6-1, is the logon method used by standalone computers and workgroup members, which authenticate users by using the local SAM database. The SAM database typically has only a few user accounts, so the large graphical

Figure 6-1 Windows Welcome logon method
Courtesy Course Technology/Cengage Learning

logon provided by Windows Welcome that displays each local user account is reasonable. In a domain-based environment with hundreds or thousands of accounts, it would not be possible to display an icon for each user account.

On the Windows Welcome screen, each user is represented by an icon and name. The name is the name of the user account. The icon is selected when the user account is created, but can be changed at any time. For home users with children, the icon can be customized to be anything from their favorite cartoon character to their own picture. This makes Windows 7 more usable for small children and more fun for parents.

Secure Logon   **Secure logon** increases security on your computer by forcing you to press Ctrl+Alt+Delete before logging on. This protects your computer from viruses and spyware that may attempt to steal your password.

The key sequence Ctrl+Alt+Delete is filtered by all Windows NT-based operating systems, including Windows 7. The key sequence is then captured by the operating system and not passed to applications. A virus or spyware never see that Ctrl+Alt+Delete are pressed. Therefore, if you press this key combination and a logon window is displayed, it is the legitimate Windows logon window.

When the computer is a domain client, then secure logon is required. When the computer is a standalone or a workgroup member, secure logon can be selected on the Advanced tab of the advanced User Accounts applet, shown in Figure 6-2.

Figure 6-2 Advanced User Accounts applet Advanced tab
Courtesy Course Technology/Cengage Learning

For domain users, this logon method has been modified to remove the domain drop-down list that was present in Windows XP. Users automatically log on to the most recently used domain unless otherwise specified.

Activity 6-1: Implementing Secure Logon

Time Required: 5 minutes
Objective: Implement secure logon for all users.

Description: Secure logon makes Windows 7 more secure by ensuring that no malicious software running in Windows 7 is creating a false logon screen and capturing usernames and passwords. In this activity, you implement secure logon, which forces users to press Ctrl+Alt+Delete before logging on.

1. If necessary, start your computer and log on.
2. Click the **Start** button, type **netplwiz**, and then press **Enter**.
3. Click the **Advanced** tab.
4. Select the **Require users to press Ctrl+Alt+Delete** check box and click **OK**.
5. Log off. Notice that the screen indicates that you must press CTRL+ALT+DELETE to log on.

You can also run control userpasswords2 from a command prompt to access the advanced User Accounts applet.

Fast User Switching Fast user switching allows multiple users to have applications running in the background on a Windows 7 computer at the same time. However, only one user can be actively using the computer at a time. For example, User1 logs on to Windows 7 and starts creating a document in Word. User1 then locks the computer before leaving for lunch with the Word document still open. User2 comes to the computer during lunch, logs on to check e-mail, and then logs out. After lunch, User1 returns, logs in, and continues to compose the Word document. Faster user switching allows this to happen. Without fast user switching, User1 would have been logged off automatically when User2 logged on. Any unsaved work in the Word document would have been lost.

In environments where multiple users share the same computer, fast user switching is a very important feature. It ensures that a second user can log on to a locked computer without logging off the first user and losing their work. This is commonly desired in lab environments and for reception computers.

Windows XP included fast user switching, but only for standalone computers and workgroup members. Windows XP could not perform fast user switching when configured as a domain client. Windows Vista and Windows 7 can perform fast user switching for standalone computers, workgroup members, and domain clients.

Automatic Logon In some environments it is desirable for the computer to automatically log on as a specific user each time it is started. This is appropriate for libraries and other public locations where users are not assigned their own logon credentials. The term kiosk is sometimes used to refer to an environment where automatic logon is desired.

Automatic logon is configured on the Users tab of the User Accounts applet, shown in Figure 6-3. When you deselect the Users must enter a user name and password to use this computer check box and click OK, you are prompted for the credentials to be used for the automatic logon. From this point forward, Windows 7 automatically logs on using the credentials you specified.

Figure 6-3 Advanced User Accounts applet Users tab
Courtesy Course Technology/Cengage Learning

When you need to do system maintenance on a computer with automatic logon enabled, you must stop the automatic logon from occurring. Holding down the Shift key during the boot process stops the automatic logon from occurring. Then you can log on with your own credentials to perform the maintenance tasks.

Naming Conventions

A naming convention is a standard process for creating names on a network or standalone computer. Corporate environments establish a naming convention for user accounts, computers, folders, network shares, printers, and servers. Names should be descriptive enough that anyone can figure out what the resource is. For example, computer names are often the same as their asset tracking number (inventory tracking number) or include the name of the person who uses the computer most often.

Using a naming convention for small networks may seem unnecessary, but even small networks benefit from resources with meaningful names. For example, in a small network with two servers named "Files" and "Email," it is easy to guess what resources are on each server. In another network where the two servers are named "Sleepy" and "Dopey," there is no logical way to know what resources are on each server. If your network grows, you will be happy you implemented a naming convention early in the process.

Some common naming conventions for user logon names are:

- *First name*—In small environments, there is little risk that two users will have the same first name. This approach is easy for users to remember.

- *First name and last initial*—This naming convention helps ensure that user logon names are not duplicated. In small and mid-sized environments, if two users have the same first name, they are unlikely to have the same last initial.

- *First initial and last name*—Most large environments use this naming convention or a variation of it. Last names are more likely to be unique than first names, so this convention reduces the risk of duplicate user logon names.

No matter which naming convention you select, you must have a plan to deal with duplicate user logon names. For example, there may be Byron Wright and Blair Wright in the same organization. If your naming convention is first initial and last name, then both users will have the same user logon name of "bwright." To fix this you could add a numeral to the end of the second user account created, to make the user logon name "bwright2." You could also use two letters of the first name, in which case the user logon names would be "bywright" and "blwright."

When creating new users, you must be aware of the restrictions imposed by Windows 7 on the user logon name, such as the following:

- *User logon names must be unique*—No two users can have the same logon name, because the logon name is used by the computer to identify the user and verify the password associated with it during logon.

- *User logon names must be 20 characters or less*—This restriction is typically not a problem, because no users want to type in a logon name of 20 characters or more.

- *User logon names are not case sensitive*—You cannot change the case of letters to create unique user logon names; Windows 7 will read any case changes as the original name. Also, users do not need to be concerned about case when they type in their user name. However, passwords are case sensitive.

- *User logon names cannot contain invalid characters*—Windows 7 uses some characters for special functions, so they cannot be used in user logon names. The invalid characters are: "/\\[]:;|=,+*?<>.

Default User Accounts

Each Windows 7 computer has an **Administrator account** and a **Guest account** that are created during installation. The Administrator and Guest accounts are called built-in accounts because they are created on every Windows 7 computer. They also have unique characteristics. In addition, a user-specified **initial account** is created during installation. The initial account is not a built-in account.

Administrator The Administrator account is the most powerful local user account possible. This account has unlimited access and unrestricted privileges to every aspect of Windows. The Administrator account can manage all security settings, other users, groups, the operating system, printers, shares, and storage devices. Because of these far-reaching privileges, the Administrator account must be protected from misuse.

The Administrator account has the following characteristics:

- It is not visible on the logon screen.
- It has a blank password by default.
- It cannot be deleted.
- It cannot be locked out due to incorrect logon attempts.
- It cannot be removed from the local administrators group.

- It can be disabled.
- It can be renamed.

To protect the Administrator account from misuse, it is disabled by default in Windows 7. However, the Administrator account is automatically enabled when you enter Safe Mode so that you can use it for troubleshooting. Safe Mode is a boot option you can use when troubleshooting Windows 7.

 Because the Administrator account is available only in Safe Mode, it is typically used only for troubleshooting or as an account of last resort when logging on.

The password for the Administrator account is blank by default. This password should be changed immediately after installation. This prevents users from starting in Safe Mode and logging on as Administrator. If users log on as Administrator, they can perform any system action such as adding software, deleting files, creating a new account with administrative privileges, or increasing the privileges of an existing account.

 Windows 7 restricts accounts with blank passwords to console access only. This means that no one can log on over the network using an account with a blank password, including the Administrator account.

The Administrator account is special because it is considered an account of last resort for logging on and troubleshooting. Therefore, the Administrator account cannot be deleted or locked out after too many incorrect logon attempts. The Administrator account also cannot be removed from the local Administrators group, because the local Administrators group is where the Administrator account derives most of its privileges.

Guest   The Guest account is one of the least privileged user accounts in Windows. This account has extremely limited access to resources and computer activities and is intended for occasional use by low-security users. For example, a company might have a computer in the lobby with Internet access for customers. The customers would log on as a guest. The guest account has no ability to change the computer settings.

The guest account has the following characteristics:

- It cannot be deleted.
- It cannot be locked out.
- It is disabled by default.
- It has a blank password by default.
- It can be renamed.
- It is a member of the Guests group by default.
- It is a member of the Everyone group.

Most organizations have no need for a Guest account. To ensure that the Guest account is not accidentally assigned privileges that are used by anonymous users, the Guest account is disabled by default. This way, even if privileges are assigned to the Guest account by accident, no one can log on as the Guest account and use those privileges.

The Guest account derives all of its privileges from being a member of the Guests group and the Everyone group. Both of these groups have very limited privileges. The Guests group is explicitly created for assigning permissions to Guest users. The Everyone group encompasses all users that have logged on as well as the guest account. Windows security has evolved so that the Everyone group has very limited privileges. Most privileges formerly assigned to the Everyone group are now assigned to the Authenticated Users group. Authenticated Users includes all users that have logged on except for the Guest account.

6

If you enable the Guest account, then the Everyone group includes anonymous users. This allows you to give users access to resources on a computer over the network without requiring a valid username and password.

Initial Account During installation, you are prompted for the information required to create a user. The user created from that information is given administrative privileges. Having administrative privileges means that the initial account created during installation is able to perform all of the same tasks as the Administrator account. The initial account can be used to configure Windows 7, including creating other user accounts.

Differences between the Administrator account and the initial account include the following:

- The initial account is visible on the logon screen.
- The initial account does not have a blank password by default.
- The initial account can be deleted.
- The initial account can be locked out due to incorrect logon attempts.
- The initial account can be removed from the Administrators group.

Despite having the same privileges as the Administrator account, the initial account is treated very differently by Windows 7, which does not protect the initial account in the way that the Administrator account is protected. As a consequence, the initial account is visible on the logon screen, has a password that is configured during installation, can be deleted, can be locked out, and can be removed from the Administrators group. Removing the initial account from the Administrators group reduces the privileges normally assigned to the initial account.

Default Groups

Groups are used to simplify the process of assigning security rights and permissions. When users are members of a group, they have access to all of the resources that the group has been given permissions to access. It is easier to assign permissions to a group and make five users a member of that group than to assign permissions directly to five users, particularly if the permissions change.

Windows has a number of **built-in local groups** that exist by default and cannot be deleted. These groups are assigned rights and permissions to Windows 7. Like local user accounts, local groups are stored in the SAM database and can only be assigned permissions to resources on the local computer.

The Windows 7 built-in groups are:

- *Administrators*—Members of this group have full access to the computer. The local Administrator account is always a member of this group. The initial account created during installation is also a member of this group by default. If the computer has joined a domain, then the Domain Admins group is a member of this group. Making Domain Admins a member of the local Administrators group provides centralized control of domain computers through a single logon.

- *Backup Operators*—Members of this group can back up and restore all files and folders on the computer. However, the ability to read and modify files is still controlled by file system security. Backup operators cannot automatically read and modify files; they must be assigned the necessary file permissions. By default, this group has no members.

- *Cryptographic Operators*—Members of this group are able to perform cryptographic operations. Only members of this group are able to modify encryption settings for IPSec in Windows Firewall when configured in Common Criteria mode. Common Criteria is a standard for security. This was a new group in Windows Vista.

- *Distributed COM Users*—Members of this group are able to run and activate Distributed COM objects on the computer. This group is relevant only when using DCOM applications, which is relatively rare. This was a new group in Windows Vista.

- *Event Log Readers*—Members of this group have the ability to read event logs on the local computer. You can add members to this group if you want them to be able to review the event logs for errors, but not have the ability to erase the logs.

- *Guests*—Members of this group have the same access to the system as members of the Users group. Members are able to log on and save files, but are not able to change system settings or install programs. The exception to this is the Guest account, which has additional restrictions.

- *IIS_IUSRS*—A group used to configure security for Internet Information Services. Only the system account NT AUTHORITY\IUSR is a member by default. The rights and permissions assigned to this group are applied to all IIS users that are not authenticated. This was a new group in Windows Vista and replaces the IIS_WPG group used by IIS 6.0 in Windows XP.

- *Network Configuration Operators*—Members can configure network components and change IP address information. This group is useful if you need to delegate the ability to change IP address configuration to other users, but do not want to give those users full administrative rights. By default, this group has no members.

- *Performance Log Users*—Members of this group are able to monitor performance counters and access performance logs on the computer. This group has no members by default. This was a new group in Windows Vista. In a domain environment, domain users and groups can be added to this group to perform remote monitoring.

- *Performance Monitor Users*—Members of this group are able to monitor performance counters on the computer, but cannot access performance logs. This group has no members by default. This was a new group in Windows Vista. In a domain environment, domain users and groups can be added to this group to perform remote monitoring.

- *Power Users*—Members of this group have almost all administrative permissions. It was common in previous versions of Windows to use this group for all users to ensure that they could make changes to their systems. In Windows 7, this group has been depreciated and Microsoft recommends using it only when necessary to support legacy applications that do not run when a user has lower privileges.

- *Remote Desktop Users*—Members of this group can log on remotely by using Remote Desktop. This group has no members by default.

- *Replicator*—This group is used by special user accounts to perform file replication between computers. This group has no members by default.

- *Users*—Members can operate the computer and save files, but cannot install programs, modify user accounts, share resources, or alter system settings. All user accounts created on the system are a member of this group by default. In addition, the system accounts NT AUTHORITY\Authenticated Users and NT AUTHORITY\INTERACTIVE are members of the group. In a domain environment, the Domain Users group is also a member.

Creating Users

Creating a user can be done from Control Panel, the **Local Users and Groups MMC snap-in**, or the **advanced User Accounts applet**. The process varies depending on which tool is used, but ultimately the same options are available in each tool. This section focuses on creating accounts from Control Panel.

User accounts can also be created by using the NET USER command at a command prompt. However, this is rarely done. For more information open a command prompt and type NET USER /?.

When an account is created from Control Panel, you are asked for very little information. As shown in Figure 6-4, you must enter in an account name and select the type of user account. The account name is typically the name of the person who is going to use the account. The type of user account is typically standard user rather than administrator.

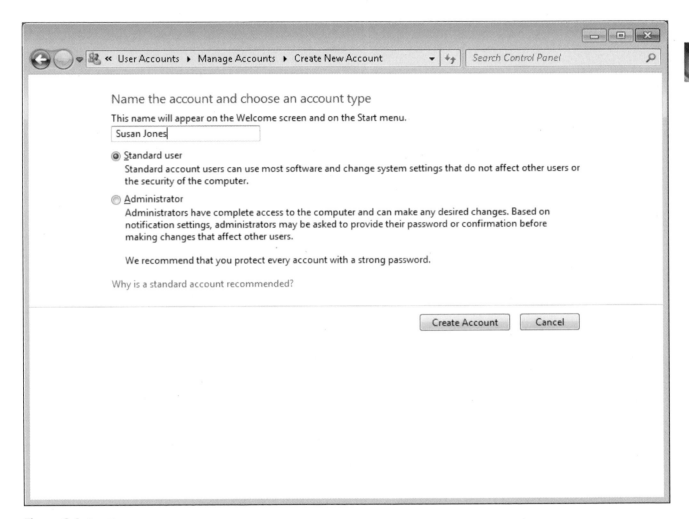

Figure 6-4 Creating a user
Courtesy Course Technology/Cengage Learning

A **standard user account** derives its privileges from being a member of the local Users group. As a member of the local Users group, a user account can use software, but not install or remove software. A standard user also is not able to change computer settings that affect other users or delete operating system files. Effectively, a standard user cannot compromise the security or stability of Windows 7.

Some older software requires administrative rights to run properly. In this case, User Account Control prompts the user for the password of a user with administrative rights. To avoid being prompted, you may want to make the user an administrative user.

An **administrator account** derives its privileges from being a member of the local Administrators group. Administrator accounts have complete access to the system. An administrator can make changes that compromise the stability and security of Windows 7, such as installing software, changing file system security, and updating device drivers.

In Windows Vista, each time an administrator performs a task that requires administrative privileges, the user is prompted to allow the action. Many administrators found this intrusive. In Windows 7, most actions that are triggered by an Administrator do not result in a prompt from User Account Control. However, changes triggered by software do result in a prompt from User Account Control. This ensures that changes are not made by malicious software.

User Accounts Applet

The **User Accounts applet** in Control Panel is a simplified interface for user management. When you access User Accounts, as shown in Figure 6-5, you are shown options to configure your own account. Users can perform basic administration for their accounts using this interface.

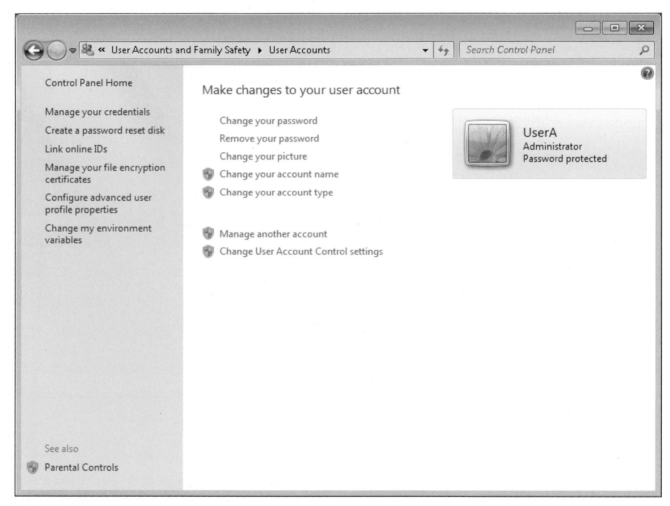

Figure 6-5 User Accounts applet
Courtesy Course Technology/Cengage Learning

The administrative options with a shield beside them are restricted to administrative users. If a standard user tries to perform these tasks, the user is prompted to provide the credentials of an administrator account.

Administrative options for user accounts include the following:

- *Change your password*—Allows users to change their own password.
- *Remove your password*—Allows users to set their password to blank.
- *Change your picture*—Allows users to change the icon that is used to represent their account on the Windows Welcome screen. The picture can be any size and will be shrunk down to the appropriate size automatically by Windows 7.
- *Change your account name*—Allows administrators to change the account name of a user.
- *Change your account type*—Allows administrators to change the user account from one type of account to another. For example, you can change a standard user to an administrative user.
- *Manage another account*—Allows administrators to select a different account to manage.
- *Change User Account Control setting*—Allows administrators to modify when prompts from User Account Control (UAC) are presented.

Additional available tasks include:

- *Manage your credentials*—This option opens the window for configuring Credential Manager. Credential Manager allows users to add, remove, and edit network locations with stored credentials. Network locations can include Web sites, FTP sites, and servers. Storing credentials avoids having to type in the credentials each time a resource is accessed. If your password for the resource changes, you need to edit the network location to change the password. In domain-based networks, this is not required to access domain resources.
- *Create a password reset disk*—This option creates a password reset disk. If a user forgets their password, the disk allows them to reset their password to a new password. Once created, a password reset disk does not need to be updated when the user password is changed. In addition to storing password reset information on a floppy disk (A:), you can also store the password reset information on a USB drive.
- *Link online IDs*—This option allows you to configure an online account, such as a Windows Live account, as a security credential that can be used for accessing information in a homegroup or logging on to your computer. To link an online ID with Windows 7, the provider of the online ID must make a provider available. You need to download and install the provider in Windows 7.
- *Manage your file encryption certificates*—This option allows users to manage the certificates used to support Encrypting File System (EFS). EFS encrypts specific files that are stored on the hard drive. Within this wizard, you can select or create a file encryption certificate, back up the certificate, configure EFS to use a smart card, and update a previously encrypted file to a new certificate.
- *Configure advanced user profile properties*—Opens the dialog box that allows you to manage user profiles. For example, you can configure a roaming user profile. This option is seldom used.
- *Change my environment variables*—Allows you to configure the environment variables for your computer that define characteristics such as the location of temporary files. This option is seldom used.

Activity 6-2: Using the User Accounts Applet

Time Required: 10 minutes
Objective: Create a local user account by using the User Accounts applet in Control Panel.

Description: Local user accounts are required to log on to Windows 7. The User Accounts applet in Control Panel provides a simplified interface for creating and managing user accounts. In this activity, you create a new user account and configure a password for the account.

1. If necessary, start your computer and log on.
2. Click the **Start** button, and click **Control Panel**.
3. Click **User Accounts and Family Safety,** and then click **User Accounts**.
4. Click **Manage another account,** and then click **Create a new account.**
5. In the **New account name** box, type **Susan Jones.** Notice that Standard user is the default account type.
6. Click **Create Account.**
7. Click **Susan Jones.**
8. Click **Create a password.** Notice that a password was not required by default.
9. In the New password and Confirm new password boxes, type **password.**
10. Click **Create password.**
11. Take note of the picture currently used for this account and click **Change the picture.**
12. Click a picture that is different from the current one and click **Change Picture.**
13. Close the Change an Account window.
14. Switch user to **Susan Jones.**
    a. Click the **Start** button, click the right arrow beside the lock icon, and click **Switch user.**
    b. Press **Ctrl+Alt+Delete.** Notice that Userx is still logged on.
    c. Click **Susan Jones,** type **password** as the password, and press **Enter.** Wait while the new profile is created. Susan can now begin using this computer.
15. Log off as **Susan Jones.**

Local Users and Groups MMC Snap-In

The Local Users and Groups MMC snap-in allows you to create and manage both user accounts and groups. The fastest way to access this snap-in is through the Computer Management Administrative Tool. The Users node contains all of the users and the Groups node contains all of the groups, as shown in Figure 6-6.

The general user tasks you can perform are:

- Create a new user
- Delete a user
- Rename a user
- Set a user password

 When you reset a user password instead of letting a user change their own password, the user's access to encrypted files is lost. A password reset disk is the preferred method to reset a forgotten password. This is **NOTE** not a concern for domain user accounts, as the EFS certificates for domain user accounts are managed differently.

Other user options can be configured in the properties of the user account. The General tab, shown in Figure 6-7, lets you view and configure the following:

- *Account name*—This information is displayed at the top of the tab but cannot be changed on this tab. To change the account name, you must right-click the user account and select Rename.
- *Full name*—The full name of the person using the account. This can be changed.

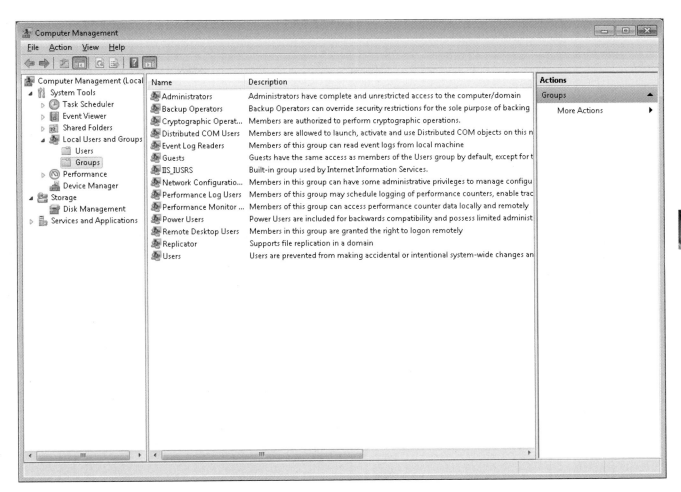

Figure 6-6 Local Users and Groups MMC snap-in
Courtesy Course Technology/Cengage Learning

- *Description*—An optional text box that can be used to describe the purpose or use of the account.

- *User must change password at next logon*—This option forces a user to change his or her password the next time he or she logs on. Forcing a password change is common in corporate environments after a temporary password has been assigned.

- *User cannot change password*—This option prevents a user from changing his or her password. Preventing a password change is often done for user accounts that are used as credentials for multiple services, such as scheduling system maintenance tasks. A password change would need to be updated on all services, and this ensures that it does not happen accidentally.

- *Password never expires*—This option exempts the user from the account policy that defines the maximum lifetime of a password. Preventing password expiry is useful for accounts that are used as credentials for services, such as scheduled tasks.

- *Account is disabled*—This option locks the account to prevent anyone from logging on and using the account. However, the account is retained and can be enabled again at any time. Disabling an account is often done when a user is away for an extended period of time. Disabling an account is also often done as an intermediary step before the account is deleted when a user leaves the organization.

- *Account is locked out*—This option is selected when an account is locked out because of too many incorrect logon attempts. When an account is locked, no one can log on by using the account. To unlock the account and allow the user to log on again, deselect this option.

UserA Properties

General | Member Of | Profile

UserA

Full name: [   ]

Description: [   ]

☐ User must change password at next logon
☐ User cannot change password
☑ Password never expires
☐ Account is disabled
☐ Account is locked out

[OK] [Cancel] [Apply] [Help]

Figure 6-7 User Properties General tab
Courtesy Course Technology/Cengage Learning

The Member Of tab, shown in Figure 6-8, lists the groups of which the user account is a member. Any rights and permissions assigned to these groups are also given to the user account. You can add and remove the user account from groups on this tab. Be aware that changes in group membership do not take effect until the user has logged out and logged on again. This is because the security token which contains group memberships and is used to access resources is generated during log on.

The Profile tab, shown in Figure 6-9, is typically not used on standalone computers or workgroup members. It is most often used in corporate environments for domain-level accounts. However, it can be used for standalone computers or workgroup members. In a workgroup, network paths can be specified to centrally store information on another computer in the workgroup.

The profile path specifies the location of the profile for this user. By default, profiles are stored in C:\Users\%USERNAME%, where %USERNAME% is a variable representing the name of the user account. If you specify a network location for the profile, then the profile becomes a roaming user profile.

Detailed information about user profiles is provided later in this chapter.

Figure 6-8 User Properties Member Of tab
Courtesy Course Technology/Cengage Learning

The logon script box defines a script that is run each time during log on. This script can be located on the local computer or another workgroup member. The logon script is typically a batch (.bat) file or VBScript (.vbs) file that is used to configure the computer with mapped drive letters for accessing network shares.

The home folder defines a default location for saving files. If a network location is used as a home folder, then a mapped drive letter is created that points to the network location. The default location for saving files is defined by the application being used. Some applications use the home folder, while others use the My Documents folder. If you do not define a home folder, it resolves to the users profile folder, for example, C:\Users\User1.

When you view the properties of a group, there is only a single tab, as shown in Figure 6-10. The General tab provides a description of the group and a list of the group members. You can add and remove users from the group here.

Activity 6-3: Using the Local Users and Groups MMC Snap-In

Time Required: 10 minutes

Objective: Manage users and groups by using the Local Users and Groups MMC snap-in.

Description: The Local Users and Groups MMC snap-in is the only management tool for creating and managing groups. It is also capable of creating and managing users. The user management options in the Local Users and Groups MMC snap-in are more detailed than in the User Accounts applet. In this activity, you create a new user, create a new group, and place the new user in the new group.

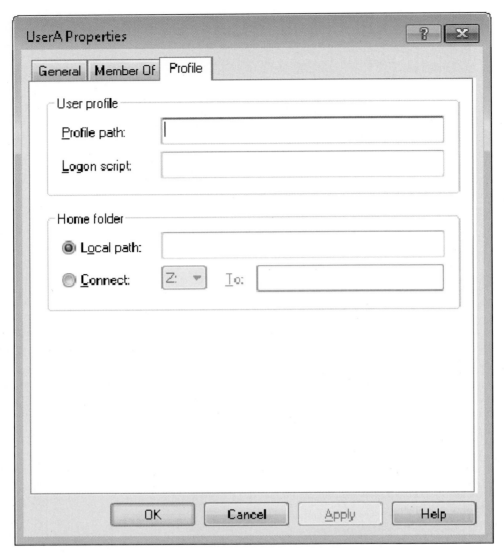

Figure 6-9 User Properties Profile tab
Courtesy Course Technology/Cengage Learning

1. If necessary, start your computer and log on.

2. Click the **Start** button, right-click **Computer**, and click **Manage**.

3. In the left pane, expand **Local Users and Groups**, and click **Users**. Notice the users that are listed here: Administrator, Bob, Guest, Susan Jones, and User**x**.

4. Right-click **Users**, and then click **New User**.

5. In the User name box, type **Jacob Smith**.

6. In the Full name box, type **Jacob Smith**.

7. In the Password and Confirm password boxes, type **password**. Notice that, by default, the User must change password at next logon check box is selected.

8. Click **Create**, and then click **Close**.

9. In the left pane, click **Groups**. Notice all of the built-in groups that exist by default.

10. Right-click **Groups** and then click **New Group**.

11. In the Group name box, type **TestGroup**.

12. Click the **Add** button.

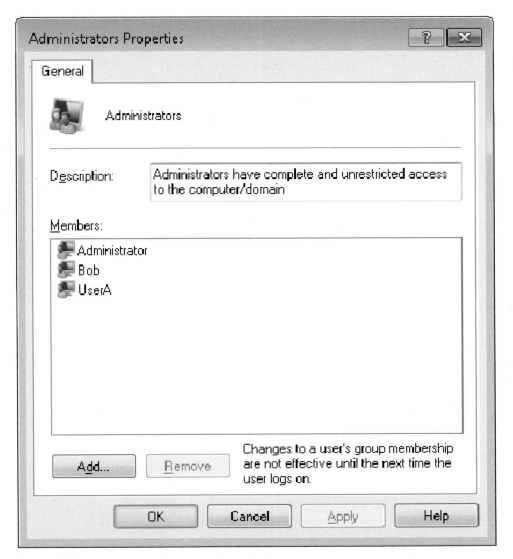

Figure 6-10 Administrators Properties General tab
Courtesy Course Technology/Cengage Learning

13. In the Enter the object names to select box, type **Jacob Smith**, click **Check Names**, and click **OK**.

14. Click **Create**, and then click **Close**.

15. In the left pane, click **Users**.

16. Right-click **Jacob Smith**, and then click **Properties**.

17. Click the **Member Of** tab. Notice that Jacob is a member of TestGroup and Users.

18. Click **Cancel** and close Computer Management.

19. Switch user to **Jacob Smith**. Notice that you are given a message indicating that the password must be changed.

20. Click **OK**.

21. In the New password and Confirm password boxes, type **password2**, and then press **Enter**.

22. Click **OK** and wait for the new profile to be created.

23. Log off as Jacob.

Advanced User Accounts Applet

Windows 7 has an advanced User Accounts applet that is available only by starting it from the command line. This User Accounts applet has some options that are not available in the User Accounts applet in Control Panel or the Local Users and Groups MMC snap-in.

To start the advanced User Accounts applet from a command line, use the netplwiz command.

The Users tab, shown in Figure 6-11, allows you to:

Figure 6-11 Advanced User Accounts applet Users tab
Courtesy Course Technology/Cengage Learning

- Configure automatic logon
- Add or remove users
- Edit user properties
- Reset user passwords

The Advanced tab allows you to:

- *Manage stored passwords on the computer*—This opens Credential Manager.
- *Perform advanced user management*—This opens the Local Users and Groups MMC snap-in.
- *Enable secure logon*—This forces users to press Ctrl+Alt+Del before logging on.

Managing Profiles

A user profile is a collection of desktop and environment configurations for a specific user or group of users. By default, each user has a separate profile stored in C:\Users.

A profile contains the following folders and information:

- *AppData*—A hidden folder containing user-specific information for applications, such as configuration settings.

- *Application Data*—A hidden shortcut to AppData for backwards compatibility with Windows 2000 and Windows XP applications.

- *Contacts*—A folder to hold contacts and their properties. Contact properties include addresses, phone numbers, e-mail addresses, and digital certificates. Contacts can be used by various applications, but the most common are e-mail applications.

- *Cookies*—A hidden shortcut to the storage location for Internet Explorer cookies. This shortcut is for backwards compatibility with previous versions of Internet Explorer.

- *Desktop*—A folder that contains all of the shortcuts and files on the user desktop.

- *Documents*—A folder that is typically the default location for saving documents. This folder appears as My Document when viewed through Windows Explorer. You can verify the name as Documents by using a command prompt.

- *Downloads*—A folder that is used to store files and programs downloaded from the Internet.

- *Favorites*—A folder that holds Internet Explorer favorites.

- *Links*—A folder that contains shortcuts that are displayed as the favorite links in Windows Explorer.

- *Local Settings*—A hidden shortcut that is included for backward compatibility with Windows 2000 and Windows XP applications.

- *Music*—A folder for storing music files. It appears as My Music in Windows Explorer.

- *My Documents*—A hidden shortcut that is included for backward compatibility with Windows 2000 and Windows XP applications.

- *NetHood*—A hidden shortcut to a location storing user-specific network information such as drive mappings. This is included for backward compatibility.

- *Pictures*—A folder for storing picture files. It appears as My Pictures in Windows Explorer.

- *PrintHood*—A hidden shortcut to a location storing user-specific printing information such as network printers. This is included for backward compatibility.

- *Recent*—A hidden shortcut to a location storing shortcuts to recently used documents. This is included for backward compatibility.

- *Saved Games*—A folder for storing saved games that are in progress.

- *Searches*—A folder that stores saved search queries so that they can easily be accessed again.

- *SendTo*—A hidden shortcut to the location storing shortcuts that appear in the Send To menu when right-clicking a data file. This is included for backward compatibility.

- *Start Menu*—A hidden shortcut to the location storing the shortcuts and folders that appear in the Start menu. This is included for backward compatibility.

- *Templates*—A hidden shortcut to the location storing application templates, such as Word document templates. This is included for backward compatibility.

- *Videos*—A folder for storing videos. It appears as My Videos in Windows Explorer.

- *NTUSER.DAT*—A file that stores user-specific registry information.

- *NTUSER.DAT.LOGx*—Files that tracks changes in NTUSER.DAT. This file is used to recover NTUSER.DAT if the system shuts down unexpectedly.

- *NTUSER.DAT{guid}.TM.blf*—A temporary file used for controlling registry changes.

6

- *NTUSER.DAT{guid}*.TMContainer*xxxxxx*.regtrans-ms—A temporary file used for controlling registry changes.
- *Ntuser.ini*—A file that controls which portions of a profile are not to be copied up to a server when roaming profiles are enabled.

In addition to the details of an individual profile, you should understand the following:

- The default profile
- Mandatory profiles
- Roaming profiles
- The public profile
- Start menu configuration

The Default Profile

The **default profile** is used when new user profiles are created. When a new user logs on for the first time, Windows 7 copies the default user profile to create a profile for the new user. The folder structure in the default profile is the same as a user profile. However, the folders are empty by default.

When you install applications, the applications often modify the default profile. You can modify the default profile to ensure that new users get consistent applications settings. For example, Microsoft Office saves documents to a default location. You may want to define the default location as a shared network location.

To configure the default profile, you configure a profile for a local user and then copy it. After this process is completed, all new users get the modified default profile the first time they log on.

Although you can see user profiles in the file system, you cannot copy them using Windows Explorer. If you copy a profile using Windows Explorer, the security permissions are incorrect, and the user experiences many errors. Previous versions of Windows, including Windows Vista, allowed you to copy an existing user profile by using the **User Profiles applet** available in Advanced System Settings, as shown in Figure 6-12, and use it as the default user profile. This

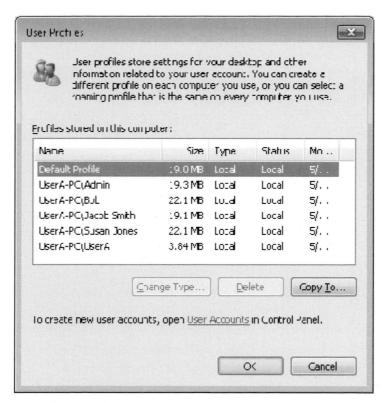

Figure 6-12 User Profiles applet
Courtesy Course Technology/Cengage Learning

process was officially unsupported starting with Windows XP and Windows 7 does not allow or support this. Instead, the default profile is configured by using Sysprep and should be performed as part of preparing a system image for distribution to users.

To configure the default profile:

1. If desired, create a new local user with administrative privileges to allow for creation of a blank user profile. Domain users are not supported.

2. Log on as the designated local user with administrative privileges.

3. Modify the user's profile as desired and delete all other user profiles. You must delete the other profiles to ensure that the correct user profile is copied.

4. Create an answer file with CopyProfile parameter set to true.

5. Run Sysprep with the /generalize option and specify the location of the answer file.

6. Image the computer and deploy the image. When the image is started after deployment, the default user profile is created from the profile of local user account used in the preceding steps.

After a default user profile is configured, you can manually copy the default user profile to the profile of an existing user. This can be useful to reset the profile of existing users to match the default configuration. However, in most cases, you would delete the existing user profile instead. The next time the user logs on a new profile is created based on the default user profile.

Editing the Default User Profile Without Using Sysprep In some scenarios, you may want to modify an existing default user profile without using Sysprep. You can do this by editing the registry settings in the default profile. You can use the Registry Editor to manually edit the user settings in the ntuser.dat file for the default user profile. You can modify individual settings or import registry keys exported from an already configured profile.

You can also update specific files in the default user profile. You can place new files into the profile or edit existing files. For example, you may want to add shortcuts on the user desktop or favorites in Internet Explorer. In this case, all that is needed is placing the files in the appropriate location in the default user profile. The files are copied when a new profile is created.

Activity 6-4: Modifying the Default Profile by Using Sysprep

Time Required: 15 minutes
Objective: Configure a profile and copy it to the default profile.

Description: A copy of the default profile is taken each time a new user profile is created. To ensure that all new users get certain settings, you can modify the default profile. To do this, you copy a correctly configured profile over the existing default profile by using Sysprep and an answer file. In this activity, you modify the default profile to provide a different desktop background.

1. If necessary, start your computer, and log on as **User***x*.

2. Right-click the desktop, click **Personalize**, and then click **Desktop Background**.

3. Click a new desktop background, and click **Save changes**.

4. Close the Personalization window.

5. Click the **Start** button, right-click **Computer**, and click **Properties**.

6. In the System window, click **Advanced system settings**.

7. In the System Properties window, on the **Advanced** tab, under **User Profiles**, click **Settings**.

8. In the User Profiles window, click **User***x***-PC\Bob** and click **Delete**.

9. Click **Yes** to confirm the delete.

10. Repeat steps 8 and 9 to delete user profiles for all users except **Userx** and **Default Profile**.

11. Click **OK** to close the User Profiles window and close all other open windows.

12. Click the **Start** button, point to **All Progams**, click **Microsoft Windows AIK**, and then click **Windows System Image Manager**.

13. If the Windows Image area does not list Windows 7 Enterprise, then right-click **Select a Windows image or catalog file**, click **Select Windows Image**, and double-click **C:\wininstall\sources\install.wim**.

14. Click the **File** menu and then click **New Answer File**.

15. In the Windows Image area, if necessary, expand **Components**, right-click **x86_Microsoft-Windows-Shell-Setup_6.1.xxx.xxxxx_neutral** and click **Add Setting to Pass 4 specialize**. If you are using a 64-bit version of Windows 7, select the amd64 version instead. Notice that the settings are now added to the answer file.

16. In the Microsoft-Windows-Shell-Setup Properties area, click **CopyProfile**, click the down arrow, and click **true**.

17. Click the **File** menu, and then click **Save Answer File**.

18. In the Save As window, browse to **C:\wininstall**.

19. In the File name box, type **unattend.xml** and then click **Save**.

20. Close Windows System Image Manager.

21. Click the **Start** button, type **cmd**, and press **Enter**.

22. At the command prompt, type **C:\Windows\System32\sysprep\sysprep.exe /oobe /generalize /unattend:C:\wininstall\unattend.xml /shutdown** and press **Enter**. The command does not copy the profile. The profile is copied later during the specialize phase after the computer is restarted. The settings of the user that is logged on at this time will be copied. The specified answer file is cached for use during the specialize phase.

23. At this point, you would typically image the computer. To simulate the image being applied to a new computer, start your computer.

24. Click **Next** to accept the default settings for Country or region, Time and currency, and Keyboard layout.

25. In the Type a user name box, type **Admin**.

26. In the Type a computer name box, type **Userx-PC** and then click **Next**.

27. On the Set a password for your account page, in the Type a password and Retype your password boxes, type **password**.

28. In the Type a password hint box, type **Just a simple password** and then click **Next**.

29. If prompted for a product key, type the product key provided by your instructor and then click **Next**.

30. Select the **I accept the license terms** check box and then click **Next**.

31. On the Help protect your computer and improve Windows automatically page, click **Use recommended settings**.

32. Click **Next** to accept the existing time zone information.

33. Click **Public network**.

34. Click the **Start** button. Notice that you are automatically logged on as Admin and the new profile has the desktop background that you configured for the default profile.

35. Log off and then log on as **Userx**.

36. If required, use the instructions in Activity 2-3 to reactivate your computer.

Activity 6-5: Modifying the Default Profile Without Using Sysprep

Time Required: 10 minutes

Objective: Modify an existing default profile without using sysprep.

Description: Sometimes you need to modify the default profile on a computer that is already deployed. In such a case, you can use the Registry Editor to modify settings. You can also directly modify the files in the default profile. In this activity, you modify the default profile to provide a different desktop background and add a desktop shortcut.

1. If necessary, start your computer, and log on as **User***x*.
2. Click the **Start** button, type **regedit**, and press **Enter**.
3. In the User Account Control window, click **Yes**.
4. In the left pane, click **HKEY_USERS**.
5. Click the **File** menu and then click **Load Hive**.
6. In the Load Hive window, in the address bar, type **C:\Users\Default** and press **Enter**.
7. In the File name box, type **ntuser.dat** and click **Open**. You are typing this name manually, because it is a hidden file.
8. In the Key Name box, type **DefaultUser** and click **OK**.
9. Expand **HKEY_USERS**, expand **DefaultUser**, expand **Control Panel**, and click **Desktop**.
10. In the right pane, scroll down and double-click **Wallpaper**.
11. In the Edit String window, in the Value data box, type **C:\Windows\Web\Wallpaper\ Architecture\img15.jpg** and click **OK**.
12. Close the Registry Editor.
13. Click **Start**, point to **All Programs**, right-click **Internet Explorer**, and click **Copy**.
14. Click Windows Explorer on the task bar.
15. In the address bar, type **C:\Users\Default\Desktop** and press **Enter**.
16. In Windows Explorer, right-click an empty area, and then click **Paste**.
17. In the Destination Folder Access Denied window, click **Continue**.
18. Close Windows Explorer.
19. Click the **Start** button, right-click **Computer**, and click **Properties**.
20. Click **Advanced system settings**.
21. In the User Profiles area, click **Settings**.
22. Click **User***x***-PC\Admin** and then click **Delete**.
23. In the Confirm Delete window, click **Yes**.
24. Close all open windows and restart your computer.
25. Log on as **Admin**. Notice that Admin now has a new profile with the modifications. There is a desktop shortcut for Internet Explorer and a new wallpaper with a white building that you specified in the registry.
26. Log off as Admin.

The .DEFAULT user profile in the registry is used by the local system. The desktop background and screen saver identified in this profile appear before any user is logged on.

Mandatory Profiles

A **mandatory profile** is a profile that cannot be modified. Users can make changes to their desktop settings while they are logged on, but the changes are not saved. This means that if there is a configuration problem, all the user needs to do is log off and log back on to get pristine settings again.

You can implement mandatory profiles for a single user that is causing problems or for a group of users. Most times, a single consistent desktop is implemented for a group of users. Most mandatory profiles are implemented as roaming user profiles.

To change a profile to a mandatory profile, you rename the file NTUSER.DAT to NTUSER.MAN. After this change is made, user modifications to the profile are not saved.

Roaming Profiles

A **roaming profile** is stored in a network location rather than on the local hard drive. The main benefit of roaming profiles is that settings move with a user from computer to computer on the network. Typically, roaming profiles are used in large corporations where users move among different computers each day.

One situation where roaming profiles are very useful is when a corporation uses Outlook and Exchange for an e-mail system. When a user runs Outlook for the first time, it must be configured to access the correct Exchange server. The configuration information for Outlook is stored in the user profile. If a user logged on to a new computer that created a new profile based on the default profile, Outlook would need to be reconfigured again. If roaming profiles are in place, the Outlook configuration moves from computer to computer as part of the roaming profile.

To configure a roaming profile, you must edit the user account to point the profile directory at a network location. Then you copy the existing user profile up to the network location.

Each time a user logs on, the roaming profile is copied to the local computer. If a user logs on and cannot contact the server with the roaming profile, then the local copy of the profile is used.

For detailed steps on how to configure a roaming user profile and a network-based mandatory user profile, see How to customize default user profiles in Windows 7 and in Windows Server 2008 R2 on the Microsoft Support Web site at *http://support.microsoft.com/?id=973289*.

The Public Profile

The **public profile** is different from other profiles because it is not a complete profile. The public profile does not include an NTUSER.DAT file and consequently does not include any registry settings. The public profile is a series of folders. The content of these folders is merged into the profiles of other users when they log on. For example, shortcuts or files placed in the Public Desktop Folder are placed on the desktop of each user.

The public profile is similar to the All Users profile in Windows XP.

The public profile includes the following folders:

- *Favorites*—Favorites stored here are available to all users.
- *Libraries*—Libraries stored here do not appear in user profiles but are available to all users.
- *Public Desktop*—Files and shortcuts stored here appear on the Desktop of each user.
- *Public Documents*—Files stored here appear in the Documents library of each user.
- *Public Downloads*—Files stored here do not appear in profiles, but the files in it are available to all users.
- *Public Music*—Files stored here appear in the Music library of each user.

- *Public Pictures*—Files stored here appear in the Pictures library of each user.
- *Public Recorded TV*—This folder is used to store recorded television programs for personal video recorder (PVR) functionality. This folder does not appear in user profiles, but the files in it are available to all users.
- *Public Videos*—Files stored here appear in the Videos folder of each user.

Activity 6-6: Modifying the Public Profile

Time Required: 5 minutes
Objective: Modify the public profile and see how it affects users.

Description: The public profile is merged into the profile of all users. Adding content to the public profile means that the content is available to all users. In this activity, you place a file in the Public Documents folder, which makes it available to all users.

6

1. If necessary, start your computer and log on.
2. Click the **Start** button and click **Computer**.
3. In the left pane, expand **Local Disk (C:)**, expand **Users**, expand **Public**, and click **Public Documents**.
4. In the right pane, right-click an open area, point to **New**, and then click **Shortcut**.
5. In the Type the location of the item box, type **C:\Windows\notepad.exe**, and click **Next**.
6. In the Type a name for this shortcut box, type **Notepad**, and click **Finish**.
7. Right-click the **Notepad** shortcut and click **Cut**.
8. In the Windows Explorer address bar, type **C:\Users\Public\Desktop** and press **Enter**.
9. Right-click an empty area and click **Paste**. Notice that even an administrative user is prompted for permission to copy files here.
10. Click **Continue**. Notice that there is now a shortcut to Notepad on your desktop.
11. Double-click the **Notepad** shortcut on your desktop to test it.
12. Close Notepad.
13. Close Windows Explorer.

The Start Menu

The Start menu is a collection of folders and shortcuts to applications. Modifying the Start menu is as simple as creating folders and shortcuts. Users all have a personal version of the Start menu that is stored in their profile. In addition, common elements of the Start menu are located in C:\ProgramData\Microsoft\Windows\Start Menu. The elements in both locations are merged and displayed to the user.

You can use Windows Explorer to access and modify the contents of the Start Menu as shown in Figure 6-13. The user specific settings are located in C:\Users\ *username*\AppData\Roaming\Microsoft\Windows\Start Menu, where *username* is the username of the user.

Network Integration

Additional considerations must be taken into account when you place Windows 7 on a network and want to interact with other network users. User logon and authorization is very different in a networked environment. A networked environment requires you to understand the configuration of the local computer and other networked computers. You need to understand

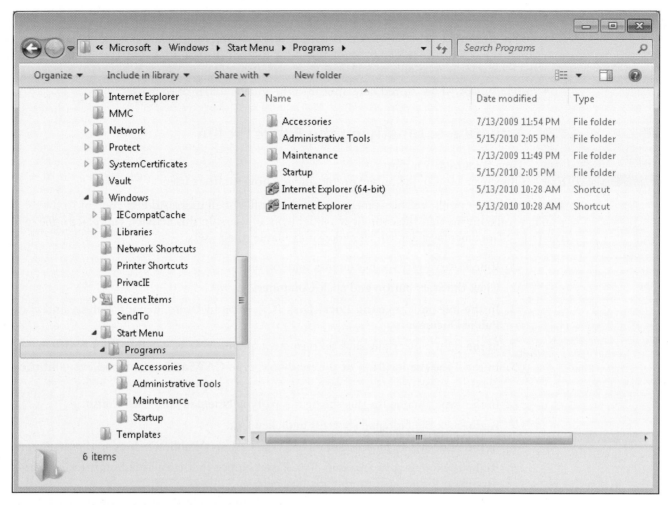

Figure 6-13 The Start menu in Windows Explorer
Courtesy Course Technology/Cengage Learning

both peer-to-peer and domain-based network types. When a domain-based network is used, you should also understand how cached credentials work on Windows 7.

Peer-to-Peer Networks

A **peer-to-peer network** (or workgroup) consists of multiple Windows computers that share information. No computer on the network serves as a central authoritative source of user information. Each computer maintains a separate list of users and groups in its own SAM database. Figure 6-14 shows a peer-to-peer network.

This type of network is most commonly implemented in homes and small offices. Windows 7 has a limit of 20 connections, which makes it impractical for sharing files and printers in larger environments.

When you access shares or printers on a remote computer, you must log on as a user that exists on the remote computer. In most cases, it is preferred that the remote computer has a user account with the exact same name and password as the local machine. This allows pass-through authentication to occur, where the local Windows credentials are used to log on to the remote computer.

Pass-through authentication is the simplest authentication method for users. However, managing the user accounts and passwords on each computer is difficult. There is no automated mechanism to synchronize user accounts and passwords between computers in a peer-to-peer network. As a consequence, security management for peer-to-peer networks is progressively more difficult as the number of computers expands.

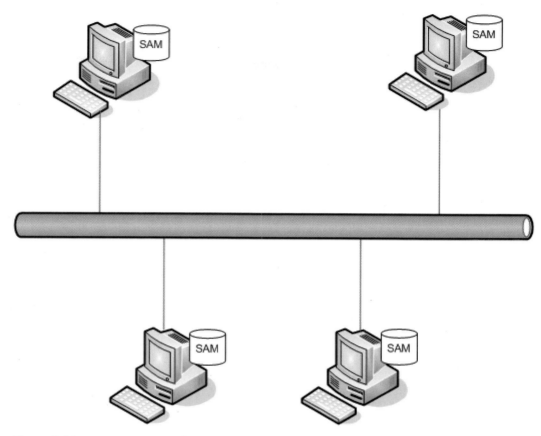

Figure 6-14 Peer-to-peer network
Courtesy Course Technology/Cengage Learning

Windows 7 includes the HomeGroup feature to simplify the configuration of peer-to-peer networks. A HomeGroup removes the need to synchronize users and passwords on each computer by using a password for the HomeGroup instead. More information about HomeGroup is available in Chapter 8 Networking.

Domain-Based Networks

User accounts for **domain-based networks** are much easier to manage than user accounts for peer-to-peer networks. A central server called a domain controller is responsible for maintaining user accounts and computer accounts. All computers in the domain share the user accounts on the domain controller. So, user accounts only need to be created once and there are no concerns about synchronizing passwords between multiple accounts. Figure 6-15 shows a domain-based network.

To participate in a domain, Windows 7 computers are joined to the domain. The joining process creates a computer account for the Windows 7 computer and integrates Windows 7 security with the domain. The Domain Admins group becomes a member of the local Administrators group to allow centralized administration by the domain administrators. The Domain Users group becomes a member of the local Users group to allow all users in the domain to log on to Windows 7.

Cached Credentials

When you use Windows 7 and log on to a domain, your authentication credentials are automatically cached in Windows 7. This is important for mobile computers that are not always connected to the domain. After credentials are cached locally, you can log on to a computer using a domain user account, even when the domain cannot be contacted.

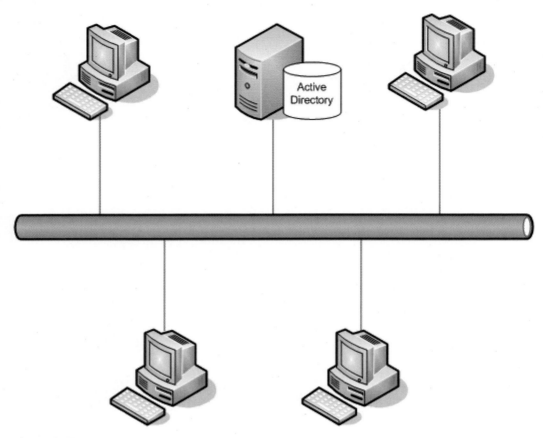

Figure 6-15 Domain-based network
Courtesy Course Technology/Cengage Learning

By default, the credentials of the last 10 users to log on are cached. However, if required, you can increase this up to 50 users, or disable cached credentials entirely. You might want to disable **cached credentials** because there are known methods for decrypting cached credentials if you are able to log on as an administrator of the local computer.

For information about modifying the number of cached credentials, see Cached domain logon information on the Microsoft Support Web site at *http://support.microsoft.com/kb/172931/*.

Cached credentials can be disabled by editing the local Group Policy object or by applying a domain-based Group Policy object.

Parental Controls

Parental Controls are a method for controlling how Windows 7 is used by specific user accounts. The accounts must be Standard user accounts. Administrator accounts are not subject to Parental Controls. In addition, Parental Controls are not available in the business versions of Windows 7; they are available only in the home versions of Windows 7 and Windows 7 Ultimate and Windows 7 Enterprise. When Windows 7 Ultimate or Enterprise is joined to a domain, the Parental Controls are unavailable.

You can perform the following tasks with Parental Controls:

- Configure time limits
- Control game playing
- Allow and block programs

 Unlike Windows Vista, Windows 7 does not include Web filtering and activity reporting functionality. However, Microsoft does make this functionality available through Windows Live Family Safety. For more information about Windows Live Family Safety see the Windows Live Web site at *http://download.live.com/familysafety*.

Time Limits

Time limits control when a user is able to log on and use the computer. Corporations have used time limits as a security mechanism for many years. For example, typical users have no need to access computer systems between midnight and 5:00 a.m., so a time restriction is implemented to prevent access during that time.

The time limits in Windows 7 allow you to restrict logons to certain times of the day. The times can vary for each day. For example, as shown in Figure 6-16, you may want to stop computer

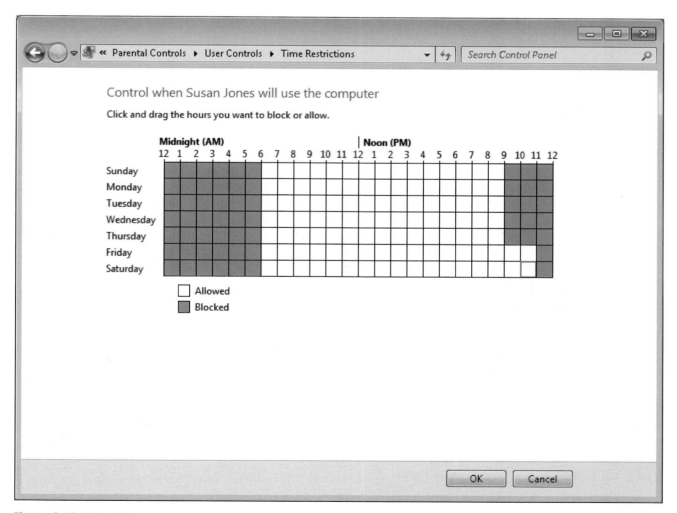

Figure 6-16 Time limits
Courtesy Course Technology/Cengage Learning

access at 9:00 p.m. on weekdays, but allow computer use until 11:00 p.m. on Friday and Saturday nights. When the time limit is reached, users are forced to log out.

Activity 6-7: Restricting Logon Times

Time Required: 5 minutes
Objective: Restrict the logon times of a user.

Description: You can configure Parental Controls to limit the times of day that a user can be logged on. This is useful to control the usage habits of a computer in a child's bedroom. In this activity, you configure and test logon time restrictions.

1. If necessary, start your computer and log on.
2. Click the **Start** button, and click **Control Panel**.
3. Click **User Accounts and Family Safety** and click **Parental Controls**.
4. Click **Susan Jones**. Notice that Parental Controls are off by default.
5. Under Parental Controls, click **On, enforce current settings**.
6. Click **Time limits** and click **OK** when warned about a FAT drive being detected.
7. Block the current time by highlighting it in blue.
8. Click **OK** twice to save the changes.
9. Close the **Parental Controls** window.
10. Switch users to **Susan Jones**. Notice that you are prevented from logging on due to the time restrictions you created.
11. Click **OK** to clear the message and click **Switch User**.

Game Controls

Game controls are used to limit access to games. Specific games can be allowed or blocked for a particular user. Blocking a specific game is appropriate when you want to prevent users from playing a game that does not meet your standards. Allowing a specific game is appropriate when a particular game you approve of is automatically blocked by the game ratings system. Figure 6-17 shows the user interface for controlling access to games.

Games can only be blocked and allowed by game controls if Windows 7 recognizes the software as a game.

You can block games based on the game rating. The default ratings source is the Entertainment Software Rating Board, but other rating organizations can be selected. You can also select whether unrated games are blocked or allowed. In addition, you can block games with certain content regardless of their rating.

Default ratings used for game controls include the following:

- *Early Childhood (EC)*—Suitable for ages 3 and older. No inappropriate content.
- *Everyone (E)*—Suitable for ages 6 and older. May contain minimal violence, comic mischief, or mild language.
- *Everyone 10+ (E10+)*—Suitable for ages 10 and older. May contain more mild violence, mild language, or suggestive themes.
- *Teen (T)*—Suitable for ages 13 and older. May contain violence or strong language.
- *Mature (M)*—Suitable for ages 17 and older. May contain mature sexual themes, more intense violence, or strong language.

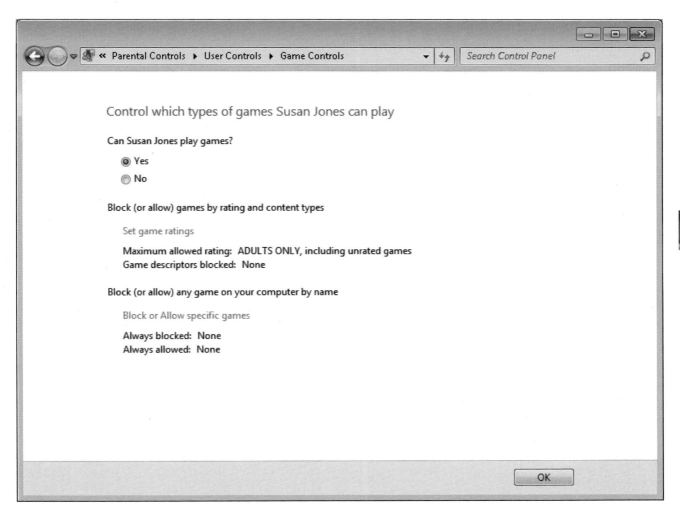

Figure 6-17 Game controls
Courtesy Course Technology/Cengage Learning

- *Adults Only (AO)*—Suitable only for adults age 18 and older. May contain graphic depictions of sex or violence.

Some of the additional categories that can be blocked:

- Online Rating Notice
- Blood and Gore
- Drug Reference
- Intense Violence
- Nudity
- Real Gambling
- Sexual Violence
- Use of Alcohol
- Use of Tobacco

Block Programs

By default, users can run all programs that are installed. However, you can restrict users to running only approved applications. This is done in corporations to restrict the use of computers to business relevant applications that have been approved by the corporate IT department. In a home environment, this is useful to ensure that a child is only using applications that are required for homework or generating a report.

When only allowed programs can be run, you are presented with a list of applications to select, as shown in Figure 6-18. This list shows most installed programs in Windows. However, sometimes an application does not have an installation that integrates into Windows, and you must manually add the application to the allowed programs list. You manually add the application by browsing and selecting the executable file.

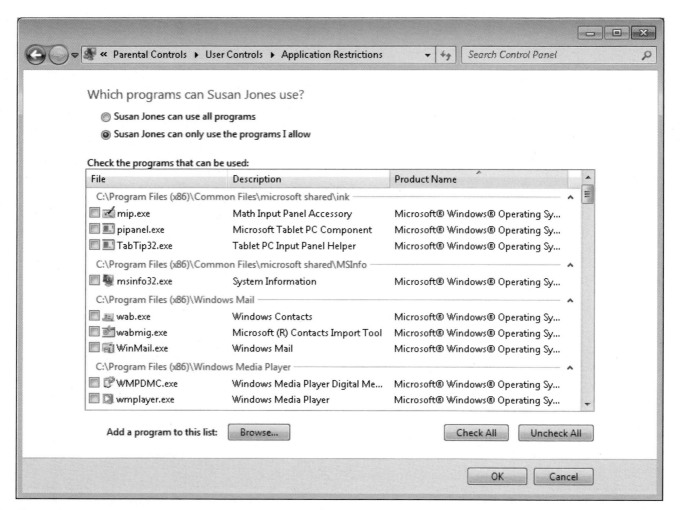

Figure 6-18 Allowed programs
Courtesy Course Technology/Cengage Learning

Chapter Summary

- User accounts are required for users to log on to Windows 7 and use resources on that computer. Local user accounts are stored in the SAM database of each computer.

- Windows 7 log on security can be enhanced by enabling secure logon.

- Fast user switching allows multiple users to be logged on to a computer at the same time. Windows 7 has been enhanced to support fast user switching in a domain-based network.

- Three default accounts are created upon installation of Windows 7: Administrator, Guest, and the initial user account. The Administrator account does not have a password but cannot be accessed remotely over the network. The initial user account is configured as an administrator.

- Groups help to simplify management by organizing users. Many built-in groups are created by default. The Administrators group and the Users group are the most commonly used.

- Users can be created from Control Panel, the User and Groups MMC snap-in, or the advanced User Accounts applet. The User Accounts applet in Control Panel is a simplified interface for managing users. The Local Users and Groups MMC snap-in allows you to manage users and groups. The advanced User Accounts applet can only be started from a command line, but has unique settings not otherwise available.

- User profiles store user-specific settings. Profiles contain a number of folders and an NTUSER.DAT file. New profiles are based on the default profile and are created the first time a user logs on. The default location for user profiles is C:\Users.

- You can modify profiles to make them mandatory or roaming. Mandatory profiles cannot be modified by users. Roaming profiles move with users when they log on to different computers. Information in the public profile is applied to all users.

- In a peer-to-peer network, each computer authenticates users by using the local SAM database. User accounts and passwords are not synchronized between computers automatically.

- In a domain-based network, user authentication is controlled centrally by a domain controller. Credentials are cached at first log on, so users can log on even if a domain controller cannot be contacted.

- Parental Controls allow you to configure time limits, control game playing, and allow or block programs. Games are controlled by ratings.

Key Terms

advanced User Accounts applet   An applet for managing users that is available only from the command line. Some options in this applet are not available in other user management utilities.

administrator account   The type of user account that is made a member of the Administrators local group and has full rights to the system.

Administrator account   The built-in account that is created during installation and which has full rights to the system. This account cannot be deleted or removed by the Administrators group.

built-in local groups   Groups that are automatically created for each Windows 7 computer and stored in the SAM database.

cached credentials   Domain credentials that are stored in Windows 7 after a user has logged on to a domain. Cached credentials can be used to log on when a domain controller cannot be contacted.

default profile   The profile that is copied when new user profiles are created.

domain-based network   A network where security information is stored centrally in Active Directory.

Fast user switching   Allows multiple users to have applications running at the same time. However, only one user can be using the console at a time.

game controls   A part of Parental Controls that is used to limit access to games.

Guest account   An account with minimal privileges intended to give minimal access to Windows 7. This account is disabled by default.

initial account   The account with administrative privileges created during the installation of Windows 7.

local user account   A user account that is defined in the SAM database of a Windows 7 computer. Local user accounts are valid only for the local computer.

Local Users and Groups MMC snap-in   An MMC snap-in that is used to manage users and groups.

mandatory profile   A profile that cannot be changed by users. NTUSER.DAT is renamed to NTUSER.MAN.

NTUSER.DAT   The file containing user-specific registry entries in a user profile.

Parental Controls   A method for configuring time limits, controlling game playing, and allowing or blocking programs.

peer-to-peer network   A network where all computers store their own security information and share data.

public profile   A profile that is merged with all other user profiles. The public profile does not contain an NTUSER.DAT file.

roaming profile   A user profile that is stored in a network location and is accessible from multiple computers. Roaming profiles move with users from computer to computer.

secure logon   Adds the requirement to press Ctrl+Alt+Del before logging on.

Security Accounts Manager (SAM) database   The database used by Windows 7 to store local user and group information.

Security Identifier (SID)   A number that is added to the access control list of a resource when a user or group is assigned access.

standard user account   A type of user account that does not have privileges to modify settings for other users. This type of account is a member of the Users local group.

time limits   A part of Parental Controls that is used to control when users are allowed to log on to the computer.

user account   User accounts are used for authentication to prove the identity of a person logging on to Windows 7.

User Accounts applet   A simplified interface for user management in Control Panel.

User Profiles applet   An applet that is used to copy or remove user profiles.

Windows Welcome   The default logon method for Windows 7. This method presents icons representing each user.

Review Questions

1. Local user accounts are stored in the SAM database. True or False?

2. Each user account is assigned a _____ to ensure that security is kept intact if the account is renamed.

3. Which logon method requires users to press Ctrl+Alt+Delete before logging on?

   a.   Windows Welcome

   b.   Secure logon

   c.   Fast user switching

   d.   Automatic logon

4. Which logon method allows multiple users to have applications running on the computer at the same time?

   a.   Windows Welcome

   b.   Secure logon

   c.   Fast user switching

   d.   Automatic logon

5. Which characters are not allowed in user account names? (Select all that apply.)

   a.   \

   b.   +

c. $

d. *

e. !

6. Because user names are case sensitive, you can use capitalization to ensure that they are unique. True or False?

7. Which characteristics apply to the Administrator account? (Choose all that apply.)

a. It has a blank password by default.

b. It cannot be deleted.

c. It cannot be renamed.

d. It is visible on the logon screen.

e. It can be locked out.

8. Which characteristics apply to the Guest account? (Choose all that apply.)

a. It has a blank password by default.

b. It cannot be deleted.

c. It cannot be renamed.

d. It is disabled by default.

e. It can be locked out.

9. Because the initial user account created during installation is a member of the Administrators group, it has all of the characteristics of the Administrator account. True or False?

10. The _____ built-in local group has been depreciated and is no longer recommended for use by Microsoft.

11. Standard users are members of which built-in local group?

a. Administrators

b. Guests

c. Remote Desktop Users

d. Users

12. Standard user accounts are more usable in Windows 7 than previous versions of Windows because User Account Control elevates privileges as required. True or False?

13. Which tasks can be performed by using the User Accounts applet in Control Panel? (Choose all that apply.)

a. Change your password

b. Change your picture

c. Change your group memberships

d. Change your account type

e. Change your name

14. A password reset disk contains _____.

15. Which user management tool is required to assign a logon script to a user?

a. User Accounts in Control Panel

b. Local Users and Groups MMC snap-in

c. Advanced User Accounts applet

d. Advanced Users and Groups MMC snap-in

6

16. What is a risk of resetting a user password?

    a. The user account becomes corrupted.

    b. EFS-encrypted files cannot be accessed.

    c. The security permissions for the user account are lost.

    d. The password is not encrypted until changed by the user at first logon.

17. Which file in a profile contains user-specific registry settings?

    a. AppData

    b. NTUSER.DAT

    c. NTUSER.MAN

    d. SYSTEM.DAT

    e. Local Settings

18. Which profile is copied to create a profile for new user accounts?

    a. Default User

    b. Public

    c. Blank

    d. Default

    e. New

19. A roaming profile is located on a network server. True or False?

20. Which profile is merged into each user profile when the user is logged on?

    a. Default User

    b. Public

    c. Blank

    d. Default

    e. New

21. In a domain-based network, each server authenticates users by using the SAM database. True or False?

22. The _____ group becomes a member of the Administrators local group when a Windows 7 computer joins a domain.

23. Which editions of Windows 7 have the option to use Parental Controls? (Choose all that apply.)

    a. Windows 7 Home Premium

    b. Windows 7 Business

    c. Windows 7 Ultimate

    d. Windows 7 Enterprise in a workgroup

    e. Windows 7 Enterprise in a domain

24. Time limits can be configured separately for each day of the month. True or False?

25. Which program or utility do you use to copy an existing user profile to the default user profile?

    a. User Profiles applet

    b. Registry Editor

    c. Sysprep

    d. Windows Explorer

    e. Robocopy

Case Projects

Case Project 6-1: Parental Concerns

Superduper Lightspeed Computers sells many computers to home users. Some of the buyers express concerns about their children accessing inappropriate content on the Internet. In addition, you are aware of some parents who will not allow children to have a computer in their bedroom because of concerns about playing games all through the night. Explain how Parental Controls in Windows 7 address these concerns.

Case Project 6-2: Network Integration

You are an IT manager at Gigantic Life Insurance. You have a new desktop support person starting today whose experience is limited to supporting peer-to-peer networks. What do you need to tell him about how Windows 7 integrates into a domain-based network?

Case Project 6-3: Public Use Computer

Buddy's Machine Shop has a lounge for customers to wait in while their parts are being retrieved. Sometimes customers arrive a little early and have to wait up to an hour for their parts to be ready. Buddy has decided that it would be nice to give waiting customers Internet access. Describe how you would configure Windows 7 for public use.

Case Project 6-4: Secure Logon

At the most recent staff meeting of Hyperactive Media Sales, the general manager gave you instructions to make the laptops used by the sales people as secure as possible. One of the changes you have decided to implement is using secure logon for the laptops. How will you explain to the general manager how secure logon makes the laptops more secure?

chapter 7

Windows 7 Security Features

After reading this chapter and completing the exercises, you will be able to:

- Describe Windows 7 Security Improvements
- Use the local security policy to secure Windows 7
- Enable auditing to record security events
- Describe and configure User Account Control
- Describe the malware security features in Windows 7
- Use the data security features in Windows 7
- Secure Windows 7 by using Windows Update

One of the main goals in the development of Windows 7 is increased security. Microsoft has made some fundamental changes to the way user security is handled to accomplish this goal, as compared to Windows XP. At the same time, security features that worked well in past versions of Windows, such as auditing, continue to be available in Windows 7.

In this chapter you will learn about the security improvements in Windows 7, how to configure security by using the local security policy, and how to enable auditing. You will also learn about User Account Control, which is a fundamentally new way for user privileges to be managed. Windows Defender, for malware protection, is also covered. Using Encrypting File System and BitLocker Drive Encryption for data protection is discussed. Finally, using Windows Update to automatically apply patches is covered.

Windows 7 Security Improvements

Security threats are constantly evolving, and Windows 7 has new features to address the new threats found on the Internet and elsewhere. Many of these features were also included in Windows Vista but have been improved or refined in Windows 7.

The major security improvements in Windows 7 are:

- Malware protection
- Easier deployment of alternative authentication methods
- Enhanced network protection
- Data protection for stolen hard drives
- AppLocker for software restriction

Malware Protection

Malware is malicious software designed to perform unauthorized acts on your computer. It is a large category of software that includes worms, viruses, and spyware. The least critical effect of malware is degraded system performance. Many times, computers with malware experience significant slowdowns and system instability. A more critical concern is that malware can steal your personal information. For example, some malware is known to capture online banking information that can be used to steal money directly from your account.

User Account Control (UAC) is one feature implemented in Windows 7 to control malware. By prompting users when software attempts to take administrative control, users are informed that software is manipulating their machine. Users can then deny the software access to make the changes. User Account Control is discussed in detail later in this chapter.

Windows Defender is a real-time spyware monitor to prevent the installation of and remove spyware. Spyware is a threat to privacy and often makes systems unstable. Windows Defender is covered in detail later in this chapter.

Internet Explorer has been modified to run in a limited state, called protected mode, in which user files cannot be modified. This means that even if an exploit is found for Internet Explorer, the exploit will not be able to manipulate the computer. A **phishing filter** has also been added to prevent unauthorized Web sites from stealing logon credentials and other personal information. Internet Explorer security features are discussed in Chapter 9, User Productivity Tools.

Windows Service Hardening Most Windows exploits that are used to install malware are the result of flaws in Windows services. Unlike applications that only run when initiated by a user, services are always running and represent a greater opportunity to attack. As well, in previous versions of Windows, services ran with high privilege levels. Windows services have been hardened in Windows 7 to reduce the impact of a flaw in a Windows service.

Windows services have been changed in the following ways to harden Windows services:

- Each service is given a SID number. Previous versions of Windows did not apply SIDs to services. With a SID assigned to each service, access to resources can be controlled for each service.

- Services run with a lower privilege level by default. In previous versions of Windows, many services ran as LocalSystem, which has full access to the local computer and operating system. Most services now run as LocalService or NetworkService, with lower privilege levels.

- Wherever possible, unnecessary privileges for services have been removed. For example, the ability to perform debugging is not required for services.

- Windows Firewall can control network access based on service SIDs. Unauthorized services are blocked from accessing the network.

- Services are isolated and cannot interact with users. Preventing user interaction stops malicious software from communicating with services and exploiting flaws.

Alternative Authentication Methods

The most commonly used method for authentication is a username and password. The combination of a username and password verifies that you are authorized to use the system. Some organizations want to use more secure authentication systems like smart cards and biometrics.

Windows 7 makes smart cards easier to manage by including tools such as a self-service personal identification number (PIN) reset tool. When a smart card is used to authenticate, the user must enter a PIN in addition to presenting the smart card. Also, many smart card devices can now be installed through Plug and Play without requiring administrative permissions.

Development of additional authentication methods for Windows, such as biometrics, has been simplified. Simpler development means that there will be a greater number of choices in the marketplace to choose from. The implementation of additional authentication methods should also be more reliable. Many laptop computers now include a fingerprint scanner for authentication.

Network Protection

Windows 7 is protected on networks by an enhanced firewall and **Network Access Protection (NAP)**. The enhanced firewall can control both inbound and outbound network packets. Controlling inbound packets prevents other computers from accessing services. Controlling outbound network packets ensures that if malicious software is installed on Windows 7, then the software cannot access the network and relay any information it might have stolen.

NAP prevents unhealthy computers from accessing the network. An unhealthy computer is one that has outdated antivirus signatures or is missing security updates. In most cases, unhealthy computers are mobile computers such as laptops used by salespeople. Detailed information about NAP and Windows Firewall is covered in Chapter 8, Local Area Networking.

Data Protection

The NTFS file system provides data protection by using permissions on files and folders. This is an effective security mechanism in a networked environment where permissions can restrict access to files. However, NTFS permissions can be easily circumvented when you have physical access to a computer. To address the risks to data stored on workstations and laptops, **BitLocker Drive Encryption** is available in Windows 7.

BitLocker Drive Encryption encrypts the contents of a partition and protects the system partition. The encrypted data is inaccessible when the system is booted using an alternative operating system or when the drive is moved to another computer.

BitLocker Drive Encryption has been enhanced in Windows 7 with the addition of **BitLocker To Go**. BitLocker To Go can be used to protect data on removable storage, such as a USB drive. Detailed information about BitLocker Drive Encryption is covered later in this chapter.

AppLocker for Software Restrictions

Windows XP and Windows Vista included software restriction policies to provide administrators with a way to limit which application could run on a computer. This functionality has been enhanced in Windows 7 with the introduction of **AppLocker**. AppLocker simplifies the management of software restrictions by implementing simpler rules than were available in software restriction policies.

Security Policies

Windows 7 includes a **local security policy**, shown in Figure 7-1, which can be used to control many facets of Windows. You can access the Local Security Policy in Administrative Tools.

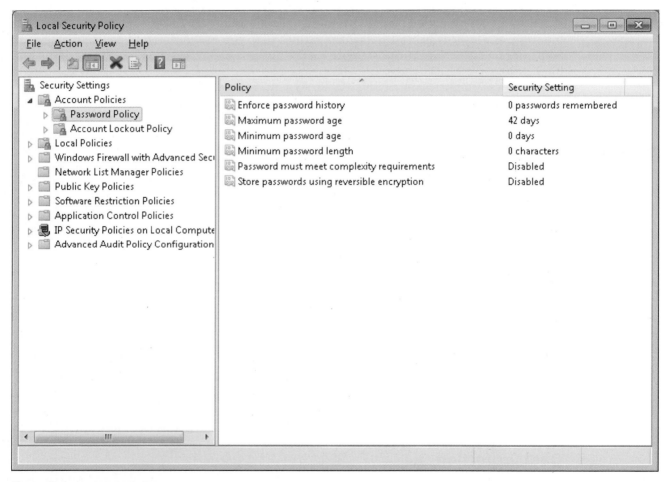

Figure 7-1 Local Security Policy
Courtesy Course Technology/Cengage Learning

The local security policy contains the following categories of settings:

- Account policies
- Local policies
- Windows Firewall with Advanced Security
- Network List Manager Policies
- Public Key Policies
- Software Restriction Policies

- Application Control Policies
- IP Security Policies on Local Computer
- Advanced Audit Policy Configuration

The local security policy is part of a larger Windows management system called Group Policy, which can be implemented on a local computer, but is typically part of a domain-based network. A variety of tools and security templates can be used to configure and analyze security policies.

Account Policies

The Account Policies category contains the **password policy** and the **account lockout policy**. The Account Policies in the Local Security Policy affect only local user accounts. The account policies do not affect domain accounts. To control domain accounts, the account policies must be configured at the domain level.

Password Policy The password policy controls password characteristics for local user accounts. The available settings are:

- *Enforce password history*—This setting is the number of password changes that must occur before a password can be reused. For example, if the setting is 3, then a password can only be reused every third time. The default value is 0 passwords remembered and the maximum is 24 passwords remembered.

- *Maximum password age*—This setting is the maximum amount of time that a user can keep the same password without changing it. Forcing password changes reduces the risk of a shared or hacked password being used over an extended period of time. The default value is 42 days.

- *Minimum password age*—This setting is the shortest amount of time that a user can use a password before changing it. A minimum password age is often used to ensure that users do not change their password several times in quick succession to continue using a single password. The default value is 0 days.

- *Minimum password length*—This setting is the minimum number of characters that must be in a password. In general, longer passwords are more secure. A minimum password length of 6 or 8 characters is typical for most organizations. The default value is 0 characters.

- *Password must meet complexity requirements*—This setting applies a number of tests to a new password to ensure that it is not too easy to guess or hack. This setting is enforced when a password change is made, but is not applied to existing passwords. The default value is Disabled. The complexity requirements include the following:

  - Cannot contain part of the user's account name
  - Must be at least six characters long
  - Must contain characters meeting three of the following characteristics: uppercase characters, lowercase characters, numerals (0–9), nonalphanumeric characters (e.g., !, @, #, $)

- *Store passwords using reversible encryption*—This setting controls how passwords are encrypted in the SAM database. By default this setting is Disabled, and passwords are encrypted in a nonreversible format. Storing passwords by using reversible encryption is required only for compatibility with specific applications, such as remote access when using Challenge-Handshake Authentication Protocol (CHAP). Enabling this option stored passwords in a less secure way.

Account Lockout Policy The account lockout policy is used to prevent unauthorized access to Windows 7. Using the account lockout policy, you can configure an account to be temporarily disabled after a number of incorrect log-on attempts. This prevents automated password guessing attacks from being successful.

The settings available to control account lockouts are:

- *Account lockout duration*—This setting determines how many minutes an account remains locked. The default value is 30 minutes, however this value is not configured until the Account lockout threshold has been configured.

- *Account lockout threshold*—This setting determines the number of incorrect logon attempts that must be performed before an account is locked. The default value is 0 invalid logon attempts, which means that account lockouts are disabled.

- *Reset account lockout counter after*—This setting determines within what timeframe the incorrect logon attempts must occur to trigger a lockout. The default value is 30 minutes, however this value is not configured until the Account lockout threshold has been configured.

Activity 7-1: Implementing a Password Policy

Time Required: 10 minutes

Objective: Implement a password policy that applies to local users.

Description: A password policy is used to control the passwords that can be selected by users. One of the most effective password policy settings for increasing security is requiring complex passwords that are difficult to hack. In this activity, you will configure a password policy to require complex passwords.

1. If necessary, start your computer and log on.
2. Click the **Start** button and click **Control Panel**.
3. Click **System and Security** and click **Administrative Tools**.
4. Double-click **Local Security Policy**.
5. In the left pane, expand **Account Policies** and click **Password Policy**. This shows all of the password policy settings that are available to you.
6. Double-click **Password must meet complexity requirements**, click **Enabled**, and click **OK**. Now all passwords must meet complexity requirements when they are changed.
7. Close all open windows.
8. Press **Ctrl+Alt+Delete** and click **Change a password**.
9. In the Old password box, type **password**.
10. In the New password and Confirm password boxes, type **simple**, and press **Enter**. You receive an error indicating that the new password is not acceptable due to length, complexity, or history requirements.
11. Click **OK**.
12. In the Old password box, type **password**.
13. In the New password and Confirm password boxes, type **S1mpl3**, and press **Enter**. This time the password is changed successfully.
14. Click **OK**.

Local Policies

The local policies are for auditing system access, assigning user rights, and configuring specific security options. Auditing lets you track when users log on and which resources are used. Details about auditing are covered later in this chapter. User rights control what system task a particular user or group of users can perform. The specific security options are a variety of settings that can be used to make Windows 7 more secure. Figure 7-2 shows some of the settings available in User Rights Assignment.

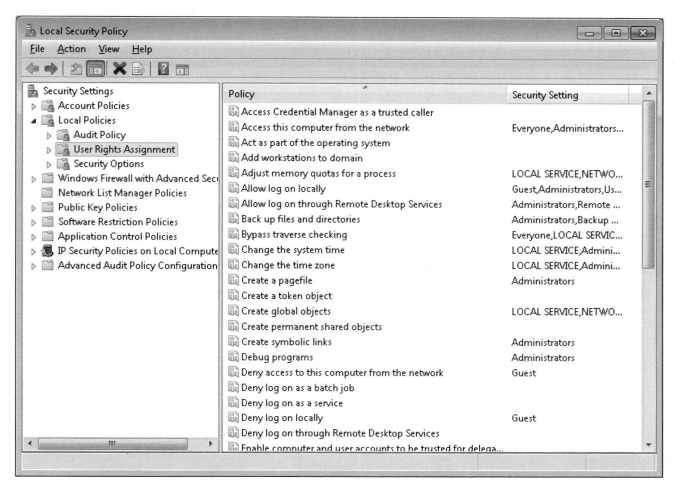

Figure 7-2 User Rights Assignment settings
Courtesy Course Technology/Cengage Learning

Some of the settings available in the user rights assignment are:

- *Allow log on locally*—This setting controls which users are allowed to log on to the computer at the console, but does not affect who can access the computer over the network. Administrators, Backup Operators, Guest, and Users are assigned this right by default.

- *Back up files and directories*—This setting controls which users are allowed to back up files, regardless of whether they have the necessary file permissions to read those files. Administrators and Backup Operators are assigned this right by default.

- *Change the system time*—This setting controls which users are allowed to change the system time. Administrators and LOCAL SERVICE are assigned this right by default.

- *Load and unload device drivers*—This setting controls which users are able to install and remove device drivers. Only Administrators are assigned this right by default.

- *Shut down the system*—This setting controls which users are able to shut down Windows 7. For a public access computer, you may restrict this right. Administrators, Backup Operators, and Users are assigned this right by default.

Some of the settings available in the security options are:

- *Devices: Prevent users from installing printer drivers*—This setting controls whether standard users are allowed to install network printer drivers. It does not affect the installation of local printer drivers. The default value is disabled, which allows all users to install network printer drivers.

- *Interactive logon: Do not display last username*—This setting allows you to remove the last username from the logon screen. This makes logon more secure by not giving away usernames to potential hackers. The default value is Disabled.

- *Interactive logon: Message text for users attempting to log on*—This setting allows you to display a message for users before they log on. The message can be instructions about how to log on or a warning against unauthorized use. By default, there is no message.

- *Shutdown: Allow system to be shut down without having to log on*—This setting allows you to enforce logon before allowing the system to be shut down. This is important for public access computers when you want to restrict which users can shut down the system. The default value is Enabled.

Activity 7-2: Configuring a Logon Message

Time Required: 10 minutes
Objective: Configure a warning message that appears for users before logon.

Description: The security policy of some organizations dictates that users are presented with a warning message about appropriate use before logon. This warning is used to ensure that users are properly informed about organizational policies. In this activity, you configure Windows 7 with a warning message that appears before logon.

1. If necessary, start your computer and log on. Remember that the password has been changed to S1mpl3.
2. Click the **Start** button and click **Control Panel**.
3. Click **System and Security** and click **Administrative Tools**.
4. Double-click **Local Security Policy**.
5. In the left pane, expand **Local Policies**, and click **Security Options**.
6. Scroll down and double-click **Interactive logon: Message title for users attempting to log on**.
7. In the text box, type **Acceptable Use**, and click **OK**.
8. Double-click **Interactive logon: Message text for users attempting to log on**.
9. In the text box, type **This computer should be used only for approved company business. Please see the acceptable use policy for more details.**, and click **OK**.
10. Close **Local Security Policy**.
11. Log off and press **Ctrl-Alt-Del**. Notice that the warning message is displayed.
12. Click **OK** to display the logon screen.

AppLocker

AppLocker is used to define which programs are allowed or disallowed in the system. Typically, AppLocker is used in corporate environments where parental controls are not able to be used to restrict software usage.

Windows XP and Windows Vista have software restriction policies that are similar in functionality to AppLocker. Software restriction policies can still be defined for Windows 7. However, if both AppLocker rules and software restriction policies are defined on a Windows 7 computer, then only the AppLocker rules are enforced. AppLocker rules can be applied only to Windows 7 Ultimate and Enterprise editions and Windows Server 2008 R2.

AppLocker provides the following enhancements over the software restriction policies:

- Rules can be applied to specific users and groups rather than all users.
- The default rule action is deny to increase security.

- A wizard to help create rules.
- An audit only mode for testing that only writes events to the event log.

You can audit or enforce AppLocker rules. When you audit an AppLocker rule, an event is logged when an action matching the rule is perfomed, but the software is allowed to run. When you enforce an AppLocker rule, software is blocked from running. If you do not define whether rules are enforced or audited, then the default is enforced. When you first implement AppLocker rules, it is a good idea to use audit rather than enforce the rules. This allows you to review the logs and verify that your rules allow all of the necessary software to run. Figure 7-3 shows the configuration of auditing and enforcement.

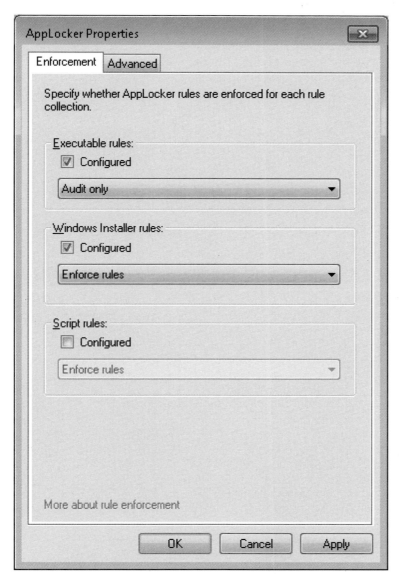

Figure 7-3 Configuring AppLocker enforcement
Courtesy Course Technology/Cengage Learning

The enforcement or auditing of AppLocker rules relies on the configuration of appropriate rules and the Application Identity service. The Application Identity service must be running for AppLocker rules to be evaluated. This service is configured for Manual startup and is stopped by default. If you are implementing AppLocker rules, you should configure the Application Identity service for Automatic startup.

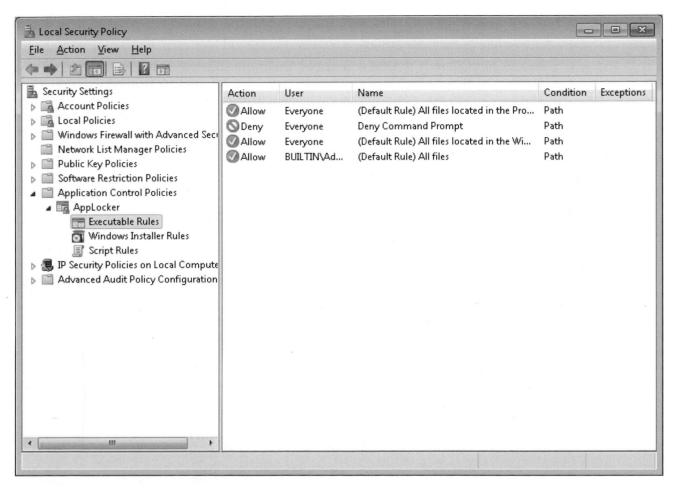

Figure 7-4 Applocker rule collections
Courtesy Course Technology/Cengage Learning

Rule Collections AppLocker rules are divided into categories called rule collections, as shown in Figure 7-4. Each rule collection applied to different types of files.

The rule collections are:

- *Executable*—These rules apply to mexe and mcom files. Use these rules to control which applications users can run.

- *Windows Installer*—These rules apply to .msi and .msp files. Use these rules to control which users can install applications and from what locations.

- *Scripts*—These rules apply to .ps1, .bat, .cmd, .vbs, and .js files. Use these rules to control which users can run scripts.

- *DLL*—These rules apply to .dll and .ocx files. Use these rules to verify that the DLLs used by applications are not modified or unknown. These rules are not enable by default due to negative performance impact.

Many Windows applications use DLL files when they are executing programs. DLL files contain code that is shared across many applications, and many DLLs are included as part of the operating system. DLL files are considered a lower risk than executable files and are not evaluated by default. Evaluating DLL files creates a significant performance impact because DLLs are accessed many times during program execution, and the DLL must be evaluated each time it is accessed. However, if performance is not a concern, you can choose to evaluate DLL files in addition to executable files to enhance security.

For each rule collection, you can:

- *Create a New Rule*—This allows you to manually specify the characteristics of a rule. To create rules in this way, you must understand the exact end results that you are trying to achieve.

- *Automatically Generate Rules*—This scans your computer and creates rules that match the current configuration of your computer. In a larger corporate environment, you can create the rules on a standardized reference computer and then apply them to all computers in the organization. You should review the rules before applying them.

- *Create Default Rules*—This creates standardized rules for a rule collection that meet the needs of many users and organizations. Because these rules are very general, they provide less security than automatically generated rules but are generally easier to manage. The default rules created vary for each rule collection.

Rule Permissions Each rule contains permissions that define whether the rule allows or denies software the ability to run, as shown in Figure 7-5. It is important to remember that until a rule is created in a rule collection, the default permission is allowed. For example, if there are no executable rules, then all executables are allowed. As soon as a single executable rule is created, then the default permission is deny and only specifically allowed executables can run. For example, if you create a rule that prevents users from running cmd.exe, then access to all other applications without an allow rule is prevented.

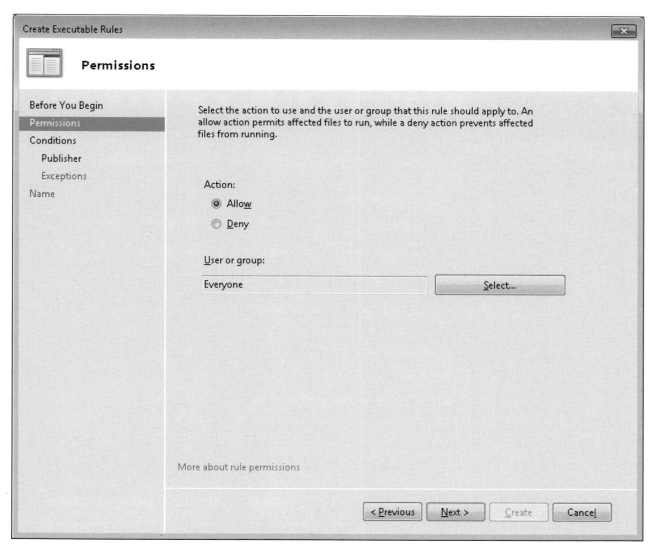

Figure 7-5 AppLocker rule permissions
Courtesy Course Technology/Cengage Learning

Permissions also define which users the rule applies to. A rule can be applied to an individual user or group, but not multiple users or groups. This means it is very important plan out which groups to use for allowing access.

In general, the best strategy for applying rules is to begin by creating rules that allow access for larger groups of users. Then you can restrict smaller groups or individuals with a rule that denies access or create an exception within the original rule. The deny permission overrides the allow permission when multiple rules apply for a user.

Rule Conditions   A rule condition defines the software that is affected by the rule. There are three conditions that can be used:

- Publisher
- Path
- File hash

The publisher rule condition, shown in Figure 7-6, identifies software by using a digital signature in the software. If the software is not digitally signed, you cannot use a publisher rule condition to identify it. Consider using a file hash rule condition instead.

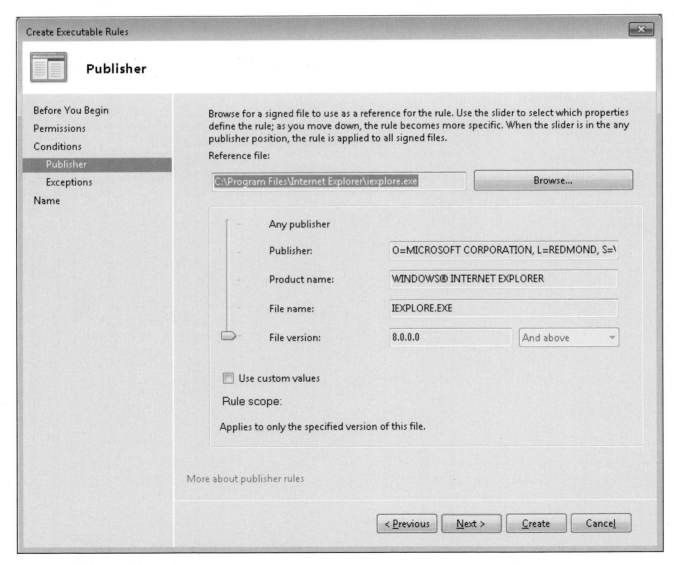

Figure 7-6 Publisher rule condition
Courtesy Course Technology/Cengage Learning

To begin configuration of a publisher rule condition, you specify a reference file. The wizard reads the digital signature from this reference file as the basis for the condition. After a reference file has been defined, you can use the slider to select the specific information that must be matched. You can make it as specific as a particular file and file version or make it more generic and restrict it only to a specific product name or publisher. You can also define custom values that do not match the information read from the reference file.

The path rule condition, shown in Figure 7-7, identifies software by file location. You can specify a single file or a folder path from which software can be run. This type of rule condition tends to be much less secure than a publisher rule condition. For example, if you use a path rule condition that allows software to be run from C:\Program Files, any malware accidentally installed by a user and located in C:\Program files can be run. At minimum, you should avoid using path rule conditions that allow executables to be run from file locations that standard users can copy files. Variables can be used as part of the path to simplify rule creation.

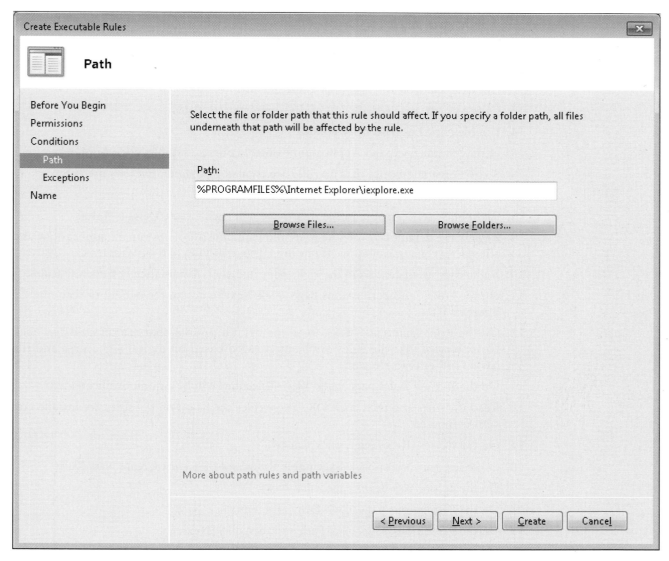

Figure 7-7 Path rule condition
Courtesy Course Technology/Cengage Learning

The file hash rule condition generates a unique identifier for the specified files called a hash value. If the file is modified in any way, the hash value no longer matches and the software no longer matches the rule. If you use a file hash rule condition, application updates will require the rule to be updated.

Rule Exceptions An AppLocker rule exception defines software that the rule does not apply to. In general, you use rule conditions to define a large set of software and then use exceptions to define a smaller set of software that the rule does not apply to. Similar to rule conditions, when you add an exception, it can be based on publisher, path, or file hash. You can add multiple exceptions to a single rule.

Activity 7-3: Configuring AppLocker

Time Required: 10 minutes
Objective: Implement AppLocker rules.

Description: Applocker rules can be used to limit which software is allowed to run on a workstation. An administrator can use this to prevent a particular piece of software from running or allow only specific software to run. In this activity, you will create and review default AppLocker rules and audit the use of cmd.exe.

1. If necessary, start your computer and log on. Remember that the password is changed to S1mpl3.
2. Click the **Start** button and click **Control Panel**.
3. Click **System and Security** and click **Administrative Tools**.
4. Double-click **Local Security Policy**.
5. In the left pane, expand **Application Control Policies** and then click **AppLocker**.
6. Scroll down and notice that no rules are created by default, but they are enforced.
7. Click **Executable Rules**.
8. Right-click an open area in the right-pane and click **Create Default Rules**.
9. Review the default rules. These rules allow administrators to run all applications and allow Everyone to run applications in C:\Program Files and C:\Windows.
10. Right-click an open area in the right-pane and click **Automatically Generate Rules**.
11. On the Folder and Permissions page, click **Next** to accept the default of scanning C:\ Program Files.
12. On the Rule Preferences page, read the default options that are selected and click **Next**. Notice that the rules are being created based on digital signatures and file hashes rather than file path.
13. On the Review Rules page, click **View Rules that will be automatically created**.
14. Read the rules and then click **OK**. These rules are based on the software installed on your computer.
15. On the Review Rules page, click **Cancel**.
16. In the left pane, right-click **Executable Rules** and then click **Create New Rule**.
17. On the Before You Begin page, click **Next**.
18. On the Permissions page, click **Deny** and then click **Next**.
19. On the Conditions page, click **Path** and then click **Next**.
20. On the Path page, in the Path box, type **C:\Windows\System32\cmd.exe** and then click **Next**.
21. On the Exceptions page, click **Next** to accept the default of no exceptions.
22. In the Name box, delete the existing name, type **Deny Command Prompt** and then click **Create**.
23. In the left pane, click **Windows Installer Rules**, right-click **Windows Installer Rules**, and then click **Create Default Rules**.

24. Review the default rules that are created. These rules allow Everyone to install digitally signed software and allow administrators to install any software.

25. In the left pane, click **AppLocker** and then click **Configure rule enforcement**.

26. Under Executable rules, select the **Configured** checkbox, select **Audit only** in the drop down list, and then click **OK**.

27. Close Local Security Policy.

28. Click **Start**, right-click **Computer**, and click **Manage**.

29. Expand **Services and Applications** and click **Services**.

30. Click the **Application Identity** service, read the description, and then click **Start**.

31. Wait a few seconds for the service to completely initialize, then click the **Start** button, type **cmd**, and press **Enter**.

32. In the left pane of Computer Management, expand **Event Viewer**, expand **Applications and Services Logs**, expand **Microsoft**, expand **Windows**, expand **AppLocker**, and click **EXE and DLL**.

33. Click the **Warning** event and read the description. Notice that cmd.exe was allowed to run because it is only being audited rather than enforced.

34. In the left pane of Computer Management, scroll down and click **Services**.

35. Click the **Application Identity Service** and click **Stop**.

36. Close all open windows.

Other Security Policies

Windows Firewall with Advanced Security is used to configure the firewall in Windows 7. This policy lets you configure both inbound and outbound rules for packets. In addition, you can configure specific computer-to-computer rules. In Windows 7, this area can also be used to configure IP Security (IPsec) rules.

The Network List Manager Policies are used to control how Windows 7 categorizes networks to which it is connected and how users can interact with the process. For example, unidentified networks can be automatically defined as either public or private, and the user can restrict the ability of other users to change it. These policies also control whether users can rename networks that they connect to.

The Public Key Policies has a settings for the **Encrypting File System (EFS)**, BitLocker Drive Encryption, and certificate services. You can add recovery agents for EFS files or BitLocker encrypted drives. A recovery agent is allowed to decrypt files protected by EFS or BitLocker. More detailed information about EFS and BitLocker Drive Encryption is provided later in this chapter.

IP Security Policies on Local Computer are used to control encrypted network communication. By default, network communication is not encrypted. However, you can configure encrypted network communication for certain hosts or communication on certain port numbers. This policy is depreciated in Windows 7 and included only for backward compatibility with Windows 2000 and Windows XP. When configuring IPsec rules, you should use Windows Firewall with Advanced Security.

Advanced Audit Policy Configuration is a simplified way to configure advanced audit policies in Windows 7. These policies first appeared in Windows Vista, but needed to be edited at a command-line. More detailed information about auditing is provided later in this chapter.

Security Templates

Security templates are .inf files that contain settings that correspond with the Account Policies and Local Policies in the local security policy. In addition, security templates can contain settings for the event log, restricted groups, service configuration, registry security, and file system security. You can use security templates to apply security settings or compare existing security settings against a corporate standard.

In a corporate environment using a domain, the security settings are typically configured by using Group Policy. Security templates can be imported into a group policy.

Security templates are edited by using the Security Templates snap-in, shown in Figure 7-8. The Security Templates snap-in automatically opens to the C:\Users\%USERNAME%\Documents\ Security\Templates folder. You can add additional locations if desired, but typically security templates are stored here.

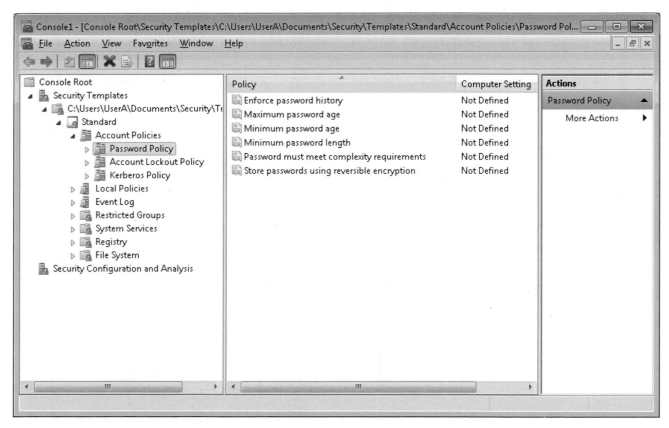

Figure 7-8 Security Templates MMC snap-in
Courtesy Course Technology/Cengage Learning

Windows 7 provides no default security templates.

Security templates are used by the **Security Configuration and Analysis tool** and **Secedit**. Both tools perform approximately the same tasks. The Security Configuration and Analysis tool is an MMC snap-in that is easy to use when working with a single computer. Secedit is a command-line utility that is better for scripting and working with multiple computers.

Tasks you can perform with the Security Configuration and Analysis tool are:

- *Analyze*—You can compare the settings in a security template against the settings on a computer. This is useful when you want to confirm that computers meet the minimum security requirements defined in a security template.

- *Configure*—You can apply the settings in a security template to a computer. This is useful to enforce the security requirements defined in a security template.

- *Export*—You can export the settings on a computer to a security template. This is useful if a computer has been properly configured and you want to apply these security settings to an additional computer.

Activity 7-4: Using Security Templates

Time Required: 25 minutes

Objective: Create a security template, analyze a computer, and then apply the security template.

Description: One method for analyzing and enforcing security settings on a Windows 7 computer is security templates. You can create your own security templates that define the security settings you require. After the security template has been created, you can use it to analyze computers or apply security settings. In this activity, you create a security template, analyze a computer, and then apply the security template.

1. If necessary, start your computer and log on. Remember that the password is changed to S1mpl3.

2. Click the **Start** button, point to **All Programs**, click **Accessories**, and click **Run**.

3. In the Open box, type **mmc**, and click **OK**.

4. In the User Account Control window, click **Yes**.

5. In the MMC window, click the **File** menu, and click **Add/Remove Snap-in**.

6. In the Available snap-ins box, scroll down, double-click **Security Templates**, double-click **Security Configuration and Analysis**, and click **OK**.

7. In the left pane, expand **Security Templates**, and click **C:\Users\User*x*\Documents\Security\Templates**. Notice that there are no templates stored here by default.

8. Right-click **C:\Users\User*x*\Documents\Security\Templates** and click **New Template**.

9. In the Template name box, type **Standard**.

10. In the Description box, type **Standard workstation security configuration**, and click **OK**. This creates a new blank security template that you can configure.

11. In the left pane, expand **C:\Users\User*x*\Documents\Security\Templates**, expand **Standard**, expand **Account Policies**, and click **Password Policy**.

12. Double-click **Password must meet complexity requirements**.

13. Select the **Define this policy setting in the template** check box, click **Disabled**, and click **OK**. Disabling password complexity is not recommended for corporate environments. In this case, it is being used as an example of one setting that can be configured using security templates.

14. In the left pane, expand **Local Policies** and click **Security Options**.

15. Scroll down and double-click **Interactive logon: Message title for users attempting to log on**.

16. Select the **Define this policy setting in the template** check box and click **OK**. You are leaving the text blank to undo the changes made in Activity 7-2.

17. Double-click **Interactive logon: Message text for users attempting to log on**.

18. Select the **Define this policy setting in the template** check box and click **OK**. You are leaving the text blank to undo the changes made in Activity 7-2.

19. In the left pane, right-click **Standard**, and click **Save**.

20. In the left pane, click **Security Configuration and Analysis**. Notice that instructions are provided in the middle pane. In this case, no database of security settings is created,

    so you are creating a new database. The database holds the security settings that are analyzed or applied.

21. Right-click **Security Configuration and Analysis** and click **Open Database**.

22. In the File name box, type **analyze** and click **Open**. This creates an empty database that security settings can be imported into.

23. In the Import Template dialog box, click **Standard.inf**, and click **Open**. This imports the security settings from the Standard security template into the database.

24. Right-click **Security Configuration and Analysis**, click **Analyze Computer Now**, and click **OK**. This compares the security settings in the database to the security settings on this computer. The comparison is then displayed in Security Configuration and Analysis.

25. Expand **Security Configuration and Analysis**, expand **Account Policies**, and click **Password Policy**. Notice that there is a red "x" beside the Password must meet complexity requirements setting because the setting in the database is different from the setting on the computer.

26. Expand **Local Policies** and click **Security Options**. Notice that there is a red "x" beside both Interactive logon: Message title for users attempting to log on and Interactive logon: Message text for users attempting to log on because the settings in the database are different from the settings on the computer.

27. Right-click **Security Configuration and Analysis**, click **Configure Computer Now**, and click **OK**. This applies the settings in the database to your computer.

28. Right-click **Security Configuration and Analysis**, click **Analyze Computer Now**, and click **OK**.

29. Expand **Account Policies** and click **Password Policy**. Notice that there is a check mark next to Password must meet minimum complexity requirements because the setting in the computer now matches the setting in the database. The setting is disabled.

30. Close the MMC and click **No** when asked to save the console settings.

31. Press **Ctrl+Alt+Delete** and click **Change a password**.

32. In the Old password box, type **S1mpl3**.

33. In the New password and Confirm password boxes, type **password**, and press **Enter**. Notice that the password was changed successfully because the requirement for complex passwords has been removed.

34. Click **OK**.

Auditing

Auditing is the security process that records the occurrence of specific operating system events in the Security log. Every object in Windows 7 has audit events related to it. Log entries can be recorded for successful events or failed attempted events. For example, logging all failed logon attempts may warn you when an attack that might breach your security is occurring. In addition, monitoring sensitive documents for read access lets you know who is accessing the documents and when.

It is more common to use auditing to monitor access to server-based resources than resources on desktop computers. However, there are some cases where you might want to know which users are logging on to a specific workstation. For example, if security logs indicate that someone was attempting unauthorized access to resources from a particular workstation, then it is useful to see which user was logged on at the time.

Windows 7 has basic auditing policy settings and advanced audit policy settings. In general, the advanced audit policy settings are more detailed than the basic audit policy settings. Using the advanced audit policy settings allows you to limit the amount of audit data that you capture. In this way, you capture only relevant data and simplify the task of reviewing the audit logs. The advanced audit policy settings are shown in Figure 7-9. Table 7-1 describes the categories for advanced audit policy settings.

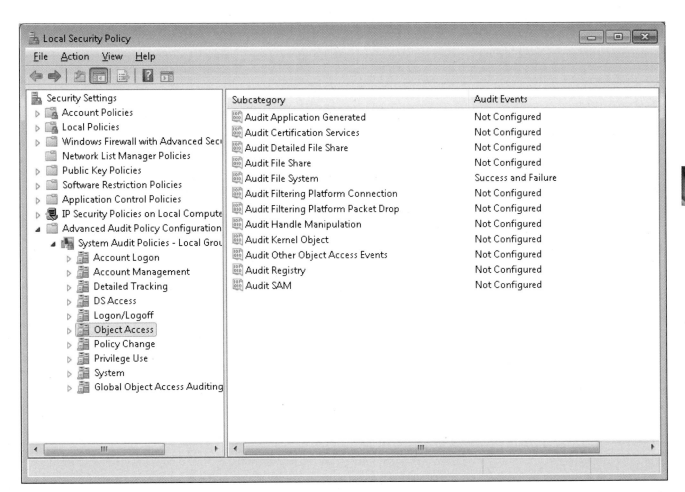

Figure 7-9 Advanced Audit Policy
Courtesy Course Technology/Cengage Learning

Basic auditing is enabled through the local security policy or by using Group Policy. The **Audit Policy** for basic auditing is located in the Local Policies node of the local security policy.

Advanced auditing is enabled through the local security policy, by using Group Policy, or by using auditpol.exe. The tool auditpol.exe provides the most accurate view of which advanced audit policy settings are applied. The advanced audit policy settings were also available in Windows Vista. However, in Windows Vista, you could configure the settings only by using auditpol.exe.

The default configuration for the advanced audit policy settings can be viewed only by using auditpol.exe. If you review the configuration in the local security policy it appears that no settings are enabled. Be aware that after you enable settings in the local security policy, the default configuration is lost and does not return if the advanced audit policy settings are removed from the local security policy. Table 7-1 describes the default configuration for the advanced audit policy settings.

Basic audit policy settings and advanced audit policy settings should not be combined as the results are unpredictable. To prevent conflicts when using the advanced audit policy settings, you can enable the security option policy setting **Audit: force audit policy subcategory settings (Windows Vista or later) to override audit policy category settings**.

Table 7-1   Event categories for advanced audit policy settings

Event Category	Description
Account Logon	Tracks when users are authenticated by a computer. If a local user account is used, the event is logged locally. If a domain user account is used, the event is logged at the domain controller. Account Logon events are not audited by default.
Account Management	Tracks when users and groups are created, modified, or deleted. Password changes are also tracked. Success events for user management are audited by default. Success and failure events for group management are auditing by default.
Detailed Tracking	Tracks how a computer is being used by tracking application activity. This includes identifying the creation and termination of processes, encryption events, and RPC events. No events are audited by default.
DS access	This category is not relevant for Windows 7 and is not audited by default. It is used only for domain controllers.
Logon/Logoff	User activity events, including local and domain logons, at the local computer. This category is similar to, but different from, audit account logon events. Logging on with a local account generates both an account logon event and a logon event on the local computer. Logging on with a domain account generates an account logon event at the domain controller and a logon event at the workstation where the logon occurred. Success event for logon, logoff, account lockout are audited by default. Failure events for logon are also audited.
Object Access	Tracks access to files, folders, printers, and registry keys. Each individual object being accessed must also be configured for auditing. Only files and folders on NTFS-formatted partitions can be monitored. Object access is not audited by default.
Policy Change	Tracks changes to user rights assignments, audit policies, and trust policies. Success events for audit policy changes and authentication policy changes are audited by default.
Privilege Use	Tracks when tasks are performed that require a user rights assignment, such as changing the system time. You can define which categories of privilege use are audited. None are audited by default.
System	Tracks when system events occur, such as restarting the system. By default success and failure events are audited for system integrity and other system events. Only success events are audited for security state change.
Global Object Access	Provides an easy way to specify that all access to files or registry keys should be audited. This avoids the need to configure auditing at the file, folder, or registry key level after enabling auditing for object access to files or registry keys. However, this must still be used in combination with auditing enabled for object access. This category does not appear when using auditpol.exe.

Once the audit policy is configured, the audited events are recorded in the Security log that is viewed by using Event Viewer. Event Viewer is available as part of the Computer Management MMC console, or as a standalone MMC console in Administrative Tools. Security events are listed by selecting the Windows Security log, as shown in Figure 7-10.

Activity 7-5: Auditing File Access

Time Required: 15 minutes
Objective: Audit file modification for users.

Description: In a corporate environment, it is useful to track all of the users that have modified sensitive files. You can use auditing to track file modification. In this activity, you will enable auditing of file modification creation, configure a file to be audited, and view user modification of that file.

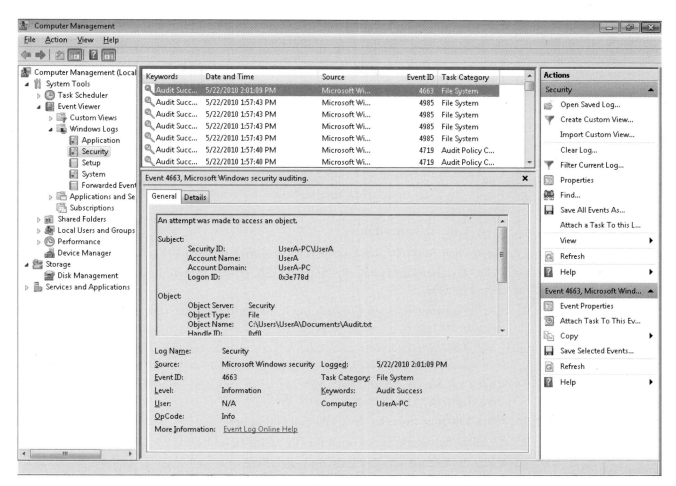

Figure 7-10 Windows Security log
Courtesy Course Technology/Cengage Learning

1. If necessary, start your computer and log on. Remember that the password is changed back to **password.**

2. Click the **Start** button, point to **All Programs,** click **Accessories,** right-click **Command Prompt,** and click **Run as administrator.**

3. In the User Account Control windows, click **Yes.**

4. At the command prompt, type **auditpol /get /category:*** and press **Enter.** This displays a list of all the advanced audit policy settings that are in place.

5. Read the list of policy settings that are enabled. This is the default configuration for Windows 7. Notice that under Object Access, File System auditing is not enabled. After you enable policy settings in the local security policy, these settings are removed and only the settings explicitly applied in the policy are effective.

6. Close the command prompt.

7. Click the **Start** button and click **Control Panel.**

8. Click **System and Security** and click **Administrative Tools.**

9. Double-click **Local Security Policy.**

10. In the left pane, expand **Local Policies** and click **Audit Policy.** Review the list of categories for basic auditing and notice that none are enabled in the local security policy.

11. In the left pane, expand **Advanced Audit Policy Configuration,** expand **System Audit Policies – Local Group Policy Object,** and then click **Object Access.**

12. Double-click **Audit File System**. This option enables auditing for file access.

13. In the Audit File System Properties window, select the **Configure the following audit events** check box and then select the **Success** and **Failure** check boxes.

14. Click the **Explain** tab, read the explanation, and click **OK**. The system is now able to track successful file access when users have permission to access a file and unsuccessful file access when users do not have permission to access a file. However, auditing must still be enabled for the individual files.

15. Close Local Security Policy and close all open windows.

16. Click the **Start** button and click **Documents**.

17. Right-click an open area in the **Name** column, point to **New**, and click **Text Document**.

18. Type **Audit** and press **Enter**.

19. Right-click **Audit.txt**, click **Properties**, and click the **Security** tab.

20. Click **Advanced** and click the **Auditing** tab. Notice that auditing information is protected by UAC.

21. Click **Continue** to open the auditing information. Notice that no auditing is configured by default.

22. Click **Add**, type **Everyone**, click **Check Names**, and click **OK**. This configures auditing to track access by all users. You can limit auditing to certain users or groups.

23. Check the **Successful** and **Failed** check boxes for **Create files/write data**. This configures auditing to track changes to the file.

24. Click **OK** four times to close all open dialog boxes.

25. Double-click **Audit.txt** to open the file and then add some content to the file.

26. Click the **File** menu, click **Exit**, and click **Save**.

27. Close Windows Explorer.

28. Click the **Start** button, right-click **Computer**, and click **Manage**.

29. In the left pane, expand **Event Viewer**, expand **Windows Logs**, and click **Security**. This displays all of the events in the security log.

30. Right-click **Security** and click **Filter Current Log**.

31. In the Event sources box, select **Microsoft Windows security auditing**.

32. In the <All Event IDs> box, type **4663** and then click **OK**. Notice that only one event is listed. This event was generated by editing the file.

33. Read the description of the event. The description indicates that a file was written by User*x*, where *x* is the number assigned to you; the file opened was Audit.txt; and the program used to write the file was notepad.exe.

34. Close Computer Management.

User Account Control

User Account Control (UAC) is a feature that was introduced in Windows Vista that makes running applications more secure. Security is enhanced by reducing the need to log on and run applications using administrator privileges. Reducing the use of administrative privileges makes it less likely that malicious software can adversely affect Windows 7.

In many organizations, all user accounts are configured as administrators on the local workstations. This is done to ensure that users are able to perform any local maintenance tasks that may be required, such as installing printers or software. In Windows 7, there have been major efforts to ensure that most tasks do not require administrative privileges. However, if users are still given administrative privileges, UAC increases security.

When UAC is enabled and an administrative user logs on, the administrative user is assigned two access tokens. One access token includes standard user privileges and the other access token includes administrative privileges. The standard user access token is used to launch the Windows 7 user interface. Therefore, all applications started by using the user interface also start with standard user privileges. This approach keeps any malicious software from having access to restricted areas like system files.

Admin Approval Mode ensures that the access token with administrative privileges is used only when required. When you use an application that requires administrative privileges, you are prompted to continue or cancel running the program with administrative privileges. If you select to continue, the program is run using the access token with administrative privileges. The Application Information Service is responsible for launching programs by using the access token with administrative privileges.

When UAC is enabled and a standard user logs on, the user is assigned only one access token with standard user privileges. If the user attempts to run an application that requires administrative privileges, the user is prompted to supply credentials for a user with administrative privileges.

Application Manifest

Newer Windows applications use an **application manifest** to describe the structure of an application. The structure includes required DLL files and whether they are shared. The application manifest can include information about UAC. An entry must be included in the application manifest to trigger the privilege elevation prompt for an application that requires administrative privileges.

Applications that are not designed for Windows 7 and which require administrative privileges do not properly request elevated privileges, generating an error. You can eliminate this error by using the Application Compatibility Toolkit.

Detailed information about the Application Compatibility Toolkit is covered in Chapter 11, Application Support.

UAC Configuration

When UAC was introduced in Windows Vista, it prompted even administrative users for just about every administrative action that was attempted. Windows 7 has reduced the number of UAC prompts presented to administrative users with a new default configuration that does not prompt if the user initiated the action. If a program initiates the action, then a UAC prompt is still presented.

Windows 7 also introduces a simplified interface for managing UAC, shown in Figure 7-11. The new interface has only four options:

- *Always notify me*—This setting is equivalent to the configuration in Windows Vista where even administrative users are prompted every time an administrative task is attempted.

- *Notify me only when programs try to make changes to my computer*—Administrative users are prompted only when a program attempts to perform an administrative task. When the administrative task is initiated by the user a prompt is not displayed.

- *Notify me only when programs try to make changes to my computer (do not dim my desktop)*—The same as the default setting except that when the UAC prompt is displayed, the screen is not dimmed.

- *Never notify me*—This disables UAC and is not recommended.

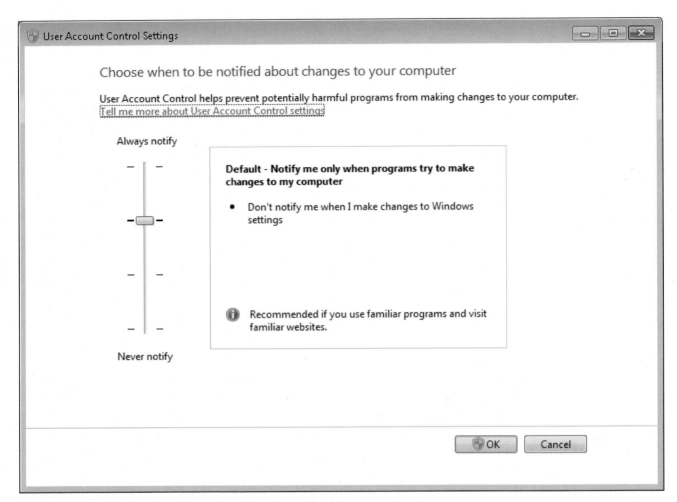

Figure 7-11 UAC settings
Courtesy Course Technology/Cengage Learning

For advanced configuration, UAC is configured by using either the Local Security Policy or Group Policy, just as it was managed in Windows Vista. The policy settings for configuring UAC are listed in Table 7-2. In most cases, it is easier to manage UAC in the simplified interface.

Activity 7-6: Configuring UAC

Time Required: 5 minutes

Objective: Identify the differences in simplified UAC settings.

Description: In most cases, UAC with the default configuration makes using a computer more secure for administrative users, since many tasks performed by administrative users do not need administrative privileges, such as reading e-mail or researching on the Internet. The default configuration does not prompt administrative users for approval when they initiate the action. However, in some cases, you may want administrators to be prompted so that they realize they are performing an administrative task. In this Activity, you will review how the simplified UAC settings modify the user experience.

1. If necessary, start your computer and log on.
2. Click the **Start** button and click **Control Panel**.
3. Click **System and Security** and click **Administrative Tools**.
4. Double-click **Local Security Policy**.

Table 7-2 UAC configuration options

Option (User Account Control:)	Description
Admin Approval Mode for the Built-in Administrator account	Used to enable or disable Admin Approval Mode for the built-in administrator account. The default configuration is disabled.
Allow UIAccess application to prompt for elevation without using secure desktop	This configuration allows UIAccess programs, such as Remote Assistance, to automatically disable the screen dimming that normally occurs when a UAC prompt is displays. This is a less secure configuration but can speed up screen drawing over slow connections. This is disabled by default.
Behavior of the elevation prompt for administrators in Admin Approval Mode	Used to configure the elevation prompt for Administrators only. The default configuration is to prompt for consent for non-Windows binaries. However, you can also configure a prompt for administrative credentials instead of a simple approval. You can also disable the prompt. Entirely disabling the prompt effectively disables UAC for administrators because applications can then request elevation to administrative privileges and are automatically approved. However, applications do run with standard user privileges until they request elevation.
Behavior of the elevation prompt for standard users	Used to configure the elevation prompt for standard users only. The default configuration is to prompt for credentials. You can also select Automatically deny elevation requests, in which case the user must manually use Runas to elevate the privileges of the application.
Detect application installations and prompt for elevation	Used to automatically detect whether an application is being installed and generate a prompt to elevate privileges. The default configuration is enabled. If this option is disabled, then many legacy application installations will fail.
Only elevate executables that are signed and validated	Used to limit privilege elevation to only applications that are digitally signed. The default configuration is disabled, which allows older unsigned applications that require administrative privileges to be elevated.
Only elevate UIAccess applications that are installed in secure locations	Used to force applications using the UIAccess integrity level in their application manifest to be located from a secure location. Secure locations are C:\ProgramFiles\ and C:\Windows\System32 and their subfolders. The default configuration is enabled.
Run all administrators in Admin Approval Mode	Used to limit all user processes to standard user privileges unless they are elevated to administrator privileges. The default configuration is enabled. When this option is disabled, UAC is disabled for administrators and standard users.
Switch to the secure desktop when prompting for elevation	Used to secure communication between the elevation prompt and other processes. When enabled, the UAC elevation prompt is limited to communication with processes that are part of Windows 7. This prevents malware from approving elevation. The default configuration is enabled.
Virtualize file and registry write failures to per-user locations	Used to enable non-UAC compliant applications to run properly. Applications that write to restricted areas are silently redirected to space in the user profile. The default configuration is enabled.

5. Expand **Local Policies** and click **Security Options**.

6. Scroll down to the bottom of the list of security options and read the options available for User Account Control.

7. Close Local Security Policy and the Administrative Tools window.

8. In the left pane of the Control Panel window, click **User Accounts and Family Safety** and click **User Accounts**.

9. Click **Change User Account Control settings**. Notice the shield symbol next to this item that indicates it is an administrative task that could be subject to UAC. Also notice that a UAC prompt was not displayed because you initiated the action.

10. In the User Account Control Settings window, move the slider up to **Always notify**, and click **OK**.

11. Click **Yes** to allow the changes. Notice that you are prompted by UAC because a program is changing the setting. Also notice that the screen is dimmed indicating that the secure desktop is being used.

12. Click **Change User Account Control settings**. Notice that this time you are prompted to elevate.

13. In the User Account Control prompt, click **Yes**.

14. In the User Account Control Settings window, move the slider down to **Notify me only when programs make changes to my computer (do not dim my desktop)**, and click **OK**.

15. Click **Yes** to allows the changes.

16. Click the **Start** button, type **diskpart** and then press **Enter**. Notice that a UAC prompt appears, but the desktop is not dimmed. Secure desktop is not being used.

17. In the User Account Control prompt, click **No**.

18. Click **Change User Account Control settings**.

19. Move the slider back to the default setting and click **OK**.

20. Click **Yes** to approve the change.

21. Close all open windows.

Malware Protection

The Internet has become an essential tool for business and home users. For many business users, the primary application used is e-mail. Many home users bought a computer specifically to access the Internet.

While the Internet is a great source of information, it is also the biggest source of malware (malicious software). Most viruses and adware come from the Internet. Protection from malware is an important feature in Windows 7.

Windows 7 includes the following features to protect computers from malware:

- Windows Defender
- Microsoft Security Essentials

Windows Defender

Windows Defender, shown in Figure 7-12, is antispyware software included with Windows 7. Spyware is software that is silently installed on your computer, monitors your behavior, and performs actions based on your behavior. Some spyware displays advertising based on Web sites you visit, others report back your Web browsing activity to a central location, and others even make system changes like changing your home page.

The most important aspect of spyware is that you do not choose to install it. Spyware is sometimes installed when you visit a Web site. Other times, spyware is installed unwittingly along with other software. For example, many of the early file-sharing programs installed spyware.

Windows Defender provides two levels of protection:

- On-demand scanning
- Real-time scanning

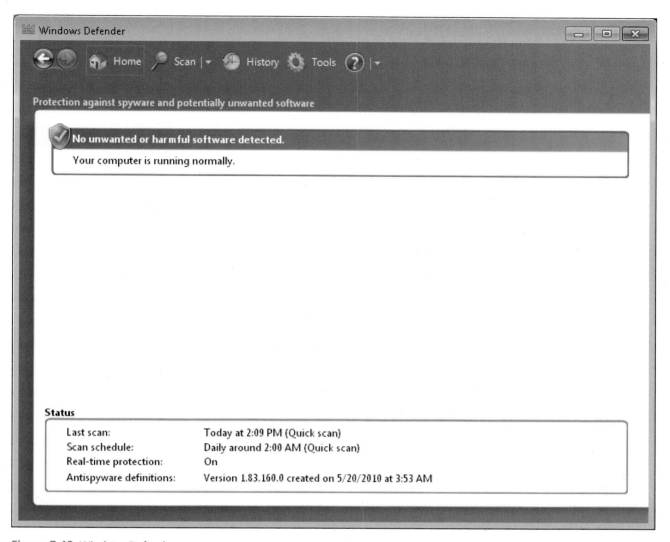

Figure 7-12 Windows Defender
Courtesy Course Technology/Cengage Learning

Both types of scanning use signatures to identify known and potential spyware. The signatures should be updated regularly to ensure you can catch the most recent spyware. By default, signatures are updated daily at 2:00 a.m. There is also an option to enable heuristics. Heuristics allows Windows Defender to identify suspicious software that does not exactly match existing signatures.

In addition to scanning, Microsoft also has an online community you can join that helps find and classify spyware. SpyNet is the online community for reporting spyware. By participating in SpyNet, you help Microsoft limit the spread of spyware.

On-Demand Scanning Windows Defender can perform ad hoc scanning when you suspect that spyware is present on your computer. In addition, you can configure Windows Defender to perform scheduled scans to ensure your computer stays spyware free on a regular basis.

A quick scan looks for spyware in the most common locations. This is the type of scan that is most commonly performed for a scheduled daily scan. When a quick scan is running, user performance is not affected.

A full scan looks at the entire disk system and running processes to find spyware. This type of scan is more complete, but will affect user performance. A full scan is typically performed when you think that spyware is on your computer. You may also want to schedule a full scan once per week or once per month.

Real-Time Scanning   Real-time spyware protection constantly monitors your computer and alerts you when spyware attempts to install or when system settings are changed. Real-time scanning is better than on-demand scanning because you are preventing the problem rather than fixing it. Real-time scanning prevents the spyware from being installed; on-demand scanning attempts to uninstall spyware after it is on your system.

Real-time scanning can protect the following areas of Windows 7:

- *Downloaded files and attachments*—This option monitor programs and files that interact with your Web browser. Programs monitored include Web browser add-ons, in addition to any files downloaded by the Web browser.

- *Programs that run on my computer*—The option monitors all applications that run on your computer and identifies software that may be running without your knowledge or permission.

Windows Defender Alert Levels   Windows Defender groups spyware into categories and provides a different alert for each category. Depending on the alert you receive, you may want to leave the software installed or allow it to install.

Windows Defender categorizes spyware in the following alert levels:

- *Severe or High*—Programs that are known to be very harmful and may damage your computer or privacy. You should remove these programs immediately when alerted.

- *Medium*—Programs that might modify your computer or collect private information. You should review the alert details to find out more about this program. After reading the alert details, you can decide whether to continue using this program.

- *Low*—Programs that might collect private information but are operating in accordance with their licensing agreement. You should review the alert details to find out more about this program. After reading the details, you can decide whether to continue using this program.

Windows Defender Actions   When malware is detected, it can be quarantined, removed, or allowed. Quarantined software is moved to a location where it can no longer run, but you can retrieve it. If you remove software, it is deleted. If you allow software, it is allowed at that specific time and added to the list of software that is allowed to run in the future without triggering an alert.

You can define default actions that are applied for severe, high, medium, and low alerts. The antispyware definitions include a recommended action for each item detected and the default configuration is to use the recommended action. If you prefer, you can override the recommended action. For example, you could specify that all severe and high alerts quarantine rather than remove. You also have the option to prompt the user with the default action rather than automatically implementing. However, in most cases, automatically applying the action is easier for the user.

Activity 7-7: Using Windows Defender

Time Required: 10 minutes
Objective: Use Windows Defender to prevent spyware on a computer.

Description: Windows Defender is used to prevent spyware installation and remove spyware. The best protection is a combination of real-time scanning and scheduled scans. In this activity, you review the default configuration and available options.

1. If necessary, start your computer and log on.

2. Click the **Start** button, type **Windows Defender**, and press **Enter**. Notice that Windows Defender is automatically protecting your computer.

3. Click **Tools** and review the available tools.

4. Click **Options**. The options for Automatic scanning are displayed. Notice that definitions are updated as part of the scanning process at 2 a.m.

5. In the left pane, click **Default Actions** and review the options selected by each alert level.

6. In the left pane, click **Real-time protection** and review the selected options. Notice that you can determine types of content are scanned.

7. In the left pane, click **Excluded files and folders**. You can indentify specific files and folder that are not to be scanned. This is useful for software that generates false positive alerts.

8. In the left pane, click **Excluded file types**. You can identify file types not to scan based on file extension in this screen.

9. In the left pane, click **Advanced** and review the available options.

10. In the left pane, click **Administrator** and then select the **Display items from all users of this computer**. This option allows you to view alerts from all users on this computer.

11. Click **Save** and then close Windows Defender.

Microsoft Security Essentials

Viruses are a different type of software than spyware. Like spyware, viruses are installed without your permission. Viruses are typically self-propagating and much more destructive than spyware. However, the important thing about viruses is not how we classify them. The important thing is to keep them off of your computer.

Some of the things viruses can do include:

- Send spam from your computer to the internet

- Capture usernames and passwords for Web sites, including online banking

- Steal enough personal information for identity theft

- Allow others to remote control your computer and use it as a launching point for illegal activities

Every computer should have anti-virus software installed. Windows 7 does not include any software to protect your computer from viruses. However, when you own a genuine version of Windows XP, Windows Vista, or Windows 7, you can download **Microsoft Security Essentials** from the Microsoft Web site at *http://www.microsoft.com/security_essentials/*. This download is free.

In an enterprise environment, you may choose to use third-party anti-virus software. Not because that software detects and removes viruses better than Microsoft Security Essentials, but because it offers better management capabilities. Most corporate anti-virus software has a centralized console for distributing signature updates and monitoring computers. Microsoft Security Essentials provided no centralized monitoring or control. Consequently, it is best suited to small environments.

Activity 7-8: Installing Microsoft Security Essentials

Time Required: 20 minutes
Objective: Install Microsoft Security Essentials.

Description: Microsoft Security Essentials is anti-virus software that can be freely downloaded for genuine versions of Windows 7. In this activity, you download and install Microsoft Security Essentials. This activity requires access to the Internet.

1. If necessary, start your computer and log on.
2. On the taskbar, click **Internet Explorer**.
3. In the Internet Explorer address bar, type **http://www.microsoft.com/security_essentials** and press **Enter**.
4. Click **Download Now**.
5. In the File Download – Security Warning window, click **Run**.
6. In the User Account Control window, click **Yes**.
7. Click **Next** to start the installation wizard.
8. On the Microsoft Security Essentials License Agreement page, click **I accept**.
9. On the Validate your copy of Microsoft Windows page, click **Validate**.
10. On the Ready to install Microsoft Security Essentials page, click **Install**.
11. When the installation is complete, click **Finish**.
12. By default the latest updates are downloaded and then a quick scan is performed. Wait until this process is complete. It may take 10 minutes or more.
13. Close Microsoft Security Essentials and Internet Explorer.

Data Security

The most basic level of data security in Windows 7 is NTFS permissions. NTFS permissions stop logged-on users from accessing files and folders that they are not assigned read or write permission to. However, NTFS permissions are only effective in protecting data when the original operating system is running.

There are many ways to work around NTFS permissions and gain access to data. The following are two examples:

- You can start a computer from floppy disk or CD-ROM and run Linux with an NTFS driver. Linux with an NTFS driver is able to read NTFS-formatted partitions, and ignores the security information. This allows you to copy or modify data on the NTFS-formatted partition without even a valid username.

- You can attach a hard drive from one Windows 7 computer to another. Local administrators always have the ability to take ownership of files and then read or modify them. When you move a hard drive, the local administrators of the new system can take ownership of files and then read or modify them.

As you can see, it is relatively easy to work around NTFS permissions when you have physical access to the computer. NTFS permissions are a very secure method of securing data when you have network access to files, but do not have physical access to the computer storing the files. This makes NTFS permissions excellent for servers, which are typically physically secured, but not as effective for desktop computers and laptops. Laptops are particularly at risk because they are more often lost or stolen.

To secure data on desktop computers and laptops, encryption is required. Windows 7 includes Encrypting File System (EFS) and BitLocker Drive Encryption to encrypt files.

Encryption Algorithms

Encryption is the process of taking data and making it unreadable. In most cases, encryption is a two-way process, where data can be encrypted to make it unreadable, then decrypted to make it readable again. The process for encrypting data is an algorithm. For computerized encryption of data, algorithms are math formulas that scramble the data into an unreadable format.

There are three main types of encryption algorithms:

- Symmetric
- Asymmetric
- Hash

Symmetric Encryption A **symmetric encryption algorithm** uses the same key to encrypt data and decrypt data. This is very similar to how a deadbolt lock works. When you leave your house, you lock the door with your key and when you return, you unlock the door with the same key. Figure 7-13 shows Bob and Susan accessing encrypted data by using the same key.

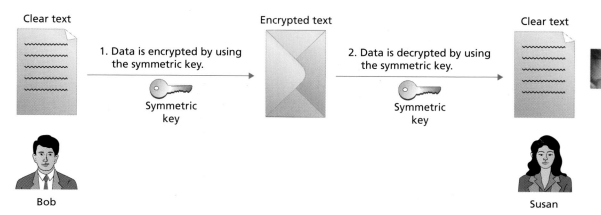

Figure 7-13 Symmetric encryption
Courtesy Course Technology/Cengage Learning

In computerized encryption, the key is a long number that is very hard to guess. The longer the key, the harder it is to guess the key. One of the most common key lengths is 128 bits. Data that is symmetrically encrypted with a 128-bit key would take years to decrypt by guessing the key. Other solutions offer stronger encryption, with longer keys up to 4096 bits.

Symmetric encryption is strong and fast. This makes it well-suited to encrypting large volumes of data such as files. Most file encryption is done with a symmetric encryption algorithm. Both EFS and BitLocker Drive Encryption use symmetric encryption to secure data.

The biggest problem with symmetric encryption is securing the key. Anyone that has a copy of the encryption key can decrypt the data. In Figure 7-13, both Bob and Susan need to have a copy of the same symmetric key. EFS and BitLocker Drive Encryption both use different methods to secure the key.

Asymmetric Encryption An **asymmetric encryption algorithm** uses two keys to encrypt and decrypt data. Data encrypted by one key is decrypted by the other key. This is similar to an electronic safe, where one person has a code that allows them to deposit money, but the other person has a code that allows them to remove money from the safe.

The keys used in asymmetric encryption are part of a digital certificate. Digital certificates are obtained from certificate authorities (sometimes also called certification authorities). Some of the better known certificate authorities are VeriSign and Thawte. Companies can also generate their own digital certificates internally. Most server operating systems, including Windows Server 2008, have certificate authority functionality as an option.

The digital certificate from the certification authority contains a public key and a private key. The public key is meant to be known to other people. The private key is protected and known only to you. By using both of these keys, encrypted data can be sent securely without the risk of transferring a symmetrical key. For example, in Figure 7-14, Bob is encrypting data for Susan. When

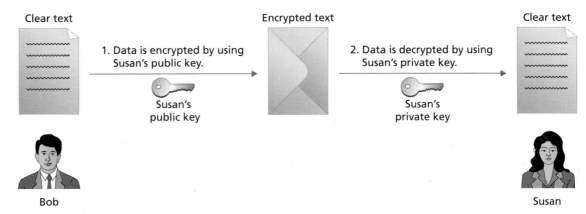

Figure 7-14 Asymmetric encryption
Courtesy Course Technology/Cengage Learning

Bob performs the encryption he uses Susan's public key. Then, only Susan can decrypt the data by using her private key. Only Susan can decrypt the data because only Susan has the private key.

Asymmetric encryption requires more processing power and is less secure than symmetric encryption. This makes asymmetric encryption unsuitable for large volumes of data. Asymmetric encryption is typically used to encrypt small amounts of data. Many systems for encrypting data use symmetric encryption to encrypt the data and then use asymmetric encryption to protect just the symmetric key because a symmetric key is relatively small compared to the data it has encrypted.

Hash Encryption   **Hash encryption algorithms** are used for a very different purpose than symmetric and asymmetric encryption algorithms. A hash encryption algorithm is one-way encryption, which means that it encrypts data, but the data cannot be decrypted.

Hash encryption is used to uniquely identify data rather than prevent access to data. Sometimes hash values for data are referred to as fingerprints. Some Web sites give you an MD5 value for downloadable software. MD5 is a hash encryption algorithm. The MD5 value is the unique value that is created when the MD5 hash encryption algorithm is run on the downloadable software. You can verify that the software has not been modified or corrupted by verifying the MD5 value after you download the software. If the software has been changed in any way, the MD5 value is also changed. Figure 7-15 shows how a hash value is used to verify software that has not been modified.

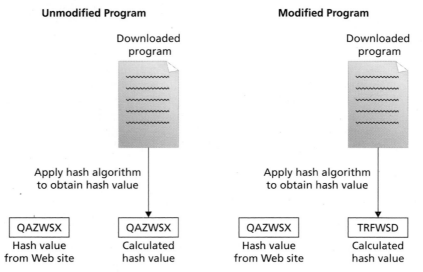

Figure 7-15 Using a hash value to verify software integrity
Courtesy Course Technology/Cengage Learning

Hash algorithms are also used for storing passwords. The actual passwords entered by users are not actually checked. The operating system verifies that the hash value of the password entered by the user matches the hash value that is stored for the user's password. When passwords are stored as only a hash value, it is impossible to decrypt the password. The password can only be guessed by brute force.

Encrypting File System

EFS is a technology that was first included with Windows 2000 Professional. It encrypts individual files and folders on a partition. This makes it suitable for protecting data files and folders on workstations and laptops. However, it can also be used to encrypt files and folders on network servers. This section focuses on encrypting local files.

To encrypt a file or folder by using EFS, the file or folder must be located on an NTFS-formatted partition. FAT- and FAT32-formatted partitions cannot hold EFS-encrypted files. FAT and FAT32 file systems are not able to hold the information required to decrypt the files.

When a file is encrypted, the data in the file is encrypted using a symmetrical key that is randomly generated for that particular file. The symmetrical key is then encrypted by asymmetric encryption, based on user-specific keys. This protects the symmetrical key from unauthorized users.

To use EFS, users must have a digital certificate with a public key and a private key. Unless specifically configured otherwise, users do not have a digital certificate by default. If a user encrypts a file and does not have a digital certificate, Windows 7 generates a certificate automatically. The public key from the digital certificate is used to encrypt the symmetrical key that encrypted the file. Only the user that encrypted the file is able to decrypt the symmetrical key because only that user has access to the private key required to decrypt the symmetrical key. The EFS encryption and decryption process is shown in Figure 7-16.

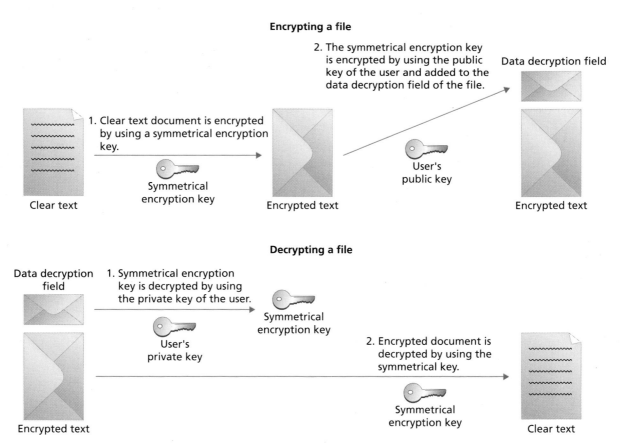

Figure 7-16 EFS encryption and decryption process
Courtesy Course Technology/Cengage Learning

Digital certificates are stored in the user profile.

From the user perspective, encryption is a file attribute like compression, hidden, or read-only. To encrypt a file, a user needs to access the Advanced attributes of the file, shown in Figure 7-17.

Figure 7-17 Advanced Attributes of a file
Courtesy Course Technology/Cengage Learning

Files that are encrypted cannot also be compressed.

Files can also be encrypted using the command-line utility Cipher. Cipher is useful for scripting or making changes to many files at once. For more information about Cipher options, run Cipher with the /? switch from a command prompt.

Lost Encryption Keys If a user loses the EFS key, then an encrypted file is unrecoverable with the default configuration. The only ways an encrypted file can be recovered is if the user has backed up their EFS key or if a recovery certificate has been created and installed.

Some ways EFS keys may be lost:

- The user profile is corrupted.
- The user profile is deleted accidentally.
- The user is deleted from the system.
- The user password is reset.

In User Accounts, there is an option for you to manage your file encryption certificates. This option allows you to view, create, and back up certificates used for EFS. You can also configure

EFS to use a certificate on a smart card and update previously encrypted files to use a new EFS certificate. Once a certificate is backed up, it can be used whenever required. This certificate can be imported back into a new user profile or even a different user.

Creating a recovery certificate allows the files encrypted by all users to be recovered if required. When a recovery certificate is in place, the symmetric key for all files is stored twice. The first copy of the symmetric key is encrypted by using the public key of the user encrypting the file. The second copy of the symmetric key is encrypted by using the public key of the recovery certificate.

The steps for creating and using a recovery certificate are:

1. *Create the recovery certificate*—This is done by running cipher with the /r:*filename* option, where *filename* is the name of the recovery certificate.

2. *Install the recovery certificate*—This is done by importing the recovery certificate into the local security policy as a data recovery agent. After this point, all newly encrypted files will include a symmetric key that is accessible to a user using the recovery certificate.

3. *Update existing encrypted files*—This is done by running cipher with the /u option. Encrypted files can only be updated by a user that is able to decrypt the files. This means that multiple users may need to update files. Updating encrypted files adds an additional encrypted copy of the symmetric key that is accessible to a user using the recovery certificate.

To recover files, you import the recovery certificate into a user profile using the Certificates MMC snap-in. After the recovery certificate is imported, that user can decrypt any files necessary.

Sharing Encrypted Files In a domain-based environment, it is easy to store encrypted files on a server and access them from multiple workstations or share them with other users. The necessary certificates are automatically created and stored on the remote server, and the files are encrypted and shared. On workstations that are part of a workgroup, the process takes more work.

For a single user to work with encrypted files on multiple computers, follow these steps:

1. Encrypt the file on the first computer.

2. Export the EFS certificate, including the private key from the first computer.

3. Import the EFS certificate, including the private key on the second computer.

4. Open the encrypted file on the second computer.

To share encrypted files with other users, follow these steps:

1. Export the EFS certificate of the first user, but do not include the private key.

2. Import the EFS certificate of the first user into the profile of the second user as a trusted person.

3. The second user encrypts the file and shares it with the first user. A copy of the symmetric key is encrypted with the public key of each user.

NOTE Encrypted files are typically not shared within a workgroup because of the complexity involved in exporting and importing certificates between computers. Sharing encrypted files is typically only done between users on the same computer or within a domain where no additional configuration is required.

Moving and Copying Encrypted Files The encryption of files and folders behaves differently than NTFS permissions and compression when files and folders are moved and copied. When files and folders are copied, they always take on the NTFS permissions or compression attribute of the folder they are copied into. However, this is not the case for encrypted files.

The following rules apply for moving and copying encrypted files:

- An unencrypted file copied or moved to an encrypted folder becomes encrypted.
- An encrypted file copied or moved to an unencrypted folder remains encrypted.
- An encrypted file copied or moved to a FAT partition, FAT32 partition, or floppy disk becomes unencrypted if you have access to decrypt the file.
- If you do not have access to decrypt a file, then you get an access-denied error if you attempt to copy or move the file to a FAT partition, FAT32 partition, or floppy disk.

Activity 7-9: Using EFS

Time Required: 10 minutes
Objective: Use EFS to encrypt and protect files.

Description: EFS is used to encrypt individual files and folders. Once a file is encrypted, only authorized users are able to read the data in the file. In this activity, you will encrypt a file and test it to ensure that only authorized users can decrypt the file.

1. If necessary, start your computer and log on.
2. Click the **Start** button and click **Computer**.
3. In the left pane, under Libraries, expand **Documents** and click **Public Documents**.
4. Right-click an open area in the **Name** column, point to **New**, and click **Text Document**.
5. Type **encrypt** and press **Enter**.
6. Double-click **encrypt.txt** to open it and type a line of text.
7. Click the **File** menu, click **Exit**, and click **Save**.
8. Right-click an open area in the **Name** column, point to **New**, and click **Text Document**.
9. Type **other** and press **Enter**.
10. Double-click **other.txt** to open it, and type a line of text.
11. Click the **File** menu, click **Exit**, and click **Save**.
12. Right-click **encrypt.txt** and click **Properties**.
13. Click the **Advanced** button, select the **Encrypt contents to secure data** check box, and click **OK**.
14. Click **OK**, click **Encrypt the file only**, and click **OK**. Notice that the file encrypt.txt is now displayed in green to indicate that it is encrypted.
15. Close **Windows Explorer**.
16. Switch user to **Susan Jones**.
17. Click the **Start** button and click **Computer**.
18. In the left pane, under Libraries, click **Documents**.
19. Double-click **other.txt**. Notice that you are able to open and read this file.
20. Close **Notepad**.
21. Double-click **encrypt.txt**. You receive an error indicating that access is denied because the file is encrypted.
22. Click **OK** to close the error dialog box and close Notepad.
23. Log off as **Susan Jones**.

Activity 7-10: Recovering Lost Encryption Keys

Time Required: 10 minutes

Objective: Back up and restore an EFS encryption key.

Description: A lost EFS encryption key means that an encrypted file cannot be accessed. To avoid this problem, you can back up the encryption key of a user. If a user's encryption key is backed up, you can restore it and then the user regains access to his files. In this activity, you will back up and restore the encryption key for a user.

1. If necessary, start your computer and log on.
2. Click the **Start** button and click **Control Panel**.
3. Click **User Accounts and Family Safety** and click **User Accounts**.
4. In the left pane, click **Manage your file encryption certificates**.
5. Click **Next** to start the Manage your file encryption certificates wizard.
6. Click **Next** to accept the default certificate.
7. If necessary, click **Back up the certificate and key now**.
8. To set the Backup location, click the **Browse** button, type **CertBak**, and click **Save**. The default location is your Documents directory. Typically, you would save the backed up certificate on removable storage and keep it in a secure location.
9. In the Password and Confirm password boxes, type **password**, and click **Next**. It is important to secure the backup with a password because it contains your private key.
10. Click **Next** to skip updating encrypted files with a new key.
11. Click **Close**.
12. Click the **Start** button, point to **All Programs**, click **Accessories**, and click **Run**.
13. In the Open box, type **mmc**, and press **Enter**.
14. Click **Yes** to start the Microsoft Management Console.
15. Click the **File** menu and click **Add/Remove Snap-in**.
16. In the Available snap-ins area, click **Certificates** and click **Add**.
17. Click **Finish** to accept managing certificates for your user account, and click **OK**.
18. In the left pane, expand **Certificates—Current User**, expand **Personal**, and click **Certificates**.
19. In the middle pane, right-click the User*x* certificate, and click **Delete**. If there are multiple certificates, delete all of them.
20. Read the warning message about losing the ability to decrypt files and click **Yes**.
21. Log off and log on again. This clears the certificate from memory.
22. Click the **Start** button and click **Computer**.
23. In the left pane, under Libraries, click **Documents**.
24. Double-click **encrypt**. You receive an error indicating that access is denied because the file is encrypted.
25. Click **OK** to close the error dialog box and close Notepad.
26. Click the **Start** button, point to **All Programs**, click **Accessories**, and click **Run**.
27. In the Open box, type **mmc**, and press **Enter**.
28. Click **Yes** to start the Microsoft Management Console.
29. Click the **File** menu and click **Add/Remove Snap-in**.

7

30. In the Available snap-ins area, click **Certificates** and click **Add**.

31. Click **Finish** to accept managing certificates for your user account, and click **OK**.

32. In the left pane, expand **Certificates—Current User**, and click **Personal**.

33. Right-click **Personal**, point to **All Tasks**, and click **Import**.

34. Click **Next** to start the **Certificate Import Wizard**.

35. Click the **Browse** button, change the file type to **Personal Information Exchange (*.pfx,*.p12)**, browse to the **Documents** library, click **CertBak.pfx**, and click **Open**.

36. Click **Next**.

37. In the Password box, type **password**.

38. Select the **Mark this key as exportable. This will allow you to back up or transport your keys at a later time** check box, and click **Next**.

39. Click **Next** to accept the default certificate location, click **Finish**, and click **OK**. Now you have a personal certificate again.

40. Close the **MMC** and click **No** to saving the console settings.

41. In Windows Explorer, double-click **encrypt.txt**. Now you are able to open the file because you have restored the certificate that contains your private key. Your public key was used to encrypt the symmetrical key that was used to encrypt the file.

42. Close Notepad and close Windows Explorer.

BitLocker Drive Encryption

BitLocker Drive Encryption is a data encryption feature included with Windows 7 that addresses some of the shortcomings of EFS. EFS is designed to encrypt only specified files. There are some files, such as the operating system files, that cannot be encrypted by using EFS. In addition, in some cases it may be possible to introduce low-level software that is able to steal EFS certificates.

An entire volume is encrypted when you use BitLocker Drive Encryption. This protects not only your data, but also the operating system. Protecting the operating system ensures that additional software is not placed on the drive when the operating system is shut down. Figure 7-18 shows the screen used to enable BitLocker Drive Encryption.

BitLocker Drive encryption is designed to be used with a **Trusted Platform Module (TPM)**. A TPM is part of the motherboard in your computer and is used to store encryption keys and certificates. TPM modules are not common on older computers and should be verified when buying a newer computer. BitLocker Drive Encryption can be used on older computers without a TPM, in which case the encryption keys are stored on a USB drive.

When a TPM is used, BitLocker Drive Encryption has two modes:

- TPM only—In this mode, the user is not aware that BitLocker is activated because the keys stored in the TPM are automatically used to start Windows 7. This option protects data from offline modification, but does not add any extra protection to the boot process to prevent password guessing.

- Startup key—In this mode, the user must supply a startup key to boot Windows 7. The startup key can be configured on a USB drive or as a PIN entered by the user. This adds additional protection because password guessing to log on to the operating system cannot be performed without first obtaining the startup key.

NOTE   For modes that require access to a USB drive, the computer BIOS must support reading and writing to the USB drive before the operating system is running. This is supported by most computers manufactured since 2005.

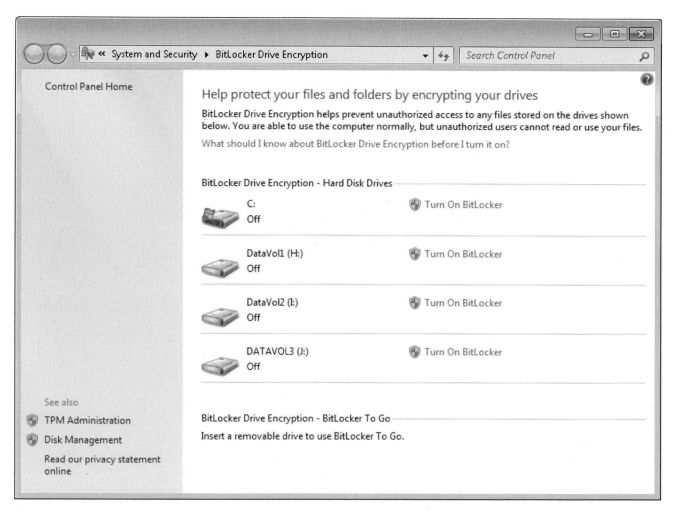

Figure 7-18 BitLocker Drive Encryption
Courtesy Course Technology/Cengage Learning

 If your computer does not have a TPM, you must use a USB drive.

BitLocker Hard Drive Configuration To use BitLocker Drive Encryption, your hard drive must be divided into two partitions. One partition is used as the operating system volume. The operating system volume is the volume that is encrypted. This volume contains both the operating system and user data.

The second required volume is the system volume. The system volume is not encrypted and contains the necessary files to boot the operating system. This volume must be at least 100 MB and formatted as an NTFS volume. Windows 7 automatically creates this volume as part of the installation process unless you specifically prevent it.

 In Windows Vista, BitLocker Drive Encryption supports encrypting only the operating system partition. In Windows 7, BitLocker Drive Encryption supports encrypting multiple volumes. However, the BitLocker feature is available only in Windows 7 Ultimate and Enterprise editions.

BitLocker Encryption Keys BitLocker actually uses two keys to protect data. The **Volume Master Key (VMK)** is used to encrypt the data on the operating system volume. The VMK is then encrypted using a **Full Volume Encryption Key (FVEK)**. This multiple-key method for data encryption makes it faster to change the encryption key. Changing the VMK would require re-encrypting all of the data, which is time consuming. Changing the FVEK requires only re-encrypting the VMK, which is very fast. Figure 7-19 illustrates how the encryption keys are used to protect data.

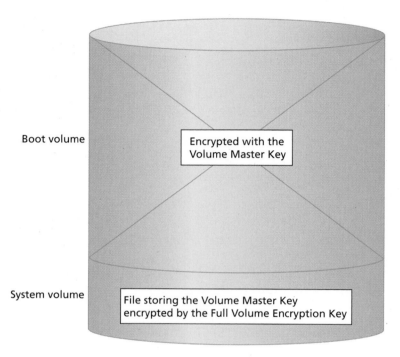

Figure 7-19 BitLocker Encryption Keys
Courtesy Course Technology/Cengage Learning

Accessing BitLocker-encrypted data is seamless for the user. A filter driver is used by Windows 7 to encrypt and decrypt data transparently as it is accessed from the hard drive. All data saved on the operating system volume is encrypted, including the paging files and hibernation file. While there is a slight decrease in disk performance, it should not be noticeable to users under most circumstances.

Recovering BitLocker-Encrypted Data When BitLocker Drive Encryption is enabled, a recovery password is generated automatically. The recovery password is a random number that you can save to a USB drive or folder, display on the screen, or print. It is important to keep the key in a secure location because it can be used to access data on the BitLocker encrypted volume.

In Windows 7, there is also an option to configure a data recovery agent for BitLocker. Like a data recovery agent for EFS, a data recovery agent for BitLocker is able to access BitLocker encrypted data even if a user forgets their PIN or password.

The recovery password is required when the normal decryption process for BitLocker Drive Encryption is unable to function. The most common reasons that the recovery password is required are:

- *Modified boot files*—If one of the boot files on the system volume is modified, BitLocker Drive Encryption stops the system from starting because the operating system has been tampered with.

- *Lost encryption keys*—If there is a problem with the TPM and the encryption keys stored in it are lost or corrupted, then the encrypted volume cannot be decrypted normally. The recovery password is also required if the encryption keys are stored on a USB drive that is lost or erased.

- *Lost or forgotten startup PIN*—If the requirement for a startup PIN is selected and the user forgets the startup PIN, then the recovery password is required to access the encrypted data.

The recovery process is as follows:

1. Turn on your computer.
2. Enter the BitLocker Drive Encryption Recovery Console.
3. Provide the recovery password by inserting a USB key or typing it in.
4. Your computer restarts and boots normally.

When typing in the recovery password, you must use the function keys. F1 represents the number 1, F2 represents the number 2, and so forth. F10 represents the number 0.

Disabling BitLocker Drive Encryption

If you no longer need BitLocker Drive Encryption, you can turn it off or disable it. Turning off BitLocker Drive Encryption decrypts all of the data on the hard drive and makes it readable again. Once BitLocker Drive Encryption is turned off, the disk can be moved to another computer and read by other operating systems.

Disabling BitLocker Drive Encryption does not decrypt the files on the volume. BitLocker Drive Encryption stores the FVEK as a clear key, which effectively removes the data protection associated with using BitLocker Drive Encryption. A clear key is one which is not encrypted or protected in any way. Disabling BitLocker Drive Encryption is not sufficient for other operating systems to read the BitLocker encrypted data.

BitLocker To Go

Windows 7 includes BitLocker To Go as a method for protecting data on removable storage such as USB drives. When you choose to enable removable storage for BitLocker To Go, you are prompted for how the storage will be unlocked. This process for unlocking the encryption keys is different for BitLocker To Go because you must be able to unlock the removable drive on multiple computers.

The options for unlocking removable storage are:

- *Use a password to unlock the drive*—When this option is selected, you enter a password that protects the encryption key for the data. When you take the removable storage to another computer, you are prompted for the password before getting access to the data on the removable drive.

- *Use my smart card to unlock the drive*—When this option is selected, you identify a smart card that will protect the encryption key for the data. When you take the removable storage to another computer, you must provide the smart card and the PIN for the smart card before getting access to the data on the removable drive. This method is the most secure, but the second computer must have a smart card reader which is not common.

When you enable BitLocker To Go for a removable drive you are prompted to save or print the recovery key, just as you are when you enable BitLocker for a fixed hard drive.

BitLocker To Go can only be enabled for a device when using Windows 7 Ultimate and Enterprise editions. However, any edition of Windows 7 can view or modify data encrypted by Bitlocker To Go. There is also a BitLocker To Go Reader that can be used on Windows Vista and Windows XP computers. The BitLocker To Go Reader is automatically included on removable storage encrypted by BitLocker To Go, and is accessible while the drive is still encrypted.

BitLocker To Go can be configured to automatically unlock a protected drive when it connects to a particular computer when a particular user is logged on. This simplifies access to the drive when used in a trusted environment, but still prompts for a password when the protected drive is used in another location.

There are many BitLocker and BitLocker To Go settings that can be managed through Group Policy. For example, you can force all removable storage to be encrypted with BitLocker To Go.

Windows Update

Scheduling automatic updates with Windows Update, shown in Figure 7-20, is the most important security precaution you can take with Windows 7. The vast majority of exploits used by viruses, worms, and other malware have updates available from Microsoft. Computers are only vulnerable to many of these threats because the necessary updates have not been applied.

When a Windows security flaw is found by a security company or ethical hacker, the flaw is reported to Microsoft. The person or company that found the flaw does not release their findings until Microsoft has created and released a update to fix the problem. Typically, this takes a few weeks or months.

After the update has been released, the person or company that found the flaw releases detailed information about the flaw. Microsoft releases the information on their Web site as well. Malware creators then begin to create software that takes advantage of the flaw. Computers that

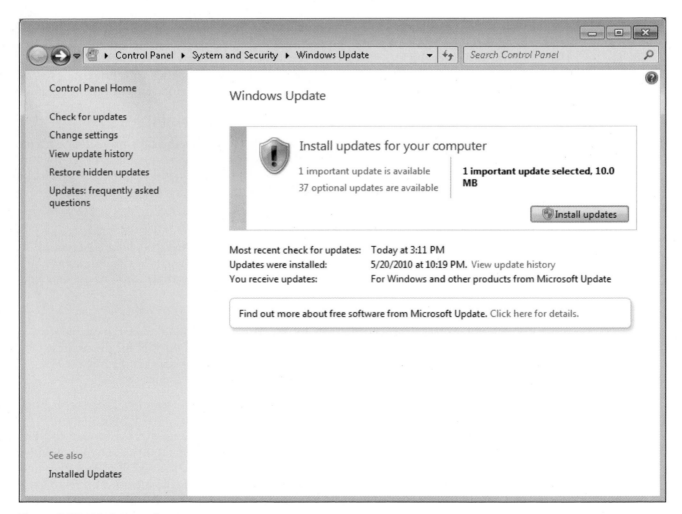

Figure 7-20 Windows Update
Courtesy Course Technology/Cengage Learning

do not apply patches in a timely way are still vulnerable to malware using the flaw. Computers that are patched regularly are not vulnerable.

Windows updates are divided into the following three categories:

- *Important*—These updates fix security and critical performance problems.
- *Recommended*—These updates fix software problems that may affect stability or features.
- *Optional*—These updates are typically updated hardware drivers and are never installed automatically.

Scheduling automatic updates is the easiest way to ensure that your computer is protected by applying the most recent updates as soon as they are available. You can configure Windows Update as shown in Figure 7-21.

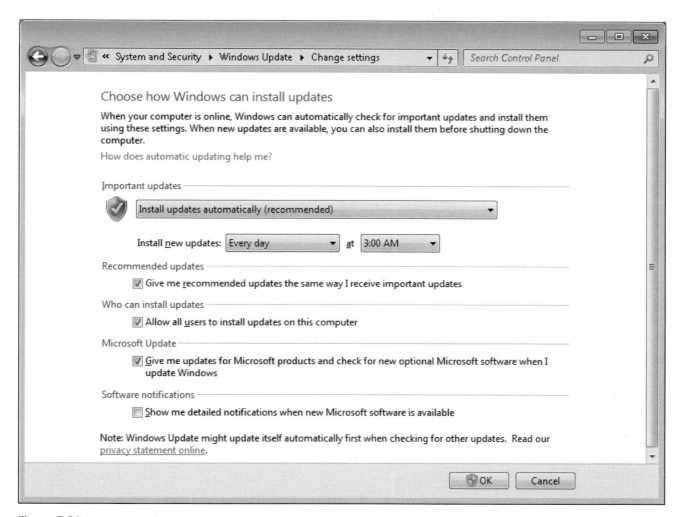

Figure 7-21 Windows Update settings
Courtesy Course Technology/Cengage Learning

The settings for important updates are:

- *Install updates automatically (recommended)*—This option downloads and installs updates automatically at a specified time without any user intervention. If the computer is turned off at the scheduled time, the updates are downloaded and installed at the next available opportunity.

- *Download updates but let me choose whether to install them*—This option lets you select which updates to install. However, most users do not have the skill set to properly evaluate which updates are best suited for them.

- *Check for updates but let me choose whether to download and install them*—This option lets you decide which updates to download and install. This option is useful when a computer is connected to the Internet by using a dial-up connection that is very slow.

- *Never check for updates (not recommended)*—When this option is selected, no updates are downloaded automatically, and you are not notified if updates are available. Selecting this option makes your computer less secure.

By default, recommended updates are automatically installed at the same time that important updates are installed. Because recommended updates can affect system stability, this you should leave this enabled.

When you allow users to install updates on the computer, they can install them before the scheduled time. It also allows standard users to install optional updates. If this option is disabled, then important and recommended updates are still installed at their scheduled time. Administrators are always allowed to install updates.

Microsoft Update is an alternative to Windows Update. Microsoft Update provides updates for Windows 7 and other Microsoft software such as Microsoft Office. Malware can take advantage of flaws in applications, not just the operating system. You should use Microsoft Update in most cases.

If you choose to not install a particular update, it becomes hidden. You can use the option **Restore hidden updates** to make it available again at a later time.

Some corporate environments are reluctant to automatically update computers because they are concerned that updates will break critical applications in their environment. Microsoft has improved the quality of their patches and critical application problems are now very rare. So, there is little risk. However, to ensure that critical applications are not affected by new updates, they should be tested.

The standard Windows Update process can be modified to use **Windows Server Update Services (WSUS)**. WSUS allows corporations to test patches before releasing them to all of the workstations in the organization. This option is not available in the standard Windows Update process. Detailed information about WSUS is covered in Chapter 13, Enterprise Computing.

If a user connects to the Windows Update Web site from Windows 7, Windows Update on the local computer opens automatically.

Activity 7-11: Protecting Your Computer by Using Windows Update

Time Required: 5 minutes

Objective: Protect your computer by configuring Windows Update for automatic updates.

Description: One of the simplest methods for protecting your computer from malware that uses known exploits is regular installation of patches and security updates. You can configure Windows Update to automatically download and install patches and security updates each day. In this activity, you configure Windows Update to download and install patches and security updates automatically.

1. If necessary, start your computer and log on.
2. Click the **Start** button and click **Control Panel**.

3. Click **System and Security** and click **Windows Update**. This screen indicates whether Windows 7 is up to date or not.

4. In the left pane, click **Change settings**.

5. Under Important updates, verify that **Install updates automatically (recommended)** is selected.

6. Configure updates to be installed **Every day** at **6:00** AM.

7. Under Recommended updates, verify that **Give me recommended updates the same way I receive important updates** is selected.

8. Click **OK**.

9. Click **View update history**. This shows only recent updates.

10. Click the **Installed Updates** link. This shows all installed updates and allows you to remove installed updates.

11. Close Installed Updates.

Action Center

Action Center, shown in Figure 7-22, is a Control Panel applet that lets you quickly check important security settings in Windows 7. This replaces the Windows Security Center that was available in Windows XP and Windows Vista. Action Center now includes a maintenance settings in addition to security settings.

The security settings monitored by Action Center are:

- Network Firewall
- Windows Update
- Virus protection
- Spyware and unwanted software protection
- Internet security settings
- User Account Control
- Network Access Protection

To ensure that you are aware of potential security problems, Action Center informs you by placing a red x icon in the system tray and displaying a text-based alert telling you what the potential problem is. Sometimes third-party software that is used for a firewall, virus scanning, or spyware protection is not properly identified.

If your third-party software is not identified properly, you can configure Action Center to not monitor that particular category. This eliminates unnecessary warning messages. For example, if you have installed a third-party firewall that is not recognized by Action Center, you will receive alerts indicating that you do not have a firewall in place. You can eliminate these alerts by indicating to Action Center that the network firewall should not be monitored.

Activity 7-12: Using Action Center

Time Required: 5 minutes
Objective: Configure Action Center.

Description: Action Center gives you a single location to view the most important security configuration information on your computer. In this activity, you will use Action Center to monitor the security on your computer.

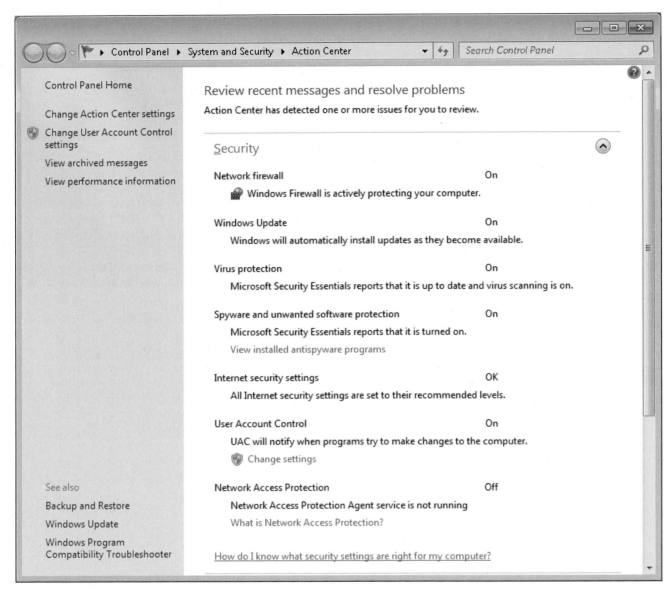

Figure 7-22 Action Center
Courtesy Course Technology/Cengage Learning

1. If necessary, start your computer and log on.

2. Click the **Start** button and click **Control Panel**.

3. Click **System and Security** and click **Action Center**.

4. Click **Security** to expand the Security area and see the current security configuration.

5. In the left pane, click **Windows Update** and click **Change Settings**.

6. Under Important updates, select **Never check for updates (not recommended)** and click **OK**. Notice that a popup appears in the system tray with a warning message.

7. In the system tray, click the Action Center icon (flag) with the red x. This gives you a summary of information in the Action Center.

8. Click **Open Action Center**. Notice that an important alert about Windows Update is displayed in red.

9. In the Windows Update alert, click **Change Settings**.

10. In the Action Center window, click **Install updates automatically (recommended)**. Notice that the alert in Action Center is gone. Also notice that the red x on the Action Center icon in the system tray is gone.

11. Click **Change Action Center settings**. Review the monitoring options that can be disabled.

12. Close all open windows.

Chapter Summary

- The major areas in which Windows 7 has improved security over Windows XP are malware protection, easier deployment of alternative authentication methods, enhanced network protection, and data protection for stolen hard drives.

- The local security policy in Windows 7 is used to configure a wide variety of security settings. Account policies control password settings and account lockout settings. Local policies configure auditing, user rights, and other security options. Software restriction policies control which software is allowed to run on a computer. Other security policies configure Windows Firewall and EFS certificates, and encrypt network communication.

- AppLocker is a new feature in Windows 7 that is used to define which programs are allowed to run. This is a replacement for the software restriction policies found in Windows XP and Windows Vista.

- Security templates can be used to configure or analyze Windows 7 security options. Security templates include account policy and local policy settings from the local security policy. Security templates also include settings for the event log, restricted groups, service configuration, registry security, and file security.

- Analyzing and applying security templates is done with Secedit or the Security Configuration and Analysis MMC snap-in. Secedit is a command-line tool that is useful for scripting mass operations.

- Auditing is used to record specific operating system events to the security log. Event categories that can be configured are Account Logon, Account Management, Detailed Tracking, DS Access, Logon/Log off, Object Access, Policy Changes, Privilege Use, System, and Global Object Access.

- UAC increases security by allowing users to log on and perform their jobs with standard user accounts. UAC also limits administrators to standard user privileges until administrative privileges are required by using Admin Approval Mode.

- Windows Defender is antispyware software. Windows Defender performs real-time scanning to prevent spyware installation and can perform on-demand scanning to remove spyware.

- Microsoft Security Essentials is free antivirus software that is available if your copy of Windows 7 is genuine.

- EFS is used to protect individual files by encrypting them. Only the person that encrypted a file can decrypt it, unless that file has been properly shared. A recovery certificate can be used to decrypt files, if the certificate is configured.

- BitLocker Drive Encryption is used to encrypt an entire partition. To use BitLocker Drive Encryption, there must be at least two partitions on the hard drive. BitLocker Drive Encryption also protects the operating system from being modified. BitLocker To Go is a new feature in Windows 7 that allows removable storage to be encrypted.

- Windows Update is used to ensure that patches are applied to Windows 7 as they are made available. It is strongly recommended to schedule updates to be installed each day.

Key Terms

account lockout policy A collection of settings, such as lockout duration, that control account lockouts.

application manifest An XML file that describes the structure of an application, including required DLL files and privilege requirements.

AppLocker A new feature in Windows 7 that is used to define which programs are allowed to run. This is a replacement for the software restriction policies found in Windows XP and Windows Vista.

asymmetric encryption algorithm An encryption algorithm that uses two keys to encrypt and decrypt data. Data encrypted with one key is decrypted by the other key.

audit policy The settings that define which operating system events are audited.

auditing The security process that records the occurrence of specific operating system events in the Security log.

BitLocker Drive Encryption A feature in Windows 7 that can encrypt the operating system partition of a hard drive and protect system files from modification. Other partitions can also be encrypted.

BitLocker To Go A new feature in Windows 7 that allows you to encrypt removable storage.

Encrypting File System (EFS) An encryption technology for individual files and folders that can be enabled by users.

Full Volume Encryption Key (FVEK) The key used to encrypt the VMK when BitLocker Drive Encryption is enabled.

hash encryption algorithm A one-way encryption algorithm that creates a unique identifier that can be used to determine whether data has been changed.

local security policy A set of security configuration options in Windows 7. These options are used to control user rights, auditing, password settings, and more.

malware Malicious software designed to perform unauthorized acts on your computer. Malware includes viruses, worms, and spyware.

Microsoft Security Essentials Free antivirus software that is available if your copy of Windows 7 is genuine.

Network Access Protection (NAP) A computer authorization system for networks that prevents unhealthy computers from accessing the network.

password policy A collection of settings to control password characteristics such as length and complexity.

Secedit A command-line tool that is used to apply, export, or analyze security templates.

Security Configuration and Analysis tool An MMC snap-in that is used to apply, export, or analyze security templates.

security template An .inf file that contains security settings that can be applied to a computer or analyzed against a computer's existing configuration.

symmetric encryption algorithm An encryption algorithm that uses the same key to encrypt and decrypt data.

Trusted Platform Module (TPM) A motherboard module that is used to store encryption keys and certificates.

User Account Control (UAC) A feature in Windows 7 that elevates user privileges only when required.

Volume Master Key (VMK) The key used to encrypt hard drive data when BitLocker Drive Encryption is enabled.

Windows Defender Anti-spyware software included with Windows 7.

Windows Server Update Services (WSUS) A service that collects and distributes patches to Windows workstations by using the automatic updates process.

Review Questions

1. Which security feature in Windows 7 prevents malware by limiting user privilege levels?

    a. Windows Defender

    b. User Account Control (UAC)

    c. Microsoft Security Essentials

    d. Service SIDs

2. The default privilege level for services is LocalSystem. True or False?

3. When compared to Windows XP, which networking features have been updated or added in Windows 7 to enhance security? (Choose all that apply.)

    a. TCP/IPv4

    b. Network Access Protection (NAP)

    c. Point-to-Point Tunneling Protocol (PPTP)

    d. Internet Connection Sharing

    e. Windows Firewall

4. When compared to Windows Vista, which data protection feature is new in Windows 7?

    a. Local security policy

    b. BitLocker Drive Encryption

    c. EFS

    d. BitLocker To Go

    e. Network Access Protection (NAP)

5. Which of the following passwords meet complexity requirements? (Choose all that apply.)

    a. passw0rd$

    b. ##$$@@

    c. ake1vyue

    d. a1batr0$$

    e. A%5j

6. Which password policy setting should you use to prevent users from reusing their passwords too quickly?

    a. Maximum password age

    b. Minimum password age

    c. Minimum password length

    d. Password must meet complexity requirements

    e. Store passwords using reversible encryption

7. Which account lockout policy setting is used to configure the time frame in which incorrect logon attempts must be conducted before an account is locked out?

    a. Account lockout duration

    b. Account lockout threshold

    c. Reset account lockout counter after

    d. Account lockout release period

8. The _____ local policy controls the tasks users are allowed to perform.

9. Which type of AppLocker rule condition can uniquely identify any file regardless of its location?

    a. Publisher

    b. Hash

    c. Network zone

    d. Path

10. How would you create AppLocker rules if you wanted to avoid updating the rules when most software is already installed?

    a. Manually create rules for each application

    b. Automatically generate rules

    c. Create default rules

    d. Download rule templates

11. Evaluating DLL files for software restrictions has a minimal impact on performance because of caching. True or False?

12. Which utilities can be used to compare the settings in a security template against a computer configuration? (Choose all that apply.)

    a. Secedit

    b. Windows Defender

    c. Security Templates snap-in

    d. Group Policy Object Editor

    e. Security Configuration and Analysis tool

13. To which event log are audit events written?

    a. Application

    b. Security

    c. System

    d. Audit

    e. Advanced Audit

14. An _____ is used to describe the structure of an application and trigger UAC when required.

15. What are you disabling when you configure UAC to not dim the desktop?

    a. Admin Approval Mode

    b. file and registry virtualization

    c. user-initiated prompts

    d. secure desktop

16. Microsoft Security Essentials requires a subscription fee after a 90-day trial period. True or false?

17. Which of the following does Action Center monitor? (Choose all that apply.)

    a. Network Firewall

    b. Windows Update

    c. User Account Control

    d. Internet security settings

    e. Virus protection

18. To prevent spyware installation, you should configure Windows Defender to perform _____.

19. Which type of encryption is the fastest, strongest, and best suited to encrypting large amounts of information?

    a. Symmetric

    b. 128 bit

    c. Asymmetric

    d. Hash

    e. Public key

20. To encrypt a file by using EFS, the file must be stored on an NTFS-formatted partition. True or False?

21. How can you recover EFS-encrypted files if the user profile holding the digital certificate is accidentally deleted? (Choose all that apply.)

    a. Restore the file from backup.

    b. Restore the user certificate from a backup copy.

    c. Another user with access to the file can decrypt it.

    d. Decrypt the file by using the recovery certificate.

    e. Decrypt the file by using the EFS recovery snap-in.

22. Which of the following is not true about BitLocker Drive Encryption?

    a. BitLocker Drive Encryption requires at least two disk partitions.

    b. BitLocker Drive Encryption is designed to be used with a TPM.

    c. Two encryption keys are used to protect data.

    d. Data is still encrypted when BitLocker Drive Encryption is disabled.

    e. You must use a USB drive to store the startup key.

23. BitLocker Drive Encryption is user aware and can be used to protect individual files on a shared computer. True or False?

24. Which is the preferred setting for Windows Update?

    a. Install updates automatically

    b. Download updates but let me choose whether to install them

    c. Check for updates but let me choose whether to download and install them

    d. Never check for updates

25. Which categories of updates can be downloaded and installed automatically by Windows Update? (Choose all that apply.)

    a. Critical

    b. Important

    c. Recommended

    d. Optional

    e. Feature update

Case Projects

Case Project 7-1: Virus Prevention

Buddy's Machine shop has been infected with a virus for the second time in six months. Several machines cannot run antivirus software because it interferes with specialized software used to carve machine parts from blocks of metal. What can you do to mitigate the risk of viruses infecting the computers?

Case Project 7-2: Home User Protection

Superduper Lightspeed Computers sells many computers to home users. Many Windows XP customers have returned to the store complaining that their computer is slow or crashes frequently. Which features can you configure in Windows 7 to increase customer satisfaction?

Case Project 7-3: Applying Security Settings

Gigantic Life Insurance has thousands of insurance brokers selling their services. The Security Officer has recently identified a list of security settings that she wants configured on all Windows 7 computers used by the insurance brokers. What is the best way to apply these security settings?

Case Project 7-4: Data Encryption

The salespeople at Hyperactive Media sales all use laptop computers so they can have easy access to important data on the road. The salespeople regularly take customer lists and other sensitive company information with them. Occasionally a laptop is lost or stolen. Which data encryption features in Windows 7 can prevent hard drive data from being used after a laptop is stolen? Which features would you implement and why?

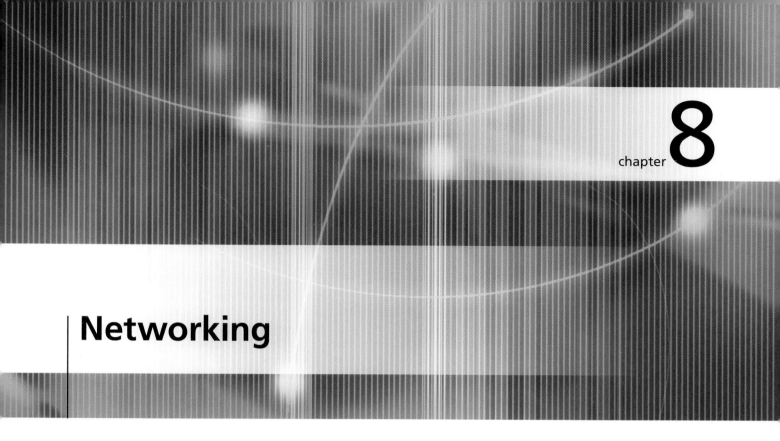

chapter 8

Networking

After reading this chapter and completing the exercises, you will be able to:

- Understand Windows 7 network components
- Understand Windows 7 network architecture
- Describe and configure Internet Protocol version 4
- Describe and configure Internet Protocol version 6
- Perform and monitor file sharing
- Connect Windows 7 to the Internet
- Describe and configure wireless networking
- Configure Windows Firewall
- Describe network bridging
- Describe ad hoc and homegroup networks

The vast majority of computers in corporations and small offices are networked. Even many homes have multiple computers that are used to share files and access the Internet. As a computer professional, it is essential that you understand how to configure Windows 7 for networking in these situations.

Windows 7 includes a wide variety of features to support different network scenarios. The basic configuration of network connectivity is similar to previous versions of Windows in many respects, but includes new features such as network location awareness.

Networking Overview

The networking configuration in Windows 7 has changed dramatically from early versions of Windows. The basic components of networking such as clients, services, protocols, and network drivers are still used, but additional features have been added. Windows 7 is network aware and can use a different configuration depending on the network you are connected to. For example, when you are at work with your mobile computer on the corporate network, you can automatically have different settings than when the same mobile computer is on your home network.

The basic components of Windows 7 that support networking are:

- Network and Sharing Center
- Networks
- Connections

Network and Sharing Center

Network and Sharing Center is a central point in Windows 7 for managing the configuration of the network you are currently connected to. The areas of Network and Sharing Center, as shown in Figure 8-1, are:

- *Network map*—This shows a summary of the network you are connected to. Three icons representing the local computer, local network, and the Internet are shown. If there are any communication problems on your network, the summary map will show whether the problem is related to the local network or the Internet. There is also a link to view a full network map.

- *Active Network details*—This area shows summary information for the network you are connected to. It displays the network you are connected to, the type of network it is, the type of access you have, and the connection being used to access the network.

- *Change your networking settings*—This area displays links to common configuration and troubleshooting wizards.

Networks

In early versions of Windows, the operating system was simply aware of a network card being physically connected (or not connected) to a cable. Windows 7 has been enhanced to be network location aware. When you move a computer from one network to another, Windows 7 is aware that it is plugged in to a different network. Previous versions of Windows would not have sensed the change.

Network location awareness allows you to configure the security settings for each **location type** differently. For example, in your office you may allow file and printer sharing, but not when you are traveling on the road in hotels and airports. The configuration settings for each location type are saved so that you do not need to reconfigure your computer as you move from one network location to another.

Developers can use the network awareness capabilities of Windows 7 to make their applications more efficient. For example, applications can query Windows 7 to ensure the Internet is available before attempting to download updates. Applications can also query Windows 7 to

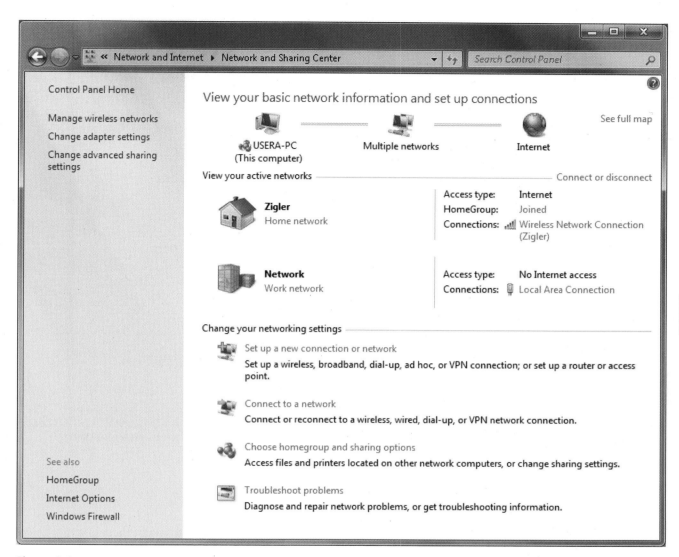

Figure 8-1 Network and Sharing Center
Courtesy Course Technology/Cengage Learning

verify that the computer is connected to a network in the proper category and ensure that an appropriate security configuration is used.

Network Management You can view and manage all of the network locations your computer has connected to. For each network location, you can configure the network location type, as shown in Figure 8-2.

Location Types Each network location must be assigned a location type. Based on the location type you select, different security settings are applied. Components that are configured include Windows Firewall and network discovery. If you modify the security settings for a network location, those settings are modified for all network locations of the same type. Security settings are tracked by location type.

The location types are:

- *Home network*—This category is used when the computer is connected as part of a peer-to-peer network in a trusted location. Typically this is used at home. The computer is able to access other network computers and you are able to share files and printers on your computer. Computers on a home network can belong to a homegroup.

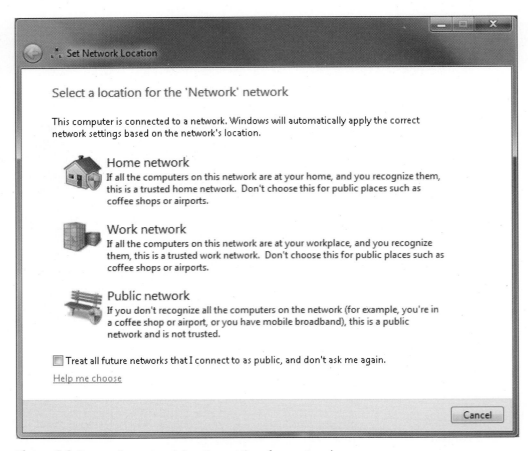

Figure 8-2 Personalize network location settings for a network
Courtesy Course Technology/Cengage Learning

- *Work network*—This category is used when the computer is connected as part of a local network in a trusted location. Typically this is used at work in a small office. In a work network, you can access other network computers and share files and printers on your computer. A computer on a work network cannot join or create a homegroup.

- *Public network*—This category is used when the computer is connected in an untrusted public location such as an airport. In a public location, you cannot be sure of who else is using the network. Other network computers have limited or no visibility to your computer on the network. Your computer can connect to publicly available network resources but you are not able to share files and printers on your computer. Connections initiated from other computers on the public network are blocked by default.

- *Domain network*—This category is used in corporate environments when your computer is part of a domain network. When Windows 7 can communicate with a domain controller, the network connection is automatically placed in this category. You cannot manually place a computer in this category. The computer settings for computers on a domain network are determined by Group Policy settings configured by the network administrator.

Network Discovery One of the network characteristics you can configure is **network discovery**. Network discovery provides you with an easy way to control how your computer views other computers on the network and advertises its presence on the network. In previous versions of Windows, you were required to modify several settings in the local security policy to get the same effect. Most users and many administrators were not skilled enough to make these choices. Network discovery settings can be reviewed or modified by selecting the **Change advanced sharing settings** task from the Network and Sharing Center.

The options for network discovery are:

- *Turn on network discovery*—You can see and access other computers and devices on the network. Other computers can also see your computer on the network and access shared resources. This is the default configuration when the network is in the Home or Work location type.

- *Turn off network discovery*—You cannot see or access other computers and devices on the network. Other computers also cannot see your computer on the network or access shared resources. This is the default configuration for networks in the Public location type.

Activity 8-1: Exploring Network and Sharing Center

Time Required: 5 minutes

Objective: Become familiar with the options that are available in Network and Sharing Center.

Description: Network and Sharing Center provides you with an overview of the network configuration on your computer. In this activity, you will explore the options available to you in Network and Sharing Center.

1. If necessary, start your computer and log on.
2. Click the **Start** button and click **Control Panel**.
3. Click Network **and Internet** and click **Network and Sharing Center**.
4. Below Network, click **Public network**. This opens a window to edit the network location configuration.
5. Click **Work Network** and then click **Close**. The location type is now Work. You can also see the network connection that is connected to this network.
6. In the upper-right corner, click **See full map**. This shows you a more complete map of your local network. The summary map in Network and Sharing Center only shows your computer, the network, and the Internet.
7. Close the Network Map window.

Connections

Connections in Windows 7 are fundamentally the same as in previous versions of Windows. For each network device installed in your computer, a connection is created to manage that network device. For example, if your computer has an Ethernet network card and a wireless network card, there will be two connections in Windows 7, one to manage each device. The properties of a connection are shown in Figure 8-3. If your computer has multiple network cards then you will see an additional Sharing tab when viewing connections properties.

Connections are composed of:

- Clients and services
- Protocols
- Network drivers

Clients and Services
Clients and **services** are the applications that use the network to communicate. A client allows you to connect to a particular service running on a remote computer. A service allows your computer to accept connections from and provide resources to a remote computer.

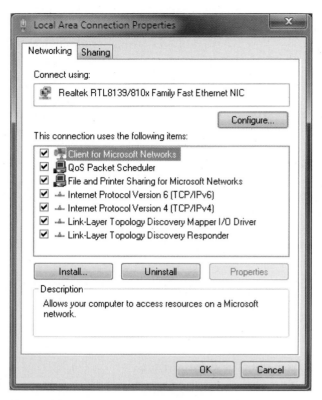

Figure 8-3 Local Area Connection properties
Courtesy Course Technology/Cengage Learning

Local Area Connection Properties   The clients and services included with Windows 7 are:

- *Client for Microsoft Networks*—This client allows Windows 7 to access shared files and printers on other Windows computers.

- *File and Printer Sharing for Microsoft Networks*—This service allows Windows 7 to share files and printers with other Windows computers.

- *QoS Packet Scheduler*—This service controls the flow of network traffic in Windows 7. It is responsible for optimizing network communication by controlling the Quality of Service (QoS). Corporate environments can use QoS policies to give certain network content types higher priority within Windows 7. For home networks, QoS incorporates Quality Windows Audio/Video Experience (qWave) to ensure that A/V streams get higher network priority than data streams, which are more tolerant of network delays.

All three client and service components in Windows 7 are installed by default.

Both the Client for Microsoft Networks and File and Printer Sharing for Microsoft Networks use the **Server Message Block (SMB)** protocol. SMB version 1.0 is included in all previous versions of Windows. Windows 7 includes support for SMB version 2.1, which is used only when communicating with Windows 7 or Windows Server 2008 R2.

Some enhancements in SMB 2.1 are:

- *Multiple SMB commands can be combined in a single packet*—SMB 1.0 performed poorly over network links with high latency due to the large number of packets required in the communication process. SMB 2.1 reduces the number of packets required and significantly speeds performance over WAN connections and VPN connections.

- *Larger buffer sizes*—On slow networks with high latency, a larger buffer size increases the overall communication speed.

- *Increased scalability*—Some characteristics, such as the number of open files allowed, have been increased to allow Windows 7 to perform more tasks at one time.

- *Higher tolerance for short network interruptions*—SMB 1.0 had a very low tolerance for interrupted network conditions. When the network experienced brief problems, often applications with open files on a remote server would generate an error and data would be lost. SMB 2.1 is more likely to reconnect to an already open file without an application error.

- *Support for symbolic links*—A symbolic link is a file that acts as a pointer to another file, similar to the way a shortcut works. Symbolic links in previous Windows versions are also known as junction points or reparse points. Previous versions of SMB could not properly follow a symbolic link, but SMB 2.1 can.

Early versions of Windows included a client for accessing Novell NetWare networks. This client has been removed from Windows 7.

Protocols Protocols are the rules for communicating across the network. They define how much data can be sent and the format of the data as it crosses the network. Windows 7 includes several protocols for network communication.

- **Internet Protocol Version 4 (TCP/IPv4)**—This is the standard protocol used on corporate networks and the Internet. This protocol is installed by default and cannot be removed. However, it can be disabled.

- **Internet Protocol Version 6 (TCP/IPv6)**—This is an updated version of TCP/IPv4 with a larger address space and additional features. It has not yet gained widespread popularity, but will in the future. Windows 7 uses this protocol for some peer-to-peer networking applications. This protocol is installed by default and cannot be removed. However, it can be disabled.

- **Link-Layer Topology Discovery Mapper I/O Driver**—This protocol is responsible for discovering network devices on the network, such as computers and routers. It is also responsible for determining the network speed.

- **Link-Layer Topology Discovery Responder**—This protocol is responsible for responding to discovery requests from other computers.

Detailed information about TCP/IPv4 and TCP/IPv6 is covered later in this chapter.

Network Drivers A **network driver** is responsible for enabling communication between Windows 7 and the network device in your computer. Each make and model of network device requires a driver specifically developed for that device, just as each printer requires a printer driver specific to that make and model of printer.

Windows 7 includes network drivers for network devices from a wide variety of manufacturers. However, if the network driver for your network device is not included with Windows 7, you can obtain the driver from the manufacturer's Web site.

Activity 8-2: Viewing a Network Connection

Time Required: 5 minutes
Objective: View the properties and status of a network connection.

Description: To configure Windows 7 for network connectivity, you need to understand the components of a network connection and how to view their status. In this activity, you view the status and properties of a network connection.

1. If necessary, start your computer and log on.
2. Click the **Start** button and click **Control Panel**.
3. Click **Network and Internet** and click **Network and Sharing Center**.
4. Under the Network heading, and to the right of Connections, click **Local Area Connection**. This shows the current connection status, including:
   - IPv4 Connectivity
   - IPv6 Connectivity
   - Media State
   - Duration
   - Speed
   - Activity
5. Click the **Properties** button. This displays all of the clients, services, and protocols that are installed. If the box is checked, then the component is enabled. Some of these components cannot be uninstalled, but they can all be disabled.
6. Click the **Configure** button. This allows you to modify the configuration of the network card or network card driver. The General tab shows you some information about the network card.
7. Click the **Advanced** tab. This tab allows you to configure many settings for your network card. The options available here vary depending on the card. However, all cards allow you to in some way configure the connection speed and duplex. These are important settings to ensure proper connectivity when connecting to some network switches in the event that autonegotiation fails.
8. Click the **Driver** tab. This tab lets you:
   - View driver details
   - Update the driver
   - Roll back the driver to a previous version
   - Disable the device
   - Uninstall the driver
9. Click the **Driver Details** button. This shows you the files used as part of the device driver as well as additional information about the driver such as version and the company that provided the driver.
10. Click **OK** to close the Driver File Details dialog box.
11. Click **Cancel** to close the network card Properties dialog box.
12. Click **Close** to close the Local Area Connection Status dialog box.
13. Close Network and Sharing Center.

Network Architecture

Windows 7 includes several interfaces that make it easier for developers to create clients, services, protocols, and network drivers. These interfaces provide a standard way for clients and services to communicate with protocols and a standard way for protocols to communicate with network drivers.

The standardization makes it easy for developers to write a client, server, or network driver that can communicate with any protocol. However, practically speaking, TCP/IP is by far the most common protocol used. The architecture of Windows 7 networking, including TCP/IP, is shown in Figure 8-4.

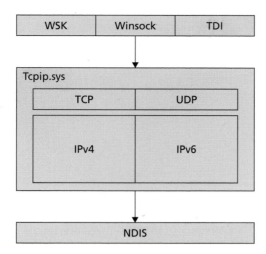

Figure 8-4 Windows 7 Network Architecture
Courtesy Course Technology/Cengage Learning

8

Interfaces for networking in Windows 7 are:

- *Windows Sockets (Winsock) user mode*—This interface supports communication between applications and the TCP/IP protocol. This interface is used by most network applications such as Web browsers, file transfer protocol (FTP) clients, and instant messaging clients.

- *Transport Device Interface (TDI)*—This interface supports communication between clients or services and protocols, including TCP/IP. TDI supports the Network Basic Input Output (NetBIOS) communication protocol used by older applications and Windows Sockets. The Windows Sockets implementation in TDI is a higher performing kernel mode that is more difficult to program and is used by services and clients, rather than applications. TDI is being phased out and is included for backward compatibility.

- *Winsock Kernel (WSK)*—This interface is a replacement for TDI and supports communication between services or clients and protocols, including TCP/IP. It provides higher performing kernel mode access and gives developers access to new TCP/IP features in Windows 7. It is relatively easy to port TDI applications to WSK.

- *Network Driver Interface Specification (NDIS)*—This interface supports communication between protocols and network drivers. NDIS 6.2, included with Windows 7, has new support for offloading network processing to specialized network cards and multi-processor capability. For backward compatibility, network drivers for earlier versions of NDIS (version 4 and up) are supported but will have support discontinued in future updates. NDIS drivers with a version number of 6.x or later are strongly recommended.

IP Version 4

TCP/IP is the most popular networking protocol in the world today. Although Windows 7 has the ability to use multiple protocols, only TCP/IP is included with Windows 7 for network communication such as file sharing or accessing the Internet. An Internet Protocol (IP) defines the methods used to send data from one computer to another over networks. Different versions of the IP methods exist, identified by a version number. A reference to the IP version, for example version four, is typically written as IPv4 in documentation. Part of the IPv4 standard defines how to specify and decipher the address of a computer that sent a piece of TCP/IP data, and the address of the computer that will receive it. The IPv4 addressing scheme works whether the computers are right next to each other or if they are located on opposite sides of the globe.

The important configuration concepts of IPv4 are:

- IP addresses
- Subnet masks
- Default gateways
- DNS
- WINS
- Methods for configuring IP
- Troubleshooting IPv4

IP Addresses

Each computer must have a unique **IPv4 address** to communicate on the network. If any two computers on the same network have the same IPv4 address, it is impossible for information to be correctly delivered to them.

IPv4 addresses are actually a binary number, 32 binary digits (bits) wide. Each binary digit can have the value 1 or 0.

IPv4 addresses are most commonly displayed in dotted decimal notation. In this format, an IP address is displayed as four decimal numbers, called octets, which are separated by periods. An example of an IP address written in dotted decimal notation is 192.168.5.66. In this example, 192 is the first octet, 168 is the second, 5 is the third, and 66 is the fourth and last octet. Each octet represents the decimal number equivalent of the 8 binary bits in that portion of the 32-bit address. An octet value can range between 0 and 255.

The value of the first octet determines the general class of an IPv4 address as shown in Table 8-1.

Table 8-1   IPv4 Address classes

First Octet Value Range	Corresponding Class
0 to 127	A
128 to 191	B
192 to 223	C
224 to 239	D
240 to 255	E

There are special cases and considerations in the IPv4 class–based system:

- If the first octet is zero, the remaining octets identify local machines on the same network as the computer sending data. The special IPv4 address 0.0.0.0 is used in routing logic to represent "all other computers."

- A first octet value of 127 identifies a destination that is local to the computer sending data. The address in this range that is commonly seen is 127.0.0.1, or the **loopback address**. Data sent to the loopback address will return to the computer that sent it and will not appear on the actual network.

- A first octet identifying a class D address represents a multicast address. Computers that belong to the same multicast group will have the same multicast address assigned to them. Data sent to that multicast address will attempt to deliver copies of the data to all multicast members with the same address. Class D addresses are not used to identify a single host computer with a unique IPv4 address.

- A first octet identifying a class E address is reserved for future use and special purposes. Class E addresses are not used to identify a single host computer with a unique IPv4 address. The special IPv4 address 255.255.255.255 is used as a **broadcast address** that represents the destination "all computers in this network." Data sent to this broadcast address cannot leave the local network through a router.

Several ranges of IP addresses are reserved for internal private network use and cannot be routed on the Internet. However, they can be routed internally on corporate networks. A proxy server or network address translation (NAT) must be used to provide Internet access to computers using these addresses. Table 8-2 shows the network addresses that are reserved for internal networks.

Table 8-2 Addresses for internal networks

IP Address Range	Network (in CIDR notation)
192.168.0.0–192.168.255.255	192.168.0.0/16
172.16.0.0–172.31.255.255	172.16.0.0/12
10.0.0.0–10.255.255.255	10.0.0.0/8

Subnet Masks

An IP address is composed of a network ID and a host ID. Using the concept of a postal address for comparison, the network ID is similar to a street name and the host ID is similar to a house number. When a packet of information is being delivered on a corporate network, the network ID is used to get the packet to the proper area of the network and the host ID is used to deliver the packet to the correct computer. The total number of binary bits used to define a network ID plus the host ID must equal 32 binary digits exactly in order to fit in an IPv4 address.

A **subnet mask** is used to define which part of an IP address is the network ID and which part of the IP address is the host ID. If the subnet mask is configured incorrectly, Windows 7 may not be able to communicate with computers on other parts of the network. Two computers cannot be active on the same local network with the same network ID and same host ID. This would cause an IP address conflict and other computers would not know which computer to communicate with.

The subnet mask is another 32-bit binary number, specified separately from the IP address itself. For discussion sake, consider this example of a subnet mask value in binary form (blank spaces inserted for readability):

Subnet mask = 1111 1111 1111 1111 1111 1111 0000 0000

The subnet mask's bits set to 1 identify what part of an assigned IPv4 address belongs to the network ID. The bits set to 0 identify what part of an address belongs to the host ID. In this example, this would be interpreted by a computer as the first 24 bits of the IPv4 address identify the computer's network ID; the last 8 bits of the IPv4 address identify the computer's host ID. For convenience, the dotted decimal notation is used to enter the subnet mask value into the IP settings of a network interface. Using dotted decimal notation, the above subnet mask binary value would be entered as 255.255.255.0.

The subnet mask octet value of 255 indicates that the corresponding IPv4 address octet belongs to the network ID. The subnet mask octet value of 0 indicates that the corresponding IPv4 address octet belongs to the host ID. For example, consider the following breakdown of an IPv4 address into its network and host ID components given a subnet mask:

IPv4 Address = 192.168.4.1

Subnet Mask = 255.255.255.0

Network ID = 192.168.4.0

Host ID = 0.0.0.1

If two computers have the same network ID in their respective assigned IPv4 address, they should be able to directly communicate on the same local network through a common device such as a network switch. If the network ID is not the same, routers must receive the data from one computer and pass it to the destination network for delivery to the target computer. For example, consider the following three IPv4 addresses and a given subnet mask:

IPv4 Address A = 172.16.4.254

IPv4 Address B = 192.168.4.254

IPv4 Address C = 172.16.4.1

Subnet Mask = 255.255.0.0

If these three IP addresses are assigned to three different computers on the same local network, it is assumed that all three computers have the same subnet mask assigned. Each computer would analyze the network ID of each address as:

Network ID of Address A = 172.16.0.0

Network ID of Address B = 192.168.0.0

Network ID of Address C = 172.16.0.0

From the perspective of a computer assigned address A, address C is reachable by sending data directly over the local network, as expected. However, the computer assigned address A considers address B to only be reachable through a router. This is because the network ID of address B does not match its own. The computers assigned address A and B do not realize that they are on the same local network. They may fail to transfer data between each other if a router is not present or not configured to relay data between the two computers.

Analyzing how subnet masks can be used to group hosts, and how to analyze subnet mask octet values other than 255 or 0, is an advanced TCP/IP design topic beyond the scope of this book.

Documenting subnet mask values with dotted decimal values is not the only way to write a subnet mask value using a shorthand notation. Another way to specify a subnet mask is to write the IPv4 address followed by a slash and a number that identifies the number of contiguous binary ones on the left-hand side of the subnet mask. For example, consider this subnet mask expressed in binary and dotted decimal notation:

Subnet mask (binary) = 1111 1111 1111 1111 0000 0000 0000 0000

Subnet mask (dotted decimal) = 255.255.0.0

In the case of the above example there are 16 ones in the subnet mask value, therefore, the IP address and subnet mask value can be written as *IPaddress*/**16**. If this subnet mask was applied to the IP address 172.16.34.1, it would be written as 172.16.34.1/16. This notation is commonly referred to as **Classless Inter-Domain Routing (CIDR) notation.**

Default subnet mask values were originally defined by the class of the IPv 4 address, as seen in Table 8-3.

Table 8-3   Class-based default subnet mask values

Class	Default subnet mask value	Default subnet mask value (in CIDR notation)
A	255.0.0.0	/8
B	255.255.0.0	/16
C	255.255.255.0	/24

For more detailed information about advanced IP addressing and deeper binary level information, see: *http://technet.microsoft.com/en-us/library/bb726995.aspx*.

Default Gateways

The Internet and corporate networks are large networks that are composed of many smaller networks. Routers control the movement of packets through the networks. An individual computer is capable of delivering packets on the local network, but not to remote networks. To deliver packets to a remote network, the packet must be delivered to a router.

A **default gateway** is a router on the local network that is used to deliver packets to a remote network. The default gateway is identified in the computer's IP settings by entering the IP address assigned to the router's local network connection. If a computer has multiple network interfaces configured for IPv4, only one should be configured with a default gateway setting. If the default gateway is configured incorrectly, then the computer cannot communicate outside the local network. This means Internet connectivity is not possible and corporate computers will likely not have access to all resources.

Windows 7 stores the default gateway setting internally as part of a larger table, called the routing table, as seen in Figure 8-5. The routing table is revisited later in this chapter.

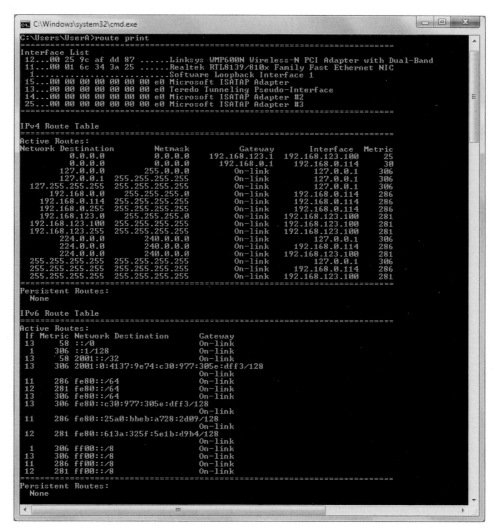

Figure 8-5 Windows networking routing table displayed with route print command

Courtesy Course Technology/Cengage Learning

DNS

Domain Name System (DNS) is essential to communicate on a TCP/IP network. The most common use for DNS is resolving host names to IP addresses. When you access a Web site, you access a location such as *www.microsoft.com*. This is a fully qualified domain name (FQDN), which is a combination of host name and domain name. Computers cannot connect to a service on the Internet directly by using a host name. Instead, they convert the host name to an IP address and then access the service by using the IP address.

DNS is essential for Internet connectivity because most people use domain names, not IP addresses, to access Internet servers such as Web sites. DNS is required to convert the name of a Web site to an IP address. As well, DNS is required for Windows 7 computers in a domain-based network to find domain controllers and log on.

A primary and secondary DNS server address can be defined for any network connection. To avoid operational problems, it must be clear how Windows 7 will use multiple DNS server entries if they are defined. When a program asks Windows 7 to translate a host name to an IP address, it picks the IP of one of the DNS servers and send it a DNS query. There is no guarantee that the primary DNS server will always be the server queried first.

When the computer receives a response from a DNS server telling it an answer has been found, or a response that no matching information is available, Windows 7 considers the DNS server active and functional. It is only when the DNS server fails to respond at all that Windows 7 sends the request to one of the other defined DNS servers. A response that a name couldn't be translated into an IP address is still a valid response and the other DNS servers will not be queried for an answer to the same question.

Windows 7 also provides a text file called HOSTS in the folder "C:\windows\system32\drivers\etc" that maps IP addresses to host names. Entries in the HOSTS file take precedence over data retrieved from DNS servers. Custom data can be entered into the HOSTS file to override DNS server data however this is a local file and can be difficult to remotely administer.

WINS

Windows Internet Naming Service (WINS) is used to resolve NetBIOS names to IP addresses. In addition, it stores information about services such as domain controllers. WINS is primarily used for backward compatibility with older NetBIOS based networks. NetBIOS names can be used to access network services, such as file shares. Windows 7 is capable of using WINS, but uses DNS as its primary name-resolution mechanism.

NetBIOS technology was originally developed to provide name resolution on local networks, not networks that span the Internet. WINS technology and NetBIOS over TCP/IP is not supported for newer standards such as IPv6 given that its practical use has become outdated and replaced with newer naming services.

Methods for Configuring IPv4

To configure IP, you can use:

- Static configuration
- Dynamic configuration
- APIPA
- Alternate IP configuration
- Scripts

All IP configuration information can be manually entered on each Windows 7 computer, but this approach is not very efficient. With each manual entry there is risk of a typographical error. In addition, if the IP configuration changes, visiting each computer to modify the configuration can be an enormous task. Manually entering IP configuration information is called static configuration. Figure 8-6 shows TCP/IP version 4 configured with a static IP address.

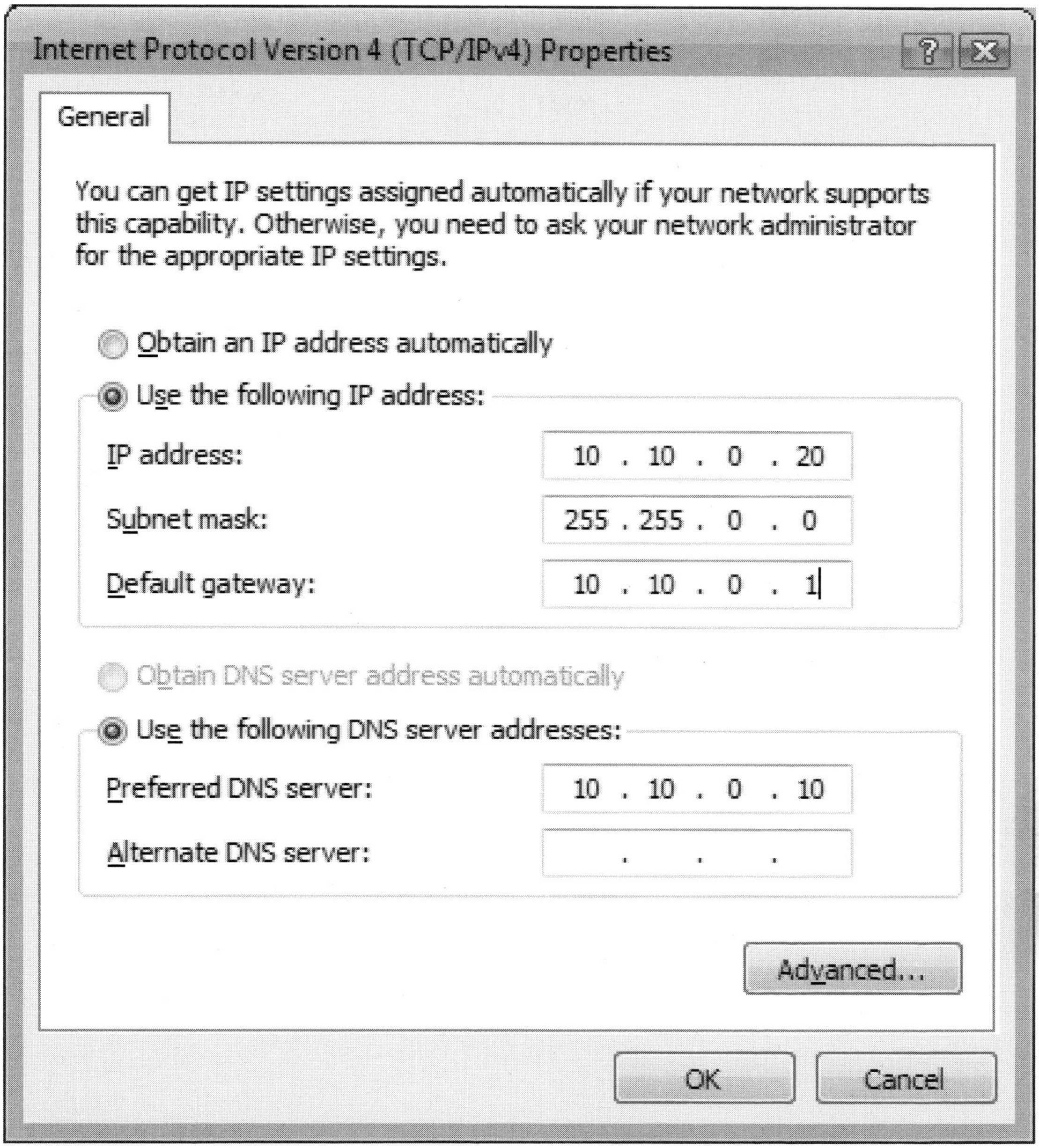

Figure 8-6 Static IPv4 configuration
Courtesy Course Technology/Cengage Learning

Dynamic Host Configuration Protocol (DHCP) is an automated mechanism used to assign IP addresses, subnet masks, default gateways, DNS servers, WINS servers, and other IP configuration information to network devices. Automating this process avoids the problem of information being entered incorrectly. If a change needs to be made to the IP address information, you modify the configuration of the DHCP server. The DHCP server can be configured with a range of IP addresses to hand out, specific exclusions to never hand out, or specific reservations that are given out to DHCP client computers with a specified MAC addresses. Obtaining IP configuration information automatically is called dynamic configuration.

If Windows 7 is configured to use dynamic IP configuration and is unable to contact a DHCP server, the default action is to use an **Automatic Private IP Addressing (APIPA)** address. These addresses are randomly chosen from the 169.254.0.0/16 network range of IP addresses (169.254.0.1 to 169.254.255.254 inclusive) with a subnet mask value of 255.255.0.0.

APIPA is designed as a solution for very small networks with no Internet connectivity requirements. When two computers generate APIPA addresses, they are able to communicate with each other on a local network.

Windows 7 also allows you to configure a static set of **alternate IP configuration** options. If a DHCP server cannot be contacted, the alternate IP configuration is used instead. When an alternate IP configuration is enabled, APIPA is not used. Figure 8-7 shows the Alternate Configuration tab for Internet Protocol version 4.

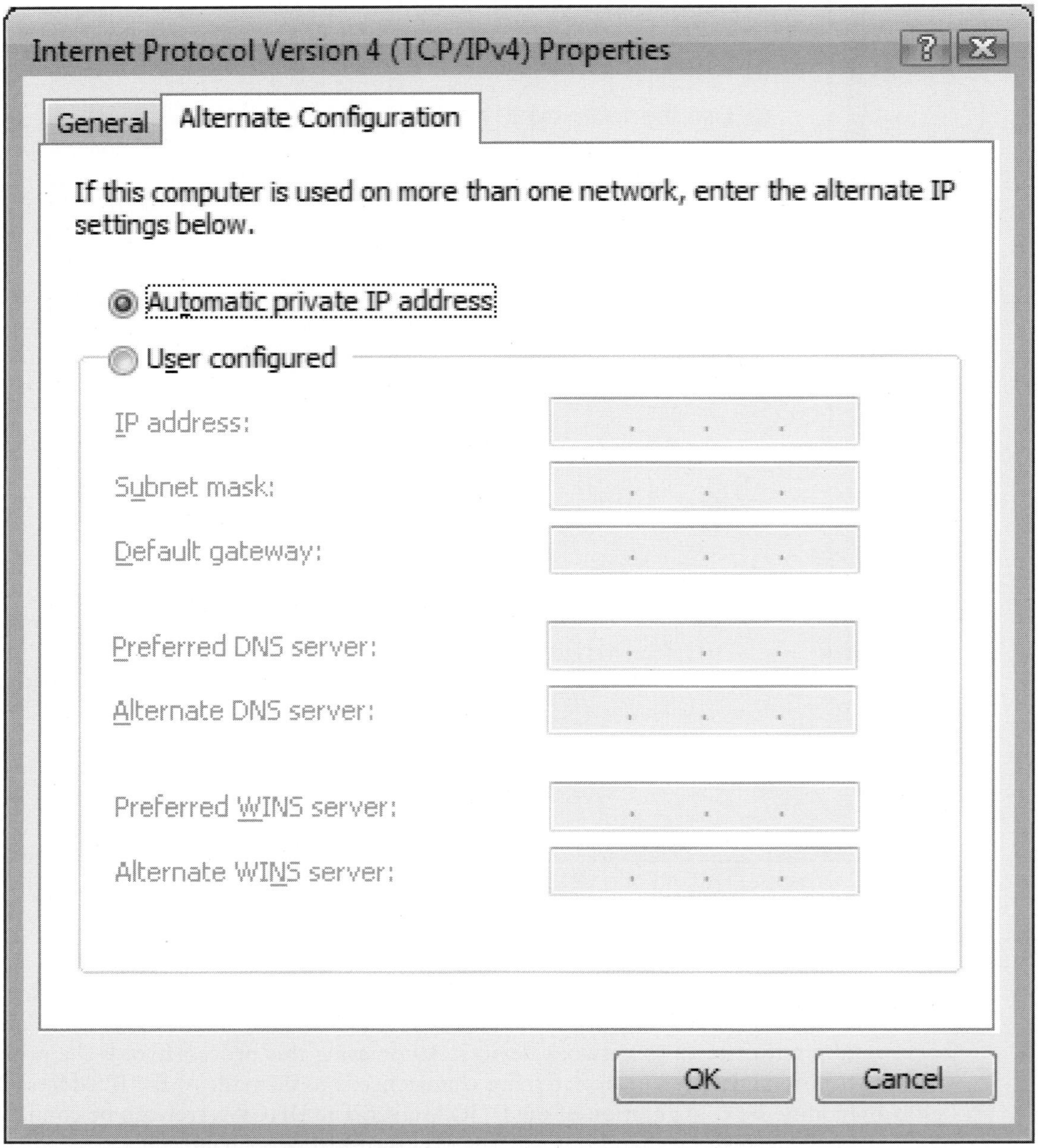

Figure 8-7 Alternate IP configuration for IPv4
Courtesy Course Technology/Cengage Learning

When an administrator is configuring many new computers or troubleshooting, scripts can be run to automatically configure, document, or reconfigure IP settings. Utilities such as netsh are powerful once their control mechanisms are mastered.

Activity 8-3: Viewing and Configuring IPv4

Time Required: 5 minutes
Objective: View and configure IPv4 settings.

Description: When you are troubleshooting network connectivity, it is essential that you understand how to view the existing IPv4 configuration to evaluate whether it is a problem. The graphical interface can be used to view and configure IPv4. In this activity, you will view and configure IPv4 by using the graphical interface.

1. If necessary, start your computer and log on.
2. Click the **Start** button and click **Control Panel**.
3. Click **Network and Internet** and click **Network and Sharing Center**.
4. Under the Network heading, and to the right of Connections, click **Local Area Connection**.
5. Under Connection, click the **Details** button. This shows you additional details about addressing for the network connection. IPv4 configuration information included here is:
   - Physical Address—Each network card has a unique identifier similar to a serial number. The physical address is the unique number. It is also sometimes referred to as the media access control (MAC) address.
   - IPv4 IP Address
   - IPv4 Subnet Mask
   - IPv4 Default Gateway
   - IPv4 DHCP Server
   - IPv4 DNS Servers
   - IPv4 WINS Server
6. Click **Close** to close the Network Connection Details dialog box.
7. Click the **Properties** button.
8. Click **Internet Protocol Version 4 (TCP/IPv4)** and click **Properties**. This shows you the basic configuration of IPv4. By default, an IP address and DNS server address are obtained automatically through DHCP.
9. Click **Use the following IP address**. This allows you to enter in a static IPv4 configuration.
10. In the IP address box, type **192.168.1.100**.
11. If necessary, in the Subnet mask box, type **255.255.255.0**.
12. In the Default gateway box, type **192.168.1.1**.
13. If necessary, click **Use the following DNS server addresses**.
14. In the Preferred DNS server box, type **192.168.1.5**.
15. Click the **Advanced** button. In the Advanced TCP/IP Settings, you can configure additional options. On the IP Settings tab, you can configure multiple IP addresses and default gateways.
16. Click the **DNS** tab. This tab allows you to control how DNS lookups are performed and whether this computer attempts to register its name with the DNS servers by using dynamic DNS.
17. Click the **WINS** tab. This tab allows you to configure how WINS lookups are performed. Some network administrators prefer to disable NetBIOS over TCP/IP to reduce network broadcasts. However, some legacy applications require NetBIOS, so test your applications before disabling NetBIOS over TCP/IP.

18. Click **Cancel** to close the Advanced TCP/IP Settings dialog box.

19. Click **Cancel** to close the **Internet Protocol Version 4 (TCP/IPv4) Properties** dialog box without saving any changes.

20. Click **Cancel** to close the Local Area Connection Properties dialog box.

21. Click **Close** to close the Local Area Connection Status dialog box.

22. Close Network and Sharing Center.

Activity 8-4: Using IPConfig and Netsh

Time Required: 10 minutes
Objective: Use IPConfig and Netsh to view and configure IPv4.

Description: Windows 7 includes IPConfig and Netsh to view and configure IPv4 at the command line. These utilities can also be used for scripting. IPConfig is used to view IPv4 configuration or release and renew IP configuration from a DHCP server. Netsh can be used to configure IPv4. In this activity, you will use IPConfig and Netsh to view and configure IPv4.

1. If necessary, start your computer and log on.

2. Click the **Start** button, type **cmd**, right-click **cmd** in the programs list, click **Run as administrator**, and click **Yes**.

3. At the command prompt, type **ipconfig** and press **Enter**. This command displays a summary of your IPv4 and IPv6 information.

4. Type **ipconfig /all** and press **Enter**. This command displays a much longer list of IP configuration information. Included here are:

   - Physical Address
   - Whether DHCP is Enabled
   - IPv4 Address
   - Subnet Mask
   - Default Gateway
   - DNS Servers

5. Type **ipconfig /release** and press **Enter**. This command releases the DHCP address on your computer. Notice that no IPv4 address is listed in the results.

6. Type **ipconfig /renew** and press **Enter**. This command renews a DHCP address on your computer or obtains a new one. Notice that the newly acquired IPv4 address is displayed.

7. Type **netsh** and press **Enter**. Netsh can be used in an interactive mode where you navigate through menu levels to view information.

8. Type **interface** and press **Enter**. This command changes to the interface context, where you can get more information about network interface configuration.

9. Type **ipv4** and press **Enter**. This command changes to the IPv4 context, where you can get more information about IPv4 configuration.

10. Type **show** and press **Enter**. This command displays a list of the information that can be displayed.

11. Type **show addresses** and press **Enter**. This command shows the IPv4 addresses that are used by this computer.

12. Type **set address** and press **Enter**. This command shows help information on how to configure an IP address for DHCP or as static. If a command is missing required information, the help screen for that command is automatically output.

13. Type **exit** and press **Enter**.

14. Close the command prompt.

Activity 8-5: Testing Alternate IP Configuration

Time Required: 10 minutes
Objective: Learn how APIPA and an alternate IP configuration can be used.

Description: By default, Windows 7 uses an APIPA address (169.254.x.x) when it is configured for dynamic IP addresses, but it cannot contact a DHCP server. However, you can configure Windows 7 to use a specific set of IP configuration information instead of using APIPA. In this activity, you will see how to configure and alternate IP configuration.

All DHCP servers in the classroom must be disabled for this activity. If you are using virtual machines, this can be accomplished by configuring the virtual machines to use a local network that does not have access to the actual classroom network.

1. If necessary, start your computer and log on.

2. Click the **Start** button, type **cmd**, right-click **cmd** in the programs list, click **Run as administrator**, and click **Yes**.

3. At the command prompt, type **ipconfig /release**. This removes the current IP address from your computer.

4. Type **ipconfig /renew** and press **Enter**. The renewal was unsuccessful and your computer is now using an APIPA address on the 169.254.x.x network.

5. Type **ipconfig** and press **Enter**. This command displays a summary of your IPv4 and IPv6 information.

6. Close the command prompt.

7. Click the **Start** button and click **Control Panel**.

8. Click **Network and Internet** and click **Network and Sharing Center**. Notice that the summary map shows you no longer have connectivity to the internet.

9. Under the Network heading, and to the right of Connections, click **Local Area Connection**.

10. Click the **Properties** button.

11. Click **Internet Protocol Version 4 (TCP/IPv4)** and click **Properties**.

12. Click the **Alternate Configuration** tab and click **User configured**.

13. In the IP address box, type **192.168.x.100**, where x is a number assigned to you by your instructor.

14. If necessary, in the Subnet mask box, type **255.255.255.0**.

15. Click **OK** to save the alternate configuration.

16. Click **Close** to close the Local Area Connection Properties dialog box.

17. In the Local Area Connection Status dialog box, click **Details**. Notice that the computer is using the alternate IP address you configured in step 13 instead of an APIPA address.

18. Click **Close** to close the Network Connection Details box.

19. Click **Close** to close the Local Area Connection Status box.

20. Close **Network and Sharing Center**.

Your instructor will enable DHCP for the classroom again once the activity has been completed by all students. You can confirm that your network connectivity is working by visiting an Internet Web site. It may be necessary to renew your IP address to obtain a valid address from the DHCP server.

Essential IPv4 Utilities

There are several key utilities that can be used at the command line or within a script to configure and diagnose IP settings. Some of these utilities make low level changes to the TCP/IP functionality. Some of these changes will be denied unless the commands are run from a command window that has Administrator privileges on the computer. The most common utilities used to troubleshoot TCP/IP are:

- hostname
- ipconfig
- ping
- tracert
- pathping
- route
- netstat
- nbtstat
- getmac
- arp
- netsh
- nslookup

Hostname

The hostname command displays the host name of the computer that it is run on. This is useful for programming a script or when a technician is sitting down at a computer and the host name of the computer is not known.

IPconfig

The **ipconfig** command entered at a command line displays the basic TCP/IP settings of all active network connections. There are several command line options that make the command versatile in troubleshooting TCP/IP settings.

Ipconfig /all displays all TCP/IP configuration settings in verbose detail.

Ipconfig /release disconnects all network connections that are configured to obtain an IP address automatically, such as through DHCP. This disables TCP/IP operations on those interfaces. Network interfaces configured with static IP settings are not be affected by this command.

Ipconfig /renew attempts to renew IP addresses for all network connections that are configured to obtain an IP address automatically. If the renewal of a network connection's current IP address is refused by the DHCP server, the IP address is lost and a new IP address must be assigned by the DHCP server.

Ipconfig /registerdns forces the Windows 7 computer to register its name and IP data with the DNS server defined on a network interface's properties. When a corporate host first connects to the network, it attempts to register its name and IP addresses with a DNS server. An administrator may review the data registered on the DNS server and discover that it was never registered or the registered values are wrong. This command will attempt to correct that error.

Ipconfig /displaydns reveals all cached DNS lookup data. DNS lookup results are cached by a service on the Windows 7 computer called the DNS Client (dnscache) service. The cache itself is called the DNS Resolver cache.

A large amount of data may scroll past the command window buffer. To limit the data displayed on the screen, use the command ipconfig /displaydns | more. The **more** command scrolls to the next screen of output only when the spacebar is pressed, or one line at a time when the enter key is pressed.

Displaying the DNS resolver cache reveals if cached DNS data from DNS server lookups is responsible for improper or unexpected operations. This can be caused by bad data stored in the DNS server hierarchy, performing the lookup against the wrong custom DNS server, or holding stale data in the cache that has since changed to different values on the DNS server.

The cached data will display positive results, where data has been returned, and negative results, where a response came back from the DNS server stating that a value matching the lookup request does not exist. Both types of responses are considered valid responses.

From these results, the technician may determine that the DNS server pointed to may be incorrect, or that data held by a DNS server may be wrong. These changes by themselves will not change the result returned by a DNS lookup for names that already exist in the DNS resolver cache. The results will persist in the cache until: the TTL (time to live) for a cache result has expired, or the DNS Client service is restarted, or the command ipconfig /flushdns is issued on the computer.

Ping

The **ping** command confirms basic IP connectivity between the computer that it is run on and a specified target host. The ping command tests the ability of network data to reach a target and return; it does not confirm that applications on the target computer are operating properly. The target host may be identified with an IP address or DNS name. By default the ping utility sends out a special type of packet called an ICMP packet. The computer that receives this packet may reply with a response ICMP packet. The ping utility measures the total time it takes for the request and response packet to get back to the computer running the ping command. This latency time is measured in milliseconds (ms). Some network devices and firewall software, such as Windows firewall, may actively block ping ICMP traffic even though the network connection is perfectly healthy.

The ping ICMP process is repeated four times by default to check if the results are consistent. The number of times the test actually runs is configurable through command line options. It can be increased to get a better profile of latency and losses over a period of time. Lost replies are tracked to reveal percent loss. Any loss could be an indication of a failing component between the computer and the target host.

To get an idea of where a problem may lie, the ping command is used to test IP connectivity from the computer outward. The typical order is:

- Ping *127.0.0.1*—If the loopback address (127.0.0.1) fails to respond, the TCP/IP software or network card is likely defective in some way. In this case, the TCP/IP software component should be removed and reinstalled for the network adapter, or the network card should be replaced.

- Ping *computerIP*—Where *computerIP* is the assigned IP address of the network adapter. If the computer cannot ping itself using its own IP address then either the routing table or the network drivers are not operating correctly.

- Ping *DefaultGatewayIP*—Where *DefaultGatewayIP* is the IP address of the local router. This device is expected to be functional and available on the established local network. If this device can be pinged then local IP communications are likely to be functional. If the ping fails, be careful to consider that the router may not be functional or may not be configured to respond to ping requests. Confirm router behavior with a known good machine.

- Ping *remotehostIP*—Where *remotehostIP* is the IP address of a computer outside the local network, only reachable through the router. If this works, then it is likely that basic IP operations are healthy on the computer and through the router. If it does not, there may be many causes that have nothing to do with the local computer's configuration. That is the reason the testing starts by testing IP connectivity to hosts closest to the computer itself. A common configuration error that can break a computer's ability to ping outside the router is a subnet mask misconfiguration.

- Ping *RemoteHostName*—Where *RemoteHostName* is the DNS name of a remote computer. If the ping by IP address of a remote host worked, basic IP connectivity is established. If the ping by name fails, host name resolution is faulty.

- Ping –a *RemoteHostIP*—The –a option asks the ping command to perform a name lookup on the *RemoteHostIP* and then perform the ping test. The resolved name can be compared to the expected host name to see if there is a match as expected. Using the wrong name or one with unexpected name resolution with a ping command always leads to unexpected results.

Tracert

The **tracert** command details an IP path through routers to a destination IP address. This command works by sending ICMP packets in a similar fashion to the ping utility. The ICMP packets test the amount of time it takes each router to respond to the computer. Note that the routers have the option of not responding or delaying a response when they are directly responding to an ICMP request. This can skew results resulting in incorrect analysis. This utility should be used together with other utilities to profile communication issues.

Pathping

The **pathping** command combines the functionality of the ping and tracert commands. The major difference is that this utility tests each router a default of one hundred times to profile packet loss and latency at each router. If there are a lot of routers in the path this command can easily take five or six minutes to complete. This disadvantage is mitigated by obtaining better analytical results.

Route

The **route** command can alter or display the IP routing table. The routing table is displayed by issuing the route print command, as seen in Figure 8-5.

The Network Destination 0.0.0.0 with Netmask 0.0.0.0 in the routing table represents the route to all other computers not described in the routing table. This is otherwise known as the default gateway setting for the computer.

Routes can be manually added or removed in the routing table using the route add or route delete commands respectively. Any custom changes that are made will be lost between reboots unless the additions are flagged as persistent with the –p command line option. Changes to the routing table are not typical for workstations. It is common to review the routing table to confirm what routing entries are present but not manage its settings directly.

Netstat

The **netstat** command can display different types of TCP/IP statistics for active software and connections. There are many options available which can be reviewed by typing netstat /? at the command line. There are several common netstat command line options which are used in troubleshooting network connections:

- netstat -a—Display all connections and active ports waiting for a connection

- netstat -e—Display statistics about total data sent and received

- netstat -r—Display the routing table

- netstat -b—Display the name of a program responsible for a connection or listening for one

- netstat -o—For each connection, display the process ID of the process that owns the connection

The netstat command is useful for documenting the network activity and connections at a moment in time. The output can be redirected to a file as part of a scripted routine. The options for the netstat command does not directly change the data it shows. Other utilities must be used to take action.

Nbtstat

The **nbtstat** command can display information about a connection using NBT (NetBIOS over TCP/IP). If an IPv4 connection has NBT enabled, this utility is commonly used to troubleshoot name resolution issues. There are several common nbtstat command line options used to troubleshooting name resolution:

- nbtstat -n—List the local NetBIOS names this computer will respond to
- nbtstat -c—List the NetBIOS names in the local name cache
- nbtstat -r—Display statistics about the NetBIOS names resolved and registered
- nbtstat -R—Purge the NetBIOS name cache and reload any preload settings from the LM-HOSTS file. Note that this option is case sensitive. The preload of cache entries will only happen if the LMHOSTS file exists in the folder C:\WINDOWS\SYSTEM32\DRIVERS\ETC. The LMHOSTS.SAM file in that folder is not a valid instance of LMHOSTS; it is only a sample file. To create a valid LMHOSTS file you must create a new file, without an extension, called LMHOSTS with the necessary content that follows the example formatting in LMHOSTS.SAM.
- nbtstat -RR—Send a command to any network adapters configured with WINS servers to notify the WINS servers to release the name data they hold for this computer and register a new set of active NetBIOS names. Note the command is case sensitive.

The nbtstat command is useful in cases where NetBIOS name resolution impacts applications operating over TCP/IP. Newer applications and servers no longer heavily use or require NetBIOS name resolution. This command is useful in configuring Windows 7 to work in legacy environments.

Getmac

The **getmac** command identifies the MAC address assigned to each adapter in the system. The MAC address is used to label a data packet's source and destination address for the next physical device that accepts or receives the packet. Identifying the MAC address is usually a task requested by network troubleshooters looking at traffic coming from, or going to, that computer in a switched network environment. The command can be run against a remote system by specifying its name (/S) and an administrative userid (/U) and password (/P) on the command line. This utility is primarily designed to be used in a scripted solution to gather information.

Because the tool relates MAC addresses to an adapter based on its coded identifier it can be difficult to interpret which adapter the MAC address applies to on a computer. To get the name of the adapter listed in the output, include the verbose command switch by typing getmac /v.

Another way to collect MAC address information for each network adapter is to run the ipconfig /all command. The problem with the ipconfig command, in this case, is that it displays a lot of unrelated data, cluttering the output and making scripted data collection difficult.

Arp

The **arp** command identifies the MAC addresses of computers that can directly communicate with the computer by displaying the address resolution protocol (ARP) table. Invalid MAC entries in the arp table will stop the successful delivery of new packets to that TCP/IP destination address. Entries in the arp table can be static or dynamic. Even though entries can be manually added, it is highly recommended that that is never done. Automatic processes do a better job of managing MAC address entries. If an entry is manually deleted from the MAC table, it will be added with a new updated value automatically as part of establishing communications with that host. Common commands available to troubleshoot the arp table include:

- arp -a—Show the address entries in the arp table
- arp -g—Same as arp –a, show the address entries in the arp table
- arp –d *HostIP*—Delete entries in the arp table that match *HostIP*. *HostIP* can be specified as a wildcard (*) to delete all hosts

Netsh

The **netsh** command is a powerful script tool that can view or modify the computer's network configuration locally or in combination with other tools remotely. For example, the command can list the IPv4 and IPv6 routing tables.

Each portion of the computer's network settings has a dedicated section of settings and syntax. To truly understand the netsh utility and its large list of features, it will require practice and research throughout the IT professional's career. Memorizing a few commands is useful for an exam, but not for real world IT skills.

Nslookup

The **nslookup** command can be used at the command prompt to lookup a DNS entry from a specific DNS server or it can provide an interactive text-based console for advanced DNS queries.

Nslookup is a powerful tool because it can query a DNS server directly, even if it is a different one that the network settings are using right now. The debug feature allows the administrator to deeply diagnose what data can be returned to the Windows 7 client and why.

To fully appreciate the utility, the administrator must have knowledge of the type of records a DNS server includes, such as:

- A—Map a host name to an IPv4 address
- AAAA—Map a host name to an IPv6 address
- PTR—Map an IPv4 or IPv6 address to a host name
- MX—Identify the mail server(s) responsible for managing email for a domain
- NS—Identify the DNS servers that authoritatively hold custom DNS data for a domain

To review nslookup commands start nslookup in its interactive mode by entering nslookup on the command line and pressing Enter. At the nslookup interactive prompt, >, type help.

Troubleshooting IPv4

To successfully troubleshoot IPv4-based communications, the technician should follow an incremental process that has proven successful in most situations. IPv4 has been in use for a very long time. Many problems are actually caused by simple problems, such as a connection being in the wrong state or a feature turned off unexpectedly.

A common approach is to perform the following in order:

- Confirm current settings
- Validate IPv4 connectivity
- Verify DNS name resolution
- Verify data connections

Confirm current settings

The existing IPv4 settings should be confirmed. Assumptions about what settings are active will lead to incorrect troubleshooting progress. The ipconfig and netsh utilities can display the current settings. If the IPv4 address settings look valid, it is possible that the default route or routing table is incorrect. The default route can be displayed with ipconfig or the route command. If all settings appear correct, the computer's connectivity with those settings must be validated.

Validate IPv4 connectivity

If all settings appear correct, the ping utility can be used to confirm that the computer can ping its own loopback address. If the command is successful, the TCP/IP IPv4 protocol is functional on the computer.

The computer keeps track of which computers it recently communicated with, and some of that information can be out of date. The IPv4 system used an ARP table to keep track of network devices it last connected to. If the ARP table data is in doubt, it can be cleared with the arp utility.

The ping command can be used to ping a local host such as the default gateway. If the local default gateway can be pinged, then connectivity to the local network and the default gateway are validated in one attempt.

If the router can be pinged, attempt to ping a remote host using its IPv4 address. If this fails, confirm the path the traffic is taking with either the pathping or tracert commands. If IPv4 communications to remote hosts work when the raw address is specified in a command, but not by name, then there is likely a DNS issue.

Verify DNS name resolution

Confirm the correct DNS servers are specified on network settings manually or automatically through DHCP with the ipconfig utility. If the wrong servers were entered, that should be corrected first. If there are multiple DNS servers specified, consider simplifying the list to just one server that you expect will have the correct data.

The DNS resolver caches data and that data may contain obsolete data or invalid responses. Once the DNS servers are corrected, the cache data can be purged with ipconfig /flushdns to provide a clean start to name resolution. The DNS data being cached can also be displayed with ipconfig /displaydns to confirm that expected answers are being correctly obtained by the Windows computer.

The DNS cached data tells you what answer the workstation received, but not from which DNS server, and not if the data the DNS server is holding is correct. The data stored on the DNS server itself should be verified. This can be verified from the workstation with the nslookup utility or you can ask the administrator of the DNS server.

A common mistake is configuring a domain joined workstation with an ISP's DNS server in addition to a corporate domain DNS server. When the workstation tries to look up DNS data to find corporate domain servers, it may ask the ISP's DNS server where they are located instead of the domain DNS server. You can specify a preferred order for Windows 7 to query DNS servers but you cannot restrict Windows 7 from using both interchangeably. The ISP DNS server will send back a valid response—the domain servers DNS data doesn't exist in its database—and the client will cache the response as a valid lookup result. As a result, domain operations will be disrupted and fail to operate correctly on the workstation. When the workstation is restarted by the user, it may go back to working with the correct domain DNS server. The workstation user will report intermittent overall failures and annoyance as a result.

Verify data connections

If basic IP communications and name resolution appear healthy, the problem may be a result of data filtering by a firewall restriction or corruption. Any computer or device between the local client and the destination may be filtering data connections, disallowing them entirely. Windows 7 has a firewall component built into filter inbound and outbound data connections, which is covered later in this chapter.

Many server based data services listen on a specific data port. The Transmission Control Protocol (TCP) portion of TCP/IP allows an application to identify itself with a specific port value. The IP address identifies the computer itself; the TCP port identifies the listening application on that computer. Many third party tools report the status of TCP ports for a given remote IP address. Windows 7 can report active port connections on the computer using the netstat command.

A crude test to check for connectivity to remote servers is to use the telnet application on the local computer to attempt a connection to a remote active TCP port. The telnet utility is available for installation as part of Windows but it is not installed by default. It can be installed by opening Control Panel, Programs and Features, and selecting the task *Turn Windows features on or off*. The telnet client can then be selected and installed.

The telnet program provides an interactive interface that normally connects to a telnet server on its default TCP port number. A different port number can be specified on the command line, one that is used by a service other than telnet. For example, the mail server protocol for the Simple Mail Transport Protocol (SMTP) is port 25. The telnet command telnet mail.example.com 25 opens an interactive session with the mail server, identified by the name *mail.example.com*, which is listening for connections on TCP port 25. If the data connection is allowed the mail server greeting should be displayed. If it is, this confirms that there is some level of data connectivity allowed.

Additional filtering or data corruption may happen after the initial TCP connection to give the impression of a data communication problem. To see the full network conversation between two computers a utility such as Microsoft's Network Monitor would have to be employed. Network Monitor is a free utility that is not included by default with Windows 7 but can be downloaded for free. Network Monitor's implementation and usage is an advanced topic beyond the scope of this book.

IP Version 6

IPv6 is the replacement for IPv4. The creators of IPv4 could not have anticipated the expansion of the Internet and, as a result, IPv4 has some serious shortcomings when used for global networking. IPv6 addresses these shortcomings.

Improvements found in IPv6 include:

- Increased address space
- Hierarchical routing to reduce the load on Internet backbone routers
- Simpler configuration through automatic address management
- Inclusion of encryption services for data security
- Quality of service
- Extensibility to support new features

In Windows 7, support for IPv6 and IPv4 (the current standard) have been built into a single TCP/IP protocol stack (tcpip.sys). In Windows XP, support for IPv4 was automatically installed (tcpip.sys), but IPv6 was an optional component that had to be installed (tcpip6.sys).

IPv6 Address Notation

The address space for IPv4 is nearing depletion; IPv6 has a significantly larger address space. IPv6 addresses are 128 bits long, while IPv4 addresses are only 32 bits long. This provides millions more addresses than are available in IPv4.

IPv6 has many more addresses than would normally be required for computing devices, but it is designed for ease of use rather than efficiency of allocation. Many of these addresses will probably never be assigned to a host. In fact, only one-eighth of the total address space is allocated for Internet-accessible addresses.

IPv6 addresses are represented in hexadecimal, with each four-digit segment separated by colons. Each hexadecimal digit can be converted to an equivalent four bit binary value. The total address length is a maximum of 32 hexadecimal digits. An example of an IPv6 address is 222D:10B5:3355:00F3:8234:0000:32AC:099C.

To simplify the expression of IPv6 addresses, any group of four hexadecimal digits can drop leading zeros, leaving at least one digit visible. The IPv6 address in the previous example can be simplified to: 222D:10B5:3355:F3:8234:0:32AC:99C.

When an IPv6 address contains a long set of zeros, the zeros can be compressed to a double colon "::". For example, the multicast address FF02:0:0:0:0:0:112A:CC87 could be shortened to FF02::112A:CC87. This type of zero compression can only be used once per address. In general, it doesn't matter if the compression is done on the right or left side of the address, what really matters is that it can only be done once.

IPv6 Address Types

The format of an IPv6 address is more complex than an IPv4 address. Depending on the purpose of the IPv6 address, understanding how to decompose the different parts of the address changes. The full decomposition of different address types is an advanced topic beyond the scope of this book.

The numbers on the left side of a written IPv6 address provide a clue as to what type of address it is, which is covered in this chapter.

Older IPv4 addresses had only two parts, the network address and the host address. The subnet mask value identified where the split between network and host bits was placed in the 32-bit IPv4 address. The IPv6 address has a similar concept, but it is not written in dotted decimal notation. Instead it uses the CIDR notation of adding a slash and a number after the slash to the end of the IPv6 address. That number indicates the number of bits on the left side of the written address that makes up the network portion of the address. This network portion of the address is referred to in general as the **address prefix**. For example, 10F0:0:0:6501::/64 is a possible IPv6 prefix.

The address prefix contains information that helps devices such as routers decide how to move data between networks and the links between those networks. When an address prefix is specified, be careful to avoid using zero compression incorrectly. The previous example of 10F0:0:0:6501::/64 is a valid address prefix that uses zero compression to shorten the full address 10F0:0:0:6501:0:0:0:0/64. A common mistake is to write the address as 10F0::6501/64, which will be interpreted incorrectly as 10F0:0:0:0:0:0:0:6501/64.

Depending on the address type, the address prefix can be composed of multiple components that are more complicated than the IPv4 network ID. It is important to recognize that IPv6 is still a young standard and it is evolving. Some of the format information current today will evolve over time.

Knowing the type of address helps to set expectations of how data can be delivered to an interface. The designers of IPv6 knew that the end point for delivery could be a physical device such as a network card, a wireless device, or some program that is receiving data and acting as an end point for IPv6 data. The end point for IPv6 data delivery is called an interface. A single computer is typically called a node, which is capable of running multiple interfaces. Each interface can have one or more IPv6 addresses assigned to it. Recognizing the address type by its address prefix (see Table 8-4) is a required skill to analyze IPv6 addresses assigned to an interface.

Table 8-4   Common IPv6 Address Prefixes

IPv6 Address Type	Address Prefix
Link-local unicast	FE80::/64
Global unicast	2000::/3
Unique local unicast	FC00::/7
Multicast	FF00::/8
Anycast	Any valid unicast address
Teredo	2001::/32

The primary types of IPv6 address types are:

- Link-local Unicast
- Global Unicast
- Unique Local Unicast
- Multicast
- Anycast
- Special addresses
- Teredo

Link-local Unicast

A unicast address defines a delivery destination that identifies a specific single interface. Data sent to or from link-local addresses are not allowed to pass through IPv6 aware routers. A link-local unicast address is automatically assigned to any active interface on the computer by

Windows 7. A link-local address allows computers in a local network to communicate with each other without requiring the use of a router. In IPv4, this same link-local behavior as provided by Automatic Private IP Addressing (APIPA), which generates IP addresses in the range 169.254.0.0/16.

The address prefix of a link-local address is FE80::/64. The last 64 bits of the address are randomly generated by Windows 7 as the host ID. An example of a link-local unicast address is FE80::F9:1435:305E:DFF2.

A computer can have more than one link-local address if it has multiple network interfaces. The address prefix for each link-local address on that computer is exactly the same. When the computer is sending to a link-local address, the routing table cannot tell which interface to use to send data to a destination link-local address. If this causes a problem, the link-local address can be extended with a zone ID.

Each network interface in Windows 7 is assigned a network interface ID, otherwise known as a zone ID. The zone ID can be used to identify what network interface is used to send the data. The syntax to specify a zone ID is *IPAddress%ZoneID*, where *IPAddress* is the destination link-local address and *ZoneID* is the interface ID of the network interface.

To see the current identifier for each network interface, open a command window and issue the command ipconfig or netsh interface ipv6 show interface. The output of the netsh command lists a column titled Idx, as seen in Figure 8-8, which identifies the interface ID for each interface listed. The ipconfig output will list it at the end of each link-local address displayed beneath each connection, but there is a lot more information displayed than necessary with the command.

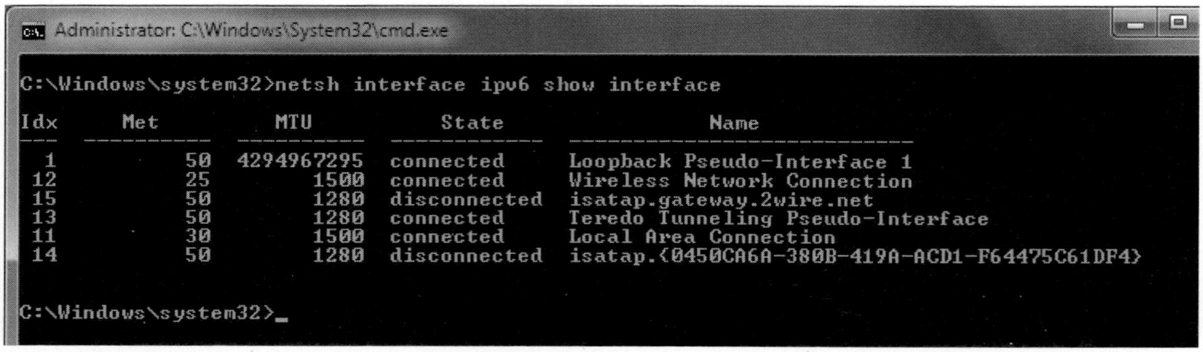

Figure 8-8 Netsh output displaying network interface ID
Courtesy Course Technology/Cengage Learning

If a command such as ping fe80::613a:325f:5e1b:d9b4 returns the error result "Destination host unreachable" or "PING: transmit failed. General failure." It may be due to the command using the wrong interface to send the ping request on. As an example, consider that the netsh command was issued to display the interface IDs and the correct one was determined to be 15. The ping command could be modified to include it as ping fe80::613a:325f:5e1b:d9b4%15.

Global Unicast

A global address can be routed as a public address on the Internet through routers and networks. Global unicast IPv6 addresses are usually assigned by an ISP or public registration authority.

Note that a global unicast address can be generally identified with the address prefix 2000::/3. Even though that is the current block of IPv6 addresses being handed out to public end points, this may change in the future. There are still large portions of the IPv6 address space that are unused. An example of a global unicast address is: 2001:0:4137:9E76:F9:1435:304E:DFF2.

Unique Local Unicast

The unique local address type is a replacement address type for the deprecated site-local address type. These addresses are intended for local communications within a private site. These addresses are similar in function to IPv4 internal private addresses (see Table 8-2) in that they are not intended to be directly routable over the Internet.

The unique local address type allows an administrator to identify a site and route internally within that private site. Routers that connect to the global Internet will drop data with this address type if it is sent directly out to the Internet. Note that a unique local unicast address can be generally identified with the address prefix FC00::/7.

Multicast

An IPv6 multicast address serves the same purpose as an IPv4 multicast address. One or more computers can be assigned a multicast address that identifies them as members of the same group of computers. When data is sent to a multicast address, all computers with an interface that belongs to that multicast group will receive a copy of the data.

The address prefix of a multicast address is FF00::/8. Multicast addresses include a scope setting that determines the distribution level of the data, such as local or global distribution. Managing multicast addresses is not a typical administration task for Windows 7, so these settings are not reviewed in detail here.

Some multicast addresses are reserved and have a special meaning. Two examples include the "all nodes" and "all routers" multicast address. The all nodes multicast address FF02::1 is used to send data to all computers on the same local network. This is the same functionality as the broadcast address for IPv4. The all routers multicast address FF02::2 is used to send data to all routers on the same local network.

Anycast

The assignment of anycast addresses to a network interface is currently restricted to routers only. The anycast address is not assigned to client computers. The anycast address has the same format as any unicast address. What makes an address an anycast address is the fact that a single unicast address is assigned to more than one network interface, and those interfaces can be on different computing devices. Multiple devices can share the same anycast address and respond to other computers without an IP address conflict. This technique allows client computers to find the closest instance of a service. The closest computer or device with a specific anycast address responds to the client.

The device configured with an anycast address must know that it is an anycast address. The format of the address does not tell a computer that an address is an anycast address. The anycast address is typically managed as part of a large enterprise or ISP managing backbone routers.

Special addresses

Two special addresses exist in IPv6, the loopback address and the unspecified address.

The loopback address in IPv6 is specified as 0:0:0:0:0:0:0:1, otherwise written as ::1 or ::1/128. The loopback address is only assigned to a virtual interface, never to a physical one. Any data sent to the loopback address for a computer will deliver in software back to the computer that sent it. The data will not be sent out on the physical network, the entire process will happen in software using the virtual interface only.

The unspecified address is 0:0:0:0:0:0:0:0, otherwise written as :: or ::/128. The unspecified address is never assigned to a computer. It indicates the absence of an address. This can be observed when an IPv6 address is unspecified in a configuration window or when a computer is sending an IPv6 packet but it doesn't have a source address yet.

Teredo

The Teredo client is built in as part of Windows 7 but it is inactive unless its services are required. Teredo is a technology that allows IPv6 data to be tunneled over an IPv4 network that is using Network Address Translation (NAT). In an IPv4 network using NAT, the identity and availability of a computer is hidden by the NAT device. This makes it difficult for a computer using IPv6 addressing to tunnel directly through an IPv4 network.

The Teredo client typically connects to two types of special servers: the Teredo server and Teredo relay server. The Teredo client connects to a Teredo server to register itself as a client. Windows 7 creates a virtual network interface called the Teredo Tunneling Pseudo-Interface.

This interface is assigned a specially formatted Teredo IPv6 address. Teredo addresses have a fixed address prefix of 2001:0/32.

The Teredo server acts a broker while a connection is being created to another computer. Control and status messages are read from the Teredo server. The bandwidth required to run a Teredo server is low, so public Teredo servers such as *teredo.ipv6.micorsoft.com* exist that can be used by any Teredo client.

The Teredo relay server connects a Teredo client indirectly to another computer on an IPv6 only network to transfer data. The Teredo relay server can send status and control messages to the Teredo server, where the Teredo client picks them up. A Teredo relay server will have a lot of data flowing through it, so there are typically no public Teredo relay servers.

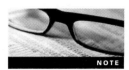

Previous versions of Windows required IPv6 to be configured by using the Netsh command-line utility. Windows 7 and Windows Vista provide a graphical interface to configure IPv6.

Methods for Configuring IPv6

A computer running Windows 7 automatically configures its network interfaces with a link-local address. These can be displayed by entering the **ipconfig** command at the command line, as seen in Figure 8-9. The link-local addresses allows the computer to interact with other computers on the local network but not through a router to other networks.

```
Administrator: C:\Windows\System32\cmd.exe

C:\Windows\system32>ipconfig

Windows IP Configuration

Wireless LAN adapter Wireless Network Connection:

   Connection-specific DNS Suffix  . : gateway.2wire.net
   Link-local IPv6 Address . . . . . : fe80::613a:325f:5e1b:d9b4%12
   IPv4 Address. . . . . . . . . . . : 192.168.123.100
   Subnet Mask . . . . . . . . . . . : 255.255.255.0
   Default Gateway . . . . . . . . . : 192.168.123.1

Ethernet adapter Local Area Connection:

   Connection-specific DNS Suffix  . :
   Link-local IPv6 Address . . . . . : fe80::25a0:bbeb:a728:2d09%11
   IPv4 Address. . . . . . . . . . . : 192.168.0.114
   Subnet Mask . . . . . . . . . . . : 255.255.255.0
   Default Gateway . . . . . . . . . : 192.168.0.1

Tunnel adapter isatap.gateway.2wire.net:

   Media State . . . . . . . . . . . : Media disconnected
   Connection-specific DNS Suffix  . :

Tunnel adapter Teredo Tunneling Pseudo-Interface:

   Connection-specific DNS Suffix  . :
   IPv6 Address. . . . . . . . . . . : 2001:0:4137:9e74:c07:3106:305e:dff3
   Link-local IPv6 Address . . . . . : fe80::c07:3106:305e:dff3%13
   Default Gateway . . . . . . . . . : ::

Tunnel adapter isatap.{0450CA6A-380B-419A-ACD1-F64475C61DF4}:

   Media State . . . . . . . . . . . : Media disconnected
   Connection-specific DNS Suffix  . :

C:\Windows\system32>_
```

Figure 8-9 IPconfig command output
Courtesy Course Technology/Cengage Learning

To configure IPv6, you can use:

- Static configuration
- Automatic configuration
- Scripts

A network connection's properties include settings for IPv6. By default the properties are configured to obtain an IPv6 address automatically. It is not common to configure an IPv6 address statically. To configure a static address, a network interface's IPv6 properties must be reconfigured to use a specific IPv6 address with a specified subnet prefix length, as seen in Figure 8-10.

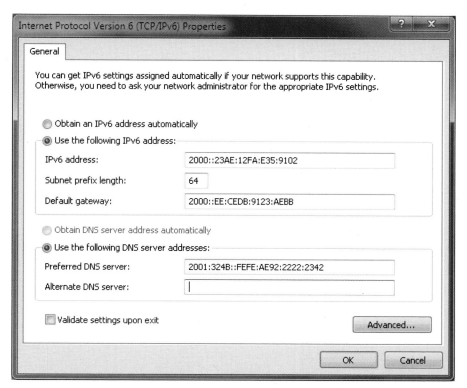

Figure 8-10 Static IPv6 Configuration
Courtesy Course Technology/Cengage Learning

The Advanced button in the IPv6 properties allows the interface to be assigned one or more default gateways, multiple IPs, and custom DNS settings. IPv6 does not implement NetBIOS over TCP/IP so there are no WINS configuration options present.

Automatic configuration can be done in two ways: stateful and stateless. To enable automatic configuration of the IPv6 address, a network interface's IPv6 properties must be configured as shown in Figure 8-11.

Stateful automatic address configuration involves one or more devices that track the state of the client in internal data tables. Traditional IPv4 address allocation through DHCP is an example of stateful address allocation. IPv6 can also obtain an address from an IPv6 DHCP server (DHCPv6) if one is configured on the local network. Windows Server 2008 or later can support IPv6 configuration as a DHCP server, but earlier versions of Windows Server cannot. A compatible IPv6 DHCP relay can also be used with IPv6 addressing to enable a client to interact with a DHCPv6 server on a different network.

In stateful address allocation, the DHCPv6 server tracks details about the client while it is operational with a leased address assigned by that DHCP server. This can restrict the mobility of a client as it has to **coordinate** its address assignment with servers and other devices while it moves from one network to another. The client and DHCP server present a DHCP Unique Identifier

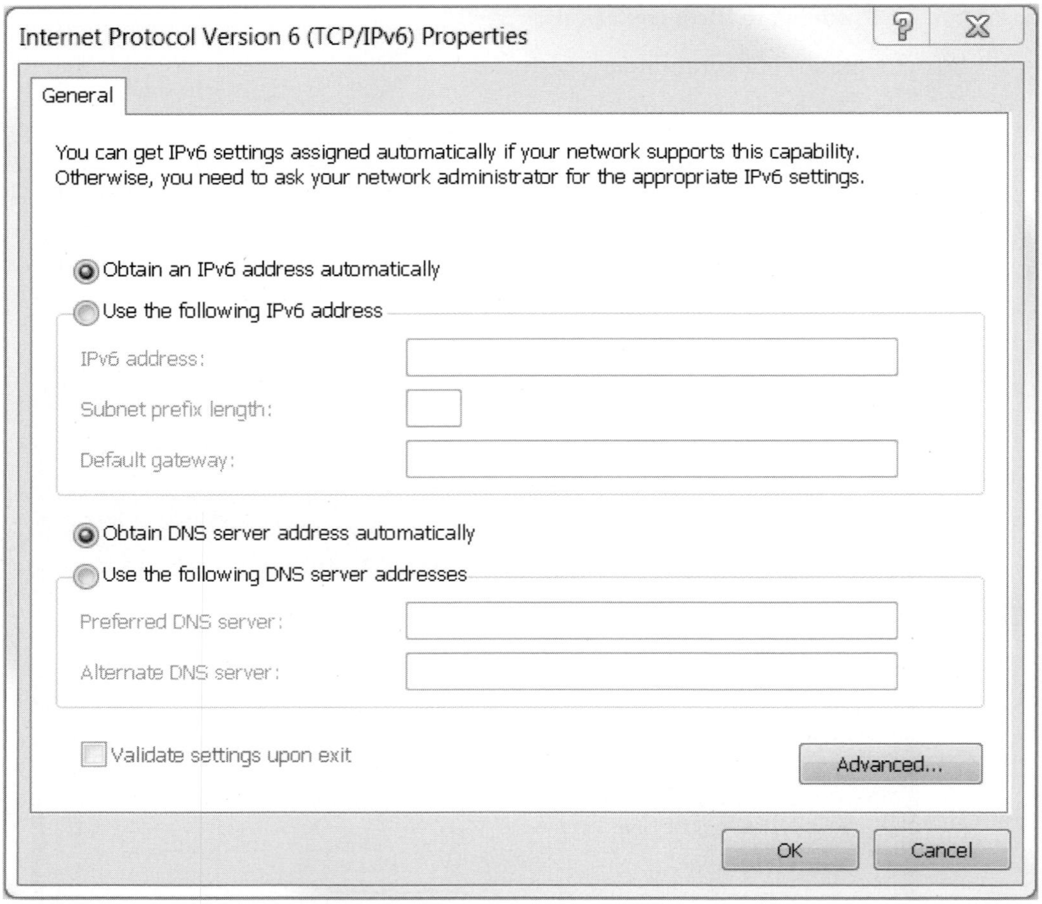

Figure 8-11 Automatic IPv6 Configuration
Courtesy Course Technology/Cengage Learning

(DUID) to identify themselves when exchanging DHCPv6 messages. The clients DHCPv6 DUID can be seen by issuing the command **ipconfig /all** at a command prompt.

Stateless configuration empowers the client to collect as many settings as possible from the network around it and have it create its own IPv6 address. The subnet address in use on a local network is advertised by an IPv6 aware router as the subnet ID. The client generates a random interface ID and combines it with the subnet ID to create its own IPv6 address. Configuration options such as DNS server settings are collected from DHCP servers or the router connected to the local network. If there is no router connected, then the interface can only automatically configure a local-link address. The advantage to stateless configuration is that less equipment and configuration effort is required to set up the IPv6 address for a network.

In small networks, even settings such as the DNS server settings may not be required. Windows 7 can resolve local client names using the **Link-Local Multicast Name Resolution (LLMNR)** protocol and related supporting services. This allows a computer to query the names of other computers on the local network using IPv4 and IPv6 without relying on NetBIOS, WINS, or DNS name resolution. This can minimize the requirement to have name configuration servers defined ahead of time and configured for clients.

The Teredo tunneling interface is a special case of address auto configuration because the computer attempts to connect to a Teredo server and obtain reply information used to create a Teredo class IPv6 address.

Script commands using **netsh** can be used to configure IPv6 settings on the computer. Changes to a network interface's settings may take multiple commands to completely configure the interface.

Troubleshooting IPv6 Settings

Because IPv6 addressing is new and there are new details of how to configure it, many people assume that troubleshooting is different. The overall troubleshooting methodology is similar to IPv4 troubleshooting with the following notable considerations in each troubleshooting stage:

- Confirm current settings
- Validate IPv6 connectivity
- Verify DNS name resolution
- Verify data connections

Confirm current settings

The existing IPv6 settings should be confirmed due to the default nature of IPv6 clients attempting to auto-configure themselves.

Validate IPv6 connectivity

If all settings appear correct, the ping utility can be used to confirm that the computer can ping its own loopback address by issuing the command **ping ::1**. If the command is successful, the TCP/IP IPv6 protocol is functional on the computer.

The computer keeps track of which computers it communicated with recently, and some of that information can be out of date. The IPv4 system used an ARP table to keep track of network devices it last connected to. IPv6 uses a neighbor and destination cache to essentially do that as well.

The neighbor and destination cache can be viewed and managed with the **netsh** utility. The neighbor cache lists known computers on the same local network as the client computer. The destination cache lists the next IPv6 address the computer should send data to reach a particular destination.

If either the neighbor or destination cache data is in doubt, they can be cleared with the netsh utility.

Verify DNS name resolution

Different types of records are registered with the DNS server depending on the IP data the client is registering. An IPv4 address and hostname are stored in the DNS server using an A record. The A record maps the name of the computer to its IP address. An IPv6 address and hostname is stored in the DNS server using an AAAA record. The AAAA record maps the name of the computer to its IPv6 address.

A DNS server may be configured to map the IP address back to the name of the computer using PTR records, but this is not commonly implemented for IPv6. IPv4 addresses are stored in a DNS server data table called in-addr.arpa. IPv6 also uses a PTR record to match an IPv6 address to a name but it uses a data table called ip6.arpa.

DNS servers may resolve a name to either an IPv4 address or an IPv6 address. There is no guarantee the DNS server will respond with IPv4 or IPv6 data in all cases. A computer may have a valid IPv4 A record stored in DNS but no IPv6 AAAA record. Some applications can be forced to use IPv6 addressing with command line options. To restrict troubleshooting to IPv6 addresses, the ping command can be forced to only use IPv6 addresses by issuing the command ping -6 TargetIP, where *TagetIP* is the target address of the remote computer. If the DNS server cannot provide an answer that is a valid IPv6 address, the command reports that the host name could not be found.

Verify data connections

Using the telnet application is a common tool for administrators to test application connectivity. The telnet utility does not guarantee it will use IPv6 to connect to a remote service unless the target address is specified as an IPv6 address. Carefully consider that specifying a target DNS host name to connect to does not guarantee that an IPv6 address will be used instead of an IPv4 address.

8

File Sharing

There are many different ways you can share files between two computers. You can copy files on floppy disk or USB drive, send files by using instant messenger software, upload files to a Web site for sharing, or send files using e-mail. However, all of these options are flawed because they do not maintain a single central copy of the file. When there are multiple copies of a file, it is difficult to track which version has the latest changes, and sometimes changes are made to multiple versions of the file which are difficult to reconcile at a later time. Due to security restrictions and firewalls, you may need to use some of these options over the Internet. However, on a LAN you can use file and printer sharing instead.

File sharing in Windows 7 allows you to share files from any folder on your computer or the Public folder with other computer users on your LAN. In a home environment, the new homegroup feature allows each homegroup member computer to share personal libraries in the home. (Homegroups are covered later in this chapter.) In a small business environment, each user may store their business files in the Public folder only, so that all users have access to the files on all of the Windows 7 computers. In a larger corporate environment, files are typically stored on centralized servers rather than shared from Windows 7 computers.

Windows 7 includes controls to allow the user and administrator to customize how much they want to share over the network, with whom, and with what access rights. When security is a concern, Windows 7 provides options to configure settings based on the convenience and knowledge level of the person making changes. In trusted environments, such as at home, shared folder security can be configured with simple wizards that can apply some or no security checks at all. In corporate environments, specific shared folder permissions can be applied that combine with NTFS file level permissions to fine tune and customize access.

If a user commutes between home and corporate networks with a portable computer, he or she may need to authenticate with several user and password combinations. Windows 7 includes the Credential Manger utility to assist with remembering those details and automating authentication.

Sharing data is an essential feature, and the most generic form of that built into Windows 7 is the idea of a shared public folder.

Sharing the Public Folder

The public folder is typically located at C:\Users\Public. Sharing the Public folder is a simplified way to perform file sharing on home and small office networks. Public folder sharing is disabled by default when a computer is joined to a domain. By default, all files in the Public folder are shared between users who log on the local computer. If a user logs on to the local computer, she or he may be restricted from seeing local data files belonging to other users of that computer. The Public folder gives those users a way to share data locally. However, the Public folder can also be shared with network users. Sharing for the Public folder is configured by using the Public folder sharing option in Advanced Sharing settings in Control Panel, shown in Figure 8-12.

The options for sharing the Public folder are:

- *Turn on sharing so anyone with network access can read and write files in the Public folder*— When this option is selected, all network users are able to read, change, delete, and create files in the Public folder. A Public folder configured this way could be used as a central storage location for business documents in a small business to ensure that files can be easily found and are able to be backed up each night.

- *Turn off Public folder sharing*—When this option is selected, only local users can access files in the Public folder.

You also have options for Password protected sharing that also apply to the Public folder, shown in Figure 8-13. Password protection offers two options. These options also apply to other shared folders and printers.

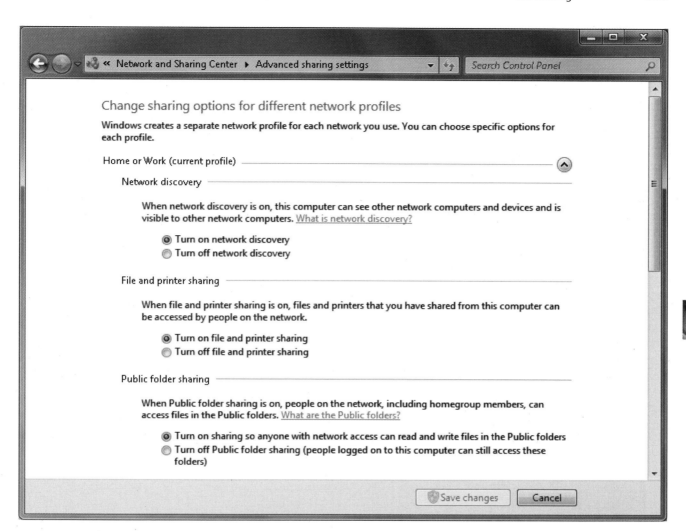

Figure 8-12 Public Folder Sharing controls from Control Panel
Courtesy Course Technology/Cengage Learning

8

- *Turn on password protected sharing*—When this option is selected, network users must log on to the sharing computer by using a user account that has been granted access to the sharing computer. The account can be either a local user account or a domain user account. This allows you to restrict access to the shared public folder to valid user accounts, but you cannot select which user accounts have access. All valid user accounts are able to access the shared Public folder.

- *Turn off password protected sharing*—When this option is selected, anyone can access the information in the public folder, even if they do not have a valid user account on the sharing computer. Effectively, this allows anonymous users access to the Public folder.

Activity 8-6: Sharing the Public Folder

Time Required: 10 minutes
Objective: Share data in the public folder with network users.

Description: Windows 7 includes a Public folder feature to make sharing files with other network users easier. Public folder sharing is performed from Network and Sharing Center. In this activity, you use Network and Sharing Center to share the Public folder.

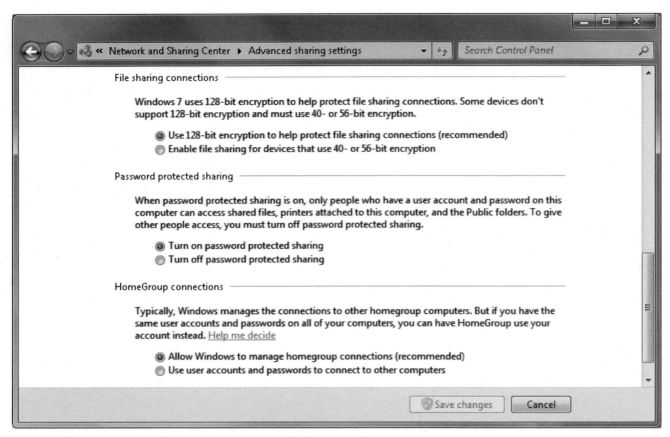

Figure 8-13 Password Protected Sharing controls from Control Panel
Courtesy Course Technology/Cengage Learning

1. If necessary, start your computer and log on.

2. Click the **Start** button and click **Control Panel**.

3. Click **Network and Internet** and click **Network and Sharing Center**.

4. Click **Change advanced sharing settings** on the left-hand side of the Network and Sharing window

5. Scroll down to **Password protected sharing** and click **Turn off password protected sharing** if it is not already selected. This allows any user on the network to access your shared folders and printers.

6. Scroll up to **Public folder sharing**, click **Turn on sharing so anyone with network access can read and write in the Public folders** if it is not already selected. This specifies the permissions given to the users specified in the previous step. Anyone on the network can create, edit, and delete files in the shared Public folder.

7. Click **Save Changes**. Notice that file sharing must be enabled to share the Public folder.

8. Click the **Start** button and **Computer** from the Start menu to open a Windows Explorer window. On the left-hand side, select **Network**. Find the computer icon with your computer name on the right-hand pane and double-click it. This opens a window that displays the shares on your computer. Users is listed as a share.

9. Double-click **Users** to display the next folder level. Double-click the **Public** folder to open it. You can see that all of the subfolders in the Public folder are available for storing and retrieving files. These folders and the files inside them are available to all

users on the network, regardless of whether they have a valid user account on your computer.

10. Double-click **Public Documents**, right-click in the empty area, point to **New**, and click **Text Document**.

11. Type **NetworkDoc** and press **Enter**.

12. Double-click **NetworkDoc.txt** and type in some text.

13. Click the **File** menu, click **Save**, and close Notepad.

14. (Optional) Test the Public folder of another computer.

   a. Click the **Start** button and click **Network**.

   b. Double-click your partner's computer.

   c. Double-click **Users**, then **Public,** and double-click **Public Documents**.

   d. Right-click in the empty area, point to **New**, and click **Text Document**.

   e. Type **RemoteDoc** and press **Enter**.

   f. Double-click **RemoteDoc.txt** and type in some text.

   g. Click the **File** menu, click **Save**, and close **Notepad**.

15. Close all open windows.

Sharing Any Folder

Sharing files from any folder on your computer gives you more options to control which users have access to your files and what those users can do to your files. You are able to set the permissions for users when you share individual folders. For example, in a small business, the users in your project team may be given permission to view and change your shared files, but your other coworkers are only able to view the files.

The ability to configure permissions may be confusing for inexperienced users, but for experienced users the level of control allows you to configure file sharing just the way you want it. In a domain-based network, you can select users from the domain to share files with. In a workgroup-based network, you must create local accounts for the users you want to share files with. For example, if you want to share files with Bob, who logs onto another computer, you must create a user account for Bob on your Windows 7 computer, and then give the local user Bob permission to access files.

In a workgroup-based network, when a user account is created for Bob on your computer, it becomes difficult for Bob to ensure that the password used for his account on his own computer and your computer remains synchronized. However, Bob can use Credential Manger to save the password for the remote account so that he does not have to remember it.

Activity 8-7: Credential Manager

Time Required: 5 minutes
Objective: Use Credential Manager to save the password for a network account.

Description: Credential Manager allows users to save the user names and password for remote systems. This avoids the requirement for users to remember many passwords on a peer-to-peer network. In a domain-based network this is not required, because the domain account can be used to access resources on all computers in the domain. In this activity, you enter a user account into Credential Manager.

1. If necessary, start your computer and log on.

2. Click the **Start** button, right-click **Computer**, click **Manage**.

3. In the left pane, expand **Local Users and Groups** and click **Users**.

4. Right-click **Users** and click **New User**.

5. In the User name and Full name boxes, type **WorkgroupUser**.

6. In the Password and Confirm password boxes, type **password**.

7. Deselect the **User must change password at next logon** option. This user account will be shared by multiple users to access this computer. Therefore, you do not want the password to change automatically.

8. Select the **User cannot change password** option. If the account is shared by multiple users, you also do not want any users to change the password.

9. Select the **Password never expires** option and click **Create**. After this user is created, it can also be used to log on to the local computer, not just access network resources.

10. Click **Close** to close the New User dialog box.

11. Close **Computer Management**.

12. Click the **Start** button and click **Control Panel**.

13. Click **User Accounts and Family Safety** and click **User Accounts**.

14. In the left pane, click **Manage your credentials**. This option allows you to configure passwords that are required for remote computers.

15. Next to Windows Credentials, click the **Add a Windows credential** link to begin adding a new account.

16. In the Internet or network address box, type the name of your partner's computer.

17. In the User name box, type **WorkgroupUser**.

18. In the Password box, type **password**.

19. Click **OK**. Now whenever you access your partner's computer, Windows 7 uses the credentials you just entered. This allows you to specify different user names and passwords than the local account you are currently logged on as.

20. Close the Credential Manager window.

21. Close all open windows.

Creating and Managing Shared Folders

There are two user interfaces for sharing folders in Windows 7:

- "Share with"
- Advanced sharing

The **"Share with"** menu option is available when the computer browser window is open to show folders and files on the local computer. It triggers a file sharing wizard that is designed for users with basic needs, users who are not trying to fine tune or tweak shared item security. It simply enables the user to get what they want—the selected file or folder shared with basic read or read/write permissions. The menu can change depending on the type of network the computer is connected to. The "Share with" menu options for a homegroup connected computer are shown in Figure 8-14. When the computer is domain joined, the homegroup menu options is not displayed.

This method simplifies folder and file sharing by controlling both NTFS and share permissions at the same time. The knowledge and complexity of what those permissions are is hidden from the user when they decide to change the sharing status of an item. The choices in the Share with menu include:

- *Nobody*—Permission to access the selected item as a general shared resource is denied. A small lock icon is placed next to the item in the computer browser window to remind the local user that shared access to that item is not allowed at that point. NTFS permission

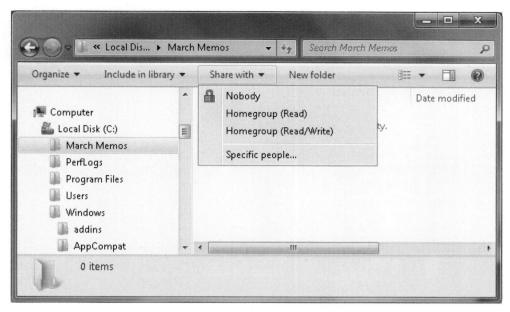

Figure 8-14 "Share with" menu
Courtesy Course Technology/Cengage Learning

inheritance on that folder or file is disabled and new permissions are applied so that only the owner of the item, members of the local Administrators group, and the operating system itself have full control permission to access it.

- *Homegroup (Read)*—This menu option only appears if the computer considers itself connected to a homegroup network location. The local HomeUsers group on the computer is granted access to only read the selected file or folder contents. This effectively gives all homegroup members this permission.

- *Homegroup (Read/Write)*—This menu option only appears if the computer considers itself connected to a homegroup network location. The local HomeUsers group on the computer is granted read and write permission to the selected file or folder contents. This effectively gives all homegroup members this permission.

- *Specific people*—This menu option opens the File Sharing wizard to select people to share the selected item with. Individual user accounts can have their permission to the selected item set to: read, read/write, or removed to discontinue access. The Owner permission is given to the person that first shares a folder. Owner status cannot be assigned to a user or groups. Owners can perform any action on the selected folders and files plus edit the permission levels for the shared resource.

The status of a shared resource can be seen by selecting an item and noting its status at the bottom of the computer browser window, as seen in Figure 8-15. Some system folders are considered protected and cannot have custom shared settings applied. The Public folder is one such example. Any attempt to modify its shared status with the "Share with" menu will only open the Advanced Sharing settings options from Control Panel.

A file or folder can be selected for sharing with the "Share with" file sharing wizard. The wizard is designed so that if a file is selected for sharing, the folder containing it is shared as well and configured with applicable permissions to access the file over the network. If the file sharing wizard was used to choose people to share the item with, after the file or folder has been shared, a dialog box with the Universal Naming Convention (UNC) path to the shared item is displayed, as shown in Figure 8-16.

You can access the "Share with" and File Sharing wizard by:

- Opening the "Share with" menu in the Computer browser window

- Right-clicking the file or folder in the Computer browser window and clicking "Share with"

- Clicking the Share button on the Sharing tab when viewing the Properties of a folder

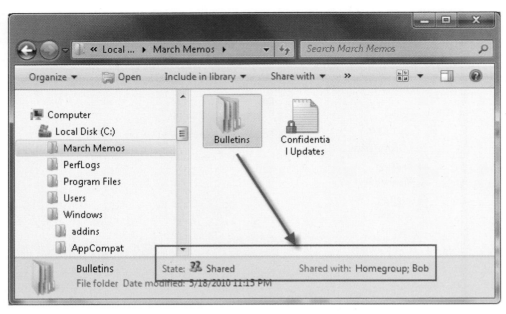

Figure 8-15 Shared folder status
Courtesy Course Technology/Cengage Learning

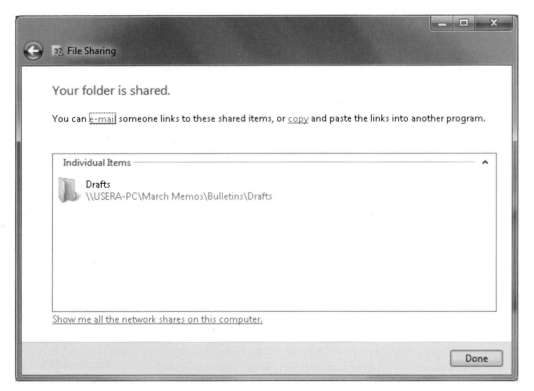

Figure 8-16 Shared folder UNC path
Courtesy Course Technology/Cengage Learning

Advanced Sharing Shown in Figure 8-17, **Advanced sharing** allows you to configure options that are not available in the simpler "Share with" interface. However, advanced folder sharing only configures share permissions; it does not configure NTFS permissions. To complete the security configuration for a shared folder created through advanced folder sharing, you must configure NTFS permissions as a separate task.

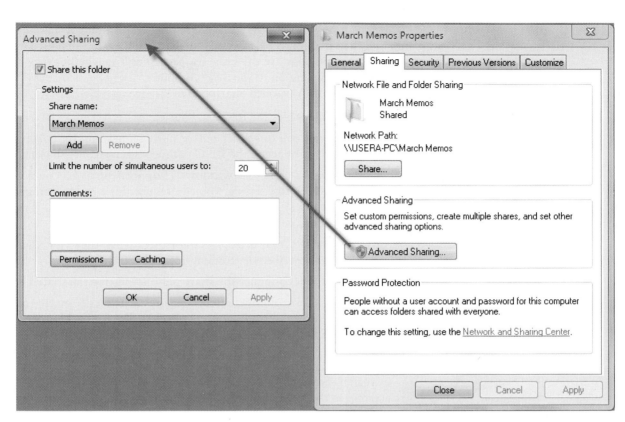

Figure 8-17 Folder properties, Advanced Sharing
Courtesy Course Technology/Cengage Learning

When shared folder permissions are combined with NTFS permissions, the most restrictive permissions are effective. For example, if a user is assigned read share permissions and full control NTFS permissions, the user will have only read access when accessing the folder over the network. If a user is assigned full control share permissions and read NTFS permissions, then the user will also only have read access. Figure 8-18 is a diagram explaining how NTFS and share permissions work together.

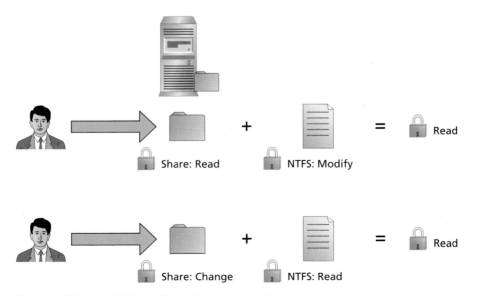

Figure 8-18 How NTFS and Shared folder permissions work together
Courtesy Course Technology/Cengage Learning

To simplify the management of permissions, you can assign the Full Control share permission to the Everyone group and then use NTFS permissions to control access to the files. This has the benefit of ensuring that user permissions are the same for accessing files whether they access the content over the network or by logging on to the local computer.

The settings you can configure in Advanced Sharing are:

- *Share this folder*—This option enables the folder as shared.

- *Share name*—This option allows you to specify one or more names that the folder is shared as. Users access the shared folder by using the UNC path\\computername\ sharename.

- *Limit the number of simultaneous users to*—Windows 7 supports up to 20 concurrent connections from network users. With this setting, you can reduce this to a lower number to ensure that the computer is not overwhelmed by network users. However, this is typically not done because sharing files has very little effect on performance.

- *Comments*—This box contains text that is displayed for users when they view the share on the network. Typically the text describes the content in the shared folder.

- *Permissions*—This button lets you configure the share permissions for the shared folder.

- *Caching*—This button lets you control how network clients cache files from this share as offline files. You can prevent file caching, allow users to select files for caching, or force file caching. Caching files for offline use is typically done only for mobile computers.

Share names ending in a dollar sign ($) are hidden shares that cannot be seen by browsing the network but can still be accessed by using the appropriate UNC path.

Advanced sharing lets you allow or deny permissions. When a permission is denied, it overrides any permissions that are allowed. For example, if the Everyone group is given Read permission and the user Bob is denied Read permission, then Bob will not have access to the share.

The share permissions available in Windows 7 are:

- *Full Control*—Allows users complete control over files and folders in the share and set permissions on files and folders in the share. In addition, Full Control allows users to configure the share permissions on the shared folder.

- *Change*—Allows users complete control to create, modify, and delete files in the shared folder, but not to set permissions.

- *Read*—Allows users to read the contents of files in the shared folder, but not to modify the files in any way.

You can access advanced sharing only by clicking the Advanced Sharing button on the Sharing tab in the Properties of a folder. This is not the same option as the "Advance sharing settings" available through the "Share with" menu.

Activity 8-8: Creating Shared Folders

Time Required: 15 minutes
Objective: Create shared folders for network users.

Description: There are multiple methods to create shared folders. To ensure that shared folders meet your needs, you need to understand the differences between the methods for creating shared folders. In this activity, you create shared folders using multiple methods.

1. If necessary, start your computer and log on.

2. Click the **Start** button and click **Documents**.

3. Right-click the empty area, point to **New**, and click **Folder**.

4. Type **SimpleShare1** and press **Enter**.

5. Click **SimpleShare1** and click the **Share with** drop-down menu on the toolbar.

6. Select **Specific people** from the drop-down menu. Click the drop-down list, click **WorkgroupUser**, and click the **Add** button. Notice that the default permission given to WorkgroupUser is Read.

7. To the right of WorkgroupUser, click **Read**, and click **Read/Write**. This allows WorkgroupUser to modify files.

8. Click the **Share** button.

9. Read the results in the File Sharing window. Notice that the UNC path for this share is long and goes through the C:\Users folder. All folders shared by using simple file sharing in your Documents folder use this long UNC path.

10. Click **Done**.

11. In the file browser window currently displaying the Documents library, double-click **Local Disk (C:)** under Computer in the left-hand pane.

12. Right-click an open area in the right-hand pane, point to **New**, and click **Folder**.

13. Type **SimpleShare2** and press **Enter**.

14. Right-click an open area, point to **New**, and click **Folder**.

15. Type **AdvancedShare** and press **Enter**.

16. Right-click **SimpleShare2**, point to **Share with**, and click **Specific people**.

17. Click the drop-down list, click **WorkgroupUser**, and click the **Add** button.

18. To the right of Workgroup User, click **Read**, and click **Read/Write**.

19. Click the **Share** button.

20. Read the results on the File Sharing window. Notice that the UNC path is directly to the shared folder when the folder is not inside your Documents folder.

21. Click **Done**.

22. Right-click **AdvancedShare** and click **Properties**.

23. Click the **Sharing** tab, and click **Advanced Sharing**.

24. Select the **Share this folder** option. Notice that the Share name setting is the same name as the folder by default, but it can be changed.

25. Click the **Permissions** button. This displays the share permissions for this share. Advanced sharing configures only share permissions, not NTFS permissions. NTFS permissions for this folder must be configured manually by using the Security tab. Using the Share with option for sharing configures both share permissions and NTFS permissions.

26. Select the **Allow** option next to the **Change** permission and click **OK**. This allows all users to modify files through the share, but not to change the share permissions.

27. Click **OK** to close the Advanced Sharing dialog box.

28. Click the **Security** tab and click the **Edit** button.

29. Click **Add**, type **WorkgroupUser**, click **Check Names**, and click **OK**.

30. In the Group or user names box, click **WorkgroupUser**.

31. In the Permissions for WorkgroupUser box, select the **Allow** option next to the **Modify** permission and click **OK**. NTFS permissions work with the share permissions to control what tasks a user is able to perform on a network share.

32. Click **Close** to close the AdvancedShare Properties dialog box.

33. Close all open windows.

Monitoring Shared Folders

Over time, you may lose track of all the folders that are shared on your computer. The most comprehensive to way monitor shares is by using Computer Management, shown in Figure 8-19. The Shared Folders System Tool has three nodes for monitoring and managing shared folders:

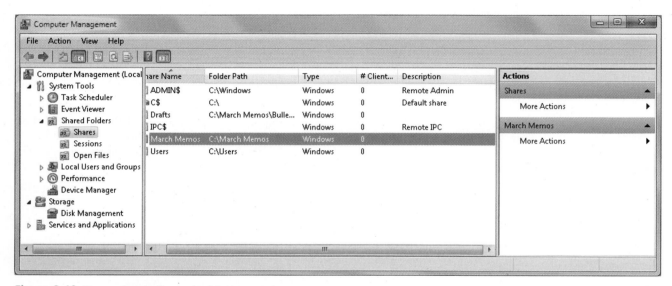

Figure 8-19 Shares view in Computer Management
Courtesy Course Technology/Cengage Learning

- *Shares*—This node allows you to create new shares, configure existing shared folders, and optionally stop sharing them. It shows all of the shared folders on this computer, including hidden shares. The summary view here even allows you to see how many clients are connected to each share.

- *Sessions*—This node allows you to see which users are connected to this computer. The summary view shows which computer each user is connecting from, how many files each user has open, and how long each user has been connected. If your system has the maximum of 20 sessions already connected and you need to allow another user access, you can disconnect an existing session from here.

- *Open Files*—This node allows you to see which files and folders are opened through file shares on this computer. You can see which users have the files open and whether the file is open for writing. Occasionally, due to system problems, users will be disconnected from files, but Windows 7 keeps the file locked. You can force a file to close here so that it can be reopened and modified.

Activity 8-9: Monitoring Shared Folders

Time Required: 5 minutes
Objective: Monitor shared folders by using Computer Management.

Description: When you share folders on your computer, it is useful to see who is using those files. For example, if you want to reboot your computer, you must be sure that no files are open. Rebooting a computer with shared files open can corrupt the files. In this activity, you will monitor shared folders on your computer.

1. If necessary, start your computer and log on.

2. Click the **Start** button, right-click **Computer**, click **Manage**.

3. In the left pane, expand **Shared Folders** and click **Shares**. This displays all of the shares on your computer, including the hidden shares. You can see the Users, SimpleShare2, and AdvancedShare shares from previous activities. You can also see the number of clients connected to each share and the folder each is sharing.

4. Right-click **SimpleShare2** and click **Properties**. The General tab allows you to configure the name of the share, description, user limit, and offline settings.

5. Click the **Share Permissions** tab and click **Everyone**. This tab allows you to configure the share permissions for the share. Notice that the Everyone group has Full Control.

6. Click the **Security** tab, and in the Group or user names box, click **WorkgroupUser**. This tab displays the NTFS permissions for the folder. Notice that WorkgroupUser has Full Control NTFS permissions. These NTFS permissions were automatically configured by the Share with sharing in the previous activity.

7. Click **Cancel** to close the SimpleShare2 Properties dialog box.

8. Click the **Start** button, and click **Computer**. Click **Network**, double-click your computer, double-click **Users**, double-click **Public**, double-click **Public Documents**, and double-click **NetworkDoc.txt** to open it. This opens NetworkDoc.txt through the UNC path and creates a network connection to your computer.

9. In Computer Management, select the Refresh button in the toolbar to update the shared folder details. Read the # Client Connections for the Users share. There is now one connection for the file you have opened. You can also press F5 to refresh the screen contents to update the # Client Connections value.

10. In the left pane, click **Sessions**. The Sessions folder shows you which users are connected to your computer and from which computer they are connected.

11. In the left pane, click **Open Files**. The Open Files folder shows you which files and folders are open on your computer and by which user.

12. Close all open windows.

Internet Connectivity

Today, almost every computer is configured to communicate on the Internet. However, depending on your needs, how your computer connects to the Internet will vary. The way you connect to the Internet will also vary depending on whether a single computer or multiple computers are using an Internet connection.

Single-Computer Internet Connectivity

Many homes have only one computer and that computer is shared by everyone in the home accessing the Internet. How that computer is configured to connect to the Internet varies depending on the type of Internet connection you have.

For all of the Internet connection types, the IP address provided to you by your Internet service provider is usually a fully routable IP address on the Internet. This means that anyone on the Internet can connect to and communicate with your computer. For this reason, it is important to enable Windows Firewall to protect your computer.

Detailed information about Windows Firewall is provided later in this chapter.

The types of Internet connections are:

- Cable
- DSL
- Dial-up
- Wireless WAN

Cable Almost all cable companies offer high-speed Internet connectivity as an option to their subscribers. In most cases, this is the simplest way to connect to the Internet.

When you subscribe to an Internet connection with your cable provider, you will be supplied with a **cable modem** that connects to the same cable that you hook up to your TV. The cable modem is responsible for converting signals from a format that travels properly over the cable provider network to standard Ethernet in your home. You connect an Ethernet cable from your computer to the cable modem. Figure 8-20 shows the components required for cable modem connectivity.

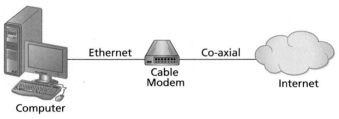

Figure 8-20 Cable Modem Connectivity
Courtesy Course Technology/Cengage Learning

By default, Windows 7 networking is configured to use DHCP to obtain IP configuration information. When you connect your computer to the cable modem, the cable provider's DHCP server provides IP configuration information to Windows 7. Moments after you plug in the Ethernet cable, you should be able to access the Internet.

For more detailed information about Internet connectivity over cable systems, see the Internet Service description at *http://technet.microsoft.com/en-us/library/cc750549.aspx.*

DSL Digital subscriber line (DSL) is a high-speed Internet connection over telephone lines. This type of Internet connectivity is often as fast as cable, but slightly more difficult to configure.

When you subscribe to DSL, you are supplied with a **DSL modem** that connects to a phone line. The DSL modem is responsible for converting signals from a format that travels properly over the phone system to standard Ethernet in your home. You connect an Ethernet cable from your computer to the DSL modem. Figure 8-21 shows the components required for DSL connectivity.

DSL connections usually use **Point-to-Point Protocol over Ethernet (PPPoE)** to secure connections. Your DSL provider supplies you with a PPPoE username and password to connect to the network. Only after you are authenticated by using PPPoE will you be able to obtain IP configuration information from the DHCP server of the DSL provider.

Windows 7 has built-in support for PPPoE. You can connect to a network requiring PPPoE by creating a Broadband connection. The options in a Broadband connection are similar to a dial-up connection.

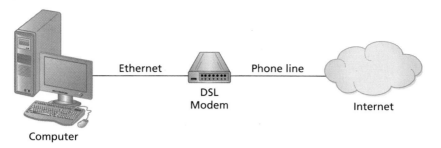

Figure 8-21 DSL Modem Connectivity
Courtesy Course Technology/Cengage Learning

For more detailed information about Internet connectivity over DSL, see the Internet Service description at *http://technet.microsoft.com/en-us/library/cc750549.aspx.*

Dial-Up Although progressively becoming less common, some people still access the Internet by using a dial-up connection over a phone line by using a **modem**, as shown in Figure 8-22. This is a much slower way to access the Internet. However, it is suitable for simple tasks such as reading e-mail and text-oriented Web pages. Windows 7 includes support for dial-up connections.

You can learn more about dial-up connections in Chapter 14, Remote Access and Mobile Computing.

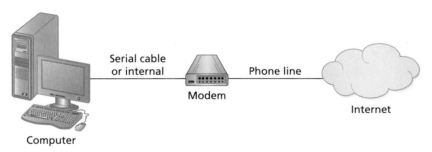

Figure 8-22 Dial-up Modem Connectivity
Courtesy Course Technology/Cengage Learning

Wireless WAN Wireless Wide Area Networking (WWAN) is fully supported by Windows 7. A mobile device such as a smartphone can connect through broadband cell towers and Wi-Fi hotspots to connect to the Internet. The portable device may offer a data card, and perhaps a specialized cable, that connects the mobile device to the computer, usually with a USB connection. The computer can access the Internet through the mobile device, treating it as a special type of modem. There are several requirements before this option works. The provider of the broadband service must enable this option for the portable device, typically for an extra fee. Most broadband vendors refer to this feature as "tethering" the computer to the mobile device. The mobile device must also be configured to recognize that this feature is active. The advantage to this technology is that broadband support for mobile devices is now widespread. The disadvantage is that the data plan contract to pay for the bandwidth used by the mobile device while it operates in this mode can be expensive. Windows 7 works with this type of connection fully aware that it is a WWAN service.

Shared Internet Connectivity

It is possible for multiple computers to share a single Internet connection. This is not commonly done for dial-up connections, but is quite common for cable modem and DSL Internet connections. For multiple computers on your network to share a single Internet connection, there must be a mechanism in place to share the single IP address given to you by your ISP. The two most common mechanisms for sharing an IP address are a **router** or **Internet Connection Sharing (ICS)**.

When multiple computers share an Internet connection, the router or computer performing ICS is assigned the IP address from the ISP. Computers on the internal network are assigned private IP addresses that are not routable on the Internet. Computers on the internal network use the router or ICS computer as the default gateway. Figure 8-23 is a diagram that describes shared Internet connectivity using a router.

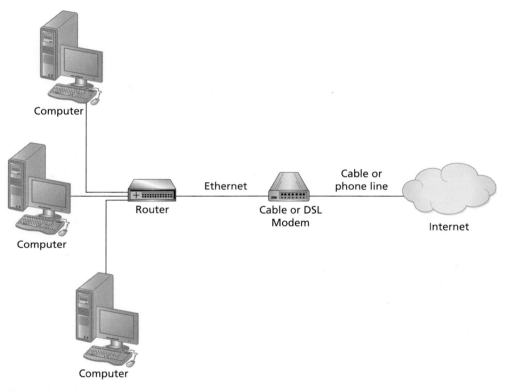

Figure 8-23 ICS Shared Networking
Courtesy Course Technology/Cengage Learning

The hardware routers sold in retail stores are actually simple firewalls that perform **network address translation (NAT)**. NAT is the process that allows multiple computers to share a single IP address. ICS also performs NAT.

Internet Connection Sharing

ICS allows a Windows 7 computer to act as an Internet router. This computer is called the host computer. To use ICS the host computer must have an Internet connection (public interface) plus one additional network connection (private interface). The public interface obtains an Internet routable IP address from your ISP. The private interface uses a private IP address to communicate with other computers that you are sharing the Internet connection with.

You use the Sharing tab in the Properties of the public interface to enable ICS. The Sharing tab, shown in Figure 8-24, is only available when there are at least two connections on the computer. To enable ICS, check the Allow other network users to connect through this computer's Internet connection check box.

ICS allows computers connected to the host's private interface to communicate through it to access information on the Internet. The host can use either IPv4 or IPv6 addressing to communicate with the private computers. The private computers should be configured to obtain an IP address automatically and their Internet Explorer LAN settings should be configured with the

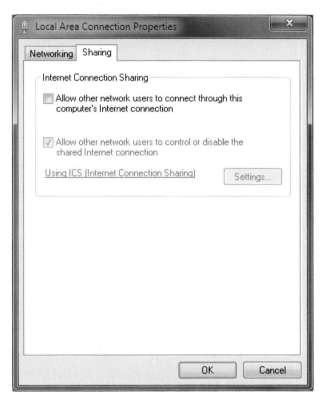

Figure 8-24 ICS Sharing Settings on network interface properties
Courtesy Course Technology/Cengage Learning

settings shown in Figure 8-25. If the host's public shared interface is actually a VPN network connection, the private computers share that VPN connection. If the VPN connection enables a connection back to the corporate office, all private computers connecting through ICS have access to the corporate network.

Wireless Networking

Network connections allow data to flow from the local computer to other computers that share that network. Many networking technologies rely on a wire-based physical data connection to the local computer. Different types of cables, connectors, and expansion equipment make up the

Figure 8-25 Recommended Internet Explorer LAN Settings to support ICS
Courtesy Course Technology/Cengage Learning

wired network. Instead of relying on wires to connect computers, a wireless network transfers data without a physical connection. The most common type of wireless technology uses radios to transmit and receive data. Many different types of radios have been developed for wireless technology.

Standards are written by organizations such as the Institute of Electrical and Electronic Engineers (IEEE) to guide the manufacturers of wireless network products and help make them functional and compatible with each other. The IEEE standard most commonly used for popular wireless networking products is IEEE 802.11.

The Wireless Fidelity (Wi-Fi) Alliance was created in 1999 as a nonprofit body to help manufacturers test and certify wireless products that would work together. Products based on the IEEE 802.11a, 802.11b, 802.11g, and 802.11n radio standards are included as part of the Wi-Fi standard supported by Windows 7. These wireless standards are summarized in Table 8-5. IEEE 802.11n performance is the fastest and it is more tolerant of interference because it can support multiple antennas working at the same time. Its maximum performance will be impacted by the number of antennas in use on both sides of a wireless radio connection. Windows 7 includes built-in support for Wi-Fi wireless networking as a unique networking technology.

Windows 7 provides a strong foundation for wireless technology, leaving the manufacturer with less responsibility for code development and a smaller chance of creating unstable software. Wireless adapters now appear as their own media type, not as an Ethernet **802.3** connection.

Table 8-5   Wireless Standard Comparison

Wireless Standard	Primary Radio Frequency	Maximum Data Throughput (Mbps)
IEEE 802.11a	5 GHz	54
IEEE 802.11b	2.4 GHz	11
IEEE 802.11g	2.4 GHz	54
IEEE 802.11n	2.4 and 5 GHz	600

Even though Windows 7 supports a range of **802.11** standards, several are becoming obsolete. For example, 802.11a and 802.11b hardware is still in use but it is getting difficult to find those technologies for sale today. Each standard defines limits on how many devices can interact at once, resistance to radio interference, how fast they transfer data, and over what range they can operate. Exceeding any of those limits can cause performance issues that Windows 7 cannot compensate for with software alone.

The computer running Windows 7 may have a wireless adapter installed in the computer. It may be installed as an add-on card, plugged into a USB port, or built-in to the system itself. If the wireless adapter is built-in, such as in a laptop, there is typically a power switch that toggles the adapter on or off to save power or ensure privacy.

The wireless adapter can communicate with a base station or other wireless adapters. A base station is commonly called a wireless access point (WAP). The WAP itself connects to the wired network and allows wireless clients to ultimately use that wired connection. The WAP may be part of a firewall device sharing access to the Internet or it may be a stand-alone unit. The WAP and wireless adapter must use the same 802.11 standard to communicate with each other. If they are not compatible, one or the other hardware component may need to be replaced.

Most WAP devices have a web server built into them that allows the device to be configured initially using a wired network connection. The manufacturer's instructions provide connection details and initial login credentials. The manufacturer identifies a default management IP address, an initial connection URL (for example, *http://192.168.0.1/admin*), and a default administrator ID and password.

The most common configuration details for a WAP include:

- *Security Set Identifier (SSID)*—The name assigned to the WAP to identify itself to clients. The SSID may or may not be configured to broadcast its identity to all wireless clients.

- *802.11 mode*—The versions of 802.11 in which the radio operates, such as 802.11n. Choices will be limited to the modes supported by the WAP hardware.

- *Security method*—The methods used to encrypt and restrict wireless client connections to the WAP

Wireless encryption methods and client connection restrictions are required because the range of a wireless signal does not have a specific boundary. A private system may be detected by clients in unauthorized and unexpected areas. Newer technology has a greater range than ever before. Simply upgrading existing wireless hardware may expose a company to risks they did not think about before. A wireless client must be configured with correct security settings to enable it to communicate with a secured WAP. If the WAP is unsecured, it is referred to as an open, or unsecured, system.

Connecting to an open system may be dangerous because your computer may be connecting to an untrusted WAP that has been configured purposely to help unauthorized users gain access to your system. If there is no choice, ensure that the connection is identified as a Public network connection to maximize the protection of Windows Firewall and to disable your computer's advertising of its identity.

Creating a Wireless Connection

Wireless network connections can be created using several methods:

- *Manually connect to a wireless network*—This wizard is available by clicking Set up a new connection or network in the Network and Sharing Center and selecting this action. All settings are manually configured.

- *Connect to a Network*—By right-clicking the network icon in the notification area of the taskbar, a list of wireless networks is displayed, as shown in Figure 8-26. Selecting a network from the list and clicking the Connect button triggers the client to attempt a connection. If a security pass phrase is requested, the user must enter a correct value before the connection is fully established.

Figure 8-26 Wireless networks displayed from Taskbar Notification area
Courtesy Course Technology/Cengage Learning

- *Copy profile from USB flash drive*—A wireless configuration profile can be saved to an USB flash drive. That USB drive stores configuration information for the wireless network, optionally including the security pass-phrase, in XML formatted data files. The XML files on the USB drive can be used to program multiple computers and devices labeled as Windows Connect Now compatible.

- *Command line*—The Network Shell command-line utility (netsh.exe) supports a command section for wireless LAN configuration (wlan). This advanced utility is not typically used in day-to-day network administration, but it is available for advanced management. More options can be seen by issuing the command netsh wlan /?.

- *Group policy*—Wireless network settings can be applied to domain computers using group policy settings defined in Active Directory. A list of allowed or denied wireless networks can be specified.

When a new wireless connection is created, the key settings used to describe it in Windows 7 are:

- *Network name*—The name of the wireless connection and its profile in the operating system

- *Security type*—The type of security methods the WAP expects the wireless client to use

- *Encryption type*—The method used to encrypt data, if a choice exists, as a customization of the selected security type

- *Security key*—A pass-phrase that acts as a password, allowing the wireless client to authenticate and connect

- *Start this connection automatically*—Identifies whether the connection starts automatically once the client detects the WAP is operating in range

- *Connect even if the network is not broadcasting*—The client attempts to connect even if it does not notice the WAP broadcasting its SSID wirelessly
- *Connect to a more preferred network if available*—The client attempts to connect to the best wireless connection it believes is currently available

Selecting the security type can be the most challenging issue in creating a wireless connection. The security type is configured as part of the WAP setup. If that configuration is not known, then Windows 7 defaults to Wi-Fi Protected Access (WPA or WPA2). The security pass-phrase must be specified correctly to establish a connection.

Some older security types are supported but not recommended. The Wired Equivalent Privacy (WEP) method is easy to crack and does not provide strong security. If you are limited to using WEP because the wireless network adapter or WAP do not support anything newer then it would be better to invest in new wireless hardware.

In corporate networks, specialized authentication servers can be used to validate users and control network access. The **802.1x** security method is one example of an enterprise authentication method. These enterprise security methods require the configuration of those network services before they can be used. When an enterprise method is selected, security methods in addition to a pass phrase can be used to help validate the user. Smart cards, certificates, and the user's Windows logon credentials can all be involved to establish a trusted connection. By default, Windows 7 uses the EAP-MSCHAP v2 authentication method to authenticate the user's Windows logon credentials. This strong authentication method avoids having the user's name or password exposed over the wireless network.

Managing Wireless Connections

The existing wireless network connections can be seen in the Network and Sharing Center. Clicking on the connections name opens the wireless networking connection's status window, as shown in Figure 8-27. This identifies the wireless signal quality, speed, Internet connectivity, and packet transmission statistics.

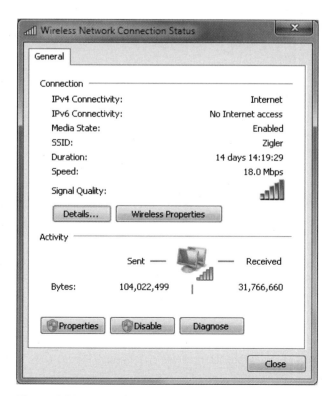

Figure 8-27 Wireless connection status
Courtesy Course Technology/Cengage Learning

Clicking the Wireless Properties button in the wireless status window displays the current settings for the wireless connection. Changes to security settings and connection preferences can be made here. Changing the SSID to connect to cannot be made here. If the SSID changes a new wireless connection profile must be created.

Troubleshooting Wireless Connections

Wireless technology is flexible, but there are several issues that commonly arise.

Wireless technologies are typically radios restricted to specific electronic signal frequencies. Other devices, such as microwaves and cordless telephones, can interfere with the signal. If the interference cannot be eliminated, the signal between the computer and WAP may need to be improved with better antennas or better antenna placement. If that does not help enough, the WAP and wireless network adapter may have to be reconfigured to use a different frequency. Each of the 802.11 standards is designed to operate on one or more frequencies. Purchasing new hardware may be a requirement in some situations where the existing hardware and its supported 802.11 settings fail to operate effectively. Options are limited by the manufacturer's support for both the WAP and wireless network adapter.

Some 802.11 standards are limited to what channels, in addition to specific frequencies, they can use to communicate with the wireless client. Channel selection may be limited by the number of active clients and sources of interference nearby. Making changes to those wireless adapter settings may require updates to the WAP configuration as well.

The SSID assigned to a WAP identifies that device. There is no automatic method to force two WAP devices in the same area to have different SSID values assigned. If they have the same SSID, the wireless client may become confused about which one to connect to and unreliable connectivity will result. This is common when WAP devices are installed with factory settings in areas where multiple offices or homes are clustered together. The only solution is to ensure that the SSID is unique.

A WAP's SSID and administrator credentials (i.e. user ID and password) should always be changed when it is installed for the first time.

Many WAP devices broadcast their SSID. That can be turned off and the wireless client is configured with a manual definition of the SSID. The client is configured so that it doesn't wait for the broadcast of the SSID to connect. Some administrators believe this is a security enhancement, but it is not. Methods exist for eavesdroppers to identify the presence of the WAP with advanced tools and an experienced skill set.

A Windows 7 client can be configured to connect to a WAP automatically when it is in range. If the same client is configured for multiple WAPs and they are all active and in range it may disconnect from one WAP and reconnect to another as the signal strength varies. This can cause the client to appear slow and unresponsive. The wireless client can be moved closer to one of the WAPs to change the signal strength or the other wireless connection profiles can have the option to Connect to a more preferred network if available turned off.

WAP devices in public places may be untrusted, even if they have a pass-phrase configured. If a computer is being connected to an untrusted network, always consider setting the network location type accordingly and perhaps updating the Windows firewall configuration.

Windows Firewall

Windows 7 includes an improved version of **Windows Firewall** to protect your computer. Like Windows Vista, Windows Firewall is enabled by default in Windows 7.

A standard firewall protects your computer by restricting which network packets that are allowed to reach your computer. A host-based firewall, like Windows Firewall, evaluates each packet as it arrives or leaves and determines whether that packet is allowed or denied. By default all packets are denied when they arrive from external sources and only a few are allowed for specific purposes. For example, when you join a domain, Windows 7 automatically configures Windows Firewall to allow the correct packets through for domain-based communication. Other packets are denied.

One way to improve security on computers is by reducing the **attack surface**. Disabling and removing unnecessary services is a common way to reduce the attack surface. Using a host-based firewall restricts communication with your computer and further reduces the attack surface. By reducing the attack surface, it is less likely that worms, viruses, and other malware are able to install on your computer.

Some of the features in Windows Firewall are:

- *Inbound filtering*—This controls incoming packets from the network and was available in previous versions of Windows. Inbound filtering protects your computer from other computers and users on the network and is enabled by default.

- *Outbound filtering*—This controls outgoing packets from your computer to the network. Outbound filtering prevents software installed on your computer from communicating on the network without your knowledge.

- *Firewall rules combined with IPsec rules*—In previous versions of Windows, IPsec rules were configured separately from firewall rules. In some cases, this resulted in conflicting rules with unexpected results. Combining firewall and IPsec rules ensures that there are no conflicts.

- *Support for complex rules*—Previous versions of Windows allowed only simple rules to control which local ports were available for communication on the network. Windows 7 supports complex rules based on:
  - Source and destination IP addresses
  - Source and destination port numbers
  - IP protocol numbers
  - Network location (home, work or public)
  - Multiple ports per rule
  - Interface types such as wireless
  - Services rather than port number
  - Active Directory groups or users (IPsec rules only)

- *Support for logging*—Logging allows you to monitor blocked packets. For example, you can look in the log and see that blocked packets are coming from a particular computer. Then you can determine whether that computer has a virus.

Basic Firewall Configuration

The Windows Firewall Control Panel window provides basic firewall configuration options. Windows 7 allows custom firewall settings for each type of network location: home, work, or public as shown in Figure 8-28. When the computer is domain joined, there are additional options only available in the advanced firewall settings window which is reviewed later in the chapter. When a network interface becomes active, it has a specified network location. The matching firewall settings for that type of network location applies to traffic through that interface. In Windows Vista, only one network location profile would be active at one time for all network interfaces. Windows 7 improves on this limitation. If a Windows 7 computer has multiple network interfaces active, each can be assigned a different network location, each with different firewall settings based on their assigned network location.

When Windows Firewall is enabled, the default configuration blocks all incoming packets except for specifically configured exceptions. This allows Windows Firewall to be configured to support applications such as instant messenger programs. Instant messenger programs, for example, typically require some exceptions on Windows Firewall to receive messages. When Turn Windows Firewall on or off is selected from the Windows Firewall Control Panel window, the firewall Customize Settings window is displayed as shown in Figure 8-29.

There is an option to block all incoming connections. When this option is selected, no exceptions are allowed. You are still able to initiate communication with other computers, but other

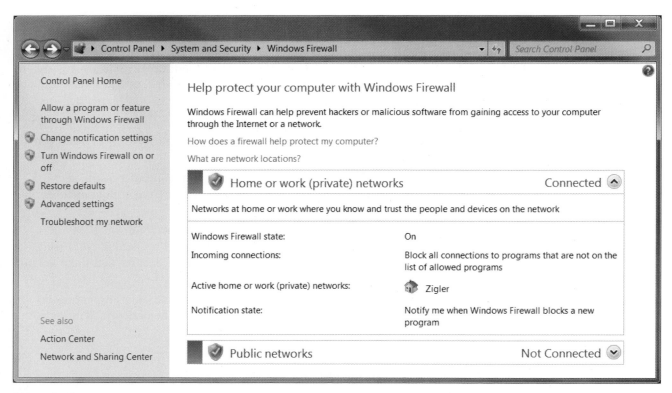

Figure 8-28 Windows Firewall, main window
Courtesy Course Technology/Cengage Learning

Customize settings for each type of network
You can modify the firewall settings for each type of network location that you use.
What are network locations?

Home or work (private) network location settings
◉ Turn on Windows Firewall
☐ Block all incoming connections, including those in the list of allowed programs
☑ Notify me when Windows Firewall blocks a new program
○ Turn off Windows Firewall (not recommended)

Public network location settings
◉ Turn on Windows Firewall
☐ Block all incoming connections, including those in the list of allowed programs
☑ Notify me when Windows Firewall blocks a new program
○ Turn off Windows Firewall (not recommended)

OK   Cancel

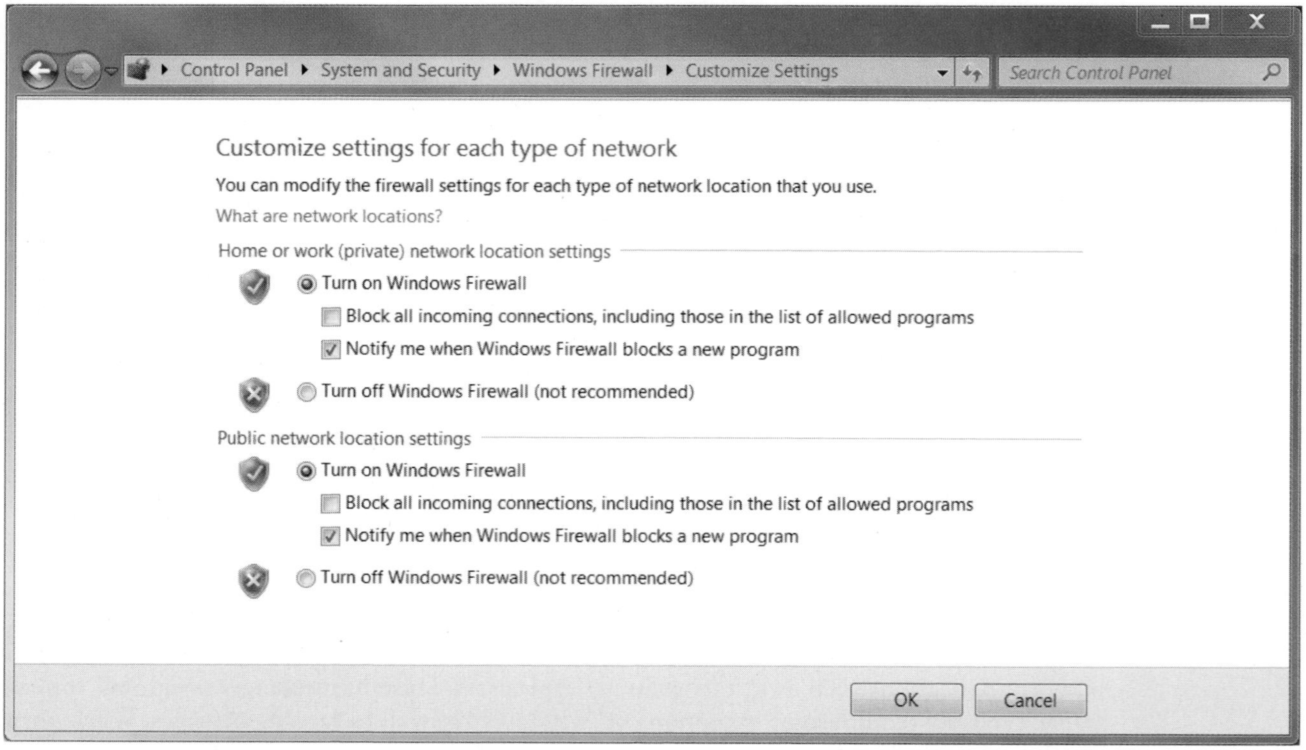

Figure 8-29 Windows Firewall, Customize Settings window
Courtesy Course Technology/Cengage Learning

computers cannot initiate communication with your computer. This is only recommended when you are connected directly to public networks, such as the wireless network in a café.

When Allow a program or feature through Windows Firewall is selected from the Windows Firewall Control Panel window, the firewall allowed programs window is displayed as shown in Figure 8-30. This allows you to configure which programs are able to accept network communication requests. A program can be allowed access through the firewall depending on the network location type, private or public. The firewall exception can be enabled for one, both, or none of the network location categories.

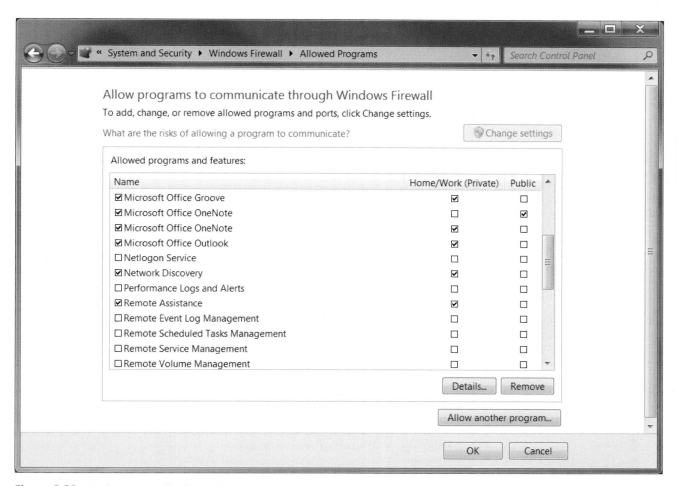

Figure 8-30 Windows Firewall, Allowed programs
Courtesy Course Technology/Cengage Learning

This allows some applications, such as Remote Assistance, to be available when the user is connected in supported situations. Many corporate offices do not want Remote Assistance enabled when the user is connected in unsupported locations, or in locations where other support methods are available. The choice of what application to make an exception for and the type of network location to enable it for are defined by situational requirements.

When you create an exception for a program, the exception applies to that program no matter what port number it uses. The exception is also only valid when the program is running. If the program is stopped, the exception poses no risk.

When Restore defaults is selected from the Windows Firewall Control Panel window, the option to restore default settings for Windows Firewall is presented. If you have performed many customized configurations and did not document them, then you may want to reset Windows Firewall back to the default configuration as part of the troubleshooting process.

Advanced Firewall Configuration

Advanced firewall configuration allows you to configure more complex rules, outgoing filtering, and IPsec rules. These cannot be configured directly with the Windows Firewall utility in Control Panel. The advanced firewall configuration is useful in corporate and enterprise computing situations. The basic Windows Firewall utility is usually sufficient in home and small business situations. The tools available to perform advanced firewall configuration are:

- *Windows Firewall with Advanced Security utility*—This utility is a graphical tool to configure all of the Windows Firewall features on a single computer.
- *Netsh*—This is a command-line utility for managing network configuration. It is also capable of configuring all of the Windows Firewall features on the local computer. This tool can be used in a script that is run on multiple computers.
- *Group Policy*—To quickly and easily manage the Windows Firewall settings in a corporate environment, you should use Group Policy. It allows firewall settings to be applied to hundreds or thousands of computers very quickly. Some Group Policy configuration options were not available for previous versions of Windows and these settings will be ignored by previous versions of Windows.

The **Windows Firewall with Advanced Security** utility is shown in Figure 8-31. By using this interface you can:

- Configure firewall properties
- View and edit rules
- Create new firewall rules
- Create new computer connection security rules
- Monitor Windows Firewall rules and connections

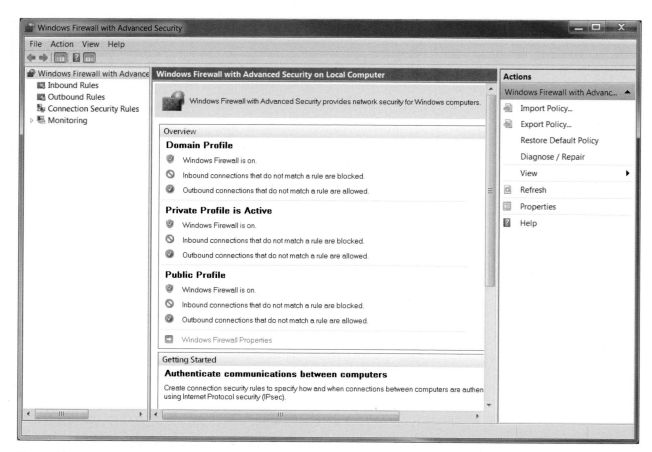

Figure 8-31 Windows Firewall with Advanced Security window
Courtesy Course Technology/Cengage Learning

Configure Firewall Properties   Windows 7 stores the firewall properties based on location types. The configuration of each location type is referred to as a profile. When the Windows Firewall with Advanced Security on Local Computer node is selected, a summary is displayed showing the configuration of each profile. You can edit the configuration for each profile as shown in Figure 8-32. The tabs for editing each profile have exactly the same options.

Figure 8-32 Windows Firewall, profile settings for network locations
Courtesy Course Technology/Cengage Learning

In each profile you can:

- Enable or disable Windows Firewall
- Configure inbound connections
  - *Block (default)*—All inbound connections are blocked unless specifically allowed by a rule.
  - *Block all connections*—All inbound connections are blocked regardless of the rules.
  - *Allow*—All inbound connections are allowed unless specifically blocked by a rule.
- Configure outbound connections
  - *Allow (default)*—All outbound connections are allowed unless specifically blocked by a rule.
  - *Block*—All outbound connections are blocked unless specifically allowed by a rule.
- Customize protected network connections
  - *Select which network interfaces this firewall state applies to*—All are selected by default
- Customize settings
  - *Display notifications to the user when a program is blocked from receiving inbound connections*—This is useful for users to be notified when something unusual is happening on the network.

- *Allow unicast response to multicast or broadcast network traffic*—Some network attackers use multicast and broadcast requests to map out the network and determine client IP addresses. Disabling this reduces that possibility.

- *Apply local firewall rules*—This option allows firewall rules from Group Policy and the local computer to both be applied. If there is a conflict between Group Policy-based rules and local rules, the Group Policy-based rules are effective. You can only configure this option in Group Policy.

- *Apply local connection security rules*—This option allows connection security rules from Group Policy and the local computer to both be applied. If there is a conflict between Group Policy-based rules and the local rules, the Group Policy-based rules are effective. You can only configure this option in Group Policy.

- Customize logging

  - *Name*—The name and location of the Windows Firewall log. By default, this is C:\ Windows\system32\LogFiles\Firewall\pfirewall.log.

  - *Size limit*—This limits the size of the Windows Firewall log to ensure you do not run out of disk space.

  - *Log dropped packets*—Specifies whether blocked packets are logged. By default, this option is off and blocked packets are not logged.

  - *Log successful connections*—Specifies whether successful connections are logged. By default, this option is off and successful connections are not logged.

IPsec is a system for securing and authenticating IP-based network connections. By using the Windows Firewall with Advanced Security utility, you can configure IPsec settings, as shown in Figure 8-33. If the settings are configured as Default, they can be overridden by Group Policy-based settings.

Figure 8-33 Windows Firewall, IPSec settings
Courtesy Course Technology/Cengage Learning

The IPsec settings you can configure are:

- *Key exchange*—This setting controls which method is used to securely transmit the keys used for data encryption between both computers.

- *Data protection*—This setting controls which methods are used to encrypt and protect the integrity of data.

- *Authentication Method*—This setting controls which method is used to authenticate the two computers creating an IPsec connection. The simplest method is a preshared key (password), but it is also the least secure. By default, Kerberos authentication is used.

View and Edit Firewall Rules

A large number of inbound and outbound rules are created by default in Windows 7. Figure 8-34 shows a list of outbound rules. In the list of rules, you can see the name of the rule, a group of rules it belongs to, profiles the rule can belong to, when the rule is enabled, and whether the rule allows or denies packets.

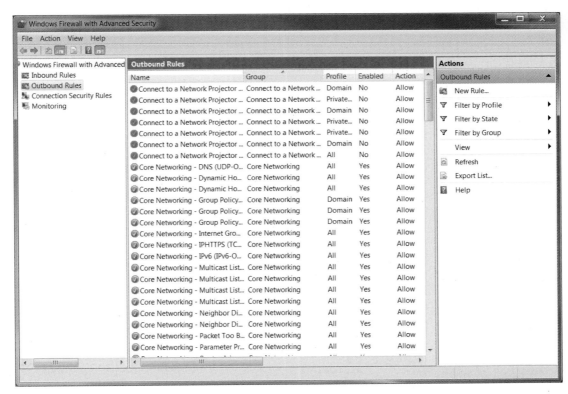

Figure 8-34 Windows Firewall, outbound rule listing
Courtesy Course Technology/Cengage Learning

The icons for each rule also give you information about that rule. Rules that allow packets have a green arrow icon. Rules that deny packets have a red circle with a slash. If the icon has a down arrow on it, then the rule is disabled.

You modify an existing rule by opening its properties. Figure 8-35 shows the properties of the Remote Assistance (TCP-Out) rule. The tabs in the properties of an outbound rule are:

- *General*—This tab allows you to configure the rule name, configure the rule description, enable or disable the rule, and choose the rule action.

- *Programs and Services*—This tab allows you to select programs and services that this rule applies to.

- *Computers*—This tab allows you to restrict connections to specific computers and groups of computers. For inbound rules, this tab is named Users and Computer and restrictions can be applied to specific users in addition to computers.

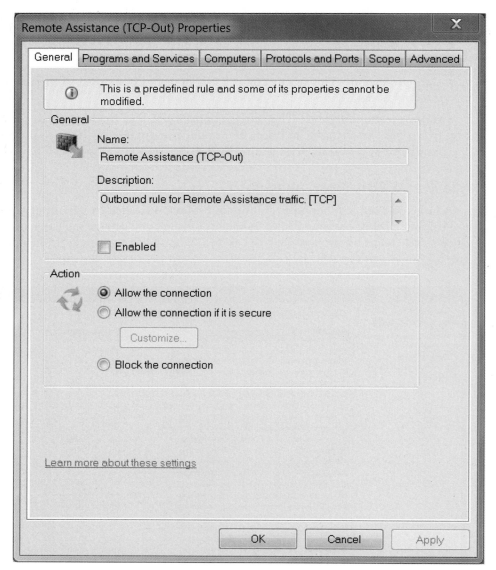

Figure 8-35 Windows Firewall, outbound rule properties
Courtesy Course Technology/Cengage Learning

- *Protocols and Ports*—This tab allows you to specify the protocol type this rule applies to, the local port this rule applies to, the remote port this rule applies to, and which ICMP packet types this rule applies to.

- *Scope*—This tab allows you to specify the source and destination IP addresses this rule applies to.

- *Advanced*—This tab allows you to specify which profiles and interface types this rule applies to.

Create New Firewall Rules When you create a new firewall rule, a wizard guides you through the process. The wizard for creating an outbound rule is shown in Figure 8-36. Using a wizard simplifies the process of rule creation because it limits the options during the creation process to only those options you need for the particular type of rule you are creating.

The rule types you can create with the Outbound Rule Wizard are:

- *Program*—A program rule allows or denies traffic for a specific program that is specified by selecting an executable file. You can specify which profiles this rule applies to.

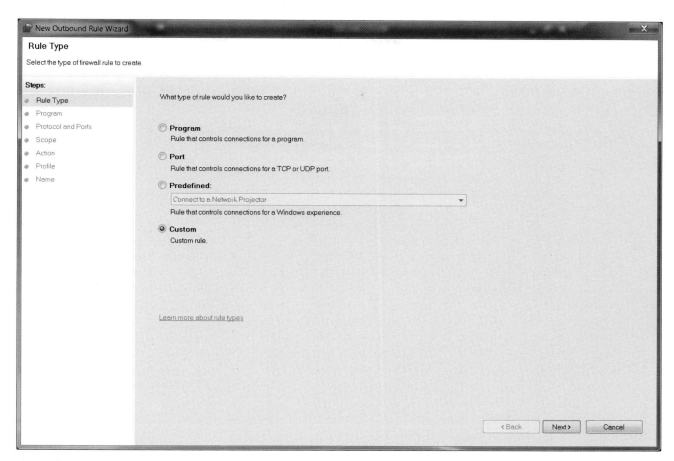

Figure 8-36 Windows Firewall, outbound rule creation wizard
Courtesy Course Technology/Cengage Learning

- *Port*—A port rule allows or denies traffic for a specific TCP or UDP port. You can specify which profiles this rule applies to.

- *Predefined*—A predefined rule creates a group of rules to allow or deny Windows functions, such as file and printer sharing or Remote Assistance. In most cases these rules are already created and do not need to be re-created. These rules allow you to define source and destination computers (endpoints) that the rule applies to. You can also specify to which profiles this rule applies.

- *Custom*—A custom rule lets you configure programs, ports, protocols, endpoints, and profiles. You can use this type of rule when the other rule types do not meet your needs.

When you define the actions for a rule, as shown in Figure 8-37, you can specify:

- *Allow the connection*—This option allows connections based on this rule.

- *Allow the connection if it is secure*—This option allows connections based on this rule only when an IPsec connection is configured. By default, this option requires that IPsec authenticates the connection and ensures integrity. However, you also have the option to require data encryption. Additionally, because a secure connection is based on an IPsec rule, you can select to have this rule override other block firewall rules.

- *Block the connection*—This option denies all connections based on this rule. However, a rule with this option selected can be overridden by another rule that allows only secure connections.

Create New Computer-Connection Security Rules Computer-connection security rules use IPsec to authenticate and secure communication between two computers. The computer-connection security rule types, shown in Figure 8-38, are:

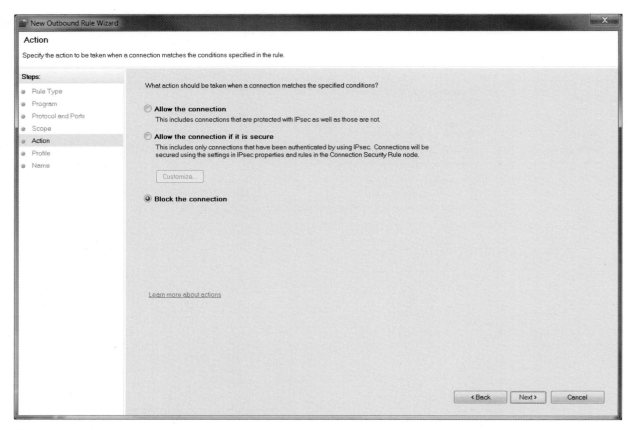

Figure 8-37 Widows Firewall, rule actions
Courtesy Course Technology/Cengage Learning

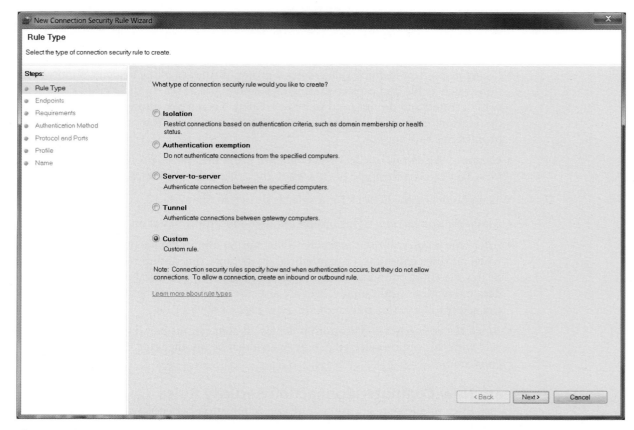

Figure 8-38 Windows Firewall, Connection Security Rule
Courtesy Course Technology/Cengage Learning

- *Isolation*—An isolation rule restricts communication with other computers to only those that can be authenticated. You can specify the method of authentication. The rule can apply to inbound connections, outbound connections, or both.

- *Authentication exemption*—An authentication exemption rule specifies IP addresses or IP address ranges that do not need to be authenticated when communicating with this computer. Effectively, this creates exceptions to an isolation rule.

- *Server-to-server*—A server-to-server rule is used to enforce IPsec settings between two computers. Typically, this type of rule is used to require encryption between two computers, such as a client and server. However, it can also be configured to apply only for certain connection types, such as wireless connections.

- *Tunnel*—A tunnel rule is used to configure Windows 7 as the endpoint of a secure communication tunnel. Other computers use the Windows 7 computer as their default gateway to secure communication through the IPsec tunnel. This type of rule is seldom used.

- *Custom*—Allows you to configure a customized rule if the standard rule types do not meet your needs.

Monitor Windows Firewall Rules and Connections
When you view the inbound or outbound rules for Windows Firewall, there is a large list of rules that includes enabled or disabled rules. The Firewall node under Monitoring in the Windows Firewall with Advanced Security snap-in, shown in Figure 8-39, allows you to see all of the rules that are enabled in one screen. This quickly shows you how your system is configured. This is also useful to see the rules that are being applied by Group Policy.

The Connection Security node under Monitoring, allows you to see the computer connection security rules that are enabled and any security associations that are active. A security association

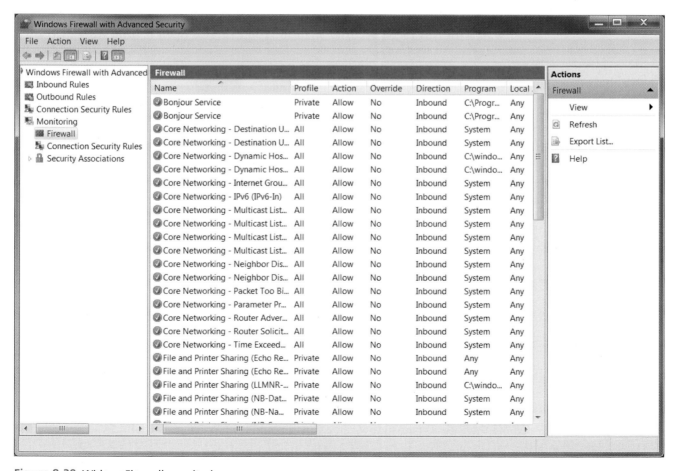

Figure 8-39 Widows Firewall, monitoring
Courtesy Course Technology/Cengage Learning

is the set of rules for communication negotiated between two computers. If two computers have a security association, they are using IPsec to communicate.

Security associations are listed in two categories:

- *Main Mode*—Used for the initial configuration of an IPsec connection, including authentication.

- *Quick Mode*—Signifies a secure IPsec communication channel has been negotiated.

Activity 8-10: Configuring Windows Firewall

Time Required: 15 minutes
Objective: Configure Windows Firewall by using the Windows Firewall with Advanced Security snap-in.

Description: Windows Firewall in Windows 7 is capable of performing outbound filtering as well as inbound filtering. In this activity, you create a rule to block access to Internet Web sites and then disable the rule.

1. If necessary, start your computer and log on.

2. Click the **Start** button, type **Internet Explorer,** and press **Enter** to start Internet Explorer.

3. In the Address bar, type **http://www.microsoft.com** and press **Enter.** When the Microsoft Web site loads, it confirms that your computer is able to connect to the Internet properly right now.

4. Close **Internet Explorer.**

5. Click the **Start** button, type **firewall,** and press **Enter.** This opens the Windows Firewall with Advanced Security snap-in. You can also open it from Administrative Tools.

6. Read the overview of Windows Firewall configuration. Windows Firewall is on for all network location profiles, inbound connections that do not match a rule are blocked by default, and outbound connections are allowed by default.

7. Click the **Windows Firewall Properties** link in the Overview. This window allows you to configure the settings for each profile.

8. Click the **Private Profile** tab. These settings apply for all Private networks.

9. In the Settings area, click the **Customize** button. Here you can configure whether notifications are displayed when inbound connections are blocked and how local firewall rules are combined with firewall rules defined in Group Policy.

10. Click **Cancel** to close the Customize Settings for the Private Profile dialog box.

11. In the Logging area, click the **Customize** button. Here you can configure logging for Windows Firewall.

12. In the Log dropped packets box, select **Yes,** and click **OK.** Now all blocked connections will be logged to C:\Windows\system32\LogFiles\Firewall\pfirewall.log.

13. Click **OK** to close the Windows Firewall with Advanced Security on Local Computer dialog box.

14. In the left pane, click **Outbound Rules.** These are the rules that control outbound communication. However, none of the default rules block outbound communication.

15. In the left pane, right-click **Outbound Rules** and click **New Rule.**

16. In the Rule Type window, click **Custom** and click **Next.**

17. In the Program window, click **All programs** and click **Next.**

18. In the Protocol type box, click **TCP**.

19. In the Remote port box, click **Specific Ports** and type 80. This rule will apply to outbound packets addressed to port 80. Port 80 is used by Web servers.

20. Click **Next**.

21. Click **Next** to select the default option of applying to all computers.

22. If necessary, click **Block the connection**, and click **Next**. This rule will block connections to port 80.

23. Click **Next** to accept the default configuration of this rule applying to all profiles. You can also limit it to specific profiles.

24. In the Name box, type **Block Web** and click **Finish**. The Block Web rule is now at the top of the list of outbound rules. Notice that it is enabled and the action is block.

25. Click the **Start** button, type **Internet Explorer**, and press **Enter** to start Internet Explorer.

26. In the Address bar, type **http://www.microsoft.com** and press **Enter**. You are unable to load the Microsoft Web site because the Block Web rule is blocking access to all Web sites.

27. Close **Internet Explorer**.

28. In Windows Firewall with Advanced Security, right-click **Block Web** and click **Disable Rule**.

29. Close **Windows Firewall with Advanced Security**.

30. Click the **Start** button, type **Internet Explorer**, and press **Enter** to start Internet Explorer.

31. In the Address bar, type **http://www.microsoft.com** and press **Enter**. When the Microsoft Web site loads, it confirms that your computer is able to connect to the Internet properly again.

32. Close **Internet Explorer**.

Network Bridging

The **network bridge** in Windows 7 allows you to connect two separate networks, with Windows 7 acting as a bridge between them. In most cases, these will be two different network types, such as wired Ethernet and wireless Ethernet. Figure 8-40 shows how the network bridge functionality in Windows 7 can be used to connect a wired and wireless network. The computer acting as a network bridge must have two network cards to connect to each network.

This technology is seldom used because in most cases, relatively cheap and simple hardware can eliminate the need for a network bridge. For example, in Figure 8-40, a wireless access point connected to the wired network would eliminate the need for Windows 7 to act as a network bridge.

Figure 8-40 Network Bridging
Courtesy Course Technology/Cengage Learning

If one of the bridged connections is actually connected to the Internet, it creates a security risk where the other bridged network is exposed to the Internet. Only one network bridge can exist at a time on a computer running Windows 7.

Ad hoc and Homegroup Networks

Networking for a small group of computers outside the corporate office is more about convenience. Security is still required but may not be as strict or feature rich. The goal is to share information without a lot of administrative knowledge or configuration steps. Two networking technologies that assist with that goal are ad hoc networking and homegroups.

Ad hoc Networking

The ad hoc network in Windows 7 allows you to configure an existing wireless network adapter on your computer as a rudimentary wireless access point (WAP). The options and features are limited in comparison to a commercial WAP but this is a quick and dirty method to set up a temporary wireless network. The range of the wireless signal is limited by the wireless adapter's antenna and restricted power levels to less than 30 feet typically.

In the Network and Sharing Center, the task Manage Wireless Networks allows you to see the current wireless network Windows 7 is connected to. You can optionally select Add to manually add a wireless network, including manually creating an ad-hoc network as shown in Figure 8-41.

In addition to specifying a SSID for the ad hoc network, the security type can be configured as open, WEP, or WPA2. More advanced security types are not supported given the limited scope of this technology. Ad hoc networking can also be combined with network bridging and Internet connection sharing to customize the computer as a gateway device if desired. Given the limited feature set and radio quality concerns, this feature is seldom used.

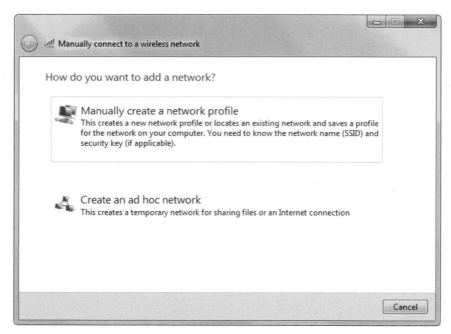

Figure 8-41 Ad hoc network creation
Courtesy Course Technology/Cengage Learning

Homegroup Networks

A Homegroup network primarily uses IPv6 and link-local addresses to enable communications between homegroup members. Discovery of computers and their names on the local network is automatic by default. This technology is designed to be used only in the home environment.

A computer can only create a homegroup when it has a network interface connected as a home network location and it is not domain joined. Windows 7 Starter and Home Basic editions are additionally restricted to not allow the creation of a new homegroup. All editions of Windows 7 are allowed to join a homegroup. A domain joined computer is not allowed to share its files on the homegroup but it can access the files shared by other homegroup members.

Security in a homegroup is simple. When a homegroup is created, a password is specified that other computers must use to join the homegroup. Homegroup settings can be managed from Control Panel with the options shown in Figure 8-42.

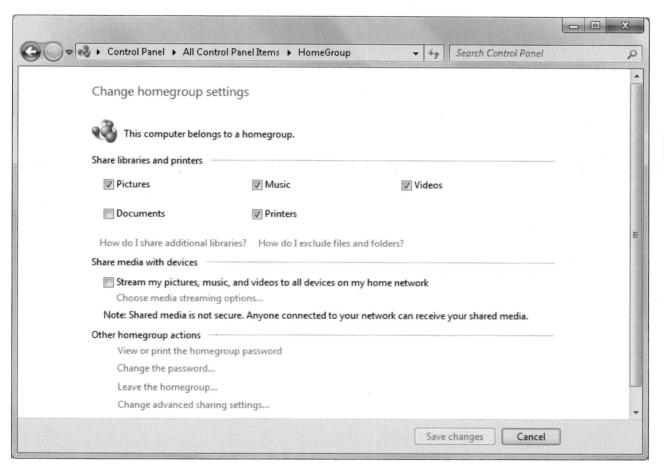

Figure 8-42 Homegroup Network Settings
Courtesy Course Technology/Cengage Learning

Each member of the homegroup can decide what to share with other members of the homegroup. Deciding what to share is a personal decision. Several libraries can be selected or deselected with only a few mouse clicks. Each library is a collection of folders on the local drive that store an expected type of content, such as pictures. Each user can manage the folders that make up a library, even if they are on very different folder locations on the local machine. This is much easier than configuring individual shared folders with older style workgroups, however it requires the use of IPv6 and several services for naming and peer management that are not available in older operating systems.

Homegroup members show up in the computer browser window as a different category of browsable locations. There is no complicated procedure to browse a homegroup resource; its intent is to just point, pick, and use.

Windows automatically manages homegroup connections; but it is possible to restrict access to known user accounts and passwords if desired. Homegroups are not a typical corporate concern for the IT administrator.

Chapter Summary

- Network Sharing Center is a central location to view and access networking information such as a network map, network status, and connection status.

- Windows 7 is network-aware and can sense which network location it is connected to and change settings accordingly. Network locations are Home, Work, Public, or Domain.

- Network connections are composed of clients, services, protocols, and drivers. Windows 7 includes both IPv4 and IPv6 protocols, neither of which can be removed.

- The Windows 7 network architecture includes Winsock, TDI, and WSK interfaces for applications and services to communicate over the network. NDIS 6.2 is used to define communication between protocols and network drivers. NDIS 6.2 is backwards compatible with previous versions of NDIS, but older drivers will experience slower performance.

- The important configuration concepts in IPv4 are IP addresses, subnet masks, default gateways, DNS, and WINS. If any of these components are configured incorrectly, network communication may be affected.

- Windows 7 can obtain IP configuration information from static configuration data, DHCP, APIPA, or an alternate IP configuration. DHCP is the most common.

- Windows 7 uses IPv6 to support peer-to-peer and general networking applications. IPv6 is becoming more common and the address types must be recognized. Teredo allows IPv6 traffic to be tunneled through an IPv4 network even when NAT is used on the IPv4 network.

- Sharing the Public folder is an easy way to share files on the network. However, access cannot be controlled per user. All files are shared with all valid users. Valid users can be defined as user accounts with access to Windows 7 or any other users.

- When you share any folder you can use "Share with"or advanced sharing. "Share with" configures sharing and NTFS permissions at the same time. Advanced sharing only configures share permissions. NTFS permissions must be configured separately.

- The primary technologies for connecting to the Internet are cable, DSL, WWAN, and dial-up. Cable and DSL are high-speed connection methods, while dial-up is slow. DSL commonly requires the configuration of PPPOE. WWAN requires a broadband device to supply Internet connectivity, a cable to tether (connect) the computer to the mobile device, and a paid contract from the broadband supplier to use the feature.

- When an Internet connection is shared by multiple computers, there must be a mechanism to share the single IP address assigned by your ISP. You can use a router or ICS. ICS configures Windows 7 as a router to share an Internet connection.

- Wireless networking in Windows 7 supports different versions of the 802.11 standard that defines how a wireless adapter in a computer connects to a Wireless Access Point (WAP). The WAP's SSID and security settings must be correctly configured to enable the wireless client to connect. Wireless clients can automatically reconnect when they are in range of a WAP. Network location settings and Windows Firewall can help secure the data connection.

- Windows Firewall is a host-based firewall included with Windows 7. Windows Firewall can perform inbound and outbound filtering. Also, IPsec rules are combined with firewall rules in Windows 7. Windows Firewall can be configured by using the basic interface, Windows Firewall with Advanced Security utility, or Group Policy.

- Network Bridging lets you connect two different network types, such as a wired network and a wireless network, as a single network.

- Ad hoc networks allow a Windows 7 computer to configure its wireless network adapter as a basic wireless access point. This is a quick and dirty method to share connectivity for small networks in a temporary capacity.

- Homegroup networking allows home users to share categories of data through libraries with each other. Homegroup networks use IPv6 addressing and specialized services to automatically track peer names and connections. Homegroup security uses a simple password to control computer membership. This technology is not intended to be used inside the corporate or typical workplace environment so there are some functional limits applied by default.

Key Terms

802.1x A IEEE standard designed to enhance security of wireless networks by authenticating a user to a central authority.

802.11 A group of IEEE standards that define how to transfer Ethernet 802.3 data over wireless networks.

802.3 A group of IEEE standards that define the transfer of data over wired Ethernet based networks.

address prefix The first portion of an IP address that allows the identification of that addresses type and therefore purpose.

ad hoc network A group of wireless computers sharing data directly with each other without the use of a wireless access point.

Advanced sharing A method for sharing folders that allows you to pick the specific options you want. NTFS permissions are not configured.

alternate IP configuration A set of static IP configuration information that is used instead of APIPA when a computer is unable to contact a DHCP server.

arp A command-line utility that can be used to display and manage the ARP table, which maps IPv4 addresses to physical MAC addresses.

attack surface Parts of the computer, applications, and operating system components that can be attacked by hackers, viruses, and malware during their attempts to intrude on a computer system.

Automatic Private IP Addressing (APIPA) A system used to automatically assign an IP address on the 169.254.x.x network to a computer that is unable to communicate with a DHCP server. A default gateway setting is not configured with APIPA.

cable modem A device that converts network signals from the cable company to a standard Ethernet.

Classless Inter-Domain Routing (CIDR) A notation technique that summarizes the number of binary bits in an IP address that identify the network an IP address belongs to, counted starting from the left-hand side of the IP address as written in binary form. The number of bits is written at the end of the IP address with a slash "/" symbol separating the two values (e.g. 192.168.1.0/24 or FE80::/64).

client A client allows you to communicate with a particular service running on a remote computer.

Client for Microsoft Networks The client that allows Windows 7 to access files and printers shared on other Windows computers by using the SMB protocol.

connection (network connection) The clients, services, and protocols that are configured for a network card.

Create A Shared Folder Wizard A wizard in Computer Management to create shared folders that does not configure NTFS permissions.

default gateway A router on the local network that is used to deliver packets to remote networks.

Digital subscriber line (DSL) A high-speed Internet connection over telephone lines.

Domain Name System (DNS) A system for converting computer host names to IP addresses.

8

domain network   The location type that is used when a computer joined to a domain is on the domain network, for example, a corporate office.

DSL modem   A device that converts DSL signals to standard Ethernet.

Dynamic Host Configuration Protocol (DHCP)   An automated mechanism to assign IP addresses and IP configuration information over the network.

File and Printer Sharing for Microsoft Networks   The service that allows Windows 7 to share files and printers by using the SMB protocol.

getmac   A command-line utility that can be used to display the MAC address for network adapters on a system.

Home network   The location type that is used for highly trusted networks where security is minimal and convenient sharing with other computers is a priority.

homegroup network   A feature that allows file sharing between computers on a hoe network without a complicated setup process.

hostname   A command-line utility that can be used to identify the name of the computer.

IEEE (Institute of Electrical and Electronics Engineers)   A professional society that promotes and nurtures the development of standards used in the application of electronic technology.

Internet Connection Sharing (ICS)   A Windows 7 feature that allows multiple computers to share an Internet connection by performing NAT.

Internet Protocol Version 4 (TCP/IPv4)   The standard protocol used on corporate networks and the Internet.

Internet Protocol Version 6 (TCP/IPv6)   An updated version of TCP/IPv4 with a much larger address space.

IP address   The unique address used by computers on an IPv4 or IPv6 network. An IPv4 address is commonly displayed in dotted decimal notation. For example, 10.10.0.50.

ipconfig   A command-line utility that can be used to display and manage IP address settings for network interfaces on a computer.

IPsec   A protocol that is used to secure and authenticate an IPv4 connection.

Link Layer Topology Discovery Mapper I/O Driver   The protocol responsible for discovering network devices on the network and determining network speed.

Link Layer Topology Discovery Responder   The protocol responsible for responding to discovery requests from other computers.

Link-Local Multicast Name Resolution (LLMNR)   A protocol that defines methods for name resolution of local neighboring computers without using DNS, WINS, or NetBIOS name resolution services. LLMNR can operate on IPv4 and IPv6 networks with the use of specially crafted multicast addresses to query client names on other computers.

location type   Describes the type of network: public, private, or domain. Different configuration settings are applied based on the location type.

modem   A device that converts computer signals to a format that can travel over phones (modulate) and also performs the reverse function (demodulate).

nbtstat   A command-line utility that can be used to display protocol statistics and current TCP/IP connections using NetBIOS over TCP/IP.

netsh   A command-line utility that can be used to display, change, add, and delete network configuration settings on a computer, including basic and advanced settings.

netstat   A command-line utility that can be used to display protocol statistics and current TCP/IP network connections.

network address translation (NAT)   A system that allows multiple computers to share a single IP address when connecting to the Internet.

Network and Sharing Center   A central location to view network status and configure network settings.

network location awareness   The ability for Windows 7 to detect when it is connected to a different network and perform actions based on the change.

network bridge A feature in Windows 7 that combines two dissimilar network types, such as wireless and wired, into a single network.

network discovery A setting that controls how your computer views other computers on the network and advertises its presence on the network.

network driver The software responsible for enabling communication between Windows 7 and the network device in your computer.

Network Driver Interface Specification (NDIS) An interface that supports communication between network protocols and network drivers.

nslookup A command-line utility that can be used to view or debug the data returned from a DNS server in response to a DNS name resolution query.

pathping A command-line utility that can be used to test IP communications between the computer running the utility and a remote target. In addition to the basic IP communication test, the pathping utility will trace the routers involved in establishing the IP communication path.

ping A command-line utility that can be used to test IP communications between the computer running the utility and a remote target.

Point-to-Point Protocol over Ethernet (PPPoE) A protocol used to secure connections over most DSL lines.

preshared keys A combination of numbers, characters, and symbols that make up a pass-phrase that both sides of an authenticated and encrypted network connection must know to decode the data delivered between them successfully.

private network The location type that is used for trusted networks where limited security is required, for example, a small office.

public network The location type that is used for untrusted networks where high security is required, for example, a public wireless hotspot.

route A command-line utility that can be used to display and manage the routing table.

router Traditionally, a network device that moves packets from one network to another. The routers sold in retail stores are used to share an Internet connection by performing NAT.

routing table A data table that is used by Windows 7 to select the next IP address data must be delivered to ultimately deliver data to a given target address.

Security Set Identifier (SSID) A unique ID that identifies a wireless access point to the wireless networking clients that send data to it.

Server Message Block (SMB) The protocol used for Windows-based file and printer sharing. Windows 7 includes SMB version 2.1.

service Provides functionality to remote clients over the network.

Share With A wizard that simplifies the setup process of sharing folders and configuring relevant share and NTFS permissions.

subnet mask A number that defines which part of an IP address is the network ID and which part is the host ID.

Teredo A system to tunnel IPv6 addressed packets over an IPv4 network, even if NAT is used on the IPv4 network.

tracert A command-line utility that can be used to trace the routers involved in establishing an IP communication path between the computer running the command and a target address.

Transport Device Interface (TDI) A legacy interface that supports the NetBIOS protocol used by many older Windows applications.

Wi-Fi Protected Access (WPA) A security protocol for wireless 802.11 networks that provides stronger security than WEP. WPA can be configured with a preshared key or with authentication from a central authority.

Windows Firewall A host-based firewall included with Windows 7 that can perform inbound and outbound packet filtering.

Windows Firewall and Advanced Security utility   An utility that is used to configure Windows Firewall and IPsec rules.

Windows Internet Naming Service (WINS)   A system used to resolve computer NetBIOS names to IP addresses.

Windows Sockets (Winsock) user mode   An interface that supports communication between user applications such as a Web browser and the TCP/IP protocol.

Winsock Kernel (WSK)   An interface that supports communication between kernel mode software, such as clients and services, and the TCP/IP protocol.

Wired Equivalent Privacy (WEP)   A security protocol for wireless 802.11 networks that provides weak authentication methods in comparison to WPA. WEP uses preshared keys that attackers have been able to decipher without much difficulty. The use of WEP is discouraged where wireless security is a major consideration.

Wireless Access Point   A device that allows wireless devices to connect through it to a wired network.

work network   The location type that is used for trusted networks where limited security is required, for example, a small office.

Review Questions

1. Your computer is configured to obtain an IPv4 address and DNS server address automatically. What utility will help you to find the IPv4 address of your computer (pick two)?

   a. tracert

   b. ipconfig

   c. nslookup

   d. netsh

2. Which location type would be most appropriate to select when using your laptop computer to access the Internet by using a wireless hot spot at a tradeshow?

   a. Trusted network

   b. Untrusted network

   c. Domain network

   d. Private network

   e. Public network

3. _____ provides you with a way to control how your computer views other computers on the network and advertises its presence on the network.

   a. Windows Firewall

   b. SMB

   c. Network Discovery

   d. NDIS

   e. Network location

4. Your computer is configured to obtain an IPv4 address and DNS server address automatically. You are concerned that the IPv4 routing table is incorrect. What utility will display the IPv4 routing table (select three)?

   a. route

   b. netstat

   c. nslookup

d.   netsh

e.   route4

5. Which components are part of a Windows 7 network connection? (Choose all that apply.)

   a.   clients

   b.   services

   c.   protocols

   d.   network drivers

   e.   cabling

6. Which protocol is used by the Client for Microsoft Networks and File and Printer Sharing for Microsoft Networks to communicate with each other and share files?

   a.   FTP

   b.   IPv4

   c.   IPv6

   d.   HTTP

   e.   SMB

7. For a Class C IPv4 address what is the correct default subnet mask value, specified as either a dotted decimal address or a CIDR value? (Pick two)

   a.   255.0,0,0

   b.   /24

   c.   255.255.255.0

   d.   C::/24

   e.   255.255.256.0

8. Which of these addresses represents a valid IPv6 link-local address?

   a.   169.254.12.1

   b.   ::1

   c.   FE80::2cab:2a76:3f57:8499

   d.   2001:0:4137:9e74:2cab:2a76:3f57:8499

   e.   FF::1:2

9. Which interface is responsible for controlling communication between network drivers and protocols?

   a.   NDIS

   b.   Winsock

   c.   TDI

   d.   WSK

10. Which IPv4 configuration options must be configured properly to communicate with Web sites on the Internet? (Choose all that apply.)

   a.   IP address

   b.   Subnet mask

   c.   Default gateway

   d.   DNS

   e.   WINS

8

11. Which of the following IP addresses can be used by a host on the global Internet? (Choose all that apply.)

   a. 192.168.0.55

   b. 172.32.0.1

   c. 169.254.99.208

   d. 38.15.222.299

   e. 99.99.99.99

12. Which method can be used to assign IPv4 configuration settings when a DHCP server is not available? (Choose three.)

   a. Static configuration

   b. DNS

   c. WINS

   d. APIPA

   e. Alternate IP configuration

13. To convert host names to IP addresses on the Internet, _____ is used.

14. Which IPv4 address below has the same network ID as 192.168.112.45 given the subnet mask 255.255.255.0?

   a. 10.0.0.45

   b. 192.168.113.46

   c. 192.168.112.257

   d. 172.16.112.45

   e. 192.168.112.5

15. Which sharing method should you use if you want to configure share and NTFS permissions for a user in a single process?

   a. Public folder sharing

   b. Share with

   c. advanced sharing

   d. Create A Shared Folder Wizard

16. Which sharing method does not allow you to pick the folder that is being shared?

   a. Public folder sharing

   b. simple sharing

   c. advanced sharing

   d. Create A Shared Folder Wizard

17. Which IPv4 address below has the same network ID as 10.16.112.45 given the subnet mask 255.255.0.0? (Choose all that apply.)

   a. 10.16.160.45

   b. 192.168.172.46

   c. 10.16.122.2

   d. 10.16.185.45

   e. 10.18.114.3

18. What is the most accurate way to view all of the shares on your system?

   a. browse your computer on the network

   b. view the shares in Computer Management

   c. use the Show me all the shared network folders on this computer link

   d. use the Show me all the files and folders I am sharing link

   e. view the shares in Network and Sharing Center

19. The Internet connection technology that requires a mobile broadband device and a data plan that activates this feature is known as a _____ connection.

   a. cable modem

   b. 802.11n

   c. DSL

   d. WWAN

   e. dial-up

20. Which Internet connection type is most likely to require the use of PPPoE?

   a. cable

   b. DSL

   c. dial-up

   d. wireless hot spot

21. Which Internet connection type is the least likely to be shared by multiple computers?

   a. cable

   b. DSL

   c. dial-up

   d. wireless hot spot

22. Which of these addresses represents a valid IPv6 global unicast address?

   a. 169.254.12.1/64

   b. 2001::1::FEA

   c. FE80::2cab:2a76:3f57:8499

   d. 2001:0:4137:9e74:2cab:2a76:3f57:8499

   e. FF::1:2

23. Which of these addresses represents a valid loopback address (pick two)?

   a. ::1/128

   b. ::/0

   c. FF::1

   d. 127.0.0.1

   e. 127::1/32

24. Which utilities can be used to perform advanced firewall configuration? (Choose all that apply.)

   a. Windows Firewall Control Panel applet

   b. Netsh

   c. Group Policy

   d. Windows Firewall and Advanced Security

25.   A computer has the IPv4 address 192.168.0.23 and a subnet mask of 255.255.255.0. Which of these addresses represents a possible default gateway address (pick two)?

   a.   192.168.0.254

   b.   193.168.0.1

   c.   0.0.0.1

   d.   127.0.0.1

   e.   192.168.0.1

Case Projects

CASE PROJECTS

Case Project 8-1: Internet Connectivity

Buddy's Machine shop has a relatively small number of computers. Until now, they have not had an Internet connection because the owner thought they didn't need it. However, many suppliers would prefer to communicate with Buddy's machine shop by e-mail. In addition, some suppliers are offering discounts for orders placed over the Internet. How would you suggest that Buddy's machine shop connect to the Internet?

Case Project 8-2: Networking Concepts

Superduper Lightspeed Computers helps many customers configure small home networks. A new staff person has started with very limited networking experience. How would you explain the basics of Windows 7 networking to the new person?

Case Project 8-3: Configuring Windows Firewall

Gigantic Life Insurance has thousands of desktop computers and has just completed a major security audit. One of the recommendations in the security audit was to implement a host-based firewall on all workstations. Explain how Windows Firewall could be used by Gigantic Life Insurance and the method you would use to configure Windows Firewall on all the workstations.

Case Project 8-4: Network Awareness

The sales people at Hyperactive Media Sales all use laptop computers so they can take data with them on the road. You are a salesperson for Superduper Lightspeed Computers talking to Hyperactive Media Sales about upgrading the laptops to Windows 7. Explain how network awareness in Windows 7 would make the laptops more secure.

chapter 9

User Productivity Tools

After reading this chapter and completing the exercises, you will be able to:

- Understand and configure Windows 7 printing
- Understand Windows Fax and Scan
- Use Windows Explorer libraries
- Find files by using Search
- Describe the features in Internet Explorer 8

Many of the changes in Windows 7 have been designed to enhance user productivity. Windows 7 printing is updated to use a new document format and printing process that increases print quality. Windows Fax and Scan is included to manage faxing from within Windows 7. Windows Explorer has been updated with libraries and new views to help you organize data. Search is integrated into almost every part of Windows 7. Finally, Internet Explorer 8 has been updated to be easier to use and more secure. In this chapter, you learn how to use all of these productivity tools.

Printing

From the perspective of a user printing documents, the printing process has not changed in Windows 7 from previous versions of Windows. However, to improve printing performance and quality, the entire printing subsystem for Windows 7 has been redesigned when compared to Windows XP. The redesign includes:

- XML Paper Specification
- The printing process
- Print drivers
- Printer management

Printing Scenarios

As a network administrator, you need to be able to troubleshoot the printing process. One of the keys to troubleshooting is understanding how printers can be connected to Windows 7. Figure 9-1 shows the physical layout of local printing, network printing to another computer, and network printing directly to a printer. This section deals primarily with local printing.

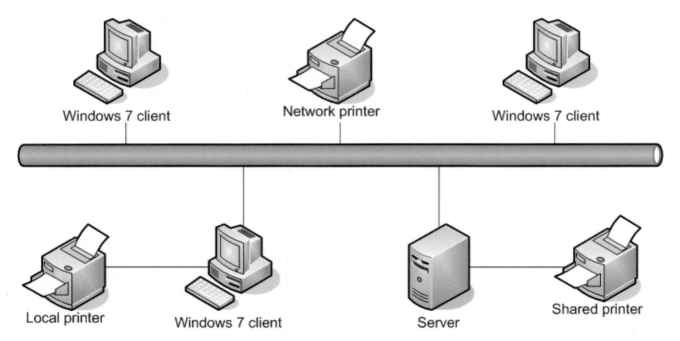

Windows 7 client   Network printer   Windows 7 client

Local printer   Windows 7 client   Server   Shared printer

Figure 9-1 Printing scenarios
Courtesy Course Technology/Cengage Learning

Local Printing Local printing requires that a printer be connected directly to a Windows 7 computer by using a parallel cable or USB cable. The type of cable you select depends on which connection type is physically available on the printer. In most cases, USB printers are automatically installed in Windows 7 when they are connected. The installation process for parallel printers must be triggered manually.

The most common reasons to use local printing are simplicity and security. The entire printing process occurs within the local computer, so troubleshooting is easier. Having a local printer makes printing secure because users are able to print sensitive documents in their office from the local printer rather than in an open area on a shared network printer where other users might see the document contents.

Printing to a Shared Printer Both Windows servers and Windows clients are capable of sharing printers on the network. When a printer is shared, multiple computers on the network can use it. Windows 7 attempts to find printers shared on the local network and install them automatically. However, if the shared printers are not on the local subnet, you need to install the printer manually.

Sharing a printer from a Windows server or client saves money in the long run. Typically, it costs less to purchase a single high capacity printer rather than many low capacity printers for many computers. The consumables cost for the high capacity printer is typically much less than low capacity printers.

In this scenario, all print jobs are queued on the computer that is sharing the printer. This allows all jobs to be controlled in a central location, which can make troubleshooting relatively simple. If jobs are not printing, you start by looking at the computer that is sharing the printer. However, the computer sharing the printer also becomes a central point of failure. If the computer sharing the printer is disabled or turned off, then it is not possible to print documents on the shared printer.

Shared printers can be connected directly to the sharing computer or be a network printer.

Printing Directly to a Network Printer Many printers can be configured to communicate directly with the network. If this feature is not built into your printer, it can be added by purchasing a print server. When a printer is connected directly to the network, computers can send it print jobs over the network. Many computers can be connected to the printer at the same time, but only one computer can be printing at a time. The costs savings of a network attached printer is the same as for shared printers.

In this scenario, print jobs are queued at the local computer and sent to the printer when the printer is not busy. This is a contention based system, and there is no specific order that print jobs are serviced in. There is no central queue to control the order or priority of print jobs. However, an additional benefit is the elimination of any single computer as a single point of failure.

XPS

XML Paper Specification (XPS) is a document format that describes how a page should be displayed. In this way it is similar to the Adobe Portable Document Format (PDF). The difference between a document in XPS format and a Word document is that the precise page layout is described in the XPS document. An XPS document will have the same page layout when printed on any printer. A Word document may vary the page layout when you select a different printer.

The XPS format was developed by Microsoft, but has been released under a royalty-free patent license. This allows Microsoft to retain control over the XPS specification, but enables other companies to use XPS in their own products without paying fees to Microsoft. Adobe makes the PDF format available under similar terms. Details of the licensing for XPS can be found at *http://www.microsoft.com/whdc/xps/xpslicense.mspx*. In 2009, XPS was also approved as a standard named OpenXPS by Ecma International.

In Windows 7, XPS is used as a document format for sharing files and as the format for spooled print jobs. A spooled print job is a document that has been printed from the application and is stored on the local hard drive in the print queue waiting to be delivered to the printer.

The Windows Presentation Foundation (WPF) is responsible for drawing the screen output in Windows 7. XPS uses a subset of the commands available in WPF to render documents. The commands allow documents to be rendered exactly as they appear on screen because no conversion to a different format is necessary.

Windows 7 includes a new XPS Viewer for reading XPS documents. This viewer gives you the ability to configure rights management or apply a digital signature. Rights management controls how users can use the document. For example, it can prevent sharing or printing. A digital signature is used to verify the authenticity of the documents.

Activity 9-1: Creating an XPS Document

Time Required: 5 minutes
Objective: Create an XPS document that can be shared with other users.

Description: The XPS document format can be used to share documents with other users. Windows 7 includes a printer driver that creates XPS documents from any application that is able to print. This can be useful for sharing documents with others when they lack the application to view the document properly. In this activity, you create and view an XPS document.

1. If necessary, start your computer and log on.
2. Click the **Start** button, type **notepad,** and press **Enter.**
3. In the Notepad window, type **This is my XPS document test.**
4. Click the **File** menu and click **Print.**
5. In the Select printer area, click **Microsoft XPS Document Writer** and click **Print.**
6. In the File name box, type **XPStest** and click **Save.**
7. Close **Notepad** and don't save the changes.
8. Click the **Start** button and click **Documents.**
9. Click the **View** menu drop-down arrow and click **Extra Large Icons.**
10. If necessary, scroll down so you can view the XPStest icon. Notice that this icon displays the content of the file.
11. Double-click **XPStext.xps.** This opens XPStest.xps in the XPS Viewer. Notice that it is displayed exactly as it would be if printed on paper. Even a header is included.
12. Close all open windows.

The Printing Process

The printing process in Windows 7 supports new XPS-based printing as well as **Graphics Device Interface (GDI)**-based printing. GDI was used to render screen drawings and print jobs in Windows XP.

GDI-Based Printing
GDI-based printing is the system that was used in Windows XP. Applications designed for Windows XP make GDI calls to print their documents. The GDI printing process is shown in Figure 9-2. This printing process is retained in Windows 7 for compatibility with older applications and printer drivers.

When GDI-based printing is used, a Win32 application uses GDI to create an **enhanced metafile format (EMF)** file for the print job. This EMF file is stored in the printer queue. Before the print job can be transferred to the printer, it must be converted from EMF to the format understood by the printer. Printers typically understand either **Postscript** or **Printer Control Language (PCL).** Converting the EMF file to the printer format is performed by the printer driver.

Figure 9-2 GDI-based printing
Courtesy Course Technology/Cengage Learning

 Additional information about printer drivers is available later in this chapter.

XPS-Based Printing When a new application designed for Windows Vista or Windows 7 prints, it uses XPS-based printing. A new XPS printer driver and printer are also required for XPS-based printing. Figure 9-3 shows the XPS-based printing process.

When XPS-based printing is used, a WPF application creates an XPS file for the print job. This XPS file is stored in the printer queue and is equivalent to the EMF file in the GDI-based printing process. If an XPS printer is used, the XPS print job can be transferred to the printer with no further conversion because the printer understands XPS and can render jobs internally. Conversion to PCL or Postscript is not required because an XPS printer uses XPS as its printer language. The printer driver is used to describe the capabilities of the printer, such as duplexing

9

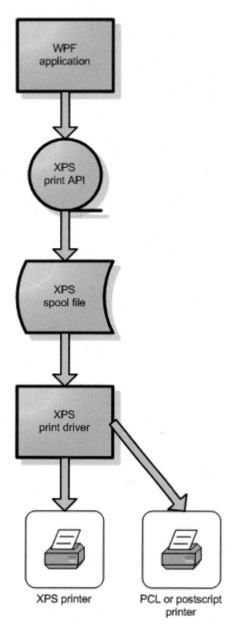

Figure 9-3 XPS-based printing
Courtesy Course Technology/Cengage Learning

(two-sided printing), print resolution, or color. If a PCL or Postscript printer is used, then the driver converts the print job to PCL or Postscript before delivery to the printer.

Backward Compatibility   The Windows 7 printing process is flexible to accommodate older applications and older printers that do not support XPS-based printing. Figure 9-4 shows how older applications can print to an XPS-based printer and how new WPF applications can print to a GDI-based printer.

When a Win32 application prints to an XPS-based printer, the printing subsystem converts the print job to XPS instead of EMF format and places it in the printer queue. This XPS file can then be sent to the XPS printer. When a WPF application prints to a GDI-based printer, then the XPS file from the WPF application is converted to EMF format and placed in the printer queue. The EMF file is then converted to the appropriate printer language by using the printer driver.

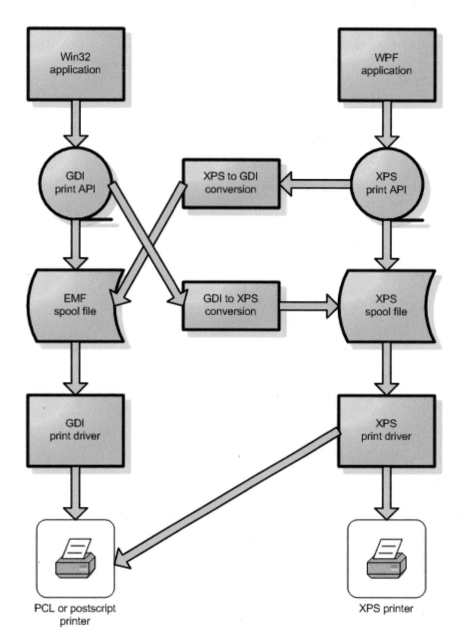

Figure 9-4 Printing compatibility with XPS-based applications and printers
Courtesy Course Technology/Cengage Learning

Benefits of XPS-Based Printing In general, XPS printing is better at handling complex graphics than GDI-based printing. The lack of a conversion step improves the accuracy of print rendering on paper compared to on screen.

Some benefits of using XPS for printing in Windows 7 are:

- *Improved color printing*—The new XPS spool files pass color information directly to the printer. This improves color accuracy. Alternatively, printer drivers can read and use the color information in the XPS spool file.

- *Improved print quality*—The XPS printing process eliminates format conversions whenever possible to prevent inaccuracies introduced during conversion. When GDI-based drivers are used, the conversion process has been significantly improved when compared to the GDI-based printing in previous versions of Windows.

- *Improved print job configuration*—XPS-based printing uses a new format to describe print job settings called **XML PrintTicket**. This format is easily readable by all components in the printing process. Ultimately, XML PrintTicket allows print job options set in applications to be more easily used on various printer makes and models.

- *Improved device configuration*—**XML PrintCapabilities** is a new system for advertising the availability of printing options for a device. Examples of these options include duplexing, page layout, and paper trays. The XML schema used by XML PrintCapabilities provides a consistent language to describe printer capabilities that can be understood by applications.

- *Improved spooling*—The processing required to spool a print job has been reduced by using XPS as the spool format rather than using EMF as an intermediary format between the operating system and the printer driver. In addition, spool files are generally smaller with XPS-based printing than in previous versions of Windows, in part because spool files are compressed using ZIP compression. Also, the XPS spool format identifies elements that are used multiple times within a document; it includes the multiple-use element as a shared element and uses pointers to refer to that single instance.

Printer Drivers

Windows 7 stores and manages printer drivers using a different process than Windows XP. In Windows 7, a **printer driver store** has been introduced to store printer drivers. Printer drivers can be added to the store before the printer is attached. This can be useful in corporate environments by preconfiguring computers with all printer drivers that may be required.

Adding Drivers to the Store
Adding a driver to the store is known as staging a driver. If a printer driver is added during the printer installation process, the driver is automatically staged as part of the process. Drivers can also be staged manually by a user with administrative rights using the pnputil.exe utility. Drivers can also be added to the store by users that have been granted device installation rights by a group policy. Table 9-1 has examples of using the pnputil.exe utility.

Table 9-1   Pnputil.exe examples

Example	Description
Pnputil.exe –a *driverINFfile*	Add a printer driver to the store
Pnputil.exe –e	Enumerate (list) all third-party drivers in the store
Pnputil.exe –d *driverINFfile*	Delete a printer driver from the store
Pnputil.exe –?	Display the help information for pnputil.exe

When drivers are added to the store, they are stored side-by-side. This means that multiple versions of the same driver can be contained in the store, which is very useful when testing new printer drivers. Occasionally, new printer drivers will result in print quality problems for specific reports or documents. When this occurs, you can simply change the printer driver back to a previous version.

Because multiple driver versions are stored side-by-side in the driver store, you should remove old versions from the driver store after you have determined that they are not required. This ensures that an obsolete version of a printer driver is not installed accidentally by a user.

Activity 9-2: Modifying the Printer Driver Store

Time Required: 10 minutes
Objective: Modify the contents of the printer driver store.

Description: The printer driver store contains all of the printer drivers that can be installed on the local computer. Printer drivers in the store can also be distributed to remote computers when shared printers are installed. In this activity, you download a printer driver package and add it to the driver store. You are doing this because you have a particular report that does not print properly with the driver included in Windows 7.

1. If necessary, start your computer and log on.
2. On the taskbar, click the Internet Explorer icon.
3. In the address bar, type **www.hp.com** and press **Enter**.
4. Click the **Support & Drivers** link.
5. In the Step 1 area, click **Download drivers and software (and firmware)**.
6. In the search box in the Step 2 area, type **universal print driver**, and press **Enter**.
7. If an autocomplete window appears, click **No**.
8. Under Select Operating System, click the version of Windows 7 that matches your operating system (32-bit or 64-bit).
9. Scroll down and next to **1 – HP Universal Print Driver for Windows PCL6**, click the **Download** button.
10. Click **Save**, and then in the Save As dialog box, click **Save**.
11. When the download is complete, click **Run**.
12. In the Internet Explorer-Security Warning dialog box, click **Run**.
13. In the Unzip to folder box, type **C:\HPDriver**.
14. Click **Unzip**, click **OK**, and click **Close**. The files are now unzipped into the C:\HPDriver folder.
15. Click the **Start** button, type **cmd**, right-click **cmd.exe**, click **Run as administrator**, and click **Yes**.
16. Type **pnputil -?** and press **Enter**. This command displays the list of available options for pnputil.exe.
17. Type **pnputil –e** and press **Enter**. This command displays the list of third-party driver packages that have been installed. The HP Universal Print Driver package is not listed.
18. Type **dir C:\HPDriver*.inf** and press **Enter**. This command displays all INF files in the HPDriver directory.
19. Type **pnputil –a C:\HPDriver\hpcu104c.inf** and press **Enter**. This command installs the printer driver package into the printer driver store. If the command prompt is not running as an administrator, this command will fail. This file may not be available in your downloaded version of the driver. If this file is not available select an alternative inf file.
20. After the package is added, type **pnputil –e** and press **Enter**. Notice that the driver is now listed and named oem*x*.inf, where *x* is a number. The INF file for each driver is renamed when it is added to the driver store. This guarantees that all INF files have a unique name.
21. Close all open windows.

Printer Driver Installation Process

For Windows XP, printer drivers were distributed as **printer driver packages** and just printer drivers. Driver packages can have functionality that extends beyond basic print job rendering, such as printer management utilities. When printers were networked, **point and print** allowed printer drivers to be distributed automatically from the print server, but not driver packages. In some cases, this limited the functionality that could be accessed in the printer.

When Windows Vista or later is used as print server, the entire driver package can be distributed by point and print, rather than just the driver. If there is an option to distribute the printer driver and the driver package, Windows Vista or later will deliver the entire driver package. The ability to deliver the entire driver package is based on the existence of the driver store.

NOTE

Windows XP is unable to take advantage of driver packages by using point and print and only receives the core printer driver files as it would with traditional point and print.

The printer driver installation process varies depending on whether the printer is local or remote and on how the client is connected to the printer. The following variations are possible:

- *Local printer*—When a local printer is installed, the printer driver package is automatically added to the driver store and the printer driver is installed.

- *Remote printer*—When a printer is installed on a remote machine, the printer driver package is added to the driver store on the remote machine and the printer driver is installed.

- *Network printer*—When a network printer on a print server running Windows Vista, Windows 2008, or later is installed, then point and print copies the printer driver package to the local driver store and the printer driver is installed.

- *Web printer*—When a network printer on a print server running Windows Vista, Windows 2008, or later is installed by using HTTP, then the printer driver package is installed in the local driver store by Web point and print, and installs the printer driver.

Web printers are printers that are installed from a Web page and use Internet Printing Protocol (IPP) to communicate with the print server.

The ability for a printer driver package to be distributed by point and print is based on settings in the printer driver INF file. The INF file must contain the PackageAware keyword. Vendors add this keyword to their INF files after ensuring that the INF file meets all necessary criteria for package-based distribution.

User Account Control (UAC) can cause problems for printer driver installations performed by using an executable file. Windows 7 recognizes printer driver installations from an INF file and automatically raises the privilege level to administrator level. When a printer driver installation is performed by using an executable file, the permission level is not automatically raised and must be controlled with an application manifest file. The application manifest file should be included by the driver vendor. However, older executables will not have an application manifest and you may need to specifically choose to run that application as Administrator.

Printer Management

Windows 7 offers two methods for managing printers. The first method, the Devices and Printers applet in Control Panel, is similar to the Printers applet offered in previous versions of Windows. The second method, the Print Management snap-in, was new in Windows Vista. Regardless of which utility you use to manage printers, you are able to perform tasks such as installing new printers, manage printer settings, and remove printers.

Devices and Printers Applet

The Devices and Printers applet in Control Panel, shown in Figure 9-5, is used to manage the printers on a local workstation. The Devices and Printers applet is not capable of installing printers on remote computers.

The major tasks you can perform in the Printers applet are:

- *Add a printer*—This option adds a new printer to the local computer. This printer can be physically attached or a network printer.

- *See what's printing*—This option allows you to see jobs in the print queue for the selected printer. Within the queue, you can pause or delete individual print jobs.

- *Set as default*—This option allows you to configure a printer as the default printer for applications. In an application, such as Microsoft Word, when you click the print button in the toolbar, the default printer is used.

- *Select printing preferences*—This option allows you to configure basic printer settings and paper configuration.

- *Configure printer properties*—This option allows you to edit all printer properties, including those for printing preferences, sharing, and security.

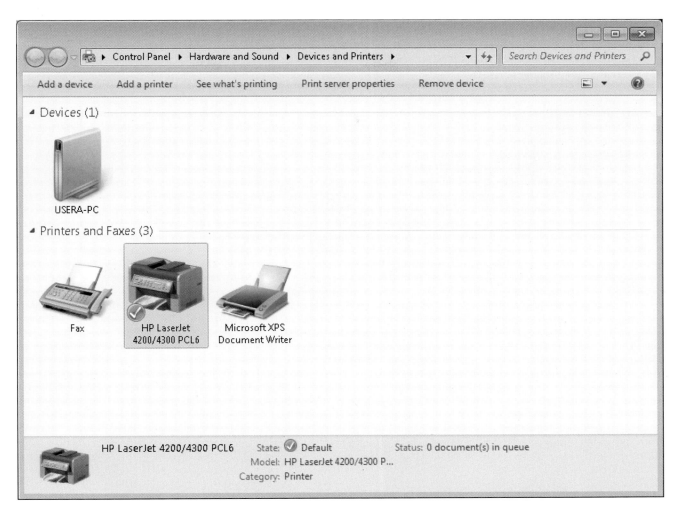

Figure 9-5 Devices and Printers
Courtesy Course Technology/Cengage Learning

- *Configure print server properties*—This option allows you edit print server properties for the local computer. This includes setting available forms (page sizes), configuring ports, and managing drivers.
- *Remove device*—This option removes the printer from your computer.

Windows 7 adds a new feature for printers and other devices called **Device Stage**. Device Stage simplifies the management of devices by bringing all of the relevant information about that device and the options for managing it into a single location. The information available for any given device is controlled by the device manufacturer. The Device Stage for a printer is shown in Figure 9-6.

Activity 9-3: Adding a Printer by Using the Devices and Printers Applet

Time Required: 5 minutes
Objective: Add a printer to the local computer by using the Devices and Printers applet in Control Panel.

Description: The Devices and Printers applet can be used to install and manage printers on the local computer. In this activity, you install an HP LaserJet 4200/4300 printer on your computer.

1. If necessary, start your computer and log on.
2. Click the **Start** button and click **Control Panel**.

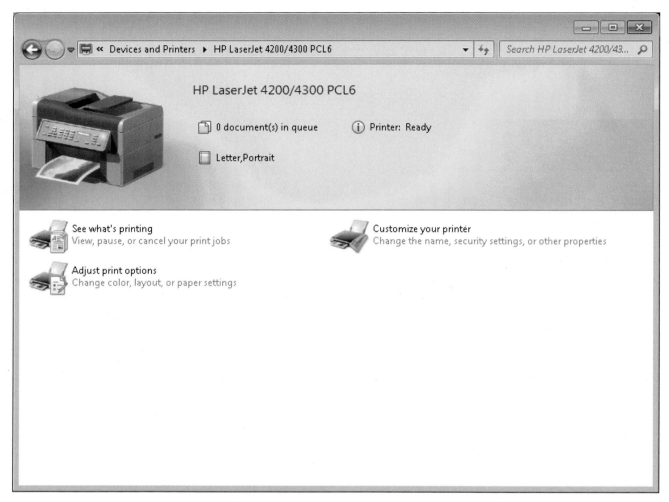

Figure 9-6 Device Stage for a printer
Courtesy Course Technology/Cengage Learning

3. Click **Hardware and Sound** and click **Devices and Printers**. You can see that two printers exist by default, a Fax printer and a Microsoft XPS Document Writer printer. You can fax documents by printing them to the Fax printer. You can create XPS documents by printing them to the Microsoft XPS Document Writer printer. Once a document is in XPS format, you can distribute it just as you would distribute PDF documents.

4. Click **Add a printer.**

5. Click **Add a local printer.** You also have the option to add a network, wireless, or Bluetooth printer.

6. In the Use an existing port list, click **FILE: (Print to File)**, and click **Next.** You are choosing this option because the classroom does not have a physical printer for you to connect to. If you have a network printer that is accessed directly by using TCP/IP, then you would create a new Standard TCP/IP port. A USB printer would be automatically detected and installed when you attach it.

7. In the Manufacturer box, click **HP**, in the Printers box, click **HP LaserJet 4200/4300 PCL6,** and click **Next.**

8. To accept the default printer name, click **Next.**

9. If the Printer Sharing page appears, click **Do not share this printer** and click **Next.**

10. Click **Finish.** Notice that this printer was automatically configured as the default printer. This is identified by the green check mark on the HP LaserJet 4200/4300 PCL 6 printer.

11. Close all open Windows.

Printers that are accessed directly by using TCP/IP are not considered network printers by the Add Printer process. They are considered local printers. Network printers are those that are shared from Windows computers.

Print Management Snap-In   The **Print Management snap-in**, shown in Figure 9-7, allows you to manage the printers for your entire network from a single workstation. This is a huge improvement over printer management in previous versions of Windows. Previous versions of Windows required that you manage printers from the console of each computer.

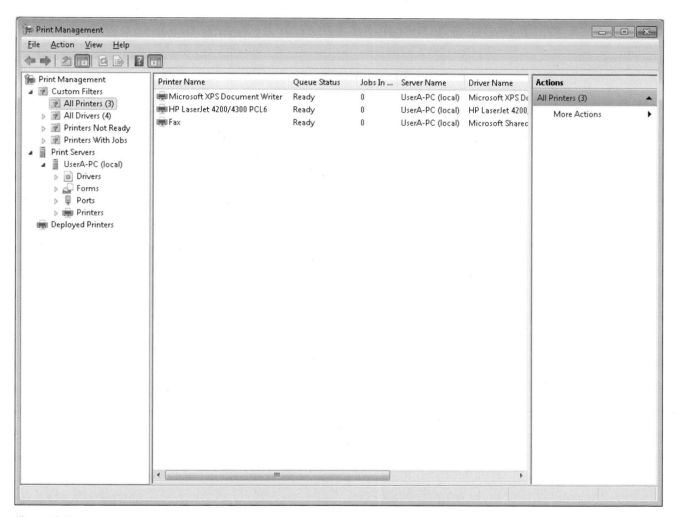

Figure 9-7 Print Management snap-in
Courtesy Course Technology/Cengage Learning

Some features of the Print Management snap-in are:

- *Manage multiple print servers*—You can manage and configure not only printers, but also print server configuration, such as adding standard TCP/IP ports or printer drivers.

- *Filter views*—You can filter views to display only the printers that you are interested in. This can include showing only printers in an error state or in one physical location. Four filters exist by default: All Printers, All Drivers, Printers Not Ready, and Printers With Jobs.

- *Automatic installation of printers on a print server*—You can trigger an automatic printer installation process that scans the local subnet for network printers. If the appropriate drivers are located on the print server, all printers will be installed automatically. This can make configuring a new print server much faster.

- *Bulk printer management*—You can perform management operations on multiple printers at one time. For example, you can pause all of the printers on a printer server before you take it down for maintenance.

- *Use Group Policy to deploy printers*—You can add printer deployment information to Group Policy objects to automatically install printers on workstations.

- *Notification*—You can configure notifications to send an e-mail when the conditions of a filter are met. For example, you can create a filter that shows only printers in an error condition and set a notification on that filter. Then, when a new printer experiences an error condition, you will be notified by e-mail.

Activity 9-4: Installing a Printer by Using the Print Management Snap-In

Time Required: 10 minutes

Objective: Use the Print Management snap-in to install a new printer on the local computer.

Description: The Print Management snap-in is capable of managing local and remote printers and print servers. In this activity, you use the Print Management snap-in to install a local printer.

1. If necessary, start your computer and log on.

2. Click the **Start** button and click **Control Panel**.

3. Click **System and Security** and click **Administrative Tools**.

4. In Administrative Tools, double-click **Print Management**.

5. If necessary, in the left pane, expand **Custom Filters** and click **All Printers**. This filter displays all of the printers installed on every print server that is being monitored. In this case, only the three local printers are displayed because only the local computer is being monitored. If you have installed additional printers or additional software such as Microsoft Office, then your number of printers will be greater than three.

6. In the left pane, click **All Drivers**. This filter displays all of the printer drivers that are installed on every print server that is being monitored. This allows you to see if different printer driver versions are installed on various print servers.

7. In the left pane, if necessary, expand **Print Servers**, expand your computer, and click **Drivers**. This node displays only the printer drivers that are installed on your computer.

8. In the left pane, click **Forms**. This node displays the forms that are configured on your computer. Forms are the paper sizes the printer is configured to use. You can add, edit, or delete forms by right-clicking on the Forms node and clicking Manage Forms.

9. In the left pane, click **Ports**. This node displays all the ports configured on your computer that can be used for printing. You can add additional ports or manage existing ports from here.

10. In the left pane, click **Printers**. This node displays all of the printers that are installed on your computer. You can manage the printers from here and install new printers.

11. In the left pane, click **Deployed Printers**. Printers that have been deployed by using a Group Policy object are listed here.

12. In the left pane, right-click **Printers**, and click **Add Printer**.

13. Click **Add a new printer using an existing port**, if necessary, click **LPT1: (Printer Port)**, and click **Next**. After printer installation, this printer will generate an error when you attempt to print because there is no printer physically attached to your computer on LPT1.

14. Click **Use an existing printer driver on the computer**, if necessary, click **HP LaserJet 4200/4300 PCL6**, and click **Next**.

15. In the Printer Name box, type **Local**.

16. Leave the option **Share this printer** checked, type **Local** in the Share Name box, and click **Next**.

17. On the Printer Found screen, click **Next**.

18. When the printer installation is finished, click **Finish**.

19. In the left pane, click **Printers**. The new printer named Local is installed here now.

20. Right-click **Local** and click **Pause Printing**.

21. Right-click **Local** and click **Print Test Page**.

22. In the Local dialog box, click **Close**.

23. In the left pane, click **Printers With Jobs**. Notice that this screen now displays the printer Local because there is a job in the queue.

24. Close all open windows.

Activity 9-5: Installing a Network Printer (Optional)

Time Required: 5 minutes
Objective: Install a network printer.

Description: In a business environment, most printers are network printers that are shared from a server. In this activity, you install a shared network printer from the computer of your partner.

Before beginning this activity, gather the following information from your partner:

- Computer name
- Username
- Password

1. If necessary, start your computer and log on.

2. Click the **Start** button, type ***computername***, where computername is the name of your partner's computer, and press **Enter**.

3. When prompted for authentication credentials, in the User name box, type ***computername\\username***, where computername is the name of your partner's computer and username is the username of your partner.

4. In the Password box, type **password** and click **OK**. The shared printers and folders from your partner's computer are displayed in Windows Explorer.

5. To install the printer, right-click **Local** and click **Connect**. The driver is downloaded from your partner's computer and the printer is installed.

6. Close Windows Explorer.

7. Click the **Start** button and click **Devices and Printers**.

8. View the list of available printers. Notice that the printer from your partner's computer is now listed.

9. Close Devices and Printers.

Printer Configuration Options Each printer you install in Windows 7 can be configured independently. Most of the options available for configuration are standardized by Windows 7. However, the Device Settings tab, shown in Figure 9-8, has device-specific settings. These settings typically indicate whether specific hardware options such as duplexers and paper trays have been installed. The Device Settings tab may not be included for all printers and in some cases may be named Configure instead.

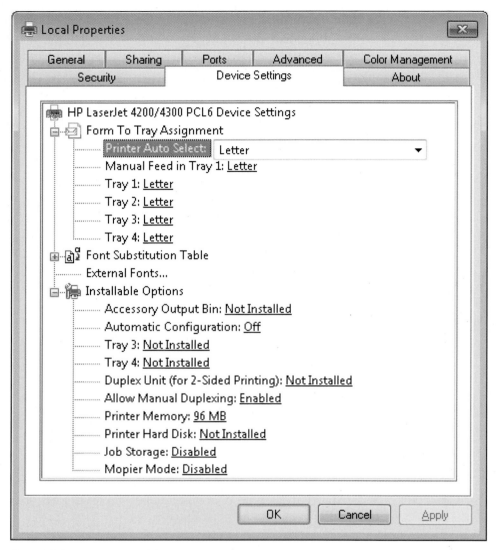

Figure 9-8 Device Settings tab of a printer
Courtesy Course Technology/Cengage Learning

The Advanced tab, shown in Figure 9-9, has a number of options that are typically only implemented for server-based printing. However, these settings are also available for Windows 7. The options on this tab are the same regardless of the printer driver that is installed.

Options on the Advanced tab are:

- *Availability*—You can schedule the time of day that the printer is available. This is typically used for large print jobs that are deferred until after regular work hours to prevent the printer from being busy for an extended period of time during the work day.

- *Priority*—Used when multiple printers are configured to use the same port. The printer with the highest priority will print first. Only when the printer with the highest priority has no jobs in its queue are other printers using that port able to print. This is used on busy print servers to give a few users faster access to the printer.

- *Driver*—You can update or change the printer driver here.

- *Spooling configuration*—Spooling allows you to begin using an application faster after printing by storing the print job as a file and sending the print job to the printer as a background process. If you print directly to the printer, you cannot begin using your application again until the print job is complete. When spooling is enabled, you can prevent printing from starting until the last page is spooled as a troubleshooting mechanism when print jobs are being corrupted.

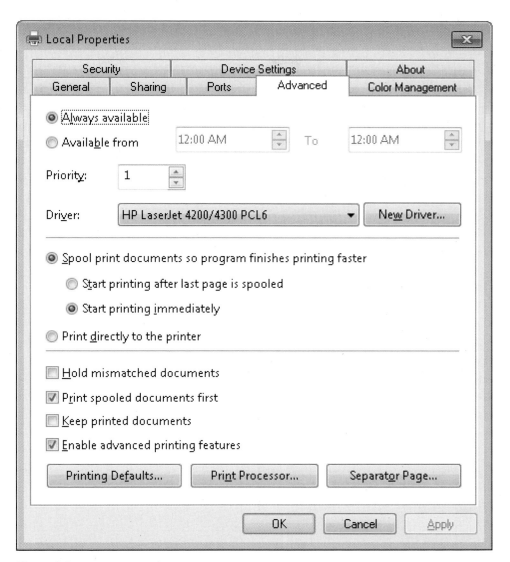

Figure 9-9 Advanced tab of a printer
Courtesy Course Technology/Cengage Learning

- *Hold mismatched documents*—Holds print jobs in the queue if the paper type of the print job is not correctly matched to the paper in the printer.

- *Print spooled documents first*—This option gives priority to print jobs that have completed spooling over those that are still spooling.

- *Keep printed documents*—Keeps a copy of each print job in the queue even after the job is complete. This allows print jobs to be resubmitted later if additional copies are required.

- *Enable advanced printing features*—Enables various advanced printing options depending on the application that you are using and the printer driver that is installed.

- *Printing Defaults*—The default configuration options for print jobs, such as duplexing, paper orientation, and print quality. These options vary based on the printer driver that is installed.

- *Print Processor*—Allows you to choose the format of the print jobs. This is typically used when troubleshooting print job corruption issues.

- *Separator Page*—Allows you to specify a separator page that is included at the beginning of each document. Large organizations sometimes include these on busy printers where the separator page includes the username of the person that printed the job.

Other standard tabs are:

- *General*—Used to view information about the printer, configure printing preferences, and print a test page.
- *Sharing*—Used to configure printer sharing.
- *Security*—Used to configure user and group permission for printing.
- *Ports*—Used to select and configure ports that are used by this printer.
- *Color Management*—Allows you to configure color profiles that are used to control how screen colors are translated to colors for printers. In some cases, color profiles for specific printers are available for download.

Printer Sharing and Security Just as you can create file shares to share files with other users and computers over the network, you can also create shared printers. This is useful in a small office when you want to share the printer attached to a workstation. Sharing is enabled and controlled on the Sharing tab, shown in Figure 9-10.

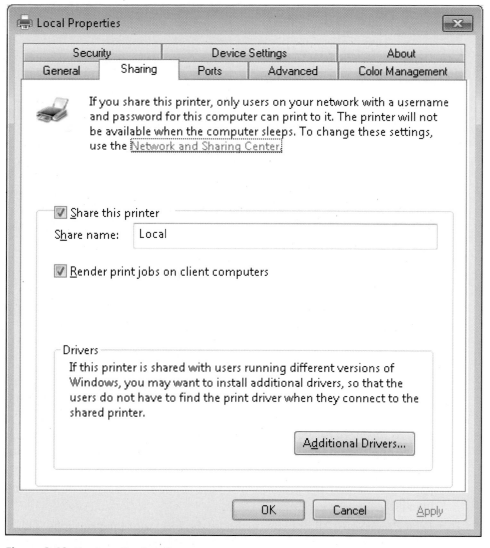

Figure 9-10 Sharing tab of a printer
Courtesy Course Technology/Cengage Learning

The Sharing tab allows you to:

- Enable sharing for the printer.
- Define the share name for the printer.
- Specify whether print jobs are rendered on the client computer or print server.
- Add drivers for other operating systems to download by using point and print.

Whether a printer is shared or local, you can also configure security on that printer to control who is allowed to use and manage the printer. The Security tab is shown in Figure 9-11. You can allow or deny user and group permissions to print, manage printers, and manage documents.

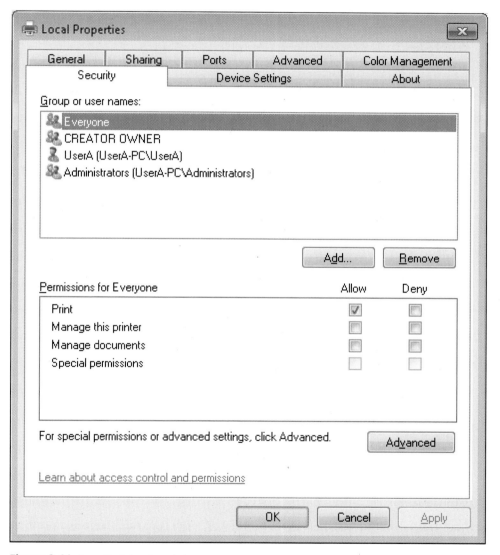

Figure 9-11 Security tab of a printer
Courtesy Course Technology/Cengage Learning

The default permissions for printing are:

- Everyone—Allowed to print.
- CREATOR OWNER—Allowed to manage documents.
- Local Administrator User (User*x*) —Allowed to print, manage printers, and manage documents.
- Administrators—Allowed to print, manage printers, and manage documents.

Location Aware Printing Windows 7 adds **location aware printing** as a new feature for computers that connect to multiple networks. One of the great annoyances for mobile users with laptop computers is selecting an appropriate printer for a given physical location. In Windows 7, you can uniquely identify a default printer for each network that your computer connects to. Figure 9-12 shows the user interface for configuring location aware printing. You access this screen by selecting Manage default printers from Devices and Printers. However, like other mobile features, this option is only displayed on computers with a battery.

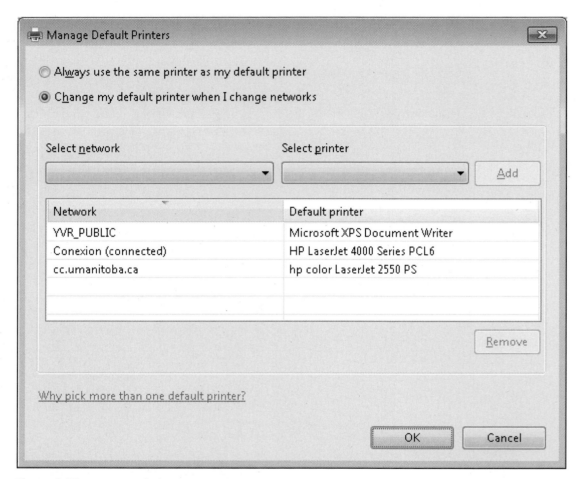

Figure 9-12 Manage Default Printers
Courtesy Course Technology/Cengage Learning

Print Job Management In addition to controlling printers, you can also manage the individual jobs in a print queue. For each print job, you can perform the following tasks:

- *Pause*—Prevents the job from printing. If a job is partially finished printing, it will stop at the end of a page.
- *Resume*—Allows a paused print job to continue printing.
- *Restart*—Restarts printing a job from the first page.
- *Cancel*—Stops a print job and removes it from the queue. The print job may not stop immediately, as it may take a few moments for the printer to remove the job from memory and complete printing the final page.
- *Edit job properties*—Allows you to change the priority of a print job or schedule the job.

Some of the situations where you might want to manage print jobs include:

- Restarting a print job when there has been a paper jam and some pages have been destroyed.
- Pausing a large print job to let several other smaller print jobs be completed.

- Raising the priority of a print job from an executive secretary to ensure that it prints next.

- Changing the schedule of a large print job to prevent it from printing during main office hours.

- Canceling a corrupted print job that is blocking other jobs in the queue.

 When printing has inexplicably stopped for a printer on a Windows computer, a reboot usually fixes the problem, unless a corrupted print job is blocking the queue. Instead of rebooting the computer, stop and start the print spooler service to accomplish the same result faster. This can be done by using the Services snap-in or opening a command prompt as Administrator and using the net stop spooler and net start spooler commands.

Activity 9-6: Managing Print Jobs

Time Required: 5 minutes
Objective: Manage print jobs.

Description: Managing individual print jobs is seldom required. However, when job management is required, it is typically for an important purpose. In this activity, you manage a print job in the queue.

1. If necessary, start your computer and log on.
2. Click the **Start** button and click **Devices and Printers**.
3. In the list of printers and faxes, double-click **Local**. The jobs list displays a job named Test Page. You created this job in Activity 9-4. Notice that the printer is paused.
4. Right-click **Test Page** and click **Pause**. Notice that the Job Status column indicates that the job is paused.
5. Right-click **Test Page** and click **Resume**. The paused status has been removed from the job.
6. Right-click **Test Page** and click **Properties**. On the General tab, you can modify the priority and schedule of the job.
7. Click **OK** to close the Test Page Properties dialog box.
8. Right-click **Test Page** and click **Cancel**.
9. When prompted, click **Yes** to confirm cancelling the job.
10. Close all open windows.

Windows Fax and Scan

Windows Fax and Scan, shown in Figure 9-13, is a utility introduced in Windows Vista that is used to control scanning and faxing documents in Windows Vista and Windows 7. Integrating these two features may not make sense to you at first, but it is logical because if you are faxing any paper documents, you must scan them first. Electronic documents are faxed by printing them to the Fax printer that is installed by default or attaching them to a fax in Windows Fax and Scan.

Windows Fax and Scan is optimized to scan documents for faxing. It should not be used to scan images such as photos for nonfaxing purposes. Images scanned for faxing will be a lower quality than desired for photo editing. Also, information scanned into Windows Fax and Scan cannot be used by other applications due to the storage format of the scans. Windows Photo Gallery is recommended for scanning and editing photos.

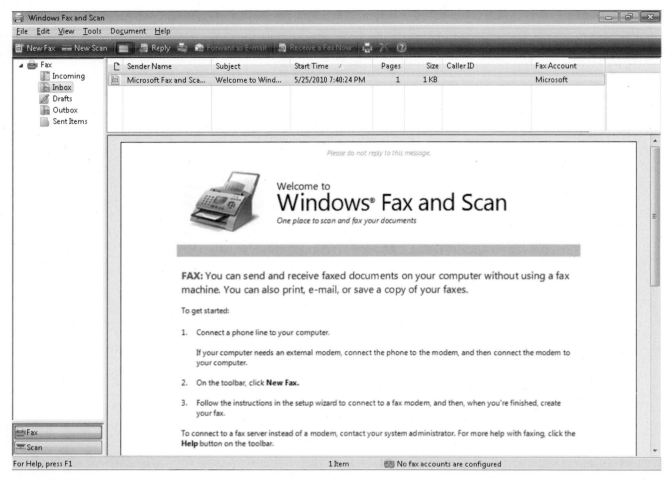

Figure 9-13 Windows Fax and Scan
Courtesy Course Technology/Cengage Learning

By using Windows Fax and Scan, you can:

- Scan documents and pictures.
- Fax scanned documents and pictures.
- Fax electronic documents.
- Receive faxes.
- Create and manage fax coversheets.
- Forward received faxes, scanned documents, and scanned pictures by using e-mail.
- Send faxes by using a central fax server.
- Maintain a contacts list that includes phone numbers for faxing.

Windows Fax and Scan requires you to have a fax modem and scanner, or a multifunction device that performs both functions. If you have just a fax modem, then you can fax electronic documents, but not scan and fax paper documents.

Most fax modems include software to fax electronic documents. Windows Fax and Scan is used instead of the fax software included with the fax modem.

Activity 9-7: Using Windows Fax and Scan

Time Required: 5 minutes

Objective: View the user interface for Windows Fax and Scan.

Description: Windows Fax and Scan allows Windows 7 to send and receive faxes when a fax modem is installed in the computer. In the classroom, your computer does not have a fax modem installed, but you are still able to review the user interface. In this activity, you review the user interface for Windows Fax and Scan.

1. Click the **Start** button, point to **All Programs**, and click **Windows Fax and Scan**.
2. If necessary, click the **Fax** button in the left pane to display the fax folders. Notice that faxes are organized into Incoming, Inbox, Drafts, Outbox, and Sent Items.
3. In the top middle pane, right-click **Welcome to Windows Fax and Scan**, and click **Properties**. This allows you to view information about a fax, such as when it was received.
4. Click **Close**.
5. In the Preview pane, right-click the fax, point to **Zoom**, and click **Fit to page**. This displays the entire fax page on the screen. You can adjust the view of a fax to whatever you are comfortable with. When faxes are received by Windows Fax and Scan, there is no need to print a fax to read it.
6. Click the **Tools** menu and click **Sender Information**.
7. Fill in the Sender Information dialog box with your information and click **OK**.
8. Click **New Fax** and click **Cancel** in the Fax Setup dialog box.
9. Read the warning message about needing a fax modem and click **OK**.
10. In the To box, type **555-1234**.
11. In the Subject box, type **Test Fax**.
12. In the text editing area, type **This is my test fax**. To include a document as part of a fax, you attach that document in this window. You also have the option to scan a document from a scanner or configure a cover page.
13. Click the **File** menu and click **Close**.
14. Click **Yes** to save the file and click **OK** to close the message dialog box indicating that the fax has been saved to the Drafts folder.
15. In the left pane, click the **Drafts** folder. Notice that Test Fax is listed here.
16. Close Windows Fax and Scan.

Windows Explorer

Windows Explorer, shown in Figure 9-14, is the interface used to view the file system in Windows 7. The way information is displayed in Windows Explorer has been changed to make browsing files easier. In the left pane, there is a Favorite Links list that gives you easy access to commonly used folders. There is also a tree view in the left pane to allow easy navigation of the file system.

Libraries

Libraries are a new feature in Windows 7 that simplifies access to data. Each library displays the files from multiple locations. This makes it easier for users to find file because they can look in a single library instead of several locations. For example, the Documents library displays the files stored in My Documents and Public Documents.

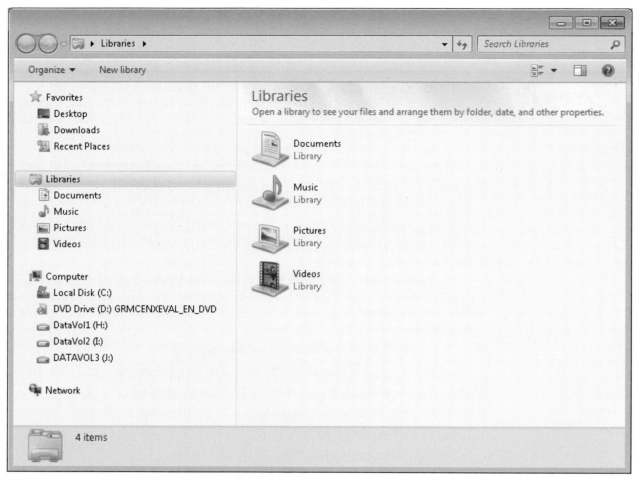

Figure 9-14 Windows Explorer
Courtesy Course Technology/Cengage Learning

You can modify the locations that are included in a library, as shown in Figure 9-15. You can add local folders, removable storage, or files shares on remote computers or servers. The only requirement for adding locations is that they must be indexed by Windows Search. This means that if you add a file share, it must be indexed by Windows Search on the computer that is hosting the file share. This requirement ensures that content can be categorized and displayed quickly. If you expand a library, the individual locations are shown and you can browse each location separately.

Some file management issues to consider for libraries are:

- When you view the root of a document library, you are seeing the combined contents in the root of all included locations. If there are two files or folders with same name in different locations, you view both items with the same name and no indication of which location it is located in. Avoid having two files or folders with the same name in multiple locations.

- When you browse down into a folder from the root of a library, you are viewing a specific location and any files created are in that specific location.

- If you are viewing the root of a library and create a new file or folder, the new item is created in the location specified as the save location in the properties of the library.

Views

Previous versions of Windows allow you to alter the Windows Explorer view to change the size of icons and control whether details about the files and folder are displayed. Windows 7 still has these options and several variations. However, Windows 7 has also introduced Arrange by options to help you organize information. The option to arrange files is only available in libraries.

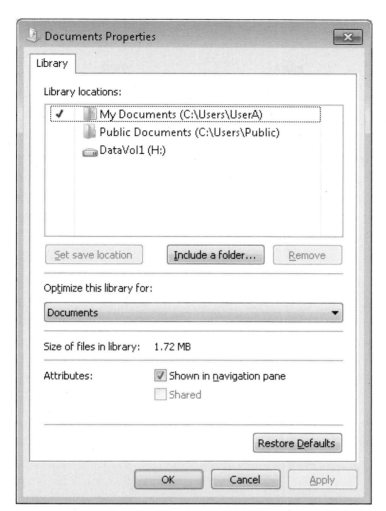

Figure 9-15 Properties of a library
Courtesy Course Technology/Cengage Learning

Arranging files sorts the files in a library based on file properties, such as author. The options for arranging files vary depending on what type of files the library is optimized for. For example, a library optimized for documents includes author, while a library for optimized for music includes genre. The file properties are indexed by Windows Search and used to create lists of files that are displayed.

Activity 9-8: Organizing Files

Time Required: 10 minutes
Objective: Use libraries to organize and view files.

Description: The libraries added to Windows 7 allows you to centralize files from multiple locations in a single virtual folder. This helps you find the files you need faster. In this activity, you use libraries to organize and view files.

1. If necessary, start your computer and log on.
2. Click the **Start** button and click **Documents**. The Documents library is displayed.
3. If your view is using extra large icons, change the view to something easier to read. For example, choose Medium icons or List.
4. In the left pane, expand **Documents**. You can see that the documents library includes My Documents and Public Documents.

5. Click **Public Documents** and note the files that are located here.

6. Click **Documents** and note the files that are located here. Notice that the files from Public Documents are listed here.

7. Right-click **Documents** and click **Properties**.

8. In the Documents Properties window, click **Include a folder**.

9. In the Include Folder in Documents window, scroll down in the left pane, click **DataVol1(F:)**, and click **Include folder**. Notice that the F: drive is now listed as a library location.

10. Click **OK**. Notice that the folder view has changed to organize the contents based on folder. Now you can create files and copy file to a specific location in the library.

11. Next to Arrange by, click **Folder** and click **Date modified**. Notice that the files from all locations, including subfolders, are now sorted by the date of modification with no indication which location they are stored in.

12. Next to Arrange by, click **Date modified** and click **Name**. Notice that the files are now sorted only by name. There are no references to locations or folders.

13. Next to Arrange by, click **Name** and click **Type**. This view organizes files from all locations into virtual folders based on file type. Each file type is in a particular virtual folder.

14. Close Windows Explorer.

Window Management

Windows 7 introduces new features for managing the windows you have opened for applications. Snap simplifies the sizing of windows by automatically sizing windows appropriately.

You can use snap to:

- *Automatically size windows the full height of the screen*—Move the mouse to the top or bottom edge of a window until the pointer becomes a double-headed arrow. Then drag the window edge to the top or bottom of the screen and release the mouse

- *Arrange windows side by side*—Click a window and drag it to the edge of the screen, until about half of the window is not visible, and then release the mouse.

- *Maximize a window*—Drag a window to the top edge of the screen and then release the mouse.

Shake minimizes all windows except the current window. To use it, click on the title bar of the current window and shake it back and forth. All other windows are minimized.

Peek allows you to see the desktop without minimizing all of the open windows. Hover the mouse over the button in the far right corner of the taskbar to make open windows transparent. Clicking this button minimizes all windows.

Other AERO specific enhancements are:

- *Live taskbar thumbnails*—When you move the mouse pointer over an application on the taskbar, a live thumbnail of that application is displayed. When many windows are open this gives you a fast visual way to find the specific window you want. For example, if you have several Word documents open, you can quickly see the contents of the documents in the live thumbnail and select the correct document without having to view the full application.

- *Live icons*—When you view files in Windows Explorer, instead of seeing a generic icon that represents the document type, such as a Word icon, you see a live thumbnail of the file content. In Windows XP, live thumbnails were available for picture files and videos. Windows 7 has improved on this and offers live thumbnails of other document types such as Word documents and Excel spreadsheets.

- *Windows Flip*—When you are changing between multiple windows by using Alt-Tab, Windows Flip shows you live thumbnails of the applications.

- *Windows Flip 3D*—When you are changing between multiple applications, Windows Flip 3D shows you the contents of each Window and organizes the windows in a lineup.

Search

Windows 7 includes a desktop search engine that is vastly improved over the file searching found in Windows XP. Search has been integrated into almost every window in the Windows 7 user interface. Search is made faster by an indexing function included in Windows 7. Finally, you can define **metadata** for files and use it to build saved searches that are displayed as virtual folders. File metadata is information about a file, also called the properties of a file.

In Windows 7, you do not choose to do searches inside or outside the index. It is context sensitive. If you are searching content that is indexed, the index will be used. If you are searching content that is not indexed, then the index is not used.

After a search is complete, you are also presented with options to further refine your search, as shown in Figure 9-16. You are given links to search again in Libraries, Computer, Custom, or Internet. Custom allows you to define the other locations. Internet uses Internet Explorer and the search provider configured for Internet Explorer to perform a search.

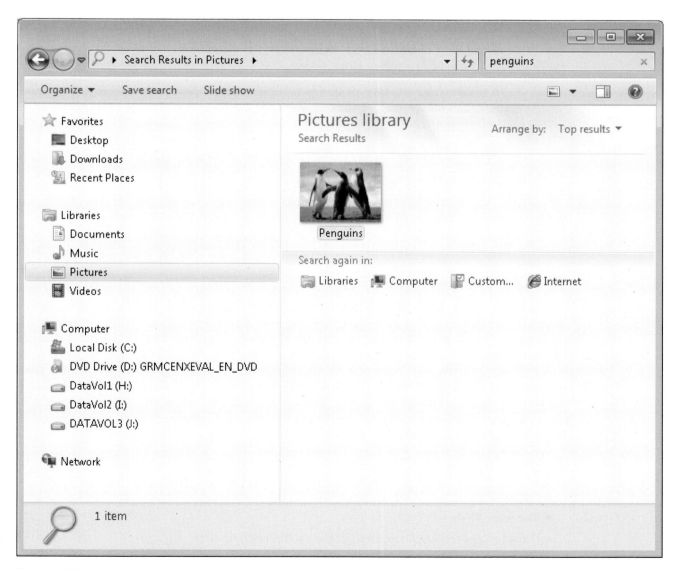

Figure 9-16 Search results
Courtesy Course Technology/Cengage Learning

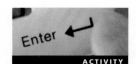

Activity 9-9: Using Search

Time Required: 10 minutes

Objective: Use the Search features in Windows 7 to find files and programs.

Description: Windows 7 integrates search into almost every part of the user interface. You can use Search to find files by name or metadata. In this activity, you use Search to find files.

1. If necessary, start your computer and log on.
2. Click the **Start** button and click **Pictures**.
3. Double-click **Sample Pictures**.
4. In the Search box, type **Desert**. Notice that the search is performed dynamically as you type. Only one file is listed because only one file name includes the word desert.
5. In the Search box, type **Corbis**. Multiple files are listed even though none of the files includes Corbis in the file name.
6. Right-click **Penguins.jpg**, click **Properties**, and click the **Details** tab. You can see that the Authors includes the word Corbis. The Search box searches file metadata in addition to the file name.
7. Click **OK** to close the Penguins.jpg Properties dialog box.
8. In the left pane, click **Local Disk (C:)**.
9. In the Search box, type **penguins** and press **Enter**. Notice that there is a warning that searching might be slow in non-indexed locations. An option is provided to add C:\ as an indexed location. Two copies of the Penguins picture are found on the C: drive.
10. Read the options available to search again in alternate locations.
11. Close Windows Explorer.
12. Click the **Start** button type **Penguins**. Notice that one indexed copy of Penguins is found here.
13. In the Start menu, in the Search box, type **Computer** and read the list of programs and administrative tasks that are displayed. This is faster than browsing in Control Panel.

The Search Index

The **indexing service** included in Windows 7 is a major improvement over the indexing service included with Windows XP. Indexing is automatically enabled so all users can immediately get the benefit of index-based searches. In addition, the index is updated each time a file is changed to ensure that search results are current.

By default, only the most common file locations are indexed. This prevents the index from incorporating less relevant files, such as operating system files, which users are unlikely to search for. Search speed is improved and indexing time is decreased by only indexing specified files. You can add additional search locations depending on your needs. Figure 9-17 shows the Indexing Options where you can configure indexed locations.

Only the following locations are indexed by default:

- Internet Explorer History
- Offline Files
- The Start Menu
- Users (except the AppData subfolder in each profile)

In addition to defining which locations are indexed, you can also define which file types are indexed and how those files are indexed. For each file type (defined by file extension) you

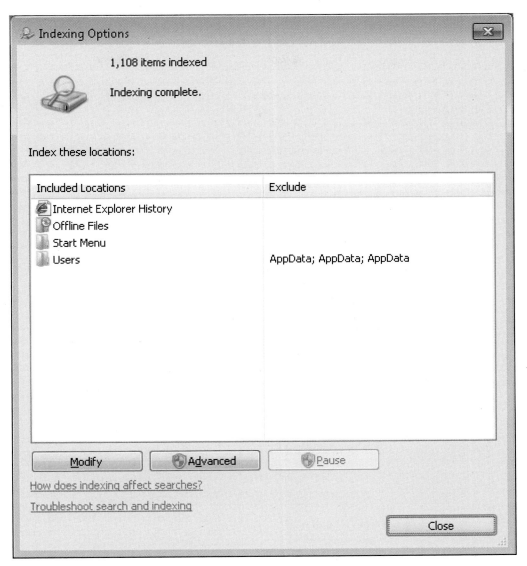

Figure 9-17 Indexing Options
Courtesy Course Technology/Cengage Learning

define whether the contents of the file or only metadata about the file are indexed. For some file types, such as pictures, the content of the files is meaningless from a search perspective and should not be indexed. Other file types such as Word documents can have their content indexed so that you can search for documents based on content. Figure 9-18 shows the configuration of file types.

You can configure the following additional index settings on the Index Settings tab that control a variety of index characteristics:

- *File Settings*—You can select whether encrypted files are indexed. You can also select whether words with different accents are treated as the same. For example, whether "resume" and "resumé" are indexed as the same word.

- *Troubleshooting*—You can rebuild the index if you believe it has become corrupted. You can also restore the default index settings.

- *Index location*—You can move the index from the default location of C:\ProgramData\ Microsoft to another location. This can be useful if the C drive is becoming full and you have free space on a different partition.

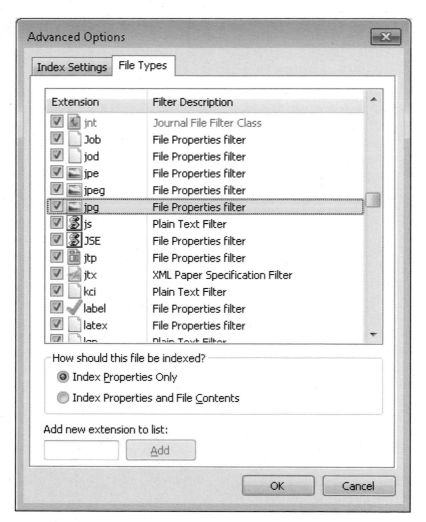

Figure 9-18 File Types for indexing
Courtesy Course Technology/Cengage Learning

Activity 9-10: Configuring Indexing

Time Required: 15 minutes

Objective: Configure how files are indexed for searching.

Description: By default, the search index only contains information about the file system locations most commonly used to store user data. If you store user data in other locations and want those files to be part of the index, you must add the file storage location to the index. In this activity, you configure indexing.

1. If necessary, start your computer and log on.

2. Click the **Start** button, type **cmd**, and press **Enter**.

3. At the command prompt, type **md C:\NewData** and press **Enter**. This command creates a new directory that you will index.

4. Type **dir C:\Windows > C:\NewData\Windows.txt** and press **Enter**. This command creates a file in your new directory.

5. Type **dir C:\NewData** and press **Enter**. If steps 3 and 4 were performed correctly, then you will see a file named Windows.txt that is about 4 KB.

6. Close the command prompt.

7. Click the **Start** button, type **Indexing**, and then click **Indexing Options**.

8. Click **Modify**.

9. Click **Show all locations**.

10. In the Change selected locations area, expand **Local Disk (C:)**, expand **Users**, and expand **User***x*. Notice that the AppData folder is not selected.

11. Select the **NewData** checkbox and click **OK**. Notice that NewData is now in the list of Included Locations.

12. Click **Advanced**.

13. Click **Treat similar words with diacritics as different words** and click **OK** to acknowledge rebuilding the index. This option means that words with varying accents will be recognized as different words.

14. Click the **File Types** tab, scroll down in the list, and click **jpg**. Notice that only properties are being indexed.

15. Scroll down in the list and click **txt**. For the text files, contents are being indexed. The filter used to analyze the file content is the Plain Text Filter.

16. Click **OK** to save your changes and close the Advanced Options dialog box. Watch as indexing is performed. Indexing may take a few minutes to complete.

17. When indexing is complete, click **Close** to close the Indexing Options.

18. Click the **Start** button and type **windows**. Notice that under Files, the Windows.txt file is listed. This search located the file in the index.

19. Click **See more results**. This opens a Windows Explorer window with more results.

20. Click in the upper-right search box, and click **Date modified**.

21. Click today's date. Notice that the list of search results is smaller because it includes only items modified today.

22. Close Windows Explorer.

File Metadata

The most basic file metadata are characteristics such as filename, creation date, and modified date. Depending on the type of file, additional metadata may be included. For example, pictures taken with a digital camera have additional metadata that is only appropriate for pictures, such as the shutter speed and lighting conditions.

Since metadata is included in the index, it is useful to create additional metadata for files. Windows 7 allows you to create **tags** that contain additional metadata for organizing your data. For example, you can add a tag to all project files so it is easy to search for them. This is particularly useful if you are using saved searches as virtual folders.

You cannot create tags for some file types. For example, you cannot create tags for txt and rtf files, but you can do so for Microsoft Office documents.

Saved Searches

A **saved search** is a virtual folder that contains the files matching a search query. For example, if you have configured a tag on all files for a project, you can create a saved search for files with the project tag. Then, any time you want to view project files, you access the virtual folder that represents the saved search. This virtual folder contains all files found in the search index that have the project tag, regardless of their location in the file system. The files listed in a saved search virtual folder are dynamically updated as new files are added to the index.

After you have completed a search, you have the option to save the search. Saved searches are stored in the Searches folder of your user profile and are also added to the favorites list in Windows Explorer.

Activity 9-11: Using Tags and Saved Searches

Time Required: 10 minutes
Objective: Add metadata to a file and create a saved search.

Description: The combination of using tags to add metadata to a file and saved searches to provide access to those files regardless of location is a powerful data organizing tool. When properly implemented, tags and saved searches increase user productivity significantly. In this activity, you create a tag for a file and then create a saved search to find files with that tag.

1. If necessary, start your computer and log on.
2. Click the **Start** button, click **Pictures**, and double-click **Sample Pictures**.
3. If necessary, arrange by **Folder**.
3. Click **Penguins.jpg**, and in the lower pane, click **Add a tag**, type **Ocean**, and click **Save**.
4. Click **Jellyfish.jpg**, and in the lower pane, click **Add a tag**, type **Ocean**, and click **Save**.
5. Click **Lighthouse.jpg**, and in the lower pane, click **Add a tag**, type **Ocean**, and click **Save**.
6. Close the **Sample Pictures** window.
7. Click the **Start** button and type **Ocean**.

    The three pictures you tagged are listed as the results of the search.

8. Click **See more results**.
9. Click **Save search**.
10. In the File name box, type **Ocean Pictures**, and click **Save**. The search is now showing more than just the tagged photos because the search is just for the keyword ocean, not specifically the tag ocean.
11. In the Search box, type **tag:**. Notice that a list of defined tags appears.
12. In the list of tags, click **Ocean**. Notice that the search now finds only files with the Ocean tag.
13. Click **Save search**, in the File name box, type **Revised Ocean Pictures**, and click **Save**.
14. Close Windows Explorer.

Internet Explorer 8

For many organizations, access to Web-based content and applications is critical. Imagine employees unable to access their Web-based applications for e-mail, sales, or accounting. Internet Explorer is how most organizations access these applications. Understanding Internet Explorer is a critical part of computer support.

Internet Explorer 8, shown in Figure 9-19, is the Web browser included with Windows 7. Critical areas of Internet Explorer to understand are:

- User features
- Security
- Privacy
- Tools

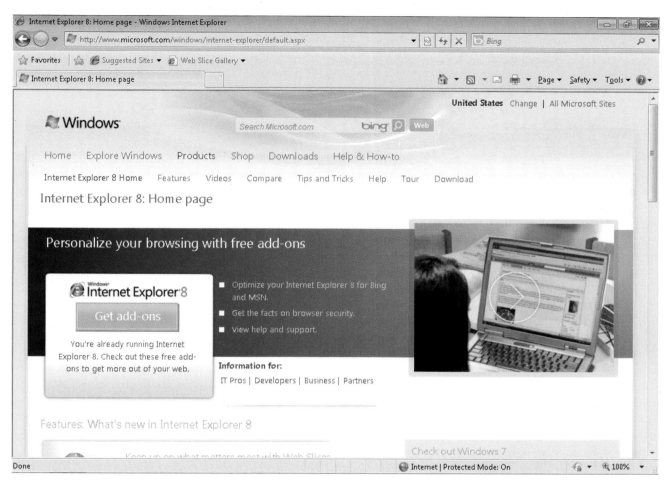

Figure 9-19 Internet Explorer 8
Courtesy Course Technology/Cengage Learning

User Features

Tabbed browsing allows Internet Explorer to control multiple Web sites being open at the same time. In older Web browsers, a separate window was required for each Web site you had open. Now each Web site gets a tab within the same Internet Explorer window. This makes it faster and easier to switch between multiple Web sites. You retain the option to open Web sites in a new window if desired.

A Search box is included in the upper-right corner of Internet Explorer 8. This Search box enhances your ability to find the information you need quickly. You are able to define the search provider used by the search box, such as Bing, Google, or Yahoo! In addition, you can have results of different searches appear in different tabs so you can easily go back to previous results as you try different search terms or providers.

Internet Explorer 8 can use **Really Simple Syndication (RSS)** feeds to display information from Web sites that you have selected. Many Web sites that deal with current topics such as news organizations or discussion groups distribute some of their content as an RSS feed. When you subscribe to an RSS feed, you get a summary of new articles in the RSS feed. If you are interested in any of the articles, you can click on the link to read the entire article. The RSS reader in Internet Explorer 8 can display whether there are new articles before you view the list. It is able to track this because it stores RSS content on the local hard drive and compares it to what it available in the feed.

Web Slices are small pieces of content from a Web site that notify you there is an update. These are useful for keeping track of content that updates or a regular basis, such as news, sports scores, or weather. Using Web Slices avoids the need to keep checking a Web site to see if it is updated. However, a web developer must include a Web Slice as part of the site for you to be able to use it. Web slices are a new feature in Internet Explorer 8.

Suggested Sites appear in the favorites bar at the top of the Internet Explorer 8 window. When you click on the Suggested Sites button, you are presented with a list of Web sites that are related to the site that you are currently viewing. Suggested Sites is a new feature in Internet Explorer 8.

Activity 9-12: Using Internet Explorer 8 Features

Time Required: 10 minutes
Objective: Learn how to use the features in Internet Explorer 8.

Description: Internet Explorer 8 includes a number of useful features. In this activity, you use several of these new features.

1. If necessary, start your computer and log on.

2. In the taskbar, click **Internet Explorer.**

3. If you are prompted to Set Up Windows Internet Explorer 8, use the following steps:

   a. On the Welcome to Internet Explorer 8 page, click **Next.**

   b. On the Turn on Suggested Sites page, click **Yes, turn on Suggested Sites.**

   c. On the Choose your setting page, click **Choose custom settings** and click **Next.**

   d. On the Choose a default search provider page, click **Keep my current default search provider** and click **Next.**

   e. On the Search Provider Updates page, click **Yes, I want to download updates** and click **Next.**

   f. On the Choose your Accelerators page, click **Keep my current Accelerators** and click **Next.**

   g. On the Compatibility Settings page, click **Yes, I want to use updates** and click **Finish.**

4. Move your mouse pointer to the right of the MSN.com tab until a new tab icon and message are displayed, and click the **New Tab** icon. A new tab opens.

5. In the address bar, type **www.microsoft.com** and press **Enter.**

6. Click the **MSN.com** tab to switch back to the MSN Web site.

7. To the left of the MSN.com tab, click the **down arrow.** This provides a list of the tabs that are open. This can be useful if there are many tabs open and the titles are difficult to read in the tabs.

8. To the left of the down arrow, click the **quick tabs** icon. This displays the content of each tab in a small version to make it easy for you to identify.

9. Click the **Microsoft Corporation** icon.

10. In the toolbar, click the **Favorites** button, click **Add to Favorites**, and click **Add.**

11. In the toolbar, click the **Favorites** button. This opens the Favorites Center, where you can view your favorites, RSS feeds, and history.

12. In the Search box, type **Windows 7** and press **Enter.** This displays the results from the Bing search engine by default. If you are prompted to turn on AutoComplete, click **No.**

13. Click the **Tools** menu and determine whether there is a checkmark beside Suggested Sites. If there is no checkmark, then click **Suggested Sites** and click **Yes** to enable them.

14. In the Favorites bar, click **Suggested Sites.** Notice that while you are on the Bing Web page, the suggested sites are other search engines.

15. In the address bar, type **http://ieaddons.com/en/webslices** and press **Enter.**

16. Read the list of Web Slices, under a Web Slice you like, click **Add to Internet Explorer.**

17. In the Add a Web Slice window, click **Add to Favorites Bar**. Notice that the Web Slice has been added to the Favorites bar.

18. Click the new Web Slice on the Favorites bar. This displays the contents of the Web Slice. This content will be periodically updated automatically.

19. Close Internet Explorer.

Security

The Security tab in the Internet Options for Internet Explorer, as shown in Figure 9-20, allows you to set Internet security options. The Web sites you connect to are grouped into zones and each zone can have different security options selected.

The zones for Internet Explorer security options are:

- *Internet*—The Internet zone includes all Internet Web sites that are not specifically assigned to another zone. The default security level is Medium-high.

- *Local intranet*—The Local intranet is meant to be all computers on the internal corporate network. The internal corporate network is defined by default as all sites in the local domain. However, this is only relevant if the workstation is joined to a domain. For workstations that are not part of a domain, the Intranet zone is treated the same as the Internet zone. The default security level is Medium-low.

- *Trusted sites*—The Trusted sites zone contains no sites by default, you must add sites that you consider trusted. This is useful when the Internet zone settings block functionality such as pop-up windows that are required for a site you know and trust. Adding the site to the Trusted sites zone allows that site to function properly. The default security level is Medium.

- *Restricted sites*—The Restricted sites zone is a specific list of sites that you do not trust. No sites are in this list by default. The default security level is High and cannot be changed except through custom settings.

The security options available for each zone control things like whether you are prompted when scripts or ActiveX controls are run. However, many security settings can be confusing to users. To make the process of selecting security options simpler, Microsoft has included predefined categories with groups of security settings. The five options are High, Medium-high, Medium, Medium-low, and Low. You also have the option to use custom settings for precise control over the security options. Table 9-2 lists the security configuration for each zone.

Internet Explorer Protected Mode All Internet Explorer zones can be configured to run in Protected Mode. Protected Mode works in conjunction with UAC to prevent malicious software from installing through Internet Explorer.

To implement protected mode for Internet Explorer, and integrity level is used. Access Control Lists (ACLs) for objects, such as files, include an integrity level in Windows 7. Running processes also include an integrity level that controls which resources they can access.

Windows 7 has three integrity levels:

- *Low (untrusted)*—The process can only write to low-risk areas. Areas designated as low risk include the Low folder in Temporary Internet Files and the HKEY_CURRENT_USER\ Software\LowRegistry key. Internet Explorer has a low integrity level in Protected Mode.

- *Medium (user)*—The process can write to user-specific areas. User specific areas include the Documents folder for the user and the HKEY_CURRENT_USER portion of the registry. Applications started from the Start menu have a medium integrity level.

- *High (administrative)*—The process can write to sensitive areas. Sensitive areas include the Program Files folder and the HKEY_LOCAL_MACHINE portion of the registry. Administrative applications that must be approved by using UAC have a high integrity level.

9

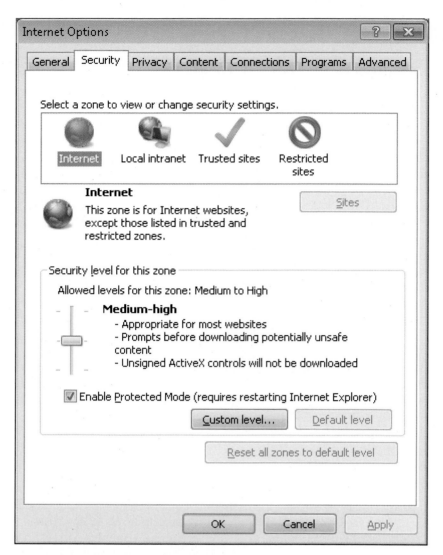

Figure 9-20 Internet Options Security tab
Courtesy Course Technology/Cengage Learning

Table 9-2   Security configuration for Internet Explorer zones

Zone	Default Security Level
Internet	Medium-high. Requires user consent for active content and restricts some active content. Most Web sites function with this security level.
Local intranet	Medium-low. Most active content is allowed without requiring user consent. Unsigned ActiveX controls are not downloaded.
Trusted sites	Medium. Same as Medium-low, but requires user consent to run some active content.
Restricted sites	High. Disables most active content.

A process can modify files and registry keys only with the same or lower integrity level. For example, Internet Explorer in Protected Mode (low integrity) can modify only resources marked as low integrity. A high-integrity process such as an MMC snap-in can modify high, medium, and low resources.

If the integrity level for files and registry keys is not specified, then it is medium. Medium is the integrity level for most files and registry keys.

Protected Mode prevents the silent installation of malicious software from Internet sites. As a low-integrity process, Internet Explorer cannot install software or modify registry keys. In addition, any process started by Internet Explorer will also be a low-integrity process. If elevation to a higher level process is required, the user is prompted.

Intranet Zone Configuration   In a domain-based network, Internet Explorer assumes that all Web sites in the local domain are part of the Intranet zone. This allows internal developers to create intranet Web sites with advanced features such as pop-up windows and scripting without worrying that Internet Explorer will block those features. The default configuration to automatically detect an intranet network, shown in Figure 9-21, gives these results.

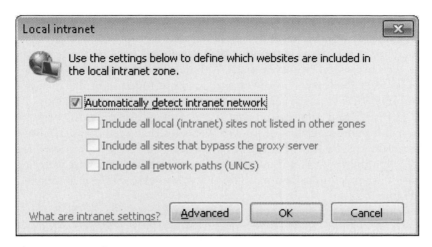

Figure 9-21 Local intranet configuration
Courtesy Course Technology/Cengage Learning

Sometimes Internet Explorer will not automatically detect all intranet sites properly in a domain. If there are only a few sites, you can add the specific sites to the list of intranet sites.

If there are multiple intranet sites, you can use the following options to detect intranet sites:

- *Include all local (intranet) sites not listed in other zones*—This option includes all Web sites that are referenced without using a dot in the host name. For example, *http://server1* does not use a dot in the host name and would be part of the Local intranet zone. The URL *http://server1.mydomain.com* does use dots in the host name and would not be part of the Local intranet zone.

- *Include all sites that bypass the proxy server*—This option includes all Web sites that are specifically configured to not be accessed through a proxy server. This is relevant only when a proxy server is being used by clients.

- *Include all network paths (UNCs)*—This option includes all files accessed by using a UNC path. For example, *\\server1\share1* is a UNC path.

Smartscreen Filter   The **SmartScreen Filter** in Internet Explorer 8 warns you when you are about to access a Web site that is known to install malicious software or is used as part of a phishing attack. The list of unsafe Web sites is maintained by Microsoft and you can report new unsafe sites.

By default the SmartScreen Filter is turned on and scans each Web site you access. This is the best configuration in most scenarios. However, if a computer does not access to the Internet, then you may want to disable the SmartScreen Filter to prevent users to seeing error messages about being unable to perform SmartScreen filtering for internal Web sites.

Privacy

Internet Explorer 8 includes a number of new features that enhance privacy. **InPrivate Browsing** allows you to access the Internet without any information being stored in cache or history. This can be useful when using a public computer and you do not want anyone to easily identify the Web sites you have been visiting. However, there are numerous other ways Web activity can be monitored, such as logging on a proxy server or firewall.

InPrivate Filtering allows you to control whether information about you is sent to advertisers that embed their content in other Web sites. When you enable InPrivate Filtering, some Web sites may not work properly. To enable proper functionality on specific Web sites, you can specify which providers are allowed to obtain your information.

Tools

Several tools are available in Internet Explorer 8 to enhance the browsing experience and increase manageability. The **Popup Blocker** prevents most popup advertisements from being displayed. Popup advertisements are not a security risk, just annoying.

Internet Explorer 8 includes strong adherence to Internet standards for Web page rendering. Previous versions of Internet Explorer included many proprietary methods for rendering Web pages. Adherence to standards is good for Web developers because their sites then work properly in multiple Web browsers. However, many Web developers targeted their Web sites for previous versions of Internet Explorer. Those Web sites may not function properly in Internet Explorer 8.

Compatibility View is a new feature in Internet Explorer 8 that provides backward compatibility for Web sites and application that were targeted for previous versions of Internet Explorer. Microsoft maintains a list of known Web sites that need compatibility view and Internet Explorer 8 automatically downloads this list. When you visit a Web site on the list of Web sites requiring Compatibility View, it is automatically enabled. If you visit a Web site, such as an internal application, that requires Compatibility View, you can enable it manually for a Web site, as shown in Figure 9-22.

Internet Explorer is extensible with Add-ons. Add-ons increase the functionality of Internet Explorer and can include toolbars or other features. Poorly written Add-ons for Internet Explorer can introduce instability to your computer. In addition, some Add-ons function as spyware or adware. Users are lured into installing Add-ons with promises of easy searching and cool icons for e-mail messages. In previous versions of Internet Explorer, it was difficult to identify and remove Add-ons. Internet Explorer 8 includes a new **Manage Add-ons** tool that makes it easier to identify, disable, and remove unwanted Add-ons.

Activity 9-13: Configuring Internet Explorer

Time Required: 10 minutes
Objective: Learn how to configure Internet Explorer 8.

Description: Internet Explorer 8 includes a number of features that you can configure for privacy and application compatibility. In this activity, you configure some of these features in Internet Explorer 8.

1. If necessary, start your computer and log on.
2. In the taskbar, click **Internet Explorer**.
3. In the address bar, type **http://www.microsoft.com** and press **Enter**.
4. Click the **Tools** menu and click **Internet Options**.
5. Click the **Security** tab and read the security configuration for the Internet zone. All Web sites are in this zone by default.
6. Click **Local intranet** and read the security configuration for the Local intranet zone. Notice that the security settings are lower.

Figure 9-22 Compatibility View settings
Courtesy Course Technology/Cengage Learning

7. Click **Trusted sites** and read the security configuration for the Trusted sites zone. Notice that the security settings for this zone are similar to the Internet zone, but Protected Mode is disabled.

8. Click the **Sites** button. Notice that by default the Web sites added to this zone must be secured by secure sockets layer (SSL).

9. Clear the **Require server verification (https:) for all sites in this zone** check box, click **Add**, and click **Close**.

10. In the Internet Options window, click **OK**. Notice that the lower status bar of Internet Explorer has changed to show the zone as Unknown Zone (Mixed). This page has content from multiple locations, not just *www.microsoft.com*.

11. Click the **Tools** menu and click **Manage Add-ons**.

12. In the Manage Add-ons window, review the Add-on Types.

13. In the Show box, select **All add-ons**.

14. Click each add-on type and review the add-ons that are installed.

15. Close Manage Add-ons.

16. Click the **Tools** menu and click **Compatibility View Settings**.

17. Click **Add** and click **Close**. Web sites for the *Microsoft.com* domain will now be renders as if by Internet Explorer 7. Notice that a new tab has opened for the Web site in Compatibility View and that protected mode is off.

18. Click the **Safety** menu and point to **SmartScreen Filter**. Read the options that are available. Notice that one of the options is to turn off SmartScreen Filter. This indicates that SmartScreen Filter is on.

19. In the Safety menu, click **InPrivate Browsing**. Notice that a new windows opens with InPrivate displayed in the address bar. This indicates that InPrivate browsing is being used and that the history is not being recorded.

20. In the address bar, type **http://www.news.com** and press **Enter**.

21. Close the InPrivate Internet Explorer window.

22. In the remaining Internet Explorer window, click **Favorites**, click **History**, and then click **Today**. Notice that *www.news.com* is not in the history list.

23. Close Internet Explorer and click **Close all tabs** when prompted.

Chapter Summary

- Windows 7 uses a new printing process that uses the XPS format for spool files. This process results in higher quality printing for graphics and color. The XPS printing process is backward compatible with GDI-based applications and printer drivers.

- Windows 7 stores printer drivers in a driver store to allow preinstallation of drivers and better support for printer drivers over the network.

- The Print Management snap-in is a new printer management tool that can be used to manage local and remote printers. Previous printer management tools could only manage local printers.

- Printers can be configured with many different options including: availability, priority, driver, spooling configuration, and a separator page. You can also share printers in a similar way to creating file shares.

- Location aware printing allows you to associated a specific default printer with different physical locations.

- When print jobs are stored in the print queue, you can manage the jobs by pausing, resuming, restarting, canceling, and editing the properties of the jobs.

- Windows Fax and Scan is used to fax and scan documents in Windows 7. A fax modem or network fax server is required.

- Windows Explorer now includes libraries to simplify access to files. Libraries can include multiple file paths.

- Search is integrated into many parts of Windows 7. You can search from the Search box or the Start menu. Search performance is increased with an index. You can also save searches and use them as virtual folders.

- Internet Explorer 8 includes Web Slices and Suggested Sites in improve the user experiences. They are added to other user features, such as tabbed browsing and RSS feeds.

- Internet Explorer divides Web sites into zones. Each zone can have different security options applied to it. By default, all Web sites are in the Internet zone. The Local intranet zone is only relevant for computers that are joined to a domain. Add known sites with lower security requirements to the Trusted sites zone.

- To enhance privacy, Internet Explorer 8 includes InPrivate Browsing and InPrivate Filtering. InPrivate Browsing prevents caching of Web content and logging of Web activity on the local computer. InPrivate Filtering prevents your information from being sent to advertisers.

- Compatibility View provides backward compatibility with previous versions of Internet Explorer.

Key Terms

Compatibility View A new feature in Internet Explorer 8 that provides backward compatibility for Web sites and application that were targeted for previous versions of Internet Explorer

Device Stage A feature for printers and other devices that displays all of the relevant information and management options for a device in a single location.

enhanced metafile format (EMF) The format used for spool files in pre-Windows Vista versions of Windows.

Graphics Device Interface (GDI) The format used for displaying screen content in pre-Windows Vista versions of Windows.

indexing service A service that indexes files in specified locations to speed up search queries.

InPrivate Browsing An Internet Explorer 8 feature that prevents caching of Web content and logging of Web activity in Internet Explorer.

InPrivate Filtering An Internet Explorer 8 feature that allows you to control which advertisers get access to your information.

Libraries Virtual folders in Windows Explorer that combine content from multiple locations to simplify file access.

location aware printing A feature for mobile computers that associates a specific default printer with a physical location.

Manage Add-ons A new tool in Internet Explorer 8 that makes it easier to identify, disable, and remove unwanted Add-ons.

metadata Information or properties for a file or other object. Windows 7 allows you to include tags as additional metadata for files.

point and print A system used by Windows to distribute printer drivers over the network when network printers are installed.

Popup Blocker An Internet Explorer feature that prevents most popup advertising from being displayed while you browse Web sites.

Postscript A common language used by printers to describe how a page is printed.

Print Management snap-in A new printer management tool in Windows 7 that allows you to manage local and remote printers.

Printer Control Language (PCL) A common language used by printers to describe how a page is printed.

printer driver Software used by Windows 7 to properly communicate with a specific make and model of printer.

printer driver package An enhanced printer driver that can contain additional software.

printer driver store A location in Windows 7 that caches printer drivers and is capable of storing multiple versions of a printer driver.

Really Simple Syndication (RSS) A format for distributing content as articles. Internet Explorer 7 is capable of reading RSS feeds.

saved search A virtual folder that contains the files matching a search query.

SmartScreen Filter An Internet Explorer 8 feature that warns you about Web sites known to install malicious software or used in phishing attacks.

Suggested Sites A list of Web sites provided by Internet Explorer 8 based on the content that you are currently looking at.

tabbed browsing A feature in Internet Explorer 8 that allows multiple Web sites to be open in the same window.

tags Additional metadata that can be added to the properties of a file.

Web Slices Small pieces of content from a Web site that notify you in Internet Explorer 8 when there is an update.

9

Windows Fax and Scan A utility in Windows 7 to manage scanning and faxing.

XML Paper Specification (XPS) A document format that describes how a page should be displayed. XPS is similar to Adobe Portable Document Format (PDF).

XML PrintCapabilities A new system to advertise the capabilities of a printer.

XML PrintTicket An XML file that describes the settings for a print job.

Review Questions

1. Which document format is similar to XPS?

   a. PDF

   b. TXT

   c. DOC

   d. RTF

2. Existing Windows applications must be updated to use XPS-based printing or print quality is not improved by using Windows 7. True or False?

3. Which of the following are languages used by printers? (Choose all that apply.)

   a. WPF

   b. XPS

   c. PCL

   d. Postscript

4. XPS-based printing uses a new format called _____ to describe print job settings.

5. Which utility is used to add printer drivers to the printer driver store?

   a. Pdriver.exe

   b. Pnputil.exe

   c. PushPrinterConnections.exe

   d. Print Management snap-in

6. Which utilities can be used to manage printers? (Choose all that apply.)

   a. the Devices and Printers applet

   b. Computer Management

   c. Device Manager

   d. Print Management snap-in

7. Which of the following are features available in the Print Management snap-in that are not available in the Devices and Printers applet? (Choose all that apply.)

   a. Manage remote printers

   b. Manage local printers

   c. Configure notifications

   d. Bulk printer management

   e. Deploy printers by using Group Policy

8. When a printer is configured with a lower priority value, the print jobs for that printer are printed first. True or False?

9. By default, all users are able to manage their own print jobs because the _____ group has the manage documents permission.

10. Windows Fax and Scan cannot be used without _____? (Choose all that apply.)

    a. a fax modem

    b. a multifunction printer with a fax

    c. a network fax server

    d. a scanner

11. When you create a new document in the root of a library, where is the document created?

    a. In the highest priority location with free space

    b. In the first location listed in the library properties

    c. You are prompted for the location

    d. In the save location of the library

12. You can only use the Arrange by option to organize files that are indexed. True or False?

13. Which file locations are indexed by default? (Choose all that apply.)

    a. Offline files

    b. the Windows folder

    c. the Start menu

    d. the Users folder

14. For each type of file, you can specify whether the contents of the file are indexed. True or False?

15. Which Windows 7 feature allows you to create a virtual folder that automatically searches for files?

    a. Saved search

    b. the Search box

    c. the Search folder

    d. tags

16. Which new feature in Windows Explorer makes sizing windows easier?

    a. Shake

    b. Snap

    c. Peek

    d. Autoconfig

17. The _____ feature is used to provide backward compatibility for Web sites targeted for previous versions of Internet Explorer.

18. Which Internet Explorer 8 security zone is only relevant if the computer is joined to a domain?

    a. Internet

    b. Local intranet

    c. Trusted sites

    d. Restricted sites

19. When Internet Explorer 8 runs in protected mode, it runs with lower privileges than the user. True or False?

20. The _____ used in Internet Explorer 8 allows multiple Web pages to be open in a single Internet Explorer window.

Case Projects

Case Project 9-1: XPS Printing

Hyperactive Media Sales prints many brochures and leaflets for salespeople to take out to clients. The sales manager heard from a friend that the printing system in Windows 7 will make his brochures and leaflets look better. He is convinced that this is the way to go, but the accounting manager needs to understand why this works before he will budget for installing Windows 7. Explain why the XPS printing in Windows 7 is better. Also explain which components they would need to buy in addition to Windows 7.

Case Project 9-2: Finding and Organizing Files

In Hyperactive Media Sales, the salespeople cache most of their customer files on their laptops by using offline files. This allows them to access their files when they are outside the office. The folder structure on the server has never been very well organized, and over the years it has become very difficult to find a specific file. Which file finding and organizing features in Windows 7 can help the salespeople?

Case Project 9-3: Phishing

Gigantic Life Insurance has thousands of insurance brokers selling their services. Recently, some of the insurance brokers have been the victim of a phishing attack that resulted in usernames and passwords being stolen. The overall cost of the attack was over a million dollars, including the time to reset passwords and verify data. Your manager would like you to come up with a short explanation of how this might be prevented in the future.

Case Project 9-4: Web Site Compatibility

Gigantic Life Insurance has many Web-based applications that are used by insurance brokers selling their services. These brokers have recently begun implementing Windows 7 and Internet Explorer 8. For most of the Web-based applications, there have been no issues. However, two of the Web-based applications are experiencing problems. Both applications are experiencing problems with buttons not working and incorrect page layouts. What are some potential solutions to this issue?

chapter 10

Performance Tuning

After reading this chapter and completing the exercises, you will be able to:

- Identify several key performance enhancements
- Describe performance tuning concepts
- Use Performance Monitor
- Use Task Manager
- Understand performance ranking
- Optimize system performance

On most Windows 7 computers, the default configuration provides acceptable performance. When users run applications, the applications respond quickly. When users access files, the files open quickly. However, on some systems, over time performance can start to deteriorate. Performance tuning lets you optimize the performance of Windows 7 to function at acceptable standards.

In this chapter, you begin by learning about the performance tuning process and how Performance Monitor allows you to find system bottlenecks. Additionally, you will learn how to use Task Manager, understand Windows 7 performance rankings, and optimize system performance.

Performance Enhancements

Windows 7 includes a number of performance and reliability enhancements that were not available in early versions of Windows. Some of these features have been discussed in previous chapters, such as faster restores from hibernation. The combination of all the new features makes Windows 7 more responsive and stable than previous versions of Windows.

Some of the performance enhancements in Windows 7 are:

- *Windows SuperFetch*—This feature tracks application utilization and ensures that the most commonly used programs are kept in physical memory rather than being swapped out to disk. To accommodate background processes, commonly used applications are swapped out and then swapped back into memory automatically. Previous versions of windows did not retrieve the application from virtual memory until you attempted to use it.

- *Low-priority I/O*—This feature allows some disk access to be designated as low priority. In this way background processes can complete tasks that require disk access without affecting performance of user applications. The indexing process for search in Windows 7 uses low-priority I/O.

- *Windows ReadyBoost*—This feature allows you to use a flash memory in a USB flash drive to boost Windows 7 performance. You can allocate a portion of the flash memory device to be used as system memory in Windows 7 that is much faster than accessing data from virtual memory on disk.

- *Windows ReadyDrive*—This feature allows Windows 7 to use flash memory embedded directly in hard disks. New hybrid disks use flash memory as a cache to enhance performance, reduce power consumption, and extend hard disk life. With a hybrid drive, recovery from sleep can be done in only a few seconds because reading data from flash memory is must faster than accessing the data from hard disk.

- *Automatic defragmentation*—The vast majority of users would not remember to defragment the hard disk in their computer. This is now performed automatically without user intervention.

Performance Tuning Overview

Performance tuning is a process rather than an event. In an ideal world, an effective performance tuning process is initiated well before problems occur. However, in most cases, performance tuning is not even considered until a performance problem exists.

The performance tuning process consists of:

- Establishing a baseline
- Recognizing bottlenecks
- Tuning performance

Establishing a Baseline

To recognize system **bottlenecks**, you must first establish a **baseline** that defines normal performance. A baseline is a set of performance indicators captured when system performance is acceptable. The values of baseline performance indicators are compared to future values of performance indicators to isolate performance problems.

Windows 7, like previous versions of Windows, is capable of reporting on a wide variety of performance indicators. Performance indicators are often called **counters** because they display values for system characteristics. Some examples of counters are:

- % Processor Time
- Disk Read Byte/sec
- Memory: Available Mbytes
- IPv4: Datagrams/sec

When you establish a baseline, it is important to ensure that you are measuring the normal state of the performance indicators. If unusual activity is occurring, then the baseline performance measurement is not valid, and it will be difficult to use the baseline to identify abnormal activity in the future.

To ensure that you are measuring the normal state when establishing a baseline, you should:

- Verify that no unusual activity is happening on the workstation—For example, ensure that no applications are performing large queries to databases or processing batch jobs, unless that is the normal state of the computer.

- Measure performance indicators over time—By measuring performance indicators over time, you can see an average value for the indicators. Average values are less volatile and more accurate than measuring with snapshots of short duration.

At the time of this writing Microsoft did not provide any specific guidance on the counters to use when monitoring Windows 7 for bottlenecks. However, information on specific bottleneck-detection counters and their acceptable values for Windows Server 2003 can be found in the Windows Server 2003 Performance Counters reference at http://technet.microsoft.com/en-us/library/cc779038(WS.10).aspx. These values should be similar to those recommended for Windows 7.

Recognizing Bottlenecks

A bottleneck occurs when a limitation in a single computer system component slows down the entire system. For any application, there is always one component in the computer system that is the limiting factor for performance. This component is the bottleneck. Performance tuning attempts to eliminate bottlenecks.

The bottleneck for each activity you perform and each application that you run may be different. For example, a database application may require fast access to the hard drive, and disk drives are a common bottleneck. A 3D-rendering program may experience limited processing power as the most common bottleneck.

The most common bottlenecks to system performance are:

- Disk
- Memory
- Processor
- Network

Disk Bottlenecks Disk bottlenecks occur when Windows 7 and running applications want to read and write information to the physical disk in the system faster than the disk can manage. This is quite a common issue on servers where many people are making requests to a single server. However, for desktop computers running Windows 7, it is uncommon. Some situations where the disk can be a bottleneck include 3D rendering and programs that use large data files, such as financial modeling software.

If required, disk performance can be increased in a few different ways:

- *Upgrade the drive controller*—For example, Serial ATA (SATA) is a faster disk technology than standard ATA. Or, upgrade narrow small computer serial interface (SCSI) to wide SCSI (also requires upgrading the disks).

- *Upgrade the disks*—Disks are rated for certain speeds of data transfer and seek time. Seek time is the time it takes for the disk to randomly locate data on the drive. If the system is accessing many different files at once, seek time is an important performance factor. A major factor in the data access is the time it takes for the surface of the drive to move under the read/write heads. Electromechanical hard drives that spin the disk faster typically perform faster. The rotations per minute (RPM) is a good indicator of expected performance. A 5,400 RPM drive (typically used in laptop computers) will perform slower than a 15,000 RPM drive, but the reduced performance will reduce noise, cost, heat generation—and power usage. To avoid the mechanical latency concerns, Solid State Drives (SSD) are now readily available. These drives are still new enough to have the advantage of no moving parts; however, they are expensive and have a specific lifetime of usage before they fail.

- *Implement RAID0 or RAID5*—Both RAID0 and RAID5 increase read and write performance by spreading data manipulation tasks across multiple drivers.

- *Move the paging file to a nonsystem disk*—By default, the paging file, which is accessed often by the system, resides on the same disk as the operating system files, which are also accessed often by the system. Putting the paging file on a different disk (not just a different partition) can increase performance by reducing the data manipulation that any one disk needs to perform. The paging file can be split over multiple disks to further enhance performance.

Memory Bottlenecks Most memory bottlenecks occur when the applications you are running require more memory than is physically available in the computer. This forces Windows 7 to use virtual memory to accommodate the memory requirements of all the running applications. Virtual memory is a system whereby memory is simulated on disk with a paging file. The least used memory areas are stored in the paging file. When information in the paging file is required, it is taken out of the paging file and placed in physical memory.

Accessing information from disk is much slower than accessing information from physical memory. Reducing the need for virtual memory can significantly improve system performance. You can recognize when virtual memory is being heavily used by a high volume of disk activity.

To reduce the use of virtual memory:

- *Increase the amount of physical memory*—Adding physical memory to a computer allows more information to be kept in physical memory, which reduces the need for virtual memory.

- *Run fewer applications at once*—If you are running multiple tasks, then more information is kept in memory. Reducing the number of applications running at the same time reduces the amount of memory used, and consequently, the need for virtual memory.

Another less common memory bottleneck occurs in systems that process very high volumes of information, such as databases or financial modeling programs. These applications can be slowed by systems where the movement of data between the processor and memory is too slow. In some cases, you may be able to add faster memory to an existing computer, but in most cases you must purchase a new computer with a faster memory system.

Processor Bottlenecks A processor bottleneck occurs when there is too much work for a processor to do. In a computer with one single core processor, the computer can only work on one task at a time. To run multiple applications and perform system tasks, the processor switches between the required tasks very quickly to give the illusion of all activities happening at the same time. When too many tasks must be performed, or an individual task requires too much processor time, the processor becomes a bottleneck.

To resolve a processor bottleneck:

- *Change to a faster processor*—Processor performance is traditionally measured by clock speed. When comparing processors with the same architecture, a processor with a higher clock speed can perform more work in a given time frame.

- *Add additional processors*—Some computers are capable of containing multiple physical processors. Windows 7 supports up to two physical processors. Having multiple processors means that tasks can be completed more quickly, because the server can work on two tasks at the same time. Be aware that two processors are not twice as fast as a single processor, because some inefficiency is introduced when the system coordinates the activity of two processors.

- *Change to a multicore processor*—Many processors are now multicore, which effectively means there are multiple processors on a single chip. A dual-core processor increases processing capacity and reduces memory consumption versus simply adding a faster processor.

 In many cases, to upgrade the processor significantly enough to notice a performance increase, a new computer is required.

10

Network Bottlenecks Network bottlenecks are more common for servers than computers running Windows 7. There are very few applications where Windows 7 requires high-speed network connectivity. In a server-based situation, multiple computers accessing a single server may overwhelm the network connection to the server.

If there is excessive network traffic coming from a single workstation, it is usually a sign of a hardware problem, an application error, or a virus. If the network card is experiencing problems and generating high volumes of traffic (jabbering), then you should replace the network card. If an application is experiencing an error, then restarting the application often fixes the problem. A virus can generate a lot of network traffic, usually directed at computers on the Internet. Having a current and reputable anti-virus product will help avoid an infection.

In the rare circumstance where the network is simply too slow, you can replace the existing network with a faster system. For example, if an old 10 Mbps network is slowing down file sharing between computers, you could replace it with a 100 Mbps or 1000 Mbps network system. This may involve replacing network cards, cabling, and switches.

Tuning Performance

The process for performance tuning is consistent regardless of the problems being experienced. In each case, you perform the following steps:

1. Create a baseline for the computer.

2. Compare the baseline to current performance indicators.

3. Identify possible causes for variations from the baseline.

4. Identify possible fixes for variations from the baseline.

5. Select a fix to implement.

6. Implement the fix and monitor for changes.

7. If the problem is not resolved, undo the fix and repeat step 5.

8. If the problem is resolved, document the solution for future reference.

When selecting a fix to implement, you should take into account the time involved and the likelihood that the fix will resolve the problem. Sometimes it is better to attempt several simple fixes, even if they are less likely to fix the problem, before attempting a complex fix that is likely to solve the problem.

Documentation during the performance tuning process is essential. As you attempt each fix, you should document the changes you are making. This allows you to undo each fix before you try the next one.

Performance Monitor

Performance Monitor is an MMC snap-in that is used to monitor system performance indicators. The utility should be run by a user logged in as an Administrator or the equivalent. The utility is commonly called "perfmon" by experienced administrators because it can be started from the command line by running perfmon.exe or starting the snap-in itself, perfmon.msc, from Administrative Tools in Control Panel or manually adding it to a custom MMC console. You can use Performance Monitor, as seen in Figure 10-1, to generate a baseline and find system bottlenecks. The first screen of Performance Monitor displays a system summary using text to summarize simple counters. The Windows 7 Resource Overview window has been moved into a separate utility called Resource Monitor, shown in Figure 10-2. Resource Monitor runs as a process spawned by Performance Monitor when you click the link Open Resource Monitor shown in Figure 10-1.

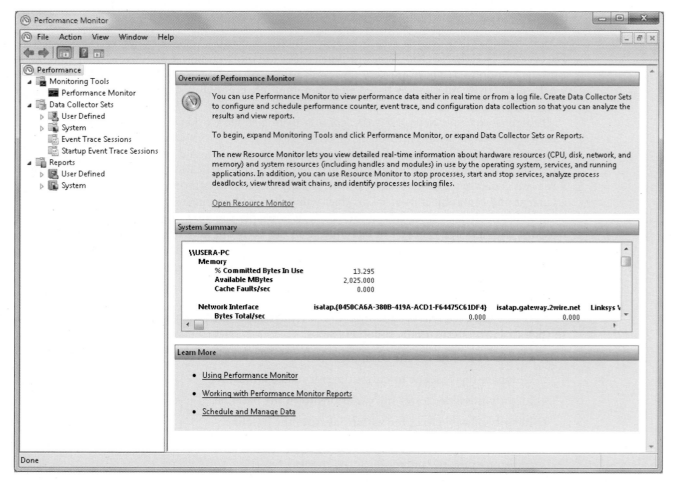

Figure 10-1 Performance Monitor
Courtesy Course Technology/Cengage Learning

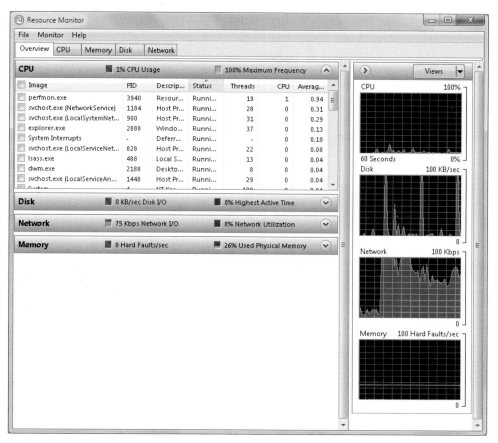

Figure 10-2 Resource Monitor, Overview tab
Courtesy Course Technology/Cengage Learning

The areas of Performance Monitor are:

• Resource Monitor

• Performance Monitor

• Data Collector Sets

• Reports

Resource Monitor

Resource Monitor, shown in Figure 10-2, provides real-time monitoring of the most common system performance indicators. The performance indicators are summarized in graphs at the side of the screen. The performance indicators are also shown in summary bars for each system area that is monitored. The displayed charts and summaries are updated in real time while monitoring is active. Monitoring can be stopped to freeze the displayed values so the information collected can be reviewed. While monitoring is stopped, new data is not collected in Resource Monitor. Monitoring can be restarted to continue data collection when desired. Each summary bar can be opened to display additional information about a specific system area. Note that the performance counters referenced in Resource Monitor are only a few key counters. Many more counters are available for advanced review and analysis in the Performance Monitor tool.

CPU   The CPU area is used to monitor processor performance and determine whether the processor is a bottleneck. The two performance indicators monitored are:

• *CPU Usage*—The percentage of CPU processing capacity that is being used. If this figure stays at 100% for extended periods of time, the processor is a bottleneck in the system.

- *CPU Maximum Frequency*—The percentage of the maximum CPU frequency that the CPU is able to use in the current configuration. In most cases, the CPU is able to operate at 100% of capacity, in which case, this value is 100%. However, some laptops reduce the processor capacity to reduce power usage when running on battery power. This is also influenced by which power plan the system is using. When processor capacity is reduced, the Maximum Frequency is less than 100%, typically 50%.

When you expand the CPU summary bar on the Overview, or switch to the CPU tab, a list of running processes is displayed, as shown in Figure 10-3. This displays the following characteristics about running processes:

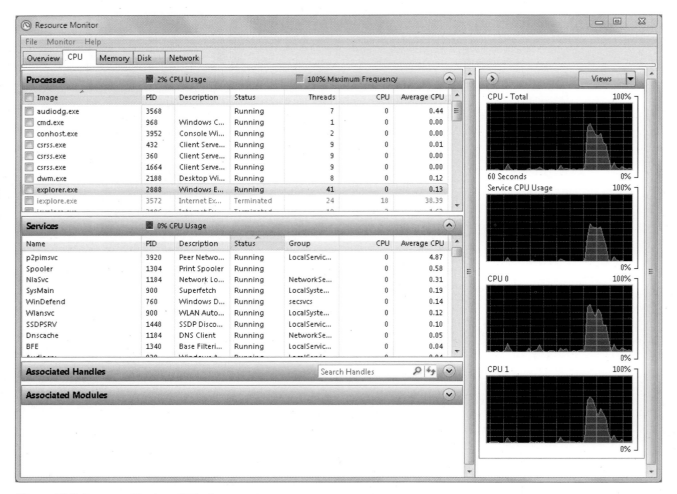

Figure 10-3 Resource Monitor, CPU tab
Courtesy Course Technology/Cengage Learning

- *Image*—The name of the executable file. System is a summary item that represents the operating system kernel and other low-level components, such as device drivers.

- *PID*—The process identifier (PID) is a number assigned to the process by the operating system when it starts. It is used by the operating system to track processes.

- *Description*—A description of the process. This description is taken from the executable file.

- *Threads*—Each process can be composed of multiple executable components called threads. A processor executes one thread at a time. An application with multiple threads can benefit from multiple processors or processor cores.

- *CPU*—Shows the percentage of CPU utilization use by each process.
- *Average CPU*—Shows the average percentage of CPU utilization used by each process.

The CPU tab displays additional information about the services running on the computer and their CPU usage as well. By right-clicking on a service, the administrator can restart, stop, or start the service. If a service name is not familiar to the administrator, the option to search online for more details about the service is available in the pop-up menu as well. This can be useful to new administrators who are not familiar with common service names.

Below the service listing are sections for handles and module listings that are associated with processes listed at the top of the screen. These are resources that a process can use to run applications. A programmer can view the handles and modules while troubleshooting his or her application.

Disk The Disk area is used to monitor disk performance and determine whether the disk subsystem is a bottleneck. The two performance indicators monitored are:

- *Current disk input/output in B/sec*—This shows the current rate of information transfer to and from the disk subsystem. This value can be compared to the theoretical maximum for the disk subsystem to determine if the disk subsystem is a bottleneck.
- *Highest Active Time*—This displays the percentage of time that the disk subsystem is active. If this percentage is very high, the disk subsystem may be a bottleneck, even if the disk subsystem has not reached its maximum theoretical transfer rate.

When you expand the Disk summary bar on the Overview, or switch to the Disk tab, a list of processes performing disk activity is displayed, as shown in Figure 10-4. This displays the following characteristics about processes performing disk activity:

10

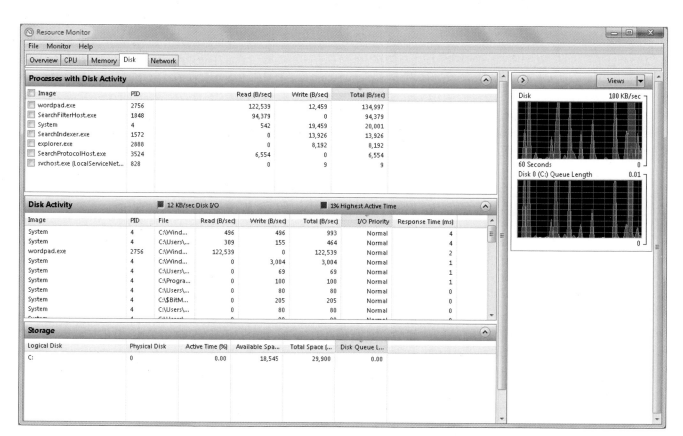

Figure 10-4 Resource Monitor, Disk tab
Courtesy Course Technology/Cengage Learning

- *Image*—The name of the executable file. System is a summary item that represents the operating system kernel and other low-level components, such as device drivers.

- *PID*—The process identifier (PID) is a number assigned to the process by the operating system when it starts. It is used by the operating system to track processes.

- *File*—The file being read or written by the process. This can be used to identify the process that accesses a particular file.

- *Read*—The current rate of data transfer from the disk in bytes per second. This can be used to identify which process is generating high amounts of disk activity.

- *Write*—The current rate of data transfer to the disk in bytes per second. This can be used to identify which process is generating high amounts of disk activity.

- *IO Priority*—The priority assigned by the application to performing the disk access task.

- *Response time*—This shows the time in milliseconds between when the disk activity is requested by the application and when the disk subsystem performed the operation. If response time is high, the disk subsystem may be a bottleneck.

The Disk tab displays additional information about disk activity and general storage attributes. The Processes with Disk Activity will report which processes have had disk activity in the last 60 seconds. The Storage section reports overall activity of each storage location, organized by logical disk. Each logical disk reports the physical disk it is on, the percentage of time that disk is active, space usage, and the number of disk operations waiting to be completed in the disk queue. A high disk queue length is usually indicative of a disk subsystem that is overwhelmed or experiencing technical issues.

Network   The Network area is used to monitor network performance and determine whether the network subsystem is a bottleneck. The two performance indicators monitored are:

- *Total current network traffic*—The current rate of data transfer to and from the network. If this number is close to the theoretical maximum for your network subsystem, the network may be a bottleneck.

- *Network Utilization*—Shows the percentage of the network capacity that is in use.

When you expand the Network summary bar on the Overview, or switch to the Network tab, a list of processes performing network activity is displayed, as shown in Figure 10-5. This displays the following characteristics about processes performing network activity:

- *Image*—The name of the executable file. System is a summary item that represents the operating system kernel and other low-level components, such as device drivers.

- *PID*—The process identifier (PID) is a number assigned to the process by the operating system when it starts. It is used by the operating system to track processes.

- *Address*—The other computer that the process is communicating with. The address can be an IP address or host name.

- *Send*—The current rate at which information is being sent to the remote computer by the process, measured in bytes per second. This helps you identify which application is causing the network bottleneck.

- *Receive*—The current rate at which information is being received from the remote computer by the process, measured in bytes per second. Receiving high rates of information may indicate that the remote computer is causing the network bottleneck, rather than the local computer.

- *Total*—The current rate at which information is being sent to and received from the remote computer by the process, measured in bytes per second.

The Network tab displays additional information about network activity and the endpoints that are generating traffic or are capable of receiving network data. TCP connection details are

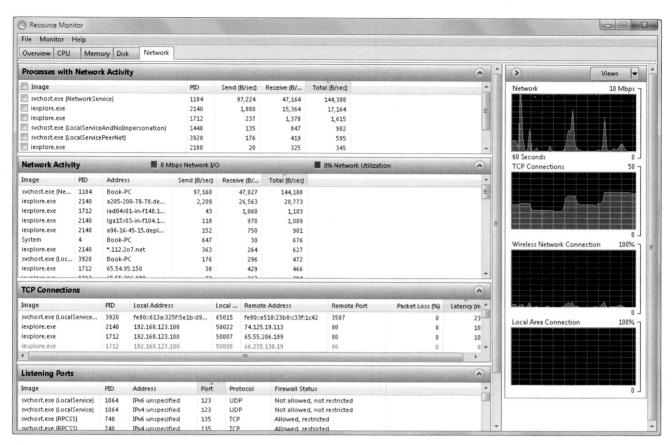

Figure 10-5 Resource Monitor, Network tab
Courtesy Course Technology/Cengage Learning

provided and include statistics about packet loss and latency in milliseconds between a listed local and remote address. Heavy packet losses or high latency is a good sign that the network connection is oversaturated or experiencing faults somewhere between the two addresses.

Listening ports are also shown to reveal which processes are listening for network data. The view provides details that include the listening address, port number, protocol, and firewall settings that apply to that port. If the expected values are not observed, the application or Windows Firewall can be reconfigured to apply correct settings. Any changes to network settings must be done outside of Resource Monitor.

Memory The Memory area is used to monitor memory performance and determine whether the memory subsystem is a bottleneck. The two performance indicators monitored are:

- *Hard Faults*—The number of times per second that a page of information is not present in physical memory and must be retrieved from virtual memory. When this value is high over an extended period of time, memory is often a bottleneck.

- *Used Physical Memory*—The percentage of physical memory that is being used. If the value is at or near 100%, memory is likely a bottleneck. Virtual memory is used by Windows 7 to ensure that physical memory does not completely run out.

When you expand the Memory summary bar on the Overview, or switch to the Memory tab, a list of running processes is displayed, as shown in Figure 10-6. This displays the following characteristics about the memory usage of the processes:

- *Image*—The name of the executable file. System is a summary item that represents the operating system kernel and other low-level components, such as device drivers.

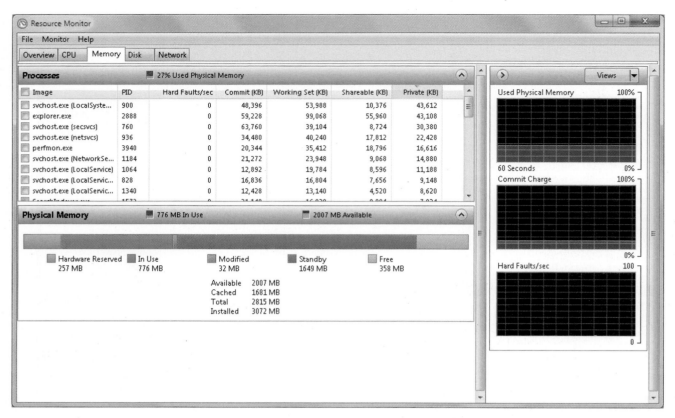

Figure 10-6 Resource Monitor, Memory tab
Courtesy Course Technology/Cengage Learning

- *PID*—The process identifier (PID) is a number assigned to the process by the operating system when it starts. It is used by the operating system to track processes.

- *Hard Faults*—The number of times per second that the process is accessing virtual memory. A large number of hard faults could indicate that an application does not have enough physical memory available for its needs.

- *Commit*—The amount of space, measured in KB, set aside for the process in the paging file. It does not necessarily mean that this amount of the page file is used; it only states what is allocated and available for use. Not all memory used by a process can be moved to the paging file. Consequently, this value is typically less than the working set.

- *Working set*—The physical memory, measured in KB, being used by the process. When a process is not actively executing, this value may fall because part of the working set is moved to the paging file. This value can be used to find which process is causing a memory bottleneck. If the process tries to access virtual memory data that is not in the working set, a hard fault occurs.

- *Shareable*—The physical memory in the working set, measured in KB, which may be shared with other applications. This is determined by the application developer.

- *Private*—The physical memory in the working set, measured in KB, which is dedicated to this specific process and cannot be shared.

The Memory tab displays additional information in a graphical form detailing how portions of memory have been allocated. The quick view can help an administrator get a general awareness of the current memory demands.

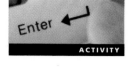

Activity 10-1: Using Resource Monitor

Time Required: 5 minutes

Objective: Use the Resource Monitor tool launched from the Performance Monitor utility.

Description: The Resource Monitor utility launched from Performance Monitor gives you a quick snapshot of what is happening on your system with regard to the CPU, disk, network, and memory. In this activity, you will use Resource Monitor.

1. If necessary, start your computer and log on.
2. Click the **Start** button and click **Control Panel**.
3. Click **System and Security** and click **Administrative Tools**.
4. Double-click **Performance Monitor**.
5. If necessary, click **Performance** in the left-hand navigation pane to display the Overview and System Summary in the right-hand pane.
6. Click the **Open Resource Monitor** link in the Overview of Performance Monitor section.
7. Review the graphs at the right side of the screen for CPU, Disk, Network, and Memory.
8. Expand the **CPU** summary bar and review the listed processes. Read the information about each process. This area provides CPU usage information for each process running on the system.
9. Click the **CPU** column header, so that there is a down arrow in the header. This sorts the processes based on their current CPU utilization.
10. Collapse the **CPU** summary bar and expand the **Disk** summary bar. Read the information about each process. This area provides disk usage information for each process running on the system.
11. Collapse the **Disk** summary bar and expand the **Network** summary bar. Read the information about each process. This area provides network usage information for each process running on the system.
12. Collapse the **Network** summary bar and expand the **Memory** summary bar. Read the information about each process. This area provides memory usage information for each process running on the system.
13. Close Resource Monitor.
14. Close all open windows.

Performance Monitor

Performance Monitor, shown in Figure 10-7, is a tool within the Performance Monitor utility that allows you to visually display the data generated by counters. For each counter that is monitored, you can view the last, average, minimum, and maximum values. These values are based on the total time that the counter has been monitored.

In addition to monitoring current activity, Performance Monitor can also be used to view logged data. In this situation, you automate the logging of data for a specific time period and then view it later. This allows you to compare the performance of different computers and review historical performance data. Performance Monitor can read data from log files and databases. Data is recorded to log files and databases by using data collector sets.

Recording performance data and data collector sets are covered later in this chapter.

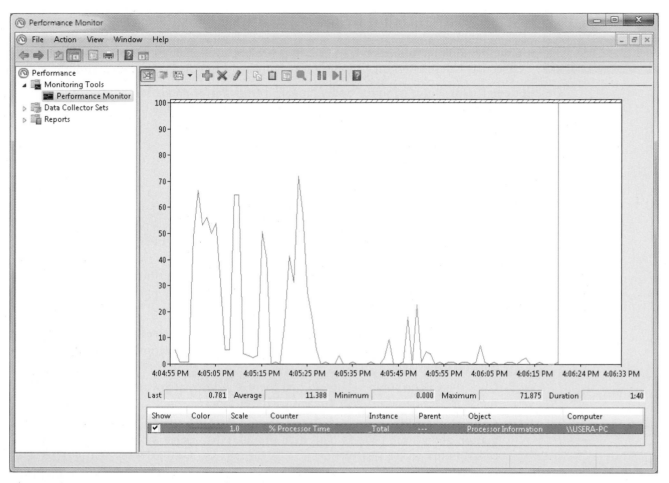

Figure 10-7 Performance Monitor Tool
Courtesy Course Technology/Cengage Learning

Counters Unlike Resource Monitor, Performance Monitor allows you to select the counters you wish to view, as shown in Figure 10-8. This helps you to focus monitoring on a specific operating system element. In some cases, after finding a general problem by using Resource Monitor, you may wish to find more detailed information by using the Performance Monitor counters.

When you add a counter, it can be from the local computer or another computer available over the network. In most cases, you will monitor the local computer. However, some counters should be monitored over the network to prevent monitoring from affecting the validity of the data. For example, if you are logging disk activity, you should monitor it over the network to ensure that the logging process is not creating disk activity that affects your results.

Counters are divided into categories. Sometimes these categories are referred to as performance objects, but that terminology is rarely seen in Windows 7. Counter categories include:

- *Cache*—Counters that monitor the file system cache in memory.

- *IPv4*—Counters that monitor IPv4 data transfer rates and errors.

- *LogicalDisk*—Counters that monitor individual partitions and logical drives on a disk.

- *Memory*—Counters that monitor virtual and physical memory use.

- *Network Interface*—Counters that monitor network card performance.

- *PhysicalDisk*—Counters that monitor the performance of each physical disk, regardless of the partitions and logical drives that are on it.

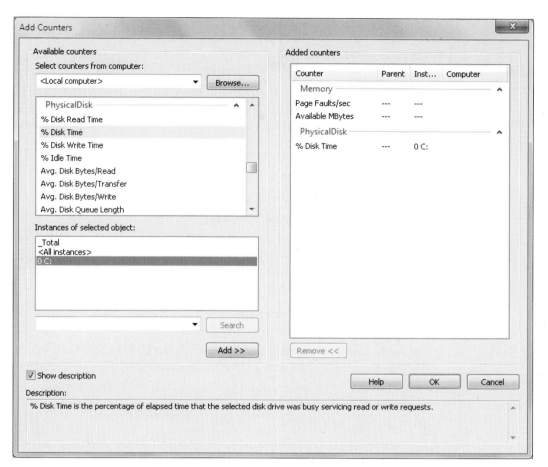

Figure 10-8 Adding a counter
Courtesy Course Technology/Cengage Learning

- *Processor*—Counters that monitor processor activity.

- *System*—Counters that monitor general system statistics that may combine elements from other categories.

For each counter, there may be multiple instances of that counter to choose from. For example, in a computer with multiple processors, each processor is an instance. This allows you to monitor the information about each processor separately. You can also view a combined total for multiple instances.

Chart Types Three different chart types are available for viewing performance data:

- *Line*—Displays a line for each selected counter. Each line is displayed in a different color to help distinguish them. This chart type allows you to visualize performance over time. This is the default chart type.

- *Histogram bar*—Displays a vertical bar for the current value of each performance counter. This chart type shows only the current status of the performance counters and does not help evaluate performance over time. However, summary data for last, average, minimum, and maximum values is displayed.

- *Report*—Displays the current value of each performance counter in decimal format. This is useful when you want to see the exact value of a performance counter rather than compare it to other performance counters. No historical information is shown in this chart type.

Activity 10-2: Using Performance Monitor

Time Required: 10 minutes
Objective: Use Performance Monitor to view counter values.

Description: Performance monitor allows you to view the value of performance counters. You can choose to display the values in several different formats. The counters allow you to monitor system performance. In this activity, you use Performance Monitor to view system activity.

1. If necessary, start your computer and log on.

2. Click the **Start** button and click **Control Panel**.

3. Click **System and Security** and click **Administrative Tools**.

4. Double-click **Performance Monitor**.

5. If necessary, in the left pane, expand **Monitoring Tools** and click **Performance Monitor**. You can see that by default % Processor Time is displayed. The default report type shown is a line chart.

6. In the tool bar, click the **plus** (+) symbol.

7. In the list of Available counters, expand **PhysicalDisk** and click **% Disk Time**. This counter monitors how often the disk is busy.

8. In the Instances of selected object box, click **0 C: F: D: E:**. This selects disk 0 for monitoring. If multiple disks were present in this computer, multiple instances would be listed.

9. Select the **Show description** checkbox to enable it. This displays a description of each counter as you select it.

10. Click the **Add** button.

11. In the list of Available counters, expand **Memory** and click **Available MBytes**. This counter monitors how much physical memory is free for use by processes.

12. Click the **Add** button and click **OK**. Notice that two new lines are added to the graph. The graph is scaled from 0 to 100 but the new counters may provide values outside that range.

13. At the bottom of the screen, click **% Disk Time**. The Last, Average, Minimum, and Maximum values now reflect what has been measured for % Disk Time. Note the average value. A small value here may not register on the scrolling line graph. A scale value will scale the counter values to better fit in the graph range of 0 to 100. The default scale value is 1.

14. Right-click **% Disk Time**, click **Properties**. Select a new color for the counter's displayed line that will be easy to see and differentiate from the other counters. This changes the color of the line in the chart. Click the **Scale** drop-down list and select **10.0** to multiply all counter values for this counter by 10 before displaying them on the line graph. Click **OK** to save your changes. Notice the changes are immediate across the graph.

15. At the bottom of the screen, right-click **Available MBytes** and click **Scale Selected Counters**. This automatically changes the scale used to measure the counter. The line for this counter was previously at the very top of the chart and did not provide useful information.

16. In the tool bar, click the **Change graph type** button. This changes the graphic to a bar chart.

17. Click the **Change graph type** button again. This changes the graph to a report.

18. In the left pane, right-click **Performance Monitor** and click **Properties**. Notice that on the General tab, you can modify the graph sample rate and the time span that is displayed.

19. Click **Cancel** and leave Performance Monitor open for the next activity.

Data Collector Sets

Data Collector Sets organize multiple counters into a single unit. This makes monitoring performance easier to manage in much the same way that assigning users to groups makes system security easier to manage. Windows 7 uses Data Collector Sets extensively to gather performance information, as shown in Figure 10-9.

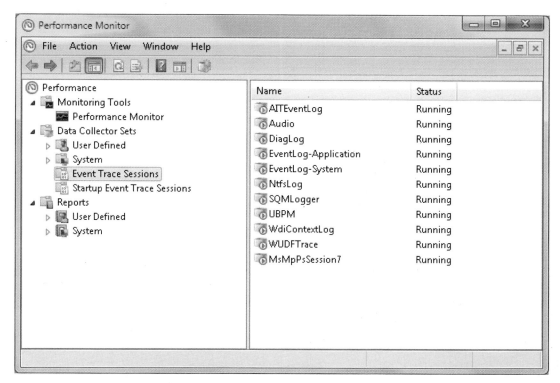

Figure 10-9 Data Collector Sets
Courtesy Course Technology/Cengage Learning

A Data Collector Set can monitor the following type of data:

- *Performance counters*—This records data on a timed basis. The value of selected performance counters is recorded at defined intervals, such as one second.

- *Event trace*—This tracks when system events occur. In this way, real-time information is collected about the system rather than samples. The information collected is based on the selection of an event trace provider. For each provider, you can select which specific events are tracked.

- *Configuration*—This tracks changes to the registry and when they occurred. You can use this to monitor changes made by application installations.

Logging When you configure a Data Collector Set, it is often to log performance information to disk. In fact, for event trace data and configuration data, the changes must be logged to disk. For each Data Collector Set you can specify:

- *Root directory*—The location all log files are stored in. The default location is %systemdrive%\perflogs\Admin*CollectorSetName*.

- *Subdirectory*—A generic subdirectory in the root directory that log files are stored in.

- *Subdirectory name format*—Used in place of a generic subdirectory, this allows you to specify an automatic naming format for the subdirectory where log files are kept. You can use this to separate files into daily logs.

For each data type being monitored, you can specify the filename used within the logging directory. For example, you can specify one filename format for performance counters and another for configuration changes.

Starting and Stopping Data Collector Sets are not always running. If they were, very large log files would be generated and system performance would suffer. You can manually start Data Collector Sets when you are performing troubleshooting or start them with an alert. If you are collecting a baseline, you will want to schedule the Data Collector Set to run at a regular time, as shown in Figure 10-10.

Figure 10-10 Data Collector Set schedule
Courtesy Course Technology/Cengage Learning

Scheduling is very flexible, allowing you to create multiple schedules based on a start date, end date, day of week, and time of day. Multiple schedules are required to start the Data Collector Set more than once per day.

Stopping a data collector set, shown in Figure 10-11, can be configured based on:

- *Overall duration*—This option allows you to specify a time period for running the Data Collector Set. This overrides any options set in Limits if specified. When the overall duration is reached, the option "Stop when all data collectors have finished" allows all the active data collectors to finish writing to the log file before the Data Collector Set is stopped.

- *Restart the data collector set at limits*—This option restarts the data collector set when a limit is reached to create a new log filename. You can use this to ensure that a new log file is started after a certain period of time or at a specific log file size.

- *Duration limit*—This is used to set a time period, after which the data collector set stops.

- *Maximum Size limit*—This is used to set a maximum log file size, after which the data collector set stops.

When the Duration limit and Maximum Size limit are used at the same time, data collection stops when either limit is reached.

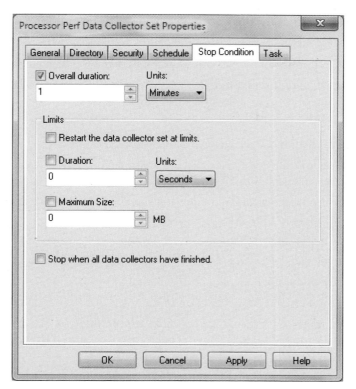

Figure 10-11 Data Collector Set stop conditions
Courtesy Course Technology/Cengage Learning

When a Data Collector Set stops, you can run a task. This can be used to process the log files after data collection is complete. For example, you may have a script that looks for specific event values within the logs. Or you may simply copy logs to a network location for further analysis.

Activity 10-3: Logging Performance Data

Time Required: 10 minutes
Objective: Log performance data by using a Data Collector Set.

Description: Data Collector Sets allow you to group counters for easier manageability. If you want to log performance data, it must be done with a Data Collector Set. In this activity, you create a Data Collector Set and log performance data to disk.

1. In the left pane of Performance Monitor, expand **Data Collector Sets,** and click **System.** You can see that two predefined Data Collector Sets are created by the system to perform common maintenance tasks.

2. In the left pane, click **Event Trace Sessions.** These are trace providers used by the system to collect system performance data.

3. In the left pane, click **User Defined.** When you create new Data Collector Sets, they are placed in this folder.

4. Right-click **User Defined,** point to **New,** and click **Data Collector Set.**

5. In the Name box, type **CPU and Disk logging** and click **Next.** This Data Collector Set will be created from a template.

6. In the Template Data Collector Set box, select each option and read the description.

7. Click **Basic** and click **Next.**

8. Accept the default Root directory and click **Next.**

9. Click **Open properties for this data collector set** and click **Finish**.

10. On the General tab, read which user the Data Collector Set will run as.

11. Click the **Directory** tab. This tab shows you where the log files will be stored.

12. Click the **Stop Condition** tab. Notice that, by default, the Data Collector Set will stop after one minute.

13. Click **OK**.

14. In the left pane, expand **User Defined** and click **CPU and Disk logging**.

15. Right-click **Performance Counter** and click **Properties**. Notice that all processor-related counters are selected by default.

16. Click **Add**, expand **PhysicalDisk**, click **PhysicalDisk**, click **Add**, and click **OK**. This adds all of the counters for the physical disk.

17. Notice that the log format is binary, and click **OK**.

18. In the left pane, click **User Defined**. Notice that CPU and Disk logging is stopped.

19. Right-click **CPU and Disk logging** and click **Start**.

20. Wait one minute for the data collection to complete.

21. In the left pane, click **Performance Monitor** and, in the tool bar, click the **View Log Data** button. Note that by hovering the cursor over each tool bar button the name of the button will be displayed as a tool tip.

22. Under Data source, click **Log files**, click **Add**, double-click the **Admin** folder, double-click **CPU and Disk logging**, double-click the folder with today's date, click **Performance Counter.blg**, and click **Open**.

23. Click **Time Range**. This displays the time range in the log file. You can select just a subset of the time range to view if you desire. The default setting is to display the entire time range.

24. Click the **Data** tab to select the counters to display from the log file, click **Remove** as required to remove any existing counters, and click the **Add** button.

25. Expand PhysicalDisk, click **%Idle Time**, and click **Add**. This adds the total % Idle Time for all physical disks that were logged.

26. Expand Processor, click **% Idle Time**, and click **Add**. This adds the total % Idle Time for all processors that were logged.

27. Click **OK**. Notice that the counters are now listed under Counters.

28. Click **OK** to save the settings and display the data on the Performance Monitor graph. If necessary, change the chart view's graph type to **Line**.

29. Click the **plus** (+) symbol in the tool bar. Notice that only the PhysicalDisk and Processor counters are available because only they were logged.

30. Expand **PhysicalDisk**. Notice that you can select any counter in the category because they were all logged.

31. Click **Cancel** to close the Add Counters window.

32. Leave Performance Monitor open for the next activity.

Alerts   For performance counters, you can configure **alerts** instead of logging to disk. After selecting the performance counter you desire for an alert, you also state a threshold value and configure whether the alert is triggered by going above or below the threshold value. For example, you can trigger an alert when the \Memory\AvailableBytes counter drops below 50 MB.

When an alert triggers, the following can be performed:

- *Log an entry in the application event log*—Placing an event in the application log allows you to search for the event later and incorporate it into your normal system monitoring process.

- *Start a Data Collector Set*—If you have an ongoing problem that you are trying to monitor, you can start a Data Collector Set when the alert is triggered. For example, if disk utilization is high, you can start a collector set with various counters that help you find the source of the problem.

- *Run a scheduled task*—Running a task can start any program. In most cases, you will want to run a batch file or VBscript. For example, if the print queue has too many jobs in it, you may want to restart the spooler service with a batch file because printing may be stalled. You could also run a script that sends the administrator an e-mail.

Activity 10-4: Creating an Alert

Time Required: 10 minutes
Objective: Create and trigger an alert.

Description: Alerts are used to notify you of system events or to start logging for further analysis. In this activity, you create an alert that starts logging when the Disk Activity is high.

1. In the left pane of Performance Monitor, click **User Defined**.
2. Right-click **User Defined**, point to **New**, and click **Data Collector Set**.
3. In the Name box, type **Trigger CPU and Disk logging**, click **Create manually**, and click **Next**.
4. Click **Performance Counter Alert** and click **Next**.
5. Click **Add**, expand **PhysicalDisk**, click **%Disk Time**, click **Add**, and click **OK**.
6. If necessary, in the Alert when box, click **Above**.
7. In the Limit box, type **50** and click **Next**. This alert will be triggered when % Disk Time is above 50%.
8. Click **Open properties for this data collector set** and click **Finish**.
9. Click the **Schedule** tab and click **Add**. The default schedule runs every day.
10. Click **OK** to add the schedule.
11. Click the **Stop Condition** tab. Notice that the duration is not limited.
12. Click **OK**.
13. In the left pane, click **Trigger CPU and Disk logging**, then right-click **DataCollector01** and click **Properties**.
14. If necessary, on the Alerts tab, in the Limit box, type **50**. Sometimes the value entered during the initial creation is not properly saved.
15. Click the **Alert Action** tab.
16. In the Start a data collector set box, click **CPU and Disk logging** and click **OK**.
17. Leave Performance Monitor open for the next activity.

Data Manager Data Manager, shown in Figure 10-12, allows you to automatically control the log files and reports that can be generated by Data Collector Sets. You can apply a policy and specify actions.

Using Data Manager, you can specify the following:

- *Minimum free disk space*—If the specified disk space is not free, the resource policy to remove log files is applied.

- *Maximum folders*—If the maximum number of folders is reached, the resource policy is applied to prevent having too many folders.

- *Resource policy*—Allows you to specify whether the oldest files or largest files are deleted to meet the minimum free disk and maximum folders requirements.

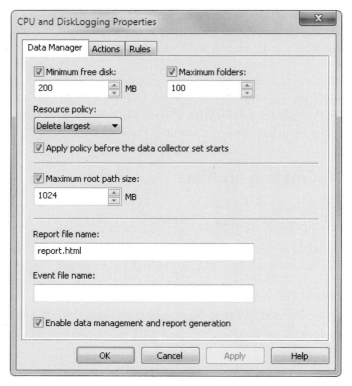

Figure 10-12 Data Collector Set Data Manager
Courtesy Course Technology/Cengage Learning

- *Maximum root path size*—If the root path for the Data Collector set is over this size, the resource policy is applied.
- *Enable data management and report generation*—When this option is enabled, the Data Manager settings are applied to manage log files and generate reports.

The Actions tab allows you to apply specific actions to log files that are a certain age or folders that are a specific size. You can apply the following actions:

- *Create cab file*—This compresses log files into a cab file to reduce disk space utilization.
- *Delete data files*—This deletes log files, often done at the same time as cab files are created.
- *Delete cab file*—This deletes cab files, typically after a certain period of time.
- *Delete report*—This deletes reports, typically after a certain period of time.

Activity 10-5: Using Data Manager

Time Required: 5 minutes
Objective: Use Data Manager to manage log file deletion.

Description: Data Manager allows you to automatically remove log files after a certain period of time or when a certain amount of disk space is used. In this activity, you configure data manager settings for the CPU and Disk logging Data Collector Set.

1. In the left pane, right-click **CPU and Disk logging** and click **Data Manager**.
2. In the Minimum free disk box, type **2000**. This ensures that log files do not result in less than 2GB of free disk space.
3. In the Resource policy box, click **Delete oldest**. This configures Data Manager to delete the oldest files first when required.

4. Click the **Actions** tab. Review the actions that are listed.

5. Click the first action and click **Edit**. This action compresses the log files into a cab file after four weeks and deletes the original log files.

6. Click **Cancel**.

7. Click the second action and click **Edit**. This action deletes the cab files after eight weeks.

8. Click **Cancel**.

9. Click the third action and click **Edit**. This action deletes all log files, cab files, and report files after 24 weeks.

10. Click **Cancel**.

11. Click **OK** to save the changes to CPU and Disk logging Properties.

12. Leave Performance Monitor open for the next activity.

Reports

Reports, shown in Figure 10-13, are used to process log file data and display it in a meaningful way. To process the data in the log files, you specify rules. A rule is an XML file that contains instructions specifying how the data is to be processed. You add rules for report processing in the properties of the Data Collector Set.

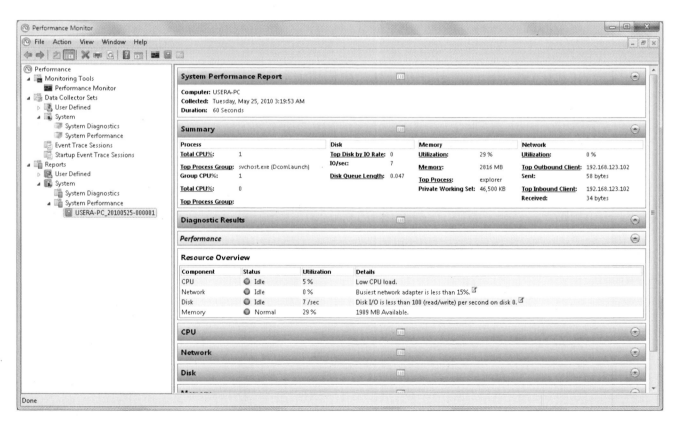

Figure 10-13 Performance Monitor Reports
Courtesy Course Technology/Cengage Learning

In theory, you could create your own rules for processing log files, but most administrators will never need to do so. Windows 7 includes the rules you are likely to need.

To generate reports covering a specific time frame, you may wish to combine smaller logs into a single large log or break a large log into multiple smaller logs. This can be done with the relog command.

Activity 10-6: Viewing Reports

Time Required: 10 minutes

Objective: View a Report generated by Performance Monitor.

Description: Performance Monitor can generate reports from log files. To do this, XML-based rules files are applied to the log data. Several system reports are available. In this activity, you view an existing system report.

1. In the left pane of Performance Monitor, under Data Collector Sets, click **System**.
2. Right-click **System Performance** and click **Start**.
3. Wait approximately one minute for System Performance to complete.
4. Right-click **System Performance** and click **Latest Report** in the pop-up menu. The left-hand navigation pane will change focus to highlight the most recent report and the report's details will be opened in the right-hand pane.
5. Review the information available in the report. Locate the Performance section and confirm that all resource components listed in the Resource Overview section have a green indicator in the Status column. If not, compare each component's status with the comments in the matching row of the Details column.
6. Close Performance Monitor and close all other open windows.

Task Manager

Task Manager, shown in Figure 10-14, provides an overview of the current state of a computer. The information provided by Task Manager is less detailed than the information found in Performance Monitor and Resource Monitor.

Figure 10-14 Task Manager
Courtesy Course Technology/Cengage Learning

You can access Task Manager several ways:

- Press **Ctrl+Alt+Del**.
- Press **Ctrl+Shift+Esc**.
- Right-click an empty area of the taskbar and select **Start Task Manager**.
- Run **taskmgr.exe** from a command prompt.

Applications

The Applications tab in Task Manager shows all user applications running on the computer. For example, the applications Administrative Tools and Performance Monitor appear in the list of active tasks in Figure 10-14 because they are actively running on that computer. The status of applications listed here will be Running or Not Responding. The Not Responding status is generated if the application has not responded to operating system requests for a period of time. However, in some cases the application will recover even when the status is listed as Not Responding. If you are concerned about data loss, you should let applications that are listed as Not Responding have additional time to recover before ending the program.

You can also view the process that corresponds with an application to find out more detailed information. To do so, right-click the task and click **Go To Process**.

Processes

The Processes tab, shown in Figure 10-15, shows the processes running on this computer. By default, only processes started by the current user are displayed. However, when you show processes from all users, all processes are displayed, including operating system processes and services.

10

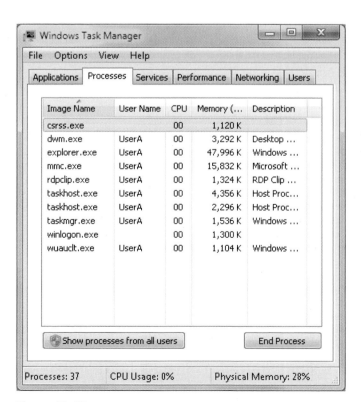

Figure 10-15 Task Manager, Processes tab
Courtesy Course Technology/Cengage Learning

For each process, you can see:

- *Image Name*—The process executable file.
- *User Name*—The user that started the process.
- *CPU*—The percentage CPU utilization of the process.
- *Memory*—The memory used exclusively by the process.
- *Description*—A brief description of the process, if available.

You can optimize the view of processes by adding additional columns and sorting based on column information. For example, if you want to find the process that is writing the data to disk, you can add the I/O Write Bytes column and then sort based on that column. Columns are added from the View menu.

For each process, you have the option to set the priority of the process. In some cases, you may be able to boost the performance of a particular application by raising the priority of the application. However, this is not recommended because raising the priority of one application can be detrimental to other applications.

You can also end a specific process or process tree. Ending a process tree stops the process and all other processes that were started by the process. Ending just the process allows other processes started by the process to continue running.

On a system with multiple CPUs or a multiple core CPU, it is possible to set processor affinity for a process. Setting processor affinity assigns a process to a particular processor. In the vast majority of situations, system performance will be better if you do not set processor affinity for a process. When processor affinity is not set, Windows 7 optimizes system performance automatically by moving processes between processors as required.

Services

The Services tab, shown in Figure 10-16, provides a list of the services running on Windows 7. The information here is approximately the same as the information found in the service portion

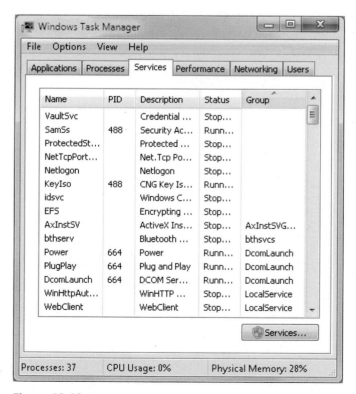

Figure 10-16 Task Manager, Services tab
Courtesy Course Technology/Cengage Learning

of Computer Management. From this tab, you can also locate the process associated with a particular service and can start and stop services.

Information displayed on this tab includes:

- *Name*—The name of the service.
- *PID*—The process identifier of the service.
- *Description*—A description of the service.
- *Status*—Displays whether the service is running or stopped.
- *Group*—Displays the group name that a service has been associated with, if applicable.

Performance

The Performance tab, shown in Figure 10-17, provides a quick overview of system performance for memory and processor utilization. The current CPU usage is shown as a bar chart, and recent CPU usage history is shown as a line graph. Also, the current physical memory usage for processes is shown as a bar chart; recent physical memory usage for processes is shown as a line graph. A button is also available to launch Resource Monitor from this tab as a convenience.

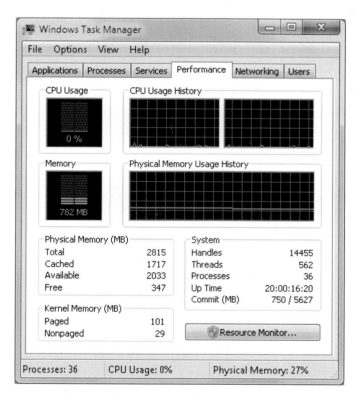

Figure 10-17 Task Manager, Performance tab
Courtesy Course Technology/Cengage Learning

The Physical Memory area displays:

- *Total*—The total amount of physical memory in the system.
- *Cached*—The amount of physical memory used to speed up file access by caching files. This value is reduced when other applications require physical memory.
- *Free*—The amount of physical memory that is not assigned for any purpose at the time.

The Kernel Memory area displays:

- *Total*—The total amount of memory used by the Windows 7 kernel. This includes physical memory and space in the paging file. The total of paged and nonpaged memory may not add up exactly to the total displayed due to rounding errors.
- *Paged*—The amount of space used by the Windows 7 kernel in the paging file.
- *Nonpaged*—The amount of physical memory that can never be swapped to the paging file by the Windows 7 kernel.

The System area displays:

- *Handles*—Internal identifiers used by processes to track system objects.
- *Threads*—The total number of threads running. Each process can have multiple threads running to perform tasks.
- *Processes*—The total number of processes running.
- *Up Time*—The amount of time since Windows 7 has started.
- *Commit (MB)*—This displays the total amount of virtual memory available and used. Virtual memory is the total of physical memory and the paging file.

Other Tabs

The Networking tab shows a line graph of recent network utilization for each network connection. This allows you to quickly see whether the network is a bottleneck when attempting a task. You can also see a summary of information for each network connection.

The Users tab has a list of users that are currently logged on to the system. If multiple users share a computer and use fast user switching to stay logged on, the users will appear in this list. If the user is accessing Windows 7 remotely by using Remote Desktop, the name of the remote computer will appear in the Client Name column. If required, you can disconnect and logoff users or send them a message.

Activity 10-7: Using Task Manager

Time Required: 10 minutes
Objective: Use Task Manager to view system information.

Description: The primary purpose of Task Manager is to provide a quick overview of system and process performance information. In this activity, you view system information and manage processes by using Task Manager.

1. If necessary, start your computer and log on.
2. Click the **Start** button, type **cmd**, and press **Enter**.
3. In the command prompt window, type **mspaint** and press **Enter**.
4. Right-click the taskbar and click **Start Task Manager**.
5. If necessary, click the **Applications** tab. You can see that both the command prompt and Paint are listed here. The status of both applications is "running".
6. Right-click **C:\Windows\System32\cmd.exe** and click **Go To Process**. This switches to the Processes tab, with the command prompt process selected.
7. Right-click **cmd.exe** and click **End Process Tree**.
8. Read the warning and click **End process tree**. This closes both the command prompt and Paint because Paint was started by the command prompt.
9. Click **Show processes from all users**. Now all processes on the system are displayed, instead of just the processes started by you.

10. Click the **CPU** column header once. This sorts the processes by CPU utilization. A down arrow indicates that the processes are sorted in descending order with the highest CPU utilization at the top of the list.

11. Click the **Services** tab. This tab displays the status of services running on the computer.

12. Click the **Performance** tab. This tab provides some basic CPU and memory utilization information.

13. Click the **Networking** tab. This tab displays an overview of network utilization and status.

14. Click the **Users** tab. This tab displays a list of all users that are logged on. Multiple users can be logged on at the same time when fast user switching is used.

15. Close Task Manager.

Performance Ranking

Windows 7 includes the **Windows Experience Index,** shown in Figure 10-18, to provide an objective measure of system performance. You can use the Windows Experience Index to decide which computer you want to buy. Depending on the rating of your computer certain Windows 7 features and software packages are recommended.

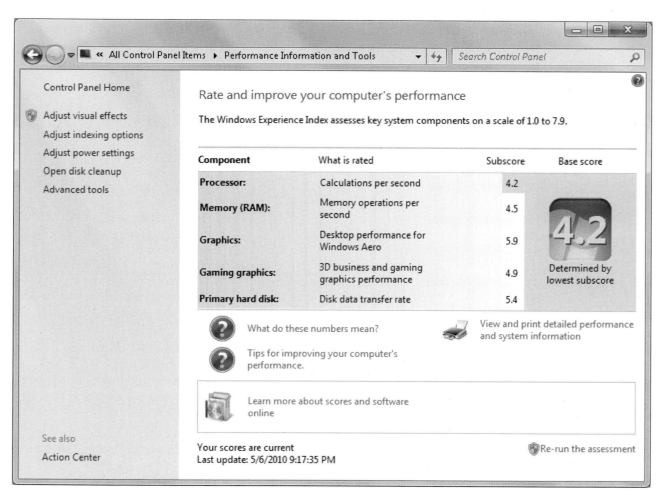

Figure 10-18 Performance Information and Tools, Windows Experience Index
Courtesy Course Technology/Cengage Learning

When evaluating your system, Windows 7 ranks five elements:

- *Processor*—The calculations per second that the processor can perform.
- *Memory (RAM)*—The memory operations per second that the system can perform.
- *Graphics*—The ability to run the Windows Aero interface.
- *Gaming graphics*—The ability to run games and 3D business applications.
- *Primary hard disk*—The data transfer rate of the C drive.

The individual **subscores** are used to create a **base score**. The base score is the primary number of concern; this is the overall ranking of your system. The ranking is from 1 to 7.9, with 7.9 being the best possible. As hardware speeds improve, higher base scores will be introduced.

The base score is not simply an average of the subscores. The base score is determined by the lowest subscore. For example, if a computer has poor graphics performance, the base score will be poor, no matter how good the other subscores are. The score for each area will help determine which areas of the computer should be considered for performance upgrades if possible.

General performance guidelines for base scores are:

- *Base score of 1 or 2*—The computer is generally able to access the Internet and run general business applications. However, the computer is generally not able to run the Windows Aero interface or advanced multimedia.
- *Base score of 3*—The computer is able to use most new features in Windows 7. However, advanced features may be limited. For example, running multimedia content may be limited in resolution.
- *Base score of 4 or above*—The computer can use all of the new Windows 7 features, including all multimedia features.

If you are not satisfied with the base score of your computer, use the subscores to identify areas to improve. In most cases, graphics performance is the cause of a low base score.

Activity 10-8: Performance Ranking

Time Required: 5 minutes
Objective: View the performance ranking for your computer.

Description: Windows 7 includes performance ranking information to ensure you have realistic expectations about which software can run on your computer. In this activity, you view the performance ranking of your computer and view software that is suitable to run on your computer. If you are running Windows 7 in a virtualized environment, you may not be able to obtain a performance rating.

1. If necessary, start your computer and log on.
2. Click the **Start** button and click **Control Panel**.
3. Click **System and Security** and, under **System**, click **Check the Windows Experience Index**. This screen displays the performance rating of your computer. This includes the base score and subscores.
4. Click **Rerun the assessment**. This recalculates your performance rating to ensure that it accurately reflects your current configuration. This may take several minutes. Note the final performance rating.
5. Close all open windows.

Performance Options

Windows 7 includes the Performance Options dialog box, shown in Figure 10-19, to optimize visual effects, processor scheduling, and virtual memory. You can access the Performance Options dialog box by clicking the **Adjust visual effects** task in the *Check the Windows Experience Index* Control Panel applet. The Visual Effects tab allows you to configure a wide variety of settings that improve how the Windows 7 interface performs.

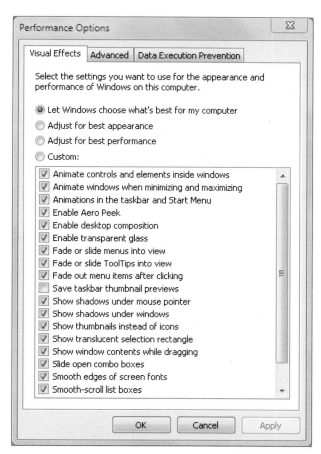

Figure 10-19 Performance Options, Visual Effects tab
Courtesy Course Technology/Cengage Learning

The Visual Effects tab has the following options:

- *Let Windows choose what's best for my computer*—When this option is selected, individual settings are enabled or disabled based on the performance of your computer. In most cases, even minimal hardware can use most of the settings.

- *Adjust for best appearance*—When this option is selected, all settings are enabled.

- *Adjust for best performance*—When this option is selected, all settings are disabled.

- *Custom*—When this option is selected, you can enable or disable specific settings.

The Advanced tab lets you select whether processor time is allocated to optimize performance for programs or background services. If Programs is selected, the program running in the active window is given a slightly higher priority than other applications. This ensures that the program you are using is the most responsive on the system. If you select Background services, all programs are given the same priority.

Virtual Memory

The Advanced tab also gives you access to the setting for **virtual memory**, shown in Figure 10-20. By default, the paging file is managed automatically by Windows. When Windows manages the paging file, the minimum size is 16 MB and the maximum size is configured as 300% of RAM. As more of the paging file is required, it is expanded from the minimum size to the maximum size.

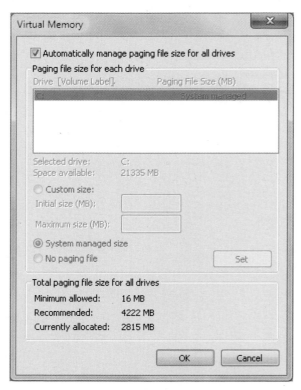

Figure 10-20 Virtual Memory settings
Courtesy Course Technology/Cengage Learning

You can manually configure the paging file if you prefer. This allows you to optimize the placement of the paging file. Moving the paging file to its own hard disk will optimize system performance because there will be less contention for disk resources when accessing the paging file. Alternatively, you can spread the paging file over multiple disks to speed access to the file.

Most Windows 7 computers have only a single hard disk, and increasing performance is not possible by adjusting the virtual memory settings. However, you may want to move the paging file to a different partition to free space on the C: drive if it is almost full.

It is also possible to specify that no paging file is to be used. However, this is not recommended as performance will suffer. Even when systems have sufficient physical memory to hold all active processes and their data, system performance suffers when the paging file is disabled.

Moving the paging file to its own partition on the same disk or multiple partitions on the same disk has no performance benefit.

Data Execution Prevention

Data Execution Prevention (DEP) is a processor feature that Windows 7 is capable of using. DEP monitors processes to ensure that they do not access unauthorized memory spaces, which is done by various types of malware, such as viruses, to take control of systems. If your processor does not support DEP, there are some software-based DEP features that can be performed by Windows 7. The tab for configuring DEP is shown in Figure 10-21.

Despite the value of DEP in preventing malware, there is a performance cost. By default, DEP is enabled for only essential Windows programs and services. This protects the core components of the operating system that are likely to be targeted by malware and preserves system performance. You can enable DEP for all programs and services (and specify exceptions), but this has a significant impact and is not recommended.

Figure 10-21 Data Execution Prevention settings
Courtesy Course Technology/Cengage Learning

Chapter Summary

- Windows 7 is a higher performing operating system than previous versions of Windows. Some features that increase performance are: Windows SuperFetch, low-priority I/O, Windows ReadyBoost, Windows ReadyDrive, and automatic disk defragmentation.

- Establishing a baseline for performance tuning allows you to recognize variations from normal system behavior and identify system bottlenecks. The four main areas that cause bottlenecks are disk, memory, processor, and network.

- Performance Monitor can be used to monitor system performance, monitor system reliability, create alerts, log performance activity, and generate reports.

- Data Collector Sets are used to control the logging of performance data and create alerts. You can schedule when Data Collector Sets are active. Data Manager is used to automatically manage the logs after creation.

- Task Manager allows you to quickly view system process information. Process information includes memory utilization and processor utilization. In addition, you can monitor network utilization.

- The performance rankings generated in the Windows Experience Index ensures that you understand the capabilities of your computer. The subscores also highlight areas for improvement.

- The Performance Options allow you to configure visual effects, processor performance, virtual memory, and Data Execution Prevention. In most cases, the default configuration for these settings is acceptable.

Key Terms

alert   An event that is triggered when a count value is above or below the specified threshold value.

baseline   A set of performance indicators gathered when system performance is acceptable.

base score   The overall rating of your computer generated from the subscores.

bottleneck   The component in a process that prevents the overall process from completing faster.

counters   The performance indicators that can be recorded in Performance Monitor.

Data Collector Set   A grouping of counters that you can use to log system data and generate reports.

Data Execution Prevention (DEP)   A primarily processor hardware-based system to prevent the installation of malware by accessing unauthorized memory spaces.

Data Manager   The component that is used to automatically manage performance logs.

Performance Monitor   A tool within Performance Monitor that allows you to visually display the data generated by counters.

performance tuning   The process for collecting system performance data, analyzing system performance data, and implementing system performance improvements.

Reports   Reports created in Performance Monitor that use XML-based rules to analyze logged data and display meaningful results.

Resource Monitor   A utility launched from Performance Monitor that provides real-time monitoring of the most common system performance indicators.

subscores   The rating of individual subsystems in your computer.

Task Manager   A utility that allows you to view overall system information and manipulate processes.

virtual memory   The combination of physical memory and the paging file.

Windows Experience Index   Scores that help you determine which applications your computer can run.

Review Questions

1. Performance Monitoring is the act of changing a system's configuration systematically and carefully observing performance before and after such changes. True or False?

2. Which of the following can Task Manager monitor? (Choose all that apply.)

   a. system CPU utilization

   b. application CPU utilization

     c.   user CPU utilization

     d.   process CPU utilization

3.   Which of the following can be used to start Task Manager? (Choose all that apply.)

     a.   Ctrl+Alt+Delete

     b.   running taskman.exe

     c.   Ctrl+Shift+Esc

     d.   running tskmgr.exe

4.   In Performance Monitor, all performance objects have the same counters. True or False?

5.   Which Performance Monitor component records log files?

     a.   Performance Monitor

     b.   Reliability Monitor

     c.   Data Collection Sets

     d.   Alerts

     e.   Reports

6.   Which Performance Monitor component analyzes logs by using XML-based rule files?

     a.   Performance Monitor

     b.   Reliability Monitor

     c.   Data Collection Sets

     d.   Alerts

     e.   Reports

7.   Each Data Collector Set can contain only a single counter. True or False?

8.   What is the most common physical symptom of insufficient memory?

     a.   excessive heat coming from the computer

     b.   graphics displayed incorrectly on the monitor

     c.   a memory error code displayed on the screen

     d.   high levels of disk activity

     e.   three short beeps from the computer

9.   Which system component is most likely to result in a poor base score for your computer?

     a.   memory

     b.   disk

     c.   CPU

     d.   video

     e.   network

10.   When a component is the slowest part of a process, it is referred to as a ___.

11.   Which actions or tasks can alerts be configured to perform? (Choose all that apply.)

     a.   Write an event to the System log

     b.   Start a Data Collector Set

     c.   Send a message to the administrator

     d.   Run a script or batch file

     e.   Restart a service

10

12. In Resource Monitor, you can stop running processes. True or False?

13. In Task Manager, you can change the priority of running processes. True or False?

14. Which memory statistic column in Resource Monitor indicates the amount of physical memory being used by a process?

    a. Commit

    b. Working set

    c. Sharable

    d. Private

15. Which Performance Monitor component is used to view performance logs?

    a. Performance Monitor

    b. Reliability Monitor

    c. Data Collection Sets

    d. Alerts

    e. Reports

16. Which chart type would you select in Performance Monitor to view data over time?

    a. pie

    b. line

    c. histogram

    d. report

17. Which command-line command will start Performance Monitor?

    a. relog

    b. taskmgr

    c. perfmon

    d. none of the above

18. In Resource Monitor, you can restart services that are currently running. True or False?

19. A network administrator has reported that your computer is generating a lot of Internet bound network traffic. You are suspicious that your machine is infected with a virus and it is responsible for the extra network traffic. You would like to quickly check your network traffic activity, the TCP connections your computer has open, and the ports your computer is listening on. The utility you can use to report this information is?

    a. Task Manager

    b. Performance Monitor

    c. Network and Sharing Center

    d. Resource Monitor

    e. netstat -a

20. Which of the following improve system performance? (Choose all that apply.)

    a. disabling virtual memory

    b. reducing the visual effects used

    c. adding an additional network card

    d. enabling Data Execution Prevention for all processes

    e. setting processor affinity for applications

Case Projects

Case 10-1: Collecting Performance Data

Gigantic Life Insurance has several batch jobs that run on Windows 7 computers overnight. The batch jobs are scheduled overnight because they require all the performance capability of the computers and must be completed by morning for staff to perform their regular work. The batch jobs always use approximately the same amount of data, but occasionally, they are not finished in the morning, resulting in lost productivity. Describe how you would determine the cause of the slow processing.

Case 10-2: Upgrading System Performance

Superduper Lightspeed Computers has been selling a large number of Windows 7 upgrade copies to retail customers. After installation, many customers find the performance of their computers is unsatisfactory. In particular, many of them are disappointed that they cannot run the Windows Aero interface. How would you determine the source of the performance problem?

10

chapter 11

Application Support

After reading this chapter and completing the exercises, you will be able to:

- Describe application architecture terminology relevant to Windows 7

- Decribe supported application environments

- Describe the Window 7 Registry and know how to manipulate it when necessary

- Understand file and registry virtualization in conjunction with User Account Control

- Know how to use the Run As Administrator feature for applications

- Understand how Windows 7 provides tweaked compatibility settings to run older applications

- Describe application compatibility research tools provided by Microsoft

- Describe application control policies that restrict which applications are allowed to run

Windows 7 is designed to be highly compatible with applications written for older Windows operating systems. However, features designed to increase security and reliability as well as new innovations in Windows 7 may prevent some older applications from functioning properly. The impact of incompatible features is minimized wherever possible to allow those older applications to run. Applications written for Windows 7 can use the newest operating system features to offer a next-generation software platform for home users and the enterprise.

Application Architecture

The **application architecture** of Windows 7 has evolved from the traditional Windows NT model. The Windows 7 operating system is designed to operate in a layered approach, where different layers provide targeted functionality. The conceptual layers add complexity, but they also allow a controlled and secure flow when processing actions requested by multiple running applications.

The Windows 7 operating system consists of two key components, the **environment subsystems** and the **Executive Services** (see Figure 11-1). The core software of Windows 7 had been revised to provide these services in a manner that is faster and more focused and that uses less convoluted code. Much of the legacy code and dependencies that persisted from one version of Windows to the next has been removed or optimized to make Windows 7 one of the best performing versions of Windows.

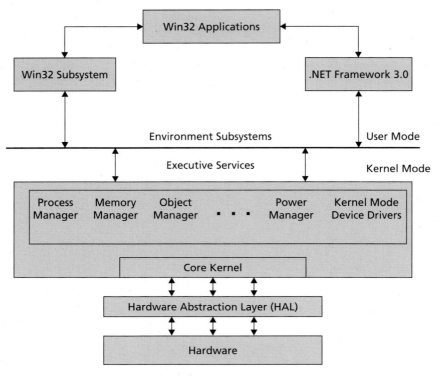

Figure 11-1 Windows Application Architecture model
Courtesy Course Technology/Cengage Learning

Executive Services provide the core operating system functionality that supports executing applications. Executive Services are made up of multiple modules, such as the core **kernel**, object manager, memory manager, and several others. Executive Services interact with each other and the computer hardware directly. Many of the services are designed to be aware of the type of computer hardware they are running on because they need to know how to work with the type of processor, memory, and disks technology present. Much of the hardware-specific knowledge is contained in the **Hardware Abstraction Layer (HAL)** service, which is specifically installed during installation of the operating system. Because the Executive Services are critical to the operation of the computer, applications are not allowed to communicate directly with it. That is the purpose of the environment subsystems.

 Using imaging to deploy previous versions of Windows across multiple hardware types (processors and motherboards) could cause compatibility problems due to the different HAL required by the varying hardware types. Windows 7 is HAL independent and can move properly from one type of hardware to another.

Environment subsystems support applications and provide indirect access to Executive Services in the Windows 7 operating system kernel. An application's view of the operating system is restricted to those methods and services exposed by the different environment subsystems.

The Executive Services operate in **kernel mode**, which allows these services full access to memory and hardware devices. This allows the kernel to configure and control hardware devices starting from the initial boot process on startup of the computer.

The environment subsystems and the applications run in **user mode**, which restricts access to memory and hardware. User mode applications and systems are assigned a specific virtual memory space to run their code and store data. Attempts to access other memory spaces are not allowed. Direct access to hardware devices is completely blocked in user mode.

 The kernel and user modes are operational modes of the computer's processor and are reviewed in Chapter 1.

The important consideration of kernel and user modes with respect to the Executive Services and environment subsystems is what happens when something goes wrong. If a program performs an operation that crashes its environment in user mode, its virtual memory space can be destroyed without affecting other systems running on the computer. If the same crash happens to a program running in kernel mode, the entire Executive Services space can crash and halt the entire operating system. The environment subsystems work together with the Executive Services to support running applications. None of the user's applications will have direct access to a service or resource that can crash the kernel of the operating system.

Supported Application Environments

Applications are written by developers to interact with a specific environment subsystem. Requests for system actions that must be performed by the Executive Services are moderated by the environment subsystems. The primary application types and special considerations to know are:

- Win32 Applications
- Net Applications
- DOS Applications
- Win16 Applications
- x64 Application Considerations

Win32 Applications

Applications designed to interact with the Win32 subsystem were the most common type of application in use with earlier operating systems, such as Windows XP. As new subsystems, such as .NET Framework, become more popular with developers the percentage of applications that use Win32 will drop.

Each Win32 application runs in its own virtual memory space and is executed by the processor in user mode. If the Win32 application crashes, it will not affect other Win32 applications or the operating system's kernel Executive Services. The number 32 refers to the binary size of the processor instructions in the applications code—32 bits.

Activity 11-1: Running Multiple Win32 Applications

Time Required: 10 minutes

Objective: Run two Win32 applications and review how they appear in Task Manager.

Description: In this activity, you will launch multiple Win32 applications to confirm how they are individually presented on the Processes tab in Task Manager.

1. If necessary, start your computer and log on.
2. Click the **Start** button, point to **All Programs**, click **Accessories**, and click **Notepad**.
3. Click the **Start** button, point to **All Programs**, click **Accessories**, and click **Paint**.
4. Confirm that Notepad and Paint are running as applications on the desktop.
5. Press **Ctrl-Shift-Esc** on the keyboard to open Task Manager.
6. If necessary, click the **Applications** tab in Task Manager and confirm that Notepad and Paint are listed as running applications.
7. Right-click the **Notepad** entry on the Applications tab in Task Manager, and click **Go To Process** from the pop-up menu.
8. Confirm that the open tab has switched to the **Processes** tab in Task Manager and that the **notepad.exe** process is highlighted.
9. Scroll through the Processes list in Task Manager and confirm that **mspaint.exe** is also listed as a running process.
10. Note that both applications are represented by two separate running processes, in this case two distinct Win32 applications.
11. Close Notepad, MS Paint, and Task Manager.

.NET Applications

The .NET Framework is the preferred method for applications to access operating system services. The .NET Framework provides a layer of abstraction that is useful for developers to perform complex tasks more simply because the .NET Framework manages the details of accessing required services.

Developers should create new applications by using the .NET Framework not only to simplify development, but also to ensure compatibility with future operating systems. Future versions of Windows may not support Win32 applications. However, the .NET Framework is likely to be supported and will continue to evolve. Using the .NET Framework 3.0 isolates applications from any changes to the Win32 subsystem.

DOS Applications

The 32-bit versions of Windows 7 support the execution of legacy DOS applications. A special Win32 process called ntvdm.exe is part of the operating system. When a legacy DOS application runs, ntvdm.exe is started to create a **Virtual DOS Machine (VDM)** environment for the DOS application. To the DOS application, it appears that it is running on a DOS computer. Access to computer hardware is virtualized through ntvdm.exe and the Win32 subsystem. A new instance of ntvdm.exe is created for each DOS application that is executed to ensure that the DOS applications do not interfere with each other. DOS was not designed as a multitasking operating system, so this is the preferred behavior.

It is common to find that DOS applications running on Windows 7 cannot run in full-screen mode. This is due to the fact that Windows 7 video drivers use a newer format that typically does not implement the video mode that DOS full-screen applications require. Users often expect such programs to work, as they did in Windows XP and Vista, after upgrading to Windows 7 and subsequently complain when these DOS programs do not run in full-screen mode. While it may be possible to downgrade the video diver on the computer to an older Windows XP version, there is no guarantee. The choice of video driver will be restricted by the computer hardware and the vendor's support for this atypical configuration on Windows 7.

Activity 11-2: Running DOS Applications

Time Required: 10 minutes

Objective: Run a DOS-based application and confirm each one is processed by ntvdm.exe.

Description: In this activity, you will launch multiple DOS applications to confirm how they are individually presented on the Processes tab in Task Manager. This activity is possible only when using the 32-bit version of Windows 7. The 64-bit version of Windows 7 does not run 16-bit applications.

1. If necessary, start your computer and logon.
2. Click the **Start** button, point to **All Programs**, click **Accessories**, and click **Run**.
3. In the Run dialog box enter the command **EDIT.COM** and click **OK**.
4. Confirm that a DOS window opens and starts the Microsoft text editor.
5. Press **Ctrl-Shift-Esc** on the keyboard to open Task Manager.
6. Click the **Applications** tab in Task Manager and confirm that EDIT.COM is listed as a running application.
7. Right-click the **EDIT.COM** entry on the Applications tab in Task Manager, and select **Go To Process** from the pop-up menu.
8. Confirm that the open tab has switched to the **Processes** tab in Task Manager and that the ntvdm.exe process is currently highlighted.
9. Minimize the Task Manager window.
10. Click the **Start** button, point to **All Programs**, click **Accessories**, and click **Run**.
11. In the Run dialog box, if necessary, type the command **EDIT.COM** and click **OK**.
12. Confirm that a second DOS window opens and starts the Microsoft text editor.
13. Restore the Task Manager window.
14. Confirm that there are now two instances of NTVDM.EXE running on the Processes tab in Task Manager, one for each running copy of EDIT.COM.
15. Close both windows that are running EDIT.COM.
16. Confirm that there are now no instances of NTVDM.EXE running on the Processes tab in Task Manager.
17. Close the Task Manager window.

Win16 Applications

The 32-bit version of Windows 7 supports the execution of legacy **Win16** applications that were originally designed to run with Windows 3.x. By default, a single Virtual DOS Machine is created to run all Win16 applications. This Win16 VDM is an instance of ntvdm.exe combined with Windows 3.x core operating system files and an application shim called wowexec.exe. Wowexec.exe is a part of the Windows 7 operating system and supports Win16-on-Win32 execution.

The 16-bit Windows applications cannot directly transfer information to the 32-bit Windows 7 operating system. All requests for service from the Win16 environment are translated to 32-bit requests and vice-versa. This specific translation situation is referred to as **thunking**.

All Win16 applications run in a single VDM by default because this is the expected behavior in a Windows 3.x environment. Note that since all Win16 applications run in the same virtual process by default, any one application that crashes can crash all other Win16 applications running with it in the VDM. It is possible to run a Win16 application in its own Win16 VDM, but this is not the default behavior and results in slower performance overall due to increased overhead.

A Win16 environment can take a lot of time to initialize the first time it is started. For this reason, once a Win16 VDM is created it is not immediately shut down when all Win16 applications terminate. Windows 7 first checks to see if any other Win16 VDMs are running. If they are, then this Win16 VDM are shut down. If there are no other Win16 VDMs, this particular one will remain running until the user logs out or shuts down the computer.

Activity 11-3: Running Win16 Applications

Time Required: 10 minutes

Objective: Run two Win16 applications concurrently and see the effect in Task Manager.

Description: In this activity, you will launch multiple Win16 applications to confirm how they are individually presented on the Processes tab in Task Manager. This activity is possible only when using the 32-bit version of Windows 7. The 64-bit version of Windows 7 does not run 16-bit applications.

1. If necessary, start your computer and log on.

2. Click the **Start** button, point to **All Programs**, click **Accessories**, and click **Run**.

3. In the Run dialog box enter the command **WINHELP.EXE** and click **OK**.

4. Confirm that the legacy Microsoft Windows Help utility opens. This is a Win16 application that is used to view older style Windows help files if necessary.

5. Press **Ctrl-Shift-Esc** on the keyboard to open Task Manager.

6. Click the **Applications** tab in Task Manager and confirm that **Windows Help** is listed as a running application.

7. Right-click the **Windows Help** entry on the Applications tab in Task Manager, and click **Go To Process** from the pop-up menu.

8. Confirm that the open tab has switched to the Processes tab in Task Manager and that the winhelp.exe process is currently highlighted.

9. Notice that the winhelp.exe process name is indented further in from the other process names.

10. Notice that next to the winhelp.exe the program name wowexec.exe (the Win16-on-Win32 shim) also appears and is indented the same amount.

11. Notice that both winhelp.exe and wowexec.exe are listed above or below ntvdm.exe on the Processes tab in Task Manager. This means that the Win16 application is running in a virtual DOS machine. If winhelp.exe and wowexec.exe are listed above ntvdm.exe then click the **Image Name** column header to sort the processes in descending order.

12. Minimize the Task Manager window.

13. Click the **Start** button, point to **All Programs**, click **Accessories**, and click **Run**.

14. In the Run dialog box enter the command **SYSEDIT.EXE** and click **OK**.

15. Confirm that the legacy System Configuration Editor for Windows 3.x opens. This is a Win16 application that was used to configure the Windows 3.x run time environment.

16. Restore the Task Manager window.

17. Confirm that the new sysedit.exe Win16 application is listed under the same ntvdm. exe instance as winhelp.exe on the Processes tab in Task manager. Both Win16 applications are running in a single ntvdm.exe shared process.

18. Close the System Configuration Editor and Windows Help windows.

19. Notice that the Win16 applications are removed from Task Manager, but the ntvdm. exe process and wowexec.exe that hosted them remain active.

20. Close the Task Manager window.

x64 Application Considerations

The x64 version of Windows 7 is designed to use applications designed for 64-bit processors. To encourage adoption of newer technologies and new application designs, application compatibility is limited to Win32 applications. DOS and Win16 applications are not supported. A **Win32-on-Win64** (WOW64) virtualized environment is created to host legacy Win32 applications.

Windows 7 Registry

Windows 7 and the applications that run on it have to maintain a record of their configuration and operational parameters. The registry is a complex and dynamic database used to store this information. The registry provides the structure and security necessary to centrally manage these settings, whether it is for core operating system components or shared third-party applications.

Older operating systems, such as DOS, used text files to store settings for the operating system (CONFIG.SYS and AUTOEXEC.BAT) and application-specific data files to store third-party application settings. A central database was not available to store any configuration information.

Windows 3.x introduced the concept of a registry, but it was not sufficiently mature as a technology to provide the required functionality. The primary method to store configuration parameters in Windows 3.x is still the use of text files that have the .INI extension. The Windows 3.x environment would use WIN.INI and SYSTEM.INI to control the user and core Windows environment. Third-party applications would use their own .INI files as designed by their application developer.

Windows 95 moved the emphasis away from the DOS and Windows 3.x methods for storing configuration information. The registry became a well defined and centrally required element in the operations of the operating system and applications designed specifically for Windows 95. With each operating system released after Windows 95, the registry has become increasingly essential and critical to the successful operation of the computer. The registry continues to be an essential component of the Windows 7 operating system.

11

To administer the registry properly you must understand:

- Registry Structure
- Registry Editing Tools
- Registry Backup and Restore Methods
- Registry Security

Registry Structure

The registry is divided into sections and levels of data. Multiple sections exist to organize data by purpose. The individual sections are called **hives**. Each hive has a specific role to play and is stored in memory while it is in use. When the computer is shut down, the memory version of the hives are written to files and folders typically found in the folder C:\WINDOWS\SYSTEM32\CONFIG.

Within a single hive the data is stored in keys and values identified by their name and position relative to each other. Figure 11-2 shows an example of the registry structure when viewed with a registry editing tool.

The left-hand navigation pane displays a hierarchical folder structure. Each hive appears as a top-level folder in the left pane. Each folder in the left pane is referred to as a **registry key**. Each registry key is identified by the hive it belongs to, its position relative to other keys in the hive, and its name. The lower level registry keys are commonly referred to as **subkeys**, or subordinate keys.

The right-hand pane shows the data values that are stored at a specific level in the registry hierarchy (i.e., within a registry key). Each registry key can store multiple data values. The data values are defined by a name that is case sensitive, a type indicating how the data is formatted (e.g., binary, string, word), and the actual data stored by the value.

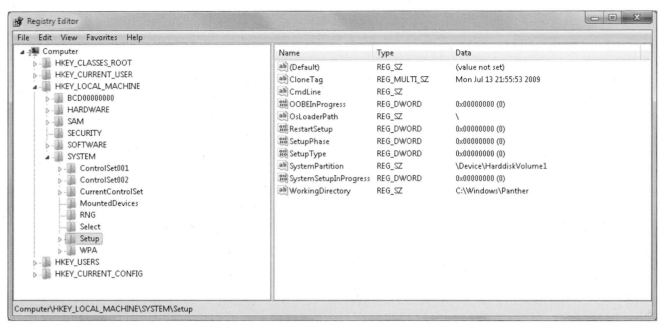

Figure 11-2 Sample view of the registry structure
Courtesy Course Technology/Cengage Learning

The notation to refer to a registry value or key is written in the format *Hive_name\key name\ subordinate key name\ . . .additional subordinate key names . . .\value_name*. For example, the value WorkingDirectory in Figure 11-2 could be referred to in printed instructions as HKEY_ LOCAL_MACHINE\SYSTEM\Setup\WorkingDirectory. It is common to abbreviate the hive name using the first letters of each word in the hive name, so that HKEY_LOCAL_MACHINE is commonly referred to as HKLM.

Registry keys can contain sensitive information that can crash the computer or damage expected functionality if they are improperly configured. The registry maintains its own security settings to restrict which entities can read or change specific keys.

Many registry keys affect other registry keys when their settings are changed. Because most keys do not operate in isolation, making changes to a single key may not yield the expected results. A simple required change to the user's environment, for example, may require a change to over 20 registry keys at the same time. The Administrative Tools and Control Panel utilities are designed to be fully aware of all the required changes—not just one or two. A simple check box in a Control Panel utility might alter many keys in a blended fashion, depending on the state of other registry information.

 The registry should never be modified directly unless it is absolutely required. Where possible, use the Control Panel or Administrative Tools to make any required changes to the computer's configuration. Direct changes to the registry may cause the system to malfunction or render it completely inoperable.

The top-level registry keys, or hives, organize registry information by purpose. The hives are not meant to be mutually exclusive and there is some overlap between hives. The primary hives found in Windows 7 are:

- HKEY_CLASSES_ROOT
- HKEY_CURRENT_USER
- HKEY_LOCAL_MACHINE
- HKEY_USERS
- HKEY_CURRENT_CONFIG

HKEY_CLASSES_ROOT Settings in this hive define the types (classes) of documents and properties associated with those types (see Figure 11-3). The information is used primarily by Windows applications to determine **COM** and **OLE** parameters for a particular file type or installed application. This hive is a merged view of data stored in two separate hives— HKEY_CURRENT_USER\ Software\Classes and HKEY_LOCAL_MACHINE\Software\ Classes—which define this type of information for the currently logged-on user and for the entire computer, respectively. The settings defined for the currently logged-on user take precedence over the settings defined for the entire computer.

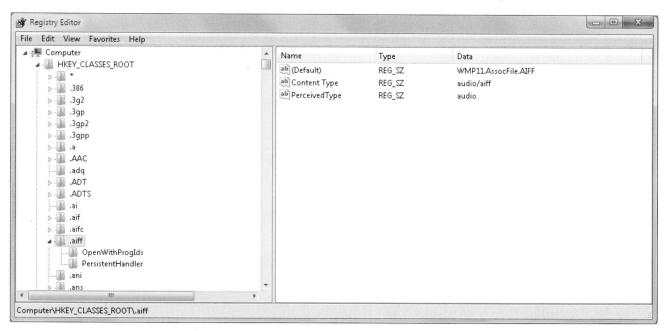

Figure 11-3 View of the HKEY_CLASSES_ROOT registry hive
Courtesy Course Technology/Cengage Learning

This view of the information is useful for deep diagnosis and inspection on the computer— but it is not user friendly. Windows 7 has a friendly view of much of the same data that can be accessed by clicking Control Panel, Programs, Default Programs, and Associate a file type or protocol with a program. Because of the complexity in updating this registry data, the Control Panel access to the information is preferred when making changes as to which program opens a particular type of data file.

HKEY_CURRENT_USER Settings in this hive define the preferences of the currently logged-on user (see Figure 11-4). These preferences include environment settings for colors, printers, and applications, to name just a few. Applications can use this hive to store user-specific preferences to be used with a specific user. Global application settings are stored in HKEY_LOCAL_ MACHINE instead. This hive is mapped to a view of a subsection of the HKEY_USERS hive. This subsection is associated with the currently logged-on user based on their **security identifier** (**SID**) and not their username. Each time this user logs on, their particular version of HKEY_ CURRENT_USER is loaded into memory as a working copy for that session.

HKEY_LOCAL_MACHINE This hive contains global settings for the entire computer and the applications installed on it (see Figure 11-5).

The hive information includes several important subordinate keys that record the state of the computer and details about the installed hardware. Some subordinate keys such as HKLM\ HARDWARE are populated when the computer is started, to reflect the hardware that is currently present and running. This information is more useful to help identify what hardware and device drivers are present when trying to diagnose other issues.

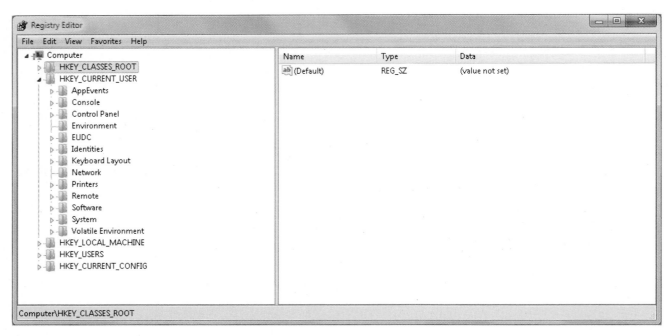

Figure 11-4 View of the HKEY_CURRENT_USER registry hive
Courtesy Course Technology/Cengage Learning

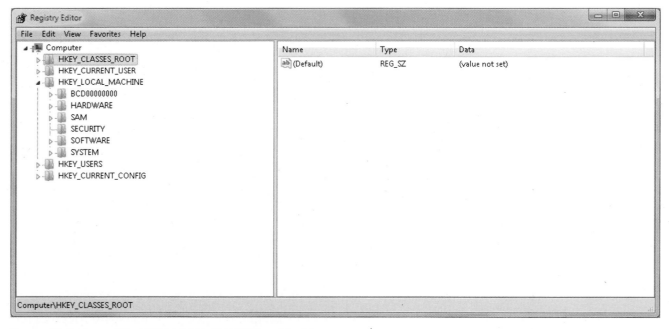

Figure 11-5 View of the HKEY_LOCAL_MACHINE registry hive
Courtesy Course Technology/Cengage Learning

Security information for user accounts defined on the computer is also stored in this hive as part of the subordinate key HKLM\SAM. The data inside this portion of the hive is not visible in a registry editing tool because it is designed to be restricted to the operating system itself. This area should not be directly modified.

Applications can store configuration settings in HKLM\SOFTWARE. Information for a specific application is usually stored in the location HKLM\SOFTWARE*Vendor**Application_Name*\. For instance, configuration data about Microsoft Office can be found in HKLM\ SOFTWARE\ Microsoft\Office.

Information to control the computer's hardware and the state of the operating system software is typically stored in HKLM\SYSTEM. The primary location for storing device driver and service control information is HKLM\SYSTEM\CurrentControlSet. More than one instance of the CurrentControlSet information is stored in the hive using the subordinate keys HKLM\SYSTEM\ControlSet001 and HKLM\SYSTEM\ControlSet002. HKLM\SYSTEM\CurrentControlSet is mapped to one of these subordinate keys. Every time the computer is successfully started, a copy of the CurrentControlSet information is saved to either HKLM\SYSTEM\ControlSet001 or HKLM\SYSTEM\ControlSet002 to provide a historic record of these critical settings. As changes are made to the HKLM\SYSTEM\CurrentControlSet, there is always an option to attempt a rollback to the last known good version of HKLM\SYSTEM\CurrentControlSet in the event a configuration error crashes the computer. To identify which of these control sets is the current one and which one is the last known good one, refer to the parameters in HKLM\SYSTEM\Select.

HKEY_USERS This hive contains multiple subsections to define user-specific settings for new users and any user that has ever logged on to the computer (see Figure 11-6).

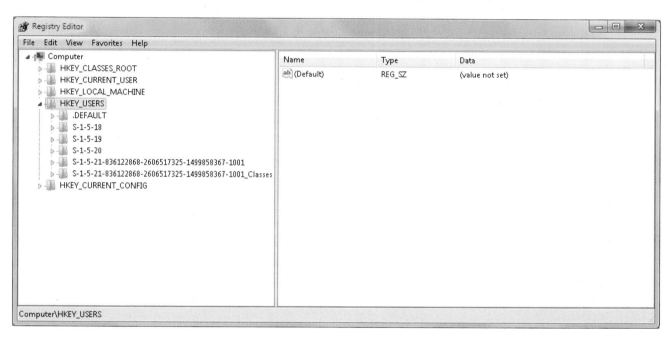

Figure 11-6 View of the HKEY_USERS registry hive
Courtesy Course Technology/Cengage Learning

This hive stores information that is mapped to HKEY_CURRENT_USER when a particular user logs in. The subsection associated with a user is marked with the security identifier (SID) of the user and not the user's name. The SID is a unique identifier that no two users share on the computer. The SID is typically formatted as a cryptic label such as *S-1-5-21-3720108926-496679219-2285711199-1000*. Each time this user logs on, their particular version of HKEY_CURRENT_ USER is loaded into memory as a working copy for that session.

If a user is logging on to the computer for the first time, a new sub key will be created for them in this hive that will be labeled with their SID. The initial settings for this key will be copied from HKEY_USERS\.DEFAULT.

HKEY_CURRENT_CONFIG This hive contains details about the current hardware profile in use. The details report the differences between the standard configuration defined in HKEY_LOCAL_MACHINE\System and HKEY_LOCAL_MACHINE\Software and those in the active hardware profile. This hive is also a mapped view to information stored in HKEY_LOCAL_MACHINE\System\CurrentControlSet\Hardware Profiles\Current. This section is not intended to be edited directly; it should only be modified indirectly through the Control Panel or Administrative Tools.

Registry Editing Tools

The registry is complex and dynamically modified by software that is running in the operating system. For many day-to-day operations, the registry should never be directly modified. The Control Panel and Administrative Tools are the preferred method to alter registry settings. However, some registry settings are not exposed to either the Control Panel or the Administrative Tools. In this case it may be necessary to directly modify the registry using registry editing tools.

Before making any changes to the registry, ensure that the following precautions are taken:

- Back up all important data on the computer before making any changes to the registry.
- Back up the portion of the registry that you will be changing (see the Registry Backup and Restore Methods section in this chapter).
- Confirm that the computer can restart properly before the change is made.
- Restrict the number of changes made at one time to limit the impact the changes have all at once.
- Confirm the effect of changes on a test system, where possible, to limit impact to production systems.
- Restart after the registry change is made to ensure that the computer can still be started.

The two main tools to directly edit the registry database are the graphical editor, REGEDIT. EXE, and the command-line editing tool, REG.EXE.

REGEDIT.EXE   An example of the graphical editor is shown in Figure 11-7. This tool allows a user to connect to the active registry database and make changes that are effective immediately. In prior versions of Windows there were two versions of this tool, REGEDIT and REGEDT32, with different capabilities for each version. In Windows 7, both REGEDIT and REGEDT32 link to the same graphical tool.

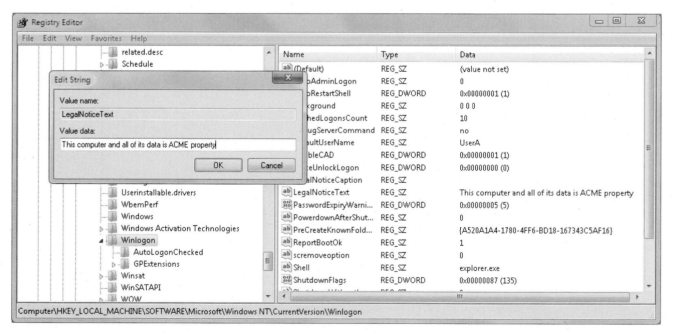

Figure 11-7 View of the REGEDIT application interface
Courtesy Course Technology/Cengage Learning

   REGEDIT does not have an undo function to remove recent changes.

Activity 11-4: View and Edit a Registry Value

Time Required: 5 minutes

Objective: Use the graphical registry editor to view and change registry information.

Description: In this activity, you will use Regedit to view and update a registry value.

It is recommended that you back up the registry before making any changes. This procedure is not being followed because this is a lab environment. Registry backup is covered later in this chapter.

1. If necessary, start your computer and log on.
2. Close any application windows which automatically open on the desktop.
3. Click the **Start** button, point to **All Programs**, click **Accessories**, and click **Run**.
4. In the Run dialog box enter the command **REGEDIT.EXE** and click **OK**.
5. If you are prompted by User Account Control for permission to allow this operation, select **Yes**.
6. Confirm that the Registry editor opens.
7. Expand **HKEY_LOCAL_MACHINE**.
8. Locate and expand **SOFTWARE** under HKEY_LOCAL_MACHINE.
9. Locate and expand **Microsoft** under SOFTWARE.
10. Locate and expand **Windows NT** under Microsoft.
11. Locate and expand **CurrentVersion** under Windows NT.
12. Locate and select **Winlogon** under CurrentVersion.
13. In the right-pane, locate and select **LegalNoticeText**.
14. Click the **Edit** menu, and click **Modify**.
15. In the Edit String window that opens, enter the text **This computer and all its data is ACME property** in the Value data field, then click **OK**.
16. Notice that the value is updated in the right-hand pane.
17. In the left pane, scroll up until you see HKEY_LOCAL_MACHINE.
18. Double-click **HKEY_LOCAL_MACHINE** to collapse it. Leave the system as is for the next activity.

Activity 11-5: Searching for Registry Values

Time Required: 5 minutes

Objective: Search for a Registry key or value.

Description: In this activity, you will use Regedit to locate a value in the registry. There may be multiple registry keys and values that have similar names, which can complicate the search process.

This activity requires that Activity 11-4 be completed. The search will begin at the point where Activity 11-4 ended.

1. In the registry editor window, click the **Edit** menu and click **Find**.

2. In the Find what box, type **LegalNoticeText**.

3. Click **Find Next**. Regedit locates the first key, value, or data containing the string. Because the registry contains many values that are similar or refer to each other, it is normal to find multiple references to a searched value. If you are modifying a registry entry, it is important that you first confirm if the search tool has found the correct one.

4. Click the **Edit** menu, and click **Find Next** (or press the hotkey equivalent, **F3**).

5. Continue searching by pressing **F3** between searches until Regedit prompts you that it has finished searching the registry. Note that the search value was found in multiple locations throughout HKEY_LOCAL_MACHINE.

6. Click **OK** and close the Registry Editor window.

REG.EXE   The command-line tool REG.EXE (see Figure 11-8) is typically used to read data from or write data to the registry from inside a scripted batch or command file. The REG.EXE tool requires intimate knowledge of the registry's hierarchy and values, so it is considered difficult, but powerful, to use.

```
C:\Windows\system32\cmd.exe

C:\Users\UserA>reg /?

REG Operation [Parameter List]

    Operation  [ QUERY   | ADD     | DELETE  | COPY     |
                 SAVE    | LOAD    | UNLOAD  | RESTORE  |
                 COMPARE | EXPORT  | IMPORT  | FLAGS ]

Return Code: <Except for REG COMPARE>

    0 - Successful
    1 - Failed

For help on a specific operation type:

    REG Operation /?

Examples:

    REG QUERY /?
    REG ADD /?
    REG DELETE /?
    REG COPY /?
    REG SAVE /?
    REG RESTORE /?
    REG LOAD /?
    REG UNLOAD /?
    REG COMPARE /?
    REG EXPORT /?
    REG IMPORT /?
    REG FLAGS /?

C:\Users\UserA>_
```

Figure 11-8 View of the REG.EXE command-line utility help screen
Courtesy Course Technology/Cengage Learning

Activity 11-6: Command-Line Registry Editor

Time Required: 5 minutes
Objective: Use the command-line Registry Editor, REG.EXE.

Description: In this activity, you will use the command-line registry editor to view the value assigned to a registry value modified in an earlier activity.

1. If necessary, start your computer and log on.

2. Click the **Start** button, point to **All Programs**, click **Accessories**, and click **Command Prompt**.

3. Type **REG /?** and press **Enter** to view the basic help screen for the command-line registry editor.

4. Type **REG QUERY "HKLM\Software\Microsoft\Windows NT\CurrentVersion\ Winlogon" /v LegalNoticeText** and press **Enter**. When entering this text there is a space between "Windows" and "NT".

5. Notice that the contents you entered in activity 11-4 are displayed.

6. Close the Command Prompt window.

Registry Backup and Restore Methods

The registry database can be preserved in multiple ways. Both the graphical registry editor and the command-line registry editor have the option of exporting the current settings from part of the registry database to a text-based file. The file has a .REG extension to signify that it is a registry file. If there are multiple registry areas that need to be exported, then each one must be individually exported to a separate .REG file.

If you want to back up many parts of the registry before making changes, the export method may be too selective. A method that backs up the whole registry may be preferred. This can be accomplished by performing a complete PC backup. The registry is a live database that is active in memory, therefore a backup method must be used that includes not only the file information but also the system state of the operating system. The system state includes dynamic settings that define individual operating system components and how they interact.

A user may import a .REG file if the user has permission to update the portion of the registry that will be modified. When the user double-clicks on the .REG file, they are prompted to confirm the action. If they respond affirmatively, the data will be imported as permissions allow.

Activity 11-7: Registry Backup

Time Required: 10 minutes
Objective: Use the Regedit application to export a portion of the registry for backup purposes.

Description: In this activity, you will use the graphical registry editor to export a portion of the HKEY_USERS hive for backup purposes.

1. If necessary, start your computer and log on.

2. Click the **Start** button, point to **All Programs**, click **Accessories**, and click **Run**.

3. In the Run dialog box, if necessary, type the command **REGEDIT.EXE** and click **OK**.

4. If you are prompted by User Account Control for permission to allow this operation, click **Yes**.

5. Confirm that the Registry editor opens.

6. Locate and expand the **HKEY_USERS** hive, and click the **.DEFAULT** subkey.

7. Click the **File** menu, and click **Export**.

8. In the left pane, click **Desktop**.

9. In the file name box, type **HKUDefaultBackup**.

10. Confirm at the bottom of the Export Registry File window that the Export range is set to Selected branch and that HKEY_USERS\.DEFAULT is listed in the text field below Selected branch.

11. Click **Save**.

12. The values and keys stored in the specified key will be exported to the file specified. Leave the registry editor tool open for the next activity.

Activity 11-8: Registry Restore

Time Required: 10 minutes
Objective: Use Regedit to restore a portion of the registry using previously exported registry information.

Description: In this activity, you will use the graphical registry editor to import a portion of the HKEY_USERS hive originally exported in the previous activity.

This application requires that Activity 11-7 be completed. This activity will begin at the point where Activity 11-7 ended.

1. In the registry editor window, click the **File** menu and click **Import**.
2. Click the **HKUDefaultBackup.reg** file you created in the previous activity.
3. Click **Open**.
4. After a few seconds a message appears stating that the import was successful. Click **OK**.
5. Close the registry editor window.

Registry Security

The registry database is protected by its own security system. Each key is assigned permissions, an owner, and optionally a list of users to audit when the key is accessed. To see the permission settings on a key, use the graphical registry editor tool, REGEDIT.EXE. The permissions window shown in Figure 11-9 is representative of what is shown when the permissions on a key are initially opened. Access to a registry key and the values it contains can be explicitly allowed or denied based on the user or the groups they belong to.

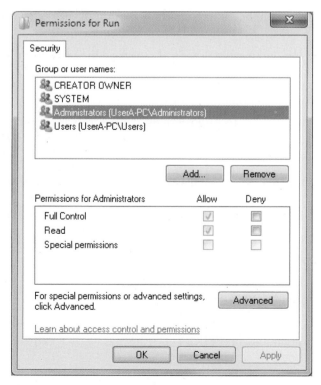

Figure 11-9 The standard registry permissions window
Courtesy Course Technology/Cengage Learning

The basic permissions usually do not reveal all of the fine security details that exist in the registry database. By clicking on the Advanced button in the standard registry permissions window, the advanced permissions window shown in Figure 11-10 is opened.

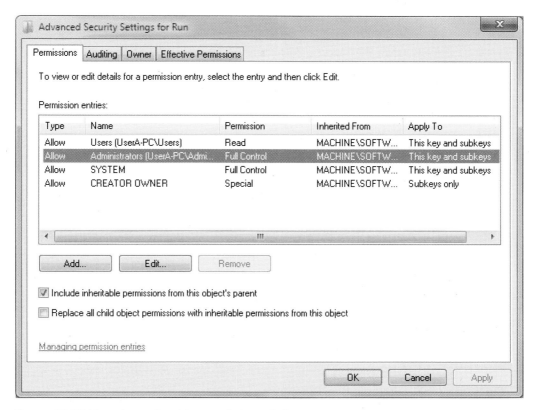

Figure 11-10 The advanced registry permissions window
Courtesy Course Technology/Cengage Learning

Security settings are inherited from the top of the hive down to the bottom of the hive. Note that in Figure 11-10 the option exists to disable permissions inherited from parent keys and to force permission settings down to child keys in the hive.

Permission inheritance and default security options should not be changed without a good reason to do so. Many of the predefined security settings include special permissions that cannot be changed without negatively impacting the computer's stability and ability to run. Permissions are not exported with registry data; they can only be preserved with a full backup that preserves the system state.

The owner of the keys is usually listed as SYSTEM—the operating system itself. This allows the operating system to modify permissions regardless of what permissions are explicitly defined on the registry keys. This can be changed to an administrative user or the built-in Administrators group, but this can also have a severe negative impact on the computer's stability and ability to run.

In Windows 7 the operating system code and services run in a user session that is not shared with any user accessible interfaces. If registry permissions are altered to restrict access or operations to users only, the registry data may not be available to the operating system at all. This will probably result in a nonbooting computer that requires a complete restore from backup.

Activity 11-9: Registry Security

Time Required: 15 minutes
Objective: View permissions on registry keys using the graphical registry editor.

Description: In this activity, you will view the basic security settings for registry values.

 Modifying registry security can have severe consequences on the stability and usability of your computer. This activity will only view existing permissions; do not make any changes to your registry's security settings.

1. If necessary, start your computer and log on.

2. Click the **Start** button, point to **All Programs**, click **Accessories**, and click **Run**.

3. In the Run dialog box, if necessary, type the command **REGEDIT.EXE** and click **OK**.

4. If you are prompted by User Account Control for permission to allow this operation, select **Yes**.

5. Confirm that the Registry editor opens.

6. In the left-hand pane, locate and expand **HKEY_LOCAL_MACHINE** to open the hive.

7. Locate and expand **SOFTWARE** under HKEY_LOCAL_MACHINE.

8. Locate and expand **Microsoft** under SOFTWARE.

9. Locate and expand **Windows** under Microsoft.

10. Locate and expand **CurrentVersion** under Windows.

11. Locate and click **Run** under CurrentVersion.

12. In the **Edit** menu, click **Permissions**.

13. Note that the local Administrators group and the SYSTEM identity have full control to the values in this key.

14. Click **Cancel** to close the Permissions for Run dialog box.

15. Close the Registry Editor.

File and Registry Virtualization

Some pre-Windows Vista application developers designed their applications to store data and configuration settings in file and registry locations that were not meant for this purpose. These selected locations were never intended to be a general access point and typically have access restricted to administrators and the operating system itself.

Prior to Windows Vista, earlier operating systems such as Windows XP allowed access to these sensitive system areas because the security environment was not as specifically designed or enforced. The user installing the application was usually given administrative rights to the entire computer; this allowed the application installer to put its data into these locations. Applications should not have used these areas in this way, but there was no easy way to enforce this before Windows Vista and User Account Control (UAC).

User Account Control in Windows 7 can distinctly recognize and control access to sensitive system areas. To provide backward compatibility for pre-Windows Vista applications unaware of UAC, Windows 7 has virtualized select system file and registry areas when UAC is enabled and active.

The key system areas that are virtualized include:

- *HKLM\Software*—A registry area that stores software configuration settings applicable to the entire computer.

- *%SystemRoot%*—A system variable that identifies the location of the Windows 7 operational files. This is typically C:\Windows.

- *%ProgramFiles%*—A system variable that identifies the location where applications are installed by default. This is typically C:\Program Files.

When an application tries to write to these areas, it is redirected to a private location that is specific to the user running the application. The application does not recognize that this virtualization is happening. Also, because the data the application is writing is actually stored in user-specific locations, the application may not operate as expected for other users. If pre-Windows Vista applications are compatible with the file and registry virtualization, they can still run until they are replaced with UAC-aware versions (if available). The proper fix for a program that requires this technique is to replace it with a new application that does not write to those areas.

UAC-aware applications can include an **XML** formatted description of application compatibility settings stored either in an application DLL, an executable, or a separate file that is called the application manifest. The application manifest can identify the application as UAC aware, which disables UAC file and registry virtualization automatically for that application.

If a non UAC aware application is run with elevated privileges, that is, allowing it to run as Administrator, file and registry virtualization is not used for that application while it is running with elevated privileges. Running a legacy application with more permission than required is not a best practice.

Run As Administrator

Applications run with the same security privileges as the currently logged-on user. In older operating systems such as Windows 2000 and Windows XP, the Run As option existed to run an application as a different user without having to log off and log on again as the other user. This Run As feature has been modified in Windows 7 to now be known as the **Run as administrator** option.

Details of the security privileges that apply to the currently logged-on user are stored in a security token that is compiled when the user first logs on. When User Account Control is active, the user may have a secondary administrative security token linked to their identity. This is true if the logged-on user is an administrator equivalent account for the local computer.

As mentioned in the File and Registry virtualization section in this chapter, some applications can automatically trigger the prompt for administrator-level access when an application is started. If an application or the operating system do not trigger this, and it is required, it can be manually initiated by right-clicking on the program and clicking **Run as administrator** from the resulting pop-up menu.

User Account Control prompts for confirmation to allow this action and, if the logged-on user confirms it, their administrative security token will be used to launch the application in a separate security space.

This is useful for the occasional time when a program must run at an elevated level. If this is required all the time and the developer cannot rewrite the application to support User Account Control, then the application's properties can be modified. By bringing up the application's properties and selecting the Compatibility tab, an option is present to **Run this program as an administrator** (see Figure 11-11). If this is selected, User Account Control always prompts for administrative access when the application is started.

Activity 11-10: Starting Applications with Run as Administrator

Time Required: 15 minutes
Objective: Start an application that requires Run as administrator.

Description: In this activity, you will try to run the DISKPART administrative tool using a regular security environment. The DISKPART tool requires administrator security privileges, so it must take advantage of the Run as administrator option.

1. If necessary, start your computer and log on.
2. Click the **Start** button, point to **All Programs**, click **Accessories**, and click **Command Prompt**.

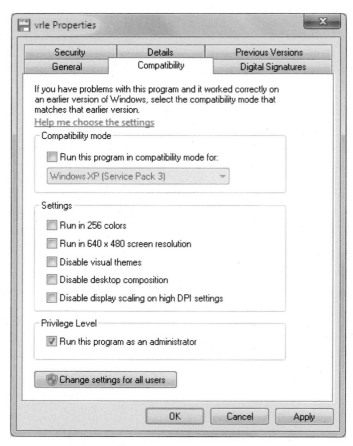

Figure 11-11 Run application as Administrator option
Courtesy Course Technology/Cengage Learning

3. Type **DISKPART** and press **Enter**. When User Account Control asks for permission to run the program, answer **No**. Note that you receive an "access is denied" error message because administrative rights are required to run this program.

4. Close the **Command Prompt** window.

5. Click the **Start** button, point to **All Programs**, click **Accessories**, and right-click **Command Prompt**, and click **Run as administrator**

6. When you are prompted by User Account Control for permission to continue, select **Yes**.

7. Type **DISKPART** and press **Enter**. Note that you now see a DISKPART prompt for the application. The diskpart application now has sufficient security privileges to run.

8. Close the Command Prompt window.

Application Compatibility

Not all applications designed to work with older operating systems will work smoothly with Windows 7. Multiple methods can be used to make older applications work successfully. Windows 7 can change how it supports an application to emulate an operating system closer to what the application was first written for. Windows 7 can try to emulate a range of older Windows operating system environments for the application. The problem is determining which compatibility setting would provide the best support for the application. This can be determined using the Program Compatibility Assistant or manually through Program Compatibility Settings. If a program cannot operate in a compatibility mode, the new Windows XP Mode environment may be a consideration. Applications that use kernel patching cannot be made compatible with Windows 7.

Program Compatibility Assistant

When an application is installed and run for the first time, Windows 7 automatically checks if the application has an issue. If Windows 7 recognizes that the application could not start, it will automatically launch the Program Compatibility Assistant the next time the same application is started and offer to fix the compatibility issues automatically. If the issues are deemed threatening to the Windows 7 operating system, the application may not be allowed to run at all. The user will be notified and directed to the Microsoft Website for further support and advice.

The Program Compatibility Assistant is designed to make it easy for users to adjust their legacy applications to work with Windows 7 without having to know a lot about compatibility settings.

A user can open a My Computer browser window to locate an application or shortcut. If the file is recognized as a program file that Windows 7 can run by adjusting its compatibility settings, right-clicking on the file opens a pop-up menu that has a Troubleshoot compatibility menu item. Data files and .msi files do not activate the Troubleshoot compatibility menu option. If a program file is already known as compatible, the menu choice will also not be displayed.

Once the Program Compatibility Assistant is started, it will check for obvious compatibility issues before displaying the main screen as seen in Figure 11-12. The user has the option of trying the resulting recommended settings or troubleshooting the program. Troubleshooting the program will trigger the wizard to guide the user through a series of questions and answers.

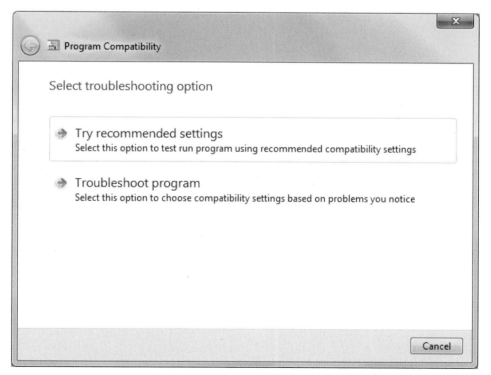

Figure 11-12 Program Compatibility Assistant starting screen
Courtesy Course Technology/Cengage Learning

Because the program cannot judge what problem the user is experiencing, it must prompt the user through guided questions. The most common trouble areas are a Windows OS version mismatch, display issues, and insufficient permissions, as seen in Figure 11-13. The user must select one or more areas the program had a problem with and the wizard will ask questions about each area to further diagnose appropriate compatibility settings.

11

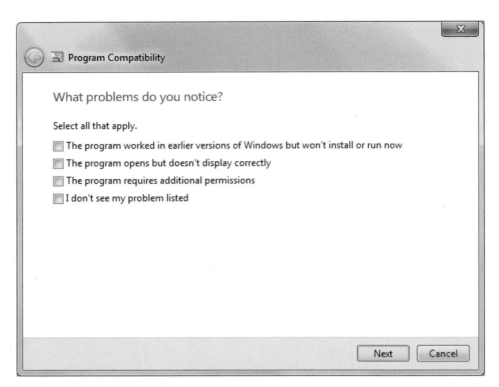

Figure 11-13 Program Compatibility Assistant asks the user to identify the problem
Courtesy Course Technology/Cengage Learning

Some applications check the version number of the operating system that it reports back. If the version number is not what the application expected, it may malfunction or fail to start. Many applications include code that adapts itself to different operating systems without requiring different application files for each operating system. An older application would see the Windows 7 version number as unexpected and may not be programmed to adjust for that contingency. In that case, Windows can be told to "lie" to the application when it starts and report a different version ID. That doesn't guarantee that the application will work, but it will stop it from failing because it doesn't know what to configure itself for. The Program Compatibility Wizard will prompt the user to pick an operating system version that the application can work with, as seen in Figure 11-14. When the application starts, it will check and be told that it is running on the selected operating system version. If the user isn't sure what version the application used to work with, the wizard will default to Windows XP SP2.

If video problems are reported, the wizard will ask the user which problems were noticed, as seen in Figure 11-15. Graphic settings will be adjusted according to the user's responses. Many older applications are not designed to use the latest graphic elements and may appear incorrectly if they run. Here, multiple options can be tried and combined to limit which graphic features are used by Windows 7 when running the application.

If the user reported problems with permissions, the wizard configures the program to Run as Administrator with respect to User Account Control. Programs should not be given elevated access unless they absolutely require it.

The wizard will then ask the user to launch the application with the settings selected by the user's answers. Once the application exits, the wizard asks if the settings are suitable. If not, the user has the option to immediately rerun the wizard and adjust the settings.

Program Compatibility Settings

Once an application is installed, it can optionally have its compatibility settings adjusted as part of the application's properties. The program's compatibility settings can be viewed and changed through the Compatibility tab in the program's Properties window (see Figure 11-16).

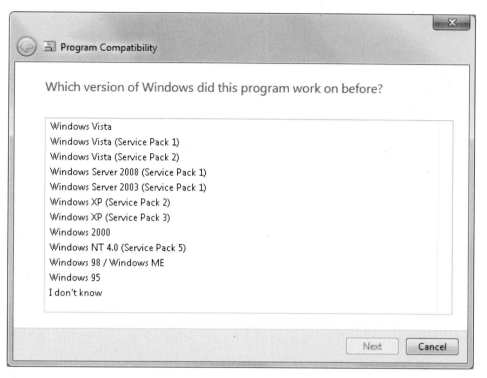

Figure 11-14 Program Compatibility Assistant asks the user what operating system the program worked with before
Courtesy Course Technology/Cengage Learning

11

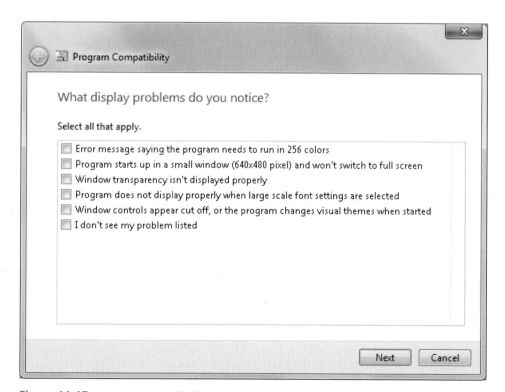

Figure 11-15 Program Compatibility Assistant asks the user what display problems were noticed
Courtesy Course Technology/Cengage Learning

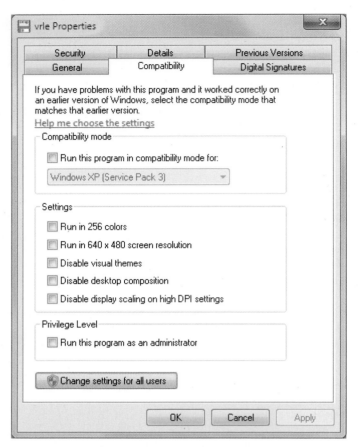

Figure 11-16 Compatibility tab for a program's properties window
Courtesy Course Technology/Cengage Learning

The compatibility settings set by the currently logged-on user are displayed unless the ***Change settings for all users*** button is clicked first. These are the same settings modified by the Program Compatibility Assistant.

XP Mode

Some applications cannot be made compatible through compatibility settings or translation software alone. If these applications are required, then there may be no choice but to run them on an older operating system, such as Windows XP. Windows 7 Enterprise, Ultimate, and Professional Editions include support for XP Mode. XP Mode installs a second virtual operating system that runs at the same time as Windows 7.

The XP Mode is made possible by installing a free copy of Virtual PC and operating system enhancements that integrate application interaction between Windows 7 and the virtual instance of Windows XP. Microsoft allows you to download and install a free copy of 32-bit Windows XP Professional SP3 and let it run inside a virtual machine. Other operating systems such as Windows Vista and Windows 7 could run in the virtual machine, but that would likely defeat the purpose of providing application support for older applications.

Windows XP mode has specific enhancements that link applications between Windows 7 and Windows XP. Icons and links to start a program in the Windows XP virtual machine can be embedded in the Windows 7 environment to hide the virtualization environment from the user running the application. The Windows XP operating system has access to most of the same local resources as the Windows 7 operating system. There may be some limits and restrictions as to what hardware is accessible, which in turn may limit the applicability of this solution.

The copy of Windows XP in the virtual machine still needs to be managed and protected; it is a full operating system that requires the same care and attention as any other workstation. This includes patches, backups, and anti-virus protection. It needs its own share of the computer's

RAM to run; therefore, it is recommended that the computer have at least 2 GB of RAM before XP Mode is installed and activated. When Windows XP reaches end of life, this virtual environment will no longer be supported. The goal is to provide short term functionality until problem applications are replaced with versions fully compatible with Windows 7 and beyond. (Some applications, however, will be "legacy" programs and not be updated.)

Kernel Patching

Kernel patching is a system whereby applications modify the core functionality of the Windows operating system to obtain low level access to the operating system and its resources. Kernel patching is considered a security risk because untrusted code, such as a root kit, could be inserted into the operating system. In addition, kernel patching can cause operating system instability if not done properly. The most common cause of system crashes in previous Windows versions is kernel patching. In Windows 7, the protection system for kernel patching is called Windows Resource Protection (WRP).

Windows 7 prevents kernel patching by untrusted applications that do not have a digital signature stamped and recognized by Microsoft. Permissions for full access to protected resources are restricted to the built-in TrustedInstaller security ID. The restriction on kernel patching does not affect most commonly used applications, such as office suites. However, some security products such as third-party firewall software may be affected. Some hardware drivers are also affected. Any attempt by an application to modify a protected registry key or operating system file will be refused. The application may realize access was denied but in several cases the default WRP action is to lie to the offending application and tell it the change was successful. This allows the computer to proceed without disturbing the user but the offending application will likely fail to operate because the data that it wrote earlier is absent.

Application Compatibility Research Tools

Many applications created before Windows 7 may or may not be compatible with it. These applications represent a significant dollar investment for many companies and individuals. For some operations these applications form a backbone for productivity that must be up and running. However, many of these applications may have compatibility issues with Windows 7.

There may be many reasons why these applications cannot be made fully compatible. Perhaps the applications cannot change without disrupting the business process for a company. Some applications could come from vendors that no longer exist. The vendor may have upgraded other applications, but the new versions have not been implemented or purchased by the user or company. If the application was developed in house, perhaps there has not been enough time and resources to train the developers in new methods and also rewrite the application.

Regardless of what the barriers to change are, they must first be revealed before anything can be done about it. This means that the critical applications must be inventoried, investigated to see if they present any operational issues with Windows 7, and a strategy to deal with the issues must be developed. To assist with this process, Microsoft has released several tools to help people and companies with researching application compatibility. The primary compatibility research tool is the Microsoft Application Compatibility Toolkit.

The Microsoft Application Compatibility Toolkit (ACT) V5.5 is currently available as a free download from Microsoft. The tool is a lifecycle management tool for the applications required by a user or company. It assists in identifying and managing which applications must be reviewed, assists in reporting and tracking application compatibility issues, and helps you deploy Windows 7 as fast as possible with the required compatibility changes. As the toolkit evolves, new editions are released to embed new knowledge and procedures to evaluate applications with newer operating systems. Even after application compatibility concerns with Windows 7 are addressed, the tool can be used to help evaluate application compatibility issues after specific Windows updates are applied. This means that, in a corporate environment, the use and maintenance of ACT will be an ongoing administrative task.

The main components of ACT include these tools:

- Application Compatibility Manager
- Compatibility Administrator
- Standard User Analyzer
- Setup Analysis Tool
- Internet Explorer Compatibility Test Tool
- Microsoft Compatibility Exchange
- Application Shim support

Application Compatibility Manager

The **Application Compatibility Toolkit** is a full suite of software that collectively operates to examine the enterprise's application environment. The Application Compatibility Manager is the administrative console that the IT administrator uses to control the overall discovery, collection, and analysis process.

Compatibility Administrator

The Compatibility Administrator is a tool for the IT administrator to collect and resolve compatibility issues. As solutions are discovered for an application they are stored in databases managed by the Compatibility Administrator. This allows them to be deployed later to the organization consistently, repeatedly, and as required.

Standard User Analyzer

The Standard User Analyzer is a tool that monitors what happens when an application is run as a user without elevated permissions. If there are problems with the application's compatibility, the Standard User Analyzer collects them and sends the findings to a log server that will centrally store the results for later analysis.

Setup Analysis Tool

Many applications are incompatible when they try to install. The Setup Analysis tool observes what steps and changes are made during the installation of an application. The findings are sent back to the Application Compatibility Manager for review by the IT administrator.

Internet Explorer Compatibility Test Tool

Many companies use corporate Web sites to operate. The Internet Explorer Compatibility Test Tool monitors what happens when a Web site is opened in Internet Explorer 7 or 8. If there are problems, the Internet Explorer Compatibility Test Tool forwards that information to the ACT logging service for later analysis by the IT administrator. This helps the IT administrator plan for custom Internet Explorer compatibility settings if required.

Microsoft Compatibility Exchange

There is no point in searching for a solution if someone else has already found it. Application compatibility solutions can be very complicated at times. The Microsoft Compatibility Exchange allows the Application Compatibility Manager to connect to external knowledge bases. This external data source includes continuously updated knowledge that is posted by Microsoft, vendors, and other ACT users.

Application Shim Support

Once there is enough data collected to identify what doesn't work—and why—what to do next is addressed. Some compatibility changes are easy and some are not. Applications may be out of date and there is no support or option to rewrite them. If the application cannot be changed, one alternative may be to change how it appears and interacts with the operating system. Application shims can be used to interact between the application and the operating system to translate operations between the two and achieve some degree of compatibility. Application shims are typically provided by Microsoft to well-known compatibility scenarios.

Application Control Policies

Getting applications to run is only part of the IT administrator's role. Sometimes it is just as important to manage what applications are allowed to run.

The control policies available to the IT administrator include:

- Software Restriction Policies
- AppLocker

Software Restriction Policies

Software Restriction Policies were implemented as part of a management strategy for Windows XP workstations that are domain-joined to a Windows Server 2003 domain. A Software Restriction Policy allows the management of what applications are allowed to run on managed computers. The customized application settings are deployed to workstations using standard Group Policy processes. With enough up-front testing and planning, the workstation environment runs more often in a known state rather than an unknown one.

Windows 7 interaction with Active Directory and Group Policy are covered in more detail in Chapter 13, Enterprise Computing.

Software restrictions are typically created using an MMC Group Policy snap-in on an Active Directory domain server to create a Group Policy Object (GPO). The GPO is associated with an Active Directory domain, site, or organizational unit. When a computer—or user—logs in to the domain that GPO object is downloaded and applied to the workstation. Computer GPO objects apply when the computer first starts. User GPO objects apply when the user first logs on. When a program or script starts, the workstation checks the Software Restriction Policies and enforce it.

A GPO doesn't have any Software Restriction Policies defined when it is first created (see Figure 11-17). The IT administrator must decide if the software restriction policy will apply to the user or computer. In addition to the implied scope of the GPO given its assignment (domain, site, OU, or local), the IT administrator can use GPO filtering to limit the application of the GPO to individual or groups of specific users and computers.

Before any software restriction policy is applied, consider that a mistake can have serious consequences to the ability of workstations to operate. All settings should first be tested in an isolated portion of the domain, such as a testing organizational unit, or in a test lab. Any domain-wide application of software restriction policies should be avoided unless stringent testing is employed.

The IT administrator must know his or her application environment to properly configure limits on it. Software restriction policies start by defining a default behavior. A default software restriction policy can be applied to deny or allow all applications by default (see Figure 11-18). Consider that if the IT administrator doesn't know what applications the users will be using, then the default should be set to allow applications to run by default.

In Figure 11-18, the default behavior is set to allow all applications to run by default. This is observed by the checkmark over the Unrestricted policy. To change it, the IT administrator can right-click the Disallowed option and select Set as default from the pop-up menu as seen in Figure 11-18. Also note that the default software restriction settings are stored in a sublevel called Security Levels. Once the default behavior is set, exceptions can be defined to specifically allow or disallow applications.

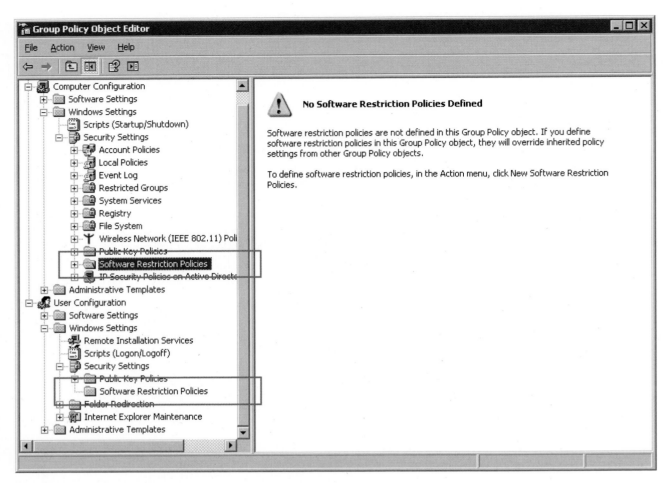

Figure 11-17 Software Restriction Policies before a default action is applied
Courtesy Course Technology/Cengage Learning

Within the GPO's Software Restriction Policies exists a sublevel called Additional Rules. New software restriction rules can be created here as shown in Figure 11-19. These provide the exceptions to the default software restriction behavior.

The additional rule types that can be created as exceptions include:

- Hash Rule
- Path Rule
- Internet Zone Rule
- Certificate Rule
- Registry Key Rule

Hash rules define a hash identifier that uniquely identifies a file and assigns it a software restriction behavior. The New Hash Rule wizard calculate the hash value. This hash ID is very specific to that exact file. The hash rule restriction behavior can be explicitly set to Disallowed or Unrestricted. This has the administrative advantage of being very specific—however, it also is a major disadvantage. Each exceptional application file must be known and identified with a hash rule in this case.

Path rules define exceptions that allow or disallow a file or folder location specified with a path value. The path value can include the wildcard characters * and ? for multiple and single character substitutions respectively.

Internet Zone rules work together with the Windows Installer. When a program is being installed from a specific Internet zone (i.e., Trusted Sites, Internet, Local Intranet, Local Computer, or Restricted Sites) the exception can allow or disallow installation.

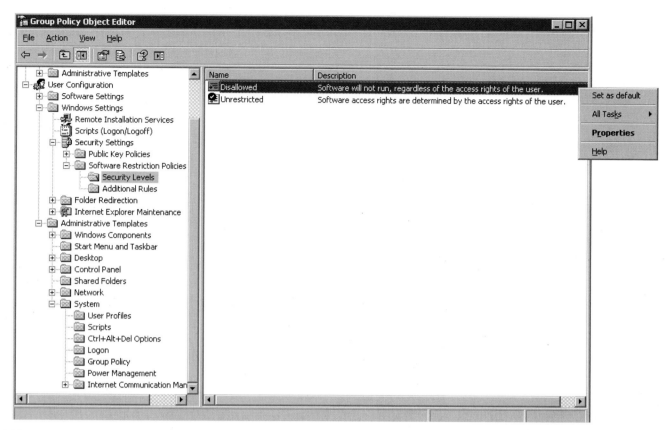

Figure 11-18 Software Restriction Policies with a default restriction applied
Courtesy Course Technology/Cengage Learning

Certificate rules define exceptions based on a digital certificate signed to an application or script. Not all applications or scripts are digitally signed. The digital certificate must be known ahead of time to create such a rule. The digital certificate is usually added by the creator of the application—it is not added by the IT administrator if the vendor did not issue one.

Registry Path rules define exceptions based on a path stored in a registry value. This customized path rule works if the IT administrator knows the location of the registry key that defines where an application was installed. The advantage with this type of rule is that it can adapt if the user has installed a controlled application in an unexpected location. Not every application will have a registry key value that can be inspected for its location.

Any rules that overlap will be applied with a specific precedence. In general, the more specific a rule is in identifying a target, the higher its priority and applicability. Rules are processed in a specific order: hash, certificate, path, Internet zone, and, finally, the default rule. The most specific match will define if the application is allowed to run or not.

Software restriction policies can be applied to all users of a computer or it can optionally apply to all users except local administrators. This is important during testing when a mistake can make a regular logon impossible.

Software restriction policies know about most executable file types based on their file extension. As new application types are introduced, the software restriction policies can become out of date. File extensions can be added to the list of executable applications as part of the policy.

Because software restriction policies are delivered by Group Policy, Group Policy troubleshooting skills are required to manage the environment's expected behavior. To ensure the workstation has the most current Group Policy data, it is common for the troubleshooting IT administrator to use the **gpupdate** utility to trigger a fresh download of applicable GPO settings from the domain controllers.

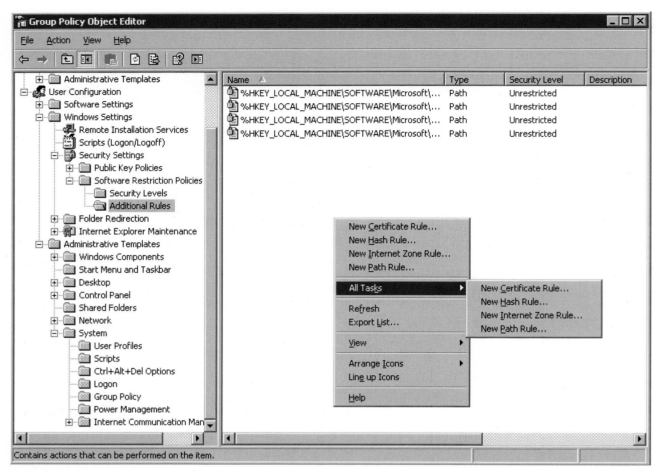

Figure 11-19 Software Restriction Policies custom rule creation menu
Courtesy Course Technology/Cengage Learning

Windows 7 fully supports Software Restriction Policies; but it is not the only technology available to the IT administrator in managing corporate applications. Windows 7 Enterprise and Ultimate versions support a new management strategy called AppLocker.

AppLocker

The choice of applications has changed with time. Since Windows XP, applications have changed to use new methods and frameworks to execute. It is difficult to add major new features to software restriction policies without breaking functionality that older Windows clients depend on. Starting with Windows 7 and Windows Server 2008 R2, AppLocker is a replacement management strategy for limiting applications allowed to run.

 AppLocker configuration and details are covered in Chapter 7, Windows 7 Security Features.

AppLocker relies on Group Policy Objects just as the older software restriction policies do. The advantage in using AppLocker with Windows 7 and future client operating systems is that it works better as a management strategy with the current application landscape. Clients older than Windows 7 do not recognize or use AppLocker controls. Because this is an enterprise application management strategy, it is only applied to Windows 7 Enterprise and Ultimate Editions. Windows Server operating systems that are earlier than Windows Server 2008 R2 are not and cannot be enhanced with AppLocker support.

Chapter Summary

- This chapter described the application architecture and its layers as they apply to the execution of the user's applications and the operating system itself. The layered approach minimizes the ability of a user application to crash or negatively affect other running applications.

- Different application environments are supported for DOS, Win16, and Win32 in the 32-bit version of Windows 7. The Win32 and Win64 application environments are supported in the 64-bit version of Windows 7. Applications can also use newer environments to interact with the operating system, such as the .NET Framework subsystem.

- The registry in Windows 7 is based on the original Windows NT registry model, but it has been enhanced to support the more dynamic functionality of software and hardware supported on Windows 7. Both graphical and command-line tools are available to modify the registry, however the preferred method to make changes is through the Control Panel or Administrative Tools. Registry settings are complicated and affect each other, which can result in an unstable or inoperable computer if a mistake is made. Registry settings can be exported or backed up as part of the operating system's system state.

- Select portions of the file system and registry are virtualized in such a way that a running application believes it is writing to those locations, but it is in fact writing to a folder location that is part of the logged-on user's profile. The virtualization allows legacy applications to run (and not crash) in the 32-bit version of Windows 7 with User Account Control enabled. The 64-bit version of Windows 7 does not support this type of virtualization because it is not encouraged behavior.

- Those applications that require administrative privileges to run properly can be granted to Run as administrator. This ability can be occasionally enabled or defined as part of the application's compatibility properties.

- Legacy applications that have trouble running natively in Windows 7 can run in a compatibility mode that simulates an older version of Windows for the application. The compatibility settings can be adjusted automatically by the Program Compatibility Assistant when Windows 7 detects a program has failed to start properly. The user can also be guided through the compatibility options and have input on their. Installed applications can have those compatibility settings modified directly as a property of the application.

- Application compatibility is not a one-time operation that is only performed when a new operating system is introduced. Microsoft has released several research tools to minimize the time and guesswork on how to make existing legacy applications compatible with new operating systems such as Windows 7. The Application Compatibility Toolkit will aid the organized lifecycle management of the applications that are important to a user or a business.

Key Terms

application architecture A logical description of how different components, services, and resources work together to run applications.

Application Compatibility Toolkit A collection of tools, advice, and methodologies that guides the IT administrator in determining which legacy applications are compatible with Windows 7 and how to help make them compatible.

COM An abbreviation for Component Object Model, which is a generalized method used by some applications to cross-link to and access each other. This is a broader method than OLE.

environment subsystems Support systems designed for specific types of applications, such as Win32 applications. The environment hides the details of how the application must communicate with lower-level operating system components such as the Executive Services. Environment subsystems operate on a user-mode basis but have awareness of kernel mode services hosted through Executive Services.

Executive Services   A collection of kernel model support modules to manage low-level duties in the operating system such as scheduling processes, managing memory, managing virtual environments, and running core kernel programming.

Hardware Abstraction Layer (HAL)   Part of the operating system that understands how to talk to the specific computer hardware on which the operating system is installed. This portion of the operating system runs at the lowest level of the application hierarchy in kernel mode.

hives   A discrete body of registry keys and values stored in files as part of the operating system.

kernel   The operating system software that runs in kernel mode on the computer's processor and which provides low-level intelligence for the operating system.

kernel mode   An access mode for applications while they are running on the CPU that allows full access to all hardware devices and memory in the computer.

OLE   An abbreviation for Object Linking and Embedding, which is a method used by some applications to cross-link to each other.

registry key   A level in a hive's hierarchy defined by its name and position relative to other keys in the hive hierarchy. A registry key can contain subkeys (other registry keys), values, or both.

Run as administrator   An option to start an application with elevated security privileges.

security identifier (SID)   A coded value assigned to a user account when it is first created to act as a unique identifier that is not duplicated for any other account. The security identifier is unique, regardless of what name is assigned to the user's account.

subkey   A subordinate or lower level registry key within a hive that can contain values and other subkeys.

thunking   A method where data and parameters passed from 16-bit software to 32-bit software is translated in a bidirectional manner.

user mode   An access mode for applications while they are running on the CPU that allows restricted access to all hardware devices and memory in the computer. This mode makes it difficult for the running application to corrupt and crash the operating system. System-level applications may need more access than is allowed and must use kernel mode instead.

Virtual DOS Machine (VDM)   A Win32 application that emulates a DOS environment for use by DOS and Win16 applications.

Win16   Applications designed to run in a Windows 16-bit instruction environment.

Win32   Applications designed to run in a Windows 32-bit instruction environment.

Win64   Applications designed to run in a Windows 64-bit instruction environment.

XML   A standard for formatting information in a self-describing way for transfer between different applications.

Review Questions

1. The HAL is designed to support specific _____.

   a. Win32 applications

   b. modems

   c. types of computer memory

   d. computer hardware

2. User applications always operate in kernel mode. True or False?

3. The Win16 subsystem provides application support for 16-bit Windows applications. True or False?

4. Environment subsystems act as intermediate processing layers between _____ and the operating system's _____. (Select two.)

   a. HAL

   b. user applications

    c.   kernel core

    d.   Executive Services

5.   x64 versions of Windows 7 will not support _____ applications.

    a.   16-bit Windows

    b.   user mode

    c.   32-bit Windows

    d.   kernel mode

6.   The 64-bit version of Windows 7 will support Win32 applications as _____ applications using WOW64.

    a.   kernel mode

    b.   .NET Framework 3.0 subsystem

    c.   Win16

    d.   legacy

    e.   VDM-based

7.   Registry information is compartmentalized into sections known as _____.

    a.   hives

    b.   thunks

    c.   key sets

    d.   vaults

    e.   values

8.   For a registry value to take effect, it must have the correct _____, _____, and _____.

    a.   key name

    b.   data type

    c.   owner

    d.   case-sensitive name

    e.   data

9.   _____ is the hive used to store global software information that applies to applications installed on the computer regardless of the currently logged-on user.

    a.   HKEY_CLASSES_ROOT

    b.   HKEY_CURRENT_USER

    c.   HKEY_LOCAL_MACHINE

    d.   HKEY_DYN_DATA

    e.   HKEY_GLOBAL_CONFIG

10.   For a registry key to be properly recognized, it must have the correct _____ and _____.

    a.   auditing configured

    b.   position in the registry hierarchy

    c.   owner

    d.   *name

11.   _____ is a hive primarily used for defining how to launch related applications based on the file extension of a data file.

    a.   HKEY_CLASSES_ROOT

    b.   HKEY_CURRENT_USER

    c.   HKEY_LOCAL_MACHINE

    d.   HKEY_DYN_DATA

12. The HKEY_CURRENT_USER hive is mapped from the _____ hive.

    a.   HKEY_CLASSES_ROOT

    b.   HKEY_USERS

    c.   HKEY_LOCAL_MACHINE

    d.   HKEY_DYN_DATA

13. The currently logged-on user is identified uniquely by their _____.

    a.   user name

    b.   security token

    c.   PIN

    d.   SID

14. The default user registry configuration is stored in the registry as part of the _____ hive.

    a.   HKEY_CLASSES_ROOT

    b.   HKEY_USERS

    c.   HKEY_LOCAL_MACHINE

    d.   HKEY_DYN_DATA

    e.   HKEY_GLOBAL_CONFIG

15. The tools available to edit the registry directly include _____ and _____.

    a.   REGMOD.EXE

    b.   REG.EXE

    c.   REGUPDATE.EXE

    d.   REGEDIT.EXE

16. The graphical registry editor can be invoked from a command window by issuing the command _____. (Select two.)

    a.   REG.EXE

    b.   REGEDIT.EXE

    c.   REG32.EXE

    d.   REGEDT32.EXE

    e.   There is only one command to start the graphical registry editing tool.

17. Registry data exported to a file will have the _____ extension.

    a.   .REG

    b.   .TXT

    c.   .BIN

    d.   .INI

18. Access to registry data can be restricted by _____ and _____.

    a.   auditing configuration

    b.   kernel mode services

    c.   assigned permissions

    d.   registry value editors

    e.   registry key owners

19. Registration files that contain previously exported registry data can be imported by double-clicking the file in Explorer. True or False?

20. File and registry virtualization is not supported by _____.

    a. Executive Services

    b. Win32

    c. the 64-bit version of Windows 7

    d. User Account Control

21. User Account Control-aware applications can include an XML file compiled in to the application to control file and registry virtualization. This XML file is also known as the _____.

    a. application manifest

    b. control limiter

    c. compatibility manifest

    d. run as administrator token

    e. There is no such file.

22. Application compatibility settings can be configured using _____. (Select all that apply.)

    a. Application Compatibility Verifier

    b. manual configuration of the program's compatibility properties

    c. Application Compatibility Toolkit

    d. Program Compatibility Assistant

    e. AppLocker

23. Application compatibility settings must always be determined by the installer who is trying to get the program to run because Windows 7 does not include an automatic tool to configure compatibility settings. True or False?

24. The key registry areas virtualized in file and registry virtualization include _____. (Select all that apply.)

    a. HKEY_USERS*SID*

    b. HKEY_LOCAL_MACHINE\\SYSTEM\\Select

    c. HKEY_LOCAL_MACHINE\\Software

    d. HKEY_CURRENT_USER\\Software

25. Applications that cannot run in Windows 7 with tweaked compatibility settings may be supported if they are installed using _____.

    a. NTVDM

    b. WOWEXEC

    c. XP Mode

    d. Software Restriction Policies

Case Projects

Case Project 11-1: Preparing to Adapt Legacy Applications

You will be deploying Windows 7 as a replacement desktop operating system for a small company with less than 40 users. The main business application is a DOS-based program that communicates with a Windows-based server and provides an interactive control screen to track inventory levels in the company's warehouse. What steps will you take to prepare for this applications compatibility testing with Windows 7?

Case Project 11-2: Registry Change Management

You have customized your Windows 7 computer with several registry changes that have tweaked the standard look and feel of your computer. After these changes were exported to registration files, you distributed them to other users within the company. Several users have called back to report that after they applied the registration files to their system, their computers will not start successfully. What steps will you take to mitigate the impact of these changes on the affected computers and ensure that such an occurrence is not likely to happen again?

Case Project 11-3: Secure Access for Applications

A user with a Windows 7 computer has complained that their system is frequently prompting them with User Account Control messages that request elevated administrative access. The user also says that he wants User Account Control disabled and that he should be given administrative rights to the entire computer. Explain why these changes are not recommended and why the existing system is a benefit to him and the organization?

chapter 12

Disaster Recovery and Troubleshooting

After reading this chapter and completing the exercises, you will be able to:

- Describe the general principles of troubleshooting
- Use Windows Backup and Restore to protect user and system components
- Describe the major tools used to repair Windows 7
- Identify systems and tools that assist in preventative maintenance operations
- Review advanced troubleshooting areas

The ability to troubleshoot problems in Windows 7 has been greatly enhanced. New and improved tools for collecting information about the status of the computer reduce the time it takes to understand what is happening with the computer. By applying common sense solution guidelines and Windows 7 specific repair utilities, the troubleshooting process is accelerated. The overall health of Windows 7 can also be managed with built-in preventative maintenance tools to minimize the time spent worrying about the computer's health.

General Principles of Troubleshooting

Troubleshooting is a process that systematically diagnoses and analyzes a situation to understand why it differs from a desired situation. Once the problem is understood, potential solutions can be suggested and investigated. Effective troubleshooting requires sufficient information collection about the problem and then applying solutions using best-practice guidelines. When performing troubleshooting use the following process:

1. Gather information about the problem, such as the errors reported by users.
2. Identify potential solutions to the problem.
3. Prioritize potential solutions based on how likely they are to fix the problem and how easy they are to implement.
4. Implement the best potential solution and verify whether the problem is resolved.
5. If the problem is not resolved, undo the fix you implemented in step 4. Then use the new information you have learned and return to step 2.
6. If the problem is solved, document the resolution for future reference.

Information Collection

Many computer users do not know how to describe a problem beyond the statement "It's not doing what I want it to."

Windows 7 is different from earlier versions of Windows, in that it has sophisticated methods to diagnose and repair as many problems as possible on its own. If it cannot diagnose or repair the problem, it can attempt to automatically connect to Microsoft and determine the best next course of action. The built-in diagnostic tools and repair wizards can work without the user having detailed and intimate knowledge of Windows 7. Windows XP and previous versions of Windows have limited methods for self-diagnosis and repair.

The automated tools in Windows 7 may fix some problems, but even these tools have limits. In these cases the person repairing the computer must resort to traditional troubleshooting tools and techniques. The first step in efficient troubleshooting is collecting of details that describe the state of the computer and information that describes the problem. The best tools to start gathering information are:

- Problem Steps Recorder
- System Information
- Computer Management
- Action Center
- Help and Support
- Microsoft Support Web site

Problem Steps Recorder   Windows 7 includes **Problem Steps Recorder** to allows users to record the exact steps required to reproduce a problem. The recorded steps can then be forwarded to help desk staff for analysis. This tool can be used to accurately capture information about how a problem is caused when help desk staff are unavailable or when it is not possible for help desk staff to remote control a computer. You can access Problem Steps Recorder by typing psr in the Start Menu search box.

Problem Steps Recorder does not capture a video of the user performing actions. Instead, a screenshot is captured each time the user clicks on a screen item. The screenshots and user actions are saved in a report that can be e-mailed or saved to a shared storage location. The report is an .mht file that contains both text and the screenshots. To keep the report size small, it is compressed in a zip file.

It is important to remember that Problem Steps Recorder does not capture anything that is typed. If information being typed is important, the user needs to add a comment that includes the information being typed.

System Information   This tool scans the current state of the computer and reports its findings in a searchable tree format, as shown in Figure 12-1. The **System Information** utility can export its findings to a text file or it can be saved to a System Information file. System Information files use the extension .NFO and store data in a compressed **binary format**.

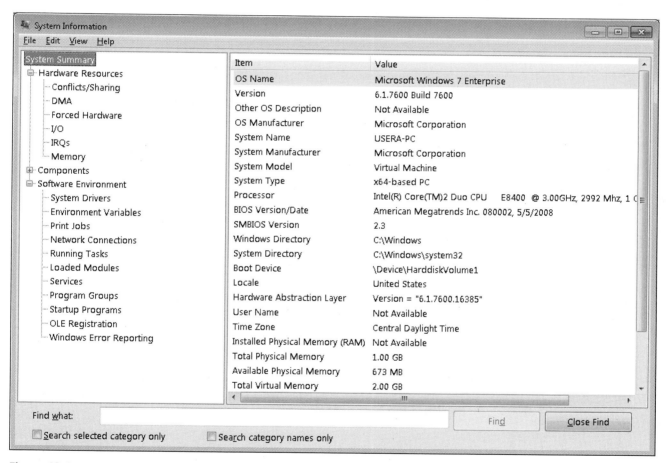

Figure 12-1 System Information
Courtesy Course Technology/Cengage Learning

A System Information file can be e-mailed to another technician and reviewed by opening the file with the System Information utility. This is an efficient way to summarize the details of the current software and hardware running on the computer. The System Information utility can also report critical observations such as what programs are started automatically and what hardware conflicts are present.

Computer Management   The Computer Management utility is an **MMC**-based utility used to manage several key systems and operations for a computer, shown in Figure 12-2. The Computer Management utility can also be used to connect to remote computers as long as the remote computer allows the communication through its **Windows Firewall** and recognizes that the user has administrative permission to interact with its systems the connection is allowed.

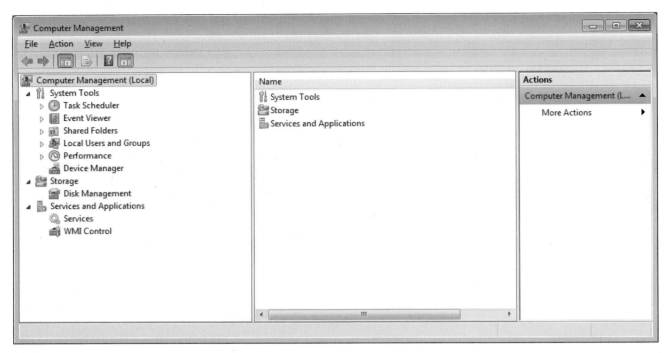

Figure 12-2 Computer Management
Courtesy Course Technology/Cengage Learning

The Computer Management utility is used for the following systems:

- Task Scheduler
- Event Viewer
- Shared Folders
- Local Users and Groups
- Performance
- Device Manager
- Disk Management
- Services
- WMI Control

Task Scheduler The Task Scheduler console is used to view the recent and current status of tasks that are started automatically. New tasks can be created and organized into a structured list called the Task Scheduler Library. The Task Scheduler Library includes a predefined structure for Windows 7 operational tasks. In addition to the predefined tasks, custom tasks can be created and organized for user-defined categories or applications, such as tasks for trigger events in Event Viewer.

Task Scheduler is covered in Chapter 3, Using the System Utilities.

The Task Scheduler in Windows 7 is very different when compared to earlier versions running in Windows NT, Windows 2000, Windows 2003, or Windows XP. The Task Scheduler in earlier versions of Windows is seldom used to perform any tasks at all.

In Windows 7, system tasks in Task Scheduler are used by Windows to perform routine maintenance and their status. The Task Scheduler console can report the status of tasks that automatically ran over a recent time interval (last hour, last 24 hours, last 7 days, last 30 days) and provide a quick way to check if any important tasks have failed to run as required. This may help identify why certain resources are impacted or it may alter the troubleshooting strategy if maintenance tasks such as periodic backups have failed.

Some tasks in Task Scheduler are configured as hidden tasks. Hidden tasks can be optionally displayed in the Task Scheduler console by selecting Show Hidden Tasks from the View menu.

Event Viewer The **Event Viewer** utility is an MMC console snap-in used to browse and manage the records of system events and messages stored in system event logs, as shown in Figure 12-3. The Windows 7 version of Event Viewer has been rewritten to offer richer reporting than the version used with Windows XP or earlier versions of Windows. The Event Viewer is also available in the Administrative Tools as a stand-alone MMC console.

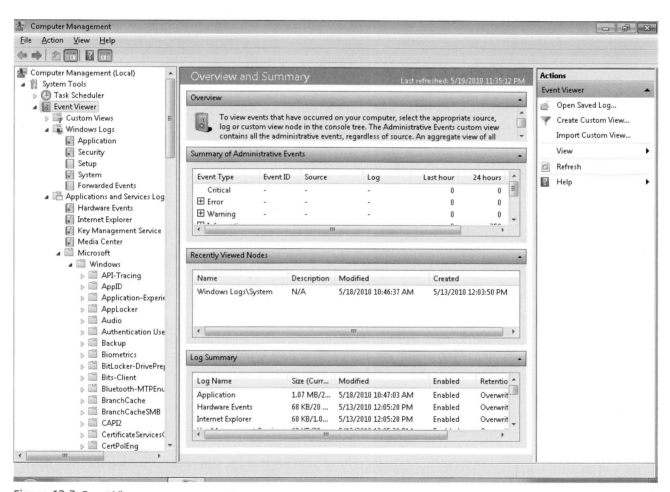

Figure 12-3 Event Viewer
Courtesy Course Technology/Cengage Learning

Windows 7 and some applications are designed to write status messages to the event logs automatically. The Event Viewer logs are primarily organized by the source of event messages:

- *Custom Views*—Filtered data from multiple event logs or event sources based on filter settings assigned to each unique custom view. The Administrative View is preset to show critical, error, and warning events from all administrative logs.

- *Windows Logs*—Reporting messages organized into general categories of application, security, and operating system messages. These logs correspond to the general log categories used by the Windows XP Event Viewer utility.

- *Applications and Services Logs*—Reporting messages organized by specific application or service. Logs for operating system applications are organized into their own folder structure within this category.

- *Subscriptions*—When configured, this manages incoming event message streams from remote computers. Remote computers are configured to deliver specific types of event messages to the local computer and store them in specific local logs.

- *Saved Logs*—Used to organize and display event logs that were previously saved to archive files and are now opened for viewing.

Operational, analytic, and debug logs can be displayed in Event Viewer. By default, only operational logs are visible. The operational logs report typical event messages. The analytic and debug logs report additional information that can be used by developers and advanced troubleshooters, but they are hidden by default. To reveal or hide these logs select Show Analytic and Debug Logs from the View menu. The analytic and debug logs do not collect data by default because this would result in a large amount of data being written to the log file and the system performance may be impacted. To enable event message recording for a specific analytic or debug log, logging must be enabled in the log's properties.

Each event log has its own properties. The properties of an event log are shown in Figure 12-4.

The event log properties General tab identifies and controls:

- *Full Name*—The name of the event log
- *Log path*—The path to the file that stores the log data
- *Log size*—The current size of the log file
- *Created*—The date and time the log file was created
- *Modified*—The date and time the log file was last modified
- *Accessed*—The date and time the log file was last accessed
- *Enable logging*—When selected, the log can be written to. If this option is not selected, corresponding events may still occur but they will not be written to the log file.
- *Maximum log size (KB)*—The limit to which the log file may grow, specified in kilobytes.

When maximum event log size is reached:

- *Overwrite events as needed (oldest events first)*—Once the log file reaches its maximum size, the oldest events are deleted from the log to make room for new information. This can result in the loss of old event information.

- *Archive the log when full, do not overwrite events*—Once the log file reaches its maximum size the current log file is archived and a new log file is started. No event information is lost using this method but disk space must be available to store the archived data.

- *Do not overwrite events (clear logs manually)*—Once the log file reaches its maximum size, the recording of event information for that log stops. The event log file must be cleared manually.

- *Clear Log*—This button erases all events in the log file. Before the log is cleared, the system will ask if the log should be saved before clearing it.

The properties of an event log also include a Subscriptions tab that can be used to manage the event log subscriptions from computers running Window 7, Windows Vista, Windows Server 2008, and Windows Server 2003 R2. In most cases, however, logs from Windows 7 computers will be centralized on a server for analysis, rather than collected on a Windows 7 computer.

Because the amount of data in a log can be rather large, it can be difficult to find the events that are of interest to the troubleshooter. The data in an event log can be filtered, as shown in Figure 12-5, to limit the display to only events that match the filter for that log.

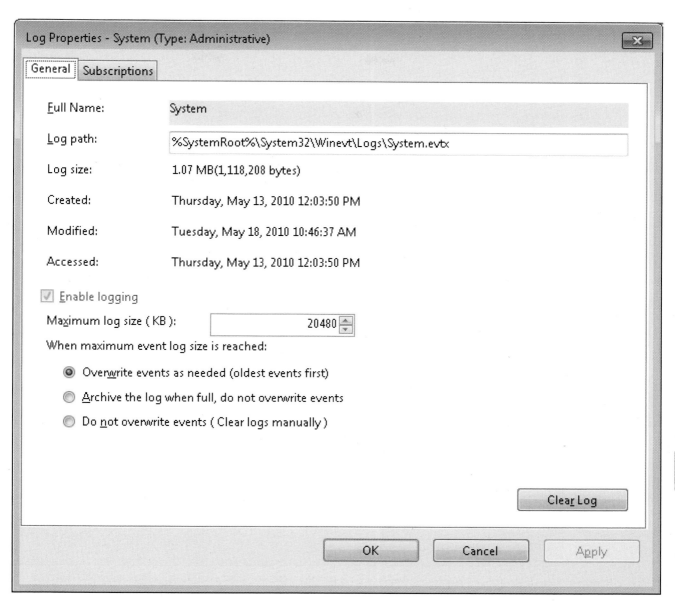

Figure 12-4 Event Log Properties
Courtesy Course Technology/Cengage Learning

The event log filter is defined separately for each log. The filter's general options include:

- *Logged*—Defines a time limit for events of interest (any time, last hour, last 12 hours, last 24 hours, last 7 days, last 30 days, or a custom range of time)

- *Event level*—Restricts the display of events to a selected event level: Critical, Warning, Error, Information, or Verbose

- *By log, Event logs*—The log the filter applies to is selected by default

- *By source, Event sources*—Select one or more event providers (applications, services, system components) that are registered to write events to the log

- *Includes/Excludes Event IDs*—Selects the events to display based on the event ID assigned to each event. Each type of event is assigned a unique event ID for general categorization purposes. If the event IDs of interest are known ahead of time, they can be specified here. If more than one event ID is to be displayed, then separate the list of IDs with commas. A range of event IDs is specified by the first and last ID in the range, separated by a dash

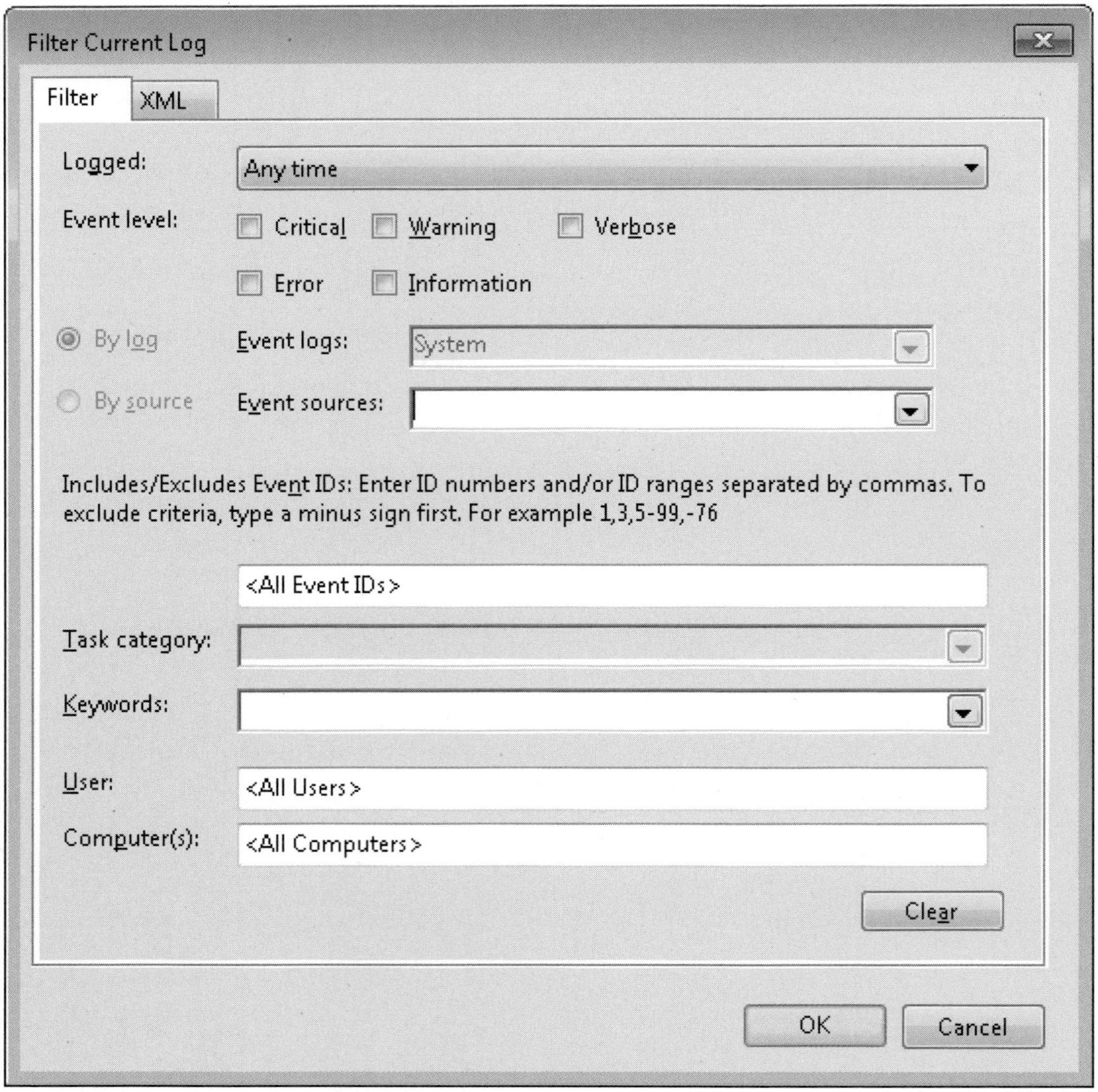

Figure 12-5 Event log display filter
Courtesy Course Technology/Cengage Learning

(e.g., 450–569). If an event ID should be specifically excluded, enter it with a minus sign in front of the ID (e.g., –458)

- *Task category*—If multiple task categories are defined for this log, selects the ones of interest here
- *Keywords*—Selects one or more predefined keywords from a list. A selected keyword must be present in the event for it to match the filter
- *User*—Selects events that are associated with a specific user name
- *Computer*—Selects events that are associated with a specific computer name

When a filter is defined for a log, any filter item that is left blank will match any event in the log. The filter can be edited in XML format by opening a log's filter and selecting the XML tab. This allows the manual editing of the XML-formatted event filter query. If a filter is applied to an event log, the Event Viewer display prefaces the event log's name with "Filtered."

To simplify the gathering of relevant event from multiple event logs, you can create a custom view. A custom view provides you with the same options for filtering as a single log, but allows you to select multiple logs. This can be very useful for monitoring an application that places events in multiple event logs.

An event log's data can be saved to a uniquely named archive file by selecting the log and then selecting Save Events As from the Action menu. The log data can be saved in a text format (.TXT), comma-separated values (.CSV), XML with language formatting (.XML), or native event log binary format (.EVTX). The native event log binary format shows all additional information reported with an event that is not shown in the other save formats. If a filter is active on the event log, then only the filtered data will be stored to the saved file.

Event log data files can be opened in Event Viewer by selecting Open Saved Log from the Action menu. The file must be formatted in the Windows 7 native event log binary format (.EVTX) or the legacy Windows NT/2000/XP/2003 binary format (.EVT).

Once a log is selected for viewing, a single event in the log can be highlighted in the upper-middle pane and its details are displayed in the lower-middle pane. This same information is displayed on the General tab when you view the properties of an event, as shown in Figure 12-6.

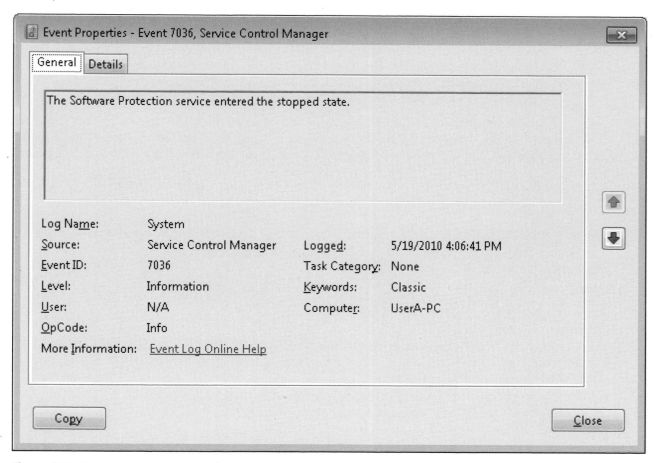

Figure 12-6 Event Properties General tab
Courtesy Course Technology/Cengage Learning

The general event details displayed for a highlighted event include:

- *General description*—A narrative that explains what the event is and why it has occurred. Information on how to respond to the event may be included in the narrative.
- *Log Name*—The name of the log that recorded the event.
- *Source*—The name of the registered event provider that generated the event.
- *Logged*—The date and time the event was recorded.
- *Event ID*—The numeric code assigned to this general type of message.

- *Task Category*—Unique identifier specified by the event provider (source). If specified, this will help identify which task being performed by the event provider was responsible for the generation of this message. For example, the Windows Update Client uses task categories to define the type of work it is performing when an event is generated. Two such task categories are: Automatic Updates and Windows Update Agent.

- *Level*—A general category to identify the significance or verbosity of an event (e.g. critical, informational).

- *Keywords*—Unique descriptive keywords assigned to the event by the event provider (source). Keywords are pre-defined and are represented by a code in the event's raw details.

- *User*—The user name or their security identifier associated with the generation of the event.

- *Computer*—The computer account associated with the generation of the event.

- *OpCode*—Label to identify the operational status (e.g. Info, Start, Stop) of the event provider.

- *More Information*—Additional information to help the user understand and determine a response to information contained in the event. The default information supplied is a link to Event Log Online Help, which will pass a summary of the event to Microsoft if the user confirms that it is allowed. The Event Log Knowledgebase will be searched at Microsoft, and any additional information or recommendations will be displayed in an Internet Explorer Web page that will open automatically.

Each event includes additional information that is not displayed on the General tab of the event's details. The extra information is visible by selecting the event's Details tab and selecting the XML View, as shown in Figure 12-7. The information that was reported on the event's

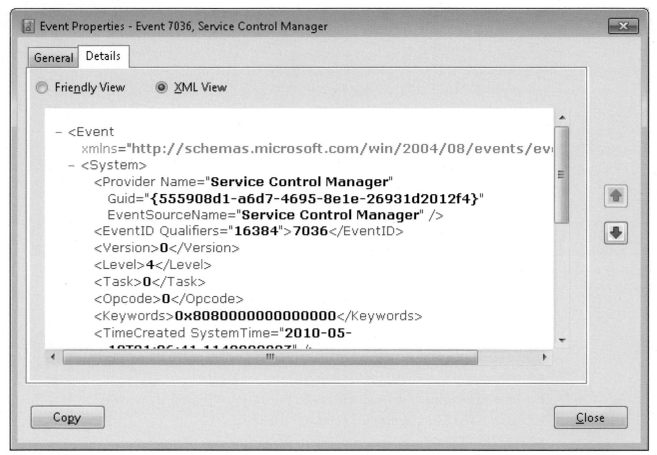

Figure 12-7 Event Properties XML View
Courtesy Course Technology/Cengage Learning

General tab is present in the XML view, but is shown in raw form. Additional details about the event source and the situation may be reported in the XML view. The Friendly View on the Details tab shows a simplified summary of the XML information.

The details of a single event can be copied to the Windows clipboard by right-clicking the event pointing to Copy, and clicking Copy Details as Text from the pop-up menu. The event details can then be pasted into a file or e-mail for further analysis.

The appearance of a specific event in an event log can also trigger a scheduled task to run by selecting the task in the event log and clicking Attach Task To This Event in the Action menu. This starts the Create Basic Task wizard, which prompts for a name and description for the task that is being created. What uniquely triggers this task is a combination of the log that the event appears in, the source of the event message, and a specific event ID. The action triggered can be the start of a program, sending an e-mail, or displaying a message. Once the task is created, it is managed through Task Scheduler.

Activity 12-1: Using Event Viewer

Time Required: 10 minutes
Objective: Use event viewer to view system events.

Description: Event Viewer allows you to see most of the system activity that is logged on your system. When applications or Windows 7 are experiencing errors, the Event Viewer is one of the first places to look and find more information. In this activity, you view the information that is available in Event Viewer.

1. If necessary, start your computer and log on.

2. Click the **Start** button, right-click **Computer**, and click **Manage**.

3. Under System Tools, expand **Event Viewer** and click **Event Viewer**. You can see the summary of events on this system over various time frames and sorted by event type. This makes it easy for you to address Critical events and Error events.

4. In the middle pane, expand **Error**. This gives you a summary of all the Error events on your system so that you can quickly scan over them. If you are not able to expand Error, it is because your system has no error events to report.

5. In the left pane, expand **Windows Logs** and click **Windows Logs**. The logs stored here are approximately equivalent to the logs in Windows XP. However, the Setup and Forwarded Events logs are new.

6. In the left pane, click **System**. This displays all of the messages in the System log.

7. In the middle pane, select an event. You can see that information about the event displayed at the bottom of the middle pane.

8. Click the **Details** tab. This tab offers a friendly view and XML view. Friendly view is best for most administrators.

9. Click **XML View** and read the event information.

10. In the left pane, expand **Applications and Services Logs**, expand **Microsoft**, and expand **Windows**. These logs are specific to particular applications and services. They were not available in Windows XP.

11. In the left pane, click **Custom Views**. Custom views filter the event logs on the local computer to make specified events viewable in a single location. You can see that the Administrative Events custom view is here by default.

12. Double-click **Administrative Events**. This view pulls all Critical, Error, and Warning events into a single location.

13. Right-click **Administrative Events** and click **Properties**.

14. Click **Edit Filter**. You cannot modify this filter because the view is created by the system. However, you can see that you can specify which event levels and which logs to include. You can also filter based on event ID, task category, keywords, user, or computer.

12

15. Click **Cancel** to close the Custom View Properties.

16. Click **Cancel** to close the Administrative Events Properties.

17. Close Computer Management.

Shared Folders The Shared Folders console identifies what folders are shared on the current computer, who is connected to those shared folders, and what files in those shared folders are open. For troubleshooting purposes, this can be useful to identify what resources are in use by users who may be connected remotely. If the computer is about to be restarted, this can identify who needs to be notified so that they can close their connections before the restart and avoid data file corruption for their open files. The shared folders' details can also be reviewed to see if the security settings or limits are correct. If they are incorrect, they can be modified from here.

Local Users and Groups The Local Users and Groups console identifies the users created on the local computer and the security groups those users belong to. For troubleshooting, this can be used to audit the groups and permission levels for a user account to see if the details match the user's expectations.

The Local Users and Groups console is covered in Chapter 6, User Management.

Performance The Performance console can be used to view real-time performance data or stored performance data from a log file. You can create Data Collector Sets to configure and schedule performance counter, event trace, and configuration data collection so that you can assess the results at a later date and view reports. Windows 7 has a new tool, called Resource Monitor, which allows you to view detailed real-time information about hardware resources (CPU, disk, network, and memory) and system resources (including handles and modules) in use by the operating system, services, and running applications. In addition, you can use Resource Monitor to stop processes, start and stop services, analyze process deadlocks, view thread wait chains, and identify processes locking files.

Performance and Resource Monitor are covered in Chapter 10, Performance Tuning.

Device Manager The Device Manager console reports the status of the currently attached computer hardware. When troubleshooting odd computer behavior, this tool can be used to address the following questions:

- Are all expected hardware devices attached to the computer?

- Are any devices disabled? If this is the problem, the device can be enabled by clicking Enable Device on the device's properties window.

- Are all devices working properly? Some listed devices may have an exclamation icon or question mark over the regular device icon to identify devices with issues. The Other devices category in Device Manager reports hardware devices that are not properly recognized by Windows 7. This can direct efforts to determine hardware that is broken, needs new drivers sourced, or is incompatible and must be replaced.

Disk Management Disk Management reports the disk configuration of the computer. For troubleshooting, Disk Management can be reviewed to:

- Determine if all disks are present as expected
- Review if any disks are reporting degraded status
- Identify drive letter assignment
- Anticipate space issues for storing additional files

The Disk Management console is reviewed in Chapter 4, Managing Disks.

Services   The Services console presents controls and reports the state of installed services that can be managed from this user interface. Services run as a process in the background within a session restricted from the user's own session for security isolation. The services do not directly communicate with the user because of this security separation, so this console is the preferred method to alter service behavior. The data that controls a service typically resides in the registry, but this data should not be modified directly from the registry.

The Services console presents a list of services on either the Extended or Standard tab. Both tabs list the same services, but the Extended tab provides a verbose description for some services.

The displayed services can be sorted by column that include:

- *Name*—The name of the service
- *Description*—The description of what the service does
- *Status*—The operational state of the service: Starting, Started, Stopping, Stopped (blank)
- *Startup type*—How the service is started (Automatic Delayed Start, Automatic, Manual, Disabled)
- *Log On As*—The user or system account security level that the service runs as

The Services console can be used in troubleshooting to identify those services that should have started automatically and should be running but are not. It can be a mistake to assume that a service set to Automatic startup should always be running. Some services only run on demand as required. Services listed as Starting may indicate a service that is taking a long time to start or has stalled completely.

In the properties of a service, the General tab, as shown in Figure 12-8, can be used to:

- *Change the startup type*—The startup type can be set to Manual, Automatic, Automatic (Delayed Startup), or Disabled. If the service is causing the computer to become unstable when it runs, the startup type can be set to Manual or Disabled. The Manual startup type still allows the service to be started as part of the diagnostic process. The Disabled setting does not allow the service to run at all. The Automatic and Automatic (Delayed Startup) option tries to start the service when the computer is started. The Delayed Startup is used to start selected services a short time after the Automatic services are started to minimize impact on the time required for the initial boot process.
- *View service status*—Report the current operational state of the service (Starting, Started, Stopping, Stopped).
- *Change the service operational state*—Buttons to Start, Stop, Pause, or Resume the operational state of the service.
- *Pass optional start parameters to the service*—Optional command-line parameters are used to start the service with modified behavior, usually for debug or diagnostic purposes. The parameters to use depend on the service and are specified by the developer of the service. Not all services can use the optional start parameters field.

The service operates as an application in its own secured session with the security credentials defined on the Log On tab of the service's properties, shown in Figure 12-9. The service can operate as

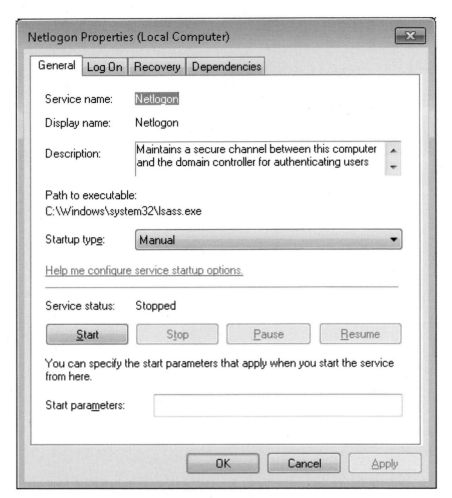

Figure 12-8 Service Properties General tab
Courtesy Course Technology/Cengage Learning

part of the operating system (Local System) security account or another specified security account. If a user account is specified for the service to authenticate itself, then the user account and password must be specified. Occasionally, the wrong account is specified for a service or the user account is deleted without updating the service properties. A frequent problem is that the user account password is changed but the password specified here is not updated to reflect the change. In many cases, the service continues to run until it is restarted and fails to authenticate as it is starting.

Services that fail or crash may be configured to restart based on the settings found on the Recovery tab of the service's properties, shown in Figure 12-10. When the service crashes, the service can be restarted, the computer can be restarted, the service can stay crashed, or a program can be run. These options can be set uniquely for the first, second, and subsequent failures so that a progressive response can be preset.

If a service is experiencing errors or issues, it may be due to the effect of other services it depends on that are having problems. The service that is being examined may in turn impact other services that rely on it. A quick way to see the coded dependencies is to examine the Dependencies tab of the service's properties, shown in Figure 12-11. This can redirect the attention for why a service is failing to a dependent service or it can explain why this service is impacting other services. The dependencies are usually defined in the registry and are not controlled through this interface. The registry settings should not be directly modified to alter the list of dependencies.

WMI Control Configures and controls the **Windows Management Instrumentation (WMI)** service. WMI allows management systems to interact with agent software running as part of the

Figure 12-9 Service Properties Log On tab
Courtesy Course Technology/Cengage Learning

Windows 7 operating system. WMI is used for reporting and configuration of application and operating system data through WMI requests, which can be made locally or remotely. Network Management software can use WMI to gather information on the status of Windows 7, such as running processes or hardware configuration.

Action Center Windows 7 includes a tool that provides you with a single location where you can identify and address any security issues, maintenance requirements, and errors that have arisen. The **Action Center** options available under maintenance, shown in Figure 12-12, are:

- *Check for solutions to problem reports*—Like Windows Vista, Windows 7 identifies when system errors occur. After a system error is identified, Windows 7 can contact Microsoft and check for solutions. If a solution is identified, you are notified by an alert in the Action Center. By default, Windows 7 automatically checks for solutions, but you can disable error reporting, exclude specific programs from error reporting, and enable prompting before Windows 7 checks for solutions. There is also a link to open Reliability Monitor.

- *Backup*—This section allows you set up backup for files that you select as well as the whole computer. This feature is discussed in detail in the next section.

- *Check for updates*—This refers to the automatic updating functionality in Windows Update, which can be set up to download and install noncritical and recommended Windows updates.

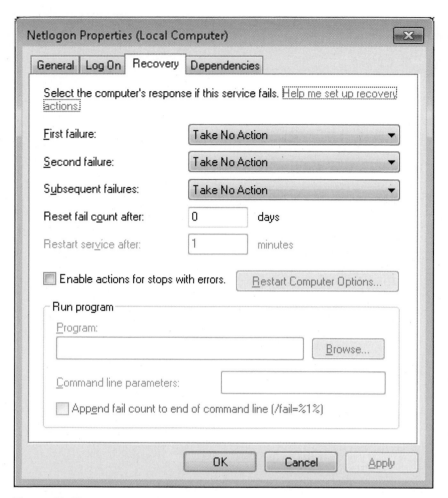

Figure 12-10 Service Properties Recovery tab
Courtesy Course Technology/Cengage Learning

- *Troubleshooting: System Maintenance*—Windows 7 actively checks the computer for maintenance problems. This section allows you to enable or disable this feature. You can also control whether users can browse the Windows Online Troubleshooting service.

Troubleshooting   Action Center contains categorized troubleshooters in the Troubleshooting area, as shown in Figure 12-13. Each troubleshooter is a wizard that can automatically identify and fix common problems. New and updated troubleshooters are obtained from the Windows Online Troubleshooting service.

The categories of troubleshooters are:

- *Programs*—This category includes troubleshooters for program compatibility, Internet Explorer performance and safety, and Windows Media Player.

- *Hardware and Sound*—This category includes troubleshooters for sound, devices, network adapters, printers, and TV tuners.

- *Network and Internet*—This category includes troubleshooters for Internet connections, shared folders, HomeGroup, and DirectAccess.

- *Appearance and Personalization*—This category includes troubleshooters for Aero and display quality.

- *System and Security*—This category includes troubleshooters for Internet Explorer safety, system maintenance, performance, power, and Windows search.

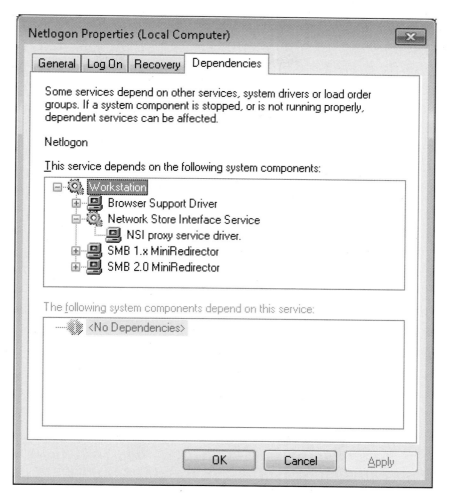

Figure 12-11 Service Properties Dependencies tab
Courtesy Course Technology/Cengage Learning

Recovery The Recovery option in Action Center is used to recover from system problems by restoring Windows 7 to a previous state. In most cases, you use **System Restore** for the first attempt at system recovery. If that doesn't resolve the problem, then you can use the Advanced recovery methods. The Advanced recovery methods are (1) Use a system image you created earlier to recover your computer and (2) Reinstall Windows. To reinstall Windows, you must have have the Windows 7 installation DVD.

Assuming that you have previously created a system image backup, the recovery from a system image restores everything on this computer, including Windows, programs, and all files saved on the system image. Reinstalling Windows performs a complete reinstall of Windows on the computer. Any files or programs that were installed have to be either restored from a backup or reinstalled using the original installation discs or files. The previous installation of Windows may remain in a Windows.old folder.

Reliability Monitor When you choose View reliability history in the Maintenance area of Action Center, you open Reliability Monitor. **Reliability Monitor** is a tool that rates the system stability of Windows 7 and lets you monitor the events that contribute to system stability. Figure 12-14 shows Reliability Monitor.

Reliability monitor collects the following data:

- *Software installs and uninstalls*—Software is often a cause of system instability. Using this information, you can correlate a decline in system stability with software installation or uninstallation. Software tracked here includes driver and operating system updates.

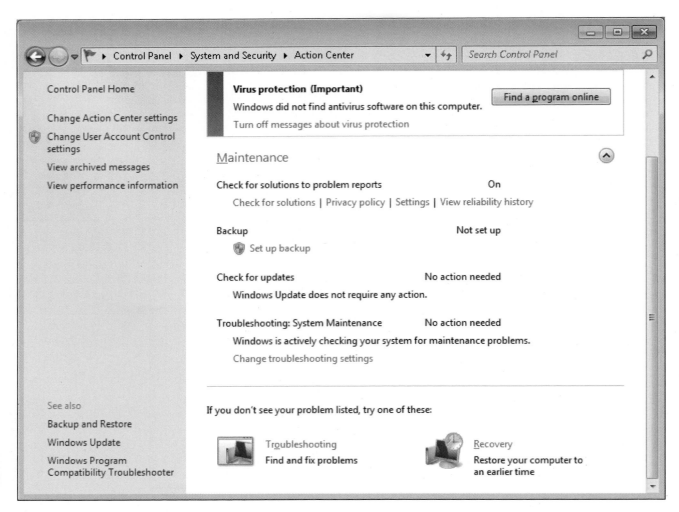

Figure 12-12 Action Center Maintenance options
Courtesy Course Technology/Cengage Learning

- *Application failures*—Application failures are one type of instability that is tracked. Any application that stops responding is logged here.

- *Hardware failures*—Hardware failures are one type of tracked instability. This is primarily for disk and memory failures.

- *Windows failures*—Windows failures are one type of instability that is tracked. This includes any system failure that results in blue screen errors (the Blue Screen of Death or BSOD) and boot failures.

- *Miscellaneous failures*—This includes any system failures not included in other categories. One type of failure recorded here is improper shutdowns.

Data collection for Reliability Monitor is automatically enabled on a new installation. However, data collection does not occur for the first time until 24 hours after installation. Data collection is controlled by the RacTask scheduled task. If this task is disabled, data collection for reliability is stopped.

Reliability Monitor provides a graphical view which is useful for a summary of system performance. You can view a list of all problem reports summarized by source by choosing to View all problem reports.

Reliability Monitor calculates a stability index for each day. The stability index is a rating from 1 (least stable) to 10 (most stable). The index is graphed over time to allow you to see when

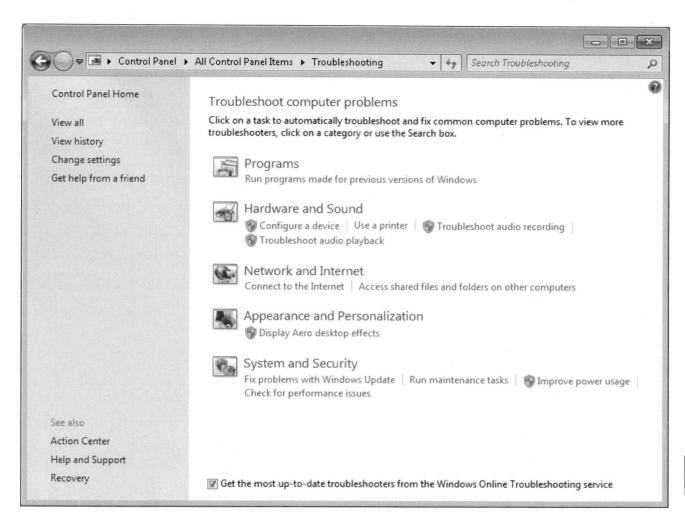

Figure 12-13 Troubleshooting
Courtesy Course Technology/Cengage Learning

12

a decrease or increase in system stability may have occurred. Icons beneath the graph allow you to drill down and view events that occurred on a particular day.

When calculating the stability index, recent failures are given more weight than past failures. As a consequence, a system with no recent failures will have a slowly improving stability index. A system with a recent failure will experience an immediate decline in the system stability index.

If a system is powered off or in a sleep state for an extended period of time, that time frame is not included in the calculation of the stability index. For example, if a computer experiences a failure and then the computer is not used again for a month, the stability index will be the same as the day it was turned off. It will not have improved slowly over the month. Significant time changes are also noted as an event.

A dotted line in the reliability graphs indicates that not enough data is available to calculate a valid stability index.

The Reliability Monitor graph lets you see the point in time at which significant reliability changes occurred. You can use the graph to drill down and find out what events occurred in that time frame, and likely correct the problem. For example, if frequent failures occur after adding a new driver, then the driver is the likely cause of the stability problem and should be removed.

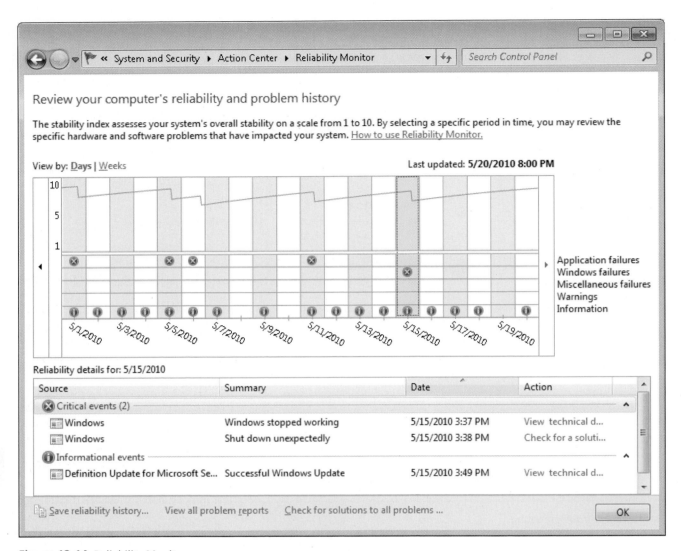

Figure 12-14 Reliability Monitor
Courtesy Course Technology/Cengage Learning

If you can see that a particular application is consistently failing, you can search for a resolution to the problem. The problem may be resolved by updating the operating system or the application. There may also be a known conflict with other applications.

If a particular piece of hardware appears to be failing, you can replace it. You can also try updating the hardware driver to ensure that hardware information is being interpreted properly by the operating system.

Activity 12-2: Using Reliability Monitor

Time Required: 5 minutes
Objective: Use Reliability Monitor to view system reliability.

Description: Reliability Monitor allows you to view overall system reliability and the events that may have made your system unreliable. You can use this tool to troubleshoot reliability problems. In this activity, you view the information in Reliability Monitor.

1. Click **Start**, type **Action Center**, and press **Enter**.

2. Expand **Maintenance** and click **View reliability history**. This is the overall reliability rating for your computer. The graph shows how reliability has increased or decreased over time.

3. If a red **x** is visible in the chart, click it. This displays the details for the error in the Reliability details section below the chart.

4. If a blue and white is visible in the chart, click it. This displays the details for the software installation or uninstallation.

5. Close Reliability Monitor.

Help and Support　The Help and Support utility is available from the Start Menu and is a useful research tool to source troubleshooting advice and develop an understanding of the affected system components. If the computer is connected to the Internet, the Help and Support utility can be used to check online for updated information or links to support resources that can provide additional advice or diagnostic services.

Microsoft Support Web Site　The Microsoft support Web site (*http://support.microsoft. com*) is available free to anyone as long as they can connect to the site. A common knowledge base is provided with searchable articles describing problems and suggested solutions. The information described in the knowledge base articles can be more detailed in describing problem scenarios and solutions than the general Help and Support utility. Each knowledge base article is assigned an article number that is usually prefaced with the letters KB (e.g. KB123456). Before applying any solution steps detailed in a knowledge base article, ensure that the article applies to the version of Windows that you are troubleshooting. For example, an article with steps to repair Windows XP might destroy the Windows 7 operating system if applied by mistake.

Solution Guidelines

Troubleshooting is a skill that can be developed over time; however there is no fixed formula that guarantees success. Troubleshooting skills can benefit by observing common solution guidelines:

- *Be patient*—Computer problems require a methodical approach to solve. If one solution does not work, another can be developed. Emotional responses to computer problems are a natural human response but the drama does not lead to a quick solution.

- *Familiarize yourself with the involved hardware and software*—Identify what hardware and software is installed. Confirm the baseline performance of the system when it is operating normally. Confirm what a user of the computer considers normal behavior. Research what the normal behavior of the hardware or software is supposed to be.

- *Limit changes*—Change only one item at a time and test the solution. The observed problem may actually be the result of multiple problems or complex systems with multiple dependencies. If multiple items are changed at once, there is no way to tell which part of the solution was responsible for a successful problem resolution. This can make it difficult or impossible to repeat or extend the solution.

- *Confirm recent changes*—Systems or components that have recently changed are the most likely suspects. Do not rely on the user to properly report recent changes. The history and order of recent changes must be verified with system utilities.

- *Attempt to isolate the problem*—The solution can be discovered faster by isolating the problem area from other parts of the computer. The scope of the problem should be limited to better identify what is broken and what impact the problem has on the rest of the system.

- *Identify past problem areas*—Items that failed in the past are likely to fail again.

- *Try the easy and quick fix first*—This approach avoids stalling the troubleshooting process while the problem is being reviewed in depth. A fix is considered quick if the repair takes little time to implement and the impact of the change does not require time-consuming disaster recovery steps.

- *Focus on the main problem area*—Many systems used in Windows 7 tie in to each other and can impact each other. Focus attention on the primary problem area to avoid losing

12

track of what needs to be repaired. Incidental systems that are impacted can be focused on once the search for problems in the primary problem area are exhausted.

- *Profile the failure*—The problem may be critical to the health of the computer, but it may not be a major issue if it rarely occurs. Determine how often the problem occurs and any reported triggers for the problem.

- *Log problems and attempted solutions*—The cause of a problem may be very subtle and difficult to detect. A history of past problems can point to a system that would otherwise not be an obvious choice for further inspection. Infrequent problems caused by the same system may reveal a trend that could help you determine if extra troubleshooting effort in that area is required. Solutions should be documented to avoid having to repeat the troubleshooting effort.

- *Learn from mistakes*—Review the success or failures of troubleshooting efforts to better understand successful and failed solutions. Reviewing the logged reports of other technicians can assist in the learning process.

- *Ask for help*—Failing to ask others for help can delay the development of a solution. Many people may have gone through the same problem and have already developed a solution. Troubleshooters do not need to know everything; interactive research tools and methods are part of the troubleshooting process.

- *Experiment*—If attempted solutions are not working, then it may be possible to reveal a problem system by placing new stressors on it. This can be accomplished with the addition or removal of hardware, software, or just the alteration of their configuration. A system that is slightly problematic might clearly reveal itself under stress or with new operational conditions.

Windows Backup and Restore

When data is lost, the only way to recover it may be from a backup copy. Waiting for a disaster to strike is the wrong time to start thinking about a backup strategy. Windows 7 includes **Backup and Restore**, shown in Figure 12-15, to provide the user the ability to set up backup regiments to back up files, restore files, create a system image, and create a system repair disc. This utility can be accessed by going to the Control Panel and selecting Backup your computer.

File Backup

When Backup and Restore is first started, you are presented with the option to set up a backup or to select a backup from which to restore files. The backup feature of Windows backup is designed to back up data files for all people who use the computer. Unlike Windows Vista, you can let Windows 7 choose what to back up or you can select the individual folders, libraries, and drives that you want to back up.

When a user first clicks on Set up backup, the Set up backup wizard is started. The wizard initially asks for where the backup data will be saved, as shown in Figure 12-16.

The backup tool makes certain assumptions about where backup data can be written:

- Backup data can be stored to hard disks (internal and external), USB flash drives, and recordable CD/DVD drives, or a network share.

- Locations used to store backup data must be formatted with either the NTFS, FAT, or UDF file system.

- A drive cannot be backed up to itself; the destination for the backup data must be a different drive.

- The system and startup disk can not be selected to store backup data. These disks are used to store the Windows operating system and start the computer respectively (they may both be the same disk or they may be two different disks in the same computer). In the event

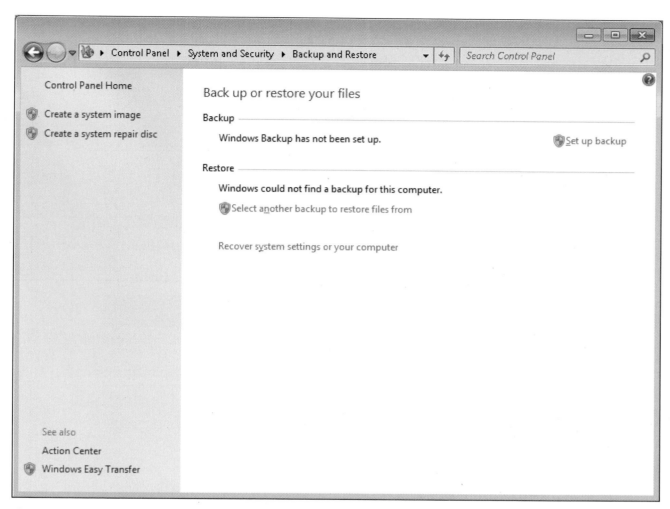

Figure 12-15 Backup and Restore
Courtesy Course Technology/Cengage Learning

that the system crashes and data needs to be restored, these disks may be unavailable or they may have to be erased and rewritten with a fresh installation of Windows 7. In this case, the backup data stored on them would be lost. To prevent this from occurring, the backup utility will not allow these disks to store backup data.

- Tape drives are not compatible with the Backup and Restore utility and cannot be used as locations to store backup data with this utility. Note that other backup software written by third-party companies may use tape drives as permitted backup devices.

- The target location selected to store the backup data must have enough room to hold all of the selected data. The Set up backup wizard will calculate the target space required and advise on how much space is required.

- The destination is not on a network location with a computer running Windows XP Home Edition. You can't save backups to these locations because setting permissions on network locations and authenticating over a network aren't supported by Windows XP Home Edition.

- The destination cannot be a recovery partition. Many computer manufacturers include a special partition with recovery tools and sometimes even a system image. Windows 7 recognizes these partitions and will not allow you to store a backup there.

- The destination cannot be locked by BitLocker Drive Encryption. If you want to store a backup on a drive that is encrypted by BitLocker then you must unlock the drive first.

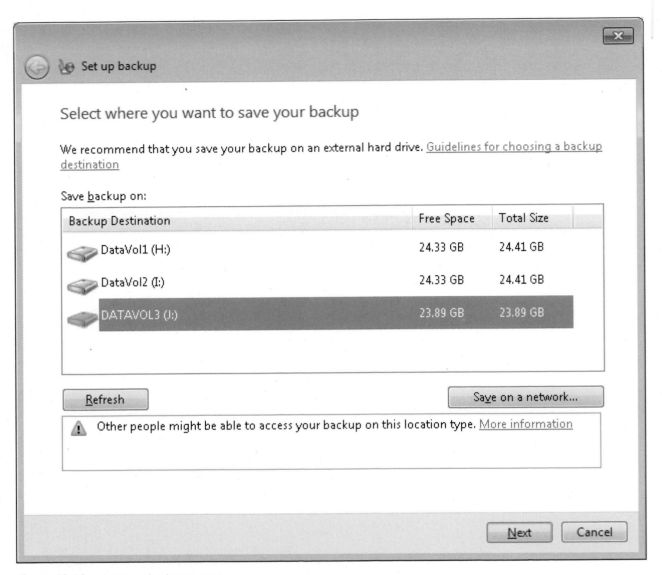

Figure 12-16 Selecting a backup target
Courtesy Course Technology/Cengage Learning

After a location is selected to store the backup data, the wizard asks the user to select what to back up. You are given the option to Let Windows choose what to back up or to Let me choose, as shown in Figure 12-17. If you select Let Windows choose, Windows will back up data files saved in libraries, on the desktop, and in default Windows folders. A regular backup schedule is also automatically set up. Furthermore, if the drive you are saving your backup on is formatted using the NTFS file system and has enough disk space, a system image of your programs, Windows, and all drivers and registry settings is also included in the backup. If you select Let me choose, Windows lets you select exactly what you want to back up as shown in Figure 12-18.

Once the items to back up are defined, a review of the backup settings is displayed and an opportunity to choose a backup schedule is also presented. This section of the wizard is shown in Figure 12-19. The schedule can be set to activate the backup engine on a fixed period:

- Daily—every day of the week
- Weekly—a specific day of the week (Sunday–Saturday)
- Monthly—a specific day of the month (1–31 or last day)

On the targeted day for the backup to run, a specific hour must be selected to activate the utility. The schedule allows the selection of a single desired hour, on the hour.

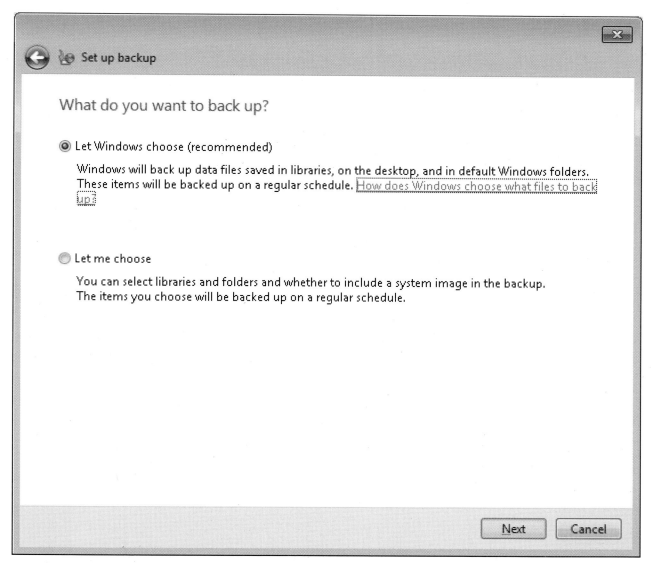

Figure 12-17 Selecting what to back up
Courtesy Course Technology/Cengage Learning

This completes the Set up backup wizard and the utility is ready to run for the first time. The Backup and Restore utility will then know where to back up data, what type of user data to include, and when to periodically check for new data to back up to that location.

When the wizard runs for the first time, the computer is scanned for data files and a full backup is created in the target location. After the initial full backup has completed, the backup utility scans only for content that has changed since the last backup. The backup uses the same shadow copy technology as previous versions of files and restore points. This allows backup sizes to be kept very small. For example, the first backup of an entire computer may be 100 GB, but each additional backup will be only the size of the changed data, which is generally very small. You could conceivably keep and entire year of daily backups on a single external disk and have access to restore all of that data as required.

 When a backup is stored in a network location, each backup is the full size of the backup. This is because shadow copy technology can be used only on locally connected disks.

The backup can automatically run as long as the computer is not turned off. The automatic check for files to back up can be suspended, or it can be forced to run from the backup utility as well.

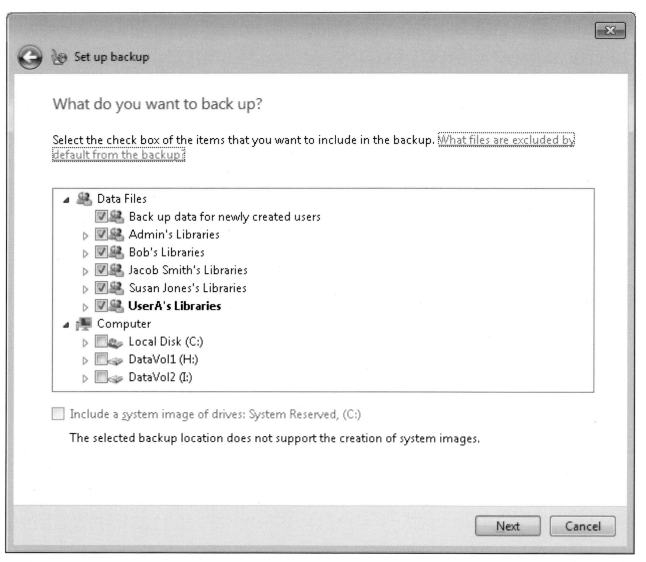

Figure 12-18 Selecting what to back up detailed version
Courtesy Course Technology/Cengage Learning

The backed-up files are stored in the target location using a complex folder structure that identifies the computer and the date and time that the data was stored. Compressed files are used to store the collected data to maximize the backup location's storage space. This backup folder structure is not to be browsed directly. The user does not have permission to view these folders and will be prompted for administrator-level permission to see their contents. The appropriate method to retrieve any data from the backup location is to use the Restore Files wizard in the Backup and Restore utility.

Restore Files

The Backup and Restore utility has an option to restore files that have previously been backed up by the utility, shown in Figure 12-20. To start the file restore process, click Restore My Files from Backup and Restore. An opportunity to restore all users' files, or to select a backup from another system or restore files is also given.

The restore files window offers you the ability to Search, Browse for files, or Browse for folders that need to be restored, as shown in Figure 12-21. The option to choose a different backup date is also given.

If the backup was stored to writeable CD or DVDs, it may span across several disks. The collection of disks will be treated as a single backup collection. The catalog that is part of the

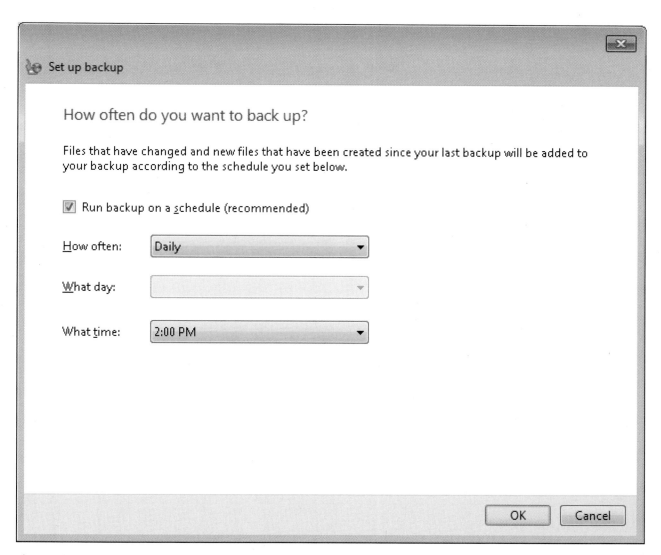

Figure 12-19 Defining a backup schedule
Courtesy Course Technology/Cengage Learning

backup will know which disk holds a particular folder or file. If a required disk is damaged or missing, the collection can still be used to recover data from the remaining healthy disks.

Files and folders can be added to the list of what data to restore. Only the data stored in the backup collection will be shown, relative to where it was originally backed up. For example, if the file to restore was originally stored in C:\USERS\KIYAG\DESKTOP, then that is the location to select for restoration.

Once the data to restore is selected, the Restore Files wizard asks where the recovered data should go, shown in Figure 12-22. The files that will be restored can go back to where they came from (the default selection) or they can optionally go to a different location.

When a file is restored, the Restore Files wizard will not just overwrite existing files. The user is prompted to confirm that the conflicting file can be overwritten, left alone, or renamed as desired, as shown in Figure 12-23.

Create a System Image

The Create a system image wizard creates a complete image of the computer that allows the operating system, applications, data, and custom settings to all be restored at one time. This is not intended to be a regular backup procedure to protect user data. It is meant as a disaster recovery strategy in the case that the computer stops working and other diagnostic tools cannot make the computer work again.

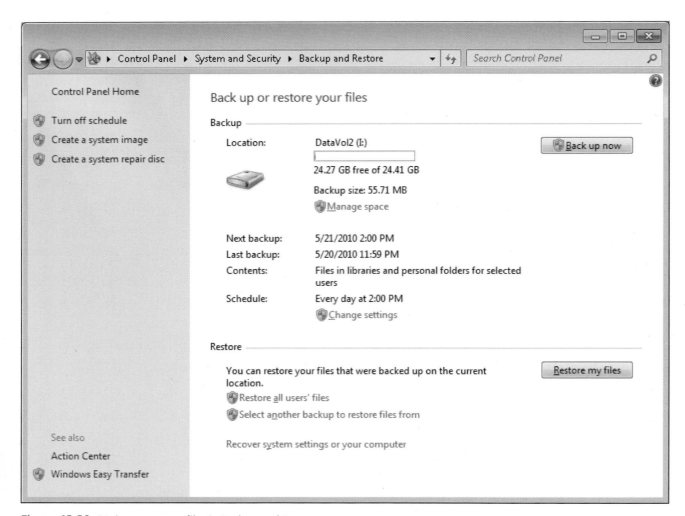

Figure 12-20 Option to restore files in Backup and Restore
Courtesy Course Technology/Cengage Learning

All versions of Windows 7 have backup and restore, but only Windows 7 Professional Ultimate, and Enterprise give you the ability to store backups and recover from backups located on a network drive.

The Create a system image wizard is accessible through the Backup and Restore tool, as shown in Figure 12-20. The system can be restored in three ways. The first method of system image restore is by using the Advanced recovery method. This can be accessed by selecting Recover system settings or your computer in Backup and Restore, then selecting Advanced recovery methods. The second is by using pre-installed recovery options on the Advanced Boot Options screen. This is discussed further later in this chapter. The last method to restore a system image is by using a Windows installation disc or a system repair disc. This method is used if you can't access the Control Panel or even the Advanced Boot Options.

The Create a system image wizard scans for devices that are capable of storing the computer image. The target location can be a CD or DVD writeable disk, a USB flash drive, or a hard drive. The user can select an appropriate device. If the target device is a writeable CD or DVD drive, there must be enough blank disks available to store the entire system's data. The wizard will warn that the target location will require a large amount of disk space. If the target device is a hard drive or a USB flash drive, it must be a basic disk formatted with the NTFS file system. Depending on the version of Windows 7 that is used, there is also an option to store on a network location.

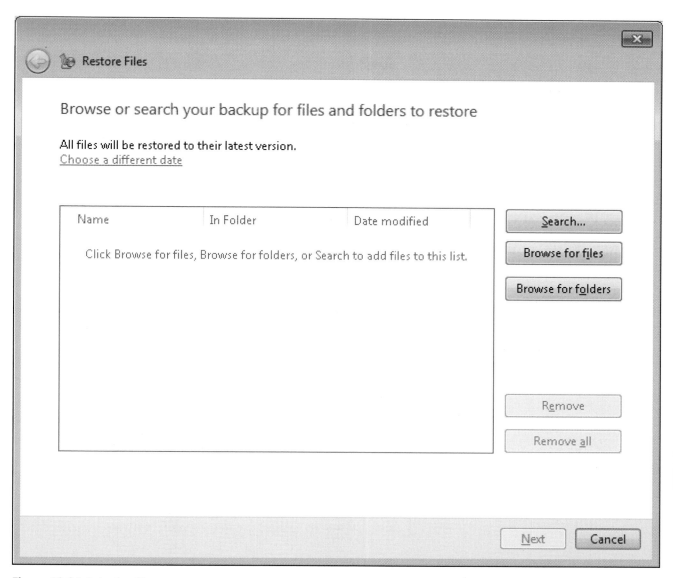

Figure 12-21 Selecting files to restore
Courtesy Course Technology/Cengage Learning

The image data is stored as a virtual hard disk image, which is stored as a .VHD file. Additional information about the image will be stored in supporting XML files and the backup catalog for that instance of the backup. If the image is spread across multiple CD or DVD disks, then all disks must be healthy and present to restore the image.

Activity 12-3: Back up User Data Files

Time Required: 10 minutes
Objective: Configure the Backup and Restore Utility to perform an automated backup of user data files.

Description: In this activity, you will launch the Backup and Restore Utility and configure a daily backup for user data files that will run every day at 2:00 PM.

1. If necessary, start your computer and log on.
2. Close any application windows which automatically open on the desktop.

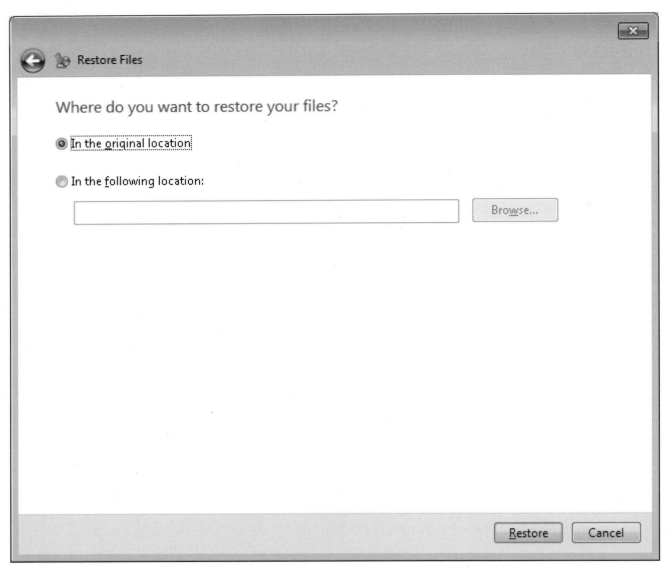

Figure 12-22 Selecting a location for restoring files
Courtesy Course Technology/Cengage Learning

3. Click the **Start** button, type **Backup and Restore** in the search tool and click Backup and Restore in the Programs section of the search results.

4. If a backup schedule has already been created, click **Change settings** under the Schedule section. Otherwise click **Set up backup**.

5. On the Select where you want to save your backup page, notice that no locations are available. Only partitions over 1 GB in size are available as a destination.

6. Use Computer Management to create a new volume that is at least **2 GB**, assign the drive letter **X:**, and set the Volume label as **Backup**.

7. In the Set up backup windows, click **Refresh**, click **Backup (X:)**, and click **Next**.

8. On the What do you want to back up page, click **Next** to accept the default option of **Let Windows choose**. Notice that Windows chooses to back up All users and a System image.

9. Click the back arrow.

10. On the What do you want to back up page, click **Let me choose** and then click **Next**.

11. Under Data Files, deselect all check boxes except for your user.

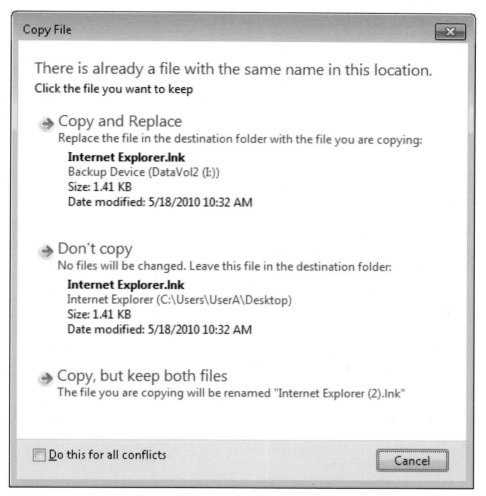

Figure 12-23 Prompt to resolve conflict during a restore
Courtesy Course Technology/Cengage Learning

12. Deselect the **Include a system image of drives: System Reserved, (C:)** check box and then click **Next**.

13. On the Review your backup settings page, click **Change schedule**.

14. Change the **How often** setting to Daily.

15. Confirm the **What day** setting is cleared.

16. Change the **What time** setting to 2:00 PM.

17. Click **OK** and then click **Save settings and run backup**.

18. Wait until the backup has finished.

19. Confirm that the Last backup was done recently and that the next backup is scheduled for 2:00 PM the next day.

20. Close all open windows.

Repairing Windows 7

Windows 7 may become unstable and behave erratically for many reasons. The cause may be an installed application, the operating system, corrupt data, faulty hardware, or one of many other root causes. The primary tools used to diagnose and repair Windows 7 in these cases include:

- Advanced Boot Options menu
- System Restore

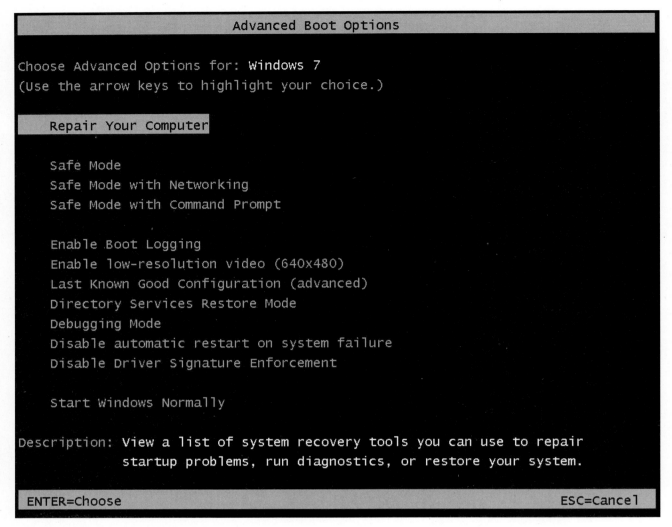

Figure 12-24 Advanced Boot Options menu
Courtesy Course Technology/Cengage Learning

- Device Driver Rollback
- Windows Recovery Environment
- Automatic Repairs

Advanced Boot Options Menu

When the computer is started, it can detect if the computer was not shut down properly the last time it was running. In this case, the Advanced Boot Options menu, shown in Figure 12-24, displayed automatically. To open this menu manually, the computer must be restarted and the F8 function key must be pressed before the Windows Logo appears: the Advanced Boot Options screen will then appear. If the Windows Logo screen appears, the computer must be restarted and the user must try pressing F8 again.

The Advanced Boot Options menu is used to select diagnostic modes that alter the startup process for Windows 7. The menu options include:

- Safe Mode
- Safe Mode with Networking
- Safe Mode with Command Prompt

- Last Known Good Configuration (advanced)
- Other Advanced Boot Options

Safe Mode   When Windows 7 cannot start properly, the next time the computer is started it may be necessary to start it in **Safe Mode**, a limited functionality mode. Safe Mode is a troubleshooting startup mode that is typically used when the regular startup mode for Windows 7 fails. Safe Mode can be enabled automatically or manually when the computer is started. To enter Safe Mode manually, the user can open the Advanced Boot Options Menu when the computer is started and select Safe Mode.

Authentication is still required to login, and an administrative user must login to perform any diagnostic or remedial action. The Administrator account that is automatically disabled when Windows 7 runs normally is automatically enabled for safe mode. If you have not configured a password for the Administrator account, the password will be blank and allow you to access and repair the system.

If you do not know the password for a local administrator account, you can download a number of password reset utilities from the Internet. Two commonly used utilities for local user password resets are the Ultimate Boot CD for Windows (*http://www.ubcd4win.com/*) and the Offline NT Password & Registry Editor (*http://pogostick.net/~pnh/ntpasswd/*).

You can determine that Safe Mode is enabled because the words Safe Mode are displayed on all four corners of the desktop background. In Safe Mode, extra applications that usually start when Windows 7 is started do not run. This limits the effect of a recently installed application that may be the cause of the computer becoming unstable.

In addition to restricting the applications that automatically start, the active hardware device drivers are restricted as well. Only device drivers necessary to operate essential computer hardware are loaded. The device drivers that are used are limited to basic Microsoft driver versions with basic settings that are very likely to function with some limited degree of functionality. This includes a Microsoft **VGA**-based driver for the video system and not the currently installed video card driver. This allows the regularly installed drivers to be replaced without crippling Safe Mode.

Because the operating system is running in this limited mode, not all of the system services are enabled. Services that support the repair or diagnosis of the computer are available, while other service cannot run in Safe Mode by design. Attempting to start the additional services will fail or produce unexpected results. Many applications can detect that the computer is running in Safe Mode and may automatically restrict their operations.

Note that in this mode the networking system is not considered essential and will not be available. All repairs and diagnoses are to be performed locally on the system. Networking requires many additional services and drivers that can limit the ability to determine base-level functionality of the system. If networking is absolutely required as part of the remedial services, then do not select this mode; instead, select Safe Mode with Networking from the Advanced Boot Options menu.

If the computer starts properly in Safe Mode, a recently installed application, device driver, or registry setting may be responsible for the problem. In this case, the suspect item can be upgraded, removed, or patched. If these update attempts fail, it may be possible to use System Restore to restore the computer's state to a prior restore point (covered later in this chapter). If the system restore fails, further action may be required, such as restoring a system image or restoring the Last Known Good configuration (also covered later in this chapter). In a worst-case scenario, the operating system may have to be reinstalled.

Safe Mode with Networking   For this mode, Windows 7 is started in the same manner as Safe Mode, but limited networking components are additionally enabled. This is not designed to support all networking features; many applications and services that support advanced networking do not work in this mode. Networking support adds the ability to connect to remote computers for diagnostic or data recovery purposes. Depending on the components that are damaged, the networking support may not work at all. Many of the automated diagnostic tools built in to Windows 7 can use the networking support to attempt a connection back to Microsoft to report the computer's errors and check if there is a suggested action from Microsoft.

Safe Mode with Command Prompt Many command line tools can be used to modify or review the state of the computer. An advanced IT administrator may want to start the computer in Safe Mode with Command Prompt to allow the tools to have direct low-level access. The Explorer interface is not started in this mode at all. Authentication is still required to login, and an administrative user must login to perform any diagnostic or remedial action.

One of the most common reasons to start this mode is to avoid the graphical environment and roll back to an earlier system restore point (covered later in this chapter) by issuing the command rstrui.exe.

Last Known Good Configuration In some cases, there may be changes made to critical system settings in the registry that may be responsible for making Windows 7 or a device driver unstable. If such changes are suspected, the best option to reverse the changes is to use System Restore to revert to a previous system restore point. If there is no suitable restore point to roll back to and the computer recently started without problems, then the Last Known Good configuration might restore functionality.

The Last Known Good configuration represents settings in the registry hive HKEY_LOCAL_ MACHINE\SYSTEM\CurrentControlSet that were in place the last time the computer was started successfully. These settings provide low-level operating system control settings, device driver control information, operational parameters for services, hardware profile information, and enumerated device information. User-based settings and global application settings are not considered part of the Last Known Good configuration.

 The Last Known Good configuration is updated when the system starts and a user is able to log on. Consequently, it is designed only for severe system errors that prevent logon. After logging on, the Last Known Good configuration cannot be used to restore settings. Logging on in Safe Mode does not update the Last Known Good configuration.

If the computer is experiencing a problem that does not involve these settings or includes other areas, then just restoring the Last Known Good configuration may not fix the problem or make the computer bootable. Changes made by restoring the Last Known Good configuration cannot be undone. By selecting the Last Known Good option on the Advanced Boot Options screen, the computer attempts to restart with the updated registry information.

Other Advanced Boot Options The Advanced Boot Menu contains several boot options that are used to modify the startup of Windows 7. These options are seldom used but are listed below:

- *Enable Boot Logging*—A record of the drivers and supporting files loaded as Windows 7 starts. The information is recorded to a file called **NTBTLOG.TXT**, which includes the last file to load before a failure. This may indicate a potential suspect area for diagnosis. When a Safe Mode start option is selected, this option is selected automatically.

- *Enable low resolution video (640×480)*—This will start the operating system with the currently installed video driver forced to use the low-resolution setting of 640×480 pixels. If the current resolution setting is too high for the currently attached monitor to display properly, this will give the user an opportunity to reset it to something that works.

- *Directory Services Restore Mode*—This does not apply to Windows 7; it is a mode used on Active Directory domain controllers to restore their database.

- *Debugging Mode*—This mode is used by developers to debug low-level operating system operations in the kernel. It is not typically used in routine diagnosis or repair procedures.

- *Disable automatic restart on system failure*—When an error occurs that stops the system, it may restart before the error is clearly identified. This option will wait for the person sitting at the keyboard to restart the system instead of restarting immediately.

- *Disable Driver Signature Enforcement*—This option allows drivers to be installed for hardware even if they do not have a valid Microsoft digital signature. This is not a recommended option. Driver signatures guarantee that the driver has not been modified since it has passed quality testing by Microsoft.

- *Start Windows Normally*—Windows 7 is started normally. The Advanced Boot Option menu may be displayed automatically as a result of the system detecting that Windows 7 was not shut down properly the last time it ran. This is commonly the result when a user turns off the computer before shutting down the operating system, the reset button was pushed, or the power to the computer was lost. In these cases, there is probably nothing wrong with the computer and there is no need to select any other option than to start Windows normally.

Activity 12-4: Using Advanced Boot Options

Time Required: 15 minutes
Objective: Use the Advanced Boot Options in Windows 7.

Description: Windows 7 includes several advanced boot options that you can use when troubleshooting and repairing Windows 7. Safe Mode loads only the minimum required files for Windows 7. Boot logging creates a log of the files that are loaded during the boot process and their load status. In this activity, you start Windows 7 in Safe Mode and enable boot logging.

1. Restart Windows 7.
2. At the BIOS screen, press **F8** until the Advanced Boot Options menu appears. You may need to press F8 repeatedly to ensure you press it at the appropriate time in the boot process. You may also need to remove any bootable DVDs from your computer.
3. Select **Safe Mode** and press **Enter**. You can see various operating system files as they are loaded.
4. After the boot process is complete, log on. When a Windows 7 computer is part of a domain, only local log ons are available at this point. Notice that Safe Mode is listed in the corners of the screen and that the resolution is 640×480.
5. Read the help topic about safe mode that opens automatically.
6. Close the Windows Help and Support window.
7. Click the **Internet Explorer** button on the taskbar to start Internet Explorer. Notice that an error is generated because networking components are not loaded in safe mode.
8. Close Internet Explorer.
9. Restart Windows 7.
10. At the BIOS screen, press **F8** until the Advanced Boot Options menu appears.
11. Select **Enable Boot Logging** and press **Enter**.
12. After the boot process is complete, log on. Windows 7 is fully functional in this mode.
13. Click the **Start** button and click **Computer**.
14. In the left pane, expand **Local Disk (C:)** and click **Windows**.
15. In the right pane, double-click **ntbtlog.txt** to open it.
16. Browse through the contents of ntbtlog.txt and then close Notepad. You can use this log to determine which driver is causing problems during the boot process.
17. Close Windows Explorer.

12

System Restore

Windows XP introduced a new feature called System Restore that is also part of Windows 7. System Restore can return the operating system to a previously saved state by reversing changes to Windows system files, the registry, and newly installed software. The System Restore will roll back the mentioned items, but it will not guarantee reversal of all changes made to the computer. The reversal is performed without changing personal files or user-specific data. The user data is preserved in case it is still required by the user.

 If the computer becomes unstable because of a recently installed application, this may not be the best method to restore stability to the computer. The application may have an uninstall program or it may be removed through Programs and Features in Control Panel instead. These methods should be attempted first before trying to recover stability through System Restore utilities.

 User data files should be protected with the Windows Backup utility, not System Restore.

System Restore also saves previous versions of files that been modified. Just before a significant system event like a driver install or Windows updates, restore points are created. These restore points are also created automatically once every seven days if no other restore points were created in the previous seven days. Furthermore, restore points can also be manually created.

System Restore relies on the same System Protection feature, shown in Figure 12-25, that is used for previous versions of files. System Protection takes snapshots of the files on a disk at a particular point in time that are called a restore point. These restore points are based on shadow copies. More than one restore point can be created, allowing the state of the system to be rolled back to different restore points.

Restore points are not useful if the information they contain is too old. Restore points are created periodically based on specific events:

- Every time Windows 7 is started (defined by the SR task in Task Scheduler)
- Daily at 12:00 am (defined by the SR task in Task Scheduler)
- If Windows detects the installation of an application
- If Windows detects the installation of a device driver
- Any time the Windows Backup utility backs up user data files
- Before an automatic Windows Update is installed
- Manually triggered

The data that is collected for a restore point is saved on the disk that holds the original copy of the data. In a default installation where all Windows files are stored on drive C, only drive C is enabled to store restore point data. Other hard disk partitions might be additionally created and used to hold installed applications. They can be enabled for system protection as well. These additional hard disk partitions must be a minimum of 1 GB in size and formatted with the NTFS file system.

The space used on a disk to collect restore point data can be adjusted from 1% all the way to 100% of the disk space available. If there is not enough disk space to create a new restore point on a disk then the oldest restore point information on the disk is deleted to make room. As long as there is enough room to hold the existing restore point data, it will remain on the disk. If a disk is de-selected for system protection, or system protection for all disks are completely turned off, then all restore point data stored on the disk is irrecoverably deleted. If system protection is re-enabled, then new restore point data will be collected.

The System Protection tab of the System Properties window allows the user to manually create a new restore point, select which disks are scanned for restore point data, and trigger the

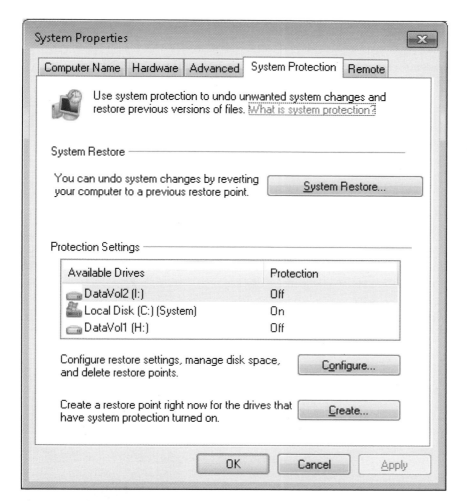

Figure 12-25 System Protection settings
Courtesy Course Technology/Cengage Learning

System Restore wizard to revert to a previously saved restore point. The System Restore wizard, shown in Figure 12-26, is also available the System Tools in the Start menu.

When the system is restored to a previous restore point, the current system state is saved first. If the selected restore point did not provide the anticipated result, then a different restore point can be tried. If none of the restore points are desirable, the state can be rolled forward to the initial configuration before the first restore point was applied.

The only time the current configuration is not saved is if the restore point is restored while the computer is in Safe Mode.

Activity 12-5: Using Restore Points

Time Required: 10 minutes
Objective: Take and restore a restore point.

Description: Restore points are your first defense against system changes that cause problems. While restore points are taken automatically when most system changes occur, you can also manually take a restore point. In this activity, you take and restore a restore point.

    1. If necessary, start your computer and log on.

    2. Click the **Start** button and click **Control Panel**.

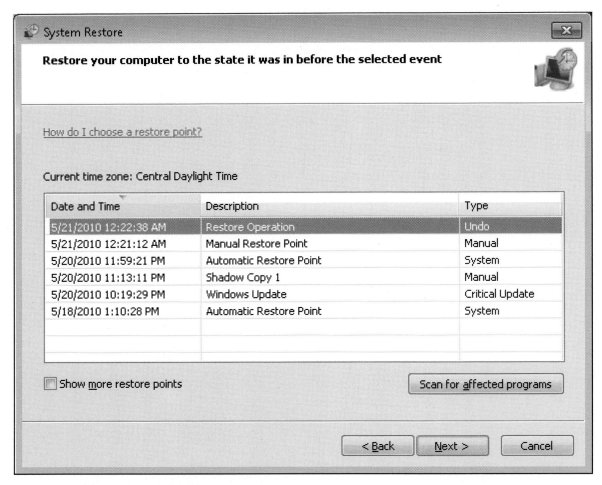

Figure 12-26 System Restore wizard
Courtesy Course Technology/Cengage Learning

    3. Click **System and Security** and click **System**.

    4. Click **System Protection** in the left panel.

    5. Click **Create**.

    6. In the text box, type **Manual Restore Point** and click **Create**. Creating the restore point will take a minute.

    7. Click **Close** in the System Protection box.

    8. Click **System Restore** and click **Next** to start the wizard.

    9. Click **Manual Restore Point** and click **Next**.

   10. Click **Finish** and click **Yes** to begin the restore. The system will reboot to perform the restore.

   11. Log on.

   12. Read the System Restore dialog box and click **Close**.

Device Driver Rollback

The computer may have been operating as usual until a recent update was made to a device driver for an installed hardware component. If this is the suspected cause, the device driver itself can be rolled back.

You can roll back a device driver on the Driver tab in the properties of a device in Device Manager. If the Roll Back Driver button is grayed out and not available, as shown in Figure 12-27, then no prior version of the device driver is installed. The computer may have to be restarted after the prior version of the device driver is restored.

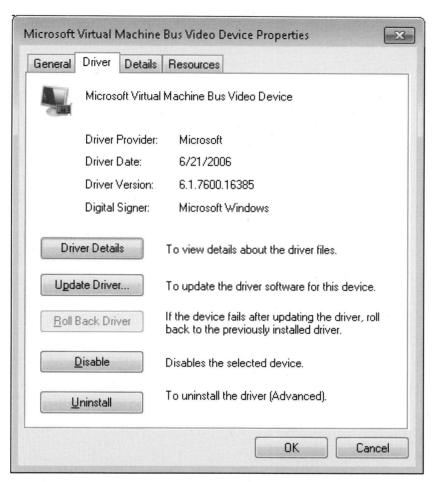

Figure 12-27 Device driver roll back option
Courtesy Course Technology/Cengage Learning

Restoring a device driver by itself may not provide the complete solution. When the problematic device driver was installed it may have been installed together with supporting or dependent applications. Once the device driver is rolled back, the applications may fail to operate or they may behave erratically. In that case, a better solution may be to try and use System Restore to recover to a previous restore point.

Windows Recovery Environment

If the current installation of Windows 7 cannot be started, perhaps not even in Safe Mode, then the Windows Recovery environment may be the solution. To start the Windows Recovery environment, manually boot from the Windows 7 DVD. When the Install Windows screen appears, do not select Install now but instead select the option Repair your computer. This will start the Windows Recovery environment and its System Recovery Center. The first step in starting the recovery environment is to scan the computer for installed operating systems to fix, shown in Figure 12-28.

Once the operating system is targeted, the main System Recovery Center menu is displayed, shown in Figure 12-29.

Figure 12-28 System Recovery Center prompt for OS to repair
Courtesy Course Technology/Cengage Learning

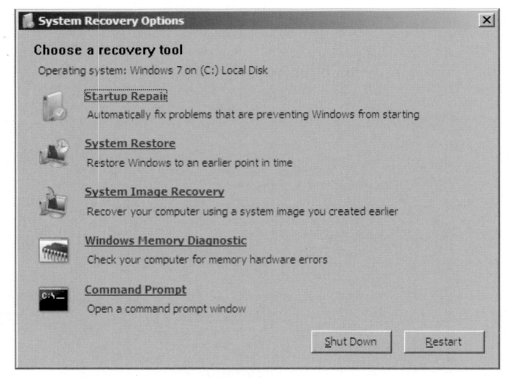

Figure 12-29 System Recovery Center repair options
Courtesy Course Technology/Cengage Learning

The System Recovery Center provides the option to run:

- Startup Repair
- System Restore
- System Image Recovery
- Windows Memory Diagnostic
- Command Prompt

Startup Repair The Startup Repair tool is used to recover a Windows 7 installation when it is unable to start. This can be caused by missing system files, a damaged boot sector, and other issues. To start the Startup Repair tool, select Startup Repair from the System Recovery Center repair options screen.

In Windows XP, repairing startup issues required a multistep manual process. In Windows 7, the Startup Repair Tool automatically fixes these problems, as shown in Figure 12-30. The tool contains built-in intelligence that can examine the operating system files, logs, and settings automatically.

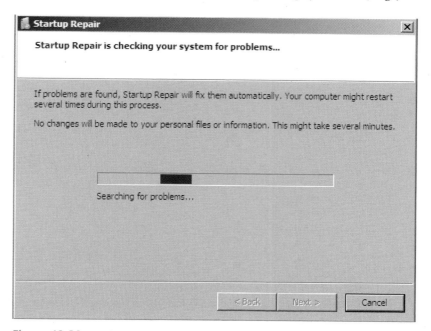

Figure 12-30 Startup Repair tool looking for issues automatically
Courtesy Course Technology/Cengage Learning

After a scan of the operating system is completed, the Startup Repair tool reports its findings, as shown in Figure 12-31. If no errors are found, the tool will report that the root cause as "The computer is starting properly."

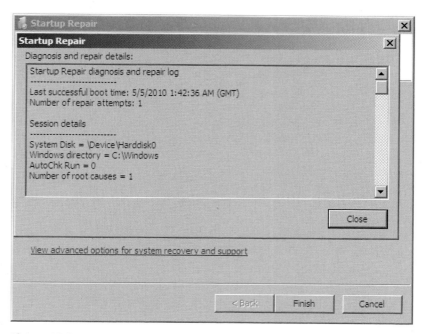

Figure 12-31 Startup Repair diagnosis and repair log
Courtesy Course Technology/Cengage Learning

Activity 12-6: Running the Startup Repair Tool

Time Required: 10 minutes

Objective: Run the Windows 7 Startup Repair tool from the installation DVD.

Description: The Startup Repair tool is used to automate the repair of Windows 7 installations that do not boot properly. This significantly simplifies the process of repairing the Windows 7 boot process. In this activity, you run the Startup Repair Tool from the installation DVD.

1. Insert the **Windows 7 DVD** in your computer.
2. Restart your computer and boot off of the DVD.
3. Press a key to boot off DVD, click **Next** to accept the default language settings, and click **Repair your computer.**
4. In the System Recovery Options window, click **Next.** This starts the recovery tools rather then restoring a recovery point.
5. Click the **Startup Repair** recovery tool. Startup Repair does not find any problems.
6. Click **View diagnostic and repair details** and view the contents of the Startup Repair diagnosis and repair log. Notice the different system components that are tested.
7. Click **Close.**
8. Click **Finish** and click **Restart.**

System Restore This option allows the computer state to be rolled back to a previous restore point, as described in the System Restore section earlier in this chapter.

System Image Recovery This option allows the computer's operating system to be restored from an image created earlier with the Windows Backup and Restore utility. The image can be stored on a hard disk, DVDs, USB flash drive, or on the network. The hard disk or the last DVD holding the image must be connected for the utility to offer to restore it. Restoring an image will replace all operating system partition files with the data stored in the image in the backup.

Windows Memory Diagnostic The Windows Memory Diagnostics Tool, shown in Figure 12-32, is built into Windows 7 and is designed to detect memory (**RAM**) that is not operating correctly. The tool will write and read data from the computer's memory to see if there are any reliability issues. By selecting Windows Memory Diagnostic from the System Recovery Options or from the Administrative Tools in Control Panel, the tool restarts the computer and activate the diagnostics tool.

The tool cannot run from within Windows 7 because no other program can be accessing memory while the diagnostics utility runs. The tool will start scanning memory automatically, but its advanced options can be modified, as shown in Figure 12-33, at any time by pressing the F1 function key.

The type of tests that can be selected are basic, standard, and extended. The standard and extended tests will increase the testing completion time, but will have a better chance of detecting any errors. The options screen also allows the CPU onboard cache to be disabled, enabled, or set depending on the test settings defined in the test groupings. The CPU cache memory may be part of the problem, so it is recommended to leave this setting set to its default setting.

The number of passes can also be set as an option, but usually one pass is sufficient to detect a failure in memory. To save the options settings and continue scanning memory, press the function key F10. Once the diagnostic has completed, it will record its findings to disk and restart the computer. The results are displayed the next time the computer is started as a notification balloon in the System Tray, as shown in Figure 12-34.

Memory is treated as a system, not just a single component. Bad memory may be detected by the tool and the boot process modified so that Windows 7 can avoid using the bad areas of memory. Memory failures may indicate that the computer is experiencing major system faults and will require additional repairs if components continue to degrade.

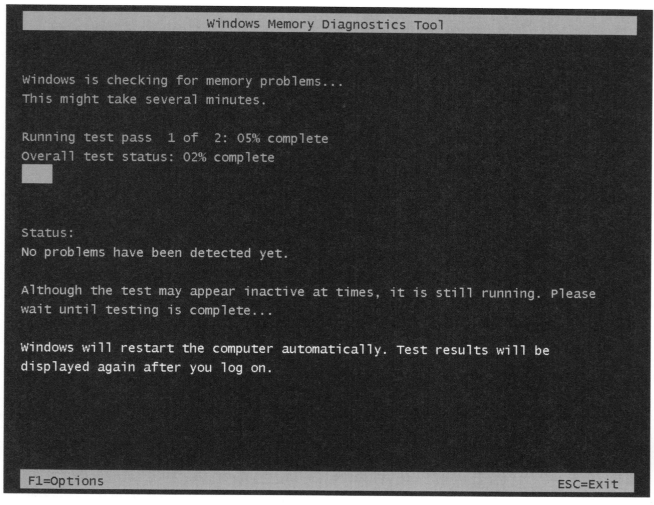

```
                     Windows Memory Diagnostics Tool

Windows is checking for memory problems...
This might take several minutes.


Running test pass  1 of  2: 05% complete
Overall test status: 02% complete



Status:
No problems have been detected yet.

Although the test may appear inactive at times, it is still running. Please
wait until testing is complete...

Windows will restart the computer automatically. Test results will be
displayed again after you log on.




 F1=Options                                                    ESC=Exit
```

Figure 12-32 Windows Memory Diagnostics Tool status screen
Courtesy Course Technology/Cengage Learning

Activity 12-7: Running a Memory Diagnostic

Time Required: 20 minutes
Objective: Run the Windows Memory Diagnostics Tool.

Description: Bad memory is a common cause of random system crashes. However, it is a difficult problem to diagnose because it only causes occasional problems. Windows 7 includes a memory diagnostics tool that you can use to test whether bad memory is a problem in your system. In this activity, you run a memory diagnostic.

1. If necessary, start your computer and log on.
2. Click the **Start** button and click **Control Panel**.
3. Click **System and Security** and click **Administrative Tools**.
4. Double-click **Windows Memory Diagnostic**.
5. Click **Restart now and check for problems**.
6. Press **F1** to view the options available. Notice that the standard test is running twice.
7. Press **Tab** twice and modify the **Pass Count** value to **1**.

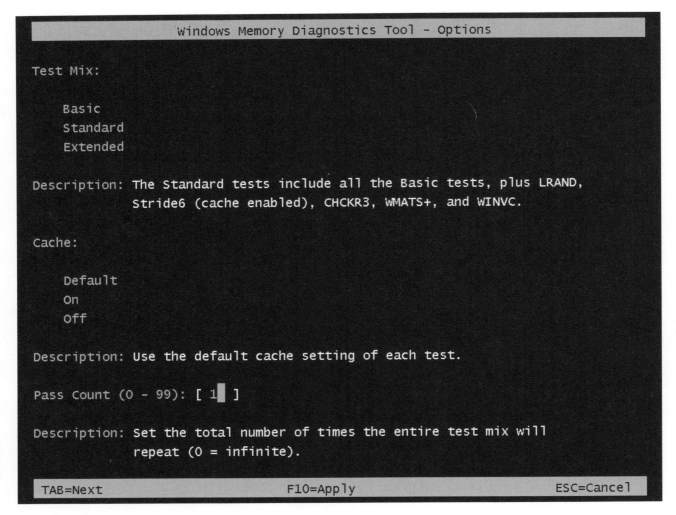

Figure 12-33 Windows Memory Diagnostics Tool options screen
Courtesy Course Technology/Cengage Learning

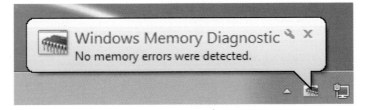

Figure 12-34 Windows Memory Diagnostics Tool results balloon
Courtesy Course Technology/Cengage Learning

8. Press **F10** to resume testing. Test completion may take 10–15 minutes.

9. After the memory diagnostic test is complete, log on. A message appears indicating that no memory errors were detected.

Command Prompt The Command Prompt option opens a command prompt window that allows command-line utilities to be used by the advanced IT administrator in repairing the computer. The benefit of this option is that it avoids many of the graphical elements that may cause problems on a corrupted system. The command prompt is used as the user interface, rather than Explorer.

Automatic Repairs

Windows 7 can automatically detect, self-diagnose, and attempt repairs for many common causes of crashes and hangs. This is an improvement over Windows XP's generalized approach to fault diagnosis that required the user to be directly involved and well versed with operational procedures. Windows 7 provides a specialized tuning system to continuously monitor the computer and recognize issues with performance or operations. Instead of waiting for the user to notice a problem and ask for help, the system attempts to take proactive steps to deal with the problem.

If a problem is suspected, Windows 7 will attempt to work around the issue and, at the same time, the user is informed and warned of the developing issue. If additional actions would be prudent, such as backing up files before a hard disk crashes, Windows 7 will try to notify the user before disaster strikes. This additional heuristic support is built into the automatic repair tools that are part of Windows 7.

Automated and advanced tools are provided to help diagnose startup, memory, hard disk, and networking issues. For example, the Startup Repair Tool can be invoked automatically when a startup failure is detected. Log files and other sources of system health information are inspected by the repair tool to determine likely causes and probable solutions. Where possible, the repair tools will attempt to apply a known solution and notify the user of what is happening. Records of the activity are stored in the event log, so that a history of the repairs is maintained.

Network Diagnostics Wizard Windows diagnostics rely heavily on built-in intelligence and tightly integrated systems that can report their status in a meaningful way to diagnostic tools. At some point, the tools themselves can run out of scripted actions or their suggested procedures may become out of date. One way to update these tools is to regularly update the computer with patches and service packs as they become available. Another option is to connect to Microsoft directly and report the problem and see if there is a better solution available. This can be invaluable for a user that is not technically savvy and is relying on the automated diagnostics for the best support possible. If there is no connection to Microsoft, those updates or online searches by the tools themselves cannot be performed.

In Windows XP, the network connectivity diagnosis was based on tearing down the Internet link and rebuilding most of it from scratch. The Windows 7 Network Diagnostics tool uses a built-in decision tree to determine a likely cause and a best course of remedial action.

If a problem is detected by Windows programs trying to link to hosts on the Internet, the Network Diagnostics wizard may start automatically and offer to diagnose and repair the problem. If the user is aware of a network issue, they can manually start the wizard. By opening the Network and Sharing Center in Control Panel and selecting the link to Troubleshoot problems, seen in Figure 12-35, the tool will scan the entire networking system of the computer. You can also diagnose a specific network connection while viewing its properties, as shown in Figure 12-36.

The Network Diagnostics wizard may find a likely error and suggest a remedial action. The wizard is designed to make the changes for the user and doesn't tell the user specifically what it is doing. If the tool cannot determine a problem, it will suggest either to explore additional options or close the troubleshooter. If Explore additional options is chosen, several options are given such as online and local support, recover using a restore point, and even requesting help using Remote Assistant.

The activities and findings of Network Diagnostics are placed in the Windows 7 event logs. They can be found in Event Viewer by navigating to Applications and Services Logs, Microsoft, Windows, Diagnostics—Networking, Operational.

Activity 12-8: Network Diagnostics Wizard

Time Required: 20 minutes
Objective: Use the Network Diagnostics wizard to diagnose all network connections and separately diagnose a single network connection.

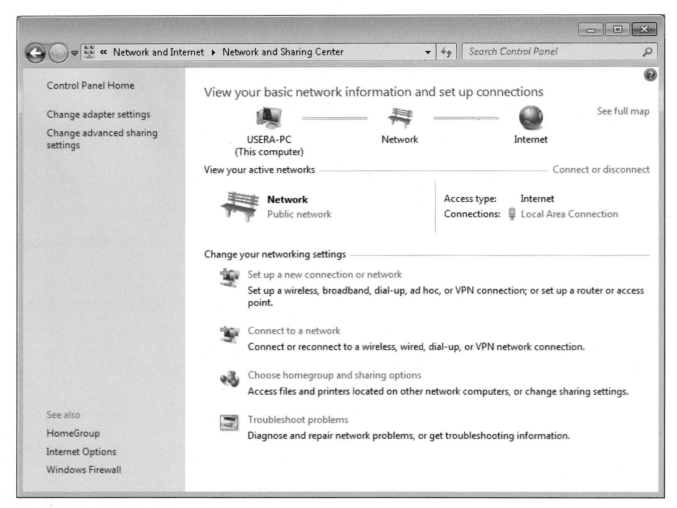

Figure 12-35 Network and Sharing Center
Courtesy Course Technology/Cengage Learning

Description: The Network Diagnostics wizard is started from the Network and Sharing window to diagnose and potentially repair all network connections available to the computer. If only a single network connection is suspect, then it can be individually diagnosed without impacting other network connections.

1. If necessary, start your computer and log on.

2. Click the **Start** button, click **Control Panel** and click **View network status and tasks** under Network and Internet.

3. Click the **Troubleshoot problems** link in the resulting Network and Sharing Center window that opens.

4. Note that if this is your first time running this utility, it may attempt to download troubleshooting packs from Microsoft.

5. Click **Network Adapter** and click **Next**.

6. When the Windows Network Diagnostics informs you that there are no problems with your connection, click the **Close** button.

Figure 12-36 Network connection status
Courtesy Course Technology/Cengage Learning

 If your computer is not connected to the Internet, you may receive a message stating that the network connection is down as a result of firewall or other connectivity issues. For the purposes of this activity, it is assumed that the lab computer has a live connection to the Internet.

7. Click the back arrow to return to Network and Sharing Center.

8. Click **Local Area Connection.**

9. Click the **Diagnose** button on the Local Area Connection Status window.

10. Click **Close** to close the Windows Network Diagnostics window.

11. Close the Local Area Connection Status window.

12. Close Network and Sharing Center.

Hard Disk Diagnostics The device drivers responsible for communicating with the disk hardware can report hard disk problems and defects to the operating system. If Windows 7 detects that a failure is in progress because of device warnings, the user is prompted to take proactive action and move or back up data that is in danger of being lost.

Preventative Maintenance

Computers are complicated systems that require hardware and the operating system to behave in predictable ways. The software code that makes up Windows 7 is reliable if it is not modified by non-Microsoft software updates and patched with any necessary updates from Microsoft. Windows 7 guarantees these points with Windows File and Resource Protection and Windows Update respectively.

Windows Resource Protection

Windows File Protection is a technology used in Windows XP to protect operating system files so that they would not be replaced with incompatible versions. A record of each operating system file is kept and, if a protected file is replaced with an unapproved version, Windows File Protection will replace the file with a validated copy of the file from %WinDir%\System32\dllcache or from the Windows installation CD.

Windows 7 includes an enhanced version of Windows File Protection called **Windows Resource Protection**. This is used to protect both critical operating system files and registry keys by restricting permissions to these resources. Administrators and the SYSTEM security principals are given only read and execute permissions. The SYSTEM security principal historically represents access levels assigned to the operating system itself.

With Windows Resource Protection, the protected files can only be modified by the **TrustedInstaller** service—a special protected operating system service designed to validate any requested changes. Microsoft or a trusted authority must digitally sign any updates that are applied by the TrustedInstaller service. The protected files and registry keys can be moved from their original locations and modified, but the modified versions cannot be put back into their original locations.

Activity 12-9: Confirm Windows Resource Protection Behavior

Time Required: 15 minutes
Objective: Confirm that Windows Resource Protection behavior will restrict changes to essential Windows 7 operating system files.

Description: In this activity, you will attempt to modify the Windows 7 executable file for the Calculator application. The security settings for the file are examined to confirm that TrustedInstaller is the only security principal with enough rights to do so.

1. If necessary, start your computer and log on.
2. Click the **Start** button, click **Computer**, expand **Local Disk (C:)**, expand **Windows**, and click **System32**.
3. In the list of files find the application calc.exe.
4. Right-click **calc.exe** and click **Rename** in the pop-up menu.
5. Type **newcalc**, press **Enter**.
6. Notice that you are prompted to try again to perform the action because it failed. Clicking the Try Again button does not allow the file to be modified.
7. In the File Access Denied window, click the **Cancel** button to close the window.
8. Right-click **calc.exe** and click **Properties** from the pop-up menu.
9. Click the **Security** tab.
10. Confirm that the SYSTEM, Administrators, and local Users security groups all have read and execute permission to the file.

11. Confirm that only TrustedInstaller has Full Control to the file.

12. Click **Cancel** to close the calc.exe Properties window.

13. Close the Windows Explorer window.

Advanced Troubleshooting

Windows 7 occasionally requires advanced knowledge of important or critical systems. This information can be useful in specific circumstances but is not commonly required. This section reviews the DirectX diagnostic testing tool and the Windows 7 boot process.

DirectX Diagnostic Testing

Windows 7 supports a rich graphical environment. Many games and media applications are written to use the **DirectX** programming specification that allows those applications to interact with sound, video, and input devices. If there is a problem with the device drivers or devices supporting DirectX, Windows 7 provides a DirectX diagnostic tool for user-based testing.

The DirectX diagnostic tool is located in %SystemRoot%\System32 and is named DXDIAG. EXE. The tool can report the current state of the computer configuration and the installed support for DirectX sound, video, and input devices. The drivers reported in the tools should be production-class drivers that are signed with Microsoft digital signatures. The tool will report any problems discovered but will not automatically repair them.

Windows 7 Boot Process

Since the early versions of x86 computers, the Basic Input Output System (BIOS) has acted as an interface between hardware and the operating system. BIOS is embedded within the motherboard, and the operating system is written to communicate with the BIOS rather than standard hardware such as IDE hard disks and keyboards.

Because it was created so many years ago, the BIOS has some design limitations. One limitation is the requirement for a 16-bit real-mode interface available only in x86 and x64 processors. To allow for different hardware architectures that do not have a 16-bit real-mode interface, a new firmware standard is required. United Extensible Firmware Interface (UEFI) is a new standard for firmware that can support additional processors such as Itanium.

UEFI allows for improved access to hardware that is currently accessed through the BIOS as well as support for additional architectures. To support UEFI as a boot firmware, the Windows 7 boot process had to be modified, as shown in Figure 12-37.

For more information about UEFI, BIOS, and Windows 7, see the Firmware and Boot Environment page on the Microsoft Web site at *http://www. microsoft.com/whdc/system/platform/firmware/default.mspx.*

Boot Components   The components used during the Windows 7 boot process are:

- *Bootmgr*—This file starts the boot process. Bootmgr reads the **boot configuration data (BCD)** and displays an operating system menu when required. Earlier versions of Windows used ntldr to accomplish these tasks.

- *Boot configuration data*—Information about how to start Windows 7 is stored in the BCD. Multiboot systems have multiple entries in the BCD. You cannot edit the BCD directly because it is formatted as a registry hive. Earlier versions of Windows used the text configuration file boot.ini for this purpose. Each entry in the BCD for Windows 7 specifies the location of Winload.exe.

- *Winload.exe*—This is the operating system loader for Windows 7. It is responsible for loading the operating system kernel, hardware abstraction layer (HAL), and boot drivers

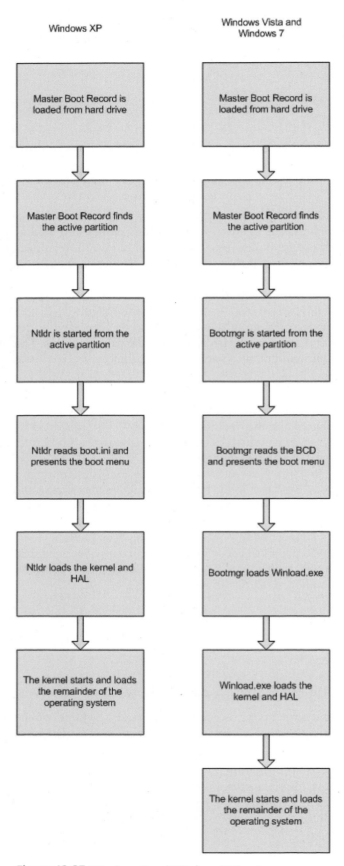

Figure 12-37 Windows 7 and Windows XP boot processes
Courtesy Course Technology/Cengage Learning

into memory. Winload.exe is stored with the operating system files, so each installation of Windows 7 in a multiboot system has its own copy of Winload.exe.

- *Winresume.exe*—This is the resume loader for Windows 7. It is responsible for starting the operating system from hibernation.

Boot Process Modification Earlier versions of Windows used the boot.ini text file to store configuration data for the boot process. You could edit boot.ini with a text editor. However, you cannot modify the BCD with a text editor and must use an appropriate tool.

Tools you can use to modify the boot process are:

- *Startup and Recovery*—You can use Startup and Recovery to modify the default operating system and how long the boot menu is displayed. This functionality was also present in previous versions of Windows, but modified boot.ini rather than the BCD.

- *System Configuration*—You can use System Configuration to modify a number of startup related settings. Modifying the advanced boot options changes configuration settings in the BCD. Other settings, such as controlling which programs run at startup, modify the registry or other locations.

- *BCDEdit*—This utility is designed specifically to modify the BCD. You can edit almost all of the data in the BCD as well as import and export data in the BCD.

- *Windows Management Interface (WMI)*—WMI is a programming interface that gives you complete access to the contents of the BCD. However, this method of modification is too cumbersome for most administrators to use.

Activity 12-10: Modifying the Boot Process

Time Required: 10 minutes
Objective: Modify the Windows 7 boot process.

12

Description: Windows 7 provides several tools to modify the boot process. In this activity, you will learn how to use Startup and Recovery, System Configuration, and BCDEdit.

1. If necessary, start your computer and log on.
2. Click the **Start** button and click **Control Panel**.
3. Click **System and Security** and click **System**.
4. Click **Advanced system settings**.
5. In the Startup and Recovery area, click **Settings**. In the System Startup area, you can control the default operating system, how long the operating system menu is displayed, and how long recovery options are displayed.
6. Click **Cancel** to close the Startup and Recovery dialog box.
7. Click **Cancel** to close the System Properties dialog box.
8. Close Control Panel.
9. Click the **Start** button, type **System**, and click **System Configuration**. You can also start System Configuration by running msconfig.
10. You can see that the General tab allows you to select from three startup options: Normal, Diagnostic, and Selective.
11. Click the **Boot** tab. This tab lets you configure advanced options for a menu entry configured in the BCD as well as boot options that correspond with the Advanced Startup menu available during the boot process.

12. Click the **Services** tab. This tab lets you disable services so that they do not start automatically.

13. Click the **Startup** tab. This tab lets you disable applications that are starting automatically when Windows starts. This is useful for disabling malware or other software that you cannot figure out how to uninstall.

14. Click the **Tools** tab. This tab provides a list of system tools that can be useful for troubleshooting and repair.

15. Click **Cancel** to close System Configuration.

16. Click the **Start** button, point to **All Programs**, click **Accessories**, right-click **Command Prompt**, click **Run as administrator**, and click **Yes**.

17. Type **bcdedit** and press **Enter**. This displays the current configuration.

18. Type **bcdedit /?** and press **Enter**. This displays the help for bcdedit.

19. Scroll through and read the help options for bcdedit.

20. Type **bcdedit /timeout 60** and press **Enter**. This changes the boot menu timeout to 60 seconds.

21. Close the command prompt.

Chapter Summary

- Several tools, such as Problem Steps Recorder, System Information, Computer Management, Action Center, Help and Support, and the Microsoft support Web site, can provide detailed information about what is happening with a computer and perhaps even explain why it is happening.

- Solution guidelines provide a basis for a common sense approach to troubleshooting problems.

- The Windows Backup and Restore utility is a method to protect user data before a loss occurs. The special case System Image Recovery is a method to image the operating system in its entirety.

- Windows 7 includes several methods to repair Windows 7. The advanced boot options allow you to start the computer in a Safe Mode, restore the last known good configuration setting, or apply additional boot options such as low resolution video settings. System Restore protection is a method to preserve the state and configuration of the operating system using restore points. You can use device driver rollback to remove recently installed drivers that are unstable.

- The Windows Recovery Environment can run the Startup Repair tool, restore a System Image, roll back system state to a prior restore point, run the Windows Memory Diagnostic, and run a command prompt for low-level diagnostic commands.

- Windows 7 protects operating system files with Windows File and Resource protection to ensure the files are not modified since Microsoft released them. Genuine updates to the operating system provide security updates and sometimes additional features.

- Advanced troubleshooting includes the DirectX diagnostic tool and the Windows 7 boot process. The DirectX diagnostic tool helps troubleshoot problems with graphical display and sound. The Windows 7 boot process has been completely updated from previous versions of Windows to support future hardware standard that do not include a BIOS. Tools you can use to modify the boot process are: Startup and Recovery, System Configuration, BCDEdit, and WMI.

Key Terms

Action Center A tool that provides you with a single location where you can identify and address any security issues, maintenance requirements, and errors that have arisen.

Backup and Restore A tool included in Windows 7 that allows you to set up backup regiments to back up files, restore files, create a system image, and create a system repair disc.

boot configuration data (BCD) A database of boot configuration data that is used during the boot process for Windows Vista and Windows 7.

binary format Data that is stored in its raw digital form as binary numbers. Data stored in this format cannot be viewed properly by text editors such as Notepad or Wordpad.

DirectX A programming standard for writing multimedia applications that interact with video, sound, and input devices such as the keyboard.

Event Viewer An MMC console snap-in used to browse and manage the records of system events and messages stored in system event logs.

Last Known Good configuration A recovery option that restores settings in the registry hive HKEY_LOCAL_MACHINE\SYSTEM\CurrentControlSet that were in place the last time the computer was started successfully and a user logged on.

MMC A standard for graphical management utilities called Microsoft Management Consoles (MMC). Management consoles can be added as snap-ins for a bare-bones MMC application.

Problem Steps Recorder A new tool included in Windows 7 that allows users to record the exact steps required to reproduce a problem. The recorded steps can then be forwarded to help desk staff for analysis.

RAM Random Access Memory, otherwise known as chip-based memory that stores instructions and data in silicon-based chips that are very quick to access but only suitable for short-term data storage.

Reliability Monitor A tool that rates the system stability of Windows 7 and lets you monitor the events that contribute to system stability.

Safe Mode A troubleshooting startup mode that is typically used when the regular startup mode for Windows 7 fails

System Image Recovery A backup option to save the current operating system partition and all of its data to an image-based file.

System Information A tool that scans the current state of the computer and reports its findings in a searchable tree format.

System Restore A recovery option that restores the operating system to a previously saved state by reversing changes to Windows system files, the registry, and newly installed software.

TrustedInstaller A special security service designed to restrict access to critical operating system files and registry settings. Administrators and the operating system only have read-only access to resources protected by TrustedInstaller. The TrustedInstaller service will not install an update unless Microsoft digitally signs the update.

VGA A standard low-resolution graphics mode that is typically used when troubleshooting incompatible video drivers or drivers set to a high resolution that is not supported by the attached monitor.

Windows Resource Protection A Windows 7 feature that protects system files and registry keys from unauthorized changes.

Windows Firewall The network filter that Windows 7 applies to restrict inbound and outbound network traffic on any network interface available to the computer.

Windows Management Instrumentation (WMI) The Windows Management Interface is a standard for accessing operating system operational status and configuration controls through remote management utilities.

Review Questions

1. Windows 7 can be restarted in several limited configurations to bypass startup applications and suspected faulty device drivers. These modes include _____. (Select all that apply.)

   a. Safe Mode with Networking

   b. Safe Mode with Microsoft Drivers

   c. Safe Mode

   d. Safe Mode Command Prompt

2. The Windows Memory Diagnostic tool can run silently in the background while the user is working with Windows 7. True or False?

3. Automatic repair wizards record their actions in event logs. True or False?

4. The Create a system image back up stores data to a _____ file.

   a. .BKP

   b. compressed

   c. XML storage

   d. .VHD

5. DXDIAG is a tool used for diagnosing _____.

   a. digital x86 instructions

   b. direct extended events

   c. disk extensions

   d. DirectX

6. The types of event logs found in Windows 7 include _____. (Select all that apply.)

   a. Analytical

   b. XML

   c. Debug

   d. Operational

   e. WMI

7. The Windows Backup and Restore utility can periodically back up selected files and folders. True or false?

8. Windows Backup and Restore can store data on _____ devices. (Select all that apply.)

   a. flash memory

   b. CD-ROM

   c. writeable DVD

   d. tape drive

   e. removable hard disk

9. The Task Scheduler _____ is used to organize the large number of operational tasks defined in Windows 7.

   a. Library

   b. Action Log

   c. service

   d. AT service

   e. Directory

10. _____ is used to restore the device driver previously in use by a specific hardware component.

    a. Windows Backup and Restore

    b. Device Manager

    c. System Restore

    d. Safe Mode

11. The _____ utility can be used to restore a system restore point from a command prompt.

    a. restore.exe

    b. srp.exe

    c. rstrui.exe

    d. FDISK /restore

12. A support contact has researched a problem that you are having with Windows 7. They have sent an e-mail referencing a document called KB84201. This document identifier is a _____.

    a. case number with Microsoft

    b. unknown, check back with the contact for clarification

    c. Microsoft knowledge base article number

    d. Help and Support lookup index

13. Common solution guidelines to follow when troubleshooting include _____. (Select all that apply.)

    a. Thoroughly research all aspects of the problem before attempting a solution

    b. If the problem cannot be quickly resolved, reinstall Windows 7

    c. Confirm recent changes to the computer system

    d. Spend time identifying past problem areas

14. When a service crashes, the action to recover can be set to _____. (Select all that apply.)

    a. run an application

    b. send an e-mail

    c. restart the computer

    d. do nothing

    e. restart the service

15. Reliability Monitor can help identify when software causing instability was installed. True or false?

16. Use _____ to verify that a service has started as expected, or start the service if required.

    a. System Information

    b. Task Scheduler

    c. Service Viewer

    d. Computer Management

    e. Service Manager

17. The operational status of an event provider can be found in a recorded event by examining the _____ value.

    a. Keyword

    b. Status

    c. OpCode

    d. Event ID

18. Services can be configured to start when the computer starts by setting their start type to _____. (Select all that apply.)

    a. Manual

    b. Automatic (Delayed Startup)

    c. Automatic (System)

    d. Automatic (Boot)

    e. Automatic

19. System image data can only be restored from the Windows Recovery Environment. True or False?

20. The advanced boot option *Enable Boot Logging* is used by Windows 7 to store a record of loaded modules to a file called _____.

    a. BOOTLOG.TXT

    b. NTBTLOG.TXT

    c. BOOTLOG.XML

    d. BOOTHIST.DOC

21. The advanced boot option *Directory services restore mode* is used by Windows 7 to _____.

    a. restore user security to the last known good configuration

    b. restore user security to the local Active Directory domain controller

    c. restore user security to the last system restore point

    d. enable the default administrator account with a password of P@$$w0rd

    e. none of the above

22. The number of unique system restore points that can be created is limited by _____.

    a. disk capacity

    b. RAM

    c. a fixed limit of 100

    d. a fixed limit of 1000

    e. no limit

23. The troubleshooters available in the Action Center can only be updated by manually downloading troubleshooting packs. True or False?

24. The management tool used to summarize the currently installed hardware and software and its operational condition is _____.

    a. Event Viewer

    b. WMI Control

    c. System Information

    d. Device Manager

25. The management console used to browse system event messages is _____.

    a. Computer Information

    b. Event Reporter

    c. System Information

    d. Event Viewer

Case Projects

Case Project 12-1: Troubleshooting a Slow Computer

You are called in as a consultant to diagnose the apparent slow down of a Windows 7 computer. What questions would be appropriate to ask as part of the initial review of the problem?

Case Project 12-2: Monitoring Events System-wide

You are the network administrator for a small supplier of precious metals. The company has four computers running Windows 7. You would like to automate maintenance tasks when specific events appear in the workstations event logs. Before you create a scheduled response to the events, you need to know how often the events occur on each computer. What can you do with Windows 7 to address these goals?

Case Project 12-3: Repairing a Startup Failure

A customer has brought in a computer with Windows 7 installed that refuses to start normally. The computer can start in Safe Mode but there are no startup applications or device drivers that seem to be responsible for the failure to start normally. Trying to restore several previous system restore points has not resolved the issue. What other actions could be considered to make the system run properly again?

12

chapter 13

Enterprise Computing

After reading this chapter and completing the exercises, you will be able to:

- Understand Active Directory
- Use Group Policy to control Windows 7
- Control device installation with Group Policy settings
- Plan enterprise deployments of Windows 7
- Describe enterprise deployment tools for Windows 7
- Use Windows Server Update Services to apply updates
- Understand Network Access Protection

In the computer industry, the term enterprise is used to describe large companies with needs that are different from smaller companies. Enterprise products typically have much better features for manageability than those used by smaller companies. Enterprise deployments of Windows 7 have unique challenges that need to be addressed.

In this chapter you learn how Active Directory and Group Policy can be used to manage hundreds or thousands of Windows 7 computers. Deployment planning and enterprise deployment tools for Windows 7 are also described. Finally, you learn how Windows Server Update Services and Network Access Protection can be used to ensure that computers on your network have appropriate updates installed.

Active Directory

Windows networks can be either workgroup-based or domain-based. A domain-based network can be centrally managed and is much more efficient than workgroup-based networks for larger environments. Windows 2000 Server and later versions include **Active Directory** to create domain-based networks. Active Directory expands on the domain concept by linking domains in logical structures named trees, and multiple trees into forests.

Domain controllers are servers that hold a copy of Active Directory information. Domain controllers are responsible for authenticating users when they log on to a workstation. After users are authenticated, they can access network resources. Domain controllers also respond to requests for other domain information such as printer information or application configuration.

 Starting with Windows Server 2008, Microsoft has rebranded several services under the Active Directory name and uses the term Active Directory Domain Services (ADDS) to refer to what has been previously known as Active Directory. The term Active Directory is still commonly used by IT professionals and is used throughout this book.

Active Directory Structure

Domains A **domain** has a central security database that is used by all computers that are members of the domain. This central database means that user accounts can be created once in the domain and then used to log on at any workstation in the domain. No matter which workstation the user logs on at, the user gains access to all of the appropriate network resources. There are no concerns about synchronizing passwords because only one central account is used.

In addition to user account information, domains also store information about computers. Each computer that is a member of the domain has an account in Active Directory. Information about applications and printers is also found in Active Directory. DNS information is often stored in Active Directory.

Active Directory uses the same naming convention for domains and objects contained in these domains as DNS. For example, an Active Directory domain can be named GiganticLife.com. However, Active Directory domains and DNS domains contain very different content. In most cases, you want to have your Active Directory domain names and external DNS domain names separate to avoid confusion. The simplest way to do this is to create Active Directory domain names with the .local extension, which is not supported over the Internet.

Organizational Units Each domain can be subdivided into **organizational units** (OUs). Using OUs allows you to organize the objects in a domain. For example, you can organize the users in a domain by department by creating an OU for each department. This makes it easier to find the user accounts that you are looking for. Figure 13-1 shows how OUs are displayed when using the Active Directory Users and Computers administrative tool on the server.

OUs can also be used for delegating management permissions. For example, you can delegate the ability to create and manage objects in the Marketing OU to an administrator assigned to the marketing department. That administrator will not be able to create and manage objects in the OUs of other departments.

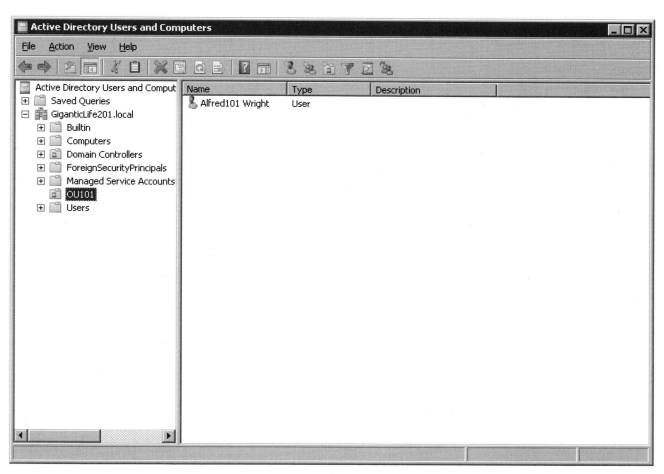

Figure 13-1 Active Directory Users and Computers
Courtesy Course Technology/Cengage Learning

Finally, OUs are used to apply Group Policies. Group Policies can be applied to a specific OU, which applies Group Policy setting to the user accounts or computer accounts in the OU. For example, you could create a Group Policy with marketing specific settings and apply it to the Marketing OU.

More information about Group Policy is provided later in this chapter.

Trees and Forests In most cases, a single domain subdivided into OUs is sufficient to manage a network. However, you can create more complex Active Directory structures by combining multiple domains into a **tree** and multiple trees into a **forest**.

Some reasons to use multiple domains are:

- *Decentralized administration*—Domain boundaries serve as security boundaries for domain administrators. In some cases, having multiple domains simplifies delegation of management responsibilities rather than using OUs.

- *Unreliable WAN links*—If the WAN links between locations are often unavailable, then separate domains minimize replication traffic across the WAN links.

- *Multiple password policies*—Unless all domain controllers in a domain are running Windows Server 2008 or later, a domain can have only a single password policy. Implementing multiple domains allows you to have multiple password policies. For example, users in a high security domain may be forced to change their password every 30 days while users in a second domain may be forced to change their password every 90 days.

If all domain controllers in a domain are running Windows Server 2008 or later, then you can use fine-grained password policies that define different password policies for individual users and groups within a domain.

The first Active Directory domain created in an organization is called the **forest root domain**. When multiple domains are needed, they are connected to the forest root domain. If all domains share the same naming structure, they are part of a single tree. If the domains have various naming structures, then each naming structure is a separate tree. For example, if GiganticLife.local is the forest root domain, then Europe.GiganticLife.local is a domain in the same tree, while EuropeLife.local is in a different tree.

When multiple domains exist in a forest, trust relationships are generated automatically between the domains. The trust relationships are transitive, as shown in Figure 13-2. An example of the transitive trust relationship is that if domain A trusts domain B and domain B trusts domain C, then domain A transitively trusts domain C.

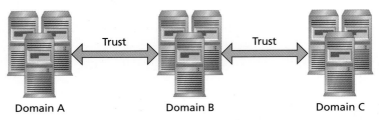

Figure 13-2 Transitive Trusts
Courtesy Course Technology/Cengage Learning

In a forest each domain trusts its own parent and subdomains. There is also a trust relationship between each tree in the Active Directory forest. Figure 13-3 shows the trust relationships between domains and trees in an Active Directory forest.

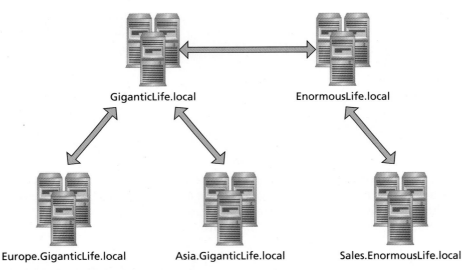

Figure 13-3 Domains, trees, and trusts
Courtesy Course Technology/Cengage Learning

Server Roles   Within Active Directory, Windows servers can be either a **member server** or a domain controller. Member servers are integrated into Active Directory and can participate in the domain by sharing files and printers with domain users. Windows 7 computers integrate into Active Directory in the same way as member servers. However, Windows 7 is a desktop operating system and is not able to function as either a member server or a domain controller.

Joining a domain with Windows 7 is covered later in this chapter.

A domain controller is a server that stores a copy of Active Directory information. When users log on to an Active Directory domain, the workstation communicates with a domain controller to authenticate the user. After users are authenticated, they can access network resources. Domain controllers also respond to requests for other domain information such as printers or application configuration.

Activity 13-1: Installing a Domain Controller

Time Required: 1.5 hours
Objective: Install a Windows Server 2008 R2 domain controller.

Description: To create a single centralized security database, you must have a Windows server configured as a domain controller. In this activity you install Windows Server 2008 R2 and configure the server as a domain controller.

Depending on hardware availability, this activity can be done as a demonstration by the instructor with students sharing the single server. However, if only a single instructor server is used, then some additional activities must also be performed as demonstrations. This requirement is noted for each of the applicable labs in this chapter. Remote Desktop Services is enabled in this activity to support sharing by multiple students.

1. If necessary, configure a second computer to boot from DVD.

2. Insert the Windows Server 2008 R2 DVD and start the computer.

3. If necessary, press a key to boot from DVD. This option appears only if there are existing partitions on the hard drive.

4. In the Install Windows window, click **Next** to accept the default settings for language, time and currency format, and keyboard.

5. Click **Install Now**.

6. On the Select the operating system you want to install page, click **Windows Server 2008 R2 Enterprise (Full Installation)** and click **Next**.

7. Select the **I accept the license terms** check box and click **Next**.

8. Click **Custom (advanced)** to install a new copy of Windows Server 2008 R2.

9. On the Where do you want to install Windows page, if there are any existing partition, click **Drive options (advanced)** and follow the on-screen instructions to delete the partitions.

10. Click **Disk 0 Unallocated Space** and click **Next**. The installation routine automatically partitions the disk with a 100 MB system partition, similar to the Windows 7 installation.

11. Wait while the installation completes. This can take up to half an hour depending on your hardware.

12. When the computer reboots and prompts you to change the password, click **OK**.

13. In the New password and Confirm password boxes, type **Passw0rd** (0 is a zero) and then press **Enter**.

14. When the password has been changed, click **OK**.

15. In the Initial Configuration Tasks window, click **Set time zone**.

16. In the Date and Time window, configure the correct date, time, and time zone for your location, and then click **OK**.

13

17. In the Initial Configuration Tasks window, click **Configure networking**.

18. Right-click **Local Area Connection** and click **Properties**.

19. Click **Internet Protocol Version 4 (TCP/IPv4)** and click **Properties**.

20. Click **Use the following IP address** and type the following information:

    - IP address: 192.168.0.y, where *y* is a number assigned by your instructor.
    - Subnet mask: 255.255.255.0
    - Default gateway: 192.168.0.1

21. Click **Use the following DNS server addresses**, in the Preferred DNS server box, type **127.0.0.1**, and click **OK**.

22. In the Local Area Connection Properties windows, click **Close**.

23. Close the Network Connections window.

24. In the Initial Configuration Tasks window, click **Provide computer name and domain**.

25. On the Computer Name tab, click **Change**.

26. In the Computer Name box, type **DC***y*, where y is a number assigned to you by your instructor, and click **OK**.

27. In the Computer Name/Domain Changes window, click **OK**.

28. In the System Properties window, click **Close** and then **Restart Now**.

29. After the server reboots, log on as **Administrator** with a password of **Passw0rd**.

30. In the Initial Configuration Tasks window, select the **Do not show this window at logon** check box and click **Close**. Notice that Server Manager starts automatically.

31. In the left pane of Server Manager, click **Roles** and click **Add Roles**.

32. In the Add Roles Wizard, click **Next**.

33. In the list of server roles, select the **Active Directory Domain Services** check box, click **Add Required Features**, and click **Next**.

34. On the Introduction to Active Directory Domain Services page, click **Next**.

35. On the Confirmation page, click **Install**.

36. On the Results page, read the results and click **Close**.

37. Click the **Start** button, type **dcpromo**, and press **Enter**.

38. In the Active Directory Domain Services Installation Wizard, click **Next**.

39. Read the Operating System Compatibility page and click **Next**.

40. On the Choose a Deployment Configuration page, click **Create a new domain in a new forest** and click **Next**.

41. In the FQDN of the forest root domain box, type **GiganticLife***y***.local**, where *y* is a number assigned to you by your instructor, and click **Next**.

42. In the Forest Functional Level box, select **Windows Server 2008 R2** and click **Next**.

43. On the Additional Domain Controller Options page, click **Next** to accept the default of configuring this server as a DNS server.

44. If prompted, click **Yes** to continue even though DNS delegation cannot be created.

45. Click **Next** to accept the default file locations.

46. In the Password and Confirm password boxes, type **Passw0rd** and click **Next**.

47. On the Summary page, click **Next**. It takes a few minutes for the wizard to complete.

48. When the wizard completes, click **Finish** and click **Restart Now**.

49. After the server reboots, log on as **GiganticLife***y***\Administrator** with a password of **Passw0rd**.

50. In the left pane of Server Manager, click **Roles** and then click **Add Roles**.

51. In the Add Roles Wizard, click **Next**.

52. In the list of roles, select the **Remote Desktop Services** check box and click **Next**.

53. Read the Introduction to Remote Desktop Services page and click **Next**.

54. In the list of role services, select the **Remote Desktop Session Host** check box, click **Install Remote Desktop Session Host anyway (not recommended)** and click **Next**.

55. Read the information about application compatibility and click **Next**.

56. Click **Do not require Network Level Authentication** and click **Next**.

57. On the Specify Licensing Mode page, click **Next** to configure later.

58. On the User Groups page, click **Next** to allow only Administrators to connect.

59. On the Configure Client Experience page, click **Next** to leave the client experience options disabled.

60. On the Confirm Installation Selections page, click **Install**.

61. On the Installation Results page, click **Close** and click **Yes** to restart.

62. Log on as Administrator to allow configuration to complete.

63. In the Resume Configuration Wizard, click **Close**.

64. Click the **Start** button, point to **Administrative Tools**, point to **Remote Desktop Services**, and click **Remote Desktop Session Host Configuration**.

65. Under Edit settings, right-click **Restrict each user to a single session** and click **Properties**.

66. In the Properties window, clear the **Restrict each user to a single session** check box and click **OK**

67. Close Remote Desktop Session Host Configuration.

Active Directory Partitions

Active Directory is not a single monolithic database with all of the information about the network. To make Active Directory more manageable, it is divided into the **domain partition, configuration partition**, and **schema partition**.

- The domain partition holds the user accounts, computers accounts, and other domain-specific information. This partition is replicated only to domain controllers in the same domain.

- The configuration partition holds general information about the Active Directory forest. Also, applications such as Exchange Server use the configuration partition to store application-specific information. This partition is replicated to all domain controllers in the Active Directory forest.

- The schema partition holds the definitions of all objects and object attributes for the forest. This partition is replicated to all domain controllers in the Active Directory forest.

In addition to the three standard Active Directory partitions, application partitions can also be created. An **application partition** is created by an administrator to hold application-specific information. The contents of an application partition are replicated to the domain controllers that are specified. Replication is not limited to just all domain controllers in the Active Directory forest or an Active Directory domain.

One special case for replication of information in the domain partition is global catalog servers. A **global catalog server** is a domain controller that holds a subset of the information in all domain partitions. For example, a global catalog has information about all users in the entire active directory forest, but only some of the information that is available about the users in each domain. Global catalog servers are used to hold the membership of universal groups and by applications such as Microsoft Exchange Server. Exchange Server uses global catalog servers to perform address book lookups and locate user mailboxes.

Active Directory Sites and Replication

Active Directory uses **multimaster replication**. This means that Active Directory information can be changed on any domain controller and those changes will be replicated to other domain controllers. This process ensures that all domain controllers have the same information. However, replication is not immediate, and the amount of time required to replicate data depends on whether domain controllers are in the same site or different sites.

An **Active Directory site** is defined by IP subnets. As administrator, you create sites and define the IP subnets in each site. In most cases, you should create an Active Directory site for each physical location in your network. However, if you have extremely fast (10 Mbps) and reliable WAN links, you can consider making separate physical locations part of the same site.

Within a site, Active Directory replication is uncontrolled. The replication process is completely automatic. When a change is made to an Active Directory object, the change begins replication to all domain controllers in the site after 15 seconds. The change is not replicated immediately because Active Directory attempts to batch multiple changes together in a single replication process to enhance network efficiency.

Between sites, Active Directory replication is controlled by site links. By default, all replication is controlled by a single site link that allows replication to occur every 180 minutes, but can be shortened to 15 minutes. You can create additional site links to have more precise control over when replication is performed. For example, you could prevent replication from happening over a slow WAN link when another process is using the WAN link.

Active Directory and DNS One of the most common configuration problems in Active Directory networks is incorrect DNS configuration on servers and workstations. Proper configuration of DNS is essential for Active Directory. Active Directory stores information about domain controllers and other services in DNS. Workstations use the information in DNS to find domain controllers in their local site and log on.

Incorrect DNS configuration can result in:

- Slow user logons
- Inability to apply group policies
- Failed replication between domain controllers

In most cases, all workstations and servers should be configured to use an internal DNS server. This ensures that all domain controllers register their information in the correct location and that all workstations have access to domain controller information. The internal DNS server can resolve Internet DNS records on behalf of clients as well. An external DNS server that is provided by an Internet service provider is typically unable to accept dynamic registration of DNS records that is required for Active Directory.

Activity 13-2: Viewing Active Directory DNS Records

Time Required: 10 minutes
Objective: View the DNS records for Active Directory.

Description: Active Directory DNS records are used to locate domain controllers and other domain services. In this activity you use the DNS management tool console to view the DNS records registered by a domain controller.

1. If necessary, log on to your Windows 7 computer.
2. Configure your computer with a static IP address and DNS server.
   a. Click the **Start** button and click **Control Panel**.
   b. Click **Network and Internet** and click **Network and Sharing Center**.

    c. In the Tasks list, click **Change adapter settings**.

    d. Right-click **Local Area Connection** and click **Properties**.

    e. Click **Internet Protocol Version 4 (TCP/IPv4)** and click **Properties**.

    f. Click **Use the following IP address** and enter the following information:

- IP address: **192.168.0.z**, where z is a number assigned to you by your instructor.
- Subnet mask: **255.255.255.0**
- Default gateway: **192.168.0.1**
- Preferred DNS server: **192.168.0.y**, where y is the number assigned to your domain controller. If students in your class are using an instructor server as the domain controller, then this IP address should be the IP address of the instructor domain controller.

    g. Click **OK** to close Internet Protocol Version 4 (TCP/IPv4) Properties dialog box.

    h. Click **Close** to close the Local Area Connection Properties dialog box.

    i. Close all open windows.

3. Click the **Start** button, type **remote** and click **Remote Desktop Connection**.

4. In the Computer box, type **DCy**, where y is the number assigned to your domain controller, and click **Connect**. If students in your class are using an instructor server as the domain controller, then this name should be the name of the instructor domain controller.

5. Click **Use another account**, select the **Remember my credentials** checkbox, and log on as **GiganticLife$y$\Administrator** with a password of **Passw0rd**.

6. Click **Start**, point to **Administrative Tools**, and click **DNS**.

7. In the left pane, expand **DCy**, expand **Forward Lookup Zones**, and click **_msdcs. GiganticLife$y$. local**. This is the domain that holds DNS records for Active Directory.

8. Expand **_msdcs.GiganticLife$y$.local**, expand **dc**, and click **_tcp**. Notice that dcy. GiganticLife$y$.local is listed for the _kerberos and _ldap services. These records are used by clients to find a domain controller for logon.

9. Expand **Sites**, expand **Default-First-Site-Name**, and click **_tcp**. Notice that dcy.GiganticLife$y$.local is listed for the _kerberos and _ldap services in this Active Directory site.

10. Close all open Windows.

11. Log off DCy.

Joining a Domain

When a workstation joins a domain, it is integrated into the security structure for the domain. Administration of the workstation can be performed centrally by using Group Policy. Also, domain administrators are automatically given the ability to manage the workstation.

The following security changes occur when a workstation joins a domain:

- The Domain Admins group becomes a member of the local Administrators group.
- The Domain Users group becomes a member of the local Users group.
- The Domain Guests group becomes a member of the local Guests group.

The process of joining a workstation to a domain creates a computer account. It is this computer account that allows the workstation to integrate with Active Directory. If the computer account is removed, then the workstation can no longer be used to access domain resources by users with domain-based accounts.

After a workstation is joined to the domain, it synchronizes time with domain controllers in the domain. This is necessary because the authentication process used by domain controllers is time sensitive. If the clock on a workstation is more than five minutes out from the domain controller then users on the workstation cannot be authenticated.

13

Activity 13-3: Joining a Domain

Time Required: 15 minutes
Objective: Join Windows 7 to an Active Directory Domain.

Description: Joining a domain integrates Windows 7 into the security system for Active Directory. In this activity, you join a Windows 7 workstation to an Active Directory domain and view the security changes.

1. If necessary, start your computer and log on.
2. Click the **Start** button, right-click **Computer**, and click **Properties**.
3. In the System window, under Computer name, domain, and workgroup settings, click **Change settings**.
4. In the System Properties window, click the **Change** button.
5. In the Member of area, click **Domain** and type **GiganticLifey.local** and click **OK**.
6. In the User name box, type **Administrator**, in the Password box, type **Passw0rd**, and click **OK**.
7. Click **OK** to clear the welcome message.
8. Click **OK** to clear the restart message.
9. In the System Properties window, click **Close**.
10. Click **Restart Now**.
11. Press **Ctrl+Alt+Delete**, click **Switch User**, and click **Other User**. Notice that the logon is using the domain by default.
12. Log on as **GiganticLifey\Administrator** with a password of **Passw0rd**. You are now logged on to the local computer as the domain administrator. You needed to include the domain name as part of the user name only because there is an Administrator account in the domain and Windows 7 local security database.
13. Click the **Start** button, right-click **Computer**, and click **Manage**.
14. Expand **Local Users and Groups** and click **Groups**.
15. Right-click **Administrators** and click **Properties**. Notice that the Domain Admins group is a member of the local Administrators group. This allows Domain Admins to manage the workstation.
16. Click **Cancel** to close the Administrators Properties dialog box.
17. Right-click **Users** and click **Properties**. Notice that the Domain Users group is a member of the local Users group. This allows all domain users to log on to the workstation.
18. Click **Cancel** to close the Users Properties dialog box.
19. Close all open windows.

Group Policy

Group Policy is a feature integrated with Active Directory that can be used to centrally manage the configuration of a Windows 7 computer. Some of the settings you can configure include:

- Desktop settings, such as wallpaper and the ability to right-click
- Security settings, such as the ability to log on locally
- Logon, logoff, startup, and shutdown scripts
- Folder redirection to store My Documents on a network server
- Software distribution

The Group Policy settings used by Windows 7 are contained in a **Group Policy object (GPO)**. A GPO is a collection of registry settings applied to the Windows 7 computer. To apply GPO settings, the GPO is linked to an OU, Active Directory site, or domain. A GPO can also be applied locally to a single computer. Configuration of Group Policy objects is performed with the Group Policy Management Console shown in Figure 13-4.

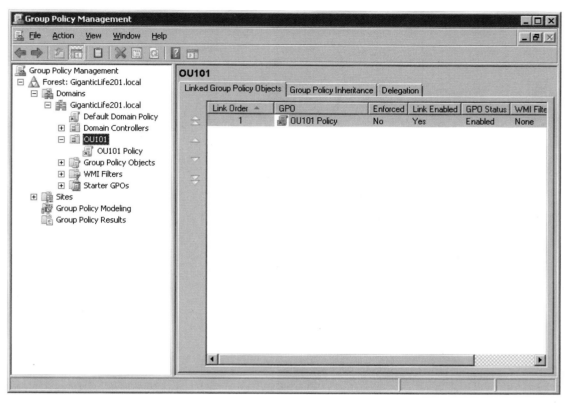

Figure 13-4 Group Policy Management Console
Courtesy Course Technology/Cengage Learning

The settings in a GPO are divided into user settings and computer settings. The user settings are applied to any user accounts in the OU to which the GPO is linked. Computer settings in the GPO are applied to any computer accounts in the OU to which the GPO is linked. In Figure 13-5, if Bob logs on to WS1, the user settings from the GPO linked to the Marketing OU and the computer settings from the GPO linked to the Head Office OU are applied.

Windows workstations and member servers download group policy settings during startup and approximately every 90 minutes thereafter. If you are testing GPO settings, you can use the gpupdate utility to trigger faster Group Policy object downloads. Domain controllers download Group Policy settings every five minutes.

Activity 13-4: Creating a GPO

Time Required: 15 minutes
Objective: Create and apply a GPO.

Description: You can create GPOs to control users and their workstations. In this activity, you create a GPO and verify that it is applied to your Windows 7 computer.

1. If necessary, start your computer and log on.
2. Connect to the server with Remote Desktop Connection.

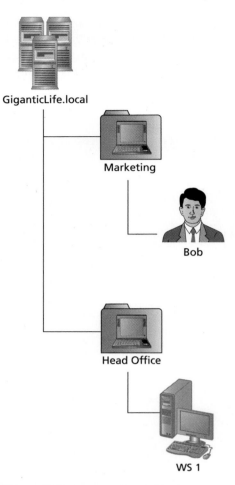

Figure 13-5 Group Policy application
Courtesy Course Technology/Cengage Learning

    a. Click the **Start** button, type **remote**, and click **Remote Desktop Connection**.

    b. In the Computer box, type **DCy** and press **Enter**.

    c. Click **Remember my credentials**, and log on as **GiganticLifey\Administrator** with a password of **Passw0rd**.

3. Click **Start**, point to **Administrative Tools**, and click **Active Directory Users and Computers**.

4. In the left pane, click **GiganticLifey.local**, right-click **GiganticLifey.local**, point to **New**, and click **Organizational Unit**.

5. In the Name box, type **OUz**, where *z* is the number assigned to you by your instructor, and click **OK**.

6. Right-click **OUz**, point to **New**, and click **User**.

7. Enter the following information and click **Next**.

    • First name: Alfred*z*

    • Last name: Wright

    • User logon name: Alfred*z*

8. In the Password and Confirm password boxes, type **Password!**. This password is required because password complexity is enforced by default in an Active Directory domain.

9. Clear the **User must change password at next logon** check box and click **Next**.

10. Click **Finish** to create the user.

11. Close Active Directory Users and Computers.

12. Click the **Start** button, point to **Administrative Tools**, and click **Group Policy Management**.

13. Expand **Forest: GiganticLifey.local**, expand **domains**, and click **GiganticLifey.local**. Notice that the Default Domain Policy is linked here. Settings in this policy apply to all users and computers in the domain.

14. Expand **GiganticLifey.local** and click **OUz**. Notice that no group policies are linked here.

15. Right-click **OUz** and click **Create a GPO in this domain, and Link it here**.

16. In the New GPO window, in the Name box, type **OUz Policy** and click **OK**.

17. Right-click **OUz Policy** and click **Edit**.

18. Under User Configuration, expand **Policies**, expand **Administrative Templates**, and click **Control Panel**.

19. Double-click **Prohibit access to the Control Panel**, click **Enabled**, and click **OK**.

20. Close the **Group Policy Management Editor**. The changes are saved automatically.

21. Close Group Policy Management and log off the remote desktop session.

22. Click the **Start** button, type **cmd**, and press **Enter**.

23. Type **gpupdate** and press **Enter**. This updates the group policy objects for the computer without performing a reboot.

24. Close the command prompt and log off.

25. Log on as **GiganticLifey\Alfredz** with a password of **Password!**. Alfred is able to log on because the Domain Users group is a member of the local Users group.

26. Click the **Start** button. Notice that Control Panel is not listed as an option.

27. Log off.

Group Policy Inheritance

Group Policy objects can be linked to the Active Directory domains, OUs, and Active Directory sites. In addition, each Windows 7 Computer can have local Group Policy objects. It is essential to understand precedence given to each of these policies. For example, when a local policy configures the home page for Internet Explorer as *http://www.microsoft.com* and a domain policy configures the home page for Internet Explorer as *http://intranet*, which one is effective? The precedence determines what settings apply when there are conflicting settings between policies.

When a Windows computer starts, GPOs are applied in the following order:

1. Local computer

2. Site

3. Domain

4. Parent OU

5. Child OU

All of the individual GPO settings are inherited by default. For example, a group policy setting on a parent OU is also applied to child OUs and to all users and computers in the child OUs. One computer or user can process many policies during startup and logon.

At each level, more than one GPO can be applied to a user or computer. If there is more than one GPO per container, the policies are applied in the order specified by the administrator. The following steps are used to determine which policy settings to apply.

1. If there is no conflict, the settings for all policies are applied.

2. If there is a conflict, later settings overwrite earlier settings. For example, the setting from a domain policy overrides the setting from a local policy.

3. If the settings in a computer policy and user policy conflict, the settings from the computer policy are applied.

Group Policy Enhancements in Windows 7

The basic process of applying group policy settings to Windows 7 is the same as previous versions of Windows. However, the details of how those policy settings are applied have been updated in Windows Vista and Windows 7. Also, many new policy settings are available for Windows Vista and Windows 7 that are not valid for previous version of Windows.

Group Policy Service
Windows 7 processes group policies with a **Group Policy service**. Windows 2000 and Windows XP used the Winlogon service to process group polices which made it less flexible.

By implementing the Group Policy service, the following benefits are obtained:

- Group Policy settings can be applied without any reboots.

- Performance is increased and resource usage is reduced for Group Policy processing.

- Group policy events are logged to the System log instead of the Application log.

- Information about Group Policy applications is logged to a Group Policy Operational log.

Group Policy Preferences
Each new version of Windows introduces new settings that can be managed by using Group Policy. As each version of Windows introduces new features, new Group Policy settings are introduced to control those features. Windows 7 also introduces Group Policy Preferences.

A typical Group Policy setting is applied to a computer and cannot be changed by the user, even if the user has full administrative privileges to the computer. A Group Policy Preference is pushed down to the computer as part of the same process as Group Policy settings; but a Group Policy Preference can be changed by the user. For example, you can use Group Policy Preferences to configure power options such as configuring the computer to sleep after 10 minutes of inactivity. The user can manually change this. However, the next time the computer is restarted the Group Policy Preference is reapplied.

Group Policy Preferences introduce a way to configure a number of Windows 7 features that may have required scripting in the past. In some cases, you may be able to use Group Policy Preferences instead of logon scripts. Some of the things you can configure with Group Policy Preferences include:

- ODBC data sources
- Enable and disable devices
- Printers
- Drive mappings
- Scheduled tasks
- Service configuration
- Internet Explorer settings
- VPN and dialup connections
- Registry keys
- Start Menu configuration

One of the unique features of Group Policy Preferences is the ability to target them. By using targeting, you can have a single Group Policy object that provides different settings for different users. For example, you can configure a drive mapping that is only applied if you are a member of the Sales group.

Activity 13-5: Configuring Group Policy Preferences

Time Required: 15 minutes

Objective: Configure and test Group Policy Preferences.

Description: One of the common tasks performed by logon scripts is creating drive mappings. Management of drive mappings can be simplified by using Group Policy Preferences to apply the drive mappings. In this activity, you create a file share and then create a drive mapping to that file share that is distributed by using Group Policy Preferences.

1. If necessary, start your computer and log on **User** *x*-**PC\User***x* with a password of **password**.

2. Connect to the server with Remote Desktop Connection.

   a. Click the **Start** button, type **remote**, and click **Remote Desktop Connection**.

   b. In the Computer box, type **DC***y* and press **Enter**.

   c. If you are not automatically logged on, then log on as **GiganticLife***y***\Administrator** with a password of **Passw0rd**.

3. Click **Start**, point to **Administrative Tools**, and click **Computer Management**.

4. Under System Tools, expand **Shared Folders**, and click **Shares**. Review the list of shares that exists by default on the domain controller. Shares ending in a $ are hidden shares that cannot be browsed, but can be connected to if you know the share name.

5. Right-click **Shares** and click **New Share**.

6. Click **Next** to begin the Create A Shared Folder Wizard.

7. In the Folder path box, type **C:\Share***z* and then click **Next**.

8. Click **Yes** to create the folder.

9. Click **Next** to accept the default share name of **Share***z*.

10. On the Shared Folder Permissions page, click **Customize permissions** and then click **Custom**.

11. In the Customize Permissions window, while **Everyone** is selected, select **Allow Full Control**.

12. Click the **Security** tab and click **Edit**.

13. In the Group or user names box, click **Users**, select the **Allow Modify** check box, and click **OK**.

14. In the Customize Permissions window, click **OK**.

15. In the Create A Shared Folder Wizard, click **Finish**.

16. On the Sharing was Successful page, click **Finish**.

17. Close Computer Management.

18. Click **Start**, point to **Administrative Tools**, and click **Group Policy Management**.

19. If necessary, browse to the **OU***z* organizational unit that you created in Activity 13-4, right-click **OU***z* **Policy** and click **Edit**.

20. Under User Configuration, expand **Preferences**, expand **Windows Settings**, and click **Drive Maps**. Notice that no drive mappings are configured by default.

21. Right-click **Drive Maps**, point to **New**, and click **Mapped Drive**.

22. In the New Drive Properties window, in the Location box, type **\\DC***y***\Share***z*.

23. In the Drive Letter area, click **Use**, and select **S**.

24. Click the **Common** tab, select the **Item-level targeting** check box, and click **Targeting**.

25. In the Targeting Editor window, click **New Item**. Read the wide variety of settings that can be used for targeting.

13

26. Click **Cancel**.

27. In the New Drive Properties window, click **OK**.

28. Close Group Policy Management Editor and Group Policy Management.

29. Log off the domain controller.

30. Click the **Start** button, type **cmd**, and press **Enter**.

31. Type **gpupdate /force** and press **Enter**. This updates the group policy objects for the computer without performing a reboot.

32. Close the command prompt and log off.

33. Log on as **GiganticLifey\Alfredz** with a password of **Password!**.

34. Click the **Start** button and click **Computer**. Notice that there is a drive mapping for the letter S. If the drive mapping for S does not appear, run gpupdate again, logoff and log back on.

35. Close all open windows and log off.

The new Group Policy settings are always available in local policies on Windows 7. To have the new Group Policy settings available at the network level, you must be using Windows Server 2008 R2.

Multiple Local Policies Windows XP and Windows 2000 allowed only a single local GPO. In domain-based networks, this was not a problem because any necessary differentiation could be made with GPOs linked to domains or OUs. However in workgroup environments, this was very limiting. With a single local GPO only one configuration could be created and it applied to all users.

Windows Vista and Windows 7 allow you to have multiple local GPOs and consequently have distinct settings for different users, even in a workgroup environment. This is very useful for public access computers that are not part of a domain. One restricted user can be used for public access, and another unrestricted user can be used for system maintenance.

Activity 13-6: Creating Local GPOs

Time Required: 10 minutes
Objective: Create local GPOs and verify their application.

Description: Windows 7 allows you to create multiple local GPOs to control users on a system. In this activity, you create multiple local GPOs and verify that they are applied as users log on.

1. Log on as **GiganticLifey\Administrator** with a password of **Passw0rd**.

2. Click the **Start** button, type **mmc**, and press **Enter**.

3. Click the **File** menu and click **Add/Remove Snap-in**.

4. In the Available snap-ins list, double-click **Group Policy Object Editor**.

5. Click **Finish** to accept the default option of editing the Local Computer Group Policy object.

6. In the Available snap-ins list, double-click **Group Policy Object Editor**.

7. Click the **Browse** button and click the **Users** tab. This shows the specific local users and groups that a local group policy object can be created for. Notice that there are also groups for Administrators and Non-administrators.

8. Click **User***x*, click **OK**, and click **Finish**.

9. Click **OK** to close the Add or Remove Snap-ins dialog box.

10. In the left pane, click **Local Computer Policy**. You can see that the policy expands and that there are computer and user settings. The user settings listed here apply to all users logging on to this computer unless another policy overrides them. Settings in more user-specific local policies and domain policies can override the Local Computer Policy.

11. In the left pane, click **Local Computer\Userx Policy**. You can see that the policy has only user settings. Computer settings can only be configured locally once in the Local Computer Policy. The user settings in this policy override the user settings in the Local Computer Policy, but the user settings at the domain level override these.

12. Expand **Windows Settings**, expand **Internet Explorer Maintenance**, and click **URLs**.

13. In the right pane, double-click **Important URLs**.

14. Select **Customize Home page URL**.

15. In the Home page URL box, type **http://www.google.com/news** and click **OK**.

16. Close the **MMC console** and click **No** when prompted to save the console settings.

17. Log off as Administrator.

18. Log on as **Userx-PC\Userx** with a password of **password**.

19. On the taskbar, click **Internet Explorer**. Notice that Internet Explorer opens with the new home page.

20. Log off as **Userx**.

Controlling Device Installation

One of the Group Policy enhancements that is of the most interest to corporations is the ability to prevent device installation in Windows Vista and Windows 7. There have been media reports of some companies physically destroying USB ports to prevent data from leaving the premises on USB drives. This may or may not be successful since so many common peripherals, such as a keyboard or mouse, are normally connected by using a USB port.

A better solution is to prevent installation of USB storage devices at the operating system level. If the device cannot be installed, then data cannot be transferred to it. You can also control removable storage as a class of devices.

While preventing device installation is most likely to be used to control USB-based storage, it can be used to control the installation of any device. For example, you could create policies that limit the installation of printers to only those that are company approved. This would prevent individual departments or users from purchasing nonstandard printers and driving up support costs.

Users with administrative privileges are able to install devices regardless of the controls put in place with Group Policy settings.

Device Identification

When a new device is installed into a Windows 7 computer, the operating system uses a **device identification string** and **device setup class** to properly install the new device. The device identification string is used to find an appropriate driver for the device. The device setup class controls how the device driver software is installed. Both the device identification string and the device setup class can be used when controlling the installation of devices.

Device Identification Strings A device often reports multiple device identification strings when queried by the operating system. A hardware ID is the most specific device identification string. When multiple hardware IDs are reported, there is typically one very specific hardware ID that includes make, model, and revision, then other less specific hardware IDs such as make and model. Figure 13-6 shows the hardware IDs for a hard disk.

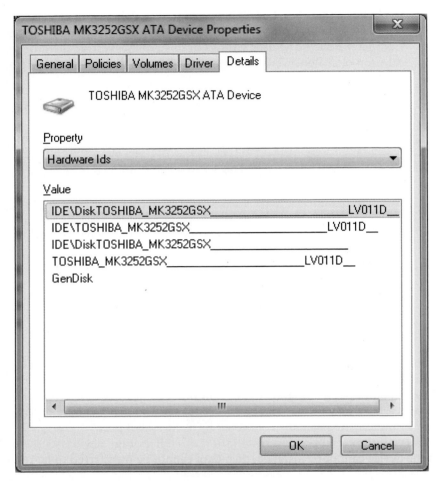

Figure 13-6 Hardware IDs for a hard disk
Courtesy Course Technology/Cengage Learning

Including multiple hardware IDs in a device allows the best available driver to be installed from those that are available. From a device installation control perspective, you can use the more generic hardware IDs to control installation rather than the very specific ones.

Compatible IDs are another device identification string that is used to find appropriate drivers. A compatible ID is less specific than a hardware ID and may allow the driver from another vendor to be used when the specific driver for the device is not available. If driver matches are made based on a compatible ID, some device functionality may be not be present.

Device Setup Classes Device setup classes are used during the installation process for a new device to describe how the installation should be performed. The device setup class identifies a generic type of device rather than a specific make or model. Each device setup class is identified by a globally unique identifier (GUID).

Some devices have multiple GUIDs defined if they are a multifunction device such as a scanner/fax/printer device. The parent device (overall device) has one GUID, and other functions (scanner, fax, printer) each have their own GUID.

Device Installation Group Policy Settings

Windows 7 includes 10 group policy settings, shown in Figure 13-7, specifically to control device installation. They control which devices can and cannot be installed. Also, you can define a default option for whether users are allowed to install new devices. All of these settings are located in Computer Configuration\Administrative Templates\System\Device Installation\Device Installation Restrictions.

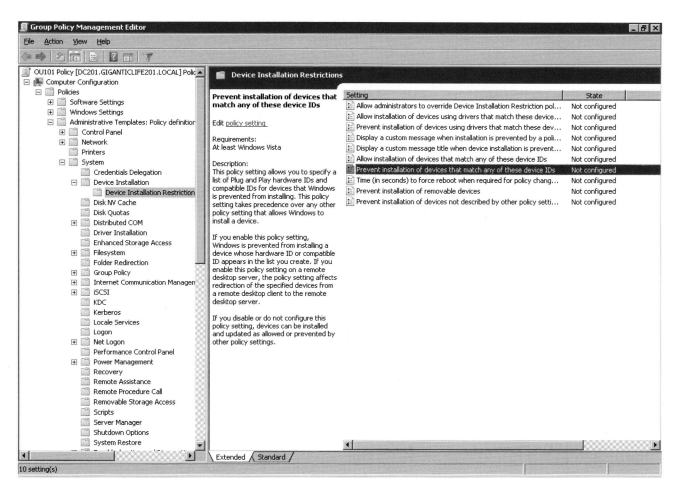

Figure 13-7 Device installation Group Policy settings
Courtesy Course Technology/Cengage Learning

The Group Policy settings that control device installation are:

- *Allow administrators to override Device Installation Restriction policies*—When enabled, members of the Administrators group are able to install and update the device driver for any device regardless of other policy settings. When this setting is not explicitly disabled, administrators can override Device Installation Restriction policies.

- *Allow installation of devices using drivers that match these device setup classes*—When enabled, devices matching the specified setup classes can be installed if the default configuration is to block device installation. If a device has multiple setup classes and one of the setup classes is specifically blocked, then this setting will not override the blocked setup class.

- *Prevent installation of devices using drivers that match these device setup classes*—When enabled, devices matching the specified setup classes cannot be installed. This setting overrides any other settings that allow device installation.

- *Display a custom message when installation is prevented by a policy setting*—When enabled, a customized message is displayed when device installation is blocked by a device installation restriction policy. This allows you to clearly indicate to users why the error is occurring.

- *Display a custom message title when device installation is prevented by a policy setting*— When enabled, a customized title is displayed in the error dialog box when device installation is blocked by a device installation restriction policy.

- *Allow installation of devices that match any of these device IDs*—When enabled, devices matching the specified device ID can be installed if the default configuration is to block device installation. If a device has multiple device IDs and one of the device IDs is specifically blocked, then this setting will not override the blocked device ID.

- *Prevent installation of devices that match any of these device IDs*—When enabled, devices matching the specified device IDs cannot be installed. This setting overrides any other settings that allow device installation.

- *Time (in seconds) to force reboot when required for policy changes to take effect*—When enabled the computers affected by this policy applies will reboot when required to apply changes to Device Installation Restrictions. When this is disabled or not configured, then a reboot is not forced.

- *Prevent installation of removable devices*—When enabled, removable devices cannot be installed. Removable devices are those identified as removable by their driver, such as USB devices.

- *Prevent installation of devices not described by other policy settings*—When enabled, all device installation is blocked unless the device ID or device setup class is specifically allowed.

Removable Storage Group Policy Settings

Since access to removable storage is a concern for many organizations, there are additional Group Policy settings, shown in Figure 13-8, that can be used to control access specifically to

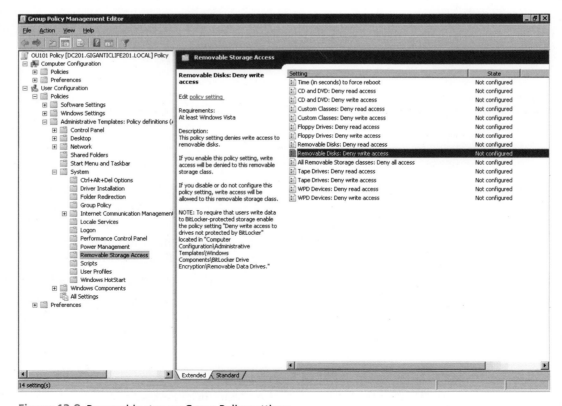

Figure 13-8 Removable storage Group Policy settings
Courtesy Course Technology/Cengage Learning

different types of removable storage, rather than preventing installation. With these policy settings, you can deny read or write access to specific removable storage types.

The types of devices you can control with the removable storage Group Policy settings are:

- *CD and DVD*—These settings control read and write access to CD and DVD drivers, including burning. Some CD and DVD burning software accesses drives in a way that this policy does not prevent. In this case, you should prevent the installation of CD and DVD burning software to ensure that CDs and DVDs cannot be burned.

- *Custom Classes*—You can control read and write access to any device setup class that you define. This is useful for future devices that are not specifically defined in the existing policy settings.

- *Floppy Drives*—These settings control read and write access to floppy drives, including USB floppy drives.

- *Removable Disks*—These settings control read and write access to all removable disks, including USB drives.

- *All Removable Storage classes*—You can deny access to all types of removable storage. This setting overrides all others for removable storage.

- *Tape Drives*—These settings control read and write access to tape drives such as those used to backups.

- *Windows Portable Devices (WPD)*—These settings control read and write access to smart devices such as media players. Many of these devices can also act as a removable disk.

Removable storage Group Policy settings can be defined by user or computer. Device installation can only be defined for computers.

In some cases, a reboot is required to enforce removable storage Group Policy settings. This is normally a problem only when a device is in use. In such a case, you can define how long the system waits to apply the changes before rebooting the system. Rebooting the system allows the policy changes to be applied.

Activity 13-7: Controlling Device Installation

Time Required: 15 minutes
Objective: Use Group Policy settings to control device installation.

Description: Windows 7 includes a number of Group Policy settings to control the installation of devices and access to removable storage. In this activity, you will use the new Group Policy settings to prevent the installation of any new disks, including portable storage devices such as USB drives.

1. Log on as **GiganticLifey\Administrator** with a password of **Passw0rd**.
2. Click the **Start** button, right-click **Computer**, and click **Manage**.
3. In the left pane, click **Device Manager**.
4. In the right pane, expand **Disk drives**. This displays the disks installed in your system.
5. Right-click one of the disks installed in your system and click **Properties**.
6. Click the **Details** tab, and in the Property box, select **Hardware Ids**. This displays the hardware IDs reported by your disk. Notice that the lowest value in the list is GenDisk. This is the least specific reference to your disk.
7. Click **OK** to close the Properties dialog box for your disk.
8. Close **Computer Management**.
9. Click the **Start** button, type **mmc**, and press **Enter**.
10. Click the **File** menu and click **Add/Remove Snap-in**.

11. In the Available snap-ins list, double-click **Group Policy Object Editor**.

12. Click **Finish** to accept the default option of editing the Local Computer Group Policy object.

13. Click **OK** to close the Add or Remove Snap-ins dialog box.

14. In the left pane, expand **Local Computer Policy**, expand **Computer Configuration**, expand **Administrative Templates**, expand **System**, expand **Device Installation**, and click **Device Installation Restrictions**.

15. In the right pane, double-click **Prevent installation of devices that match any of these device IDs** and click **Enabled**.

16. Click the **Show** button, in the Value box, type **GenDisk**, and click **OK**. This device ID prevents the installation of all disk devices, including portable USB drives.

17. Click **OK** to close the Prevent installation of devices that match any of these device IDs dialog box.

18. Close the **MMC** console, and click **No** when prompted to save the console settings.

Deployment Planning

In many smaller organizations, Windows 7 is introduced when new systems are purchased. This means that there is often a mix of old and new operating systems. As each computer is installed, Windows Easy Transfer can be used to migrate user settings and files to the new computer. This is a time-intensive process, but is acceptable if only one or two machines are being migrated at a time.

In larger organizations, there is a greater need for operating system standardization. Typically, the change to a new operating system is a large project with a formal planning process. This is essential in larger organizations to keeps support costs down.

The formal process for implementing Windows 7 should include the following steps:

1. Define the scope and goals of the project.

2. Assess the existing computer systems.

3. Plan the new computer system configuration.

4. Determine a deployment process.

5. Test the deployment process.

6. Deploy Windows 7.

Scope and Goals

Organizations should not change computer systems for the sake of change. To justify the expense of changing to Windows 7, there must be significant benefits to the organization. The project plan must attempt to quantify the benefits migrating to Windows 7; simply listing features is not enough.

The scope of any migration project must be defined as well. The scope for a Windows 7 migration project defines which computers should be upgraded to Windows 7. Also, the scope should define the data that is to be migrated from the old operating system to Windows 7. In many cases, users want to retain existing files and application settings in the new operating system. However, this adds a significant amount of work to the migration process.

Existing Computer Systems

The existing computer systems in the organization must be evaluated to ensure that they support Windows 7. This evaluation is composed of two parts:

- *Hardware evaluation*—The existing computer hardware must be evaluated to ensure that it is powerful enough to run Windows 7 and support any desired features such as the Aero interface. Hardware that does not support Windows 7 must be replaced or excluded from the migration project.

- *Software evaluation*—The existing applications must be evaluated to ensure that they run properly in Windows 7. Any application that does not run properly in Windows 7 must be replaced or accommodated by running an older operating system. An older operating system can be run in a virtual machine or by configuring the computer to dual-boot the older operating system and Windows 7.

New Configuration

In some cases, the default configuration of Windows 7 is sufficient for organizational needs. However, in many more cases, the organization customizes the default configuration of Windows 7 to match its needs. Security settings, power management configuration, and many other settings can be customized. Many configuration settings can be applied after installation by using Group Policy objects.

The applications must also be selected as part of the configuration planning. Changing to a new operating system is often a good time to introduce a new office suite. Making multiple changes at the same time reduces the number of times users are impacted by change.

Deployment Process Selection

When existing computers have sufficient hardware capacity to run Windows 7, you can choose to either upgrade the existing operating system or perform a clean installation. An upgrade retains all of the existing computer settings possible including user files, applications, and application settings. Performing a clean installation allows you to standardize your configuration rather than using existing settings. A clean installation requires you to reinstall applications and migrate any desired user settings or files.

 The Windows 7 upgrade process is different from Windows XP because of the image-based installation process. When you upgrade to Windows 7, all applications and user configuration settings are captured, the image is applied, and then the settings are reapplied.

The potential installation methods are:

- *Boot from DVD*—This method is simple, but not well suited to large migrations. Clean installs and upgrades can be performed.

- *Run an unattended setup from a network share or DVD*—This method requires creating an Unattend.txt file with installation instructions. A network startup disk is required if no operating system is configured on the computer. This can be used for large migrations, but is not the most efficient method. Applications are not included as part of the installation. Clean installs and upgrades can be performed.

- *Imaging*—This method allows you to perform the installation in a single step including applications. This is well suited to large migrations. However, only clean installs can be performed. A network startup disk is required to perform the imaging operations.

- *Windows Deployment Services*—This method automates the deployment of images by booting computers from a Preboot eXecution Enviroment (PXE) network card. A PXE network card is able to retrieve an operating system across the network to perform the imaging process. Only clean installs can be performed.

- *System Center Configuration Manager*—This method uses System Center Configuration Manager (SCCM), a Microsoft network management package to install Windows 7 automatically over the network.

Test Deployment

Before attempting to perform any mass migration of workstations to Windows 7, you must thoroughly test the deployment process. The first part of the testing process should be done in a test lab that is completely separate from the rest of the network. The test lab should mimic your real network as closely as possible. In this case, you should ensure that the workstations have similar hardware to production workstations and the same software.

13

After the deployment process is working in a lab environment, you should perform a test pilot to designated users within the organization. This further tests the deployment process on a small scale to identify any issues that were missed in the lab environment. The users and computers selected for the test deployment should be representative of the users and computers in the overall organization. For example, a few users should be selected from every department with various applications. Selecting only users from within the IT department is not representative of the overall organization.

Deployment

After deployment testing is complete, Windows 7 can be deployed to the overall organization. In most cases, deployment will not be done over a single night or a single weekend. In an organization with thousands of users, it is not realistic to migrate all of those computers to Windows 7 and respond to user concerns the next day.

In most cases, deployment will be done by department, region, building, or floor. Breaking the deployment into smaller phases reduces the risk of failure. If there are problems during migration that were missed by testing, then only the current phase is affected rather than all users. Also, using multiple phases makes dealing with user concerns and training users more manageable.

Enterprise Deployment Tools

Many tools are available to help in the deployment of Windows 7. Chapter 2 discussed how tools, such as ImageX, Sysprep, Windows System Image Manager (WSIM), Windows PE, and Windows Easy Transfer, can be used as part of the deployment process. Many of these tools are still used in enterprise deployments. However, additional tools, such as the **User State Migration Tool (USMT)** and **Windows Deployment Services (WDS)**, are often used in enterprise deployments. **System Center Configuration Manager (SCCM)** and the **Microsoft Deployment Toolkit (MDT)** can also be used to help automate the deployment. Finally, you have the option to boot Windows 7 from a VHD file.

User State Migration Tool

USMT performs approximately the same tasks as Windows Easy Transfer. USMT migrates user settings, documents, and application configuration settings from the previous operating system to Windows 7. This allows users to keep a consistent work environment from the old operating system to Windows 7 and results in better productivity.

The biggest difference between USMT and Windows Easy Transfer is the user interface. Windows Easy Transfer has a graphical interface with a wizard that leads you through the migration process. USMT has a command-line interface and a graphical interface. Configuration of USMT is done by editing XML files. The command-line interface of USMT makes it possible to use scripted migrations and is more suitable for large organizations.

The XML files used to control USMT are:

- *MigApp.xml*—Used to include or exclude the setting for specific applications.

- *MigUser.xml*—Used to control which file types, user folders, and desktop settings are included in the migration.

- *MigSys.xml*—Used only when migrating operating system and browser settings to a Windows XP computer.

- *Config.xml*—A custom configuration file that allows you to control the migration process in detail. For example, it can control which operating system component settings or which specific applications settings are migrated.

USMT Migration Process The migration process performed to move settings from the old operating system to Windows 7 is the same regardless of whether a new computer is being used or an older computer is having a clean install performed. Figure 13-9 shows the USMT migration process.

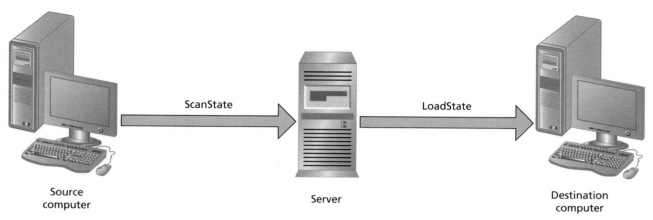

Figure 13-9 USMT migration process
Courtesy Course Technology/Cengage Learning

The steps in the USMT migration process are:

1. Use ScanState on the source computer to collect settings and files.

2. Install Windows 7 on the destination computer.

3. Use LoadState on the destination computer to import settings and files.

When ScanState is used to collect settings and files, they are stored in an intermediate location such as a network server. The settings and files cannot be transferred directly to an existing Windows 7 computer.

All applications should be installed on the destination computer before LoadState is used. This ensures that the installation of the application does not overwrite any of the imported configuration settings. Using LoadState before the necessary applications are installed can have unpredictable results.

Using Config.xml Config.xml does not exist by default. It is generated by running Scan-State.exe with the /genconfig option. This option captures all of the settings that are being migrated. You can then edit this file to control which of the settings are actually migrated when ScanState.exe is run.

To create a single Config.xml file that includes all possible application settings, install a workstation explicitly for this purpose. On this workstation, install each application used in your organization for which you want to migrate the settings. Then after all applications are installed, you can create the Config.xml file based on this workstation. This single Config.xml file can be used to migrate settings and applications for all computers in the organization, rather than maintaining separate Config.xml files for computers with a specific set of applications.

You can use multiple Config.xml files to control the migration process in different ways for users with different needs. For each component listed in the Config.xml file, you can specify yes or no to migrating the component.

Windows Deployment Services

Windows Deployment Services (WDS) is an updated version of the Remote Installation Services (RIS) found in Windows 2000 Server and Windows Server 2003. Both applications allow you to automate the installation of Windows clients. WDS is part of Windows Server 2008 and Windows Server 2008 R2.

WDS can be managed by using the WdsMgmt administrative tool. In addition, the WDSUTIL command-line tool can be used.

WDS Requirements
The following are required for successful installation and use of WDS:

- *Active Directory*—The WDS server must be a member server or domain controller in an Active Directory domain.

- *DHCP*—DHCP is used by client computers to obtain an IP address and communicate with the WDS server.

- *DNS*—DNS is used by client computers to resolve the hostname of the WDS server.

- *An NTFS partition on the WDS server*—The images must be stored on an NTFS-formatted volume on the WDS server.

- *Windows Server 2003 SP1 with RIS installed*—This is only required when deploying WDS on Windows Server 2003.

- *Administrative credentials*—To install WDS on a server, you must be a local administrator on the WDS server.

WDS Image Types
WDS uses different image types to accomplish different tasks in the deployment process. The four types of images are:

- *Install image*—These are WIM images that include the operating system and may include applications that are deployed to workstations. You can use an unattend file to modify the operating system as part of the deployment process.

- *Boot image*—These are WIM images that include Windows PE. They are used to run ImageX and deploy install images. The default boot image (boot.wim) displays a menu that allows you to select which install image to deploy.

- *Capture images*—These images are used to automate the collection of a deployment image from a computer that has been configured as a reference image. Sysprep is run on the computer before the image is captured. The capture image uses Windows PE as an operating system and runs ImageX to collect the image.

- *Discover image*—These images are used to deploy the deployment images on computers that do not support PXE. Discover images are ISO files that can be burned to CD or DVD. At the client, you can boot from CD or DVD to connect to the WDS server and download images.

WDS Deployment Process
WDS uses a combination of technologies to load an image onto a workstation. Some of the most important technologies are PXE and DHCP. Figure 13-10 shows the WDS deployment process.

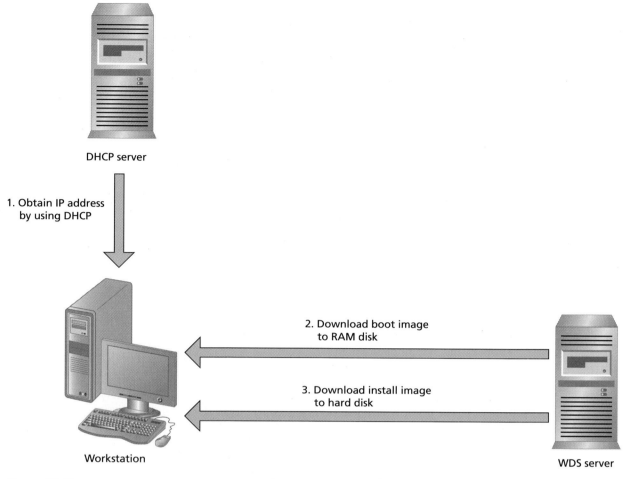

DHCP server

1. Obtain IP address
   by using DHCP

2. Download boot image
   to RAM disk

3. Download install image
   to hard disk

Workstation

WDS server

Figure 13-10 WDS deployment process
Courtesy Course Technology/Cengage Learning

13

When deploying an image by using WDS, the following process is used:

1. Enable PXE in the client computer and configure it to boot from network first.

2. Reboot the workstation and press F12 to perform a PXE boot.

3. The workstation obtains an IP address from a DHCP server and contacts the WDS server.

4. Select a PXE boot image if required. This is used to select boot images for various architectures such as ×86 or ×64. The boot menu is only displayed if a client has multiple options to select from. An ×64 client will see this menu because it can select either ×86 or ×64 images. An ×86 client will not see the boot menu because only one option is available. You may create additional boot images to support network drivers not available in the default Windows PE configuration.

5. The boot image is downloaded to a RAM disk on the client computer and Windows PE is booted.

6. Select an install image to deploy from the menu.

7. ImageX runs to deploy the install image.

By using customized boot images and answer files, the installation process can be controlled to minimize user intervention. Also, additional tasks such as disk partitioning can be performed.

For more information about WDS, visit the Microsoft TechNet Web site (*http://www.microsoft.com/technet*) and search for Windows Deployment Services.

System Center Configuration Manager

SCCM is a solution from Microsoft to control the configuration of Windows computers. The main tasks you can accomplish with SCCM are:

- Inventory
- Standardized configuration
- Software deployment
- Operating system deployment
- Software updates

When you use SCCM to deploy operating systems, you can completely automate system deployment to the point where you do not need to physically touch the computer. After you deploy the operating system, you can also push out any required applications. It is a complete desktop management solution.

Microsoft Deployment Toolkit

The MDT is a solution that helps you configure scripted installations of operating systems and applications. You can use MDT with SCCM or on its own. If you use MDT with SCCM you can perform zero touch installations that are completely scripted. If you do not use SCCM then MDT can configure light touch installations.

A light touch installation requires someone to start the remote computer from a boot image. However, after the boot image is started, the entire installation process for the operating system and applications can be automated.

In addition to tools that configure scripted installations of Windows 7 and applications, the MDT includes a wide range of documentation about the deployment Windows 7. This guidance on best practices for deployment is as valuable as the scripted installations.

The MDT is available from the Microsoft Web site at *http://www. microsoft.com/downloads/details.aspx?familyid=3bd8561f-77ac-4400- a0c1-fe871c461a89&displaylang=en.*

VHD Boot

A typical installation of Windows 7 is located on a hard drive partition. In most scenarios this is the best way to install Windows 7. A new feature in Windows 7 allows the operating system to be installed to and booted from a virtual hard disk (VHD) file instead of a disk partition. When the boot process begins, the VHD file is mounted and used just like a physical disk.

Large enterprises with a virtualized desktop environment may find the ability to perform a VHD boot useful for power users. In a virtualized desktop environment, Windows 7 is run as a virtual machine on centralized servers. Each user has a virtual machine on the centralized servers. Each virtual machine shares the resources available on the centralize servers. Some power users may need an instance of Windows 7 with more resources than can be provided by the centralized servers. In such a case, the standarized VHD file used in the virtualized environment can be copied to a physical computer and configured to boot.

VHD boot can also be used to simplify dual booting. Normally dual booting a computer requires a separate disk partition for each operating system. When VHD boot is used, there can be a single disk partition with multiple VHD files. However, only Windows 7 and Windows Server 2008 R2 can be used with VHD boot. Other operating systems, such as Windows XP cannot be installed to a VHD file and used for VHD boot.

To view a demonstration of how to configure VHD boot, see the How Do I: Windows 7 VHD Boot Demonstration? Page on the Microsoft TechNet Web site at *http://technet.microsoft.com/en-us/windows/dd758779.aspx*.

Windows Server Update Services

One of the most effective ways to prevent security problems is to ensure that all clients are up to date with the latest security updates. One of the most common ways this can be accomplished is by configuring Windows clients to use Automatic Updates to download security updates directly from Microsoft. This is a reasonable solution for smaller environments, but it is inefficient for larger environments.

Windows Server Update Services (WSUS) is a server component for Windows Server 2003 SP1 and later. WSUS contacts Microsoft Update and downloads updates rather than each client computer downloading updates. This is very efficient for network utilization because each update is downloaded only once and stored on the WSUS server. You can even organize multiple WSUS servers in a hierarchy so that WSUS servers can obtain updates from another WSUS server.

Client computers are configured to contact a WSUS server for updates rather than contacting Microsoft Update directly. This can be configured by editing the registry or by using a Group Policy object.

13

WSUS Update Process

WSUS is significantly more flexible than Automatic Updates downloaded directly from Microsoft Update. You can organize computers into groups to control the update process and generate reports to view which computers have been updated and which have not. The ability to test updates before they are generally applied to workstations significantly reduces the risk of an updates causing system down time. The WSUS update process is shown in Figure 13-11.

The WSUS update process is as follows:

1. Updates are downloaded by the WSUS server.

2. The WSUS server notifies the administrator by e-mail of available updates.

3. The administrator approves updates for a test computer or group of computers.

4. The administrator verifies correct application of updates to the test computer or group of computers.

5. The administrator approves updates for the remaining computers.

6. The administrator verifies correct application of updates to the remaining computers.

The WSUS update process still relies on the client computers to trigger the installation of updates. After updates are approved for a specific computer, the update is downloaded by that computer from the WSUS server the next time Automatic Updates is triggered.

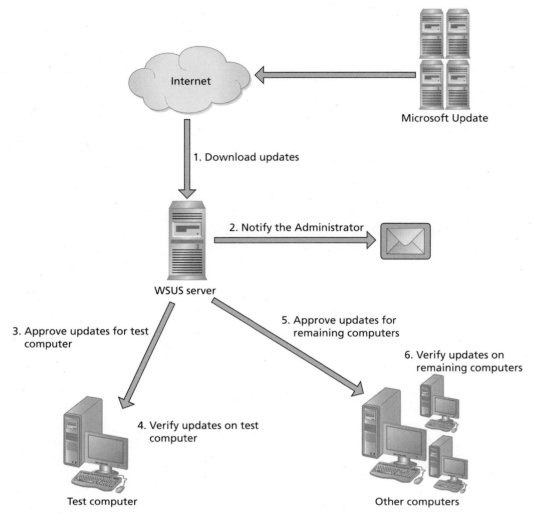

Figure 13-11 WSUS update process
Courtesy Course Technology/Cengage Learning

You can configure rules on the WSUS server to automatically approve some updates for specific computers. For example, you may want to automatically approve all updates for your test computers to reduce administrative work.

WSUS Updates

WSUS obtains updates from Microsoft Update. The products with updates available on Microsoft Update include:

- Windows clients and servers(including 64-bit)
- Exchange Server
- SQL Server
- Microsoft Office
- Microsoft Data Protection Manager
- Microsoft ForeFront
- Windows Live
- Windows Defender

The updates downloaded automatically from Microsoft Update can be controlled by product, product family, update classification, and language. For example, you can choose to download only English updates or only critical updates. You can manually specify to download any updates that are not configured to download automatically.

Network Access Protection

Network Access Protection (NAP) is a system that enforces requirements for client health before allowing client computers to connect to the network. Client and server components are required for NAP. The client components are included in Windows XP SP3, Windows Vista and Windows 7. The server components are included in Windows Server 2008 and Windows Server 2008 R2.

It is important to note that NAP is not intended to block network intruders or protect the network from malicious users. The purpose of NAP is to enforce client configuration requirements such as appropriate update levels and current antivirus signatures.

Enforcement Mechanisms

Client access can be limited only when the client connects to the network by using an enforcement mechanism that is integrated with NAP. When a client connects by using an enforcement mechanism, the client configuration must match the requirements of any health policies that are applied. Clients that meet the health policy requirements are allowed unlimited access to the network. Clients that do not meet the health policy requirements are restricted. Restrictions can include IP filters, static routes, or being placed on a restricted network.

The enforcement mechanisms integrated with NAP are:

- *IPsec*—IPsec is used to encrypt and authenticate network traffic. When IPsec is used as an enforcement mechanism, the ability to create an IPsec connection is denied until the health policy requirements are met.

- *802.1X*—802.1X is an authentication mechanism used on switches and wireless access points. Access to the network via the 802.1X device is restricted until the health policy requirements are met.

- *VPN*—Access to a VPN connection is restricted until the health policy requirements are met.

- *DHCP*—An IP address on a restricted network is leased to the client until the health policy requirements are met.

- *RADIUS*—RADIUS is an authentication mechanism that is used by various devices and applications to authenticate users to active directory. RADIUS can integrate with NAP to restrict access for any device authenticating users with RADIUS.

13

For more information about NAP, see the NAP page on the Microsoft Web site at *http://www.microsoft.com/nap*.

Chapter Summary

- Active Directory is a database of network information about users, computers, and applications. A network based on Active Directory is far more scalable than workgroup-based networks. The components of Active Directory are domains, OUs, trees, and forests.

- Computers in an Active Directory domain can be either a member server or domain controller. A member server is integrated into the security structure of the domain. A domain controller holds a copy of the Active Directory information for the domain.

- Active Directory is composed of a domain partition, configuration partition, and schema partition. The replication of the information in each partition is controlled by Active Directory sites.

- Clients use DNS to locate domain controllers. If DNS is not configured properly, client performance suffers and group policies may not be applied.

- Group Policy is used to configure and control workstations. Group Policy settings are stored in Group Policy objects. The order of application for group policy objects is: local, site, domain, parent OU, and child OU. If there is a conflict, the last applied policy has the highest priority.

- Group Policy has been enhanced in Windows 7. The application of Group Policy is controlled by a stand-alone Group Policy Service. Windows 7 includes Group Policy Preferences with a range of configuration options not available in previous versions of Windows. Finally, multiple local Group Policies can be created to apply to various users.

- You can use Group Policy settings to control device installation and the use of removable storage devices. Both of these enhance the ability of organizations to control data leaving the organization.

- Deploying Windows 7 in an enterprise requires a formal planning process. The process should include defining the project scope and goals, assessing the existing computer systems, planning the new configurations, determining a deployment process, testing the deployment process, and deploying Windows 7.

- USMT has a command-line interface that is appropriate for scripting in large scale deployments, unlike Windows Easy Transfer, which has similar capabilities, but does not have a command-line interface. ScanState and LoadState are used to migrate user settings, files, and application settings.

- WDS is used to apply images to workstations with minimal user intervention. WDS is an update to RIS, which is found in Windows 2000 Server and Windows Server 2003. Clients connecting to WDS must support PXE.

- SCCM is a software package that can perform inventory, implement a standardized configuration, deploy software, deploy operating systems, and deploy software updates.

- MDT can be used to configure automated installations of Windows 7. When used with SCCM, the deployment can be completely automated.

- WSUS downloads updates from Microsoft Update and controls their application to Windows clients. Network utilization is reduced because clients download their updates from the WSUS server. Control is increased because updates are approved by an administrator before being installed on the clients.

- NAP was introduced in Windows Vista and Windows Server 2008. It can be used to ensure that client computers are healthy before connecting to the network. The enforcement methods for NAP are IPsec, 802.1X, VPN, DHCP, and RADIUS.

Key Terms

Active Directory A directory of network information about users, computers, and applications that links multiple domains together.

Active Directory site A set of IP subnets representing a physical location that are used by Active Directory to control replication.

application partition An Active Directory partition created by an administrator to hold and replicate application-specific information. It is replicated only to specified domain controllers.

configuration partition The Active Directory partition that holds general information about the Active Directory forest and application configuration information. It is replicated to all domain controllers in the Active Directory forest.

device identification string One or more identifiers included in a hardware device that is used by Windows 7 to locate and install an appropriate driver for a hardware device.

device setup class An identifier included with a hardware device driver that describes how the device driver is to be installed.

domain A logical grouping of computers and users in Active Directory.

domain controller A server that holds a copy of Active Directory information.

domain partition The Active Directory partition that holds domain-specific information, such as user and computer accounts, that is replicated only between domain controllers within the domain.

forest   Multiple Active Directory trees with automatic trust relationships between them.

forest root domain   The first domain created in an Active Directory forest.

global catalog server   A domain controller that holds a subset of the information in all domain partitions for the entire Active Directory forest.

Group Policy   A feature integrated with Active Directory that can be used to centrally manage the configuration of Windows 2000 and newer Windows computers, including Windows 7.

Group Policy object (GPO)   A collection of Group Policy settings that can be applied to client computers.

Group Policy service   The service responsible for retrieving and applying GPOs for a Windows 7 computer.

member server   A server that is joined to an Active Directory domain, but does not hold a copy of Active Directory information.

Microsoft Deployment Toolkit (MDT)   A set of best practices, scripts, and tools to help automate the deployment of Windows operating systems.

multimaster replication   A replication system where updates can be performed on any server and are replicated to all other servers.

Network Access Protection (NAP)   A system that enforces requirements for client health before allowing client computers to connect to the network.

organizational unit (OU)   A container within a domain that is used to create a hierarchy that can be used to organize user and computer accounts and apply group policies.

schema partition   Holds the definition of all Active Directory objects and their attributes. It is replicated to all domain controllers in the Active Directory forest.

System Center Configuration Manager (SCCM)   A software package that can perform inventory, implement a standardized configuration, deploy software, deploy operating systems, and deploy software updates.

tree   A group of Active Directory domains that share the same naming context and have automatic trust relationships among them.

User State Migration Tool (USMT)   A utility with both a command-line and graphical interface that is used to migrate user settings, files, and application configuration from a source computer to a destination computer.

Windows Deployment Services (WDS)   A Windows Server service that is used to simplify the process of applying images to computers.

Windows Server Update Services (WSUS)   A Windows Server application that is used to control the process of downloading and applying updates to Windows 2000, Windows XP, Windows Vista, and Windows 7 clients.

13

Review Questions

1. Which type of server is used to log on clients that are joined to an Active Directory domain?

    a. Domain controller

    b. Member server

    c. Global catalog server

    d. RADIUS server

2. Which type of server is used by Microsoft Exchange to generate address lists?

    a. Domain controller

    b. Member server

    c. Global catalog server

    d. RADIUS server

3. Which Active Directory partitions are replicated to all domain controllers in the Active Directory forest? (Choose all that apply.)

    a. Domain partition

    b. Configuration partition

    c. Schema partition

    d. Application partition

4. The _____ partition contains the definition of the objects and their attributes that can exist in Active Directory.

5. It is recommended that domain names never end with the .local extension. True or False?

6. What are multiple Active Directory domains that share the same naming context referred to as?

    a. Branch

    b. OU

    c. Forest

    d. Tree

7. Active Directory uses _____ replication, which allows data to be updated on any domain controller.

8. Which network service is used by workstations to find domain controllers?

    a. Active Directory

    b. DHCP

    c. DNS

    d. NetBIOS

9. Group Policy can be used to distribute software to a Windows 7 computer. True or False?

10. Approximately how often does a Windows 7 computer download Group Policy objects?

    a. Every 5 minutes

    b. Every 90 minutes

    c. Only at shut down

    d. Only at start up

11. Which group policy setting location has the lowest priority and will always be overridden by other GPOs when there is a conflict?

    a. Local

    b. Site

    c. Domain

    d. Parent OU

    e. Child OU

12. Which of the following are benefits provided by the Group Policy service in Windows 7? (Choose all that apply.)

    a. Group Policy settings can be applied without any reboots.

    b. Multiple local policies can be used.

    c. The Internet Explorer Administration Kit is no longer required.

    d. USB storage device installation can be blocked.

    e. Group Policy events are now logged to the system log as well as a Group Policy Operational log.

13. A hardware device includes multiple _____ to help Windows 7 identify the appropriate driver to install for the device.

14. You can display a customized error message when device installation is blocked. True or False?

15. The IT department is a good department to use for a test deployment of Windows 7 because it is representative of the larger organization. True or False?

16. Which configuration file for USMT does not exist by default and must be created by running ScanState with the /genconfig option?

    a. MigApp.xml

    b. MigUser.xml

    c. MigSys.xml

    d. Config.xml

17. Which utility or software package can completely automate the deployment of Windows operating systems?

    a. SCCM

    b. WDS

    c. USMT

    d. MDT

    e. WSUS

18. Which WDS image type is used by workstations to connect to the WDS server and select an image to install?

    a. Install image

    b. Boot image

    c. Capture image

    d. Discover image

19. Which of the following products can be updated by WSUS? (Choose all that apply.)

    a. Windows 7

    b. Windows Vista

    c. Office 2003

    d. Windows Server 2003

    e. Windows Defender

20. Network Access Protection is used to prevent malicious users from damaging network resources. True or False?

Case Projects

Case 13-1: Enterprise Group Policy Application

Gigantic Life Insurance is planning to implement Group Policy to control user desktops. Some of the desired settings are to be implemented for the entire organization, while other settings apply only to particular regions or departments.

Gigantic Life Insurance is organized as a single domain. The network manager is concerned that dividing into multiple domains to apply individual Group Policies will be a lot of work and disrupt users. Explain why this is not a concern.

Case 13-2: Small-Office Group Policy Application

Buddy's machine shop has a kiosk computer located in the lobby for customers to use. The kiosk computer has recently been updated to Windows 7 from Windows XP and is not part of a domain. The local computer policy created for Windows XP has been applied to Windows 7. This policy severely restricts the use of the computer, so that customers can only use the Web browser.

Occasionally, an administrator needs to log on to the kiosk computer to perform maintenance and update software. However, this is awkward because the administrator needs to disable settings in the local policy before performing any task. Then, when the tasks are complete, the administrator needs to re-enable the settings in the local policy. Explain how this system can be improved upon when using Windows 7.

Case 13-3: Deployment Planning

Enormous Financial Corporation has 10 offices across the United States. Each of those offices has 100 or more computers. You have recently obtained approval from upper management to migrate all existing computers from Windows XP to Windows 7. None of the Windows XP computers contain any user data that needs to be saved. Create a plan for deploying Windows 7.

Case 13-4: Controlling Software Updates

Currently, all computers at Enormous Financial Corporation download updates directly from Microsoft. You have heard that many other companies use WSUS to download and apply updates. You would like to use WSUS in your organization. To justify implementing WSUS, you must plan how it will be implemented and describe the benefits of using WSUS.

chapter 14

Remote Access

After reading this chapter and completing the exercises, you will be able to:

- Understand remote access and remote control features in Windows 7
- Understand virtual private networking features in Windows 7
- Describe DirectAccess technology as an alternative to virtual private networking
- Understand how Remote Desktop is used
- Understand how Remote Assistance supports users
- Describe BranchCache technology to minimize WAN traffic for remote branch users
- Understand Sync Center
- Describe Mobility Center

Some resources required by the user are not local to the user's computer. Some solutions created to address this issue connect the user over foreign networks to directly access the remote resource. Other solutions provide tools to remotely control computers in the same location as the resource. The network connection itself may be across hostile networks, troubled by slow connections, and potentially spied on by people and computers that should not see the information. This chapter will look at how Windows 7 addresses the need for remote access, the connections it supports, and the security it offers.

Remote Access and Remote Control Overview

Mobile and remote users do not have direct access to the network resources, such as printers and applications, which are located at the main office. The lack of a direct network connection is a barrier to accessing those resources. Public networks allow traveling users to obtain a remote network connection, but the security of that connection is suspect and a threat to the safety of the resources being accessed by mobile workers. To address these issues, computer operating systems have developed remote access and remote control technologies. Remote access and remote control are two different solutions to the problem.

Remote access consists of a dedicated computer acting as a remote access server and other computers (the mobile computers) configured to link to the server. This allows remote access clients to access resources local to the remote access server as if the remote client was on the same network as the remote access server. Typically, the remote access client establishes a link for network traffic to the remote access server across a public network, using varying levels of security to guard the data passing between them. Files, print jobs, database access, and other network resources are transferred across the link between the remote access client and server. In Windows 7 this link can be established over a dial-up connection or a TCP/IP network. Dial-up connections can be made over an **Integrated Service Digital Network (ISDN)** line or phone line. The TCP/IP network connection can be a private system, such as a corporate network, or a public one through wireless or broadband (cable or DSL) technology.

Remote control technologies are different from remote access. All resource access and data processing is performed on a remote server that is remote controlled. The remote client uses remote control software to send keyboard and mouse commands to the computer being remotely controlled. These commands are processed on the remote controlled computer, not on the remote client computer. The remote client is sent a visual update of the screen from the remotely controlled computer. This solution requires much less bandwidth between the remote client and server than remote access does. Windows 7 includes a Remote Desktop client and Remote Desktop Web Access. Figure 14-1 compares the data flow for remote access and remote control.

Choosing between remote control and remote access depends on many factors, some of which include the following:

- Where should data be kept, on a central server or distributed among clients?

- How many copies of the data are allowed to exist? Version control of each copy may be an issue.

- Each instance of the data needs security; can the security of the data on a client be protected?

- How much bandwidth exists between the remote client and server? Is the bandwidth guaranteed?

- What time is required to transfer data? Is it fast enough to meet business needs or will customers be waiting?

- How many clients need to access the data? How large does the remote access or remote controlled server have to be to service all of the clients?

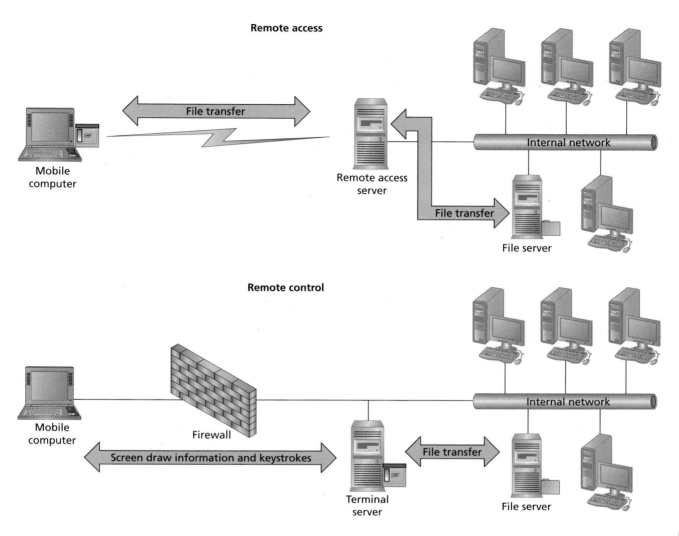

Figure 14-1 Comparison of remote access and remote control
Courtesy Course Technology/Cengage Learning

14

These are network architecture questions that are usually considered when a remote access or control solution is first crafted. Each situation with a customer or site is different and has distinct priorities with respect to these considerations. The general characteristics of remote access and remote control are listed in Table 14-1.

Table 14-1 Remote access and remote control client/server characteristics

Considerations	Remote Access	Remote Control
Special client software required	Part of operating system's networking software	Yes, included with Windows 7
Potentially high bandwidth requirements from a single client	Yes	Not likely
Information transfer between client and server is secure	Yes	Yes
Application data is processed by client CPU	Yes	No
Applications to process data installed on client	Yes	No
Data must be transferred to client for processing	Yes	No
Applications to process data installed on server	No	Yes

Table 14-1   continued

Considerations	Remote Access	Remote Control
Only keyboard, mouse, and screen updates are typically transferred between clients and servers	No	Yes
Additional clients require faster server CPU and extra RAM on server	No	Yes
Server configuration required before clients can be serviced	Yes	Yes
Client can disconnect from server and reconnect without losing connections to network resources opened on the remote network	Generally No	Yes

Once a decision has been made to use either remote access or remote control, the server side is implemented and configured first. This book does not cover the implementation or configuration of a remote access server, which is typically implemented on a server class operating system, such as Windows Server 2008 R2 running **Routing and Remote Access (RRAS)**.

For more information on configuring remote access services for Windows Server 2008 see the Microsoft Web site at *http://www.microsoft.com/ras.*

Remote Access Dial-Up Connectivity

Remote clients connect to a remote access server through a **Wide Area Network (WAN)** connection of some type. Specific protocols are used in Windows 7 to securely manage data sent over a dial-up connection. Windows 7 supports both **analog** and ISDN dial-up connections.

Dial-Up Protocols

Windows 7 supports the industry standard **Point-to-Point Protocol (PPP)** for end-to-end communications between a remote client and remote server using dial-up connections. PPP has the ability to carry different protocols within PPP data packets, including TCP/IP data.

Serial Line IP (SLIP) and **X.25** are supported by Windows XP but are no longer supported by Windows 7. This may present backward-compatibility issues with remote access servers that still use these communication protocols. However, SLIP and X.25 are not used by most organizations.

Analog Dial-Up Connections

The remote client and the remote access server both connect to a common WAN infrastructure. This WAN infrastructure for analog dial-up is usually the **Public Switched Telephone Network (PSTN)**, which is also known as the **Plain Old Telephone System (POTS)**. The PSTN is designed to carry human voices from one phone to another as an analog signal. The analog dial-up modem in a computer converts the computer's digital information into an analog form that is compatible with delivery over the PSTN. Analog dial-up modems are connected to computers as an internal card or via an external connection port such as a serial or USB port.

The analog dial-up connection strategy is not as popular as it once was. The main advantage of analog dial-up technology is that it is a mature technology that is available in many locations where no other WAN solution exists. The main disadvantage of analog dial-up is that it is slow, transferring below 100,000 bits of data per second when compared to solutions such as cable or DSL modems that transfer more than a megabit (1,000,000 bits) of data per second. The most common reason that dial-up still exists today is that, in some geographical regions, it is the only practical low cost option to access the Internet.

A remote access server must have one modem per dial-up client that is connected at the same time to the server. Each modem requires a separate phone line. The monthly expense of each phone line, and the need to service a bank of modems, have stopped many companies from hosting a dial-up remote access server within their own company. One reason to accept the cost and deploy the remote access server in-house would be to keep control and security over all data passing through the server. If security and control are not major concerns, many companies will purchase a connection to an ISP offering dial-up access for a monthly fee. This allows the remote client to connect to the ISP and obtain a general network connection to a public network such as the Internet. In this case, layering another technology such as a **virtual private network (VPN)** on top of the dial-up network connection can provide data security. VPN connections are covered later in this chapter.

Regardless of where the remote access dial-up server is located, configuration of the dial-up networking in Windows 7 requires the following to be completed:

1. Install an analog dial-up modem in the client computer.
2. Configure dialing rules for phone and modem options.
3. Create a connection to a remote access server.
4. Review dial-up connection properties.
5. Configure optional advanced settings.

Install an Analog Dial-Up Modem Analog dial-up modems must be installed and their supporting hardware driver must be fully functional before any other configuration steps are performed. Follow the device and driver installation steps that are provided by the manufacturer of the modem.

Activity 14-1: Install a Modem

Time Required: 10 minutes
Objective: Confirm that a dial-up modem is correctly installed in your computer.

Description: In the lab environment, you do not have access to modems for every computer. In most cases, modems are plug and play and drivers will be installed automatically. In this activity, you install just a modem driver. This allows you to complete other activities in this lab.

This activity assumes a modem is not physically installed or attached to your computer.

1. If necessary, start your computer and log on.
2. Click the **Start** button and click **Control Panel**. Change the *View by:* option from Category to **Large Icons** in Control Panel. This will change the Control Panel view to a list of control applets. For convenience this view will be used for the following activities.
3. Click the **Phone and Modem** applet. Notice that you are immediately prompted for location information.
4. If necessary, in the What country/region are you in now box, click **United States**.
5. In the What area code (or city code) are you in now box, type **555**, and then click **OK**.
6. Click the **Modems** tab, click the **Add** button.
7. Select the **Don't detect my modem; I will select it from a list** check box and click **Next**. If your computer has a physical modem installed do not select this box when installing it.
8. In the Models box, scroll down and click **Standard 56000 bps Modem** and then click **Next**.
9. Click **COM1** and click **Next**.
10. After the modem installation is complete, click **Finish** and click **OK**.
11. In Control Panel, click **Device Manager**.
12. In the list of device categories, find and expand **Modems**.

13. Verify that Standard 56000 bps Modem is listed.

14. Double-click **Standard 56000 bps Modem** to open its properties window.

15. On the **General** tab verify that the Device status is reported as "This device is working properly."

16. Click the **Modem** tab. This tab allows you to configure the speaker volume, port speed, and whether to wait for dial tone before dialing.

17. Click the **Diagnostics** tab. This tab allows you to query the modem and verify it is working.

18. Click the **Advanced** tab. This tab allows you to add additional commands that are used during modem initialization.

19. Click the **Cancel** button.

20. Close Device Manager and Control Panel.

Configure Dialing Rules for Phone and Modem Options Windows 7 can control the dialing process based on where a user and computer are physically located by using dialing profiles. Multiple dialing profiles are used to control how a phone number to a remote access server is dialed based on the location of the user and computer. For example, consider a traveling salesman that works from a home-based office and a temporary desk at several company branch offices around the globe. One dialing profile would be configured for the home office and another for each branch office.

You must define at least one location-based dialing profile, and optionally add additional dialing profiles for other locations, before a dial-up connection can be established. If you try to create a dial-up connection and the profile information is not entered, you are prompted to complete it before being allowed to proceed with the connection setup.

Dialing rules are defined through the Phone and Modem Control Panel applet on the Dialing Rules tab. See Figure 14-2 for an example of the Phone and Modem Options Control Panel applet.

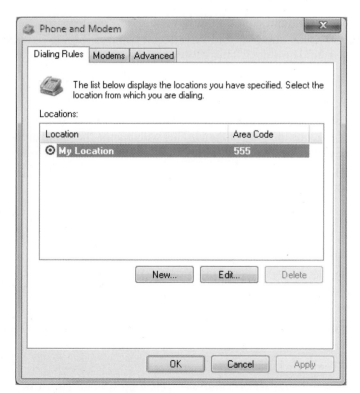

Figure 14-2 Dialing Rules for Phone and Modem options
Courtesy Course Technology/Cengage Learning

Additional locations can be added and existing locations on the Dialing Rules tab can be edited to modify the dialing behavior. The dialing rules take into account the user's current area code, dialing prefixes to access outside lines, disabling call-waiting, and special case treatment for target area codes and calling cards. See Figure 14-3 for an example of the Edit Location window.

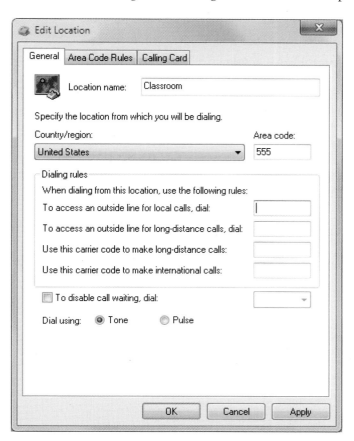

Figure 14-3 Edit Location Dialing Rules
Courtesy Course Technology/Cengage Learning

Activity 14-2: Create Dialing Rules Based on Your Location

Time Required: 5 minutes
Objective: Create a new dialing rule based on your current location.

Description: In this activity, you will create a dialing rule to identify your location in the classroom.

1. If necessary, start your computer and log on.
2. Click the **Start** button and click **Control Panel**.
3. Click the **Phone and Modem** applet.
4. On the Dialing Rules tab click the **New** button to create a new location.
5. In the Location name box type **Classroom**.
6. In the drop-down beneath Country/region, click your country from the list.
7. In the Area code box, type your local area code and read the remaining options on the General tab.
8. Click the **Area Code Rules** tab. This tab allows you to configure area code and dialing prefix combinations that specify whether you dial a number to gain long distance access or an area code.

9. Click the **Calling Card** tab. This tab allows you to configure calling card information to be automatically used when a connection is made.

10. Click **OK** to save your changes.

11. Note that the location you have just created is listed in the Dialing Rules tab and is marked as the current location that you are dialing from.

12. Click **OK** to close the Phone and Modem window.

13. Close the Control Panel window.

Create a Connection to a Remote Access Server   Once the modem is installed correctly and the location dialing properties are configured, Windows 7 is ready to make a dial-up connection to the remote access server. The connection requires the phone number and usually a username and password to authenticate the connection.

To define the dial-up connection you must activate the Set Up a Connection or Network wizard. This wizard can be started from the Network and Sharing Center. See Figure 14-4 for an example of the Set Up a Connection or Network window.

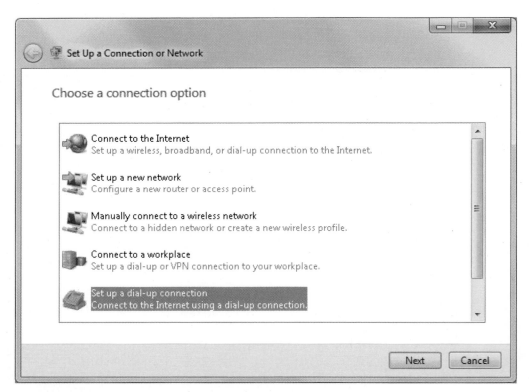

Figure 14-4 Set Up a Connection or Network window for a dial-up connection.
Courtesy Course Technology/Cengage Learning

Before a dial-up connection can be created, the remote access server's dialing information must be known. In the Set Up a Connection or Network wizard, select Set up a dial-up connection to define the dial-up properties for the target remote access server. See Figure 14-5 for an example of the Create a Dial-up Connection window.

When the connection is being configured, the phone number to the remote access server is mandatory. All other fields are optional and can be updated later.

Activity 14-3: Create a Dial-Up Connection

Time Required: 5 minutes
Objective: Create a dial-up connection using the built-in connection wizard.

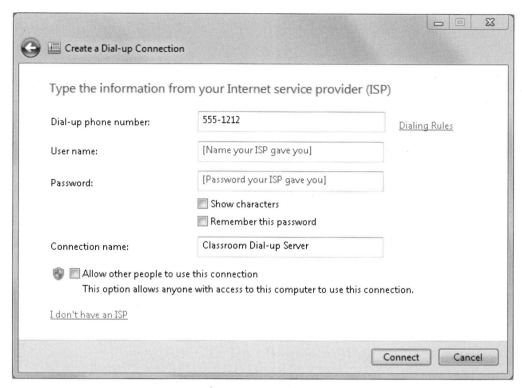

Figure 14-5 Create a Dial-up Connection window
Courtesy Course Technology/Cengage Learning

Description: In this activity, you will create a dial-up connection to connect to a classroom dial-up server.

1. If necessary, start your computer and log on.
2. Open **Control Panel** and click the **Network and Sharing Center** applet.
3. Click the **Set up a new connection or network** link in the middle of the window.
4. Select **Set up a dial-up connection** and click **Next** to proceed.
5. If necessary, click **Set up a connection anyway**. This may be required because your computer does not have a modem.
6. If your instructor has not supplied different settings, type **555-1212** in the Dial-up phone number box.
7. In the Connection name box, change the text to **Classroom Dial-up Server**.
8. Click the **Connect** button to save the information and create the dial-up connection. Windows 7 will try to establish a connection, which will fail if there is no real modem connected to your computer. For the purposes of this activity, this is acceptable.
9. After the dial-up connection fails, if necessary, click **Set up the connection anyway**, and then click **Close**.

Review Dial-Up Connection Properties Once a dial-up connection has been defined through the Set up a dial-up connection wizard, there are additional settings that are available to refine the connection's properties. To access the properties of the dial-up connection, you can access the Network and Sharing Center from Control Panel and follow the link to Change adapter settings. See Figure 14-6 for the location of the Change adapter settings link as found in the Network and Sharing Center window.

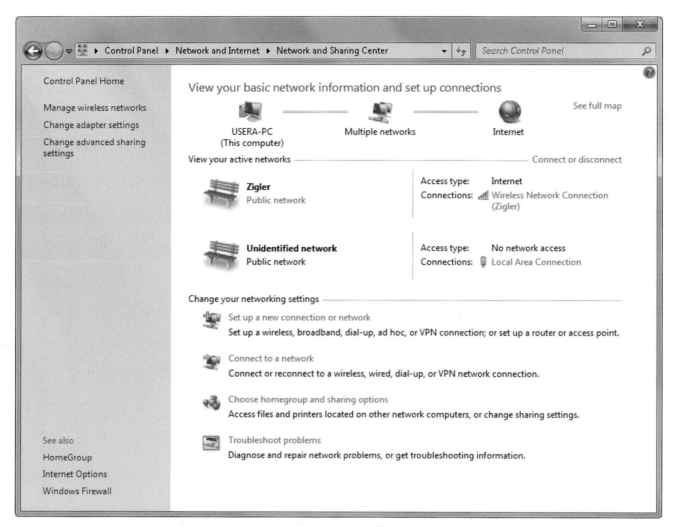

Figure 14-6 Change adapter settings link in the Network and Sharing Center window
Courtesy Course Technology/Cengage Learning

This link opens the Network Connections window, which shows the network connections defined on the computer. See Figure 14-7 for an example of the Network Connections window. Note that the icon for the dial-up connection in Figure 14-7 has a picture of a phone in the bottom right and the LAN connection icon shows an RJ-45 plug.

The properties of the dial-up connection in the Network Connections window are shown in Figure 14-8. The General tab is used to configure devices for the connection and phone numbers used to dial the connection. The Connect using field lists the installed communication device that will be used for the dial-up connection. The Phone number area includes settings for the area code, phone number, country/region code, and dialing rules.

Options Tab The Options tab (see Figure 14-9) changes the behavior of the dial-up connection while it is connecting.

The following are the settings for Dialing options on the Options tab:

- *Display progress while connecting*—Provides a status report of the connection as it is being established. This is selected by default.

- *Prompt for name and password, certificate, etc.*—Prompts the user to verify or enter credentials before the connection is attempted. This is selected by default.

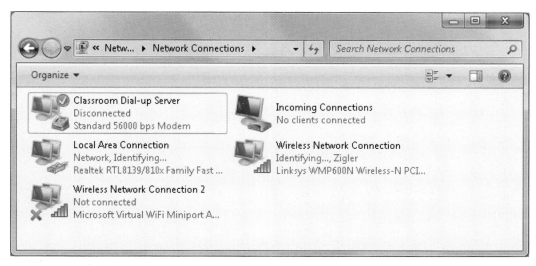

Figure 14-7 Network Connections window showing multiple connections, including a dial-up connection
Courtesy Course Technology/Cengage Learning

Figure 14-8 Dial-up connection properties, General tab
Courtesy Course Technology/Cengage Learning

14

- *Include Windows logon domain*—Prompts the user for a domain name that is passed to the remote access server as part of the user credentials for this remote access connection. This is not selected by default.

- *Prompt for phone number*—Prompts the user to verify or enter a phone number for this connection before the connection is attempted. This is selected by default.

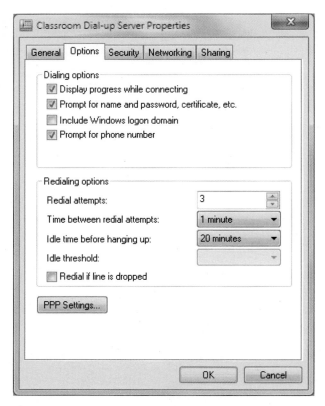

Figure 14-9 Dial-up connection properties, Options tab
Courtesy Course Technology/Cengage Learning

The following are the settings for Redialing options on the Options tab:

- *Redial attempts*—The number of retries the system makes when a connection cannot be established before the connection attempt is aborted. The default setting is three retries.

- *Time between redial attempts*—The time the system will wait to retry the connection if the last attempt was not successful. The default is one minute between retries. This delay must be long enough for the modem and phone line to reset between retries. Do not make this time too short or attempts to dial-out will fail when a retry is attempted.

- *Idle time before hanging up*—The time the system will keep the connection alive when no activity over the connection is detected. The default is 20 minutes, but it can be set to never to disable this feature.

- *Idle threshold*—The minimum level of data communication below which the connection is considered idle. This control is necessary because there will always be a small amount of network chatter across the connection, even when no actual data is being transferred.

- *Redial if line is dropped*—Forces the system to attempt a reconnect if the link is broken for any reason. This is not selected by default.

The following are the PPP Settings available from the Options tab:

- *Enable LCP extensions*—The PPP Link Control Protocol (LCP) extensions negotiate link and PPP parameters dynamically for the data link of a PPP connection. This option should be enabled when Windows 7 is communicating with a Microsoft-based remote access server. This setting is enabled by default.

- *Enable software compression*—This setting enables the dynamic configuration of parameters to configure and enable or disable data compression between PPP peers. This option should be enabled when Windows 7 is communicating with a Microsoft-based remote access server. This setting is enabled by default.

- *Negotiate multi-link for single link connections*—This setting enables the connection to request that the remote access server consider this link as one part of a multiple-link connection from this computer. This setting is disabled by default.

Security Tab The Security tab (see Figure 14-10) controls the behavior of the dial-up connection while it is connecting.

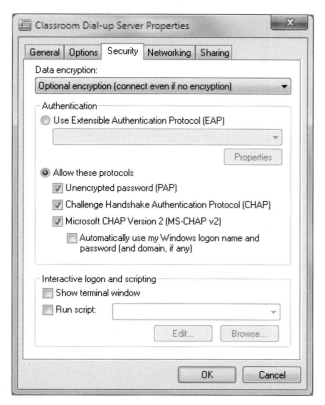

Figure 14-10 Dial-up connection properties, Security tab
Courtesy Course Technology/Cengage Learning

14

The Data encryption setting in the Security Settings window offers the following options:

- *Optional encryption (connect even if no encryption)*—This is selected by default.

- *No encryption allowed (server will disconnect if it requires encryption)*—If the remote access server has been configured to only talk to clients that encrypt data, the remote client will abort the connection.

- *Require encryption (disconnect if server declines)*—The remote client requires data encryption and if the remote access server cannot reciprocate, the remote client will abort the connection.

- *Maximum strength encryption (disconnect if server declines)*—The remote client requires data encryption using the strongest (most secure) method it knows, and if the remote access server cannot match it, the remote client will abort the connection.

The Authentication settings on the Security Settings window can use Extensible Authentication Protocol or a predefined list of **authentication protocols.**

If **Extensible Authentication Protocol (EAP)** is enabled, then EAP-MSCHAP v2 is the default logon security method. EAP allows the use of extra credential information to securely authenticate the user. It can optionally use the user's Windows logon credentials, certificates, and smart cards to identify the user and the connection as trusted.

EAP offers a high degree of security between the remote client and remote access server, but it can be difficult to implement.

For more information about implementing certificate solutions and smart cards, see the Microsoft Web site at *www.microsoft.com/pki* for additional information.

It is best practice to disable the authentication methods that are not required and that have low security. **The Password Authentication Protocol (PAP)** transfers user credentials in plain text and is not a secure authentication protocol. Anyone monitoring the communication stream will see the username and password for the connection. PAP may still be required for compatibility with older remote access servers that do not offer a compatible authentication method, but it is not a recommended authentication protocol.

CHAP authentication is still used by older remote access servers. It is an improvement over PAP in that the password is not sent over the wire in plain text. The server will create a challenge token using the password it knows, and the client must correctly prove that it has the same password by correctly updating and returning the challenge. The limitation to this method is that the password must still be known locally on the server and client. Memory scanners and background programs may spy on the process and reveal the password. An additional problem with CHAP is that the server is not required to prove its identity. A bogus remote access server can impersonate the real one and the remote client cannot verify the fact.

To address the limitation of CHAP, MS-CHAP v1 was created to use a hash of the password instead of the actual password in calculating the challenge. The hash represents a calculated value that returns a unique value for a given password. This removed some of the risk with having the actual password in memory, but it did not address the fact that the remote access server could still be impersonated.

To address the limitation of MS-CHAP v1, MS-CHAP v2 was implemented to allow validation of both the client and the server. MS-CHAP v2 is the recommended authentication protocol for dial-up connections.

Networking Tab The Networking tab (see Figure 14-11) shows the network communication components used by the connection. Note that both TCP/IPv6 and TCP/IPv4 are enabled for the dial-up connection, but the Client for Microsoft Networks is not. The dial-up connection is used to route network traffic between the remote client and the remote access server.

Configure Optional Advanced Settings
In some specialized situations, you may need to configure additional advanced dial-up connection options. These options can enhance security or provide additional client configuration. The advanced dial-up connection options are not used frequently, but when required they are valuable.

The advanced dial-up connection options are:

- Remote Access Preferences
- Operator-Assisted Dialing
- Interactive Logon and Scripting

Remote Access Preferences
To set remote access preferences, you must open the Network and Sharing Center from Control Panel and follow the link to "Manage network connections." This link opens the Network Connections window. Once the Network Connections window is open, press the Alt key to reveal a menu bar. Notice the Advanced menu option shown in Figure 14-12.

When Remote Access Preferences is selected from the Advanced menu, the screen in Figure 14-13 is displayed. The Autodial tab defines which connection will automatically be triggered if the computer is trying to connect to a network that is not currently available but could be reached through a dial-up connection.

Some traveling users find it expensive to dial in to a central server, typically from a hotel that charges premiums for outgoing phone calls. It may save traveling users money to have the

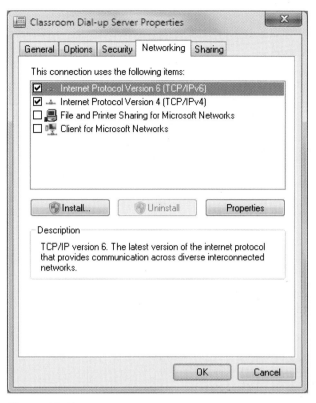

Figure 14-11 Dial-up connection properties, Networking tab
Courtesy Course Technology/Cengage Learning

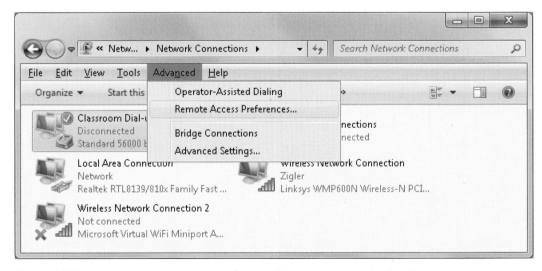

Figure 14-12 Networking Connections window with Advanced menu displayed
Courtesy Course Technology/Cengage Learning

remote access server call them back. The Callback tab (see Figure 14-14) allows the user to configure how their client requests or responds to offers of a callback from the remote access server.

The default callback setting is to ask the user during dialing if the server offers the option. The remote access server must be preconfigured to offer this option or no callback will be available.

The Diagnostics tab is visible as shown in Figure 14-15. You can use the diagnostics tab to enable logging for a dial-up connection. You can use the log files to perform troubleshooting. Additionally, Windows 7 can generate a report based on the log files to simplify analysis of log file information.

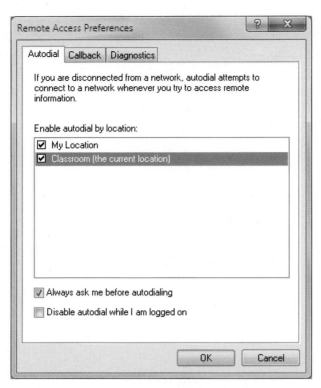

Figure 14-13 Remote Access Preferences window
Courtesy Course Technology/Cengage Learning

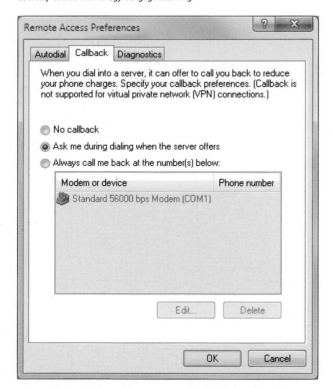

Figure 14-14 Remote Access Preferences window, Callback tab
Courtesy Course Technology/Cengage Learning

Operator-Assisted Dialing A modem may not be able to make a connection even with the help of dialing rules and custom dialing settings. For example, sometimes international dialing must be performed by an operator. After the phone operator has established a connection, the modem can take over. In the Advanced menu of the Network Connections window (see Figure 14-12) there is a menu option to enable or disable operator-assisted dialing. If it is enabled, there will be a check mark next to that menu item.

While operator-assisted dialing is enabled, any network connection that is activated will first display a connection window (see Figure 14-16). This gives the user time to contact the operator

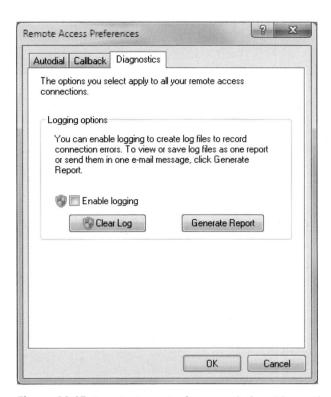

Figure 14-15 Remote Access Preferences window, Diagnostics tab
Courtesy Course Technology/Cengage Learning

Figure 14-16 Dial-up connection waiting for operator assisted dialing to begin
Courtesy Course Technology/Cengage Learning

and prepare the phone connection. Once the phone line is ready, the user clicks the Dial button in the connection window and the connection proceeds normally.

Interactive Logon and Scripting This is a seldom-used feature found in the properties of a dial-up connection. It is found on the bottom of the Security tab (see Figure 14-10).

The "Show terminal window" option opens a terminal window when the connection is being established to allow the user to enter commands and settings directly to the remote access server. This may be required for older non-Microsoft remote access servers that require additional settings not included in the connection's properties. The remote access server must support this option.

The "Run script" option is used to define a script that runs as part of the connection process. This can be useful with remote access servers that require navigating a menu or other additional steps beyond providing a username and password. The script is not required with Microsoft remote access servers. Generic examples of scripts are provided in C:\WINDOWS\SYTEM32\RAS but are not supported by Microsoft.

Activity 14-4: Customize a Dial-Up Connection

Time Required: 10 minutes
Objective: Customize an existing dial-up connection.

Description: In this activity, you will customize the classroom dial-up connection created in the previous activity. Not all dial-up settings are configured individually for each connection. The global callback property is also configured for dial-up connections.

This activity assumes a modem is installed and previous activities in this chapter have been completed successfully.

1. If necessary, start your computer and log on.
2. Click the **Start** button and click **Control Panel**.
3. Click **Network and Sharing Center**.
4. Click the link **Change adapter settings** to open the Network Connections window.
5. Right-click the **Classroom Dial-up Server** icon and click **Properties**.
6. Click the **Options** tab in the Classroom Dial-up Server Properties window.
7. In the Time between redial attempts box, click **2 minutes**.
8. In the Redial attempts box, type **1**, and then click **OK**.
9. In the Network Connections window, click the **Classroom Dial-up Server** icon to select it, then press the **Alt** key.
10. Notice that a hidden menu is revealed at the top of the window. Click the **Advanced** menu and click **Remote Access Preferences**. Notice that on the Autodial tab you can configure settings that control when autodial occurs.
11. Click the **Callback** tab in the Remote Access Preferences window.
12. Click the **No callback** option and click **OK** to save the change.
13. Close the Network Connections window.
14. In the notification area of the taskbar, click the network icon to display a list of network connections.
15. In the list of networks, notice the Classroom Dial-up Server connection is listed as a potential dial-up connection.
16. Click the Desktop to close the list of network connections.

Remote Access VPN Connectivity

A resource might be separated from a client because there is no direct network connection available to the resource or because there is a security barrier, such as a firewall, between the client and the resource.

A remote user without a direct network connection may use a dial-up or network connection through a public network such as the Internet to connect to a private system that also has a connection to that public network. The problem is that data transmitted over the public network can be recorded or modified by individuals with criminal or mischievous intent.

Some resources, such as databases, are valuable because of the data they contain. Even users in the same building using a local area network cannot obtain direct access to the resource. Firewalls are put up as barriers between the resource and any computer network that is not completely trusted.

A secure point-to-point connection can be created using VPN technology. VPN technology is similar to remote access in that a server and client form the two endpoints of a connection. The VPN link is different from a remote access connection in that it protects the data transferred between its endpoints; the remote access solution only tries to get the data from one point to another.

A VPN server accepts connections from VPN clients, and optionally from other VPN servers. Any data that enters either the VPN server or the VPN client is encrypted and passed over whatever network connection joins the two. The VPN connection emulates a private link. As long as the data encryption is not compromised, the data is secure—even if it is transmitted over a public network. Once the data reaches the other side and leaves the VPN connection, it regains its original form. Figure 14-17 shows the design of a VPN solution.

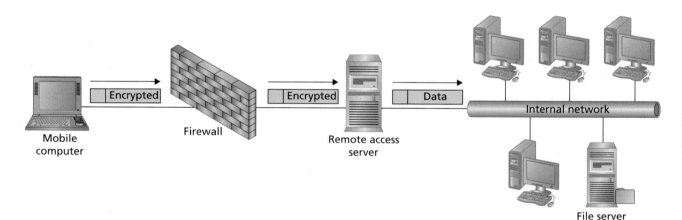

Figure 14-17 VPN Design
Courtesy Course Technology/Cengage Learning

VPN Protocols

Communication protocols, called tunneling protocols, manage the virtual private link and encrypt the data it carries. The tunneling protocols which are supported by Window 7's VPN software, are separate from the actual network protocols that join a VPN client or server to a physical or wireless network. Tunneling takes a data packet and places it inside another packet. In most cases, this is done to encrypt the data in the original packet. Figure 14-18 shows how tunneling works. For a single secure data connection, Windows 7 can implement PPTP, L2TP, SSTP, or IKEv2 as a choice of VPN tunneling protocols.

PPTP Tunneling Protocol
Point-to-Point Tunneling Protocol (PPTP) allows IP-based networks to deliver PPP packets by encapsulating them in IP packets. The IP packets can be routed through public networks and remote access dial-up connections.

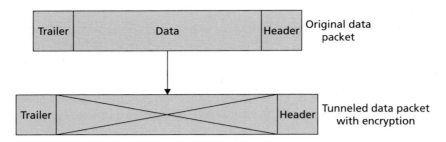

Figure 14-18 Tunneling
Courtesy Course Technology/Cengage Learning

When data needs to go from one end of the VPN link to the other, the VPN endpoint acting as a sender creates a stream of PPP packets to carry the data. Each PPP packet is encapsulated in a different IP packet. When the IP packet arrives at the other end of the VPN link, the PPP packet is extracted and interpreted by the receiver. A PPP response packet is encapsulated in a different IP packet and sent back to the other end of the VPN link.

PPTP can theoretically be used with IPv4 and IPv6 networks and is distinguished in literature as PPTPv4 and PPTPv6, respectively. Windows 7 does not implement PPTPv6, therefore ,PPTP is only used with IPv4.

The connection state between two PPTP endpoints is created, maintained, and terminated using a version of the Generic Routing Encapsulation (GRE) standard. GRE is slightly modified to help encapsulate PPP packets over IP packets.

The PPP packets contained in the IP packets are compressed and encrypted using standard PPP techniques. User authentication and data encryption use the same security mechanisms used by dial-up remote access.

L2TP Tunneling Protocol   Layer 2 Tunneling Protocol (L2TP) also encapsulates PPP packets to be sent over IP network connections. L2TP started as a combination of PPTP and Layer 2 Forwarding (L2F) tunneling protocols. L2F was originally proposed by Cisco Systems Inc. as a competing tunneling protocol. L2TP performs the tunneling function required for a VPN connection, but is not designed to provide the data security required for a VPN connection.

IPSec provides encryption for L2TP connections. IPSec is a set of standardized security protocols for encrypting and authenticating information. This provides a strong foundation for user authentication, data authentication, data integrity, encryption, and mutual computer authentication. IPSec uses stronger encryption methods than those available with PPTP.

L2TP can be used with TCP/IPv4 and TCP/IPv6 networks and is distinguished in literature as L2TPv4 and L2TPv6, respectively.

SSTP Tunneling Protocol   Secure Socket Tunneling Protocol (SSTP) allows IP-based networks to deliver traffic through firewalls that would otherwise block PPTP and L2TP traffic. SSTP was first introduced with Windows Vista SP1 to the workstation environment.

PPP traffic is encapsulated inside packets formatted with the **HyperText Transport Protocol Secure (HTTPS)**. The HTTPS protocol allows traffic to flow through a firewall on port 443, which is commonly allowed in many firewall implementations.

IKEv2 Tunneling Protocol   Internet Key Exchange v2 Tunneling Protocol (IKEv2) standardizes the use of the IPSec protocol to establish a **Security Association (SA)** between the VPN client and server. Earlier versions of Windows supported the original IKE standard; however, these early implementations were not always stable, many features and their implementations provided a poor experience. Windows 7 fully supports the new IKEv2 standard. This new standard has been rewritten to support the best of IKE and add new features such as **MOBIKE** (an industry term for the **IKEv2 Mobility and Multihoming Protocol**). The MOBIKE protocol extension allows a VPN client to lose its network connection and still reconnect to its original SA once network connectivity is restored. This allows the user to tolerate network changes without corrupting the applications and data that they are working with.

Creating a VPN Connection

A computer or device must be configured as a VPN client to connect to a specific VPN server. The VPN server must be configured before the VPN client can establish a connection. The main points to consider before creating a VPN client connection in Windows 7 include:

- The VPN server must identify if it is using a IKEv2, SSTP, PPTP, or L2TP connection.

- The encryption and authentication methods used by the VPN client and server must be compatible.

- An IP connection path, such as the Internet, must exist between the VPN server and the VPN client to carry the tunneled packets. If a dial-up remote access connection is required to establish an IP connection to the VPN server, then that connection must be up and stable before the VPN connection is established.

- The VPN client must know the address of the VPN server on the IP network. The client's IP address can be dynamic and does not need to be statically assigned.

More than one VPN connection can be defined. Any single VPN connection can be activated to connect to a specific VPN server. Multiple VPN connections, each to a different VPN server, can be active at the same time if required. Each active VPN connection provides a virtual private IP network connection to the remote VPN server's network. Windows 7 includes a network connection wizard to create and define a VPN connection to a specific VPN server.

To define a VPN connection, you must activate the "Set up a new connection or network" wizard. This wizard can be activated from the Network and Sharing Center in Control Panel by selecting the link there. See Figure 14-19 for an example of the Set Up a Connection or Network window which can be used to create new connections, including a new VPN connection (typically to a VPN server located at a workplace).

The Connect to a Workplace window, (see Figure 14-20) offers the following options:

- *Internet address*—The VPN server's identity on the IP network. The VPN server's IPv4 address, IPv6 address, or DNS name must be specified.

- *Destination name*—A text name to uniquely identify this connection.

- *Use a smart card*—Option to specify whether a smart card is used as part of the authentication process.

- *Allow other people to use this connection*—Option to specify whether other computer users on the computer's local network can share this VPN connection to the remote VPN server's network.

- *Don't connect now; just set it up so I can connect later*—Option to specify whether this connection should be activated when the wizard is completed.

Once this information is entered and you click Next, the following screen prompts for the user's identity (see Figure 14-21). This information is optional and can be entered when the connection is established, rather than in this window. In most cases, users will enter this information when the connection is established to limit access to cached credentials. If the user id and password are stored with the VPN settings these credentials will be used automatically to authenticate. This screen offers the following fields and options:

- *User name*—The username used to verify the user connecting to the VPN server.

- *Password*—The password used to verify the user connecting to the VPN server.

- *Show characters*—Reveal the characters typed in the password field.

14

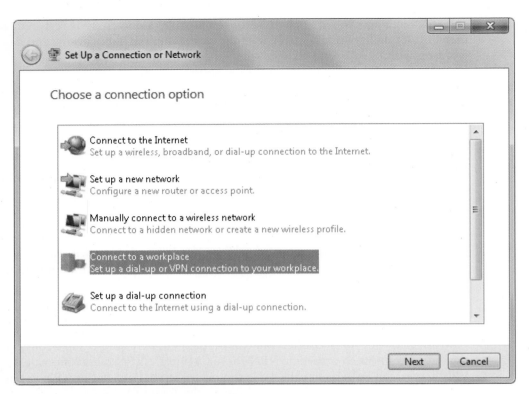

Figure 14-19 Set Up a Connection or Network window for a new VPN connection
Courtesy Course Technology/Cengage Learning

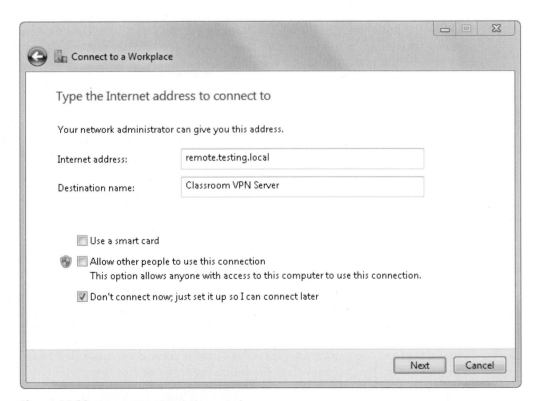

Figure 14-20 Connect to a Workplace window
Courtesy Course Technology/Cengage Learning

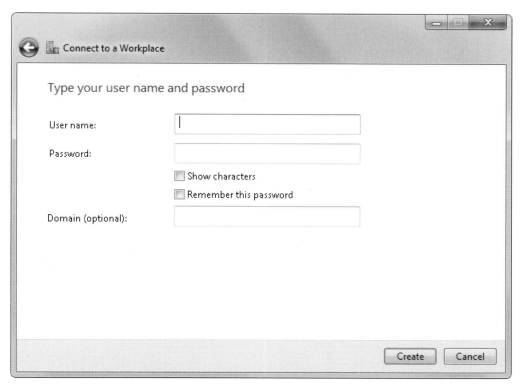

Figure 14-21 Connect to a Workplace window, user identity
Courtesy Course Technology/Cengage Learning

- *Remember this password*—The password entered for the connection will be remembered as part of this connection's settings. If this connection is going to be shared with other users on the computer's network, this option should be enabled.

- *Domain (optional)*—The authentication domain to be contacted to verify the username and password specified in the other fields.

Once the user identity is entered, the connection is created and connected—or just created but not immediately connected. The choice depends on the optional setting found on the initial VPN wizard window.

Configuring a VPN Connection

Once a VPN connection has been defined through the new connection wizard, additional settings are available to refine the VPN connection's properties. To access the properties of the VPN connection, you can access the Network and Sharing Center from Control Panel and follow the link to "Change adapter settings."

The Change adapter settings link opens the Network Connections window that shows the network connections defined on the computer. See Figure 14-22 for an example of the Network Connections window that contains a VPN connection. Note that the icon for the VPN connection in Figure 14-22 has a picture of a computer in the bottom right.

By bringing up the properties of the VPN connection from the Network Connections window, the behavior of the VPN client can be configured in ways that the initial wizard does not expose. The properties of the VPN connection in the Network Connections window are shown in Figure 14-23.

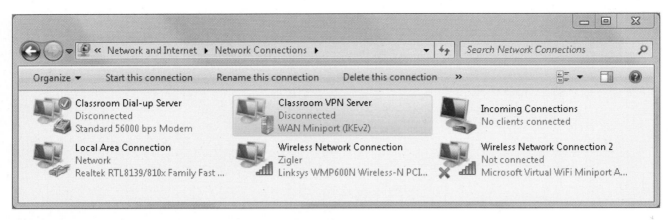

Figure 14-22 Network Connections window showing a VPN connection
Courtesy Course Technology/Cengage Learning

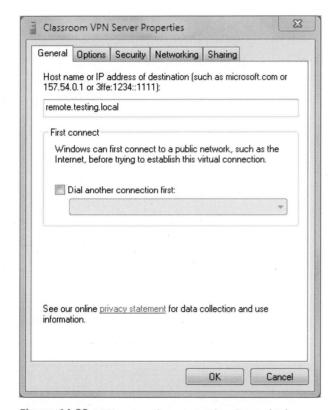

Figure 14-23 VPN connection properties, General tab
Courtesy Course Technology/Cengage Learning

NOTE The options available for configuring a VPN connection are exactly the same as for a dial-up connection. To see detailed information about settings on the Options tab, see the dial-up connection information earlier in this chapter.

The General tab of the VPN connection's properties is used to configure:

- *Host name or IP address*—The host name or IP address of the VPN server that is the target of this connection.

- *Dial another connection first*—An option to select if a dial-up connection must be established before the VPN connection is attempted.

- *Dial-up connection list*—A drop-down list of all dial-up connections defined on the computer. The selected dial-up connection will be made if the option to dial another connection first is selected and the VPN connection is activated.

The Security tab (see Figure 14-24) has similar options to the dial-up Security tab; however, it also has the option of specifying the type of VPN tunneling protocol to use for a connection. The tunneling protocol used for this connection is configured under "Type of VPN" as Automatic, PPTP, L2TP, SSTP, or IKEv2.

If the VPN connection type is configured as Automatic, the VPN client uses each protocol in turn until it successfully connects. The protocols are attempted in this order: IKEv2, SSTP, PPTP, and L2TP. Note that PPTP is the least secure protocol but it is tried before L2TP by design. PPTP is more common in real-world implementations therefore Microsoft decided to attempt a PPTP connection immediately after the preferred protocols of IKEv2 and SSTP.

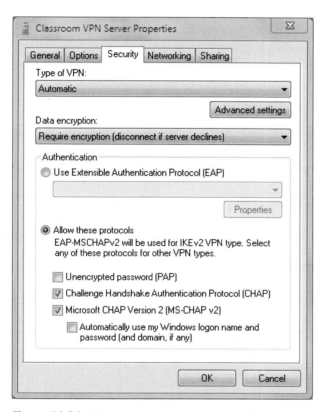

Figure 14-24 VPN connection properties, Security tab
Courtesy Course Technology/Cengage Learning

If the name of the VPN server is specified as a host name, the DNS server may return an IPv4 or IPv6 address, or both. IPv6 addresses take precedence in VPN connection attempts and will be used where possible. Note that PPTP does not support IPv6 in Windows 7, so it will only use the IPv4 address.

If the connection is configured as Automatic or L2TP, the Advanced settings button (seen in Figure 14-24) will open an Advanced Properties window (see Figure 14-25) which allows for the entry of a preshared key when this is required by the VPN server or the use of a trusted certificate.

If the connection is configured as Automatic or IKEv2, the Advanced settings button (seen in Figure 14-24) will open an Advanced Properties window (see Figure 14-26) which allows the user to identify a mobility setting that allows the VPN to reconnect. The VPN reconnect feature is supported by Windows 7 and RRAS servers built with Windows Server 2008 R2 and later. When the IKEv2 VPN connection is made with a VPN server that supports the Mobility feature, a service called Mobility Manager automatically starts on the workstation. This service detects when the network connection has failed and it keeps the client connection from terminating for the amount of time specified in the VPN connection's Advanced properties (see Figure 14-26).

Figure 14-25 VPN connection properties, Type of VPN advanced settings for L2TP
Courtesy Course Technology/Cengage Learning

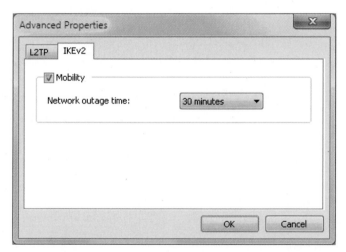

Figure 14-26 VPN connection properties, Type of VPN advanced settings for IKEv2
Courtesy Course Technology/Cengage Learning

When the workstation regains a network connection, it does not have to be the same as the one it used to start the VPN connection. Windows 7 resumes the old secure association it had with the RRAS server before the network connection was lost or changed. The maximum time you can specify to keep the connection alive is eight hours. Note that this will only work if the VPN is established with IKEv2, the mobility option is configured, and the RRAS VPN server is able and configured to support the feature as well.

Specifying Automatic for the type of VPN may be convenient and robust; but it can also slow down the time required for the VPN client to discover the correct tunneling protocol and connect. If the exact connection settings for a particular VPN connection are known, the client may connect much faster. In that case, the type of VPN should be configured manually.

The Networking tab (see Figure 14-27) identifies the network communication components used by the connection.

Note that both TCP/IPv6 and TCP/IPv4 are enabled for the VPN connection, along with the Client for Microsoft Networks and File and Printer Sharing. This allows resources on the remote VPN server and its network to be accessed as if they were local resources.

The Sharing tab (see Figure 14-28) allows the VPN connection to be shared and controlled by other users on the computer's local network.

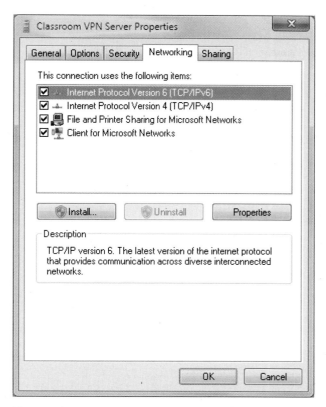

Figure 14-27 VPN connection properties, Networking tab
Courtesy Course Technology/Cengage Learning

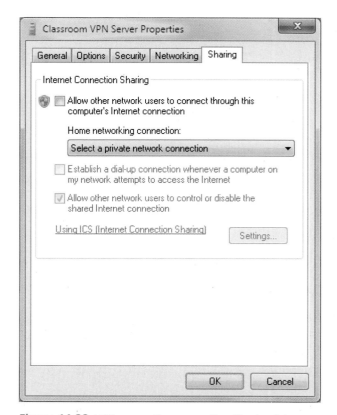

Figure 14-28 VPN connection properties, Sharing tab
Courtesy Course Technology/Cengage Learning

14

The options on the VPN properties Sharing tab are:

- *Allow other network users to connect through this computer's Internet connection*—When this option is enabled, the VPN connection can be shared by other computers on this computer's local area network. Resources on the remote VPN network will be shared with local workstations connected to the network interface specified under "Home networking connection."

- *Establish a dial-up connection whenever a computer on my network attempts to access the Internet*—If this option is selected and a resource on the VPN network is accessed, this connection will be activated.

- *Allow other network users to control or disable the shared Internet connection*—If this option is enabled, the status of this connection can be controlled by local network users.

Activity 14-5: Create a VPN Connection

Time Required: 10 minutes
Objective: Create and customize a VPN connection.

Description: In this activity, you will create a new VPN connection to a fictional VPN server. The VPN connection will be customized to support only IKEv2 and not PPTP connections.

1. If necessary, start your computer and log on.
2. Click the **Start** button and click **Control Panel.** Click **Network and Sharing Center.**
3. Click the **Set up a new connection or network** link in the middle of the window.
4. Select **Connect to a workplace** and click **Next** to proceed.
5. If necessary, click **No, create a new connection** and click **Next.**
6. Click **Use my Internet connection (VPN).**
7. In the Internet address box, enter the address provided by your instructor. If your instructor does not specify an address, type **remote.testing.local** in the field.
8. In the Destination name box, type **Classroom VPN Server.**
9. Select the option **Don't connect now; just set it up so I can connect later.**
10. Click **Next** to continue.
11. Click **Create.** Leaving these options empty forces you to enter a username and password during the connection process.
12. Click **Close** to close the Connect to a Workplace window.
13. In Network and Sharing Center, click the link **Change adapter settings** to open the Network Connections window.
14. Right-click the **Classroom VPN Server** icon and click **Properties.**
15. Click the **Security** tab in the Classroom VPN Server Properties window.
16. In the Type of VPN box, click **IKEv2.**
17. Click **Advanced settings.**
18. Confirm that the **Mobility** feature is enabled to allow the VPN to reconnect. Change the **Network outage time** to its smallest value, five minutes. Click **OK** to close the Advanced Properties window.
19. Click **OK** to close the Classroom VPN Server Properties window.
20. Close the Network Connections window.

21. Click the **Start** button and click **Control Panel**. Change the *View by:* option from Large Icons to **Category** in Control Panel. This changes the Control Panel view back to its original setting.

22. Close all open windows.

DirectAccess

When a VPN solution is not practical for a client to access corporate resource outside the corporate intranet, Windows 7 can work together with Windows Server 2008 R2 to optionally use a new technology called DirectAccess. Users are provided with the same experience working remotely as they would have working in the office. While the user is out of the office, they have access to the same corporate data sources and resources without the use of a VPN. This is useful when intermediate firewalls and conflicting applications installed on the Windows 7 computer do not allow the use of a VPN connection.

The Windows 7 computer must have DirectAccess enabled, and corporate servers must be configured to support DirectAccess clients. DirectAccess is configured on the client using either Group Policy or netsh commands.

Once it is configured, DirectAccess activates itself before the user logs on the computer. The computer uses its own identity credentials to establish a secure connection with a DirectAccess server. When that is complete, the user can log on and a second connection is established to the DirectAccess server. This allows administrative policies to apply to the computer and user the same as when the user is in the office. DirectAccess connections are established automatically once they are configured and the user does not have to trigger the connection.

IT administrators can remotely manage these computers, even though there is no VPN connection. The data connection is bidirectional. DirectAccess is built to use IPSec for security and IPv6 for transport. A dedicated Windows Server 2008 R2 computer is configured as a DirectAccess server, which will act as a gateway to the corporate intranet. Because the technology requires IPv6 communication to function, technologies such as Teredo or 6to4 are required to encapsulate IPv6 traffic over IPv4 networks. If these connection types fail, the client can also attempt to use **IP-HTTPS**, which encapsulates IPv6 traffic over HTTPS.

The DirectAccess server is not just a gateway server; it can limit which applications and resources the user is allowed to access. Application servers that interact with the DirectAccess server must be running a minimum of Windows Server 2008 and be configured properly with IPv6 and, optionally, IPSec.

DirectAccess is only supported on Windows 7 Enterprise and Ultimate Editions. DirectAccess is primarily configured server side, so its configuration is not covered in this chapter.

14

Remote Desktop

Dial-up and VPN connections establish a connection that allows data to flow between a remote client and a remote network. Once the connection is made, applications can send and receive data over the link. A common problem with this scenario is that the resulting link over the dial-up or VPN connection is too slow to carry the data in a timely fashion. Remote users end up waiting for operations to complete, or even worse, operations that fail to complete if they are time-limited.

One possible solution is to eliminate the need for application data to traverse the link at all. A workstation or server can be configured to be remotely controlled using a remote control application. Keyboard and mouse commands are sent from the client to the remotely controlled server and screen updates are returned to the user to show the results of the user's actions. The amount of data to transfer user commands and screen updates is typically much lower then if the actual application data had to move across the link.

Instead of using a tunneling protocol such as PPP, PPTP, or IKEv2 to carry data between the remote control client and remotely controlled server, the **Remote Desktop Protocol (RDP)** is used. The RDP protocol is designed to carry remote control session data efficiently and securely between the client and server involved in a remote control session.

The Remote Desktop client is the software that is used to remotely control a Windows 7 computer. It is available as a stand-alone client application or it can be triggered from a Web site through Remote Desktop Web.

Stand-Alone Remote Desktop Client

The most commonly used version of the Remote Desktop client is the full stand-alone application. A full IP network connection must be available between the computer running the remote desktop client and a computer configured as a remotely controlled server. Earlier versions of the Remote Desktop client support Windows 95 and later operating systems. This version of the remote desktop client, version 7.0, is a new version designed specifically for Windows 7 and Windows Server 2008 R2. An updated version of the older remote desktop client is available for Windows XP SP3 and later operating systems. Older operating systems can continue to use the older client without some of the new enhancements found in the version of the client released with Windows 7, but the upgrade is recommended.

The new remote desktop client improvements include:

- Support for Network Access Protection client updates to ensure remote clients are using the latest software updates and settings
- Bidirectional audio allowing recording and processing from client devices such as a microphone
- Remote application task scheduler can automatically start remote applications
- The ability to support up to 16 multiple monitors at the remote client
- Support for Aero glass in a remote session as long as it is not combined with multiple monitor support at the same time
- The ability to redirect Window Media Player to the client computer for decoding and improved quality

General Settings   The Remote Desktop client is found in the Start menu as a menu item in the Accessories subfolder. When the remote desktop client is started from the Start menu it does not immediately connect to a remote server. By clicking the Options button, several optional settings are available to adjust the remote control experience. The first tab visible is the General tab, as shown in Figure 14-29.

The General tab is used to identify the remote server to connect to and identifies what user credentials will be passed to the remote desktop server. The server is identified by its IPv4, IPv6, or DNS host name. The user is prompted for credentials when they first connect to the remote server, so that no user credentials are displayed by the options screen.

The General tab also allows the current option settings to be saved to a settings file for later use. The file that is created has the file extension RDP. Multiple RDP files can exist in the file system for different settings to different servers or different custom settings to the same server. By opening an existing RDP file from the General tab, the saved settings are restored prior to making a connection.

Display Settings   Before the connection is established, you can configure the screen settings to set the local experience during the remote control session. The Display tab allows the remote control window to be sized from a minimum of 640 by 480 pixels to the full client screen resolution. The color depth for the remote control screen can be configured from a minimum of 15-bit color depth to the maximum color depth supported by the local client video system.

Increase the resolution and color settings with caution, as the amount of data that must be transferred between the remotely controlled server and the remote client increase with increasing

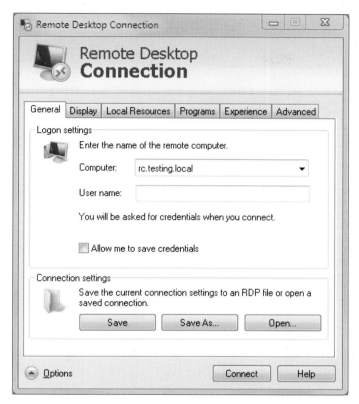

Figure 14-29 Remote Desktop Client connection properties, General tab
Courtesy Course Technology/Cengage Learning

resolution and color depth. The remote client's experience may become unacceptably slow and difficult to work with. If this is a suspected cause for poor performance, a lower resolution or color depth may improve the screen update performance for what the remote user sees.

If the user is operating the remote control connection in full-screen mode, they can optionally see a connection bar at the top of the screen that reminds them that they are using a remote control connection and not the local operating system window.

Local Resource Settings Beyond what the remote users see on the screen, their local computer resources can be included as part of the remote session. The Local Resources tab allows the remote user to define which local resources are available inside the remote control session (see Figure 14-30).

The options included on the Local Resources tab are:

- *Remote audio settings*—The sound generated by the remotely controlled computer can be played locally (Play on this computer), remotely (Play on remote computer), or not at all (Do not play). The default setting is "Play on this computer." Audio from the local client can also be recorded by the computer being remote controlled. The default setting is to disable recording audio from the local client.

- *Keyboard*—Special windows keyboard shortcuts such as Alt-Tab are applied at the local client (On this computer), the remotely controlled server (On the remote computer), or only in the special case that the local client is operating in full-screen display mode (Only when using full screen). The default setting is "Only when using full screen."

- *Local devices and resources:*

  - *Printers*—If this option is selected, the client's local printers are automatically created on the remote computer for the duration of the remote connection. When the remote connection is logged out, the printers that were created are automatically removed. This allows application on the remotely controlled computer to print to the printers attached

Figure 14-30 Remote Desktop Client connection properties, Local Resources tab
Courtesy Course Technology/Cengage Learning

to the remote client as if they were attached to the remote computer. The remotely controlled computer must have the appropriate print driver for the printer, and the print driver must be compatible with the remote control software. If this is not the case, the printer that does not meet these conditions will not be automatically created in the remote control session. This option is enabled by default.

- *Clipboard*—If this option is selected, any data saved to the clipboard on either the remote client or the remotely controlled computer is available to the other side of the remote control session. Data can be cut and pasted between the remote and local operating systems. This option is enabled by default.

- *More button*—This button opens a window with additional local resource settings. The settings on this window allow local client smart cards, serial ports, specific drive letters, and certain types of plug and play devices to appear as resources inside the remote control session. Plug and play devices that work with this setting are restricted to those devices that state explicit support for this purpose. Local resources such as drive letters are visible on the remotely controlled computer, but the data is still stored on the remote client. If an application on the remotely controlled computer reads a file from the local computer, it must completely transfer the file's data from the remote client to the remote computer. If the network connection between the client and remote computer is slow, the file transfer performance may be unacceptable. By default, local client drives are not selected to appear in the remote control session.

Program Settings   When the remote desktop client makes a connection to a remote computer, the default behavior is to open a remote control session showing the desktop of the remote computer being controlled. If there is one specific program that should run each time the connection is established, it can be entered on the Programs tab.

Having a specific application run each time the connection is started is useful for special purpose applications. The remote user might only use a single application to take customer orders, input data, or some other focused task. To save this setting for later use, save the settings to an RDP file using the controls on the General tab.

Experience Settings Many professions use remote control sessions, but the session must meet performance requirements to be an effective business tool. To make the remote control session faster, some elements of the interactive experience can be restricted or eliminated to adjust performance closer to expectations. In some situations, a richer user experience is required and performance is a secondary consideration. The Experience tab shown in Figure 14-31 is used to adjust factors that impact the remote control session experience.

Figure 14-31 Remote Desktop Client connection properties, Experience tab
Courtesy Course Technology/Cengage Learning

The options on the Experience tab include:

- *Choose your connection speed to optimize performance*—This option lists possible connection speeds between the remote client and the remote computer. Depending on which connection speed is selected, the performance options are automatically selected or deselected. The suggested performance settings for a specific connection speed can be overridden individually.

- *Desktop background*—If this option is selected, the desktop wallpaper is shown; otherwise, the desktop is blank.

- *Font smoothing*—If this option is selected, the fonts are smoothed to improve their readability and appearance.

- *Desktop composition*—If this option is selected, some of the graphics rendering is offloaded from the server to the client computer. This allows advanced graphics such as the Aero glass interface to function over remote desktop.

- *Show contents of window while dragging*—If this option is selected, the contents of a window are redrawn continuously as it is moved from one spot to another.

- *Menu and window animation*—If this option is selected, the opening, closing, and moving of windows is fully animated.

- *Visual styles*—When selected, optional visual theme elements are shown.

- *Persistent bitmap caching*—If this option is selected, common graphical elements that are drawn more than once are buffered locally to accelerate screen redraws.

- *Reconnect if the connection is dropped*—When selected, the remote session tries to automatically restore the connection if the connection between the remote client and remote computer appears broken. This option is selected by default.

Advanced Settings The Advanced tab, shown in Figure 14-32, includes a section for server authentication. This feature is only supported if the remote client and the remotely controlled computer use Network Level Authentication. Network Level Authentication is a security protocol used by clients and servers to prove their identity before a data connection is established. If the server identity is not trusted, the connection is refused.

Figure 14-32 Remote Desktop Client connection properties, Advanced tab
Courtesy Course Technology/Cengage Learning

The server authentication options available on the Advanced tab that use Network Level Authentication include the following:

- *Warn me*—This is the default setting, which will warn the user if the remote computer the user is connecting to cannot adequately prove its identity using Network Level Authentication.

- *Connect and don't warn me*—This setting allows a connection with those remote computers that do not support Network Level Authentication without generating a warning message for the user.

- *Do not connect*—This setting will refuse the connection to the remote computer unless it adequately proves its identity using Network Level Authentication. Authentication methods that are part of Network Level Authentication are based on DNS names, not IP addressing, therefore names are the preferred information for identifying which remote computer to connect to.

The Advanced tab also contains a section titled Connect from anywhere with a Settings button. When the Settings button on the Advanced tab is clicked, the window shown in Figure 14-33 is visible.

Figure 14-33 Remote Desktop Client connection properties, Advanced tab, RD Gateway Server settings
Courtesy Course Technology/Cengage Learning

14

The Gateway Server Settings shown in Figure 14-33 are used to configure how the remote client interacts with **Remote Desktop (RD)** Gateway servers. Remote Desktop server services were formerly called **Terminal Services**. The Remote Desktop Gateway server is part of Windows Server 2008 R2. The RD Gateway server is usually configured at the perimeter of the network, with one network connection to a public network and one to the private corporate network. The remote client creates a secure connection to the RD Gateway server's public connection using secured HTTP (HTTPS) for the initial server connection. The advantage of using HTTPS to carry remote control data is that firewalls do not need custom port rules and settings to allow RDP traffic on TCP port 3389 through the firewall. Most firewalls will allow HTTPS traffic to pass without issue. If the RD Gateway authorizes the connection, the user is allowed to pass through the RD Gateway and connect to remotely controllable servers behind the RD Gateway.

The default connection options to a RD Gateway server are set to automatic detection, which is the recommended setting. The RD Gateway connection can be explicitly set or completely disabled if desired.

Command-Line Options Some remote connection options are not present on any of the property pages. Several options are available only by running the remote desktop client program MSTSC.EXE directly from the command line.

The command-line options for MSTSC include:

- */v:server[:port]*—Used to identify the remote computer to connect. A port number other than 3389 can be specified by using a colon after the IP address or DNS name of the server.

- *admin*—Used to connect to the same interactive desktop that a user sitting at the remote keyboard would see. This replaces the old remote desktop client option of /console. This special type of connection opens a special connection specifically to administer the remote computer.

- */h:# and /w:#*—Used to set nonstandard screen resolutions for the remote session.

- */public*—Used to configure the remote client with the assumption that it does not have a private location to store information, such as the registry. The local computer is treated as a public access computer.

- */span*—Used to enable multiple monitor spanning support on the local client so that a single remote session can span multiple monitors on the local client. The monitors must each be the same vertical resolution and be arranged side-by-side in a horizontal arrangement. The local client will try to match the remote desktop height and width by spanning across local monitors as necessary.

- */multimon*—Used to enable multiple monitor support where the remote desktop session monitor layout is matched to the current client-side configuration. A maximum of 16 monitors are supported.

- */f*—Used to start the remote session in full-screen mode.

- *"connection file"*—The path and name of an RDP file can be specified to launch a remote session using the optional settings inside the RDP file.

- */migrate*—Used to convert a connection file created by using Client Connection Manager to an .rdp file.

- */edit*—When specified with an RDP file, the settings in the RDP file are opened for editing.

RemoteApp and Remote Desktop Web Access

Running an RDP file is one way a user can connect to a remote system and run an application. Windows Server 2008 allows the publishing of these remote applications through a feature called RemoteApp. On the server side, an administrator can publish applications to make them available as a RemoteApp. Those applications can show up on the user's Start menu as if they were locally installed. The administrator centrally maintains the applications in one place. The user's list of available RemoteApps is updated regularly by a local scheduled task. When the user runs the RemoteApp it can appear to have full local access to the client, as if it was installed locally.

Remote Desktop Web Access presents RemoteApps and remote connections to the user in one Web-based resource. This allows the user to see and use the resources they that requires, even if the local computer being used is not part of the corporate network and not administered by the corporate IT administrator. The IT administrator will grant or deny access to RemoteApps and remote connections accordingly via Remote Desktop Web Access.

Activity 14-6: Create a Remote Control Connection

Time Required: 15 minutes
Objective: Start the remote desktop connection application and use it to create a custom remote connection preference file.

Description: In this activity, you will verify the remote control settings of your local computer. The Remote Desktop Application is started and a customized remote control connection is created. The custom settings are saved to their default location as a remote control preference file.

1. If necessary, start your computer and log on.
2. Click the **Start** button and click **Control Panel**.
3. Click **System and Security** and click **System**.

4. Click the **Remote settings** link in the list of Tasks.

5. Note that the System Properties window appears and that the Remote tab is selected.

6. In the Remote Desktop section, click the option **Allow connections from computers running any version of Remote Desktop.**

7. Click **Select Users.**

8. Note which users currently have permission to connect to this computer.

9. Click **OK** to close the Remote Desktop Users window.

10. Click **OK** to close the System Properties window.

11. Close the **System** window.

12. Click the **Start** button, point to **All Programs**, click **Accessories**, and click **Remote Desktop Connection.**

13. Click the icon in the top-left corner of the Remote Desktop Connection window and click **About** in the pop-up menu.

14. Confirm that the About screen indicates the remote desktop client supports Network Level Authentication. Click **OK** to close the About Remote Desktop Connection window.

15. In the Remote Desktop Connection window, click **Options.**

16. On the General tab, in the Computer box, type **rc.testing.local** as the remote computer name to connect to.

17. Click the **Experience** tab and in the Choose your connection speed to optimize performance box, click **Satellite (2Mbps – 16 Mbps with high latency).**

18. Click the **Local Resources** tab and in the Local devices and resources section deselect Printers and Clipboard.

19. Click the **Advanced** tab and in the Server authentication area, click **Connect and don't warn me.**

20. Click the **General** tab and in the Connection settings area click **Save As.**

21. This will create an RDP connection file. Note the default name, location, and file extension of the remote control preference file.

22. Click **Save** to save the RDP connection file. If the file already exists, you may be prompted to replace it. In this case, click **Yes.**

23. Close the Remote Desktop Connection window.

Remote Assistance

If a user is having difficulty operating their computer, they can ask someone else they trust to help them. This feature allows a user to send an invitation file to a remote user using e-mail or any other method that transfers the file between the two computers. The invitation file invites the helper to remotely connect to the local computer. If the remote user accepts the invitation, they can establish a secure remote connection to view what is happening on the desktop. If the remote user is also using Windows 7, they can connect remotely through Easy Connect.

Easy Connect is a service provided through Microsoft that allows two Windows 7 computers to connect through IPv6 tunnels over the Internet. This will not work if access to the Internet is limited for either computer, or if a firewall in the path of the conversation doesn't support Easy Connect traffic passing through it.

The local user can electronically chat with the person providing remote assistance, which allows the help session to be interactive without granting the remote user full access to the user interface. If the remote user is highly trusted, they can optionally be granted complete keyboard and mouse control during the remote assistance session.

14

The Windows Remote Assistance wizard is accessed by clicking the *Windows Remote Assistance* link in Help and Support or from the Troubleshooting Control Panel applet by clicking the *Get help from a friend* link. Once the Remote Assistance wizard is started, you can ask someone to help you or offer to help someone else.

Remote Assistance can potentially give a remote user the ability to access sensitive information and settings on a computer. An offer asking for remote assistance is limited to only be valid for a limited period of time, with a default of six hours. Once the need to use remote assistance has passed, the overall ability to use remote assistance on the local computer can be disabled. If the need for remote assistance arises again, remote assistance on the local computer can be re-enabled. The main on/off control for remote assistance is found as a property of the System in Control Panel. If remote assistance is not enabled on the local computer, the Remote Assistance wizard will offer to open the System properties Remote tab so that remote assistance can be enabled (see Figure 14-34).

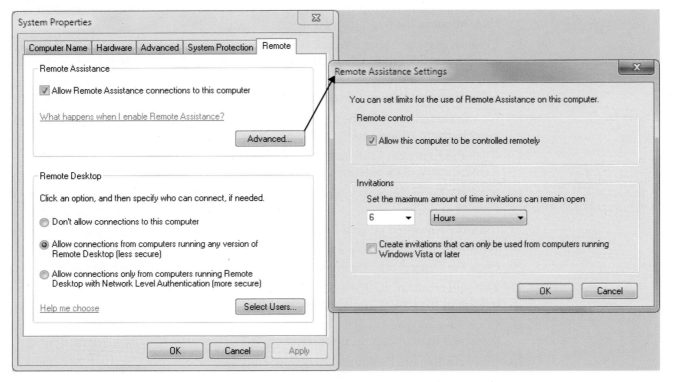

Figure 14-34 Remote Assistance controls on the local computer's System Properties
Courtesy Course Technology/Cengage Learning

An invitation to use remote assistance is password protected with a unique password selected for that specific invitation. Once the remote user receives the invitation, they can open it and use it to initiate a connection to the computer offering an invitation. There must be an IP network connection between the two computers that does not block the connection attempt from the remote user. Network firewalls and administrative policies may prevent the connection attempt, even with a valid invitation.

The remote client that is processing the invitation can be running Windows XP or Windows Server 2003 at a minimum. The Windows XP ability to talk over a remote assistance connection is not supported in Windows 7. Remote assistance clients previous to Windows XP are not supported when communicating with Windows 7. The preferred remote assistance client used to open an invitation is Windows 7.

Once the remote assistance invitation is sent out, a window will open waiting for the remote assistance client to accept the invitation (see Figure 14-35). If this window is closed, the invitation will not work.

Figure 14-35 Waiting for a Remote Assistance connection via Easy Connect
Courtesy Course Technology/Cengage Learning

The remote assistance control window has button controls to activate a chat window, log the session, and control sharing of the desktop. If the remote assistance user is given the ability to remotely control the desktop and they perform any task that is undesirable, their control can be revoked by canceling the remote assistance session, pressing the Esc key, or clicking on the Stop Sharing control.

If the remote assistance user is not given the ability to remotely control the computer and there is sensitive data they should not see, make sure the data is not visible before the invitation for remote assistance is sent out.

Activity 14-7: Create a Remote Assistance Request

Time Required: 10 minutes

Objective: Enable remote assistance for your computer and create an invitation for help.

Description: In this activity, you will confirm that the system properties allow remote invitations to be sent from your computer. The user who will connect to offer remote support must be limited to using a remote assistance client that is fully compatible with Windows 7. The invitation for remote assistance will be saved to a file on your local system.

 This activity does not establish an actual remote assistance connection between two computers. As an optional exercise, the invitation file may be copied to a second workstation and an actual remote assistance session can be started. Confirm this optional activity with your instructor.

1. If necessary, start your computer and log on.
2. Click the **Start** button and click **Control Panel**.
3. Click **System and Security** and click **System**.
4. Click the **Remote settings** link in the list of Tasks.
5. Note that the System Properties window appears and that the Remote tab is selected.
6. Verify that the option **Allow Remote Assistance connections to this computer** is enabled.
7. Click the **Advanced** button in the Remote Assistance area.
8. To make sure the version of Remote Assistance used by the remote contact is fully compatible with Windows 7, select the option **Create invitations that can only be used from computers running Windows Vista or later** in the Remote Assistance Settings window.
9. Click **OK** to save the change and close the Remote Assistance Settings window.
10. Click **OK** to close the System Properties window.

14

11. Close the System window.

12. Click the **Start** button and click **Help and Support**.

13. Click the **More support options** link on the bottom of the main page of the Help and Support window.

14. In the More support options display, click **Windows Remote Assistance**. Click **Invite someone you trust to help you** in the Remote Assistance application.

15. Click the option to **Save this invitation as a file**.

16. In the Save the invitation as a file window, notice the default path and filename for the invitation file.

17. Click on the **Save** button.

18. If the file already exists, you may be prompted to replace the invitation file. Select **Yes** in this case.

19. Notice that the Windows Remote Assistance application window opens with the status message Waiting for incoming connection. An automatically generated password is displayed that the remote helper must specify to connect to your system.

20. In the Windows Remote Assistance application window, click **Settings**.

21. In the Windows Remote Assistance Settings window, move the **Bandwidth usage** control to its minimum (Low) and maximum (High) settings. Note how the list of optimizations beside the control changes as the position of the control changes.

22. Close the Windows Remote Assistance Settings window.

23. Close the Windows Remote Assistance window. You will be asked if you are sure you want to close Remote Assistance. Click **Yes**.

24. Close the Windows Help and Support window.

BranchCache

Many corporations store critical data in a central location, typically the company's head office. Users can be spread throughout the company, even if they are located in a branch office. The branch office commonly has a custom network connection back to the head office, but its Internet connection is typically low bandwidth in comparison to the connection at head office. These remote office users can take advantage of BranchCache with Windows 7 to speed up their access to information.

BranchCache technology requires that the Windows 7 clients interact with servers running Windows Server 2008 R2 as a minimum. Data that is read from the head office is cached locally at the branch, using local servers or other Windows 7 workstations. Only the first client to access the data must wait for the content to fully transfer to a local branch cache location. Other Windows 7 clients can access the local copy of the data once they are authenticated and authorized.

BranchCache can operate in two modes, Hosted Cache mode and Distributed Cache mode. Hosted mode stores cached data on a local Windows Server 2008 R2 server. Distributed mode does not use a local server, the Windows 7 clients in the branch cooperate to cache content. The distributed mode is only practical for 50 or less clients, where all clients operate on a single IP subnet. Cached content can be impacted by clients that get turned off, hibernate, or lose their network connection. The advantage to distributed mode is that a server is not required. When it is impractical to use distributed mode, an advantage of the hosted cache mode is that the server does not need to be dedicated to caching data and can be tasked as an all purpose server.

The servers at head office track the content of cached data using identifiers and metadata describing the content. In the hosted mode, the servers tracking content at head office can inform remote clients that the data that they are seeking is stored on a local server. In distributed mode, when the client is informed that the data is locally cached, the client will issue a multicast request on the local subnet to identify the location of a copy on the local network. Data transfers between local clients are encrypted and verified to make sure the local client receives the version of the data that they are looking for.

Because BranchCache is a technology to buffer data, it operates over IPv4 and IPv6 equally well. Data connections to servers can use either **SMB** or HTTP protocols. Data transfers are securely encrypted with the use of HTTPS and IPSec, while users must authenticate before they are granted access. BranchCache is typically enabled on clients using Group Policy or netsh commands. BranchCache configuration is primarily a server-side exercise so its configuration is not covered in this chapter.

Sync Center

When a computer is portable, one of the problems is making sure a user still has access to his/her data. The earlier sections of this chapter looked at how the connection back to the data could be made through remote access, remote control, VPN or DirectAccess. Another option is to keep a local copy of the data on the computer itself. When the user returns to their main network location, the cached data on the computer can be synchronized back to its original location. Operating systems such as Windows XP offered similar technology, such as Offline files for caching file information. The problem with these earlier caching methods is that they can be very complex to configure and maintain. The average user found it difficult to manage and therefore many people avoid using it.

To address the ease of use for cached data, Windows 7 also provides the Sync Center as a central control mechanism. The Sync Center is accessible from the Control Panel and from the Mobility Center (covered later in the next section). The Sync Center window lists all of the data sources that need to be cached on the local computer (See Figure 14-36).

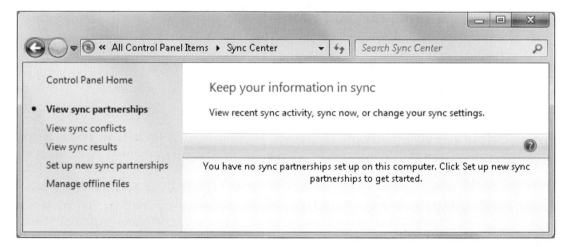

Figure 14-36 Sync Center Window
Courtesy Course Technology/Cengage Learning

A resource must be compatible with the Sync Center to be available as an item to track and synchronize. If there are no suitable sources to synchronize with, the Sync Center will not offer to manage any defined synchronization sources. Data sources suitable for setting up synchronization are not arbitrary; they must be supported by Sync Center and Windows 7.

Windows 7 supports data synchronization with certain mobile devices, network folders (offline file support), and applications designed to work with the Sync Center. Network folder synchronization is not supported with Windows 7 Starter, Windows 7 Home Basic, or Windows 7 Home Premium.

The current status of resources that are being tracked by Sync Center is shown on the main screen of the Sync Center. Before a user disconnects from the network and goes on the road, they can trigger the Sync All option from the main screen to make sure the user has the latest content. When the user returns, the local copy of data is synchronized with the original data source. Any version conflicts for updated content are stored on the computer and listed in the Sync Center.

Mobility Center

Windows 7 places controls for mobile computer features in one single window, the Mobility Center found in the computer's Control Panel. If the computer is not a mobile computer, this item will not show up in Control Panel. A mobile computer is detected by looking for the presence of a battery.

The controls available in the Mobility Center can all be configured from other locations in Control Panel. The point of Mobility Center is to bring all of these options into a central location and make it easier for mobile computer users to manage their systems, as they are more likely to change system settings than a desktop computer user. For example, mobile computer users are more likely to change screen resolution to match display projectors when giving presentations.

Mobility Center includes some standard controls provided by Windows 7, but mobile computer vendors can add additional specialized controls. Typical controls found in the Mobility Center include:

- *Battery status and power management*—This control allows you to view the charge level of the battery and change the power management plan.

- *Wireless network configuration*—This control allows you to connect to wireless networks and configure wireless networking options.

- *Display configuration*—This control allows you to change your display configuration, including enabling external display.

- *Synchronization settings*—This control gives you quick and easy access to synchronization settings used by Sync Center.

- *Presentation settings*—This control allows you to preconfigure presentation profiles that control settings such as the sound level and desktop background used when giving a presentation.

Chapter Summary

- Windows 7 supports both remote access and remote control. Remote access allows you to access data remotely by using a dial-up or VPN connection. Remote control allows you to control a desktop remotely and run applications on the remote computer.

- Dial-up remote access can be done with a modem and regular phone line or ISDN. You can use dialing rules to how phone numbers are dialed based on location and other characteristics. There are many options that can be configured including those for redialing and security.

- VPN connections allow you to securely access data over the Internet. When combined with high-speed internet, a VPN allows you much faster access to data than a dial-up connection. VPN connections can use either PPTP, L2TP, SSTP, or IKEv2 to secure data. Most of the configuration options are the same as for a dial-up connection. An advanced feature of IKEv2 is the Mobility option to automatically reconnect the VPN, optionally, up to several hours after a client has lost a network connection—without losing the work the client had open beforehand.

- DirectAccess allows Windows 7 Enterprise clients to connect to corporate intranet resource without a VPN while they are outside the corporate network. DirectAccess requires a dedicated Windows Server 2008 R2 server and IPv6 support between the client and server. Communication with the client is bidirectional and IT administrators can manage the client as if it was locally on the corporate intranet.

- Remote control client functionality has been enhanced to support server authentication and offer more control over which remote client resources are included and accessible as part of the remote control session. IT administrators can also centrally manage remote applications by configuring RemoteApps and Remote Client Web Access.

- Remote Assistance is a software tool to ask trusted users to connect over the network and provide help. The remote users can see and optionally make changes to the local computer.

- BranchCache helps speed up performance for users in remote branch offices that do not have the same access to corporate data as other users in the main office. Data retrieved by local Windows 7 users can be buffered on a local server (Hosted mode) or other Windows 7 computers (Distributed mode). Data transfers are secure and encrypted using either IPv4 or IPv6 transports.

- Sync Center allows mobile users to quickly and easily synchronize network content on the mobile computer. The mobile users can modify data while on the road and synchronize the changes when they return to the office.

- Mobility Center is a feature available only on Mobile computer. It brings together the most commonly used features for mobile computers into a single location.

Key Terms

analog Information transmitted in a continuously variable form. Phone systems are an example of an information system that uses analog data.

authentication protocols Routines used by servers to establish the identity of a remote client attempting to connect and communicate with the server.

BranchCache Technology that allows user data from the corporate data center to be buffered on branch servers or workstations for local client use. Local clients can access cached data instead of retieving it over the WAN again.

certificate Digital information that describes the identity of a user or computer. A user or computer can inspect the certificate and decide if its validity can be trusted. Certificates are issued by special servers called Certification Authorities (CA). If a user or computer trusts a CA, then they typically trust the certificates issued by the CA.

Challenge-Handshake Authentication Protocol (CHAP) A more secure authentication protocol than PAP. CHAP is used to periodically identify the client identity without sending the actual password over the client and server data stream. CHAP passwords are simple by design and do not support strong security methods. This presents a security risk and therefore this authentication protocol is discouraged unless the risk from communication eavesdropping is considered low.

DirectAccess A replacement for VPN access to corporate intranet data sources and applications utilizing bidirectional IPv6 communication with a specialized DirectAccess server. Workstations and users connect separately, allowing corporate IT administrators to manage both.

Extensible Authentication Protocol (EAP) A modular standard for defining authentication protocols that can be used to validate a computer or user. A product developer can introduce a custom authentication protocol for their product if it is not already included with Windows 7. EAP is available as an authentication standard with dial-up, VPN, and wireless connections.

hotspot A geographic area where a Wi-Fi wireless signal from a Wireless Access Point is available to wireless networking clients to enable network and/or Internet access.

HyperText Transport Protocol Secure (HTTPS) An application protocol commonly used to transfer TCP data in a secured session between a client and server. Because this is a common protocol used with Web servers, many firewalls allow this protocol to pass without blocking it.

IKEv2 Mobility and Multihoming Protocol (MOBIKE) A protocol designed to work together with IKEv2 to allow a host involved in a secure IKEv2 initiated SA to change its IP address, switch to a different network interface, or recover from a network outage.

14

Integrated Service Digital Network (ISDN)   A direct, digital dial-up connection to a PSTN that operates at 64 KB per channel over regular twisted-pair cable between a subscriber and the PSTN office.

Internet Key Exchange version 2 (IKEv2)   An authentication protocol that identifies the identity of both the client and server to each other. Once the identity of both sides is established, one or more IPSec based SAs are established between them for data transfer. IKEv2 is considered a strong authentication protocol.

IP-HTTPS   A protocol that allows a secure IP tunnel to be established with a secure HTTP connection for the purpose of transporting IPv6 packets. A IP-HTTPS client must initiate a connection to a configured IP-HTTPS server. The connection between client and server is not likely to be stopped by a firewall because the HTTPS protocol is not commonly blocked.

IPSec   A protocol that is used to secure and authenticate IP connections.

Layer 2 Tunneling Protocol (L2TP)   A protocol used to carry PPP packets through IP networks.

MOBIKE   See IKEv2 Mobility and Multihoming Protocol.

MS-CHAP-v1&2   A Microsoft version of the Challenge-Handshake Authentication Protocol (CHAP). MS-CHAP-v1 adds features to change the password during a session, as well as limit authentication retries, between a client and server. MS-CHAP-v2 added the ability for both sides to confirm each other's identity instead of just the server confirming the client's identity.

Password Authentication Protocol (PAP)   A simple authentication method that establishes the identity of a remote client with the authentication password sent in the data stream between the client and server. This presents a security risk and therefore this authentication protocol is discouraged unless the risk from communication eavesdropping is considered low.

Plain Old Telephone System (POTS)   See Public Switched Telephone Network (PSTN).

Point-to-Point Protocol (PPP)   A network-layer transport protocol that manages connectivity over serial or modem lines. PPP can negotiate any transport protocol used by both systems involved in the link and can automatically assign TCP/IP settings.

Point-to-Point Tunneling Protocol (PPTP)   A protocol used to carry PPP packets through IP networks.

Protected Extensible Authentication Protocol (PEAP)   An enhancement of EAP that encrypts the entire EAP process. This protects all EAP communication before authentication is performed.

Public Switched Telephone Network (PSTN)   Provides a connection to subscribers for dial-up devices such as analog or ISDN modems. Originally developed to connect telephones and allow people to make analog phone calls.

remote access   A system where clients are able to remotely connect to a network and access resources as though the remote client is connected directly to the network.

remote control   A system where clients are able to remotely connect to a server to run applications and access data. Applications and files are accessed at the server and only screen drawing commands are sent back to the client.

Remote Desktop Protocol (RDP)   A protocol used to carry remote control data between the remote control client and the remotely controlled computer.

Remote Desktop (RD)   Terminal Services has been rebranded as Remote Desktop Services in Windows Server 2008 R2.

Routing and Remote Access (RRAS)   A service installed and configured on Windows Server 2003 to allow remote clients and networks to connect to network services local to the server. The Routing and Remote Access service must be configured to support VPN connections, dial-up connections, and routed IP traffic from routers.

Secure Socket Tunneling Protocol (SSTP)   A protocol that allows secure communication between a VPN client and server using the SSL based encryption methods of HTTPS. The connection between client and server is not likely to be stopped by a firewall because the HTTPS protocol is not commonly blocked.

Security Association (SA)   A connection established between two computers for the purpose of securely exchanging data. The connection is only allowed if both sides of the connection know how to find each other on the network, agree on how to authenticate their identities, and agree on how to encrypt and decrypt the data sent between them. Any aspect of the SA connection may be renegotiated periodically to ensure that the other side of the connection is still a valid communication partner.

Serial Line IP (SLIP)   An implementation of the IP protocol over serial lines. SLIP has been made obsolete by PPP.

smart card   A small physical card that contains a processor and memory. The processor is capable of interacting with a computer in which the card is plugged. The most common use of a smart card is to store and validate personal security credentials for a computer or user. The smart card can be physically removed and stored in a small space, such as a wallet.

Terminal Services (TS)   A service that can be installed on a computer running a server-based operating system. Depending on licensing limits, multiple users can connect to the Terminal Server and run applications on the Terminal Server using only a remote control client. Each remote user is unaware that other users are also remote controlling applications on the Terminal Server.

virtual private network (VPN)   A remote access technology that creates an encrypted tunnel for communication between the VPN client and a remote access server. VPN connections are commonly used over the Internet to secure communication when accessing office data from home.

Wide Area Network (WAN)   A geographically dispersed network connected by routers and communication links. The Internet is the largest WAN.

X.25   A networking technology standard that defines packet switching networks used for WAN connectivity.

Review Questions

1. The device most commonly connected to a PSTN is a _____.
   a. wired network card
   b. wireless network card
   c. dial-up modem
   d. printer

2. The remote desktop application is used to establish remote VPN connections to another computer's desktop. True or False?

3. A VPN connection can be established over dial-up, wired, and wireless networks. True or False?

4. When Windows 7 is configured to connect to a remote VPN server, it is referred to as a _____.
   a. VPN client
   b. remote access client
   c. VPN server
   d. remote access server

5. When Windows 7 is configured to connect to a remote access server, it is referred to as a _____.
   a. VPN client
   b. remote access client

    c.   VPN server

    d.   remote access server

6.   A remote control session requires a _____ between two computers.

    a.   PPP VPN

    b.   dial-up connection

    c.   IP network connection

    d.   L2TP IPSec VPN

    e.   PPTP VPN

7.   A remote access server can use a single modem to service _____ connected dial-up clients at the same time.

    a.   one

    b.   two

    c.   three

    d.   four

    e.   unlimited

8.   A remote access client with three installed modems can connect to _____ remote access servers at the same time.

    a.   one

    b.   two

    c.   three

    d.   four

    e.   unlimited

9.   Dial-up networking supports the _____ protocol to manage its connection.

    a.   IP

    b.   PPTP

    c.   L2TP

    d.   PPP

    e.   RRAS

10.   VPN network traffic is sent between two endpoints of the VPN connection using the _____ protocol. (Select all that apply.)

    a.   IP

    b.   PPTP

    c.   L2TP

    d.   PPP

    e.   SSTP

11.   When using Remote Desktop Connection a user wants to make sure their local printers are included as part of the remote control session. This is configured as an option on the _____ tab of the remote control application.

    a.   General

    b.   Local Resources

    c.   Experience

    d.   Printers

12. When using Remote Desktop Connection, a user wants to make sure their remote control session automatically reconnects if the network connection is dropped. This is configured as an option on the _____ tab of the remote control application.

    a. Advanced

    b. Display

    c. Experience

    d. General

13. A remote user is trying to connect from a Windows XP computer to your Windows 7 computer using Remote Desktop Connection. The remote user is unable to connect. You suspect the problem is that the Windows XP client does not support _____.

    a. IPv6

    b. IPSec

    c. Network Location Awareness

    d. Network Location Authentication

14. Windows 7 can connect to a VPN server specified by its _____. (Select all that apply.)

    a. machine address

    b. IPv6 address

    c. reverse IP address

    d. IPv4 address

    e. DNS name

15. To check if a modem is installed correctly, use _____.

    a. Connection Manager

    b. RRAS console

    c. Network and Sharing Center

    d. Device Manager

16. Dialing rules alter the connection process for _____ connections.

    a. IP

    b. VPN

    c. PPTP

    d. remote control

    e. dial-up

17. Operator-assisted dialing requires the operator to have _____.

    a. an invitation for remote assistance

    b. the IP address of the remote access server

    c. remote control access to your computer

    d. the phone number of the remote access server

18. Logon authentication protocols not supported by VPN connections in Windows 7 include _____ and _____.

    a. CHAP

    b. MS CHAP-v1

    c. MS CHAP-v2

    d. SPAP

    e. PAP

19. The remote desktop client application can transfer remote control session information over a public network such as the Internet without requiring a VPN connection. True or False?

20. You must configure a laptop for a company salesman's trip. The salesperson requires access to corporate files to edit a presentation being delivered by another salesperson in another city next week. The laptop will have intermittent Internet access through wired hotel networks, airport wireless hotspots, and wireless WAN broadband. The gap between available connections will not be longer than six hours. You decide to implement a VPN. What type of VPN should you select so the salesperson can tolerate network connection losses without losing their work?

   a. IKEv2

   b. SSTP

   c. L2TP

   d. PPTP

   e. Mobility

21. The command-line utility to run the remote desktop client application is _____.

   a. REMOTE.EXE

   b. RCON.EXE

   c. NETSH.EXE

   d. MSTSC.EXE

   e. SSH.EXE

22. The strongest authentication protocol that uses password-based authentication is _____.

   a. PAP

   b. CHAP

   c. MS CHAP-v1

   d. MS CHAP-v2

   e. smart cards

23. VPN connections created in Windows 7 do not support IPv6 connections. True or False?

24. A remote assistance invitation is valid for a default time period of _____.

   a. 15 minutes

   b. 30 minutes

   c. one hour

   d. six hours

25. A _____ can establish a secure network communication link with a VPN server. (Select all that apply.)

   a. remote access client

   b. remote access server

   c. VPN client

   d. VPN server

Case Projects

CASE PROJECTS

Case Project 14-1: Provisioning Network Services for Traveling Staff

The president of a small company selling collectible sports items, LFO Inc., is traveling from North America to factory locations in China, South Korea, and Japan to arrange bulk purchases. He will take a laptop with both a dial-up modem and a wired network card installed. During the trip, he will require access to the Internet to access e-mail stored in a Web account provided by their North American Internet service provider. Not all locations offer direct wired network access, but all locations offer dial-up connectivity. How many remote access servers would be required to support his trip? Where should they be located? What alternatives might exist to avoid implementing a remote access server as a company resource?

Case Project 14-2: Remote Access to Important Data

A medium-sized survey company stores sensitive government data that is used as part of a study. A security requirement from the government requires that all sensitive data must remain stored at the company's head office. All staff and the head office network have undergone a security audit and have received clearance to store and access the data.

The application that uses the sensitive data can be installed on any computer and can access data from local hard drives or a shared folder location. The application and the data must be accessible to a remote branch office with 30 users, traveling staff using dial-up connectivity, traveling staff using public wired/wireless Internet connectivity, and specific users operating from home.

What solution would you recommend to allow all staff to run the application with the government data and still meet the government security requirements? The solution must be proposed to the government auditor for review.

14

MCTS 70-680 Exam Objectives

The following tables correlate the MCTS Windows 7 (70-680) exam objectives to the corresponding chapter and section title where the objectives are covered in this book.

Installing, Upgrading, and Migrating to Windows 7

Objective	Chapter Section
Perform a clean installation	Chapter 1: Hardware Requirements and System Hardware Support Chapter 2: Deployment Enhancements in Windows 7 Chapter 2: Windows 7 Installation Methods Chapter 2: Windows 7 Installation Types Chapter 2: Attended Installation Chapter 2: Unattended Installation Chapter 2: Image-Based Installation
Upgrade to Windows 7 from previous versions of Windows	Chapter 2: Windows 7 Installation Methods Chapter 2: Windows 7 Installation Types Chapter 2: Attended Installation
Migrate User Profiles	Chapter 2: Deployment Enhancements in Windows 7 Chapter 2: Windows Easy Transfer Chapter 13: Enterprise Deployment Tools

Deploying Windows 7

Objective	Chapter Section
Capture a system image	Chapter 2: Image-Based Installation Chapter 13: Enterprise Deployment Tools
Prepare a system image for deployment	Chapter 2: Image-Based Installation Chapter 13: Enterprise Deployment Tools
Deploy a system image	Chapter 2: Image-Based Installation Chapter 13: Enterprise Deployment Tools
Configure a VHD	Chapter 2: Image-Based Installation Chapter 4: Disk Technology Chapter 4: Virtual Disk Management Tasks Chapter 13: Enterprise Deployment Tools

Configuring Hardware and Applications

Objective	Chapter Section
Configure devices	Chapter 3: Hardware Management
Configure application compatibility	Chapter 11: File and Registry Virtualization Chapter 11: Application Compatibility Chapter 11: Application Compatibility Research Tools
Configure application restrictions	Chapter 7: Security Policies Chapter 11: Application Control Policies
Configure Internet Explorer	Chapter 9: Internet Explorer 8

Configuring Network Connectivity

Objective	Chapter Section
Configure IPv4 network settings	Chapter 8: Networking Overview Chapter 8: Network Architecture Chapter 8: IP Version 4
Configure IPv6 network settings	Chapter 8: Networking Overview Chapter 8: Network Architecture Chapter 8: IP Version 6
Configure network settings	Chapter 8: Internet Connectivity Chapter 8: Wireless Networking Chapter 8: Network Bridging Chapter 8: Ad hoc and HomeGroup Networks
Configure Windows Firewall	Chapter 8: Windows Firewall
Configure remote management	Chapter 14: Remote Desktop Chapter 14: Remote Assistance

Configuring Access to Resources

Objective	Chapter Section
Configure shared resources	Chapter 8: Networking Overview Chapter 8: File Sharing Chapter 8: Ad hoc and Homegroup Networks Chapter 9: Printing
Configure file and folder access	Chapter 5: Supported File Systems Chapter 5: File and Folder Attributes Chapter 5: File and Folder Permissions
Configure user account control	Chapter 7: User Account Control
Configure authentication and authorization	Chapter 6: User Accounts Chapter 6: Creating Users Chapter 6: Network Integration Chapter 7: Windows 7 Security Improvements Chapter 11: Run As Administrator
Configure BranchCache	Chapter 14: BranchCache

Configuring Mobile Computing

Objective	Chapter Section
Configure BitLocker and BitLocker To Go	Chapter 7: Data Security
Configure DirectAccess	Chapter 14: DirectAccess
Configure Mobility Options	Chapter 14: Sync Center Chapter 14: Mobility Center
Configure Remote Connections	Chapter 13: Network Access Protection Chapter 14: Remote Access and Remote Control Overview Chapter 14: Remote Access Dial-Up Connectivity Chapter 14: Remote Access VPN Connectivity

Monitoring and Maintaining Systems that Run Windows 7

Objective	Chapter Section
Configure updates to Windows 7	Chapter 7: Windows Update Chapter 13: Windows Server Update Services
Manage disks	Chapter 4: Disk Technology Chapter 4: Partition Styles Chapter 4: Types of Disk Partitions Chapter 4: Disk Management Tools Chapter 4: Disk Management Tasks Chapter 4: Partition and Volume Management Chapter 14: Controlling Device Installation
Monitor systems	Chapter 10: Performance Monitor Chapter 10: Task Manager Chapter 10: Performance Ranking Chapter 11: General Principles of Troubleshooting
Configure performance settings	Chapter 10: Performance Enhancements Chapter 10: Performance Tuning Overview Chapter 10: Performance Options

Configuring Backup and Recovery Options

Objective	Chapter Section
Configure backup	Chapter 12: Windows Backup and Restore
Configure system recovery options	Chapter 12: Repairing Windows Vista
Configure file recovery options	Chapter 5: Previous Versions Chapter 12: Repairing Windows Vista

Glossary

8.3 file name A standard for naming files first introduced with MS-DOS operating systems. The numbers indicate the maximum number of characters that can be used for that part of the name, eight characters and three characters respectively. The period is a separator character between the two names. The three-character field is also known as the file extension.

802.11 A group of IEEE standards that define how to transfer Ethernet 802.3 data over wireless networks.

802.1x A IEEE standard designed to enhance security of wireless networks by authenticating a user to a central authority.

802.3 A group of IEEE standards that define the transfer of data over wired Ethernet based networks.

Access Control Entries (ACE) A specific entry in a file or folder's ACL that uniquely identifies a user or group by its security identifier and the action it is allowed or denied to take on that file or folder.

Access Control List (ACL) For those file systems that support ACLs for files and folders, such as NTFS, the ACL is a property of every file and folder in that file system. It holds a collection (that is, list) of ACE items that explicitly defines what actions are allowed to be taken on the file or folder to which it is attached.

account lockout policy A collection of settings, such as lockout duration, that control account lockouts.

Action Center A tool that provides you with a single location where you can identify and address any security issues, maintenance requirements, and errors that have arisen.

Active Directory A directory of network information about users, computers, and applications that links multiple domains together.

Active Directory site A set of IP subnets representing a physical location that are used by Active Directory to control replication.

active partition A primary partition that is indicated in the partition table as the partition to use when loading the rest of the operating system. If a basic disk has multiple primary partitions, only one primary partition can be marked as active at a time. The primary partition's boot sector is used to load the rest of the operating system.

ad hoc network A group of wireless computers sharing data directly with each other without the use of a wireless access point.

address prefix The first portion of an IP address that allows the identification of that addresses type and therefore purpose.

Administrative Tools A group of MMC consoles that are used to manage Windows 7. Computer Management, Event Viewer, and Services are the most commonly used.

Administrator account The built-in account that is created during installation and which has full rights to the system. This account cannot be deleted or removed by the Administrators group.

Advanced Configuration and Power Interface (ACPI) The current standard for power management that is implemented in Windows 7 and by computer manufacturers.

Advanced sharing A method for sharing folders that allows you to pick the specific options you want. NTFS permissions are not configured.

advanced User Accounts applet An applet for managing users that is available only from the command line. Some options in this applet are not available in other user management utilities.

Aero Glass A visual effect that is part of the Aero theme of Windows 7. Many graphical elements have a semitransparent appearance to allow users to see other windows under the active one. This is done to allow the user a better feel for what other applications are doing in the background without being too distracting.

alert An event that is triggered when a count value is above or below the specified threshold value.

alternate IP configuration A set of static IP configuration information that is used instead of APIPA when a computer is unable to contact a DHCP server.

analog Information transmitted in a continuously variable form. Phone systems are an example of an information system that uses analog data.

answer file An answer file is used during an unattended setup to provide configuration to Setup. exe. Windows 7 answer files are in an XML format and are created by using Windows System Image Manager.

applet A tool or utility in Control Panel that is focused on configuring a particular part of Windows 7.

application architecture A logical description of how different components, services, and resources work together to run applications.

Application Compatibility Toolkit A collection of tools, advice, and methodologies that guides the IT administrator in determining which legacy applications are compatible with Windows 7 and how to help make them compatible.

application manifest An XML file that describes the structure of an application, including required DLL files and privilege requirements.

application partition An Active Directory partition created by an administrator to hold and replicate application-specific information. It is replicated only to specified domain controllers.

Application Programming Interface (API) A set of rules and conditions a programmer follows when writing an application to allow the program to interact with part of the operating system. The program is guaranteed to work if they follow the API rules published by the authors of a feature in the operating system.

AppLocker A new feature in Windows 7 that is used to define which programs are allowed to run. This is a replacement for the software restriction policies found in Windows XP and Windows Vista.

arp A command-line utility that can be used to display and manage the ARP table, which maps IPv4 addresses to physical MAC addresses.

asymmetric encryption algorithm An encryption algorithm that uses two keys to encrypt and decrypt data. Data encrypted with one key is decrypted by the other key.

attack surface Parts of the computer, applications, and operating system components that can be attacked by hackers, viruses, and malware during their attempts to intrude on a computer system.

attended installation An installation when a network administrator must be present to answer configuration questions presented during Windows 7 installation.

audit policy The settings that define which operating system events are audited.

auditing The security process that records the occurrence of specific operating system events in the Security log.

auditSystem configuration pass This configuration pass is performed before user logon when Sysprep triggers Windows 7 into audit mode.

auditUser configuration pass This configuration pass is performed after user logon when Sysprep triggers Windows 7 into audit mode.

authentication protocols Routines used by servers to establish the identity of a remote client attempting to connect and communicate with the server.

Automatic Private IP Addressing (APIPA) A system used to automatically assign an IP address on the 169.254.x.x network to a computer that is unable to communicate with a DHCP server. A default gateway setting is not configured with APIPA.

AutoPlay Automatically performs a configurable action when new removable media is inserted into the computer.

autounattend.xml An answer file that is automatically searched for during the windowsPE, offlineServicing, and specialize configuration passes.

Away Mode An instant-on power saving mode that keeps the system in the S0 state.

Backup and Restore A tool included in Windows 7 that allows you to set up backup regiments to back up files, restore files, create a system image, and create a system repair disc.

Backup DC (BDC) A specialized Windows NT server that is responsible for holding a read-only copy of the domain security database.

base score The overall rating of your computer generated from the subscores.

baseline A set of performance indicators gathered when system performance is acceptable.

basic disk An older, IBM-originated method used to organize disk space for x86 computers into primary, extended, and logical partitions. Basic disk technology is supported by many legacy operating systems and may be required in certain multiboot configurations.

binary format Data that is stored in its raw digital form as binary numbers. Data stored in this format cannot be viewed properly by text editors such as Notepad or Wordpad.

Biometric Devices applet A Control Panel applet that is used to configure biometric devices and the authentication data associated with them.

BitLocker Drive Encryption A feature in Windows 7 that can encrypt the operating system partition of a hard drive and protect system files from modification. Other partitions can also be encrypted.

BitLocker To Go A new feature in Windows 7 that allows you to encrypt removable storage.

blue screen of death (BSOD) A common term used to describe an error condition in the operating system that has resulted in a full halt of the operating system due to a critical error. The error screen is usually white text on a blue background, hence the name.

boot configuration data (BCD) A database of boot configuration data that is used during the boot process for Windows Vista and Windows 7.

boot partition The partition or volume used to load the operating system from a hard disk. The system partition is processed before the boot partition. The boot partition can be the same partition as the system partition.

boot sector A term used to describe a special-purpose block of data on a disk or partition essential to the boot process of an x86 computer. The computer's BIOS will process the boot sector of the MBR initially to find a partition to continue the boot process. The first sector of that partition or volume contains a boot sector with code responsible for beginning the operating system load process from a partition or volume.

bottleneck The component in a process that prevents the overall process from completing faster.

BranchCache Technology that allows user data from the corporate data center to be buffered on branch servers or workstations for local client use. Local clients can access cached data instead of retieving it over the WAN again.

built-in local groups Groups that are automatically created for each Windows 7 computer and stored in the SAM database.

cable modem A device that converts network signals from the cable company to a standard Ethernet.

cached credentials Domain credentials that are stored in Windows 7 after a user has logged on to a domain. Cached credentials can be used to log on when a domain controller cannot be contacted.

catalog file WSIM uses catalog files to read the configurable settings and their current status for an WIM image.

CD-ROM File System (CDFS) A file system introduced with Windows 95 and Windows NT to organize files and folders on a CD-ROM disk. The CDFS file system is considered adequate for older CD-ROM disks but not for rewritable CD-ROMs or newer DVD media formats. For those newer media technologies, UDF is the preferred file system.

Central Processing Unit (CPU) A device responsible for the actual execution of instructions stored in applications and operating system code. Windows 7 supports 32- and 64-bit CPUs.

certificate Digital information that describes the identity of a user or computer. A user or computer can inspect the certificate and decide if its validity can be trusted. Certificates are issued by special servers called Certification Authorities (CA). If a user or computer trusts a CA, then they typically trust the certificates issued by the CA.

Challenge-Handshake Authentication Protocol (CHAP) A more secure authentication protocol than PAP. CHAP is used to periodically identify the client identity without sending the actual password over the client and server data stream. CHAP passwords are simple by design and do not support strong security methods.

This presents a security risk and therefore this authentication protocol is discouraged unless the risk from communication eavesdropping is considered low.

Classless Inter-Domain Routing (CIDR) A notation technique that summarizes the number of binary bits in an IP address that identify the network an IP address belongs to, counted starting from the left-hand side of the IP address as written in binary form. The number of bits is written at the end of the IP address with a slash "/" symbol separating the two values (e.g. 192.168.1.0/24 or FE80::/64).

clean installation An installation that is performed on a new computer, or does not retain the user settings or applications of an existing computer.

Client for Microsoft Networks The client that allows Windows 7 to access files and printers shared on other Windows computers by using the SMB protocol.

client A client allows you to communicate with a particular service running on a remote computer.

cluster A unit of storage for reading and writing file data in a file system. The cluster size is determined when a partition or volume is first formatted with a file system. Cluster size is based on the sector size of a disk and the number of sectors used per cluster. Cluster sizes typically range from 512 bytes to 64 KB.

color depth The number of bits that are used to store the color information for each pixel in the display.

COM An abbreviation for Component Object Model, which is a generalized method used by some applications to cross-link to and access each other. This is a broader method than OLE.

Compatibility View A new feature in Internet Explorer 8 that provides backward compatibility for Web sites and application that were targeted for previous versions of Internet Explorer

Computer Management One of the most commonly used Administrative tools. This MMC console contains the snap-ins to manage most Windows 7 components.

configuration partition The Active Directory partition that holds general information about the Active Directory forest and application configuration information. It is replicated to all domain controllers in the Active Directory forest.

configuration set The subset of files from a distribution share that are required for a particular answer file. A configuration set is more compact than a distribution share.

connection (network connection) The clients, services, and protocols that are configured for a network card.

Control Panel A central location for Windows 7 Management utilities. Most system settings are configured here.

cooperative multitasking A method for applications to share the CPU. All applications rotate access to and do not monopolize the CPU. If an application does not release control of the CPU, the computer may appear stalled or other applications appear very sluggish.

counters The performance indicators that can be recorded in Performance Monitor.

Create A Shared Folder Wizard A wizard in Computer Management to create shared folders that does not configure NTFS permissions.

Data Collector Set A grouping of counters that you can use to log system data and generate reports.

Data Execution Prevention (DEP) A primarily processor hardware-based system to prevent the installation of malware by accessing unauthorized memory spaces.

Data Manager The component that is used to automatically manage performance logs.

Data Sources (ODBC) Used to configure data sources for applications that require access to a database.

default gateway A router on the local network that is used to deliver packets to remote networks.

default profile The profile that is copied when new user profiles are created.

defragmentation The process of ordering data on the hard disk in a contiguous fashion to minimize the delays in reading or writing data. This attempts to minimize the mechanical delay caused by having to move read/write mechanisms from one region of the disk to another.

Deployment Image Servicing and Management (DISM) A command-line tool that can be used to service Windows 7 images offline or online.

device driver Software that manages the communication between Windows 7 and a particular hardware component.

device driver signing A system that ensures that a device driver is from a known publisher and that the device driver has not been modified since it was signed.

device identification string One or more identifiers included in a hardware device that is used by Windows 7 to locate and install an appropriate driver for a hardware device.

Device Manager An MMC snap-in that is used to manage hardware components and their device drivers.

device setup class An identifier included with a hardware device driver that describes how the device driver is to be installed.

Device Stage A feature for printers and other devices that displays all of the relevant information and management options for a device in a single location.

Digital subscriber line (DSL) A high-speed Internet connection over telephone lines.

DirectAccess A replacement for VPN access to corporate intranet data sources and applications utilizing bidirectional IPv6 communication with a specialized DirectAccess server. Workstations and users connect separately, allowing corporate IT administrators to manage both.

DirectX A programming standard for writing multimedia applications that interact with video, sound, and input devices such as the keyboard.

Disk Management console An MMC console snap-in used to administer hard disks in Windows 7.

disk partition Hard disks are subdivided into logical units called partitions. Each partition is then formatted and represented as a drive letter in Windows.

Disk quota A system of tracking owners for file data within an NTFS-formatted partition or volume and the total disk space consumed by each owner. Limits or warning can be established to restrict disk space usage.

Display applet A Control Panel applet that gives you links to adjust the screen resolution, calibrate color, change display settings, adjust ClearType text, and set a custom text size

distribution share A share configured through WSIM to hold drivers and packages that can be added to Windows 7 during installation.

distribution share installation An installation of Windows 7 that is started by running Setup.exe over the network from a distribution share.

domain A logical grouping of computers and users in Active Directory.

domain controller A server that holds a copy of Active Directory information.

Domain Name System (DNS) A standard service in the TCP/IP protocol used to define how computer names are translated into IP addresses.

domain network The location type that is used when a computer joined to a domain is on the domain network, for example, a corporate office.

domain partition The Active Directory partition that holds domain-specific information, such as user and computer accounts, that is replicated only between domain controllers within the domain.

domain-based network A network where security information is stored centrally in Active Directory.

Drive letter A letter of the alphabet assigned to a formatted partition or volume as a reference point for future access by the user or their applications.

driver store A central location in Windows 7 where drivers are located before they are installed. A large set of drivers is included with Windows 7.

DSL modem A device that converts DSL signals to standard Ethernet.

dual boot installation A computer with two operating systems installed at the same time. The user selects an operating system during start up.

duplexed mirror A RAID 1 implementation that uses one hardware controller for the first disk in a RAID 1 pair, and a second different hardware controller for the second RAID 1 disk. This increases fault tolerance in the case where a disk controller fails instead of a single disk. IDE and SCSI implementations of RAID 1 would typically use one hardware controller to manage both RAID 1 members. In this case the hardware controller would be a single point of failure.

DVD boot installation An installation of Windows 7 that is started by booting from CD or DVD to run Setup.exe.

dynamic disk A method used to organize disk space into volumes. First introduced with Windows 2000, the dynamic disk method is seen as an improvement over basic disk technology. Not all operating systems support the dynamic disk method of organizing disk space. This may restrict multi-boot configurations. Dynamic disk technology supports simple, spanned, striped, mirrored, and RAID 5 volumes.

Dynamic Host Configuration Protocol (DHCP) An automated mechanism to assign IP addresses and IP configuration information over the network.

Dynamic Link Library files (DLLs) A file that holds application code modules. These modules are shared among applications, so the file is also called a library. DLL files can be replaced to update an application without having to replace the entire application.

Ease of Access Center applet A collection of settings to make Windows 7 easier to use for those that have visual or hearing impairment.

EDID (Extended Display Identification Data) A standard that defines how the monitor hardware can pass details about its abilities to the graphics card and ultimately the operating system. Details such as preferred refresh rate and screen resolution can be set by the monitor manufacturer and EDID will allow this information to be passed to the operating system.

Encrypting File System (EFS) An encryption technology for individual files and folders that can be enabled by users.

enhanced metafile format (EMF) The format used for spool files in pre-Windows Vista versions of Windows.

environment subsystems Support systems designed for specific types of applications, such as Win32 applications. The environment hides the details of how the application must communicate with lower-level operating system components such as the Executive Services. Environment subsystems operate on a user-mode basis but have awareness of kernel mode services hosted through Executive Services.

Event Viewer An MMC console that is used to view messages generated and logged by Windows 7, applications, and services.

Executive Services A collection of kernel model support modules to manage low-level duties in the operating system such as scheduling processes, managing memory, managing virtual environments, and running core kernel programming.

Extended File Allocation Table (exFAT) A proprietary Microsoft file system used with external storage media to organize files and folders using a technology similar to FAT but without the space limitations of FAT32. Volume sizes over 32 GB are fully supported.

extended partition A reserved block of space on a basic disk. No more than one extended partition can exist on a single basic disk. Logical partitions are created within the extended partition. Extended partitions cannot be formatted with a file system directly.

Extensible Authentication Protocol (EAP) A modular standard for defining authentication protocols that can be used to validate a computer or user. A product developer can introduce a custom authentication protocol for their product if it is not already included with Windows 7. EAP is available as an authentication standard with dial-up, VPN, and wireless connections.

Extensible Firmware Interface (EFI) A standard initially created by Intel to replace the BIOS based computer firmware.

eXtensible Markup Language (XML) A standard for formatting data that is exchanged between applications. By using a standard, application developers do not have to write custom data translators for every product with which their applications share data.

Fast user switching Allows multiple users to have applications running at the same time. However, only one user can be using the console at a time.

FAT A generic term that refers to early versions of the FAT file system (FAT12, FAT16) or to any FAT file system in general, also see File Allocation Table.

File Allocation Table (FAT) An older method of organizing files and folders in a hard disk partition. Files are stored in blocks of data that point to each other in a chain-like structure. The blocks that are used in the partition and the link from one to another are stored in a master table called the FAT.

File and Printer Sharing for Microsoft Networks The service that allows Windows 7 to share files and printers by using the SMB protocol.

File extension Typically a three-character name at the end of a file name that is used to indicate the type of data contained in the file. Common extension examples include DOC for documents and EXE for executable programs.

File Signature Verification utility A utility that verifies the digital signature on operating system files and device drivers.

Folder Options applet Configures the behavior of Windows Explorer, including whether file extensions are hidden for known file types, and whether hidden files are displayed.

Foreign Disk A dynamic disk that is recognized as not belonging to the computer it is currently installed in. Until the disk is imported, to change its dynamic disk computer membership, the volumes it contains are not accessible.

forest Multiple Active Directory trees with automatic trust relationships between them.

forest root domain The first domain created in an Active Directory forest.

Full Volume Encryption Key (FVEK) The key used to encrypt the VMK when BitLocker Drive Encryption is enabled.

game controls A part of Parental Controls that is used to limit access to games.

generalization A process performed by Sysprep to prepare a computer running Windows 7 for imaging. The computer SID, computer name, user profiles, and hardware information are removed during generalization.

generalize configuration pass This configuration pass is performed when Sysprep is run to generalize Windows 7.

getmac A command-line utility that can be used to display the MAC address for network adapters on a system.

global catalog server A domain controller that holds a subset of the information in all domain partitions for the entire Active Directory forest.

Graphical Processing Unit (GPU) A hardware component, similar to the CPU, that is added to video cards to calculate how to draw complex shapes on the screen. Because the GPU can perform the complex operations on its own, the CPU is free to work on other tasks.

Graphics Device Interface (GDI) The format used for displaying screen content in pre-Windows Vista versions of Windows.

Group Policy A feature integrated with Active Directory that can be used to centrally manage the configuration of Windows 2000 and newer Windows computers, including Windows 7.

Group Policy Object (GPO) A collection of Group Policy settings that can be applied to client computers.

Group Policy service The service responsible for retrieving and applying GPOs for a Windows 7 computer.

Guest account An account with minimal privileges intended to give minimal access to Windows 7. This account is disabled by default.

GUID (Globally Unique Identifier) A label that identifies an item with a unique name or code that is used to tell it apart from similar items. Software typically uses a coded number or value to represent a unique identifier.

GUID Partition Table (GPT) A disk partitioning style that allows more partitions and advanced partition information when compared to the older MBR style disk partition scheme. Desktop computers only use GPT in specialized and limited cases due to its limited applicability.

Hardware Abstraction Layer (HAL) Part of the operating system that understands how to talk to the specific computer hardware on which the operating system is installed. This portion of the operating system runs at the lowest level of the application hierarchy in kernel mode.

Hardware Compatibility List (HCL) A legacy method of determining if hardware is compatible with the operating system. This has been replaced by the Windows Catalog and the Windows Marketplace Web site.

hash encryption algorithm A one-way encryption algorithm that creates a unique identifier that can be used to determine whether data has been changed.

hibernate See S4 state.

hives A discrete body of registry keys and values stored in files as part of the operating system.

Home network The location type that is used for highly trusted networks where security is minimal and convenient sharing with other computers is a priority.

HomeGroup A new feature in Windows 7 that is used to configure file and printer sharing for small peer-to-peer computer networks.

hostname A command-line utility that can be used to identify the name of the computer.

hotspot A geographic area where a Wi-Fi wireless signal from a Wireless Access Point is available to wireless networking clients to enable network and/or Internet access.

hybrid sleep The sleep method used by Windows 7 that combines the S3 state and S4 state. When the computer moves to the S3 state, it also saves the memory file required for the S4 state.

HyperText Transport Protocol Secure (HTTPS) An application protocol commonly used to transfer TCP data in a secured session between a client and server. Because this is a common protocol used with Web servers, many firewalls allow this protocol to pass without blocking it.

Hyper-Threading A technique used in certain Intel processors to improve their overall performance by working on more than one thread at a time. When one thread is waiting for an operation to complete a second thread can use some of the processor's hardware instead of the processor just idling. This extra work is done inside the processor's hardware and is specific to the design of the processor itself. Programmers writing application threads and the operating system that schedules those threads to run must be aware of the benefits and limits of the Hyper-Threaded processor to take best advantage of any performance gain that might be possible.

IEEE (Institute of Electrical and Electronics Engineers) A professional society that promotes and nurtures the development of standards used in the application of electronic technology.

IKEv2 Mobility and Multihoming Protocol (MOBIKE) A protocol designed to work together with IKEv2 to allow a host involved in a secure IKEv2 initiated SA to change its IP address, switch to a different network interface, or recover from a network outage.

image A collection of files captured using ImageX and stored in an image file.

image file A file that stores one or more images. The size of an image file is minimized through the use of single-instance storage when a file exists in multiple images.

image-based installation An image-based installation that uses ImageX to apply an image of an operating system to a computer. The image can include applications as well as the operating system.

ImageX A command-line tool for managing WIM images.

indexing service A service that indexes files in specified locations to speed up search queries.

Industry Standard Architecture (ISA) A legacy standard for connecting expansion cards to the motherboard in computers.

initial account The account with administrative privileges created during the installation of Windows 7.

InPrivate Browsing An Internet Explorer 8 feature that prevents caching of Web content and logging of Web activity in Internet Explorer.

InPrivate Filtering An Internet Explorer 8 feature that allows you to control which advertisers get access to your information.

Integrated Service Digital Network (ISDN) A direct, digital dial-up connection to a PSTN that operates at 64 KB per channel over regular twisted-pair cable between a subscriber and the PSTN office.

Internet Connection Sharing (ICS) A Windows 7 feature that allows multiple computers to share an Internet connection by performing NAT.

Internet Key Exchange version 2 (IKEv2) An authentication protocol that identifies the identity of both the client and server to each other. Once the identity of both sides is established, one or more IPSec based SAs are established between them for data transfer. IKEv2 is considered a strong authentication protocol.

Internet Options Settings to control Internet Explorer, including security settings.

Internet Protocol Version 4 (TCP/IPv4) The standard protocol used on corporate networks and the Internet.

Internet Protocol Version 6 (TCP/IPv6) An updated version of TCP/IPv4 with a much larger address space.

IP address The unique address used by computers on an IPv4 or IPv6 network. An IPv4 address is commonly displayed in dotted decimal notation. For example, 10.10.0.50.

ipconfig A command-line utility that can be used to display and manage IP address settings for network interfaces on a computer.

IP-HTTPS A protocol that allows a secure IP tunnel to be established with a secure HTTP connection for the purpose of transporting IPv6 packets. A IP-HTTPS client must initiate a connection to a configured IP-HTTPS server. The connection between client and server is not likely to be stopped by a firewall because the HTTPS protocol is not commonly blocked.

IPSec A protocol that is used to secure and authenticate IP connections.

iSCSI A protocol for transferring files between a computer and external disk storage over an Ethernet network.

kernel The operating system software that runs in kernel mode on the computer's processor and which provides low-level intelligence for the operating system.

kernel mode An access mode for applications while they are running on the CPU that allows full access to all hardware devices and memory in the computer.

Last Known Good configuration A recovery option that restores settings in the registry hive HKEY_LOCAL_MACHINE\SYSTEM\CurrentControlSet that were in place the last time the computer was started successfully and a user logged on.

Layer 2 Tunneling Protocol (L2TP) A protocol used to carry PPP packets through IP networks.

Libraries Virtual folders in Windows Explorer that combine content from multiple locations to simplify file access.

Link Layer Topology Discovery Mapper I/O Driver The protocol responsible for discovering network devices on the network and determining network speed.

Link Layer Topology Discovery Responder The protocol responsible for responding to discovery requests from other computers.

Link-Local Multicast Name Resolution (LLMNR) A protocol that defines methods for name resolution of local neighboring computers without using DNS, WINS, or NetBIOS name resolution services. LLMNR can operate on IPv4 and IPv6 networks with the use of specially crafted multicast addresses to query client names on other computers.

local security policy A set of security configuration options in Windows 7. These options are used to control user rights, auditing, password settings, and more.

local user account A user account that is defined in the SAM database of a Windows 7 computer. Local user accounts are valid only for the local computer.

Local Users and Groups MMC snap-in An MMC snap-in that is used to manage users and groups.

location aware printing A feature for mobile computers that associates a specific default printer with a physical location.

location type Describes the type of network: public, private, or domain. Different configuration settings are applied based on the location type.

logical partition A reserved block of space on a basic disk. Logical partitions can only be created within an extended partition. As long as free space exists in an extended partition, a new logical partition can be created. Logical partitions can be formatted with a file system directly.

Long file names File names that can be a maximum of 255 characters in length.

malware Malicious software designed to perform unauthorized acts on your computer. Malware includes viruses, worms, and spyware.

Manage Add-ons A new tool in Internet Explorer 8 that makes it easier to identify, disable, and remove unwanted Add-ons.

mandatory profile A profile that cannot be changed by users. NTUSER.DAT is renamed to NTUSER.MAN.

Master Boot Record (MBR) The Master Boot Record exists at the very first sector of an IBM-formatted hard disk. It contains code to start the load process for an operating system from a partition or volume on the disk, a partition table to indicate what space has been reserved as partitions, and a signature sequence of bytes used to identify the disk to the operating system. When the disk is used as a basic disk, the partition table is used to identify primary, extended, and logical partition types. When the disk is used as a dynamic disk, the partition table is filled with placeholder values and the volume information is actually held in a 1 MB dynamic volume database at the end of the drive.

member server A server that is joined to an Active Directory domain, but does not hold a copy of Active Directory information.

metadata Information or properties for a file or other object. Windows 7 allows you to include tags as additional metadata for files.

Microsoft Deployment Toolkit (MDT) A set of best practices, scripts, and tools to help automate the deployment of Windows operating systems.

Microsoft Management Console (MMC) A graphical interface shell that provides a structured environment to build management utilities.

Microsoft Security Essentials Free antivirus software that is available if your copy of Windows 7 is genuine.

mirrored volume A RAID 1 implementation using dynamic disks.

MMC A standard for graphical management utilities called Microsoft Management Consoles (MMC). Management consoles can be added as snap-ins for a bare-bones MMC application.

MMC console A collection of one or more snap-ins that are saved as an .msc file for later use.

MMC snap-in A small software component that can be added to an MMC console to provide functionality. An MMC snap-in typically manages some part of Windows.

MOBIKE See IKEv2 Mobility and Multihoming Protocol.

modem A device that converts computer signals to a format that can travel over phones (modulate) and also performs the reverse function (demodulate).

mount point An empty folder in an NTFS-formatted file system that is used to point to another FAT, FAT32, or NTFS partition.

MS-CHAP-v1&2 A Microsoft version of the Challenge-Handshake Authentication Protocol (CHAP). MS-CHAP-v1 adds features to change the password during a session, as well as limit authentication retries, between a client and server. MS-CHAP-v2 added the ability for both sides to confirm each other's identity instead of just the server confirming the client's identity.

multimaster replication A replication system where updates can be performed on any server and are replicated to all other servers.

multiple monitors Attaching two or more displays to a single computer. The information can be exactly the same on each display, or each display can be used independently by using extended mode.

multiprocessor A term used to refer to a computer with more than one CPU.

multitasking A term used to describe the appearance of more than one application sharing the CPU of the computer. To the user, the applications all seem to be running at the same time.

nbtstat A command-line utility that can be used to display protocol statistics and current TCP/IP connections using NetBIOS over TCP/IP.

netsh A command-line utility that can be used to display, change, add, and delete network configuration settings on a computer, including basic and advanced settings.

netstat A command-line utility that can be used to display protocol statistics and current TCP/IP network connections.

Network Access Protection (NAP) A computer authorization system for networks that prevents unhealthy computers from accessing the network.

network address translation (NAT) A system that allows multiple computers to share a single IP address when connecting to the Internet.

Network and Sharing Center A central location used to view network status and detailed network information.

network bridge A feature in Windows 7 that combines two dissimilar network types, such as wireless and wired, into a single network.

network discovery A setting that controls how your computer views other computers on the network and advertises its presence on the network.

network driver The software responsible for enabling communication between Windows 7 and the network device in your computer.

Network Driver Interface Specification (NDIS) An interface that supports communication between network protocols and network drivers.

network location awareness The ability for Windows 7 to detect when it is connected to a different network and perform actions based on the change.

Network Location Awareness Service (NLA) A service that allows applications to track the state of the network connections available to the computer. An application can track how much data can be sent over a connection, if it is available, or if new connections appear. Based on this information, the application can modify its attempts to communicate over the network.

New Technology File System (NTFS) A file system introduced with Windows NT. NTFS supports advanced features to add reliability, security, and flexibility that file systems such as FAT and FAT32 do not have. NTFS is the preferred file system for use with Windows 7.

nslookup A command-line utility that can be used to view or debug the data returned from a DNS server in response to a DNS name resolution query.

NTFS See New Technology File System.

NTUSER.DAT The file containing user-specific registry entries in a user profile.

offline update An offline update is applied to Windows 7 during installation before Windows 7 is started. The packages used for offline updates are supplied by Microsoft.

offlineServicing configuration pass The second configuration pass that is performed after the Windows image has been copied to the local hard drive. This configuration pass applies packages such as security updates and service packs before Windows 7 is started.

OLE An abbreviation for Object Linking and Embedding, which is a method used by some applications to cross-link to each other.

oobeSystem configuration pass The final configuration pass before installation is complete. This configuration pass is typically used in conjunction with Sysprep and ImageX.

organizational unit (OU) A container within a domain that is used to create a hierarchy that can be used to organize user and computer accounts and apply group policies.

Parental Controls A method for configuring time limits, controlling game playing, and allowing or blocking programs.

partition table A data structure contained in the MBR that is used to identify reserved areas of disk space for hard disks formatted for x86 computers. The partition table holds a maximum of four entries originally tasked to point to a maximum of four primary partitions, or three primary and one extended partitions.

Password Authentication Protocol (PAP) A simple authentication method that establishes the identity of a remote client with the authentication password sent in the data stream between the client and server. This presents a security risk and therefore this authentication protocol is discouraged unless the risk from communication eavesdropping is considered low.

password policy A collection of settings to control password characteristics such as length and complexity.

pathping A command-line utility that can be used to test IP communications between the computer running the utility and a remote target. In addition to the basic IP communication test, the pathping utility will trace the routers involved in establishing the IP communication path.

peer-to-peer network A network where all computers store their own security information and share data.

Performance Monitor An MMC console used to monitor and troubleshoot the performance of your computer.

performance tuning The process for collecting system performance data, analyzing system performance data, and implementing system performance improvements.

Peripheral Component Interface (PCI) A current standard for connecting expansion cards to a computer motherboard. PCI devices are plug and play.

ping A command-line utility that can be used to test IP communications between the computer running the utility and a remote target.

pixel A single dot on the display.

Plain Old Telephone System (POTS) See Public Switched Telephone Network (PSTN).

Plug and Play technology A general term used to describe hardware that can be plugged in to the computer system and removed at any time. The computer will recognize the hardware dynamically, load a device driver for it, and make it available to the user in a short period of time.

point and print A system used by Windows to distribute printer drivers over the network when network printers are installed.

Point-to-Point Protocol (PPP) A network-layer transport protocol that manages connectivity over serial or modem lines. PPP can negotiate any transport protocol used by both systems involved in the link and can automatically assign TCP/IP settings.

Point-to-Point Protocol over Ethernet (PPPoE) A protocol used to secure connections over most DSL lines.

Point-to-Point Tunneling Protocol (PPTP) A protocol used to carry PPP packets through IP networks.

Popup Blocker An Internet Explorer feature that prevents most popup advertising from being displayed while you browse Web sites.

Postscript A common language used by printers to describe how a page is printed.

power plan A set of configuration options for power management. The Balanced, Power save, and High performance power plans are created by default.

Preboot eXecution Environment (PXE) A standard used by network cards to boot directly to the network and download an operating system. Once that operating system is started, tasks such as imaging can be performed.

preemptive multitasking A method for applications to share a CPU and appear that they are all running at the same time. This method adds time limits and priority levels to determine how long an application can use the processor and which application gets to go next. An application can also be preempted by another application if it has a higher priority level.

preshared keys A combination of numbers, characters, and symbols that make up a pass-phrase that both sides of an authenticated and encrypted network connection must know to decode the data delivered between them successfully.

Primary DC (PDC) A specialized Windows NT server that is responsible for holding a writeable copy of the domain security database.

primary partition A reserved region of disk space on a basic disk that is capable of loading an operating system. The first sector of the primary partition is also known as a boot sector and stores the code for beginning the operating system load process from that primary partition.

Print Management snap-in A new printer management tool in Windows 7 that allows you to manage local and remote printers.

Printer Control Language (PCL) A common language used by printers to describe how a page is printed.

printer driver Software used by Windows 7 to properly communicate with a specific make and model of printer.

printer driver package An enhanced printer driver that can contain additional software.

printer driver store A location in Windows 7 that caches printer drivers and is capable of storing multiple versions of a printer driver.

private network The location type that is used for trusted networks where limited security is required, for example, a small office.

Problem Steps Recorder A new tool included in Windows 7 that allows users to record the exact steps required to reproduce a problem. The recorded steps can then be forwarded to help desk staff for analysis.

process A term used to describe the files, memory, and application code that combine together to form a single running application. Each application running on a multitasking system is referenced by a single process.

processor affinity A standard in which a process that starts in a computer with more than one CPU is usually assigned to that CPU again the next time it runs.

product activation A process put in place by Microsoft to reduce piracy. Unique information about your computer is sent to Microsoft to ensure that the package of Windows 7 purchased is installed on only a single computer.

Protected Extensible Authentication Protocol (PEAP) An enhancement of EAP that encrypts the entire EAP process. This protects all EAP communication before authentication is performed.

public network The location type that is used for untrusted networks where high security is required, for example, a public wireless hotspot.

public profile A profile that is merged with all other user profiles. The public profile does not contain an NTUSER.DAT file.

Public Switched Telephone Network (PSTN) Provides a connection to subscribers for dial-up devices such as analog or ISDN modems. Originally developed to connect telephones and allow people to make analog phone calls.

quantum The amount of time allocated to a program running in a preemptive multitasking environment. Once a program's quantum has expired, it must wait for the next available quantum.

RAID 0 A collection of disks that combine their storage capacity by striping data across all drives. Data is written in a fixed block size, typically sized in KB, in a sequential fashion to each disk. The first block of data for a file is written to the first disk, the second block of data to the second disk, and so on until the last drive is reached. The next block of data starts over with the first drive and the process continues with each subsequent block of data written to the next disk. This type of storage is not fault tolerant and the failure of a single disk will result in the loss of all file data. This type of storage will generally improve write and read performance when compared with a single disk. The number of disks that can be pooled this way is limited by the operating system or hardware controller used to pool the disks.

RAID 1 Two disks are used to store a single copy of file data in a fault-tolerant fashion. An exact copy of the data is written to each disk. If one disk fails, the other copy allows continued operation. Performance is similar to a single disk where reads are generally faster and writes can be slower. Both disks can be on a single controller, which introduces a common point of failure. If the hardware used to control each disk is fully duplicated into independent channels, the system is referred to as a duplexed mirror.

RAID 5 A collection of disks that combine their storage capacity by striping data and error-correcting parity information across all drives. The parity information is calculated from the data itself and can be used to identify and regenerate damaged or missing data. The data and parity information is striped in the same fashion as RAID 0 data. RAID 5 is fault tolerant in that a single disk in the collection may fail and the missing data can be calculated from the remaining data and parity information distributed across the remaining disks. A multiple disk failure will result in the loss of all data in the collection. The disks space cost for parity information is approximately the same as the size of disks space contributed from one disk member. For example, if five 10 GB disks are collected into a single RAID 5 solution then the space of one disk, 10 GB, is consumed by parity information. The remainder of 40 GB is available for file storage. A minimum of three disks is required to build a RAID 5 solution.

RAM Random Access Memory, otherwise known as chip-based memory that stores instructions and data in silicon-based chips that are very quick to access but only suitable for short-term data storage.

Really Simple Syndication (RSS) A format for distributing content as articles. Internet Explorer 7 is capable of reading RSS feeds.

Redundant Array of Independent Disks (RAID) Also known as Redundant Array of Inexpensive Disks. A standard reference to a collection of disks grouped to store data. The RAID level indicates the type of grouping and is indicated by a number following the term RAID. Common RAID levels are RAID 0 striped storage, RAID 1 mirrored storage, and RAID 5 striped storage with error-correcting information.

Region and Language Options applet Used to configure display and input options to support different languages and regions. Settings include time, date, and number formats.

registry key A level in a hive's hierarchy defined by its name and position relative to other keys in the hive hierarchy. A registry key can contain subkeys (other registry keys), values, or both.

Reliability Monitor A tool that rates the system stability of Windows 7 and lets you monitor the events that contribute to system stability.

remote access A system where clients are able to remotely connect to a network and access resources as though the remote client is connected directly to the network.

remote control A system where clients are able to remotely connect to a server to run applications and access data. Applications and files are accessed at the server and only screen drawing commands are sent back to the client.

Remote Desktop (RD) Terminal Services has been rebranded as Remote Desktop Services in Windows Server 2008 R2.

Remote Desktop Protocol (RDP) A protocol used to carry remote control data between the remote control client and the remotely controlled computer.

Remote Installation Services (RIS) The server-based system available in Windows Server 2003 SP2 and later versions for deploying desktop operating systems automatically over the network.

removable disk storage A mass storage device that can be removed from the computer, either by powering down the computer first or while the computer is running. This includes floppy disks, portable hard disks, and cartridge-based disk storage.

Reports Reports created in Performance Monitor that use XML-based rules to analyze logged data and display meaningful results.

Resource Monitor A utility launched from Performance Monitor that provides real-time monitoring of the most common system performance indicators.

ring level A security level in the CPU that is used to determine a program's degree of access to memory and hardware. The ring levels are used to set user and kernel mode access in the operating system.

roaming profile A user profile that is stored in a network location and is accessible from multiple computers. Roaming profiles move with users from computer to computer.

route A command-line utility that can be used to display and manage the routing table.

router Traditionally, a network device that moves packets from one network to another. The routers sold in retail stores are used to share an Internet connection by performing NAT.

Routing and Remote Access (RRAS) A service installed and configured on Windows Server 2003 to allow remote clients and networks to connect to network services local to the server. The Routing and Remote Access service must be configured to support VPN connections, dial-up connections, and routed IP traffic from routers.

routing table A data table that is used by Windows 7 to select the next IP address data must be delivered to ultimately deliver data to a given target address.

Run as administrator An option to start an application with elevated security privileges.

S0 state An ACPI power saving mode that disables power to specific devices as requested by the operating system, but keeps the overall system running.

S3 state An ACPI power saving mode that disables power to all devices except RAM.

S4 state An ACPI power saving mode that saves the contents of RAM to disk and then disables power to all devices including RAM.

Safe Mode A troubleshooting startup mode that is typically used when the regular startup mode for Windows 7 fails.

saved search A virtual folder that contains the files matching a search query.

schema partition Holds the definition of all Active Directory objects and their attributes. It is replicated to all domain controllers in the Active Directory forest.

screen resolution The number of pixels that are displayed on your display.

Secedit A command-line tool that is used to apply, export, or analyze security templates.

sector A single unit of storage for a hard disk that represents the smallest block of data that can be read or written to the disk. The typical hard disk sector size is 512 bytes.

secure logon Adds the requirement to press Ctrl+Alt+Del before logging on.

Secure Socket Tunneling Protocol (SSTP) A protocol that allows secure communication between a VPN client and server using the SSL based encryption methods of HTTPS. The connection between client and server is not likely to be stopped by a firewall because the HTTPS protocol is not commonly blocked.

Security Accounts Manager (SAM) database The database used by Windows 7 to store local user and group information.

Security Association (SA) A connection established between two computers for the purpose of securely exchanging data. The connection is only allowed if both sides of the connection know how to find each other on the network, agree on how to authenticate their identities, and agree on how to encrypt and decrypt the data sent between them. Any aspect of the SA connection may be renegotiated periodically to ensure that the other side of the connection is still a valid communication partner.

Security Configuration and Analysis tool An MMC snap-in that is used to apply, export, or analyze security templates.

security identifier (SID) A coded value assigned to a user account when it is first created to act as a unique identifier that is not duplicated for any other account. The security identifier is unique, regardless of what name is assigned to the user's account.

Security Identifier (SID) A number that is added to the access control list of a resource when a user or group is assigned access.

Security Set Identifier (SSID) A unique ID that identifies a wireless access point to the wireless networking clients that send data to it.

security template An .inf file that contains security settings that can be applied to a computer or analyzed against a computer's existing configuration.

Serial Line IP (SLIP) An implementation of the IP protocol over serial lines. SLIP has been made obsolete by PPP.

Server Message Block (SMB) The protocol used for Windows-based file and printer sharing. Windows 7 includes SMB version 2.1.

service A Windows application that runs in the background without user interaction. Provides functionality to remote clients over the network.

Services administrative tool An MMC console used to manage Windows services.

Shadow copy A snapshot of the file system that tracks changes to files and allows the restoration of previous file versions.

Share With A wizard that simplifies the setup process of sharing folders and configuring relevant share and NTFS permissions.

simple volume A reserved area of space on a single dynamic disk. A simple volume can be formatted with a file system. The areas of space reserved for a simple volume do not have to be contiguous on the dynamic disk.

smart card A small physical card that contains a processor and memory. The processor is capable of interacting with a computer in which the card is plugged. The most common use of a smart card is to store and validate personal security credentials for a computer or user. The smart card can be physically removed and stored in a small space, such as a wallet.

SmartScreen Filter An Internet Explorer 8 feature that warns you about Web sites known to install malicious software or used in phishing attacks.

Software Assurance (SA) An option when purchasing Microsoft software that allows you to automatically receive the latest version of a product. For example, if you purchased Windows XP with Software Assurance you would automatically be able to upgrade to Windows 7.

Sound applet Configures the properties for the audio devices in your system and configures a sound scheme.

spanned volume A reserved area of space combined from two or more dynamic disks. A spanned volume can be formatted with a file system. Files are written to each disk's reserved area of space until that area is full. Additional file data is then written to the next available reserved area of space on the next disk that is part of the spanned volume. The capacity of the spanned volume is the total of all reserved areas of space from each disk that is a member of the spanned volume. Loss of a single disk that holds part of the spanned volume will result in the total loss of the volume.

specialize configuration pass The configuration pass that is performed after hardware has been detected. This is the most common configuration pass to apply settings.

Speech Recognition Options applet Configures how Windows 7 performs speech recognition, and allows you to train speech recognition for your voice.

standard user account A type of user account that does not have privileges to modify settings for other users. This type of account is a member of the Users local group.

standby See S3 state.

Startup Repair Tool A tool provided in Windows 7 to help users determine why their computer failed and what they should do to repair it.

striped volume A RAID 0 implementation using dynamic disks.

subkey A subordinate or lower level registry key within a hive that can contain values and other subkeys.

subnet mask A number that defines which part of an IP address is the network ID and which part is the host ID.

subscores The rating of individual subsystems in your computer.

Suggested Sites A list of Web sites provided by Internet Explorer 8 based on the content that you are currently looking at.

symmetric encryption algorithm An encryption algorithm that uses the same key to encrypt and decrypt data.

Sysprep A tool that is used to generalize Windows 7 and prepare computers for imaging.

System applet Shows basic information about your computer, such as Windows edition, performance rating, and activation status. Links are provided to configure system properties.

System Audit Mode cleanup action An option in Sysprep that triggers the computer to enter Audit mode and run the auditSystem and auditUser configuration passes on reboot.

System Center Configuration Manager (SCCM) A software package that can perform inventory, implement a standardized configuration, deploy software, deploy operating systems, and deploy software updates.

System Configuration The Administrative Tool that gives you access to control the boot configuration, service startup, application startup, and system tools.

System Image Recovery A backup option to save the current operating system partition and all of its data to an image-based file.

System Information A tool that scans the current state of the computer and reports its findings in a searchable tree format.

System Out-of-Box Experience cleanup action An option in Sysprep that triggers the computer to run the oobeSystem configuration pass and start Windows Welcome on reboot.

system partition The partition or volume used to initiate the boot sequence for a computer from a hard disk. The system partition is processed before the boot partition, which loads the remainder of the operating system. The system partition can be the same partition as the boot partition.

System Restore A recovery option that restores the operating system to a previously saved state by reversing changes to Windows system files, the registry, and newly installed software.

tabbed browsing A feature in Internet Explorer 8 that allows multiple Web sites to be open in the same window.

Tablet PC Settings applet Configures settings that are specific to tablet PCs such as screen menu locations and handwriting recognition.

tags Additional metadata that can be added to the properties of a file.

Task Manager A utility that allows you to view overall system information and manipulate processes.

Task Scheduler A utility that allows you to schedule tasks to run at a particular time or based on specific events occurring.

Taskbar and Start Menu applet Configures the behavior of the taskbar and Start menu, including which toolbars are displayed on the taskbar.

Terabyte A unit of data that consists of 1024 gigabytes. Commonly abbreviated as TB.

Teredo A system to tunnel IPv6 addressed packets over an IPv4 network, even if NAT is used on the IPv4 network.

Terminal Services (TS) A service that can be installed on a computer running a server-based operating system. Depending on licensing limits, multiple users can connect to the Terminal Server and run applications on the Terminal Server using only a remote control client. Each remote user is unaware that other users are also remote controlling applications on the Terminal Server.

thread A piece of code that performs a specific single task. An application is written as one or more threads, each of which performs a specific task within the application. The thread is typically seen as a unit of work for the CPU to perform.

thunking A method where data and parameters passed from 16-bit software to 32-bit software is translated in a bidirectional manner.

time limits A part of Parental Controls that is used to control when users are allowed to log on to the computer.

tracert A command-line utility that can be used to trace the routers involved in establishing an IP communication path between the computer running the command and a target address.

Transport Device Interface (TDI) A legacy interface that supports the NetBIOS protocol used by many older Windows applications.

tree A group of Active Directory domains that share the same naming context and have automatic trust relationships among them.

Trusted Platform Module (TPM) A motherboard module that is used to store encryption keys and certificates.

TrustedInstaller A special security service designed to restrict access to critical operating system files and registry settings. Administrators and the operating system only have read-only access to resources protected by TrustedInstaller. The TrustedInstaller service will not install an update unless Microsoft digitally signs the update.

unattend.xml An answer file that is automatically searched for during the generalize, auditSystem, auditUser, and oobeSystem configuration passes.

unattended installation An installation that does not require any user input because all necessary configuration information is provided by an answer file.

Unified Extensible Firmware Interface (UEFI) An open standard that builds on the proprietary EFI standard started by Intel to replace the legacy BIOS firmware design.

Universal Disk Format (UDF) A third-party standard that defines how data is stored on removable media such as DVD disks.

Universal Naming Convention (UNC) A naming system used by windows computers to locate network file shares and network printers. The format is \\servername\sharename.

upgrade installation An installation that migrates all of the settings from a preexisting operating system to Windows 7.

user account User accounts are used for authentication to prove the identity of a person logging on to Windows 7.

User Account Control (UAC) A feature in Windows 7 that elevates user privileges only when required.

User Accounts applet A simplified interface for user management in Control Panel.

user mode An access mode for applications while they are running on the CPU that allows restricted access to all hardware devices and memory in the computer. This mode makes it difficult for the running application to corrupt and crash the operating system. System-level applications may need more access than is allowed and must use kernel mode instead.

User Profiles applet An applet that is used to copy or remove user profiles.

User State Migration Tool (USMT) A set of scriptable command-line utilities that are used to migrate user settings and files from a source computer to a destination computer. USMT is typically used by large organizations during deployments of desktop operating systems.

VGA A standard low-resolution graphics mode that is typically used when troubleshooting incompatible video drivers or drivers set to a high resolution that is not supported by the attached monitor.

Virtual DOS Machine (VDM) A Win32 application that emulates a DOS environment for use by DOS and Win16 applications.

Virtual Hard Disk (VHD) Disk space that stores files and folders in a formatted file system. The disk space is not an actual physical device; it is actually stored in a single file. That file will have the extension ".vhd". Once the vhd file is created it can be attached, or opened for use. The operating system can use the space inside the file as if it was an actual disk device, but it is really a virtual disk. The vhd file itself is stored on a real physical device.

virtual memory The combination of physical memory and the paging file.

virtual private network (VPN) A remote access technology that creates an encrypted tunnel for communication between the VPN client and a remote access server. VPN connections are commonly used over the Internet to secure communication when accessing office data from home.

virtualization software Software that allows you to run multiple operating systems on a single computer at the same time. One operating system functions as the host, while others are guest operating systems that run on the host.

volume A term used to refer to a region of disk space reserved to store file data. The term is used to generically refer to both dynamic disk volumes and basic disk partitions.

Volume Master Key (VMK) The key used to encrypt hard drive data when BitLocker Drive Encryption is enabled.

Web Slices Small pieces of content from a Web site that notify you in Internet Explorer 8 when there is an update.

Wide Area Network (WAN) A geographically dispersed network connected by routers and communication links. The Internet is the largest WAN.

Wi-Fi Protected Access (WPA) A security protocol for wireless 802.11 networks that provides stronger security than WEP. WPA can be configured with a preshared key or with authentication from a central authority.

Win16 Applications designed to run in a Windows 16-bit instruction environment.

Win32 Applications designed to run in a Windows 32-bit instruction environment.

Win64 Applications designed to run in a Windows 64-bit instruction environment.

Windows 7 Compatability Center A list of software or hardware and associated device drivers that have been tested with Windows 7.

Windows Automated Installation Kit (WAIK) A collection of utilities and documentation for automating the deployment of Windows 7.

Windows Defender Anti-spyware software included with Windows 7.

Windows Deployment Services (WDS) A server-based system for deploying desktop operating systems automatically over the network. PXE is used to connect the computers to WDS.

Windows Display Driver Model (WDDM) A standard API for writing device drivers that are compatible with the newer graphical subsystem that is part of Windows 7.

Windows Driver Foundation (WDF) A standard for writing device drivers that interact with Windows 7. This standard replaces WDM and adds new features such as support for user mode device drivers.

Windows Driver Model (WDM) An older standard for writing device drivers that interact with Windows. Device drivers that use this standard are still supported, but should be replaced with drivers that use the new WDF architecture.

Windows Easy Transfer A graphical wizard for migrating user files and settings from Windows 2000 Professional, Windows XP, or Windows Vista to a new Windows 7 computer.

Windows Experience Index Scores that help you determine which applications your computer can run.

Windows Fax and Scan A utility in Windows 7 to manage scanning and faxing.

Windows Firewall A host-based firewall included with Windows 7 that can perform inbound and outbound packet filtering.

Windows Firewall with Advanced Security utility An utility that is used to configure Windows Firewall and IPsec rules.

Windows Flip Displays a live thumbnail of each open Window as you use ALT-Tab to select a window.

Windows Flip 3D Displays each open Window in a three-dimensional list and allows you to scroll through the windows using the mouse wheel.

Windows Hardware Quality Labs (WHQL) A service provided by Microsoft to hardware developers and vendors to test their hardware with different versions of Windows. This testing only validates that a device works with Windows; it does not compare devices.

Windows Imaging Format (WIM) A format to store images of applications and operating systems in image files. These images represent customized installations that can be distributed to other computers and installed using a scripted solution.

Windows Internet Naming Service (WINS) A system used to resolve computer NetBIOS names to IP addresses.

Windows Management Instrumentation (WMI) The Windows Management Interface is a standard for accessing operating system operational status and configuration controls through remote management utilities.

Windows Memory Diagnostics Tool A utility used to perform tests on the physical memory of a computer.

Windows Mobility Center A single location that you can use to configure the mostly commonly used settings on mobile devices.

Windows PE A limited version of Windows that can be used to perform recovery tasks and install Windows 7.

Windows PowerShell An enhanced command-line interface that can be used to perform administrative tasks.

Windows Resource Protection A Windows 7 feature that protects system files and registry keys from unauthorized changes.

Windows Server Update Services (WSUS) A Windows Server application that is used to control the process of downloading and applying updates to Windows 2000, Windows XP, Windows Vista, and Windows 7 clients.

Windows Sockets (Winsock) user mode An interface that supports communication between user applications such as a Web browser and the TCP/IP protocol.

Windows System Image Manager (WSIM) A utility that is used to create answer files for Windows 7 unattended installations. WSIM can also create distribution shares and configuration sets.

Windows Update A service that automatically downloads and installs service packs and security updates.

Windows Welcome The default logon method for Windows 7. This method presents icons representing each user.

windowsPE configuration pass The first configuration pass performed during setup, which can be used to perform tasks such as disk partitioning and entering the product key.

Winsock Kernel (WSK) An interface that supports communication between kernel mode software, such as clients and services, and the TCP/IP protocol.

Wired Equivalent Privacy (WEP) A security protocol for wireless 802.11 networks that provides weak authentication methods in comparison to WPA. WEP uses preshared keys that attackers have been able to decipher without much difficulty. The use of WEP is discouraged where wireless security is a major consideration.

Wireless Access Point A device that allows wireless devices to connect through it to a wired network.

work network The location type that is used for trusted networks where limited security is required, for example, a small office.

X.25 A networking technology standard that defines packet switching networks used for WAN connectivity.

x64 A generic term used to refer to Intel and AMD CPU processors capable of 64 bit operations that are compatible with the Windows operating system.

x86 A generic term used to refer to computers based on Intel CPU processors. These CPUs include 8086, 80286, 80386, 80486, the Pentium family and Pentium compatible processors from other companies such as AMD.

XML A standard for formatting information in a self-describing way for transfer between different applications.

XML Paper Specification (XPS) A document format that describes how a page should be displayed. XPS is similar to Adobe Portable Document Format (PDF).

XML PrintCapabilities A new system to advertise the capabilities of a printer.

XML PrintTicket An XML file that describes the settings for a print job.

Index